www. wadsworth.com

wadsworth.com is the World Wide Web site for Wadsworth and is your direct souce to dozens of online resources.

At *wadsworth.com* you can find out about supplements, demonstration software, and student resources. You can also send e-mail to many of our authors and preview new publications and exciting new technologies.

wadsworth.com
Changing the way the world learns®

Becoming an EC-4 Teacher in Texas

A Course of Study for the Pedagogy and Professional Responsibilities (PPR) TExES

Edited by

JANICE L. NATH
University of Houston—Downtown

MYRNA D. COHEN
University of Houston—Downtown

THOMSON

WADSWORTH

Australia • Canada • Mexico • Singapore • Spain • United Kingdom • United States

THOMSON

WADSWORTH

Education Editor: Dan Alpert
Development Editor: Tangelique Williams
Editorial Assistant: Heather Kazakoff
Technology Project Manager: Barry Connolly
Marketing Manager: Dory Schaeffer
Marketing Assistant: Neena Chandra
Advertising Project Manager: Shemika Britt
Project Manager, Editorial Production: Trudy Brown

Print/Media Buyer: Doreen Suruki
Permissions Editor: Bob Kauser
Production Service: Matrix Productions
Copy Editor: Jill Saxton
Cover Designer: Bill Stanton
Compositor: Bookcomp, Inc./Nighthawk Design
Text and Cover Printer: Webcom, Ltd.

For more information about our products,
contact us at:
Thomson Learning Academic Resource Center
1–800–423–0563
For permission to use material from this text,
contact us by:
Phone: 1-800-730-2214   **Fax:** 1-800-730-2215
Web: http://www.thomsonrights.com

ISBN 0-534-60300-9

Wadsworth/Thomson Learning
10 Davis Drive
Belmont, CA 94002–3098
USA

Asia
Thomson Learning
5 Shenton Way #01–01
UIC Building
Singapore 068808

Australia/New Zealand
Thomson Learning
102 Dodds Street
Southbank, Victoria 3006
Australia

Canada
Nelson
1120 Birchmount Road
Toronto, Ontario M1K 5G4
Canada

Europe/Middle East/Africa
Thomson Learning
High Holborn House
50/51 Bedford Row
London WC1R 4LR
United Kingdom

Latin America
Thomson Learning
Seneca, 53
Colonia Polanco
11560 Mexico D.F.
Mexico

Spain/Portugual
Paraninfo Thomson Learning
Calle/Magallanes, 25
28015 Madrid
Spain

Contents

COMPETENCY 2   22

Chapter 2   Appreciating Human Diversity   23
Eileen R. Westerman
Janice L. Nath
Myrna D. Cohen
Emiliano Gonzalez
Gena Jerkins

COMPETENCY 3   43

Chapter 3   Part I—Designing Effective Instruction   44
Janice L. Nath

Chapter 13 Part 2—Motivating Learners 261
Sandy Cmajdalka

COMPETENCY 9 279

Chapter 14 Using Technology in the EC–4 Classroom 280
Mary E. Parker
Janice L. Nath

COMPETENCY 10 307

Chapter 15 Part 1—Using a Variety of Appropriate Assessment Techniques to Monitor Student Progress 308

Pam Lindsey

DOMAIN IV FULFILLING PROFESSIONAL ROLES AND RESPONSIBILITIES 347

Preface

Over the past few years, teacher certification in Texas has seen a series of rapid changes. The certification structure now offers three rather than two certificate levels, so current candidates must choose either early childhood (EC–4), middle school (4–8), or high school (8–12) certification. The current Pedagogy and Professional Responsibilities (PPR) Texas Examination of Educator Standards (TExES) requires teacher candidates to have deeper knowledge of more specific age groups than did the former standards and ExCET examinations. This book addresses the knowledge and responsibilities required of teachers taking the PPR state certification test in Pre-K through fourth grade.

In 2000, *Becoming a Teacher in Texas* was published to address the former state-mandated competencies (which addressed criteria for grades 1–12) that were in place at that time under the ExCET (Examination for Certification for Educators in Texas). In the following year, the State Board of Educator Certification (SBEC) revised certification levels and structured new standards and competencies for certification in Texas. In an effort to continue to help teacher candidates prepare for the new PPR, we began to work toward specifically addressing information for new testing requirements for EC–4 candidates. Because Texas still focuses on many of the learner-centered ideas that were established in the former standards, much the same philosophy expressed in *Becoming a Teacher in Texas* is found in this book—yet now applied to young learners.

Structure

You will find that concepts appear and reappear throughout these 20 chapters. This resurfacing of concepts is intentional, as it is in the Texas standards and competencies. The overlapping reflects the nature of the competencies for, although the competencies are divided into distinct statements, each is interlaced into the complexities of effective teaching. For example, a teacher cannot assess students without referencing the objectives of a lesson, the circumstance of the learner(s), and so forth. The redundancies of this book are important and they highlight the interdependencies of these competencies.

As you glance through the table of contents, you will see that this book is organized around the 13 state PPR competencies for EC–4. However, what is not readily visible is that each author first addressed the set of state *standards* for this age level certification prior to developing each competency. Therefore, be assured that you are studying not only the competencies for the state test, but also the standards on which the competencies and the examination are based. You will note that the number of chapters for each competency can vary, depending upon its complexity. All chapters share the same structure: a selection of important terms that test-takers should commit to memory, a discussion of information on which the standards and competencies were developed, a glossary to define the terms as applicable to the chapter, activities to help further develop the concepts for the chapter, practice test items with discussion, related Web sites, and references. The final chapter, differently formatted, offers advice on study skills, information on how to register, and suggestions for the test day.

The authors offer a wide range of expertise, representing urban and rural areas, large and small institutions, and public and private colleges and universities throughout Texas and beyond. All authors are dedicated to teacher education and are committed to helping teacher candidates pass this important examination. Most importantly, the authors are also committed to helping each candidate gain ideas that will help foster the best of teacher practices.

As you begin to study to become a teacher in Texas, we trust that you will remember that however frustrating it might be to prepare for this test, these competencies have been thoroughly researched and reflect the best in teacher practice. Although we know there is more to being an excellent teacher than passing a particular examination, we also feel that when you follow these competencies in your classroom, many Texas children will grow in knowledge and in the love of learning. It is our hope that you will give your children your very best every day.

Acknowledgments

Dr. Janice Nath would like to acknowledge and dedicate her part of this work to her mother, Esther Faseler Huff, who taught in Texas classrooms for 28 years and who continues to teach her daughter much of her wisdom. "It is because of her support and her values that I am able to work for those who are seeking to teach in Texas."

Dr. Myrna Cohen would like to acknowledge and dedicate her part of this work to her past students, who have taught her so much over the years. It is her wish that the candidates preparing for their Texas certification will enjoy and learn similarly from their future students.

It is with great thanks that we also acknowledge the following people for their time and suggestions in reviewing our chapters: Joy Edwards, Texas Wesleyan University; Robert C. Peters, Howard Payne University; Dorothy Smith, St. Mary's University, San Antonio; Linda Ann Weeks, Lamar University; J. Helen Perkins, Southern Methodist University; and Shari Mills, LeTourneau University.

We would also like to thank those at Wadsworth Publishing and their associates, who helped to make the vision a reality, particularly Dan Alpert, Editor.

About the Editors

Dr. Janice Nath currently serves as a University of Houston—Downtown faculty member in the Department of Urban Education. *Becoming a Teacher in Texas: A Course of Study for the Professional Development ExCET* was her first co-edited book on the professional development aspect of Texas teacher certification for elementary and secondary education. Currently she is also co-editing a book for the EC–4 Generalists Texas test in content and pedagogy and another for research in Professional Development Schools, *Forging Alliances in Community and Thought*. She served as the Coordinator for Elementary Education, Director of the PUMA TRACS Program for Post Baccalaureate Teacher Certification, Assistant Director of the Internship Program, and headed a Professional Development School (PDS) site in her former position at the University of Houston. She has been actively involved in field-based teacher education for many years, formerly serving as the chair and program chair of the AERA PDSR SIG (American Educational Research Association Professional Development School Research Special Interest Group). At this time, Dr. Nath serves as president of the Teacher Coordinators for Teacher Certification Testing (formerly, the ExCET Coordinators Association of Texas). She thanks the many children whom she has taught, especially those in kindergarten through fourth grade, and her many new teachers for their parts in helping this book to become a reality.

Dr. Myrna D. Cohen is a faculty member in the Department of Urban Education at the University of Houston—Downtown and serves as the Director of the Center for Professional Development and Teaching. She is the president of Texas Directors of Field Experience, and is an officer and board member of the Consortium of State Organizations of Texas Teacher Educators (CSOTTE). She also served for several years as co-editor of the *Texas Teacher Education Forum* and as a board member of Texas Teacher Educators (TTE). Dr. Cohen was Director of Field Experiences and Coordinator of Secondary Education in her previous position at the University of Houston—Main Campus. Her areas of interest include teacher education, second language education, and student-centered strategies such as cooperative learning. She has been published in various journals, such as *Bilingual Research Journal, The Teacher Educator,* and *Teacher Education and Practice.* She is also a co-author of the assessment monograph for the *Restructuring Texas Teacher Education Series* published for the Texas State Board for Educator Certification. In addition to undergraduate and graduate university-level teaching, Dr. Cohen has had 15 years of classroom teaching experience, encompassing grades 2–12.

About the Contributors

Isela Almaguer is a faculty member at The University of Texas—Pan American at Edinburg, Texas, where she teaches undergraduate courses in elementary education. Ms. Almaguer is currently an Ed.D. candidate at The University of Houston, where she is pursuing a doctorate in Curriculum and Instruction with an emphasis in teacher preparation and literacy. She has a Bachelor's of Interdisciplinary Studies degree in bilingual education and is a certified reading specialist. Ms. Almaguer has extensive teaching experience as a bilingual early childhood classroom teacher. Her dissertation is a study of the literacy development of early childhood English language learners through the use of peer-mediated instruction.

Dr. Terry Brandt is an associate professor who serves as the coordinator of undergraduate teacher education and the director of gifted education at the University of St. Thomas in Houston, Texas. Before joining the faculty of St. Thomas, he was a teacher and administrator in Texas schools for 32 years. Dr. Brandt teaches the introductory courses in educational psychology and classroom management to undergraduate and post-baccalaureate students who are preparing to become teachers. At the graduate level, he teaches theories of learning and courses in gifted education.

Dr. Lillian Chenoweth is a professor in the Department of Family Sciences at Texas Woman's University, where she currently teaches undergraduate and graduate courses in family studies. Her research interests include home/school collaboration, parent education, families and money, and families and technology. She has published numerous articles in these areas.

Diane Clay, Ph.D., is an associate professor of reading at the University of St. Thomas in Houston, Texas. Her main areas of interest are emergent literacy, teacher modeling, and the importance of using children's literature in the reading program. She is a co-author of the assessment monograph for the *Restructuring Texas Teacher Education Series* published in 1998 for the Texas State Board for Educator Certification and "Enhancing Student Achievement" that appears in *Becoming a Teacher in Texas: A Course of Study for the Professional Development ExCET* (2001), edited by Cynthia Henry and Janice Nath.

Dr. Gary Clay is an associate professor in Education at Houston Baptist University (HBU). He also serves as chair of the Department of Education at HBU and teaches both graduate and undergraduate courses. His interests include district and campus leadership and administration, curriculum development, technology integration, distance education, and action research. One of the courses he currently teaches is an online course dealing with the use and integration of the Internet as an instructional tool. Dr. Clay coordinates the preparation and delivery of review sessions for state certification exams for HBU. Dr. Clay served for 30 years in the public schools of Texas. His experiences include teaching in elementary schools, serving as principal in elementary and intermediate schools, and holding positions in district administration for 15 years, including 7 years as superintendent. He has served in a variety of leadership roles in professional education associations and attempts to share his experiences by helping future teachers to become effective leaders in the classroom.

Dr. Sandy Cmajdalka received her Ph.D. in Curriculum and Instruction from Texas A&M University with a major area of study in bilingual education. She is an assistant professor in the Department of Urban Education at the University of Houston—Downtown and is a coordinator for bilingual field-based experiences. She teaches courses in educational psychology, bilingual education, and early childhood education. Her current research activities explore problem-solving difficulties in mathematics for Hispanic students with limited English proficiency.

Dr. Donna Cunningham is an associate professor, an undergraduate program director, and director of field experiences and of student teaching in the Department of Teacher Education, College of Professional Education, at Texas Woman's University (TWU) in Denton. She has developed expertise as an ExCET/TExES trainer specializing in ExCET/TExES testing strategies. As a consultant to universities in Texas, she assists faculty and administrators in developing individual training plans and aligning professional development courses with state standards. She also provides sessions for students to help improve their ExCET/TExES scores. Dr. Cunningham has taught both graduate and undergraduate courses. Her current focus is on the professional development of preservice teachers, course development, and online instruction. Dr. Cunningham is a Texas certified teacher and vocational supervisor with a combined total of 28 years of teaching experience at the junior high, high school, and university level.

Dr. Jo Ann Engelbrecht is a professor in the Department of Family Sciences at Texas Woman's University, where she currently teaches undergraduate and graduate courses in child development and family studies. Her research include home/school collaboration, parenting, parent education, care of young children, and education of young children. She has published numerous articles in these areas. Dr. Engelbrecht is a Certified Family Life Educator (CFLE) and Certified Family and Consumer Sciences (CFCS). She has taught for 29 years in preschool, middle school, high school, university, and adult education settings. For 10 years, she served as director of the Texas Woman's University Child Development Center.

Veronica Lopez Estrada is an assistant professor at The University of Texas-Pan American (UTPA) at Edinburg, Texas, where she specializes in language, literacy, and culture. She received her Ph.D. from The Ohio State University in 1997. Her research has focused on resiliency theory, beginning teacher induction, online technology preservice teacher education, and diversity issues in education. Dr. Estrada teaches undergraduate and graduate courses in reading and research methods courses for doctoral students. Currently she is program coordinator of the Master of Education in Reading program and the Master Reading Teacher (MRT) certification program at UTPA.

Emiliano Gonzalez is currently a faculty member at the University of Saint Thomas in Houston. He serves as the Director of Field Experience and is in charge of the Masters in Bilingual Education Grant and the Partnership Quality Education Grant (PQE) from his department. Emiliano graduated from Indiana University in 1998 with a Ph.D. in Curriculum and Instruction. After studying with leading experts in their fields, such as Christine Bennett in Multicultural Education and Carlos Ovando in Bilingual Education, he pursued those areas of research. Other areas of interest are issues of poverty, equity, and social justice. While living and working in South Texas, Emiliano gained extensive experience with the instruction of language to minority students living in abject poverty.

Dr. Cynthia Henry is a preschool director in Atlanta, Georgia. She was formerly a professor in the Department of Curriculum and Instruction at the University of Houston and served as the coordinator for the Teacher Internship Program there. She has been actively involved in field-based teacher education. Dr. Henry has been an elementary classroom teacher and has worked extensively with gifted and talented and ESL students. She is co-editor of *Becoming a Teacher in Texas: A Guide for the Elementary and Secondary Professional Development ExCET.* Her research interests include teacher education, gifted and talented education, and parent involvement.

Gena Jerkins received both her Bachelor of Arts degree with certification and her Masters of Education from Texas A&M University. Her doctoral degree is in Educational Administration from the University of Houston. Her interest centers on multicultural issues, and she is the author of *Stand Tall,* a book that delves into diversity concerns. Currently, she is working as an assistant principal in Houston area schools.

Dr. Stephanie L. Knight is Professor in the Department of Educational Psychology at Texas A&M University, and the Houston Endowment, Inc. endowed chair in Urban Education. She also directs the Center for the Study and Implementation of Collaborative Learning Communities in the College of Education at Texas A&M. Her research interests include the impact of classroom processes on student outcomes and the use of teacher research as professional development. She has published numerous books, chapters, and journal articles in these areas and was named a University Faculty Fellow in 2001 in recognition of her scholarship. Dr. Knight teaches graduate and undergraduate courses in educational psychology and received the Association of Former Students university award for outstanding teaching in 1998.

Dr. Pam Lindsey is an associate professor at Tarleton State University and is a member of both the graduate and undergraduate faculty. She is the director of the Educational Diagnostician program at Tarleton State. Prior to her tenure there, she directed the diagnostician program at Texas Tech University and was instrumental in reinstating the undergraduate special education teacher training program. Dr. Lindsey was a classroom teacher in special and general education for 13 years and a full-time educational diagnostician for 5 years. She continues to work as a diagnostician for several local school districts. Because of her extensive background and interest in assessment issues, she has accumulated a wealth of expertise, emphasizing the important link between effective assessment strategies, program planning, and student learning.

Dr. Jennifer Martin is Associate Dean for Graduate Studies at Texas Woman's University. In addition, she is Professor in the Department of Family Sciences, where she has taught graduate and undergraduate family studies courses since 1986. Her research interests include family/school collaboration, parent education, work and family, and family resource management. She has published numerous articles in these areas. Dr. Martin is Certified in Family and Consumer Sciences (CFCS) and has taught for 26 years in secondary and higher education settings.

Dr. Lin Moore is a faculty member in the College of Professional Education at Texas Woman's University. She teaches undergraduate and graduate courses in teacher education, early childhood development and education, and research methods. She presents reviews for the TExES Region X Education Service Center and Dallas Public Schools.

Dr. Moore holds a bachelor's degree in Home Economics Education, a master's degree in Child Development and Family Living, and a doctorate in Child Development and Marriage and Family Counseling from Texas Woman's University. Her numerous presentations at state, regional, national, and international conferences have focused on high-stakes testing, developmentally appropriate practices, mixed-age grouping, home-school partnerships, children's social skills, parenting behaviors and family routines, school climate, and school-based services. She currently serves as an external evaluator for grants focusing on young children's language development, early literacy and math skills, and programs for mentoring beginning and veteran teachers. She is a member and past chair of the Research Committee of the Association for Childhood Education International and a member of the Head Start/Public School Transition National Research Consortium. Previously Dr. Moore taught child development courses in Texas community colleges, established and directed a child development laboratory school, and directed Title XX Child and Family centers.

Dr. Mary E. Parker is an assistant professor at West Texas A&M University in Canyon, Texas, where she coordinates the secondary Professional Development School and teaches secondary methods. She is also a member of the A&M University System Regents' Initiative Academy of Educators. She is counselor for the Iota Theta chapter of Kappa Delta Pi and chairs the national membership committee. Iota Theta has coordinated the Celebration of Teaching conferences on the WTAMU campus for three years as a result of grant monies awarded by Kappa Delta Pi. Iota Theta is a six-year winner of the ACE award, Kappa Delta Pi's national recognition for outstanding chapters. Dr. Parker's research interests include topics emerging from teaching online classes, the historical aspects of early education on the Llano Estacado, partnership research through the PDS, and professional portfolio development. She also presents Professional Development ExCET reviews for the Division of Education and is currently involved in maintaining a Web site (http://makingtransitions.wtamu.edu) constructed as a result of a Regents' Initiative grant.

Robin A. Rackley teaches educational psychology at the undergraduate level at Texas A&M and is affiliated with the Center for the Study and Implementation of Collaborative Learning Communities through her research interests. She taught in Texas public schools for eight years and focuses her research on early childhood teachers and students. In particular, she is interested in the development of teacher leadership among early childhood educators.

Angela Spaulding is an associate professor of Educational Leadership at West Texas A&M University in Canyon, Texas, where she coordinates the educational leadership program and teaches courses in leadership and curriculum. She is also the project director of the A&M University System Regents' Initiative at WTAMU. She is a sponsor for Alpha Chi, an academy member of the Regents'

Initiative for Excellence in Education, and has been the recipient of the WTAMU Outstanding Professor award. Dr. Spaulding's research interests include topics emerging from leadership and group dynamics, communication, conflict management, and the micropolitics of life in the classroom. She has numerous publications and presentations in these areas. Dr. Spaulding has been an early childhood classroom teacher and administrator.

Eileen R. Westerman received her Bachelors of Science degree from The Ohio State University and a Masters in Supervision from the University of St. Thomas. She also holds Endorsements in Gifted and Talented and Mid Management/Principalship in the state of Texas. Eileen is a Licensed District Trainer of Trainers for TRIBES TLC. She has developed a Module for Teaching Multicultural Education to undergraduate students. Teacher Education has been her main focus area; she has been a University of Houston, Professional Development Site Cluster Coordinator for the undergraduate teacher education program for the past five years, a supervisor of student teachers and interns, and a mentor to many students. She is also the ExCET Coordinator for the University of Houston and the Counselor for Kappa Delta Pi.

Test Framework for Field 100:

Pedagogy and Professional Responsibilities EC–4

Domain I   **Designing Instruction and Assessment to Promote Student Learning (approximately 31% of the test)**
Standards Assessed:
Pedagogy and Professional Responsibilities Standard I:
The teacher designs instruction appropriate for all students that reflects an understanding of relevant content and is based on continuous and appropriate assessment.

Domain II   **Creating a Positive, Productive Classroom Environment (approximately 15% of the test)**
Standards Assessed:
Pedagogy and Professional Responsibilities Standard II:
The teacher creates a classroom environment of respect and rapport that fosters a positive climate for learning, equity, and excellence.

Domain III   **Implementing Effective, Responsive Instruction and Assessment (approximately 31% of the test)**
Standards Assessed:
Pedagogy and Professional Responsibilities Standard I:
The teacher designs instruction appropriate for all students that reflects an understanding of relevant content and is based on continuous and appropriate assessment.
Pedagogy and Professional Responsibilities Standard III:
The teacher promotes student learning by providing responsive instruction that makes use of effective communication techniques, instructional strategies that actively engage students in the learning process, and timely, high-quality feedback.
Technology Applications Standards I–V:
All teachers use technology-related terms, concepts, data input strategies, and ethical practices to make informed decisions about current technologies and their applications.
All teachers identify task requirements, apply search strategies, and use current technology to efficiently acquire, analyze, and evaluate a variety of electronic information.
All teachers use task-appropriate tools to synthesize knowledge, create and modify solutions, and evaluate results in a way that supports the work of individuals and groups in problem-solving situations.
All teachers communicate information in different formats and for diverse audiences.
All teachers know how to plan, organize, deliver, and evaluate instruction for all students that incorporates the effective use of current technology for

teaching and integrating the Technology Applications Texas Essential Knowledge and Skills (TEKS) into the curriculum.

Domain IV Fulfilling Professional Roles and Responsibilities
(approximately 23% of the test)
Standards Assessed:
Pedagogy and Professional Responsibilities Standard IV:
The teacher fulfills professional roles and responsibilities and adheres to legal and ethical requirements of the profession.

Becoming an EC-4 Teacher
in Texas

A Course of Study for the Pedagogy and

Professional Responsibilities (PPR) TExES

Domain I

Designing Instruction and Assessment to Promote Student Learning

Competency 1

The teacher understands human developmental processes and applies this knowledge to plan instruction and ongoing assessment that motivate students and are responsive to their developmental characteristics and needs.

The beginning teacher:

- Understands the lifelong impact of the experiences provided in early childhood through grade 4 on individual development and on society.

- Knows the typical stages of cognitive, social, physical, and emotional development of students in early childhood through grade 4.

- Recognizes the wide range of individual developmental differences that characterizes students in early childhood through grade 4 and the implications of this developmental variation for instructional planning.

- Recognizes factors affecting the physical growth and health of students in early childhood through grade 4 (e.g., nutrition, sleep, prenatal exposure to drugs, abuse) and knows that students' physical growth and health impact their development in other domains (e.g., cognitive, social, emotional).

- Recognizes factors affecting the social and emotional development of students in early childhood through grade 4 (e.g., lack of affection and attention, limited opportunity for verbal interactions, changes in family structure) and knows that students' social and emotional development impact their development in other domains.

- Knows the stages of play development (i.e., from solitary to cooperative) and the important role of play in young children's learning and development.

- Demonstrates knowledge of developmental changes in children's thinking (i.e., from primarily concrete thinking to the ability to reason and think logically, to understand cause and effect, and to organize information systematically).

- Analyzes how developmental characteristics of students in early childhood through grade 4 impact learning and performance.

- Recognizes the importance of helping students in early childhood through grade 4 to apply decision-making, organization, and goal-setting skills (e.g., selecting learning centers, putting materials away in the appropriate places, completing a self-initiated project).

- Uses knowledge of the developmental characteristics and needs of students in early childhood through grade 4 to plan meaningful, integrated, and active learning and play experiences that promote the development of the whole child.

- Understands how development in any one domain (i.e., cognitive, social, physical, emotional) impacts development in other domains.

- Recognizes signs of developmental delays or impairments in students in early childhood through grade 4.

Chapter 1

Understanding Human Development

STEPHANIE L. KNIGHT
ROBIN A. RACKLEY

Texas A & M University, College Station

TERMS TO KNOW

Accommodation

Adaptation

Assimilation

Assisted learning

Cognitive development

Concrete operational

Conventional moral reasoning

Development

Developmentally appropriate

Disequilibrium

Egocentrism

Equilibration

Formal operational

Guided participation

Industry versus inferiority

Information processing theories

Initiative versus guilt

Maturation

Metacognitive ability

Physical development

Preconventional moral reasoning

Preoperational

Private speech

Psychomotor domain

Readiness

Scaffolding

Schemata (the plural of schema)

Sensorimotor

Social development

Zone of proximal development

This chapter focuses on Competency 1, tested in the EC–4 Pedagogy and Professional Responsibilities Examination, although the information contained within is integrated throughout this book. The competencies are linked to a specific state test, but they represent knowledge and skills that teachers in any state might need to know in order to be effective in a variety of EC-4 classrooms.

EXPLANATION OF COMPETENCY 1

Students' developmental and background characteristics affect what and how they learn. Effective decision making about instructional content and methods considers intellectual, social, physical, and emotional development as well as skills, interests, and needs. A teacher in Pre K–4 must be very knowledgeable about cognitive, social, physical, and developmental stages, for many changes occur during these years. We now know through research that children are not "little adults," but think in very different ways as they grow. Teachers should be aware of these expected developmental progressions and understand cultural and socioeconomic differences. In addition, teachers need to know how to motivate students to succeed. Teachers should apply the knowledge of children to instructional design and should implement instruction that helps students at various developmental levels and with varied backgrounds make connections between their current skills and understandings and those that are new to them.

Can you think of teachers you have had in the past who appeared to know their content areas very well but had difficulty getting information across to students because they failed to give concrete examples or applications? Or perhaps you know teachers who experienced classroom man-agement problems because they required relatively young students to remain seated and inactive for long periods at a time. These teachers may know their content very well. They may have a repertoire of instructional strategies at their command. Nevertheless, effective teaching requires more than just knowledge of content and instructional strategies. Teachers also need knowledge about developmental levels and the variation in developmental levels that might be expected from students in their classes in order to design appropriate learning experiences. Although many teachers acquire the knowledge and skills to provide **developmentally appropriate** instruction in their classrooms by observing and interacting with students over time, beginning teachers typically have not had sufficient experience with students to acquire this knowledge. The study of child and adolescent developmental theory in advance of or concurrent with field experiences provides a more efficient means of enabling teachers to integrate their knowledge of students, strategies, and tasks needed for effective instructional decision making.

This chapter examines several areas that inform prospective teachers about childhood developmental progression and the implications for teaching children in Texas classrooms. Areas of emphasis include cognitive, social, physical, and emotional development and the range of characteristics that children in certain grade levels exhibit in these areas.

THEORIES OF GROWTH AND DEVELOPMENT

How many times have you heard—in formal education courses as well as in informal discussions with teachers—that you have to "know" your children in order to match your teaching to their learning needs and interests? One way to know them involves recognizing the physical, intellectual, social, and personal characteristics that occur as humans develop capacities in these areas.

Development refers to systematic, lasting changes that take place over the course of the human life span. There has been a great deal of controversy over the source of these changes, but most educators recognize that development takes place as a result of both internally determined change, referred to as **maturation,** and the interaction of the individual with the environment, an external influence. The relative importance of the internal and external (or "nature and nurture") varies, depending on the area of development we are discussing. For example, variations in **physical development** (changes in the human body), depend to a large extent on genes. On the other hand, **social development** occurs as humans interact with others. These two types of development ("nature and nurture") are related and are often difficult to separate. Inherent personality or physical traits may influence the nature of human interactions.

Environmental Influences on Development

Because development and learning can be affected by outside factors, early childhood teachers must be aware of these influences—especially those that they can help control. Environmental influences such as nutrition, lack of sleep, physical or emotional abuse, and exposure to certain chemicals can impact growth. For example, prenatal exposures to teratogens (environmental agents that can cause abnormalities) are not limited to physical damage. A birth defect resulting from drugs taken by a mother during pregnancy can impact reactions of others to the child as well as the child's ability to move about in the environment. Over time, parent-child interactions, peer relations, and other opportunities to explore may suffer. The experiences can have far-reaching consequences for cognitive, emotional, and social development (Friedman, 1996). In all develop-

mental areas, the environment appears to be an important factor.

Early childhood educators should take particular precautions to reduce the risk of biological and physical hazards. Biological hazards include viruses, bacteria, and fungi. A number of early childhood diseases of these types are common, yet serious (chicken pox, pink eye, ringworm, strep throat, etc.), and can cause a number of children to be absent from instruction unless care is taken to prevent the spreading of the disease. More serious diseases such as Hepatitis B, HIV, and tuberculosis are concerns, so universal precautions (wearing gloves, immediate cleanup, etc.) should always be taken in working with bodily fluids. Keeping a very clean room and helping children learn about disease prevention should also be a goal to help avoid any type of illness, including the numerous colds that children develop. Careful handwashing (and drying with paper towels) should be a part of early childhood rooms for both children and teachers. For very young children, play materials should be disinfected often. If a teacher is not sure that tables are being disinfected, he or she should do it weekly (or daily during outbreaks of illness). Early childhood teachers should also be aware of arthropods (such as head lice and scabies) along with the possibilities of insect stings that can cause pain and allergic reactions. Teachers must also be concerned with plant and animal allergens and should be certain that classroom plants and pets are not causing allergic reactions. A note at the beginning of the year (or when a child transfers in) describing the types of lessons involving sensory experiences will give parents the opportunity to inform teachers of any known allergies. However, teachers should be alert to any reactions during these types of "tasting/smelling/touching" lessons. In addition, teachers must also remember never to medicate children. Often it is the early childhood teacher who first notices symptoms of illnesses, disease, or other health-related problems, and those teachers who are vigilant can make sure that children receive medical aid from the school nurse and/or parents.

Physical hazards include noise, temperature extremes, radiation, and hazards in the classroom and playground. In Texas, for example, young children can become too hot very quickly, and sunburn on young skin can occur if children are outside during the day too long without protection. Classrooms and playgrounds must be checked constantly for possible hazards. Teachers should also make their classrooms "childproof" by checking under cabinets or in school furniture for possible poisons, including cleaners, certain types of paints, glues, aerosol sprays, and so forth. All classroom toys should be carefully selected and maintained so as not to cause injury. A teacher can be found liable if he or she notices something that could easily hurt a child and does nothing to prevent it.

Variation in Developmental Progression

Certain principles apply to *all* types of development (cognitive, social, personal, and physical), despite the differing influences of nature and nurture. In general, developmental changes are continuous and gradual rather than sudden, although periods of rapid physical growth can often make teachers and parents remark that a certain child has "sprouted overnight." Some changes are highly visible, as in physical development, while others, such as **cognitive development** or changes in mental processes, are less readily observed. Even a classroom with children of exactly the same age would contain a rather broad range of developmental levels because children develop at different rates and bring with them different experiences. In a kindergarten classroom, the difference can vary from children who are reading and comprehending to students still working on letter recognition. This variation may be attributed to developmental differences in cognition or differences in experiences with print. Being aware of the differing needs of these students is an important component of instructional planning. Although this potential diversity may seem initially overwhelming to the novice teacher, developmental theory helps us recognize changes in children and make predictions about behavior that can guide our teaching.

Although theorists often argue about the nature and order of stages, humans appear to develop in similar, orderly stages. This orderly progression enables teachers to make predictions about "typical" characteristics and behaviors at certain grade levels that, in turn, help teachers plan appropriate instruction. Children who do not match these characteristics may be cause for concern. For example, children with developmental delays or impairments may demonstrate difficulties in academics; exhibit poor coordination for their age; have difficulty paying attention, organizing information, or synthesizing information presented visually or orally; and may require further screening to determine appropriate instructional goals (Hallahan & Kauffman, 2000). Students who seem to learn easily, retain information quickly, exhibit more knowledge than their peers, recognize relations among problems, and make creative connections may also require testing to determine whether their possible "giftedness" needs are being met. Therefore the role of the teacher is to be aware of the range of possible developmental levels and characteristics that children exhibit at these levels and to provide developmentally appropriate instruction in a way that allows learning experiences to lead to optimal development for each child. Children in class will certainly not all be at the same point on a developmental continuum. However, theories of students' cognitive, social, emotional, and moral reasoning development provide tools that help teachers to become proficient in identifying general stages so that proper instruction can be employed. Using the knowledge of characteristics of different levels in combination with knowledge about the cognitive, social, or physical demands placed on a student in specific tasks or activities enables teachers to assess student **readiness** for various learning experiences.

PIAGET'S STAGE THEORY OF COGNITIVE DEVELOPMENT

Anyone who has worked with children recognizes that children do not think like adults. The difference is not solely a matter of capacity. For example, sunflowers grow from seeds but not by becoming very large seeds. Likewise, the cooing and babbling of infants change to adult language but only after progressing through various stages that are qualitatively different.

A Swiss biologist, Jean Piaget, noted the qualitative differences between adults and children in their cognitive development—and how their knowledge, thinking, and problem solving change over time (Piaget, 1963, 1970, 1985). Piaget devised a theory that explains the way people make sense of their environments and how their cognitive processes change as they grow older. According to Piaget, maturation, social experiences, actions on the environment (activity), and the process of equilibration interact to impact our cognitive development. Humans innately engage in the constant combination and arrangement or organization of actions and thoughts into systems or structures that he called **schemata** (the plural of **schema**). Schemata enable us to understand our world and help guide our interactions with objects and events. As we mature and encounter new information through interaction with objects and people, the way thought is organized in these schemata changes. For instance, changes occur through the process of **adaptation,** the adjustment of existing knowledge structures in a schema through the two processes of assimilation and accommodation. When we perceive that a current experience and our prior mental structures (or schemata) that represent understanding of the environment are consistent, we merely incorporate the new knowledge into our existing knowledge through the process of **assimilation.** In other words, to make sense of the new information we use an existing schema. For example, if there is a recognition schema for birds based on characteristics such as "has feathers and flies" and a robin is seen for the first time, one could easily assimilate the fact that a robin is a bird and is similar to others already identified (such as wrens, blue jays, or other such birds in the "bird" schema). In some cases, the new knowledge may have to be somewhat distorted in order to make

sense of new information. This distortion may result in a misconception. An example is the misconception held by some children that a whale is a fish because it swims.

On the other hand, when we perceive that the information received from interaction with the environment is not consistent with our prior representation of events or objects, dissonance or **disequilibrium** is experienced. To alleviate the incongruity between what we know and conflicting new information, we must change our existing structure to accommodate the new information through a process called **accommodation.** For example, if an animal that has feathers and flies is seen, it fits well with our notion of birds. However, when another animal (perhaps one with scales and fins that swims) is introduced for the first time, it does not fit into our bird schema. A new category is required to accommodate this new experience—a fish schema. The constant search for a balance between what we know and what we are learning through activity or social experiences is known as **equilibration.** Humans experience equilibrium when our schemata and our categories all "make sense" and nothing has occurred to disrupt them. When they are disrupted, we experience disequilibrium. We then are driven to make new sense of the world by adjusting and changing our schemata to reach equilibrium again. Equilibration helps us understand why children enjoy "brain teasers" and why they persist at challenging tasks even without the promise of some external reward. Motivation stems from the child's internal desire to balance what he or she already knows with novel events or information.

From this perspective, teachers would want to design experiences that result in some disequilibrium to motivate children to pursue puzzling situations. They might provide information or experiences that challenge children's existing beliefs. For example, in science a teacher might conduct an experiment using two glasses of clear liquid—one water and the other alcohol. When the teacher places an ice cube in one glass, it floats as students expect. But when she or he places an ice cube in the other glass, which is actually filled with alcohol, the ice sinks to the bottom. Children become curious about a situation that challenges their previous understanding of the way objects in the natural world act. They become motivated to learn about scientific principles. However, if new information is too far in advance of a child's current knowledge, the child may choose to ignore it.

With these processes in mind, Piaget suggested specific differences in the way children's thinking evolves as they develop. He proposed four stages of cognitive development: **sensorimotor, preoperational, concrete operational,** and **formal operational.** Although children may enter these stages at different ages, each child goes through the same sequence of developmental stages (according to Piaget). Furthermore, these stages can be represented by a typical range of ages that helps teachers predict and verify the range that might exist in a particular grade level, remembering that an individual child may enter a stage earlier or leave a stage later than others. Piaget developed a series of tasks to determine the developmental stage of a child, and these tasks can be used by new teachers to become familiar with characteristics of children representative of the grade levels they will teach. Although current research has modified our thinking about cognitive stages in relation to information processing capacity, knowledge and expertise, and cultural influences (Case, 1985; Rogoff, 1990; Siegler, 1991), the cognitive stages still serve as a useful guide for thinking about the kinds of experiences that will benefit children at various grade levels. In this chapter, only the first three stages are presented in detail because early elementary children are unlikely to be at the last stage of development—the formal operational stage of cognitive processing.

Sensorimotor Stage. During infancy (from birth to approximately 2 years of age), humans rapidly develop the ability to act on their environment. As a result, they form initial schema from their physical interactions with the objects and people around them. Their primary accomplishments during this period include the following: understanding that objects exist even when not in sight or sound range (object permanence); imitation of the actions of others, combination of simple actions into more complex routines; the ability to reverse an action (reversibility); and evidence of goal-directed or intentional behaviors tied to physical actions. Infants can dump objects from a container over and over, producing a pleasing effect or reaction. In fact, caregivers of infants and toddlers quickly recognize that many of their young charges have developed a schema for dropping a spoon from their highchair—expecting it to be retrieved for them—only to be dropped and retrieved again and again.

Preoperational Stage. During early childhood, which includes the early elementary school years (2 through 7 years), children move from the development of schemata that are tied to physical actions to actions that are carried out mentally by thinking them through (operations). In other words, this stage marks the transition to symbolic thought. There are two substages of preoperational thought: the *symbolic function stage,* in which children from about 2 through 4 years of age gain the ability to mentally represent an object with which they have had experiences but that is not "there now," and the *intuitive thought substage,* from about 4 through 7 years of age, in which children begin to use primitive reasoning, asking many "why" questions. They intuitively know much but do not know how they know (Santrock, 2001). Children in the first substage begin to scribble pictures that symbolize real life, but they are limited by egocentrism (children see only from their own perspective) and animism (inanimate objects are "alive"). Focusing on one aspect or characteristic to the exclusion of all others (*centration*) in sorting, for example, is typical of this age. Children who are 3, for instance, might line up pebbles on a beach "in *a linear order* because that is a form of order typical of 3-year-olds; a 4- or 5-year-old might place the pebbles in a one-to-one correspondence, one pebble next to one shell, for instance; and a 6-year-old might arrange the pebbles into two lots of six, or six lots of two, or three lots of four" (Athey, 1990, pp. 40–41).

Despite the ability to use symbols, children at this stage cannot yet perform the mental experiments (or operations) characteristic of later cognitive development. For example, children in this stage do not yet realize that a change in the appearance of an object does not necessarily change the characteristics of the object (a tall glass of water can have the same volume as a short, wider glass). They also may be able to think operations through in one direction but not mentally reverse the operations. This is another example of limitations that cause young children, when confronted with a task or problem, to focus on one aspect of the situation and ignore others.

As noted above, preoperational children also are considered egocentric in that they are unable to view situations from the perspectives of others. Other aspects of this concept are important for a teacher to understand. For example, try asking a young child if he or she has a sibling (brother or sister). If the answer is *yes,* ask him if his brother or sister has a brother or sister. The answer to the second question is typically "No" because preoperational children have difficulty putting themselves in their sibling's place. Preoperational children also tend to play side by side in groups, chattering happily about what they are doing but without direct interaction or dialogue with other children.

Teachers can provide a range of experiences through field trips and invited guests to enable preoperational children to transition to the next stage. Teachers should encourage preoperational children to make comparisons often, put things in order in different ways, draw with perspective, and justify their answers. Decision making, goal setting, and organization strategies should all be taught during this cognitive stage and children should have opportunities to use these skills at school. For example, to help facilitate the completion of a task, a teacher might ask students to verbalize the next step, prompting them to think about the goal of the activity and engaging them in planning for the next steps. Teachers can use

prompts such as "I am so pleased that you are helping me set the table for our snack! I see that you have already put a plate on the table for the cookies. What else do we need for snack time? What do you think should go next?" To develop organization, students might be asked to separate toys or art supplies in labeled bins. Activities such as putting materials away correctly, completing a self-initiated project at an activity center, and selecting from a variety of learning centers encourage this development.

Given the limited use of symbolic language at this stage, the use of concrete items, visuals, and role-playing are desirable. For example, when teaching a unit on touch in kindergarten, a teacher might bring in cotton balls to demonstrate the concept of "soft," sandpaper for "rough," toothpicks for "sharp," and silk for "smooth." Experiences that help preoperational children see other viewpoints also benefit those on the verge of moving to the next stage. Therefore, social interactions are beneficial. For example, rather than lecture children about the importance of sharing with others, demonstrate what it would look like if you were sharing the crayons with someone else. Then have students provide demonstrations of sharing other objects in other settings.

Providing children with hands-on practice in basic skills and manipulation also provides the background they will need for the development of more complex skills in language, math, and reading later. Teachers can use large magnetized felt or Velcro® letters to build words. They also can have students divide the morning snack into equal portions to concretely demonstrate sharing with others. Piaget found that young children in this stage could not perform operations such as categorization, but more recent research indicates that preoperational children may exhibit operations in areas of greater knowledge (e.g., Chi & Koeske, 1983; Siegler, 1991). Thus even young children may be able to classify dinosaurs in different related groups if they have a relatively large knowledge base about them. However, these same children may be unable to use this skill in other areas.

Concrete Operational Stage. During a large part of elementary school (7- through 11-year-olds), children exhibit characteristics at a concrete operational stage of cognitive development. They can now perform mental experiments, but their operations are constrained by what they have actually experienced. During this stage, when confronted with a task or problem, they can consider more than one aspect of the task simultaneously and solve hands-on problems logically. They now also understand cause-and-effect relationships. They can group objects according to common characteristics (*classification*) as well as arrange objects in an orderly fashion using a quantitative dimension such as size (*seriation*). The major accomplishment of this period is development of *conservation*—the realization that a change in the appearance of an object does not necessarily change the characteristics of the object (a ball of clay can have the same mass as a pancake of clay). The development of conservation requires use of three other reasoning skills acquired during this same period: *identity*—when nothing is added or subtracted, the material is not changed; *compensation*—a change in one dimension or direction can be balanced by a change in another dimension or direction; and *reversibility*—the ability to conjecture what would happen if an action were reversed or undone. Despite these accomplishments, concrete operational children are normally unable to deal with abstract concepts.

Teachers of concrete operational children most likely have to continue to use concrete objects and visuals to help children understand complex concepts and procedures. To continue to encourage perspective-taking, children should work in groups. Although children have more complex mental skills than in the previous stage, long readings and presentations are difficult for concrete operational children to follow, and teachers should break these into more manageable segments separated by periods of activity. Graphic organizers (charts, diagrams, webs, time lines, etc.) and models are helpful for the presentation and learning of complex information and serve two purposes: to help the teacher organize material for presentation to students so that it is clear and logically arranged, and to provide students with opportunities to analyze and compare objects and ideas at a more complex level. For example, when teaching a lesson on perspective, a first grade teacher might compare *The Three Little Pigs, The Fourth Little Pig,* and *The True Story of The Three Little Pigs,* using a story web or Venn diagram. Children are able to see the commonalities and the differences among the stories based on who told the story more clearly.

As in the previous stage, opportunities for activity enable children to explore the world and to make connections between what they know and the new material. Simple science experiments, opportunities to act out historical or fictional events, and manipulation and crafting of objects representative of time periods provide the experiential base that concrete operational students need. Likewise, the use of familiar examples to explain unfamiliar material helps them make connections between the known and the unknown. When introducing a new denomination during a mathematics unit on money, the new denomination should be explained in terms of denominations already mastered. For example, if children know that a nickel is five pennies, the teacher should introduce a dime as ten ones or ten pennies before the more abstract concept of two nickels (also equaling a dime) is taught.

Concrete operational tasks such as beginning mathematical procedures, ordering numbers and lengths, and reversing of operations are important concepts for the operational child. Teachers should not introduce topics that require the higher reasoning skills of later stages until children exhibit some capability in that area. For example, mathematics problems that involve fractions or decimals are difficult to teach until children have some ability to reason proportionally. Even then, the teacher should enable children to understand proportions by providing objects or props such as slices of pie, candy bars, fruit, or rods that can be broken into smaller pieces. Manipulations are a must for children in the concrete operational stage.

In summary, Piaget's theory provides the basis by which teachers at all levels can design active learning environments that fit with children's active construction of knowledge. Teachers can help students acquire new information by relating it to something students already know. Likewise, as students advance, they will encounter information that does not fit with their simpler conception of the world. In this case, teachers should provide discrepant events that challenge or slightly contradict students' existing conceptions and motivate them to reconcile the two opposing beliefs. Students at all levels can benefit from hands-on manipulation of concrete objects to form a bridge between preoperational and concrete operational stages or between concrete and formal operational stages. Finally, the opportunity for children to interact, whether through play at lower levels or through academic discussions at upper levels, contributes to the development of expanded perspectives (for more on play, see Competency 3, Part 2, Chapter 4).

VYGOTSKY'S SOCIOCULTURAL THEORY OF COGNITIVE DEVELOPMENT

Vygotsky, a contemporary of Piaget, provides a somewhat different view of the cognitive development of children (Vygotsky, 1978, 1986). In contrast to Piaget's focus on the individual's construction of meaning through activity, Vygotsky emphasizes the role of social interaction and the development of language in cognitive development. Piaget viewed self-talk (the oral directions children often give themselves while working through a task) as an example of self-centeredness **(egocentrism)** exhibited by young children in the preoperational stage; Vygotsky interpreted this characteristic differently. He described **private speech,** his term for self-talk, as a critical factor in guiding and monitoring the thinking and problem solving of young children. More complex tasks require more use of private speech. Piaget believed

that young children's solitary play is the result of their inability to use two-way logic. He saw young children playing side by side with independent conversation as a forerunner to the next stage, in which they could utilize two-way logic and then begin cooperative play. Vygotsky, however, viewed this solitary play stage as the "trying out" of language. In contrast to Piaget, Vygotsky emphasized the role that adults and more capable peers play in children's learning through scaffolding and assisted learning. He suggested that children operate within a **zone of proximal development.** This refers to the difference between the intellectual tasks that children can perform alone and those that they can perform with the assistance of an adult or a more skilled peer.

The classroom implications of Vygotsky's theory emphasize the importance of determining the zone of proximal development for children and providing instruction within that zone. In other words, teachers provide tasks that students would not be able to perform without some assistance. That assistance is typically given in the form of questions, hints, or clues. Teachers also may give some type of structure or procedural facilitator such as a checklist to provide a prompt. For example, a teacher in mathematics watching a child struggling with a problem might say, "Ruben, look at your chart. What step are you on now? What will you need to do next?" Children might have checklists on their desks or on the wall reminding them to: check that your name is on your paper, check that each sentence begins with a capital letter, and check that each sentence ends with a period. **Scaffolding,** or the appropriate guidance and support from adults or peers that is gradually withdrawn as competence improves, arises from the notion that children develop cognitively when they are involved in tasks that are more difficult than they could accomplish alone but which are attainable with varying degrees of help from others. The terms **assisted learning** and **guided participation** describe the process a teacher might use when providing scaffolding within a student's zone of proximal development. For example, a child may not be able to generate all the causes of the Texas Revolution on her own after reading a chapter in a book. However, if the teacher provides a concept map with some of the causes provided, the child may be able to fill in the remainder. In mathematics, the teacher could provide examples that are partially completed and have students complete the remainder of the problems. Story maps or other kinds of webs may provide prompts when reading fictional text, that result in student understanding of themes or character and plot development. Likewise, the teacher may direct children to keep cue cards for complex processes such as long division or factoring that can be used as they work.

Teachers also can plan instructional groupings involving cooperative learning or paired problem solving to take advantage of guidance provided by peers who are more skilled in certain areas. Children can collaborate with adults or peers when performing particularly challenging or novel tasks. In addition, instructional strategies such as reciprocal teaching, in which the teacher first models and then children gradually assume the role of teacher, also enable children to advance gradually beyond their zone of proximal development. In all cases, "thinking out loud" while doing complex tasks, that is, talking about what you are thinking and doing as you solve a problem, provides a model for students to use in accomplishing tasks, particularly when they encounter difficulties. The teacher, as well as other students, can model the use of language as a means of organizing thinking.

SOCIAL AND EMOTIONAL DEVELOPMENT

Although we think of school as primarily a place for cognitive development, schools foster other kinds of development and the reverse is also true—other kinds of development have an impact on how children learn. Students develop personally in areas of self-concept and emotions, socially in their relationships with others, and morally in their sense of what is right and wrong. These areas

of development occur as a result of the combination of certain maturations and experiences (nature and nurture). Lack of attention by the primary caregiver(s), limited verbal interactions, and changes in the family structure are all factors affecting the social and emotional development of children. We often refer to the sum of these areas as "psychosocial development." Abraham Maslow established a hierarchy of needs in which he stated that humans' lower-level or "deficiency" needs must be met before their upper-level or "being" needs can be realized. Maslow identified deficiency needs as physiological needs, safety needs, belongingness and love needs, and esteem needs. Only when these needs are met can being needs (need to know and understand, aesthetic needs, and self-actualization needs) be addressed. The implication of Maslow's theory is that a student who is suffering socially or emotionally will not be concerned with academic endeavors (Maslow, 1970). Teachers have to be aware of the needs of their students. More details on Maslow's theory are addressed in Competency 5, Part 2, Chapter 8 and Competency 8, Part 2, Chapter 13.

Just as Piaget described a stage theory of human cognitive development, Erik Erikson proposed a stage model of psychosocial development based on critical periods for the development of certain personality characteristics (Erikson, 1963, 1968). In this theory, social or societal demands interact with individual needs and bring about a conflict that must be successfully recognized and resolved or the individual will have difficulty in personality development at later stages. Prior to school, infants and toddlers encounter conflicts that determine whether they learn to trust or mistrust people (trust versus mistrust—ages birth to 18 months) and whether they develop personal autonomy or end up doubting their abilities to cope with the world (autonomy versus shame and doubt—ages 18 months to 3 years). The results of these stages influence school-age children's later development (either in a negative or a positive way). According to this theory, if a child has not resolved these stages positively, an early childhood educator may encounter children who are very mistrustful and self-doubting. The teacher may need to focus on helping individuals develop more fully in these areas. The stages that usually apply most to early elementary teachers include the two stages that span the years from the ages of 3 to 12. Although many of the influences on personality development occur within the family, teachers are in a position to foster healthy social and emotional development within the classroom.

Initiative versus Guilt. During the stage of **initiative versus guilt,** children from about 3 until 6 years of age test their independence and explore their environment as they master language, cognitive, and social skills. If children are provided with opportunities to try out new behaviors and are successful, they develop initiative. On the other hand, if these attempts are limited or punished too frequently, children may develop a sense of guilt and become overly dependent on adults. Teachers of preschool, kindergarten, and first grade students can support early efforts of children as they plan and implement activities. They can also create a safe environment by encouraging children to take risks and explore new ideas without fear of "failure."

Industry versus Inferiority. From the ages of 6 to 12, children engage in attempts to develop the academic and social skills and abilities needed for successful societal and social interaction **(industry versus inferiority).** When they see themselves as incompetent in dealing with social situations and with their peers, a sense of inferiority or worthlessness may emerge. This feeling of incompetence may be self-fulfilling in the sense that a child who has a self-view of incompetence may approach new situations in a manner that builds in failure. This may be a key stage for children's success. Children in elementary schools benefit from success at academic tasks and genuine praise from teachers for this success. Teachers can provide realistic opportunities for successful attainment of skills coupled with the guidance toward mastery needed during this period.

Because comparison with peers is a powerful indicator of success, teachers should downplay *continuous* competition with classmates. Instead, teachers can place more emphasis on individual criteria and progress toward individual goals.

Teachers play an important role in recognizing and helping children and their caregivers seek help for developmental problems that emerge during school years. Although there is a very broad range of differences that teachers and other adults should accept and encourage, unusual or serious problems may require consultation and special attention of counselors or school psychologists. Even when problems are not serious enough for outside intervention, students who have not emerged as successful in previous stages may need further opportunities to develop trust, autonomy, and initiative. Teachers can involve students in opportunities to choose activities, assume classroom responsibilities, and work independently at all levels of schooling.

STAGES OF MORAL DEVELOPMENT

In addition to his work on cognitive development, Piaget studied children's moral reasoning in relation to their ideas of right and wrong and their understanding of the rules of games they played (Piaget, 1965). By posing moral dilemmas and observing the reasoning of children, Piaget proposed a stage theory of moral development that begins with a premoral period in which children are unaware of rules or standards of right and wrong. Children then progress through a stage of moral absolutes at about the time they enter school. At this stage, children believe that rules are not to be broken despite possible motives or circumstances justifying changes in certain rules. There are no gray areas. Teachers of young children must establish general rules as opposed to narrow, specific rules with no room for flexibility. By having broad rules such as "respect others," teachers can help students differentiate between accidentally bumping into someone and purposefully pushing a classmate. At the end of the elementary years, children enter a stage of autonomous morality. Children now begin to recognize motives or circumstances as an important factor. For example, a school-age child in the moral absolute stage would think that a child who spilled paint while trying to help his teacher should be punished in the same way as a child who spilled paint as a result of playing with the paint jars. In contrast, the child in the stage of autonomous morality would consider that the first child intended to do something good and that the spilling of the paint was an accident. Therefore, the first child would not be as "guilty" as the second.

Kohlberg posed a similar, but more elaborate, stage theory of moral development based on reasoning about moral dilemmas presented in the form of stories. Using the justifications provided by children for what children in the stories should do, Kohlberg proposed his stage theory of moral reasoning with three levels of moral reasoning: **preconventional, conventional**, and postconventional. Students at a preconventional stage of moral reasoning (who define right and wrong in terms of the consequences that they would receive) choose a course of action because they will receive certain punishments or rewards for doing so. Preschool children, most elementary age children, and a few junior and senior high school students exhibit this level of moral reasoning.

Students at a conventional level focus on gaining the approval of others as a result of a particular course of action. They often view societal rules and laws as guidelines that should be followed inflexibly. A few older elementary students and some junior high school students may exhibit this level of moral reasoning but it is seen primarily in high school students.

The last level, postconventional, reflects moral decision making in light of the interests of the majority and the rights of the individual and moves in its last stage to the establishment of a personal code of ethics. Laws are seen as flexible and subject to change when they no longer fulfill their purpose in society. This level is rarely seen in students younger than college age, and most people never reach the highest stage of this level.

Kohlberg's theory was based on males only and has not proven to be an adequate portrayal of female moral reasoning because females tend to base moral decisions on relationships and attitudes of caring (Gilligan, 1982). Nevertheless, the stage theories of both Piaget and Kohlberg provide some useful implications for teachers. Children develop morally through opportunities to play and interact with others. Social play also provides opportunities for children to acquire social skills, such as the importance of taking turns when having a conversation. Children recognize the necessity of making and adhering to rules in interactions with others on the playground and in the classroom and learn to use social skills rather than aggression. For older students, providing real life experiences in which moral decisions may be encountered often serves as a catalyst for more mature moral reasoning and behaviors. Interaction with others at higher levels of moral reasoning may provide the catalyst for transition to a higher level. Opportunities to hear moral reasoning at a higher level challenge the reasoning of children at lower levels. These theories can be combined with other theories that encourage students to think of the perspectives of others as a basis for moral decision making and behavior (Selman, 1980).

Teachers can model appropriate behaviors for children and reinforce appropriate classroom behavior. At lower levels of schooling, teachers may want to describe how children should behave in class ("I like the way everyone is working together so quietly.") and apply the consequences of misbehavior consistently. Students at preconventional stages may be preoccupied with how "fair" the teacher is, requiring the teacher to provide similar opportunities for all students to the greatest extent possible. Children at this level in elementary classrooms might be given opportunities to share materials, enabling them to understand why following guidelines for equitable use might be desirable. Opportunities for playing the roles of others and discussing how they feel in particular situations may also encourage development in perspective-taking.

PHYSICAL DEVELOPMENT DURING EARLY CHILDHOOD

Changes in body size, proportions, and muscle strength develop during early childhood and contribute to an explosion of new gross motor skills (Berk, 2000). As children's bodies become more streamlined and less top-heavy, their center of gravity shifts downward toward their trunk. This shift improves balance greatly, making way for new motor skills involving large muscles of the body (gross motor skills). Young children's gaits become smoother and more rhythmic between the ages of 3 and 6. Most children also have added hopping, galloping, and skipping to their increasing repertoire of skills during this period. Upper- and lower-body skills eventually combine into more fluid actions (Getchell & Roberton, 1989). At age 3, children throw a ball rigidly; however, by age 4 to 5, they use their shoulders, torso, and legs in a more coordinated manner to accomplish this motion.

During the school years, improved balance, strength, agility, and flexibility support refinements in running, jumping, hopping, and ball skills. Early childhood teachers can accent this development through developmentally appropriate activities such as simple creative movements to music; imitation of animals or machines; playground games where there is running, jumping, hopping, skipping; and so forth. For younger children, calisthenics-type group exercises are not appropriate, although they enjoy "copy-me" movement games.

Fine motor skills (involving finely tuned muscle movements) also develop during early childhood. Children become better able to manipulate writing instruments in continuous writing as they move to the basic lines of print. Finger plays are an excellent way to help them increase the control of small movements. Teaching these skills is important to teachers of the early grades, and

teachers should allow for a great range of development in this area.

Instruction related to learning physical skills falls under the **psychomotor domain,** consisting of seven sequential levels (Simpson, 1972; Cruickshank, Bainer, & Metcalf, 1999):

1. Perception: Children must attend to what is asked and perceive desired behavior through their senses (for example, learners watch as the teacher shows students how to hold a crayon for the best control).
2. Set: Children are able and ready to try physically, mentally, and emotionally.
3. Guided response: Children make the first attempt(s) as the teacher watches and guides performance (for example, children practice making "perfect" circles on their desk covered with shaving cream).
4. Mechanism: Enough practice is given that children begin to "internalize" the skill.
5. Complex or overt response: The skill is refined and automatic, with a high degree of proficiency.
6. Adaptation: Children take the skill and, building upon it, are able to perform related skills easily.
7. Origination: Children take the skill and create new varieties to which they have not been exposed.

Understanding how children move through these seven levels can assist teachers in planning skills and instruction that relate to physical skills.

INFORMATION PROCESSING THEORIES OF DEVELOPMENT

Information processing theorists tend to disagree with the stage theory proposed by Piaget (e.g., Case, 1985). In contrast, they suggest that cognitive development occurs through more gradual processes involving increasing capability and capacity of attention, learning strategies, knowledge, and metacognition. Younger children are more distractible than older ones and less purposeful in their goals of learning. As children progress, they are better able to direct their attention to learning despite outside interference and can begin to focus on specific aspects of materials while ignoring others.

Furthermore, older students have strategies they can apply to help them learn material (Gagne, Yekovich, & Yekovich, 1993). Children use more complex strategies as they increase in age and knowledge, and they use the strategies more effectively. For example, kindergarten students rarely use a rehearsal strategy spontaneously to remember information. They may use mnemonics and repetition such as "Thirty days hath September . . . ," or "*i* before *e* except after *c*." During elementary years, they spontaneously use rehearsal more frequently and with better results as they progress through school. The same students also tend to organize information in meaningful categories that aid memory as they continue through elementary school. As they reach puberty, the elaboration of information (adding information they already know to new information) develops as a learning strategy. However, high-ability adolescents tend to utilize elaboration to aid learning more than do lower-ability students, despite similarities in age.

Concurrent with the development of more effective learning strategies is expansion and integration of the knowledge base. As children progress through school, they acquire more and more information that becomes interrelated with existing knowledge. Because we learn best by relating new information to existing information, the more knowledge a person has, the more she or he can acquire. Younger children may have knowledge bases consisting of isolated facts; older students are more likely to have better-organized systems of concepts and ideas.

Finally, differences between younger and older learners exist in **metacognitive ability**—their knowledge about their own cognitive thinking processes and their use of these processes to facil-itate learning. Older children are better able to predict how well they can learn material and identify what they know and do not know, whereas younger learners are typically too optimistic in their predictions and descriptions. In addition, as children progress through school, they become increasingly aware of the advantages of some strategies over others and are more likely to use strategies effectively. Teachers can aid in this process by gradually adding direct instruction and practice in a number of strategies for learning in various subject areas.

Although the information processing theory represents a somewhat different conception of cognitive development than that proposed by Piaget, many of the implications are similar. Consistent with Piagetian theory, teachers need to remember that younger children are not as effective or efficient in the performance of learning tasks as their older counterparts. In particular, distractions may pose more of a challenge to younger students than to older ones. Teachers must be explicit in directing children's attention and in minimizing distractions caused by competing materials or activities. Also consistent with a Piagetian perspective, teachers should enable students to see connections between new material and information they already possess because new learning builds on existing knowledge. Information processing theories build on Piagetian approaches by suggesting that teachers may have to teach learning strategies directly to some students, model their use for all students, and point out the advantages of using particular strategies for learning. Furthermore, children should be encouraged to determine how well they know material and to examine discrepancies in their predictions of accuracy and their actual performance.

SUMMARY

This chapter focused on Competency 1, on the EC–4 Pedagogy and Professional Responsibilities text. This set of indicators highlights teachers' needs to understand variations in developmental levels, background, needs, and interests that might be expected from students in their classes in order to create appropriate lessons.

Appropriate instruction considers the physical, intellectual, social, and personal characteristics that occur as humans develop capacities in these areas. Piagetian, Vygotskian, and information processing theories sensitize teachers to differences in the cognitive processes and capacities of students as they progress through school and suggest instructional practices that enable students to progress intellectually. Psychosocial developmental theories that describe the ways students develop personally and socially provide a framework for understanding internal and external influences on intellectual development. Students develop personally in areas of self-concept and emotions, socially in their relationships with others, and morally in their sense of what is right and wrong. Finally, children rapidly develop physical skills during early childhood. Although schools may emphasize cognitive development, these other kinds of development influence how students learn academic content and are important when we consider the development of the disposition for lifelong learning as an important educational outcome. With the knowledge of cognitive, social, and emotional developmental theories and the range of characteristics that students exhibit in these areas, teachers can better design learning experiences that are appropriate for the grade and age levels they teach.

GLOSSARY

accommodation   a process through which change is made to an existing knowledge structure (schema) to accommodate new information.

adaptation   the adjustment of existing knowledge structures (schemas) through either of the two processes of assimilation or accommodation.

assimilation   incorporating new knowledge from existing knowledge frames (schemas).

assisted learning   the process a teacher might use when providing scaffolding within a student's zone of proximal development.

cognitive development   changes in mental processes.

concrete operational stage   the third of Piaget's stages, covering ages 7 through 11; characterized by the ability to consider more than one aspect of an object or problem, conserve and classify, and demonstrate the concept of seriation (placing items in a series).

conventional moral reasoning   the focus on gaining approval of others as a result of a particular course of action.

development   systematic, lasting changes that take place over the course of the human life span.

developmentally appropriate   instruction in a way that considers the stage of the child and the capabilities in the developmental stage, providing learning experiences that lead to optimal development.

disequilibrium   occurs when dissonance after interaction with the environment is not consistent with our prior representation of events or objects.

egocentrism   the inability to take the perspective of others.

equilibration: the constant search for a balance between what we already know and a new activity, skill, or social experience.

formal operational stage   the last of Piaget's stages, covering ages 11 to adult; characterized by the ability to deal with abstract concepts.

guided participation   the process a teacher might use when providing scaffolding within a student's zone of proximal development.

industry versus inferiority   the engagement by children from the ages of 6 to 12 in attempts to develop the academic and social skills and abilities needed for successful societal and social interaction.

information processing theories of development suggest that the development of cognitive processes occurs through more gradual processes involving increasing capability and capacity of attention, learning strategies, knowledge, and metacognition.

initiative versus guilt   testing by children from about 3 until 6 years of age of their independence and exploration of their environment as they master language, cognitive, and social skills.

maturation   internally determined change.

metacognitive ability   the ability to think about one's own cognitive thinking processes and to use these processes to facilitate learning.

physical development   changes in the human body (dependent to a large extent on genes).

preconventional moral reasoning   right or wrong is decided by punishment or rewards to be received after an action.

preoperational stage   Piaget's second stage, covering ages 2 through 7; it marks the transition to symbolic thought characterized by the child's focus on a single aspect of a situation while ignoring other aspects, and the child's ability to think operations through in one direction but not the reverse.

private speech   Vygotsky's term for young children's talking themselves through tasks aloud; this develops as we grow older into mentally talking ourselves through tasks.

psychomotor domain   levels in which children learn physical skills.

readiness   the assessment of student's ability to complete tasks.

scaffolding   guidance and support from adults or peers that is gradually withdrawn as competence improves.

schema   according to Piaget, building blocks of thought that enable us to understand our world and help guide our interactions with objects and events.

sensorimotor stage   Piaget's initial stage, covering ages birth to 2 years; primary accomplishments during this period include understanding that objects exist even when not in sight or sound range (object permanence), imitation of the actions of others, the combination of simple actions into more complex routines, the ability to reverse an action (reversibility), and evidence of goal-directed behavior(s) or intentional behavior(s) tied to physical actions.

social development   occurs as humans interact with others, although inherent personality traits may influence the nature of these interactions.

zone of proximal development   the difference between intellectual tasks that children can perform alone and those that they can perform with the assistance of an adult or a more skilled peer; the place in learning at which a child could succeed with the help of a more skilled peer but could not succeed alone.

SUGGESTED ACTIVITIES

1. Interview students at the age and grade levels you will teach, using one of Piaget's tasks (available in most college-level educational psychology or child development texts). How do students respond to the questions or tasks? What stage do they exhibit? How might this impact the way you teach them?

2. Conduct a similar set of interviews for students at the level you will teach, using one of Kohlberg's moral dilemmas. How do students respond to the questions? What stage do they exhibit? How might they respond to different approaches to classroom management or discipline as a result?

3. Observe children on the playground or in the school cafeteria. Describe their interactions with peers or adults. Analyze these interactions in terms of Erikson's psychosocial stage model of personality development.

4. Summarize the major changes brought about by cognitive and psychosocial development during early childhood and elementary school. Construct profiles of students at different levels in school.

5. Make a list of activities you could do to encourage (a) initiative in preschool children and (b) industry in elementary school children. Ask someone familiar with these ages to comment on your list.

6. Shadow a student at the grade level you will teach. What do you notice about this student in relation to cognitive, social, and emotional development?

7. Scan the newspapers for several days for stories about children at the age level you will teach. What societal pressures or challenges do they depict that might endanger their social and emotional development? Are these similar to the challenges you faced at that age?

8. Consult one of the Web sites listed below for additional information about students' cognitive, social, or emotional development.

9. Look at the table of contents of a text at the level you will teach. At what cognitive level must students in your classes be in order to be able to learn this material as presented? What can you do to make the concepts more concrete for students?

10. Ask teachers at the level at which you plan to teach about the range of developmental levels in their classes. How do they deal with the diversity?

11. Watch several popular children's TV shows or videos. How has the structure been designed to appeal to young children, based on cognitive, social, or emotional development?

12. Observe a lesson in which writing or pre-writing skills are being taught. Compare the stages of the lesson to the levels listed in the psychomotor domain.

PRACTICE QUESTIONS

1. John Anderson has just accepted a position as a second grade teacher in a large suburban school district. As a member of a grade level team, he will be responsible for developing the math activities for the entire second grade team. From a cognitive developmental per-spective, when Mr. Anderson is planning these activities he should incorporate:

   A. opportunities for students to interact with their peers during math.
   B. hands-on activities using concrete materi-als/manipulatives.
   C. competitive games to increase interest level.
   D. packets of worksheets for each math skill taught.

2. Sally is in the stage Erikson calls "initiative versus guilt." Her parents supervise her closely and direct all of her activities. The danger is that Sally may:

   A. develop an exaggerated sense of her own abilities.
   B. eventually grow to mistrust her parents.
   C. have difficulty trusting her own judgment.
   D. not learn that some things should never be done.

3. Curriculum coordinators in the Walton ISD have designed a curriculum to be used by teachers in their classes to enhance children's decision-making capabilities. For one of the activities, they include "Heinz's Dilemma," a story about a man who couldn't get the money to pay a druggist's exorbitant prices for a drug that would cure his dying wife and who subsequently stole the drug in order to save her life. Children are asked to discuss whether Heinz was right in what he did. Which of the following responses might teachers expect from a typical elementary school student?

   A. "I think what Heinz did wasn't so bad because his wife is more important to him than the druggist's money. But if he gets caught, he could go to prison. I would do it so no one would ever know it was me."
   B. "Although I have a hard time blaming Heinz for wanting to save his wife, he has to think about what others would say about stealing—I mean, think how embar-rassed he would be in church and all that."
   C. "Heinz was right in what he did in this particular situation because he had exhausted all other alternatives, and she would have died if he hadn't. Sometimes the laws don't fit certain situations."
   D. "Nothing justifies breaking the law. What if everyone did that? Our society would be a mess!"

4. Six-year-old Nathan is shown two balls of Play-Doh® that he identifies as equal in quan-tity. One of the balls is then rolled into a cylin-der shape. Nathan is asked to point to the shape that has more Play-Doh®. A typical response from Nathan at this level might be to indicate the cylinder shape as containing more Play-Doh®. What would be the best response by the teacher to Nathan?

   A. Repeat the process, pointing out that the shape has changed but because no Play-Doh® was added or taken away, the amount of Play-Doh® is the same.
   B. Ignore his answer and just let him play with the Play-Doh® until he loses interest.
   C. Tell him he's incorrect, give him the right answer, and have him repeat it back to you.

D. Repeat the process, but have Nathan make animal shapes with the Play-Doh® this time, to get his attention and make it meaningful.

Answers and Discussion

Answer 1: Students at the lower elementary level are most likely in the concrete operational stage of cognitive development. For this reason, Mr. Anderson would want to provide concrete experiences for students to facilitate their understanding of abstract math principles. Teachers may want to incorporate the use of groups or provide practice in basic skills for other reasons, but from the standpoint of cognitive development, the answer is B.

Answer 2: Applying Erikson's guidelines for psychosocial development, we know that if children are not allowed to do things on their own, a sense of guilt may develop; they may come to believe that what they want to do is always wrong. Adults must provide supervision without interference. The answer is C.

Answer 3: Most elementary age children are at a preconventional stage of moral reasoning characterized by concern over the consequences that breaking a law will have for them (Answer A). Answers B and D reflect conventional morality based on pleasing authority figures and maintaining a law-and-order stance. Answer C is characteristic of postconventional morality. As an aside, these types of scenarios are good ways of discovering children's stages of moral development but can be confusing to young children in discussion, because there is no concrete answer that they can grasp. The answer is A.

Answer 4: Preoperational children (2 to 7 year olds) lack the concept of conservation, the understanding that some properties of an object or substance remain the same even when its appearance is altered in some superficial way. Therefore a child in this stage will likely indicate that the cylinder shape contains more Play-Doh® because it now looks bigger. In this scenario, the student is making the transition from preoperational thought into concrete operational. The teacher is helping the student develop the concept of conservation by explaining to the student that unless something is added or removed, the quantity of an object stays the same. The answer is A.

WEB LINKS

Remember that Web site locations may change. If any of these sites have moved or cannot be located, use terms in the index to search for further information.

http://ericps.ed.uiuc.edu/eece/ed2link.html

Development in the early childhood and elementary grades

http://snycorva.cortland.edu/~ANDERSMD/ERIK/sum.HTML

Erikson's psychosocial theory of development

http://www.ed.gov/pubs/schoolinvolvement/issues.html

Key issues for professional development in early childhood education

http://www.piaget.org/

Jean Piaget Society home page

http://www.piaget.org/biography/biog.html

Piaget's biography

http://teach.fhu.edu/technology/psy306/kohlberg.html

Kohlberg's theory of moral development with classroom dilemmas and applications

http://mathforum.org/mathed/vygotsky.html

Put in a site search for Vygotsky.

www.vanderbilt.edu/kennedy

Research in human development

REFERENCES

Athey, C. (1990). *Extending young thought in young children: A parent-teacher relationship.* London: Paul Chapman Publishing Ltd.

Berk, L. (2000). *Child development* (5th ed.). Boston: Allyn & Bacon.

Case, R. (1985). *Intellectual development: Birth to adulthood.* New York: Academic Press.

Chi, M., & Koeske, R. (1983). Network representation of a child's dinosaur knowledge. *Developmental Psychology, 19,* 29–39.

Cruickshank, D., Bainer, D., & Metcalf, K. (1999). *The act of teaching* (2d ed.). Boston: McGraw-Hill.

Erikson, E. (1963). *Childhood and society.* New York: Norton.

Erikson, E. (1968). *Identity, youth and crisis.* New York: Norton.

Friedman, J. (1996). *The effects of drugs on the fetus and nursing infant: A handbook for healthcare professionals.* Baltimore: Johns Hopkins University Press.

Gagne, E., Yekovich, C., & Yekovich, F. (1993). *The cognitive psychology of school learning.* New York: Harper-Collins.

Getchell, N., & Roberton, M. A. (1989). Whole body stiffness as a function of developmental level in children's hopping. *Developmental Psychology, 25,* 920–928.

Gilligan, C. (1982). *In a different voice: Psychological theory and women's development.* Cambridge, MA: Harvard University Press.

Hallahan, D., & Kauffman, J. (2000). *Exceptional learners: Introduction to special education.* 8th ed. Boston: Allyn & Bacon.

Maslow, A. (1970). *Motivation and personality* (2nd ed.). New York: Harper and Row.

Piaget, J. (1963). *Origins of intelligence in children.* New York: Norton.

Piaget, J. (1965). *The moral judgment of the child.* New York: Free Press.

Piaget, J. (1970). *The science of education and the psychology of the child.* New York: Orion.

Piaget, J. (1985). *The equilibrium of cognitive structures: The central problem of educational development.* Chicago: University of Chicago.

Rogoff, B. (1990). *Apprenticeship in thinking.* New York: Oxford University Press.

Santrock, J. (2001). *Educational psychology.* Boston: McGraw-Hill.

Selman, R. (1980). *The growth of interpersonal understanding: Developmental and clinical analyses.* New York: Academic Press.

Siegler, R. (1991). *Children's thinking.* Englewood Cliffs, NJ: Prentice-Hall.

Simpson, E. (1972). *The classification of educational objectives: Psychomotor domain.* Urbana: University of Illinois Press.

Vygotsky, L. (1978). *Mind in society: The development of higher mental processes.* Cambridge, MA: Harvard University Press.

Vygotsky, L. (1986). *Thought and language.* Cambridge, MA: MIT Press.

Competency 2

The teacher understands student diversity and knows how to plan learning experiences and design assessments that are responsive to differences among students and that promote all students' learning.

The beginning teacher:

- Demonstrates knowledge of students with diverse personal and social characteristics (e.g., those related to ethnicity, gender, language background, exceptionality) and the significance of student diversity for teaching, learning, and assessment.

- Accepts and respects students with diverse backgrounds and needs.

- Knows how to use diversity in the classroom and the community to enrich all students' learning experiences.

- Knows strategies for enhancing one's own understanding of students' diverse backgrounds and needs.

- Knows how to plan and adapt lessons to address students' varied backgrounds, skills, interests, and learning needs, including the needs of English language learners and students with disabilities.

- Understands cultural and socioeconomic differences (including differential access to technology) and knows how to plan instruction that is responsive to cultural and socioeconomic differences among students.

- Understands the instructional significance of varied student learning needs and preferences.

Chapter 2

COMPETENCY 2

Appreciating Human Diversity

EILEEN R. WESTERMAN
University of Houston
JANICE L. NATH
University of Houston—Downtown
MYRNA D. COHEN
University of Houston—Downtown
EMILLIANO GONZALEZ
University of St. Thomas
GENA JERKINS
University of Houston

TERMS TO KNOW

Ability group
Acculturation
Assimilation
Bidialectism
Bilingual
Biracial/multiracial
Cultural deprivation
Cultural pluralism
Culturally relevant teaching
Culture
Differently-abled
Discrimination

Empowerment
English as a Second Language
  (ESL)
Ethnicity
Ethnocentric behavior
Exceptionality
Gender
Hidden curriculum
Human/student diversity
Inclusion
Macro culture
Melting pot

Micro culture
Minority
Monocultural
Multicultural
Physically challenged
Prejudice
Race
Salad bowl
Social class/status (SES)
Stereotyping

As we prepare education students to become teachers, it is necessary to understand the significance of social directions created by an increasingly diverse Texas population. More than ever before, professionals must understand the effects of diversity on early childhood practices and adapt their curriculum and teaching behaviors to new socialization patterns. Diversity requires that early childhood professionals gain respect for various cultures of children and their families and teach in an atmosphere that creates mutual respect for all (de Melendez & Ostertag, 1997).

Interestingly, many of the things that represent distinction and a sense of uniqueness for various cultures are often the same components that form a common strand or "meeting porch" where *all* groups can emphasize that which is common. Art, literature, foods, fads, styles, music, special holidays, traditions, and rituals provide a wealth of information that foster greater understanding of those who are different, and they also remind us that all humans have the same needs and wants.

Teachers of young children who are sensitive to areas of **human/student diversity** (areas of distinction for identifying various groups) can be instrumental in facilitating classrooms where pluralistic student groups can learn from one another. Such a teacher recognizes the strengths that diversity can bring to a classroom and emphasizes mutual respect for all, regardless of ethnicity, race, age, gender, religion, social class, disability, and other distinguishing categories. Professionals who work with young children and their families must ensure that no cultural biases creep into classrooms. This can easily occur when teachers view their own cultural group as setting the standard against which other groups are to be measured. When this happens, teachers are guilty of exhibiting **ethnocentric behavior,** wherein they view their own cultural group's characteristics as cor-

rect or superior and the ways of other groups as odd or inferior. Teachers should model a sincere appreciation for different cultures and sensitivity to social problems and injustices created by prejudices. Teachers should engage in finding solutions with regard to differences rather than shifting blame. Although the responsibility of being such a teacher may seem immense, the consequences of not being one could create discriminated student groups with a cost that may be detrimental to all involved. **Discrimination** in teaching is the use of negative responses or the absence of positive responses that can deny success for certain groups of students.

The question in a teacher's mind may be, "So, how do I accomplish this?" This chapter provides insightful, thought-provoking, and challenging discourse for teachers. Perhaps many of the ideas presented will stimulate teachers to examine their present mindset. This may cause some discomfort, yet perhaps if teachers allow it to happen, they may be forced to challenge some personal beliefs and grow. This self-challenge may help a teacher realize the richness that all children and their families bring to the classroom. It may also help students grow into people who continue to help create a good and just society in which all have equal opportunities.

DEMOGRAPHIC DYNAMICS

In any given classroom, educators across this country must interact with diverse student groups. Schools consisting of one type of student group are becoming increasingly rare. The United States is expected to become a nation with no racial or ethnic majority during the twenty-first century (Riche, 1991). Today the population of children below the age of 6 years is becoming increasingly diverse (Clark, 1995). Interestingly, in 1988, 3.2 million students attended Texas public schools, with the majority of students falling into the category of Anglo. However, within 10 years, the numbers of students in Texas public schools increased to 3.9 million, with more than half of this number consisting of students from minority groups. In Texas, **minority** typically refers to any ethnic group (Hispanic, African American, Native American, Asian, and so forth) other than Anglo, even though in some areas of our state Anglos are already the minority population. Historically, *minority* has referred to those groups who have been disenfranchised. Sharp increases in growth within "minority" student groups and the relatively small growth within the Anglo group present Texas with a host of cities and counties, and thus school systems, that consist of diverse student groups. This equates to major ethnic diversity in most Texas classrooms. Children notice differences of race and gender by at least age 3, and by age 4 or 5 they are already engaging in behaviors that isolate children whom they perceive as different. Texas wants all children in its classrooms to have a sense of belonging, so early childhood is a time for helping children learn about and appreciate others who are different.

According to the TEA Academic Excellence Indicator System for the 2000–2001 school year, there were 4 million students attending Texas schools. This population was made up of 14.4 percent African American, 40.6 percent Hispanic, 42 percent White, 2.7 percent Asian, and 0.3 percent Native American. In contrast to this diverse student population, the teacher population continues to have a preponderance of Anglo females. The Texas teacher population of 274,816 is made up of 8.8 percent African American, 17.1 percent Hispanic, 73.2 percent White, 0.6 percent Asian, and 0.3 percent Native American. The changing demographics of Texas students is a trend that is predicted to continue for years to come.

Statistics show that we must also pay attention to differences in **SES** (socioeconomic status). Children raised in poverty-stricken neighborhoods will come to school with very different life experiences from those in middle-class areas, no matter what their ethnicity. Statistics show that many Texas children live in poverty and that most of them are minority populations as well.

Educators must conscientiously help *all* students pursue their own dreams by empowering them to transcend social and economic barriers to become productive and successful citizens. Very young children recognize differences and perceive that color, language, gender, dialect, and physical ability differences are connected to privilege and power. Teachers must not underestimate the ability of children to comprehend what they see and hear. Young children can be taught antibias identity and attitude. (Richey & Wheeler, 2000).

Becoming a teacher in Texas requires an embracing and a celebration of human diversity rather than only an acceptance of differences. This is not taken lightly in certification testing and in Texas schools. At times there is a resistance to the idea of accepting multiculturalism due to the misunderstanding or myth that diversity is synonymous to division. The fear of this concept is also heightened by the belief that multiculturalism negates those traditions and values that mainstream Americans hold dear. An accurate perception of multiculturalism, however, is based on the understanding that in order to create a bond that extends beyond surface tolerance, the positive contributions of diverse groups must be viewed as an enriching and valuable addition to American culture rather than a subtraction.

INTEGRATING MULTICULTURALISM IN THE SCHOOL COMMUNITY

Teacher Roles

Learning about culture and cultural diversity at the early childhood level is an important step in developing a sense of pride and awareness about one's culture and an acceptance of others. It is also the first step toward a child's realization of the existence of diversity (de Melendez & Ostertag, 1997). According to a statement presented jointly in 1991 by the National Association for the Education of Young Children (NAEYC) and the National Association of Early Childhood Specialists in State Departments of Education (NAECS/SDE), multiculturalism should be embedded in every program for young children.

Empowerment is a student's personal belief that the factors that make up his or her identity (including language, culture, and other factors) are vital contributions to society. Society, in general, sends strong messages to children, who, when given certain expectations over a long period of time, can assimilate those expectations into self-fulfilling prophecies. Recently a preservice teacher asked a young minority student where he was thinking of going to college. His answer was, "Hispanics don't belong in college, Mister." It is distressing when a child limits his or her options based on ethnicity alone.

To provide students with empowerment, a teacher must examine the role that she or he has in personally shaping ways that students perceive their worth and the messages conveyed through student-teacher interactions (Cummins, 1989). A teacher's self-examination of his or her roles and influence can provide insight into messages that teachers send to children, messages that serve to perpetuate failure or encourage images of success in the minds of students. A teacher should be equally careful of telling children in so many words that they need to be doctors or lawyers or be in a high income bracket to be successful. This type of statement tells them that anyone who is not financially prosperous (including, perhaps, the students' own families) is somehow lacking. Yet teachers should encourage children to understand that each one has the power to open doors to success in many areas, and that pride and success come from doing one's very best work and going as far as one can and wants to go. For empowerment to become a reality in the classroom, the early childhood teacher, who has made a commitment to teach in a multicultural way, must verify developmentally appropriate practices, analyze the curriculum, and take an inventory of the classroom environment to see that all children can open many doors.

Although simple in description, examining oneself is often difficult, as many teachers come from middle-class backgrounds and operate with the cultural knowledge of that class—the same knowledge that is essential for functioning successfully in the school system and in business society. **Social class or social status** refers to one's economic status. Teachers in Texas rarely come from extreme poverty. Most teachers are of the middle class and implicitly recognize "rules" that generate success in mainstream society, including most schools and greater America. For example, this knowledge provides "the ticket" into a good interview for a scholarship because one understands that dressier, business-type clothes, rather than casual dress or fad clothing, are appropriate for corporate interviews. In the context of schools, this knowledge allows teachers and students from certain backgrounds to understand the dynamics of appropriate language or discourse to solve a problem, of appropriate attire, and so forth. Such information is often so common for a group that it is taken for granted. A teacher may never recognize that some students are even unaware of proper school language (e.g., saying "please," "excuse me," and "thank you," or even refraining from using street terms or vulgarities). Too often a teacher does not allow the child to shine through before labeling the culture from which he or she comes as "less than" that of the teacher's. A teacher who is sensitive to cultural differences recognizes that these actions and beliefs can also be associated with ethnic and cultural norms with academic levels, gender, religion, and other differences. It is important to recognize that what may be common knowledge and behavior for some children may be unknown to others.

In light of these differences in background cultural knowledge, teachers must take the time to explain desired or appropriate behaviors for specific situations, procedures for performing those desired behaviors, and consequences and/or benefits for doing so. For example, a teacher of young children may have students practice the correct way to get someone's attention when that person is already conversing with someone else. The teacher might have two students engage in a mock conversation; then the teacher can walk up to them and politely wait for a moment within eyesight until being noticed and acknowledged. Modeling, many social skills in the classroom will help students operate not only in their neighborhood with its culture, should it be different, but also in business situations as they begin to grow and venture out into the world.

To understand this concept better, teachers should think in terms of their own comfort level in various cultures. For example, one would, perhaps, like to feel comfortable walking into a five-star French restaurant in Paris, ordering a meal (and knowing what is actually going to be served), using the correct utensils, and enjoying the ambiance. Many of us, however, would not be entirely comfortable doing that unless, for example, a kindly waiter took the time to carefully explain the menu to us, offered suggestions, and cued us about which utensil to use as the food arrived. Children who come from different cultures with different sets of behaviors may in certain circumstances feel very much the same in our classrooms. Think again of the restaurant and how an arrogant waiter might make us feel about our experience—perhaps as if we didn't really belong there, that we were inferior to his other customers, and so forth. In addition, even though an adult might be excited to be able to operate well in another culture without a faux pas, most would want to come back home and casually enjoy a favorite home-cooked meal with parents and friends (knowing that one wouldn't dare set the table with four forks in that particular setting). We also would never want family and friends to believe we were too good to eat with them in a home-style manner. It would be ideal to be able to operate in both cultures, without being forced to leave one behind and/or without seeing one as better or more valuable than the other—just different.

Although certain behaviors are definitely more appropriate for certain settings and/or spe-

cific times, the teacher must not use this fact as an opportunity to emphasize assimilation but instead should provide opportunities for acculturation. **Assimilation** refers to taking on the ways of the dominant culture at the expense of losing the ways of native culture and language. In contrast, **acculturation** is the successful application of new knowledge from another culture while maintaining one's own native culture and language (Nieto, 1996; Ovando & Collier, 1998). Bicultural or **multicultural** means to be able to operate in more than one culture comfortably and successfully.

In fact, **culturally relevant teaching** (CRT) theory underscores teacher practices grounded in the understanding of culture and experiences that shape students' ways of knowing the world (Ladson-Billings, 1992a, 1992b, 1992c, 1995; Lipman, 1995). **Culture** is simply a way of life, or it can be thought of as the habits, attitudes, and values of a group of people. This group can be either large **(macro culture)** or small **(micro culture),** and people can be a part of a macro culture and a micro culture at the same time. This concept should not be confused with **ethnicity** (a shared national heritage) or **race** (the association of skin color with a person's identity). The term "ethnicity" has generally replaced "race" (which was originally used to describe physical characteristics of a group of people such as Mongoloid, Caucasoid, and so forth). Many Texas students may be classified as **biracial** or **multiracial,** children whose ancestors are from two or more different racial groups.

Culture can change, based on a person's way of life at a specific time or place; ethnicity is stable. A person may also coexist in numerous cultures simultaneously. For example, at this moment you may be a part of a student culture, you are also a part of the culture of women or men, and you are a part of a seeing and literate culture. You may belong to the culture of a certain religion or be a part of the culture of a particular sports group. After you pass the certification test, you will join the culture of certified educators. Yet, your ethnicity in the first cultures will be the same ethnicity that you bring to your later cultures or way of life. Each of these groups has accepted learned behaviors, or norms, that define us as a part of that particular culture. The successful norms one exhibits as part of a religious culture may differ greatly from the norms of a sports culture.

A teacher who has a clear understanding of these two concepts—culture and ethnicity—is less likely to fall into the trap of stereotyping in the classroom. Such a teacher clearly understands that children share common physical attributes such as skin color, but that does not mean that they also share common ways of life (culture). Within each culture there are many patterns, yet each child truly is an individual. **Stereotyping** is the assumption that certain beliefs based on skin color or other forms of physical, religious, or other cultural identifiers are true for all people of that type. For example, teachers must recognize that two African-American students, while sharing a similar skin color, may have two totally different cultural experiences. One child's family may come from the Bahamas with its British-based culture, while another comes from an urban neighborhood in a large American city. Socioeconomic class may, in fact, make more of a difference than ethnicity. Two girls, one Hispanic and one Anglo, from the same community or social class or status may feel more connected culturally due to their similar status in a middle-class neighborhood (where both girls participate in weekend sports activities, dance and piano lessons, and shop at the same mall). Also, although many Asian groups have similar physical features, families of Chinese descent, for example, have cultures or ways of life that are very distinct from those of Japanese, Vietnamese, Korean, Thai, and other Asian descendents. (As a side note, the term "oriental" does not refer to a culture of people but is an adjective associated with artifacts such as rugs, pottery, and jewelry.)

Through the use of culturally relevant teaching theory, a teacher not only demonstrates within the classroom an appreciation for the diversity of children's cultures but also centers teaching and learning around his or her students and the diversity they bring into the environment. For example, a teacher who has students who are recent arrivals from another country (or even another region or state) may want to include the heritage, customs, beliefs, favorite pastimes, practices, and other interesting concepts that provide opportunity to value the new students while facilitating relationships between them and the rest of the class. It behooves teachers to find out about the children they teach, and they can do so easily. International business and travel books contain information on both acceptable and unacceptable or rude behaviors for almost any country in the world. The Internet also provides this type of information.

Other practices based on culturally relevant teaching (Brewer, 2001; Derman-Sparks & the A.B.C. Task Force, 1989; Ladson-Billings, 1992a, 1992b, 1992c, 1995) that may be beneficial for the classroom include the following:

- The inclusion of numerous opportunities for all students to experience academic success in areas of literacy, numeracy, technology, social and political arenas, arts and music, and other areas. This is important for developing active, lifelong learners.

- The inclusion of opportunities for students to develop and maintain their cultural heritage through vehicles such as music, poetry, community artists, role models, family traditions, home language, and other areas that depict the diversity within the classroom. Teachers should learn and use children's names, even though the pronunciation may be strange or difficult.

- The careful examination of teaching materials and methods for ethnic and gender bias and stereotyping. For example, are different genders and ethnicities equally represented in pictures and information, and are all treated with respect? Are various types of people represented in wall posters and decorations in the classroom? Do available stories and books feature stereotypical sex roles (only about boys' adventures while girls look on, and so forth)? Are these materials about one ethnicity? Do any of the books in a center have derogatory remarks about genders or ethnicities or make fun in some way? Are crayons, Play-Doh®, construction paper, and so on available with multiple skin tones? Are dolls of various skin tones and facial features in the play centers? Are differently-abled dolls (which can be specially purchased) available? Are there dolls that can represent various types of families and family members, including grandparents, for example? Does the curriculum include music and games of various cultures?

- The inclusion of discussions that foster and develop a critical consciousness through which students challenge the status quo of the current social order with issues such as stereotyping, inequalities, social problems, and prejudices. **Prejudices** are the mindset and resulting action that consistently thrust negative responses on a particular person or identified group of people.

- The inclusion of multicultural educational experiences into the learning environment, even if only one ethnic group is represented within a given classroom. Although a particular classroom may be **monocultural** (ethnically the same), larger society is not. It is probable that students, outside the classroom, will have the opportunity to work and interact with people of many ethnicities and backgrounds. Teachers should recognize and utilize instructional modes that create and foster an environment in which differences are respected, valued, and enhanced through optimal teaching and learning exchanges.

- The focus on similarities among people through their differences. "Everyone laughs, cries, eats, works, and plays because we are all human beings, *and* people do all these activities in different ways" (Derman-Sparks & the A.B.C. Task Force, 1989, p. 58).

- The inclusion of the developmental approach on which current social studies

teaching is based: Learn about that which is closest to children first (themselves and their families and other children in the class and their families) before branching out into the larger community.

Because the definition of culture, or a way of life, incorporates more than ethnicity, teachers must also expand their scope regarding the different categories that make up diversity within their classroom. This results in different needs and mandated practices. Several factors that may influence a child's culture, or way of life, include ethnicity, gender, language background, religion, physical challenges, and exceptionalities. Each factor will be discussed as the chapter continues.

Ethnicity is a significant area of diversity within many school environments. Even with good intentions or positive beliefs associated with a particular ethnicity, teachers must safeguard the well-being of children. For example, Asian students are generally perceived as high achievers, particularly in areas of math and science. By stereotyping these students with a blanket of positive attributes, teachers often miss the opportunity to help those Asian students who do not excel.

Gender Differences

Gender, the distinction between male and female, creates another area of concern as it relates to multiculturalism. By age 4, preschoolers are strongly influenced by societal norms for gender behavior and accept that girls and boys are supposed to act differently and do different things. Theory suggests that, despite some biological differences, differential treatment by parents, teachers and society as a whole creates more differences. Many of these are positive, yet others eventually work in concert to "shut doors" for some girls *and* boys. How can teachers create classrooms that open doors for both genders? One of the requirements for effective teaching is to encourage play choices in classroom centers. For example, boys should play in the housekeeping center, and girls need opportunities to build with blocks, and so forth. As models, teachers should make sure they also go to each center, despite their own gender.

Teachers must also be careful to avoid actions based on stereotypical assumptions of females and males. For example, it is a common belief that boys are better or more apt to succeed in areas of mathematics and science. Research indicates that teachers are more likely to challenge their male students with higher-level questions than their female students. Teachers also offer more detailed and constructive criticisms to males. Studies emphasize the tendency of both male and female teachers to attribute more attention to male students. Teachers often allow boys to shout out answers while reprimanding girls for this action. Without realizing it, teachers often compliment girls for their appearance while praising boys for academic accomplishments (Sadker & Sadker, 1994). The subliminal message is that the academic success of female students is not valued or emphasized. It is increasingly important for teachers to generate environments whereby all students, regardless of gender, experience success in all areas of academia. With a changing society, both male and female students need opportunities to participate actively in mathematics, science, technology, and other areas that generate financial success and independence for participants.

Different Language Backgrounds

Language background presents a distinct area of concern, especially within many of the southern regions of Texas. Students who are ESL **(English as a Second Language)** speakers are unfamiliar with the English language but fluent in another. ESL speakers sometimes experience discrimination because they are viewed as problematic by unprepared classroom teachers. Teachers sometimes erroneously equate English language proficiency with intelligence and come to invalid judgments about the abilities of their ESL students. In fact, many times teachers are even responsible for "silencing" ESL students. For example, a teacher may assign a problem-solving task to be completed in a cooperative group. As

he or she walks around the room and monitors the students, the teacher may notice that a particular group is working together but speaking in a language other than English. The teacher, not understanding this language, may command that the students speak only in English. This may also happen with children speaking in heavy dialects, and it may cause such students to assume that the use of their birth language is unacceptable. This conclusion also may be transferred to other areas associated with students' culture. More often than not, these children begin to withdraw from participating or speaking in the learning environment. It must be noted that it can be totally appropriate for the non–English speaking group to attempt to solve problems in their own language. A university student may experience this type of phenomenon in a college classroom as a professor attempts to explain a lesson in a technical language. After leaving the classroom in confusion, the student can experience clarity and understanding by speaking with a peer in "casual terms" that are familiar or common among his or her group. The prevention of such peer discussion at their level would hinder the student's understanding.

If there is a lack of communication, it may become easy for teachers to fault students or react toward them with frustration. Such practices serve only to hinder the positive involvement of these students in the learning environment. An alternative practice for the teacher could be to utilize the unique knowledge and experiences of the ESL or bilingual students within the classroom. For children with strong dialects (for example, those found in some African-American children), the teacher can encourage **bidialectism,** in which children are encouraged to keep and value their home and neighborhood dialects but learn that "newscaster" English is a successful norm for business situations and school. This simple action serves to reinforce the value of embracing the diversity of all students within the classroom and school environment. Teachers should also be familiar with **bilingual** programs in their schools and districts. Bilingual classrooms provide instruction in students' native language *and* in English. ESL programs provide placements in a regular classroom with "pull out" reinforcement in English. Instruction is all in English because students who speak many languages may be in one classroom.

The classroom teacher can help ESL children who are mainstreamed into the class by employing several techniques that, while imperative for the success of ESL students, may be beneficial for all other children in the class as well. One consideration is for the teacher to include as many contextual (nonlinguistic) clues as possible. For example, while talking about the Northern and Southern Hemispheres in social studies class, the words alone may not be comprehensible to an ESL child. An oral explanation about the hemispheres may leave an ESL student completely confused. However, if the teacher uses a broad gesture to encircle the location of each hemisphere on a globe or map while explaining about each, the ESL child has an additional contextual clue to help him or her figure out the meanings of the words. While discussing the bitter cold climate of northern Canada, the teacher can add to the meaning of "bitter cold" by exhibiting shivering and chattering teeth. These simple types of nonverbal clues provide contextual clues to words that may be incomprehensible by themselves to children learning English as a second language. The repetition of language reinforces vocabulary and concepts for all children, especially those designated as ESL students. Songs sung routinely, skits or plays that are rehearsed, or games in which lines are constantly repeated (for example, in the game "Go Fish," each time one's turn comes, the words, "Do you have any . . . ?" are repeated). These are all natural ways to add the repetition of language into the classroom. Singing songs when performing routine procedures such as, "This is the way we all line up . . ." is another popular example. Games such as "Simon Says" provide both repetition and physical contextual clues. Obtaining concrete items and pictures with which to teach should be a priority, and "labeling" the classroom for emerging readers increases literacy skills for all children—particularly those who are ESL.

A safe, nurturing classroom environment is important for all children, but it is crucial for ESL students, who are often experiencing the discomfort of culture shock. Those who feel culturally different from others in the class need to feel emotionally safe in order to take the risk of expressing themselves in a new language. Every effort needs to be made to make ESL children feel welcome and accepted. Having books with the home language available can encourage literacy and add familiarity. Having a "buddy" translator for ESL children, when possible, is effective because in addition to language support, it may help foster friendships and a feeling of belonging. Teachers can also set up centers with two or more children, where the task involves play and discussion (phone center, store center, and so forth) to encourage the development of friendships between first- and second-language learners. Technology is proving to be an excellent tool for teachers with ESL students.

Differently-Abled Learners

Exceptionalities are another component of multiculturalism. Many classrooms today have children with special educational needs. Children may have hearing impairments, visual impairments, emotional disabilities, and so forth. It is necessary to remember that today's trend is toward the most **inclusion** possible, an approach in which children with exceptionalities are placed in education settings with children without exceptionalities and receive services alongside them (Richey & Wheeler, 2000). Thus, by law, special needs children must be placed in the least restrictive environment. More is discussed in Competency 13, Chapter 19 on the specific laws regarding children who are designated with special needs.

Although children may be challenged in some manner, because of the actions that they *are* able to perform, a new terminology is evolving: **differently-abled.** Emphasizing the things that these children *can* accomplish recognizes that they are not handicapped but, in fact, are able to accomplish tasks in a different way.

Children who are **physically challenged** are those who possess some type of bodily condition that prevents them from performing certain actions such as moving, speaking, hearing, and seeing. Young children are often curious and ask questions about children whose bodies are different from theirs. A teacher should answer these questions rather matter-of-factly for young children rather than discourage curiosity. For example, when Tron asks, "Why does Megan wear that thing on her leg?" the teacher replies, "That is a brace that helps Megan keep her balance better. She can walk much better with it on.""But why?" Tron may continue. "When Megan was born, her right leg was a little shorter instead of both being the exact same length."

Young children may also want to touch something that is different, which should be encouraged if the special needs child agrees. Being able to touch takes much of the fear and curiosity away for young children. However, teachers must teach young children not to touch expensive specialized equipment that could endanger children with special needs, should it be broken or settings be changed. Teachers must also support kindness to children with visible differences by telling students that it is acceptable and good to notice differences and to want to know about them, but it is never acceptable to make hurtful remarks or exclude the child. The classroom teacher's job is to ensure safety and mobility for any children with special needs, so the teacher must be responsible for the classroom setting, materials placement, and so forth. However, the teacher should also encourage problem solving to help the class determine ways that children with special needs can be included somehow in all activities in which a class engages. Rather than solving a dilemma, the teacher can have children come up with solutions. On a day when there was a fire drill, for example, a child with a hearing impairment had not heard the bell and was alarmed when everyone jumped up. In a problem-solving conversation, the teacher reviewed the situation and asked children what they should do next time (Derman-Sparks & the A.B.C. Task Force, 1989). In another example,

several children were playing kickball as Kevin watched in his wheelchair. The teacher noticed and asked the children to consider how Kevin could be included. "Well, he can't kick," one boy remarked. "Yes," said the teacher, "so how could we modify that part so Kevin can play?" "He could be allowed to throw," said Michael, "and maybe because he can't go fast in this chair, we could count, like one-thousand-one, one-thousand-two, before we throw the ball." "Those are good ideas! Let's see, Kevin, what do you think?"

Continuing Derman-Sparks's (1989) recommendations, a teacher may obtain equipment such as a wheelchair and have students use it to determine how to better arrange the classroom so that a child in a wheelchair in their class can navigate better. A teacher can also help with inclusion by centering on what all children in a class have in common and setting up situations in which the strengths of a child with special needs are at an advantage.

Exceptional children may be those who have mental differences that either far exceed or fall short when compared to the typical mental or intellectual capacities of other children in their general age range. Gifted and talented students, autistic students, and students with academic disabilities are all part of this category. These students are often mainstreamed into regular classrooms and participate in some or all subject areas. Teachers who have specialized training in working with exceptional students help regular classroom teachers best serve these children in mainstreamed classrooms. Creating a team with special education teachers can create success for exceptional children.

A teacher who promotes a community of acceptance of diversity by his or her actions encourages students to interact with others who are culturally different. Remember that the teacher serves as the most important model in the classroom because he or she is the authority figure of the group. Students conclude that a teacher's modeled behavior is what is acceptable. A culturally sensitive teacher must be willing to put forth the extra effort needed to accommodate the needs of exceptional students. Young children receive cues from the teacher's behavior and use those to guide theirs. If a teacher "isolates" a child, so will the class. If a teacher shows frustration, so will the class. Improving the social acceptance of those who are differently-abled is a critical task of inclusion and is best accomplished by teacher modeling. Using group activities has been shown to be effective with special needs children as well as providing "buddy systems" and peer tutoring. Special education teachers may be key elements in helping an entire class understand and accept differently-abled children. Regular classroom teachers should work in close contact with them and use them as resources. Numerous other resources such as specialized materials and supplies, equipment, and trained support aides are available to assist children who are differently abled. Teachers must be willing to seek out the resources necessary to benefit these students.

FACILITATING POSTIVE CLASSROOM ENVIRONMENTS BY RECOGNIZING CULTURAL DIFFERENCES

Teachers are responsible for the creation of a multicultural environment in which all learners feel safe and secure. Teachers should consider the ideas listed below:

- Ignoring cultural differences can inhibit student learning and achievement; bias may result from a teacher's ignorance. Reacting to a child's cultural difference (of which a teacher may not even be aware) may cause that teacher to treat a student in a very different manner from a child of the teacher's cultural group. Teachers who reflect carefully on their beliefs, feelings, and actions may treat children more fairly.

- Be aware of the **"hidden curriculum"** (that is, what students learned that a teacher didn't explicitly teach) with regard to cultural differences. Perhaps the teacher doesn't ask higher-level questions of certain students, so children internalize that those types of students must not be smart enough to handle them. The teacher may be a bit afraid of or doesn't like being near certain students, so these children are always seated at the back of the room where the teacher doesn't go. The teacher may not understand an accent well and is impatient for students to answer, so children never get an opportunity to talk.

- Treating every child the same way is called "color blind" bias because it denies a child the clear differences in skin color and heritage from which he or she may come. A teacher should indicate that he or she *does* see differences and that those differences are to be valued, not ignored.

- In the **"salad bowl"** analogy to multiculturalism, one can easily see that, although the flavors blend nicely, each is still a separate piece. In the **"melting pot"** analogy of past decades, all dissolve into one and the individual flavors are lost.

- **Cultural deprivation** assumes that students have no culture and that is why they do poorly in school. This is not so. All children have a culture. However, their culture may be very different from white middle class culture or the cultures teachers bring to the classroom with them. Cultural deprivation sets up the idea that students are lacking—that they come to school "half empty." These boys and girls, most often seen as economically deprived, communicate very well in their own world. However, children are not going to want to learn the "standard way" of reading and talking unless they feel that what they can say is important and makes a difference. One reason, it is believed, that poor children (or minority children) do not do well in school is that they have been treated as if their background, their family, their culture, their neighborhood, their habits, and/or their way of talking are less valuable than that of others, and that they "had to be cured" before learning could take place. Ruby Payne (1995) promotes the direct teaching of hidden cues of the middle class because it opens doors for children later in life but does not force children to leave their home cultures and relationships in other ways. They are thus able to operate multiculturally.

- Be sure that **ability groups** are not used to create ethnic tracks. Ability groups are those small groups where all children are roughly at the same academic level. Too often this type of placement results in ethnic tracking.

- Acculturation to American culture, or to any culture, is a gradual process. Teachers should recognize that the families of their students may be at different places in that process. Furthermore, a child may be more acculturated than his or her family and may be confused by this discrepancy. A teacher may find that there are ethnically different families who match U.S. culture exactly and others who are very different. In addition, many subcultures exist within a "main culture." For example, Hispanic culture may include cultures from Mexico (and, within Mexico, the many Native-American tribes who live there), Central America, the Philippines, Puerto Rico, the many countries of South America (which also have European and Native-American cultures), and so forth. Not all children coming from these Hispanic families may know or care much about Cinco de Mayo (a Mexican holiday) or the many traditions attached to that celebration and observed in most Texas schools. The same could be said for Chinese New Year, although most, but not all, Asian cultures celebrate this holiday in a fairly similar manner. Furthermore, isolating one holiday to celebrate for a population only excludes a culture from feeling a part of the rest of the year. These celebrations offer exciting opportunities to examine some cultures, but inclusion should occur all year long.

- Failing to teach children to respect people who are different from themselves does not bode well for the future of our country. Many educators feel that unless we are able to positively influence the education of our poor and minority children, our ability to compete in world markets will be lost.

Recognizing Various Communication Differences

Following are some ideas that may inform teachers about cultural differences manifested in their students:

- Many Asian and Hispanic children, as a culturally learned sign of respect, do not look a teacher in the eyes even when asked. Teachers may see this as being sly or an indication of lying.

- Some African-American and Middle Eastern children may look a teacher directly in the eye for a long time without breaking eye contact. This may be seen as threatening or defiant to some teachers. Many African-American children can listen very intently without maintaining direct eye contact. Teachers who are not of these cultures may see this as not paying attention.

- In many Asian families, expressing conflict or high emotions is not appropriate. Teachers may see this lack of visible emotion in children as passive or dull. Silence can be a sign of respect in the Asian culture.

- Hispanic children may learn better in a social context (groups), while Asian and White children may learn better individually. Varying groupings throughout the day to accommodate all preferences is recommended.

- Native-American children may rarely wish to compete against one another; thus, cooperative methods are best with many of these students.

- Some Hispanic, Asian-Indian, and lower SES families have a different view of time and timeliness than middle-class White cultures. Asian families, in general, also view promptness as a sign of respect.

- Loudness of conversation and interrupting may be a part of the culture of Jewish, Asian-Indian families and in families in poverty.

- Some Asian and Hispanic families may see the teacher as a true professional; therefore the teacher and school know best, and the family will not tread upon their expertise (and may not understand the concept of home-school involvement).

- The idea of lining up is very English and American. In many other cultures throughout the world, it is every person for him- or herself, in terms of getting to the front.

- Personal space is different for many Hispanic, Greek, and Middle Eastern cultures. In these cultures, people communicate in a space that is much closer than is comfortable for most Americans. This may be seen by Americans as pushy or inappropriately intimate, while the American need for space is seen by those cultures as cool and aloof.

- Many White, middle-class teachers place great value on expression through the spoken or written word, while many African-Americans place greater value on nonverbal communication.

- Teachers are regarded as employees of the state. Students whose parents are illegal immigrants may not wish to communicate with teachers for fear that they may be discovered and reported.

- Some students of different cultures may have large families and no money to pay baby-sitters while parents attend conferences. Teachers should be prepared to have young children or babies in their classrooms during these conferences. Preparing a corner with toys for very young children can help amuse toddlers during these times.

CURRICULUM RESTRUCTURING

Teachers of young children can begin to restructure their curriculum for multiculturalism by examining the topics and units and then using the process of infusion recommended by James Banks (1992).

Steps for multicultural content infusion:

1. If you use an emerging curriculum (built around the interests of the child) or if you follow a teacher-made curriculum, go through lesson plans and find topics, or themes, to be taught. Those should be listed. If using a prescribed curriculum, you should check your guides and list all of the topics, themes, or units already there.

2. Review the profile of the classroom and look for traits that are descriptive of cultural diversity (ethnicities, religion, languages, social class, and exceptionality).

3. From the list of topics, themes, or units, circle or highlight those that lend themselves best to the infusion of diversity. Begin by incorporating the characteristics that are found in your classroom, and then consider others.

4. Brainstorm on how to incorporate diversity into the selected topics. Begin by asking what other views could help young children expand their understanding of this topic. Write down all plausible ideas.

5. Gather all of the ideas and rewrite a list of themes or units, including the additional diverse perspectives. The only way to know whether one's approach will work is to try it with children, so the next step is to implement these ideas!

6. Keep notes during the lessons on children's reactions. This will help you assess the success of this venture and offer constructive information for revisions.

There are other effective instructional techniques to use as well. As mentioned, cooperative learning has proved to work in diverse classrooms.

A number of different strategies with different goals work with younger and older elementary students. Some of these include peer tutoring (students take turns teaching each other for one-on-one help), Student Teams Achievement Division (STAD), group inquiry, and Jigsaw. The idea is to provide opportunities for students to work together on one goal with individual accountability. Competency 3, Chapter 4, delivers more information on cooperative learning. Mastery learning (children must master a small section of material at their level before they continue to the next level) also has much positive research indicating success with diverse populations, particularly for children in different achievement levels. Basically a teacher first pretests for prerequisite skills, then introduces information in a whole-class format. Children are then assigned materials at their level, which they work through at their own pace with formative feedback. Children who complete all subunits early are provided enrichment activities. At the end, all children are tested together.

To provide a well-rounded and inclusive education, teachers of every discipline should integrate multiculturalism into the areas they teach. Subject areas such as mathematics and English provide exemplary opportunities to explore diversity in problem solving and literature interpretation. Such areas emphasize the importance of alternative viewpoints, perspectives, and actions, while demonstrating that there is more than one correct approach. Gollnick and Chinn (1990) warn that multicultural education is not simply tasting ethnic food and learning ethnic dances; it is much more complex and pervasive than setting aside an hour, a unit, or a month. Derman-Sparks (1989) bemoans this as a deterioration into the tourist curriculum rather than a serious effort at understanding. A multicultural, antibiased approach should influence the whole curriculum. Multicultural concepts and activities must be included in the curriculum throughout the year. For example, often schools designate October as Hispanic Heritage month, February as Black History month, March as Women's History month, and so forth. Although these types of activities do give credence

to certain groups, as mentioned, they may also prove detrimental in perpetuating images of non-necessity or "extra" in the minds of students. Thus when students encounter such practices only once a year, they may conclude that other than at a specific time, the celebrated groups are not very important. Additionally, celebration of certain groups without the celebration of others may institute a sense of hostility or mockery among children. A more productive approach would incorporate, throughout the year, the addition of materials and instructional resources that are inclusive of all cultural groups. Early childhood educators should seize every opportunity to teach from multiple perspectives. Although every lesson does not provide the opportunity to discuss certain persons or events, many do provide the opportunity to address a topic from multiple perspectives, brainstorm for various ideas, incorporate the viewpoint of more than one person, and solve or share from different insights and life experiences.

To further restructure curriculum with regard to multicultural considerations, the different voices or multiple perspectives surrounding a given event must be allowed to enrich and enhance a lesson. For example, there are alternative views to much of history. The diversity of the perspectives helps students to develop critical thinking skills while fostering an awareness of self, social issues, and global perspectives of inequalities, injustices, power struggles, oppression, and other societal concerns (Wink, 1997).

Early childhood educators should work toward a restructuring of mindsets. One such mindset that must remain constant is the assumption that parents from different cultural groups *do* care about the well-being of their children. Of course, not *every* parent cares as much as teachers would want, but it is easy to assume that parents do not care when their responses are not what the teacher desires or contradict expectations. For example, it is easy to believe that when parents of children in poverty do not show up for parent conferences or open house events, they are not concerned with the education of their children. Likewise, it is easy to draw such a conclusion when parents of ESL or bilingual students do not respond to a note sent home or a phone call. Teachers must understand that many of these parents may have immediate needs that are different from that of the teacher and school. Teachers who are sensitive to issues of diversity, however, will consider that perhaps the parents of the children in poverty did not have transportation to the school site, or perhaps the hours that the teacher suggested for parent conferences or other school events conflicted with parents' work schedules. Parents who have basic needs for food and shelter for their families may not be able to miss work, even for what is considered an important school conference. Likewise, for the parents of ESL and bilingual students, the teacher may consider sending notes or leaving messages in the home language using an interpreter. Furthermore, many parents are intimidated by the thought of venturing upon school grounds, the territory of the teacher, to address concerns. Alternative sites for conferences and meetings (such as a local restaurant or community center) may have to be utilized to provide adequate comfort for all involved.

SUMMARY

Good teachers provide all students with equal opportunities for success. To do this we must adjust our teaching to include the cultural backgrounds of students. The further teachers move into multicultural education, the more they must know about the children in their classrooms and communities. Applying multicultural concepts in everyday classroom practices is not difficult. The best hope for a world community is for people to function well in a multicultural society, working with many other types of people **(cultural pluralism).** Using a variety of teaching methods, teachers can teach children about cultural differences and what to expect. Teachers should examine their own reactions to student differences and be sure that they are not creating bias in their classrooms. This requires treating others as they want others to treat them, their children, or their loved ones who have specific traits that define their individuality. Multiculturalism also requires giving active and constant respect and consideration for all, and dedication to achieving the best education and life for each and every student. The issues of diversity are as significant and permanent as the diverse people who create them. Key educators for the millennium recognize, accept, embrace, and celebrate this fact as they pursue ways of cultivating diversity within the domains of classrooms and schools for which they are accountable.

GLOSSARY

ability groups   a grouping in which all children in a small group are roughly the same in academic level. Too often, this type of placement results in ethnic tracking.

acculturation   the successful application of new knowledge from another culture while retaining one's own native culture and language.

assimilation   taking on ways of the dominant culture at the expense of losing ways of one's native culture and language.

bidialectism   being able to speak a home/casual and a school/business English dialect when appropriate.

bilingual   being able to speak two languages with the facility of a native speaker.

biracial/multiracial   people whose ancestors are from two or more different racial groups.

cultural deprivation   assumes that students have no culture and that is why they do poorly in school. This is not so. All children have a culture—yet it may be very different from the culture from which teachers come.

cultural pluralism   an aspect of a society in which many different cultural groups are valued and respected and share power.

culturally relevant teaching   a theory that underscores teaching practices grounded in the understanding of culture and experiences that shape students' ways of knowing the world.

culture   a way of life; the habits, values, and attitudes of a group of people.

differently-abled   a term used to describe exceptional students who accomplish tasks in ways different from those of most other students.

discrimination the use of negative responses or the absence of positive responses that can deny success for certain groups of students.

empowerment one's personal belief that the factors that make up his or her identity (including language, culture, and other factors) are vital contributions to society.

English as a Second Language a program or category pertaining to students whose native language is not English but who are learning English for academic purposes.

ethnicity a shared national heritage or race; the association of skin color with a person's identity.

ethnocentric behavior actions wherein people view their own cultural group characteristics as correct or superior and the ways of other groups as odd or inferior.

exceptionality attributes that make a child different from most others.

gender pertaining to male or female.

hidden curriculum what students learn that the teacher doesn't teach explicitly.

human/student diversity areas of distinction for identifying various groups.

inclusion: an approach in which children with exceptionalities are placed in educational settings with children without exceptionalities and receive services alongside them.

macro culture large cultural group.

melting pot metaphor for many cultures blending together so that each one loses its original identity and becomes something new.

micro culture small cultural group.

minority term typically referred to as any ethnic group.

monocultural of only one culture.

multicultural more than one culture.

physically challenged those who possess some type of bodily condition that prevents them from performing certain actions such as walking, speaking, and seeing.

prejudice the mindset and resulting action that consistently thrust negative responses on a particular person or group of people.

race the association of skin color with a person's identity.

salad bowl metaphor for many cultures blending together so that each one retains its original identity while simultaneously becoming part of something new.

social class/socioeconomic status (SES) term referring to one's economic status (lower class, middle class, etc.)

stereotyping the assumption that certain beliefs based on skin color or other forms of physical, religious, or other cultural identifiers are true of all people of that type.

SUGGESTED ACTIVITIES

1. Examine the textbooks of different subject areas and analyze the positive integration of people from diverse cultural groups. For example, recognize whether those from various ethnic groups and of a specific gender are consistently depicted in subservient or negative roles. Are women consistently depicted as aides or secretaries while men take on the roles of doctors, fire fighters, and astronauts? Are boys making all of the important decisions? Are boys allowed to have emotions? Are people of color important in such roles or totally absent from the pages? Are differently-abled children pictured? What is the implicit message given to children by the textbook that you are examining?

2. Examine a preschool or early childhood classroom environment. Analyze the decor (posters, displays, notes, and advertisements) to determine whether it presents messages of inclusion for all students.

3. Visit a preschool, public school, or childcare center that mainstreams children with developmental disabilities. For 30 minutes, observe in a mainstream class one of the children who has a disability. Record the social skills the child displays. Analyze your observations and list the social skills you believe the child has and lacks in terms of his or her age and developmental level. Record also how many times the teacher attends to this child and in what ways.

4. Select three children from those that you teach or in your field placement, and begin learning about their individual characteristics. Examine their files to find data about physical traits, their families, and the elements of diversity (religion, ethnicity, language, social class, exceptionality, gender) that characterize them.

5. Create an alternative plan to the traditional open house or parental conference utilized by many schools. Your plan should promote ways of reaching and including parents from various ways of life. When designing the plan, specify your intended audience and explain how the plan will benefit those in that group.

6. Generate a list of possible resources and activities that would be beneficial for utilizing multicultural concepts within the Early Childhood–4 classroom.

7. Design a layout for your classroom that will accommodate the needs of physically challenged or exceptional students.

8. Considering the developmental needs of children in your class, design two experiences targeting differences that will help apply prosocial skills (interacting with others, establishing relations with others, making friends, showing empathy toward others).

9. Ask how your mentor makes modifications in his or her plans for differently-abled students. How does a teacher who has children in a "pull-out" program accommodate children who leave and return to class? Do these children feel completely a part of the classroom? Why or why not?

10. Do an *honest* evaluation of certain beliefs and stereotypes that you hold regarding different types of people. Explore these beliefs through objective input or interaction with the people about whom they are held. Reevaluate these beliefs for truths or fallacy. Be open! Examine your classroom behavior to see whether those beliefs affect your interactions with children who belong to those groups.

11. Have a colleague observe a lesson you teach and mark how many times you call on different genders, different ethnicities, and so forth, in your class, and what kinds of questions you ask (high level, low level, and so forth). Reflect on possible changes in your teaching that may create a more equal opportunity for all children.

PRACTICE QUESTIONS

1. Ms. Sheree notices that during the selection of instructional supplies for the upcoming school year, the majority of resources chosen have little or no representation of other cultures. To address this situation, Ms. Sheree should:

   A. Recognize that it is impossible for resources to represent every culture.

   B. Accommodate for diversity by utilizing resources from the community, including parents and children from her classroom.

   C. Find a special day that the diversity of persons can be celebrated in a program.

   D. Assume that the absence of diversity is a good thing because diversity helps to illuminate differences and, thus, could increase conflict.

2. Ms. Sheree notices that different ethnic groups within her third grade classroom are remaining isolated and are not intermingling with other groups within the class. She wants to promote multicultural educational concepts in her ethnically mixed class. Which of the following activities would likely be most effective in promoting cross-cultural interaction?

   A. Have each ethnic group learn about a different culture group and present the information to the rest of the class.

   B. Give the class a lecture discussing the dynamics that she is seeing and her disapproval of such developments.

   C. Allow students to form natural bonds where they may, and let them develop others in their own time.

   D. Regroup students by having everyone with pants, shorts, long socks, tennis shoes, or other distinguishing marks work together, switching the indicator often to make new groups.

3. Mr. Gregory notices that the upcoming units in social studies do not include books on the many diverse cultures that make up his first grade classroom. He also recognizes the fact that he must follow the plan set out for his

grade level. Mr. Gregory should address this concern by:

A. Strictly sticking with the curriculum and not concerning himself with the diversity issue.

B Having a two-week period when books about other cultures will be explored.

C. Assigning additional readings on other cultures as extra credit to read at home with parents.

D. Integrating books about other cultures into the planned curriculum.

4. Five-year-old Gladys is a Hispanic child who is learning English as a second language. One day as her teacher, Ms. Pope, is reading a book to a group of children, Gladys points to a picture of a hat and says, *"el sombrero,"* the Spanish word for hat. Ms. Pope recognizes the word and responds by asking the class, "Who can tell Gladys how we say that in English?" Which of the following is the best analysis of Ms. Pope's response?

A. She should have told Gladys directly that the English word is "hat" rather than asking the other children to do so.

B. She should have acknowledged Gladys's appropriate use of her native language before introducing the English word.

C. She should have ignored the Spanish and encouraged Gladys's production of the word in English before asking the other children to supply it.

D. She should have waited to see whether the other children reacted to Gladys's statement before doing so herself.

Answers and Discussion

Answer 1: It is the teacher's responsibility to seek alternative ways of providing exposure and representation of diverse cultures from other sources. A practical source would be the parents and children from other cultures within a given community

(B). Ignoring the lack of diversity by justifying that it is impossible *(A)* or that it prevents the acknowledgment of differences and decreases conflict *(D)* does not depict an accurate understanding of multicultural ideals and concepts. Celebrating through a special program or day *only* gives messages of extra or nonessentialism to the multicultural concept *(C)*. The answer is *B*.

Answer 2: The teacher should not draw unnecessary attention to a natural phenomenon in the classroom. She should instead find alternative means of regrouping that will afford students opportunities to learn and work together based on simple concepts such as color of socks, or those who brought their lunch, and that will not emphasize tensions or differences between groups until a more appropriate or desired time. The answer is *D*.

Answer 3: Remember, integration is the key to utilization of multicultural resources. The other solutions of ignoring diversity and of specialty treatment are a disservice to the scholarship of multicultural education. The answer is *D*.

Answer 4: The early childhood teacher understands how having a home language other than standard English affects English language development and knows how to use young children's diverse linguistic and cultural backgrounds to facilitate their English language development as well as to enhance all children's awareness of the diversity of languages and cultures. Choices *A, C,* and *D* do not respect and acknowledge first language proficiency. The correct answer is *B*.

WEB LINKS

Remember that Web site locations may change. If any of these sites have moved or cannot be located, use Terms to Know in this chapter to search for further information.

http://community-1.webtv.net/SoundBehavior/DIVERSITYFORSOUND

This site includes an outstanding compilation of links to sites that have information related to such topics as culture, diversity, immigration, languages, multicultural education, and multicultural organizations. It also includes useful listings of sites with content related to individual ethnic groups.

http://www.ael.org/eric/digests/edorc942.htm

Blueprints for Indian Education: Improving Mainstream Schooling, by Robin Butterfield, is a wonderful link for information on Native Americans.

http://www.libraries.rutgers.edu/rul/rr_gateway/ research_guides/history/afrores.shtml

Information at this site organizes resources related to the history of African Americans. Included are numerous links to individual documents as well as to entire collections of texts and other key resources.

www.yahoo.com

Information about Native-American education is available through this site by choosing the subject Education K–12 and entering Indian Education.

www.asiasociety.org

This site offers information on Asia and Asian Americans. It provides cultural understanding of some Asian groups.

http://www.census.gov

This site provides thorough statistics on the issue of poverty, broken down by race and ethnic groups.

http://www.mhhe.com/socscience/education/ multi/activities.html

This link has been developed and refined for multicultural education courses and workshops for preservice and in-service teachers. All activities that lead to dialogue on issues such as oppression, prejudice, stereotypes, and discrimination should be closely examined and appropriately modified for the target audience.

http://education.indiana.edu/cas/tt/v2i2/ cultural.html

This issue of "Teacher Talk" examines how diversity issues influence what goes on in the classroom and what teachers can do to provide all students with opportunities to be successful learners.

http://www.dec-sped.org/

The Division for Early Childhood (DEC) of the Council for Exceptional Children (CEC) is a non-profit organization advocating for individuals who work with or on behalf of children with special needs, of ages birth through 8, and their families. Founded in 1973, the Division is dedicated to promoting policies and practices that support families and enhance the optimal development of children. Children with special needs include those who have disabilities or developmental delays, are gifted and talented, and are at risk of future developmental problems.

http://www.naeyc.org/

The National Association for the Education of Young Children (NAEYC) is the nation's largest and most influential organization of early childhood educators and others dedicated to improving the quality of programs for children from birth through third grade.

REFERENCES

Banks, J. (1992 November/December). Reducing prejudice in children: Guidelines from research. *Social Education,* 3–5.

Brewer, J. A. (2001). *Introduction to early childhood education: Preschool through primary grades.* 4th ed. Boston: Allyn and Bacon.

Clark, P. (1995). Culturally appropriate practices in early childhood education: Families as the resource. *Contemporary Education, 3*(66), 154–157.

Cummins, J. (1989). *Empowering minority students.* Sacramento, CA: California Association for Bilingual Education.

de Melendez, W., & Ostertag, V. (1997). *Teaching young children in multicultural classroom issues, concepts, and strategies.* Albany, NY: Delmar.

Derman-Sparks, L., & the A.B.C. Task Force. (1989). *Anti-bias curriculum.* Washington, D.C.: National Association for the Education of Young Children.

Gollnick, D. M., & Chinn, P. C. (1990). *Multicultural education in a pluralistic society.* Upper Saddle River, NJ: Merrill Prentice Hall.

Ladson-Billings, G. (1992a). Culturally relevant teaching: The key to making multicultural education work. In

C. A. Grant (Ed.), *Research and multicultural education* (pp. 106–121). London: Farmer Press.

Ladson-Billings, G. (1992b). Liberatory consequences of literacy: A case of culturally relevant instruction for African American students. *Journal of Negro Education, 61,* 378–391.

Ladson-Billings, G. (1992c). Reading between the lines and beyond the pages. A culturally relevant approach to literacy teaching. *Theory into Practice, 31,* 312–320.

Ladson-Billings, G, (1995). But that's just good teaching! The case for culturally relevant pedagogy, *Theory into Practice, 34*(3), 159–165.

Lipman, P. (1995). Bringing out the best in them: The contribution of culturally relevant teachers to educational reform. *Theory into Practice, 34(3),* 202–208.

Nieto, S. (1996). *Affirming diversity: The sociopolitical context of multicultural education.* White Plains, NY: Longman.

Ovando, C. J., & Collier, V. P. (1998). *Bilingual and ESL classrooms: Teaching in multicultural contexts.* Boston: McGraw Hill.

Payne, R. (1995). *Poverty: A framework for understanding and working with students and adults from poverty.* Baytown, TX: RFT Publishing.

Riche, M. F. (1991). We're all minorities now. *American Demographics, 13,* 26–43.

Richey, D., & Wheeler, J. (2000). *Inclusive early childhood education.* Albany, NY: Delmar Publishers.

Sadker, M., & Sadker, D. (1994). *Failing at fairness.* New York: Touchstone.

Wink, J. (1997). Critical pedagogy: Notes from the real world. New York: Longman.

Competency 3

The teacher understands procedures for designing effective and coherent instruction and assessment based on appropriate learning goals and objectives.

The beginning teacher:

- Understands the significance of the Texas Essential Knowledge and Skills (TEKS) and of prerequisite knowledge and skills in determining instructional goals and objectives.

- Uses appropriate criteria to evaluate the appropriateness of learning goals and objectives (e.g., clarity; relevance; significance; age-appropriateness; ability to be assessed; responsiveness to students' current skills and knowledge, background, needs, and interests; alignment with campus and district goals).

- Uses assessment to analyze students' strengths and needs, evaluate teacher effectiveness, and guide instructional planning for individuals and groups.

- Understands the connection between various components of the Texas statewide assessment program, the TEKS, and instruction, and analyzes data from state and other assessments using common statistical measures to help identify students' strengths and needs.

- Demonstrates knowledge of various types of materials and resources (including technological resources and resources outside the school) that may be used to enhance student learning and engagement, and evaluates the appropriateness of specific materials and resources for use in particular situations, to address specific purposes, and to meet varied student needs.

- Plans lessons and structures units so that activities progress in a logical sequence and support stated instructional goals.

- Plans learning experiences that provide students with opportunities to explore content from integrated and varied perspectives (e.g., by providing an integrated curriculum, employing play as one learning mode, permitting student choice of activities, involving students in working on projects, designing instruction that supports students' growing ability to work cooperatively and to reflect upon other points of view when appropriate).

- Allocates time appropriately within lessons and units, including providing adequate opportunities for students to engage in reflection, self-assessment, and closure.

Chapter 3

COMPETENCY 3 – PART 1

Designing Effective Instruction

JANICE L. NATH

University of Houston—Downtown

TERMS TO KNOW

Age-appropriateness

Analysis level

Application level

Authentic activities

Closure

Comprehension level

Evaluation level

Focus

Goals

Interdisciplinary integration

Knowledge level

Long-range goals

Long-range plans

Miniclosures

Objectives

Observable behaviors

Prior knowledge

Rationale

Scaffolding

Scope

Sponge activity

State/District goals

Student background

Student interests

Synthesis level

TAAS

TAKS

Teacher input

TEKS

Touching on the community

Transition

Numerous hours in a teacher's life are spent thinking about lessons that she or he will teach to children. In that process many questions arise. What do children need in order to learn, appreciate, and understand? Will children like the lessons that are selected or created? Will lessons be challenging enough? Will all children in the class be able to succeed? Where can enough activities and resources be found to fill the time and ensure learning? How will I know that children have learned? Will they learn enough to do well on the state tests? All of these—and many, many more—are questions that teachers ask themselves as they begin to set goals and plan for their days in the classroom. This chapter addresses goal setting and lesson planning, while the following chapter (Part 2 of this competency) completes the remainder of the indicators for this competency that work to enhance effective instruction.

BEGINNING WITH A GOAL

An instructional **goal** can be defined as a broad, general idea of what the teacher and others interested in education want children to learn. Goals may evolve from several different sources. One source, normally referred to as the *formal curriculum,* comes from curriculum guides and other materials from various levels in education: the grade and/or school level, the district level, the state level, and the national level. These types of goals may also be joined with local, state, and national standards devised by subject area specialists and coupled with (and often overlapping with) a teacher's own beliefs about teaching and learning. All of these aims for educating children originate from three primary directions: the need to enhance students' developmental factors, the need to prepare students for real life, and the needs

of the academic discipline itself. Educators, for instance, may believe that an important part of teaching young children is related to helping them progress through the stages of the cognitive, social, personal, and physical domains. Those educators may also have extensive knowledge about childhood development. If that is so, many goals for a teacher's classroom may be driven by developmental factors. General goals for teaching lessons developed from this inclination may appear as "I want children to learn to cooperate with others to enhance their social development," or "I want children to develop good fine motor skills to enhance drawing and writing," or "Students should begin to develop higher-level thinking skills," along with many other examples of developmental growth.

A second belief that may drive goals for children is learning as a preparation for life. General desires for teaching from this perspective involve readying children with skills they will need or want in the "real world" and as a part of society. Goals driven by this belief are often logical and supply their own rationale: "I want children to understand map skills," or "I want children to appreciate good music," or "I want students to understand the rights and responsibilities of a good citizen."

The subject or the academic discipline itself may drive goals from a third direction. There are certain basics in every subject area that either "form the essence" of that subject or provide essential prior knowledge or readiness for later skills in those areas. Goals such as these may include "Children should understand the relationship between cause-and-effect," or "Children should know why the Pilgrims left England," or "Children need to know basic shapes."

As teachers articulate goals, they take the first step toward purposeful learning. If a teacher thinks not only of his or her general aim in designing a lesson but also about the direction from which the goal originates, three purposes are attained. First, lessons will reflect a variety of student learning and skills over time. Thus children will receive a better balance in curriculum between subject and content driven goals, societal driven goals, and human development driven goals. Second, by understanding what a teacher's own broad reasons are for wanting to teach a lesson, the process of planning will begin in a much more purposeful manner. Goal statements will also assure that a classroom is not being activity driven—that is, teachers are not just teaching a lesson because they found the "cutest thing for children to do." Finally, by understanding the origin of their goals, teachers can more easily defend the purpose(s) for their teaching.

Researchers such as Brophy (1987) believe that it is teachers who determine the curriculum for children no matter what type of standards or goals are in place, so carefully considering one's teaching goals and aims is a huge responsibility and should be made with forethought, reflection, and professionalism. Once again, balancing sound reasoning for teaching a lesson based on the goal directions given above (the development of the child, the needs of real life/society, and subject area/disciplines) will provide children with a better learning year. As an additional check for teachers who are designing goals, the following questions should be asked at each step in planning goals (note indicators from Competency 3 in italics): (a) Is this goal *clear, relevant, meaningful, and age-appropriate*? (b) Is this goal *responsive to students' current skills and knowledge, background, needs, and interests*? (c) Is it *in alignment with campus and district goals*? and (d) Can it be *assessed* in some way?

Many lessons have multiple goals that lead, in turn, to a specific lesson plan. For example, Ms. DuLaney, a Pre-K teacher, began to plan a lesson with the goal or purpose of having her young children learn "big and small" (driven by the goal of readiness in the academic discipline of mathematics). "Let's see," she told herself, "I also want to be sure that children work on their motor skills

and listening skills" (driven by child development), "and our district grade level requires learning about animals in their science curriculum for Pre-K" (local mandate derived from national standards). Driven by goals in these three directions, Ms. DuLaney began to design a specific lesson in which children would discriminate between big and small animals in several ways and, while listening to circus music, move in ways that depicted large and small animal movement.

LONG-RANGE GOALS AND PLANS

The success of a teacher's year depends upon developing **long-range goals** as well as goals and plans for each day. The state of Texas and school districts want all of their teachers to have a long-range goal statement **(state/district goals)** or a general "map" of their entire school year in every subject that they teach. It is normally required that these goal statements be on file at one's school. This long-range goal statement or plan may be one of the first tasks a new teacher undertakes as the school year begins in those first few in-service days before children arrive. Teachers will revise this statement every year, however, as goals for children change—driven by changes in the national, state, and local curriculum; events; the growth of knowledge about children; and a teacher's own changing beliefs. These statements are often completed collaboratively in grade-level meetings, although teachers may, depending on the school and/or district, be free to design their own. The state of Texas helps teachers in this process, as it has developed curriculum guidelines for Texas Essential Knowledge and Skills (the **TEKS**) for all grade levels and subject areas. Thus new teachers are not faced with guessing what is fundamental for their children to be taught.

Teachers usually take a very broad goal and then begin to divide it into subgoals that, in turn, become long-range plans. A broad goal might be, "I want children to communicate well in writing at a fourth-grade level by the end of the year." To help develop broad goals, teachers may want to start with some of the following terms:

Table 3.1 Terms for Broad Goals

know	appreciate	love	understand
value	believe	grasp	think
enjoy	like	cope with	learn

Long-range plans can be divided into plans for the year, a semester, quarters, a six-week period, or other smaller thematic units. Developing long-range goals and plans for the entire school year is important for many reasons. First, teachers must know in general (and in each subject area they will teach) what they want children to learn during the year. One rationale behind this type of planning is that, of course, one cannot teach everything for every subject area. Therefore, setting long-range goals and planning for each subject helps in understanding **scope.** Scope refers to how much or how deeply into a topic teachers can delve in a particular time period.

A most important concern in setting goals in a Texas classroom and designing a yearly plan is the state learning requirements in the TEKS (Texas Essential Knowledge and Skills) for each grade level. As mentioned, the TEKS provide a logical, age-appropriate scope and sequence to guide teachers in planning their curriculum for their current grade level (and for gaining knowledge about expectations for learning in past and future years).

Another reason to design a long-range plan is assessment. Competency 3 requires teachers to ask, "Can my goals and objectives be assessed?" Teachers use assessment constantly, not only to determine whether children are matching expectations of their own goals and objectives, but the state of Texas also places much importance on testing children to assess whether they are meeting state curriculum goals and objectives. In elementary schools, mathematics and reading TEKS goals and objectives are assessed through the **TAAS** test (Texas Assessment of Academic Skills [to become the **TAKS**—Texas Assessment of Knowledge and Skills]). Currently, these tests involve third and fourth graders, and a writing TAAS (or TAKS) is

added to the tests for fourth graders. Other tests are anticipated in time. Texas holds schools (and thus teachers) accountable for student achievement on TAAS (or TAKS) scores, so it is essential for teachers to include knowledge and skills from the TEKS curriculum guide as part of their goals and to map out carefully how and when required skills and knowledge will be introduced. Even if teachers are not assigned to a "TAAS (TAKS) grade level," they must remember that third and fourth grade teachers are counting on them to have readied children by planning for and teaching the TEKS in earlier grades. If one does teach in a grade level in which children are tested, he or she must ensure that the TEKS goals and objectives are covered in long-range plans and daily lessons.

Arranging goals and plans for the entire school year can help teachers make important decisions in other ways. Because having children pass the TAAS (or TAKS) test is an important goal, teaching those particular skills before the test is given must be a part of decision making. Special reviews for skills needed on TAAS (or TAKS) tests are often "an event" in many Texas schools, so if a teacher has a third or fourth grade, for example, it is necessary to take this into account in one's long-range goals and plans. Teachers also must consider, for instance, that some textbooks are not arranged so that important TAAS elements are taught before testing. A teacher may, therefore, conclude that working sequentially through a particular text is not appropriate for one or more subject areas.

Planning for the year can also remind teachers to look ahead for ideas and collect materials that will enrich lessons they will teach in the coming months. If a teacher knows what topics are coming up, he or she has opportunities to search resource closets, libraries, the Web, and so forth, hunting down supplemental resources and ideas to make lessons more exciting and meaningful. In addition, setting up long-range plans can help a teacher arrange important units of study so as not to be disrupted by holidays or school breaks, thus increasing the likelihood that children will not leave a project half completed or forget important concepts over a break.

Teachers may also want to arrange certain topics or activities to match the seasons in mapping the year. If a class is to study animals in science, for instance, field trips to a farm or to the zoo can be arranged in the more pleasant months of late fall or spring, or a teacher may want to connect a weather chapter with hurricane season in Texas. In this way, goals and plans often become richer and more relevant to children. Finally, a school may participate in district or community activities that could affect the way teachers plan. Earth Week, Rodeo Week, and so forth, may provide special opportunities to tie subject matter to activities for long-range plans. Special holidays or multicultural events such Black History Month or Cinco de Mayo may also help the "map of the year" by tying the curriculum to special happenings that enhance learning.

As one can see, setting goals and planning for the year can be compared to a jigsaw puzzle. To put the pieces together more easily, teachers can do the following: (a) make a list of goals and objectives mandated by the state TEKS and local mandates, along with any necessary national standards for a subject area; (b) add those to personal goals for one's class(es); (c) find or make a large calendar on which all of the weeks of the school year can be seen; (d) mark down school breaks and special events (including testing) taken from the district and school calendar; (e) ask experienced teachers at the school whether other events come up during the year that might not be on the calendar but that could affect long-range plans. For example, experienced teachers who have taught at Oak Leaf Elementary know that all classes must design a game for their Fall Carnival and that in the spring all children must contribute their best art to a local "Mall Show." These teachers at Oak Leaf integrate goals for those particular events logically into their overall long-range goals and plans in various subject areas before the events.

Now teachers should be ready to begin to map their long-range goals and plans. They can begin to fill in each week of their calendar with a list of needed skills and knowledge, keeping logical sequencing in mind and thinking in terms of all of the areas mentioned above. Using a pencil is best because changes and rearrangement will have to be made as one works through "the jigsaw puzzle." Remember also that if a teacher is part of a grade-level team, he or she will need to negotiate with all members of the team to accomplish this task—particularly if a school asks that all teachers in a grade level generally be "on the same page" during the year. If new teachers are completing long-range goals and plans alone, it is well worth the time to ask for a copy from the previous year in the same grade level for a guideline. Then, after having completed a plan for the current year, have an experienced teacher and/or an administrator double-check to see that everything children should learn during the school year has been included. With this long-range plan in hand for each subject to be taught, teachers are ready to focus upon smaller units (semester, quarter, six-week unit, weekly, and/or daily plans), and they now know that the course mapped out addresses children's needs for the year. Figure 3.1 shows how planning often takes place.

DAILY GOALS AND OBJECTIVES

Yearly plans are further divided into smaller units, as noted above—perhaps by semester, by quarter, by six-weeks, by week or unit, and ultimately by day and subject area. Let us move to the daily plan for a subject area, remembering that a teacher who is responsible for multiple subjects each day must design plans for each of those time slots. It is easier to write plans on the computer, where cutting and pasting are easily managed. At least use a pencil because writing a lesson plan is a continuously changing process—discursive in nature. Most parts of the lesson plan are revamped as the teacher writes, then reflects, and rewrites—throughout the process of finalizing a plan.

It is difficult to start a daily plan without knowing generally what a teacher has in mind; instructional goals answer the question "What is it that I really want children to learn in my lesson(s) today?"

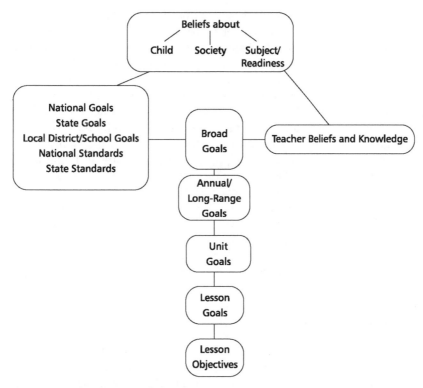

FIGURE 3.1   The Elements of Planning.

A first step is thus selecting an overall goal for children. For example, a teacher might select a goal of, "I want children to understand how to develop a character in their writing," or "I want children to know about the regions of Texas." As the lesson begins to develop, thoughts continue as to what strategies would work best to attain that goal. Keep in mind that the requirements or indicators listed at the beginning of this chapter from this competency dictate that at every step a teacher should ask, "Are my goals and objectives *clear, relevant, meaningful, and age-appropriate? Are they responsive to students' current skills and knowledge, background needs and interests, in alignment with campus and district* (and state) *goals,* and can they be *assessed?* Communicating educational purposes and pathways for children is serious business. Children and their parents (as well as colleagues, principals, the school district, and the public in general) want to know where students are going (and where they have been) in learning.

If teachers cannot defend their goals or purposes in teaching a lesson from an educational standpoint, they must go back and begin again. Unfortunately, too many children have been taught lessons that were not firmly grounded in educational rationale and purposes, causing the general public to question teachers' professionalism.

When a general purpose has been established, teachers may begin to look at the intricacies of other elements that make a good lesson. As teachers begin to think of goals for lessons, several great activities for children may flash into their heads—even before they have thought of other necessary lesson components. As noted earlier, designing a plan can involve writing various parts of the lesson at different times, then visiting and revisiting these parts of the plan throughout the process, ensuring a good "fit" between all. However, there is a still a beacon that must guide this process. Effective teachers clearly know what they want children to accomplish (Berliner, 1985). The beacon used in planning is a concise statement of those particular **objectives** that the teacher wants students to accomplish, either for learning content or for performing skills. The effective teacher also wants to establish a way to determine *how well* children have achieved in a particular area.

What other reasons are there for taking the time to formulate good objectives? One important purpose is that objectives are most likely to help teachers maintain their focus on the exact learning that they want children to accomplish. Teachers who write their goals and objectives in their plans are much more likely to stay on course and, thus, not skip over needed knowledge and skills. Like goals, objectives help to formulate a lesson that is realistic in scope and addresses timing constraints. Good objectives also help teachers decide precisely how they want to assess the skills or knowledge so that they know whether to move on to the next step or to go back and reteach. This logical organization helps maintain clarity for learners. Educational research has found, too, that stating objectives helps children know what is expected. When children understand the expectations for learning, they can match their performance to those expectations more easily. Children also can self-assess their learning as the lesson progresses.

Armed with a list of TEKS for a grade level, a teacher can be sure to include all state required objectives for children along with those objectives that help support and round out a lesson and lead to higher levels of thinking. At first it seems like a daunting task to combine all of these elements. It is certainly another puzzle with many pieces. However, as with many skills, writing objectives becomes much easier with practice.

WRITING A GOOD OBJECTIVE

Considering the Learner

When traveling, it is rare that one does not use some sort of planning to ensure a safe arrival. Good objectives can be compared to a map for children who are "traveling through" a lesson. A good map has a key, shows directions, shows the types of conditions of the roads, and thus provides us with a way to determine our destination. A good objective, like a map, provides: (a) a key to *who* the learner is; (b) directions, or the *desired behavior* that will help the learner get to a desired destination; (c) the *conditions* for travel or the circumstances of the task; and (d) the destination, or the *degree of accomplishment.* By analyzing these elements further, teachers can see how each fits together to provide a clear picture of what will happen in a lesson or a "journey of learning." First, teachers should decide *who* the learner should be for an objective. This sounds a bit odd at first because, obviously, it should be a class. But looking more closely, teachers may have to discriminate further. For example, at times they may want to use *flexible grouping* (ability groups formed for a short time to work on a specific skill), so a particular group may be listed as "the learner" for an objective. By law, teachers are also required to modify for children with exceptionalities, so these special individual children (differently-abled, gifted, bilingual, etc.) will often need to have special objectives. By including the grade level in the objectives as part of the learners' identity, teachers are always reminded to examine their objectives for **age-appropriateness.** Thus, specified skills and tasks (and the quantity to be given) should be able to be accomplished both physically and mentally by a child at a particular age and/or stage of development (see Competency 1, Chapter 1). In addition, the information to be taught should be suitable in terms of interest for an age group, and topics and presentations judged suitable for young children. Occasionally, for example, teachers exhibit poor judgment and present movies, computer materials, topics, and reading materials that are not age-appropriate due, in particular, to violence and/or "scariness," language, adult themes, or other unsuitable areas. In extreme cases, parents may lobby for removal of a teacher who does not adhere to age-appropriate materials.

Other hints ensure that objectives are written well. For example, if a teacher has a question about a skill or task, he or she should quickly consult the TEKS, childhood development materials, and other relevant standards for the age group. Remember that focusing upon exactly "who the learner is" is an important part of designing an effective plan. A number of questions come to mind concerning **students' backgrounds** and/or **prior knowledge.** Thus, a teacher may want to consider the following questions:

Exactly who is/are my learner(s) for this objective?

At what level are they (is she/he)?

Does the learner come to these objectives with the proper foundation or readiness?

How many levels are in my class?

Do I have special learners for whom objectives must be different?

Upon what subject area(s) am I focusing in this lesson (an important area when working with thematic units for balance of subject areas)?

Therefore, objectives might begin with:

Third grade science students will . . .

In science, 3rd graders will . . .

Group A will . . .

Group B will . . .

Madison will . . .

Inez will . . .

A good formula for writing objectives might be: *the exact learner + observable/measurable behavior + circumstance/condition under which the behavior will be measured + assessment of the behavior.*

Considering the Behavior Aspect of a Performance Objective

The next step in formulating objectives is to look closely at the behavior(s) required to accomplish the goal of the lesson for a content area (remem-

bering again that each behavior considered must be *clear, relevant, meaningful, and age-appropriate*). "Children will manipulate cubes to find the correct sum of 10 addition problems of single-digit numbers" is such an example. When reading this objective, a teacher knows exactly what behavior children will exhibit and how much is required. Every objective must also measure whether learning took place or not. The later part of an objective is termed *assessment,* or, by using our map analogy, deciding a way to determine whether children have arrived at the planned learning destination. Consequently, we see that an important part of writing objectives is ensuring that a stated behavior must be observable—that is, it must be able to be seen or heard.

Why must objectives be written with **observable behaviors?** Teachers must have something to observe in order to be able to measure how much learning took place. Unfortunately, teachers are unable to use X-ray vision to look inside children's brains to see how well they accomplish "understanding a concept," "knowing about a topic," or "being able to perform a skill." Because learning cannot actually be seen, teachers must make deductions based on what *can* be seen and/or heard in a student's performance. From a student performance of some type, teachers can thus infer whether or not a child has learned specific skills or content. Knowing how well students learned determines the course of the next lesson. Teachers will also want to give feedback to children and their caregivers on the progression of learning. To determine this, teachers need to have something tangible to measure—something that can be observed.

To see how the concept of observable, measurable objectives unfolds in the classroom, let us examine a simple incorrect objective: "First graders will know two-column addition." But how is it that a teacher could look inside a child's mind to determine whether that child actually knows this? This "objective" is really more of a general goal. On the other hand, what judgments could a teacher make from the following objectives: "First-grade mathematics students will review the steps of two-column addition by correctly singing a related numbers song, completing at least three problems by participating in a team relay game, and passing a test of 15 problems on two-column addition with 70 percent accuracy." Each segment is a clear, observable behavior that allows assessment of how well or how much was done. Teachers observe children singing the correct words, and they measure how correctly and how rapidly children work in the game. Finally test scores are easily measured numerically. Teachers know about children's learning because there is an observable behavior or product in each case. They can then use this information to make decisions. What kinds of decisions are there to make? What would teachers want to do, for example, if the results of a test revealed that more than half the class did not accomplish 70 percent? Of course they must go back and revisit this concept in detail. Also, children and their caregivers can be informed of poor performance so that more focus can be placed upon this concept. If 95 percent of a class achieved this objective, however, teachers would also know that, in general, children "got it," and the class could safely move on to the next logical goal in mathematics (while individual remediation is put in place for those few who did not attain an acceptable degree of success). When examining objectives for even younger children, the same would transpire: "Kindergarten students will color a picture of three shapes with no more than five marks outside the lines." If children are able to match these expectations the teacher would know that a class already has on-level fine motor skills, and, thus, should continue on to develop more detailed work. If not, the teacher would have to introduce other tasks to help develop that skill more fully.

Behaviors: Creating Various Levels of Thinking in Objectives through Bloom's Taxonomy

Yet another purpose of good objectives is to have teachers examine the type or level of thinking that children are doing. Are children just recalling facts day after day, or is the teacher providing objectives and activities that require deeper thinking? Because of this question, Bloom's Taxonomy is an important tool for writing objectives. Bloom et al. (1956) developed a taxonomy that categorizes behavioral terms into a hierarchy of thinking, beginning with lower-level thinking (knowledge, comprehension, and application) and moving to higher-level thinking (analysis, synthesis, and evaluation). These categories are listed in Table 3.2 later in this chapter.

Let's look now at what happens when this concept is applied to objectives. What if an objective for a lesson began with, "Students will tell orally who the first president of the United States was." How much thought does that take? Very little, really! Children must only recall a memorized **knowledge level** answer—George Washington. To measure knowledge level is simple—either children know it or they don't. Low-level objectives are important, however, because children initially need some information, vocabulary, or facts with which to build on a topic. This is referred to as cognitive or "simple knowledge" (Cangelosi, 1992). However, what if another objective were added to a plan to "explain what the term *first President of the United States* means"? Children must now know not only who it was but also what significance it had to our country (the leader of our country after independence). This would be a **comprehension level** objective. This level demonstrates an understanding of knowledge. If a third objective were added to list and classify the traits of the first president of the United States, children would have to first recall who it was, list all the important features and traits of that president, and sort them into categories (perhaps physical descriptions, personal traits such as honesty, etc.). Children are now thinking on the **application level,** or they are asked to apply or use the knowledge they have learned. So far, only lower-level objectives have been used in this plan.

Let us continue to examine how higher-level thinking can be built, one idea on top of another. When teachers move to higher-level objectives, knowledge and skills become much more relevant to learners. Children are no longer only recalling and repeating, but actually employing information or skills in a contextual situation. Let's examine some higher-level objectives with this thought in mind. "The student will analyze reasons why the first president of the United States was seen as one of our best presidents" could be a fourth objective at the **analysis level** (breaking a complex problem into parts). What must children do now? They must take apart components to see how they are interrelated. First the name of the first president must be recalled and positive attributes listed. Then descriptions of other leaders and situations must be made, classified, and compared to identify Washington as a good model. Finally children must support their answers with evidence. This is quite a distance, in terms of thinking, from the first objective of "telling who the first President was."

What thoughts are needed if objectives are at the **synthesis level** or the level that applies concepts in creating something new? Note the objective: "Predict what type of person would be the most successful president for the United States today." What are the thought processes required here? Children must recall who other successful presidents were, list traits that made each successful, compare each by analyzing all possible failures with all positive traits remembered by the American people, consider the difference in time and issues facing the nation today, and finally, "create" a new image for a future successful candidate.

The highest level of thinking in Bloom's Taxonomy is the **evaluation level,** involving making and supporting judgments. The following objective is at this level: "From possible current candidates, recommend the nominee who would be likely to have the most successful presidency." Once more, let us look at the thought processes needed: (a) recall those presidents most remembered for being successful, and list their traits; (b) classify successful traits and events that contributed to their success; (c) keeping these traits in mind, develop a "model" for a president in this era; (d) considering events and concerns in our times, decide what type of person would be even more successful; (e) compare that

model to candidates on the horizon; and (f) finally, make a judgment as to which candidate might fit that model in the best manner.

Building thinking skills through good objectives is like constructing a building. A foundation must be constructed at low levels, but what good is a foundation by itself? However, as one can see, there is a world of difference in the thought processes from the recall or knowledge level to the evaluation level. If teachers work toward designing objectives and activities in lower *and* upper levels of thinking, children will form solid thinking skills needed in all subject areas to be successful. These types of objectives can and should be written in every subject area and for every grade level. As a word of caution, do not underestimate young children's ability to use higher-level processes. Children are excellent creators and judges—just ask caregivers of young children who hear excellent, creative reasons and judgments, often in the middle of a store, of why certain products or toys should be purchased and taken home. It is up to teachers to refine these skills. For example, using the previous example, objectives for young children might be as follows:

- The student will tell who the first president of the United States was and recognize his picture.

- The student will orally compare a picture of the first president with a picture of our current president, specifying at least one trait both have in common and one trait that is different.

- The student will orally give two examples of why the first president was a good president and will think of someone whom they know who has the same character traits.

- In groups of three, students will decide what attributes might make a good president and tell why.

- The student will create or design and illustrate his or her own short flip book, showing the life of George Washington (the student must decide on the events he or she will use), including at least four events of Washington's life.

- In an oral question-and-answer session, the student will recommend a person in his or her family (or an adult friend) who would make a good president and give at least two reasons why.

Thoughtful teachers of all levels and subjects can find higher-level objectives for their students. They may, however, have better success with higher-level thinking by keeping objectives as close to the young child's world as possible. For example, in the evaluation level objectives above, very young students were asked to compare (and make judgments on) a famous figure from history to a family member or close adult friend rather than to another political figure about whom they would know little, if anything.

What problems hinder the process of taking children to higher levels of thinking? Higher-level objectives take more time. Therefore, obtaining success for children in higher-level thinking requires that "thinking time" be built into a teacher's plan. Another issue arises when teachers do not keep a Bloom's Taxonomy chart in their plan book. This more than likely means that plans are not inclusive of various levels of thinking in their objectives, so children will receive a hefty dose of lower-level objectives (which research shows is normally the case). Also, teachers may not have a good understanding of the behavioral terms under each of the categories. The state of Texas firmly believes that teachers must have a working knowledge of the terms and activities (as shown in Table 3.2) that are a part of each of Bloom's levels to formulate objectives, create activities, and ask questions at higher levels. To endorse this, Texas has previously included questions in its certification tests that require a working knowledge of Bloom's Taxonomy. This table shows a list of many observable behaviors and activities related to the six levels of thinking according to Bloom et al. (1956). To use the table easily, take a behavior verb from the first column and match it to any appropriate activity in the second column. The activity column represents the condition or circumstance under which the behavior will be completed. Teachers must decide what would be an appropriate circumstance for the behavior or skill to be learned (for example, "state facts," "recall steps," "interpret the graphs on page 10," "draw diagrams," and so forth, according to the needs of learners). Be sure that that there is an appropriate match to the goal that you are attempting to achieve. These are a few suggestions, but there are many more.

Considering the Degree for Assessment

There is yet another consideration in designing a good objective. We know already that good objectives include which learners are being targeted (the audience), exactly what behavior the teacher wants children to perform, and how children will demonstrate specific learning (the condition). The teacher, in designing an objective, must also think about one more factor: the *degree of proficiency,* or "how much" would be needed to say that, indeed, a student has learned. To get to the base of this, a teacher might ask him- or herself questions such as "What would be 'passing' on this objective?" or "How could I know if they really 'get it'?" The rationales for including this assessment component are crucial, as previously mentioned. First, teachers make judgments about what to teach next after they see how well children do. Second, teachers have to give feedback to children and others concerned with learning. Third, giving feedback fulfills yet another purpose—that of helping children become better self-evaluators. When children know what the expectations are for learning, they can often judge for themselves what progress is being made and act accordingly to self-correct.

Other elements are important in setting up the degree of proficiency. For instance, all parts of an objective must fit together tightly. The condition (discussed above) and the degree of proficiency in objectives should have a direct link to or synchronization with the goal. For example, in the objective, "The student will describe the causes of the

Table 3.2 Using Bloom's Taxonomy *(continued)*

Knowledge Level (Memorization/Gathering Information)	
Terms to Use (The student will . . .)	**Activity/Condition**
state	facts
recall	steps of a method
define	procedure
describe	definitions
name	information about/names of people
identify	events, places
memorize parts	facts from a speech, filmstrip, magazine article,
label	recording, play, television show, book, etc.
recognize	
locate	
draw	
select	
write	
recite	
list	
tell	
point to	

Comprehension Level (Understanding Knowledge)	
Terms to Use (The student will . . .)	**Activity/Condition**
explain	conclusions or implications
illustrate	a summary
paraphrase	an outline
restate	graphs, tables, etc., based on data
compare	diagram
match	analogies
change	causal relationships
transform	speeches
express	tape recordings
defend	cartoons
distinguish	stories
predict	dramas
relate	own statements
generalize	skits
infer	photographs
interpret	
convert	
extend	
put in order	
summarize	
trace	

continued

decline of the cotton industry in Texas on a true/false quiz," it can be seen clearly that there is not an appropriate match between the desired behavior and the assessment. "Describe" could mean many things, but it does not fit a true/false quiz. Also, using goal-like terms confuses commu-nication about assessment. Think what questions might be asked if an objective were to "know the regions of Texas" for a quiz tomorrow. Children (and likely their parents) would ask some hard questions: What exactly should be known about these regions? The names of these regions alone?

Table 3.2 Using Bloom's Taxonomy *(continued)*

Application Level
(Using Knowledge)

Terms to Use (The student will . . .)	Activity/Condition
(These activities will be exact representations rather than creating something new, as you see in synthesis.)	

Terms to Use (The student will . . .)	Activity/Condition
apply	questions
change	projects
report	solutions
solve	problems
choose	lists
interpret	paintings
draw	maps
show	cartoons, mobiles
modify	illustrations
put together	projects
paint	pictures of . . .
dramatize	meetings/events
collect	photographs
discover	diagrams
make	sculptures
prepare	paper that follows outline
construct	diorama
demonstrate	forecast

Analysis
(Breaking a Complex Problem into Parts)

Terms to Use (The student will . . .)	Activity/Condition
analyze	a questionnaire
classify	a part of a propaganda statement identified
examine	a graph
survey	an argument broken down
research	a survey
compare	a conclusion
contrast	a model
point out	a report
distinguish	a syllogism (deductive, inferential doctrine) broken down
investigate	
subdivide	
differentiate	
infer	
separate	
select	
subdivide	
construct	
take apart	
show the interrelation	
evaluate the relevancy of information	
recognize unstated assumptions	

continued

Their locations? Their main landforms? Their importance historically or now? Their main economies? Teachers must make absolutely sure that objectives communicate a clear picture and that assessment is clearly stated as a match (for example, "Fourth graders, given a map with the regions drawn in, will label and color each with a different colored map pencil"). Writing clear

Table 3.2 Using Bloom's Taxonomy *(continued)*

Synthesis
(Putting Together or Applying New Concepts in a Different Setting)

Terms to Use (The student will . . .)	Activity/Condition
combine	articles
role-play	plays
hypothesize	plans with an alternative
speculate on	courses of action
add to	songs
invent	games
decide what if	formulation of hypotheses or questions
write or rewrite (something new)	inventions
plan	reports
formulate	poems
create	rebus stories
organize	sets of rules, principles, or standards
develop	cartoons
design	books
produce	themes
originate	short stories
construct	plans
rearrange	new schemes
compose	
devise	
generate	
predict	

Evaluation
(Judging the Outcome or the Merits)

Terms to Use (The student will . . .)	Activity/Condition
appraise	conclusions
compare	self-evaluations
recommend	recommendations
critique	group discussions
weigh	court trials
solve	surveys
evaluate	evaluations
criticize	compared standards
summarize	established standards
relate	valuing/value of a work
consider	editorials
judge	
conclude	
justify	
assess	
choose	
debate	
measure	
prioritize	
rank	
rate	
score	

objectives helps map the way to a learning destination that teachers and children can easily follow. Writing obscure objectives does not benefit anyone in the educational process, least of all children.

In considering the degree of proficiency, motivation theory (in Competency 8, Chapter 13) tells us that appropriately designed objectives are those in which moderate difficulty is provided for children. Thus, some challenge should be offered, yet children should still be able to complete objectives and/or tasks and, most importantly perhaps, attribute their success to a good effort on their part. Being able to attribute success to one's own efforts is termed *locus of control*—an important concept in keeping children engaged. Setting inappropriate objectives that are too difficult or too easy can cause children to give up or become bored. Individual observation will tell a teacher whether his or her objectives and tasks are motivating and engaging for each child in the classroom and indicate that objectives are responsive to students' current skills and knowledge levels (another criteria for this competency).

The following formula revisits the elements of a good objective:

the exact learner + observable/measurable behavior + circumstance/condition under which the behavior will be measured + assessment of the behavior

Reflection on Objectives

Of course a teacher is not finished with goals and objectives after writing them. These objectives must now be taught. It is good teaching practice, as noted earlier, to communicate objectives to children for each lesson and to refer to the objectives during the lesson so that children know what they need to do in order to meet performance standards. Teacher appraisal instruments often require that a teacher tell children what the lesson objectives are. For this reason, many teachers of elementary children both tell and write objectives on the board so that children clearly understand what is expected of their learning. After the lesson has been taught, the teacher must then go back through each objec-

tive and reflect upon its usefulness toward the learning process and modify it for next time, if necessary. A teacher may want to ask some of the following reflective questions:

Did the objectives meet the needs of each learner?

Did the objectives turn out to be a good match for the desired goal?

How well were children able to meet the expectations of these objectives?

Were students' products or performances able to be assessed well under the degree set forth in the objectives?

Were objectives clear, relevant, and meaningful to students and others who might see them?

Can I continue tomorrow's objectives, or must I reteach?

LESSON PLAN FORMAT

Table 3.3 illustrates the beginning of a good lesson plan format. Although this format is quite exttensive, knowing and using this format well will help teachers completely understand the elements for this competency. In addition, a teacher's appraisal should be excellent, since this plan coalates with Texas teacher appraisal, and teachers will know that students are barraged with elements of good learning theory. Goals and objectives have already been discussed in detail. The remaining parts of the plan are discussed in more detail in Table 3.3.

CREATING RELEVANT, MEANINGFUL, AND AGE-APPROPRIATE GOALS AND OBJECTIVES

In the indicators for Competency 3, the words *relevant, meaningful,* and *age-appropriate* are emphasized, but how do teachers really accomplish these things in designing plans for young children? One way to accomplish this is by relating the content

Table 3.3 Lesson Plan Format

Overall Daily Goal	In general, what is it that I really want for children to learn/accomplish by my teaching this lesson? How will this lesson fit into the bigger picture of the unit/six-weeks/semester/year?
TEKS	Which of the TEKS requirements is being taught or strengthened? Is it the correct level for the child(ren)? Is it the correct sequence of knowledge and skills?
Time Constraints **Objectives**	Time anticipated to teach this lesson. Formula = who is the learner + what is the task/behavior + what is/are the condition(s) + what is the degree of accomplishment? Should be stated in "Bloom's terms." Should be observable and measurable. State "The student or learner will . . ." (do not state that the learner understands, appreciates, etc. These can't be seen to be measured [not observable].) —Lower-level objectives only are not acceptable. —Check to see that each thing children will do has a corresponding objective—almost all lessons have multiple objectives. —Put all objectives in the order in which the teacher anticipates they will happen in the lesson. —All four parts of a good objective given in the formula should be included.
Integrated Subjects	Remember that all lessons should include at least three subjects somewhere within the same lesson (for example: math, language arts, and music; science, art, and social studies, etc.). This will help create a more interesting plan and push the teacher to show how knowledge of one subject does not exist in a vacuum (shows authenticity).
Possible Sponge Activity	When children enter a room and the lesson will not begin for a moment (all children are not there yet, the teacher needs to take lunch count or attendance, etc.), the teacher may plan for an individual or group activity that can be done independently to help children begin to focus and remain in their seats until the lesson formally begins.
Focus (Anticipatory Set, "Hook")	This is an event that creates interest and ties into the lesson to be presented. It should entice students into the lesson. Thus using only questions for discussion is not usually acceptable, because they are often not as motivating and enticing for children as the teacher believes. It can be used to enhance the relevance of new knowledge to interest children.
Connection of Prior Knowledge	How will you find and tie what children may know already to what they will learn here? Or how will this knowledge apply to future knowledge? Touch on prior or future learning.
Touch on Community	Where would you find and tie this learning to children's known world? Begin nearest to children first (i.e., home, neighborhood, city, and so forth).
Culture	Is there any way to relate this lesson or knowledge to the cultures near the school? Is there a multicultural element that you could reference?
Student Interest	How can you relate this concept or information to something that is interesting to children? What does the child do in his/her spare time? What are the favorite movies, television shows, hobbies, and sports activities of children right now?

continued

Table 3.3 Lesson Plan Format *(continued)*

Rationale	What *good* reason should a student have for learning this lesson from you? (The mother of memorization is necessity.) Answer the question, "Teacher, why do I have to learn this stuff?" State in students' terms (not that it's going to be on the TAAS (or TAKS) test.
Materials	List everything you need to teach this lesson, plus all that students will need (students' needs/supplies and teacher's list of things needed for this lesson). List where teacher and student materials are located for ease of use. Check this list the last thing before leaving school in the afternoon and the first thing before school each morning.
Activities or Instructional Input	What will you do to get students through the objectives above? What seating arrangements are necessary? List steps you will follow and the teaching skills and strategies you will use. Identify how you will model content and/or tasks. Tell why you are choosing the methods you are using.
Guided Practice	What will students do, activity-wise, as you "hold them by the hand" to get them started through the materials to be learned? List steps: (The teacher will. . .)
Independent Practice	What activity will students perform all by themselves to exhibit that they have learned the objectives?
What Will Students Do If They Finish Early?	Decide and tell students exactly what you expect them to do if they finish early (as a reinforcer and/or a management tool).
Assessment	List not only the activity you will evaluate but also select one or more of the following questions to answer: How will you be able to tell whether a student "got it" and how well they "got it"? Tell what a child must do on an activity (criteria) to get an A, B, C, D, F (or an S/U)? What are the teacher's expectations for the achievement of these grades? What is a passing grade? How will the activity be graded? Provide a rubric, if appropriate (see Competency 10). Give the rubric or expectations to children in advance for objectivity and student success.
Closure	How will you reinforce what children have learned one last time? (For mini-closures, how and when will you close on information given throughout the lesson?)
Transition	Think about moving to the next lesson or next setting. Decide in advance how to do that (singing a song, changing seating arrangements, referencing the past lesson, etc.).
Environmental Concerns	Sometimes lessons are better when taught at a certain time of year, during certain weather conditions, etc. Note these concerns here.
Any Anticipated Problem(s)	Special seating, getting materials to students at the same time, grouping, etc.
Modifications	Any modifications for special needs students must be included in a plan (see Competency 13, Chapter 19).

Remember that everything should tie together in a "neat package"—all parts work together to make sense as a whole.

to the need for actually learning the information or skill(s). Another way is relating the information to the real world, which is closely knit with the part of a lesson plan that deals with rationale and providing for interdisciplinary studies.

Rationale

In presenting a **rationale**, teachers engage children in reasons that the information and/or skills that are contained in the lesson are important.

"Necessity is the mother of memorization (or acquisition)" is a phrase that teachers should keep in mind. If there is a good reason to know or be able to do, children will be much more inclined to interact with the knowledge or skills than when they believe there is little or no reason for retaining the information or drilling the skills. Think about how many times you may have sat in a class as a student and wondered, "When will I ever use this?" The information or skill may be remembered long enough for a test, and then it is gone. When there is relevance, however, learners are much more motivated to acquire and retain the information or skill. Such statements as, "You will need to know this some day," or "It will be on the test," are not engaging rationales. Teachers may say instead, "There is a need to know this or be able to do this because . . ." or "This concept or skill is tested because . . ." A rationale should have solid substance in the real world. The closer teachers can relate a rationale to what the child knows or can do now, the more relevant the information will seem to the child.

There are several ways to engage children in a rationale. A teacher may simply *tell* children why the material is important to them and exactly when and/or where they can use the information or skill. Or the teacher may design the lesson to help children discover that information for themselves. For example, a class project may ask children to find "25 Ways to Use Math in Real Life." Finally, teachers may ask children to predict when the information or skills may be used either now or in their futures and then help them to verify or encourage the logic of their predictions. By doing so, teachers are trying to "beat students to the draw" on the question that will certainly be asked if they do not bring it up first: "Teacher, why do we have to learn this stuff?"

Integrated Subjects

Relating content to the need for having the information or skill(s) and to the "real world" is closely knit with the rationale for providing for interdisciplinary studies, or working across the curriculum. Let us first examine the part that providing

for interdisciplinary studies plays. When schools departmentalize by giving teachers only one or two subjects to teach, these subjects often become disconnected from other subjects in the grade level. This occurs, too, when self-contained elementary teachers say, "It's time for math now, boys and girls." Unfortunately, science and language arts rarely meet in a lesson, and the same occurs with mathematics and social studies. Yet, in the real world, many topics invariably overlap. Statistics and experiments play a huge part in health; social studies depend on graphs and mathematical skills; language arts are essential for communication in the sciences. Teachers must make these connections concretely clear.

To engage children in seeing connections that each subject area has in the real world, Texas asks teachers to cross over the boundaries that have been long established in subject specialization and to reference and use subject areas together. Thus, **interdisciplinary integration** means to make connections between and among other subject areas somewhere within each lesson or within integrated thematic units. In both self-contained and departmentalized schools, curriculum can be integrated easily. In both, teachers can often and easily reference how one subject area can be a part of another. Self-contained classrooms can promote this concept through thematic units (see Competency 3, Chapter 4). If a teacher is departmentalized (teaches only one or two subjects), collaboration between teachers at his or her grade level can increase the relevance of curriculum for children by connecting learning throughout the grade level. For example, departmentalized fourth-grade teachers plan that when they are studying the development of the cattle industry in Texas history, children will also be singing western songs of that era in music, reading stories of the Old West with their language arts teacher, and working on math problems that deal with distances and speed (two concepts that helped the development of rail lines to connect to trail heads during this period of history). In addition to strengthening these relevant and significant connections, the lesson will turn out to be much more interesting for students.

Touching on the Community, Culture, and Student Interest

Relevance is also closely related to **touching on the community,** local culture, and/or bringing the subject matter into the realm of **student interests.** These areas are also important in thinking about student background, because a teacher considers *all* of a child's experiences in school and out. A teacher should (somewhere in the lesson) relate concepts or skills to the child's world and to what he or she already knows. The best place to begin relating a lesson to a child's world is to think of where connections can be made between the information or skills that will be taught and the homes or neighborhoods of children. If the concept or skill cannot be used or seen there, move out a bit to the city or state in which the child lives and try to make a connection there. Finally, expand to the nation or the world. In other words, think of the information or skill in terms of how closely a child can already relate to it. Developmentally, we know that young children often cannot relate to abstract concepts, so by concretely tying information to the world with which they are familiar, teachers increase understanding. The more concretely the reality for using the concept or skill is explained, the more likely it is to be seen by the child as relevant and thus be stored in the child's memory. For example, when children begin to learn subtraction skills, teachers should design objectives that help them understand that these skills are needed for ensuring correct change at the store or fast-food drive-in (given by name) where they are often taken to purchase after-school treats. Perhaps teachers can ask local establishments to contribute items for props that can be used in role-playing these skills. If older elementary students are beginning to learn about force, have them see videotapes of a local flood or storm, where natural forces are shown in a neighborhood in their own town, city, or state. This is another way of showing relevance to the real world of the child. Many children live in towns that are diverse. Relating skills and knowledge to diverse groups, when possible, also makes information more relevant to children.

If a classroom has little diversity, it is a good opportunity for a teacher to demonstrate how diversity can contribute to a community.

Age-appropriateness and relating to students' interests are also important elements for lessons. Pay close attention to not only what children are generally able to do but also what will motivate children in their age group. If a teacher is uncertain about objectives that might be inappropriate for children's abilities, he or she should check Competency 1, Chapter 1, for information on Piaget's Stages of Development and/or the grade level TEKS.

To continue to examine meaningful lessons, we can look again at Competency 1 to determine what the child's world is like and what children are seeking at each developmental level. Generally, younger children are interested in the latest toys and movie theme items, while older elementary children, although also interested in these aspects, can relate to poetry through song lyrics they enjoy, and are interested in various sports activities. Teachers must pay close attention to what children say they do away from school and bring those ideas into lessons. It is profitable for teachers to see the latest popular children's films or television shows because they usually spawn a variety of toys, games, and books that children enjoy and to which they relate. Providing objectives that induce children to share their own experiences also makes lessons more meaningful and provides relevance. Research shows, for example, that exemplary teachers working in inner-city schools emphasized the appreciation of cultural diversity and enhanced children's self-esteem by providing opportunities for children to relate personal experiences to the content being learned (Cabello & Terrell, 1994).

Prior Knowledge

Relating prior knowledge to new information can also help relevancy and meaningful application, along with another element to be considered—those prerequisite skills and knowledge necessary for success. Prerequisite skills and/or knowledge should be reviewed before new learning. It is very difficult for children to see that new information and skills are meaningful when they have not been properly sequenced and tied to past learning—that is, they seem to appear "out of the blue." How meaningful, for example, would the following description of a slide picture be? "Localization of GFP-tagged H2Kb (an MHC class I molecule and mannosidase II, a medial Golgi marker) in L-M mouse fibroblast cells. H2Kb assembles in the ER and traffics to the cell surface through the secretory pathway." Unless one has a biology background, it is probably meaningless and sounds "Greek" without prior knowledge. Let's see, though, what a bit of background knowledge can do to help **scaffold** this to make it more relevant for us to engage with the information. If we were reminded that GFP is a "Green Fluorescent Protein" isolated from a jellyfish that can be genetically expressed in other cells (even whole organisms) as part of a larger protein (or proteins) and that H2Kb is an MHC particular class of molecule (it stands for "Major Histocompatibility Class" of proteins), we have some information, but we still might not be willing to engage. If we knew that this type of protein plays an essential role in an immune response (obviously, quite important in the development of vaccines for diseases), we might begin to understand why we should be interested. Finally, we may be told that it is a major present-day research goal to try to understand how a cell responds to antigen exposure, so this picture of an experiment shows the pathway. Although one may not be able to function in a microbiology lab, it can be seen that with just a bit of background knowledge, participation and a bit more motivation to engage are now more likely.

The job of teachers is to try to provide a link to students' schemas (as discussed in Competency 1, Chapter 1) so that knowledge can be more easily attained and retained. Teachers do not want to be "speaking Greek" or to introduce concepts "out of the blue" to children. Their plans should reflect how they will scaffold the information so that children can work upward in their thinking

processes from what they know to what they will know. One way to do this is to remind children of what they already know. For example, a teacher might say, "We are going to begin division with remainders today, boys and girls, but do you know how easy it will be? Half of the problem is subtraction—something you are already good at!" A teacher might also provide some supplemental information up front, saying, "Our story today is about a family in Japan. Before we read, let me tell you about some different customs that you will find in this story, so that you will better understand as the story unfolds." Yet another method is to simply review, as in "Class, let's review what we learned about plants yesterday, and then we will continue to learn about their seeds today. Now who can tell one thing you remember?"

Bruner's approach to learning states that knowledge is constructed by relating incoming knowledge to a store of knowledge that has already been acquired—or a person' unique model of his or her world. As new information enters, it is categorized, based upon what the person already knows (Rosser & Nicholson, 1984). This is covered earlier in Competency 1, Chapter 1, where children who have attained a category (or schema) for "a bird" as something with feathers and a beak can easily add a parrot, for example, to their category the first time they see one. Without a category, there can be difficulty identifying and retaining the new knowledge. A teacher's job is to try to provide a link to students' possible known categories so that knowledge can be better "hooked on" and retained. Much of this can be done in advance if teachers think about ways to link new knowledge to prior knowledge throughout their plans.

Focus

Even the **focus** activity (sometimes called an "anticipatory set," "hook," or "stage setting") can work to make lessons meaningful and relevant, and it has the function of connecting new knowledge with the interests of children. A focus activity is an introducing event that a teacher plans so as to "entice" children into the lesson in some manner. "Take out your math book and turn to page 25," certainly focuses attention on the fact that it is time for mathematics, but it does nothing to create an open door for learning. What a difference in a lesson on storms or electricity, for instance, if a teacher shows a short video clip of *Back to the Future,* when lightning hits a clock tower, winds its way down through town, and starts a time-machine car! Reading short, relevant books or a page of a diary, constructing inquiry activities, selecting video clips, dressing as a character, using a sensory experience, playing a game or singing a related song, having children role-play, and a host of other activities can increase the chances that children will be drawn into the lesson from the start.

The Role of the TEKS in Lesson Planning

As a teacher continues the lesson design, he or she must think about activities that match skills. For instance, a teacher might ask, "What are the skills involved in fourth-grade writing, and is there a sequence to those skills?" Then the teacher would arrange the skills logically and sequentially. For example, writing an organized paragraph correctly should come before writing a good persuasive argument. The TEKS provide logical and sequential guidelines. Most often a teacher can use the TEKS to answer questions such as, "Are there prerequisite skills and knowledge that children should have before I can teach this?" As noted above, the TEKS have been designed to provide an age-appropriate outline for what children should be able to do at every grade level and in most subject areas. TEKS can be accessed for each grade level online at the address at the end of the chapter. The following information quoted from the listed Web site demonstrates the importance of the TEKS in Texas (www.utdanacenter.org/ssi/teksforleaders/):

■ TEKS are the center of the curriculum and, as such, define the basic content of the instructional program in Texas.

■ TEKS outline the knowledge and skills required of every student by the statewide accountability system.

■ Successful implementation of TEKS is dependent upon school staff having a thorough understanding of TEKS.

■ Increased student achievement is best assured by high-quality classroom instruction with a TEKS focus.

A continuous reminder flows through this book: schools test children on TEKS through the TAAS (or TAKS) test, and schools and teachers are held accountable for these scores. Though planning around TAAS (or TAKS) may at first seem burdensome to a new teacher, TEKS really are an excellent starting point for lessons with skills that children need for preparation and readiness, for testing, and for life. TEKS also provide a map for long-range planning that is developmentally sequential. This is extremely important for children in levels Pre-K–4 because of their many developmental differences (described in Competency 1, Chapter 1). For example, remember that Pre-K and kindergarten children who may be in Piaget's preoperation stage may not yet be able to perform tasks that involve seriation (placing objects in size order), classification, conservation (quantities remain the same despite changes in their appearance), centering (concentration on one dimension of an object, such as height, and ignoring others, such as width), reversibility, animism (inanimate objects are believed to be alive), and so forth. It is certain that the educators who have designed TEKS have carefully thought through these developmental levels for Pre-K–4 children and have devised skills and knowledge criteria that are appropriately sequenced for optimum learning.

TEKS can provide an excellent base for beginning sequential planning, but there is more to remember about sequencing. Each skill taught has a sequence that is easier to learn if children "walk before they run." For example, in methods classes, teacher candidates should have already learned about the sequence in which children understand and master handwriting skills. Every subject area has certain knowledge or skills that are prerequisites to understanding. School texts also have been written to follow logical sequences of learning. Thus, social studies texts often begin with an introduction of map skills. Each year these skills will repeat and advance slightly through a spiraling curriculum. To follow the idea of sequencing based on a spiral curriculum, note that after very young social studies students have mastered a few basic age-appropriate map skills, they are normally asked to apply those skills to investigate a part of the school, then a neighborhood situation. In each year that follows, these basic skills are reviewed and more advanced map skills are added. The learners in upper grades are asked to widen their horizons increasingly by using the skills first to examine the state, then the nation, and finally the world with map skills.

In viewing the importance of sequencing it should be remembered that each lesson should also maintain proper sequencing as it is introduced to children. Consequently, activities and information in each lesson should begin at the simplest, most concrete level and build upward to complex skills or knowledge. Teachers should also move from the introduction of skills or knowledge to guided and supported work and finally to independent work. Often we say that a lesson should move from parts to whole, indicating that a teacher should break down skills or information to its most simple for introduction purposes and build to the whole during the lesson. A lesson on a particular landform (a mountain, for instance) could begin with the introduction and include many picture examples of various types of mountains (and perhaps some nonexamples), along with a clear definition. The lesson would then move to guided practice with manipulatives. For instance, children should first follow the teacher's exact example of making the landform with clay; then the teacher should direct them to construct their own examples of the landform. Children next complete guided practice on paper, where the teacher helps children to identify the landform on

a map key. Finally children move to independent work on paper, where they complete a map key with the landform on which they have worked. This attention to sequence in many aspects of instruction will help children gain the knowledge and skills that teachers want them to learn.

Teacher Input

Teacher input is the main section of the lesson. It provides children with opportunities to engage new skills and/or knowledge in activities. It is in this part of the lesson plan that teachers decide what strategies and activities they will use to help children learn the objectives. A *strategy* deals with "how" a teacher will go about having children gain knowledge or skills. Popular teaching strategies include lecture presentations, Computer-Assisted Instruction, discussion, seatwork, learning centers, cooperative groups, and so forth. *Activities* are what children actually do. Therefore, if children are asked in cooperative groups to fill a brown bag with pictures that have the "b" sound, the strategy is the group work and the activity is the "B Bag."

Teachers must be careful to sequence activities in such a way as to guide children carefully through new steps. To review, one should think of a child who is learning any new skill—perhaps, even how to walk. Children must "crawl before they walk and walk before they run" in learning. If activities "take children by the hand and lead them through information/skills" little by little and in correct sequence for understanding, when children reach independent practice, they should be ready to attempt the skill or use the knowledge alone. For example, in introducing subtraction, what would happen if a teacher gave children ten written subtraction problems to do for the first activity? Success would be minimal at best. However, if the teacher first had children "act out" some subtraction "situations" in front of the class, demonstrated subtraction on the felt board with felt objects, provided manipulatives for each child or group to do subtraction at their desks, and finally (for independent practice) presented children with a written page of problems—would learners be more successful in understanding this concept? More than likely so. This is the sequence that teachers should take into consideration in designing the order of activities within a lesson.

Planning for **authentic activities** and authentic conditions also helps to support real-world connections. When designing objectives and strategies, teachers should therefore search for strategies that allow for products and performances that are more "real world." For example, will a child learn more about operating in a democratic society by just reading about democracy or by participating in activities that simulate democratic principles? Will a child learn more about the reason for knowing addition and subtraction facts correctly by doing sheets of problems or by keeping his or her own checkbook? Will a student be more motivated to write a "form" friendly letter to be turned in for a grade or to write to a real pen pal on the Internet who will send an answer? Searching for real-life applications helps teachers to become experts in relevancy. Another part of creating authenticity involves performances and products that are unfragmented from the whole. Practicing components of correct punctuation for letter writing, for instance, may have its benefits, but if never used in the context of actually writing letters, it loses its relevance quickly for children.

Assessment

In designing objectives, an assessment component was already included. Why have another assessment area in the lesson plan? At times, assessment is very clear cut in the objectives (for example, "Students will correctly answer 70 percent of 10 problems"). However, at other times teachers have to consider much more as they are planning. For example, in the subject of writing, objectives might state that "The student will write a paragraph," yet that statement certainly does not give children clear expectations on how it will be assessed. Providing a rubric or clear details for children ahead of time on writing assignments,

projects, presentations, and so forth, helps children match those expectations much better and helps teachers be more objective in their grading.

It may also seem very easy for teachers to compare children's work if no assessment standards are set before certain types of assignments. For example, Mrs. Littleton sat down to grade her third graders' paragraphs that she had assigned that day. "My," she noted, "Josh wrote a pretty good one! Five sentences! He also has a topic sentence and a closing sentence. I'll give him an 'A'!" But next she picks up Darla's paragraph and sees that Darla has filled the page with details, along with the correct formatting. Now the teacher, who did not set expectations ahead of time (for herself or for children), is tempted to go back and give Josh a "B." Yet both children may really have met the requirements that the teacher vaguely encouraged. In addition, when the teacher hands back the papers, she may end up in an argument with LeTosha (who receives a "C-" for her three sentences), who correctly states, "Well, you just said you wanted a paragraph with a topic and closing sentence!" Children will feel that assessment is much more meaningful and fair if criteria needed for a grade are developed and specified ahead of time. For more details on rubrics, see Competency 10, Chapter 15, on assessment. The more a teacher can tell children about what is expected on a task or skill, the better return he or she will have, and when children do not match the expectations, there will be no question in their minds as to why their assessment was lower. This helps create a locus of control, where children see themselves as controlling what happens in the classroom with their learning rather than seeing their grades as a teacher's whim or a subjective opinion.

Teachers may not want to record a grade for each objective. However, they will always want to know whether children "got it" or not. Therefore teachers should decide how they will know, being sure to consider the circumstances. Lilah Brown, for example, wrote that she would know that her students had achieved success through oral questions at the end of the lesson. However, she didn't allow enough time at the end of the lesson; thus only about a third of the class received a question. That circumstance would not help her know whether the class in general "got it" and certainly not whether many of her individual learners understood the material. Teachers who go back over their plans to ensure that all parts work in concert are better prepared to make judgments on children's learning.

Closure and Reflection

Many times teachers end their lessons with, "Oops! It's time to go to lunch!" or "Put your things away quickly. The bell is about to ring!" Yet allowing time for reflection at the end of each lesson and unit can be extremely valuable to the process of learning. It is easy to write this into your lesson plan(s) as **miniclosures** and/or a final **closure.** After information has been presented, it is a simple but important matter to have children reflect upon the most important things they have learned. This is an excellent time to ask for or make connections to other learning as well. ("How is our butterfly unit like the one that we have just finished in health?") This can also be done in the middle of any lesson or unit, as a teacher pauses and asks children, "Now who can tell what the steps are that we have just learned?" "Let's remind ourselves of the story line once again," "Give me a very quick definition of the most important terms that we learned today," and so forth. Teachers who maintain clarity in learning seek time to reiterate what learning is important. Making time to let this information "sink in" can help bring attention back to what is truly important throughout the lesson. One reason that reflective closure is so significant to learning is the rehearsal and/or focus factors—that is, children hear information and its importance several times, and their attention is directly and purposefully focused. For researchers, repetition and focus are both elements that help set information in long-term memory. Even when one or more miniclosures have been accomplished during the lesson, teachers should still use a closure at lesson completion, for the brain often picks up on the first and last parts of a study session. Directly and clearly stating the objectives at the beginning sets the aim of the lesson, while closure gives children an opportunity to reflect again on the most important aspects of what they have learned. Closure should also help to bring to children's minds the answer to the "all important" question at home at the end of the day: "Well, what did you learn today in school?"

Other Details of the Plan

Time constraints. Teachers must consider their time constraints carefully when designing lessons of substance. Being able to anticipate how quickly or slowly a lesson will proceed is not always easy for new teachers, but teachers should consider that a lesson that allows time for *reflection, self-assessment,* and *closure* will be more meaningful for students. Planning lessons with enough activities to last through the allotted time is also important for management. Children will very rarely "just sit quietly for five minutes" until it is time for lunch, music, or so forth.

Sponge activity. A **sponge activity** is an optional part of the plan, but it can be an important activity for the teacher and students. Often individual children enter the room at different times, with no assignment. The teacher may not be quite ready to begin formal instruction until all students have arrived. Teachers may also need a few moments, for example, to complete attendance and lunch count or other paperwork, to set up equipment or labs, and so forth. Without something to occupy them, children may begin to talk loudly or move about the room. However, if a teacher has an independent activity (usually put on the board in the same place each day as a routine), children know to come into the classroom and begin work quietly. Sponge activities should be short and can tie to the current lesson or review a previous lesson or concept in some manner. An example for a sponge activity in math, for instance, is to draw a picture that uses only triangles; for language arts: list all the words that you can think of that rhyme with ____ or have the same long or short vowel, etc,; for social studies: draw a store that you like to visit; and for science: draw three animals that you know live in the jungle.

Materials. When teachers plan for an exciting lesson, they look for materials and resources that will enhance meaningful connections and learning. Matching and finding resources are discussed in Competency 3, Part 4, Chapter 2. Without fail, a teacher must be sure to list on the lesson plan all of the materials and equipment that he or she wants to use in a lesson. The job is not done yet, however, because the teacher must also be sure to check this list the day before a lesson and the first thing in the morning before teaching. More than one exciting lesson has failed because the teacher forgot to check out equipment in time, go by the store to pick up a special item, or remind children to bring specific supplies. Other typical obstacles could be that a book that the teacher intended to read as a focus activity was checked out, there was a long line at the copy machine (so an activity was not copied in time), the school ran out of red construction paper, the sheet that a teacher thought was in the file cabinet couldn't be found, and so forth. In addition, classroom management can wane when a teacher turns his or her back to search for items. Writing down these materials and locating them ahead of time ensures that children have a richer learning experience.

Transitions. When teachers are closing one lesson, they may be immediately opening a new one. A teacher who thinks ahead to make a link between one lesson and the next can create more relevance in learning for children. Teachers who plan for good **transitions** between lessons can think ahead about how to make these links and about the need for movement to different seating arrangements, putting away of previous materials, getting out new materials, and so forth. Visualizing these arrangements and planning for them also helps maintain good management. Within the lesson, teachers can also make decisions about how students will move easily from one activity to another.

Modifications

Teachers are required by law to follow modifications for special needs students (see Competency 13, Chapter 19). These modifications should be written in teachers' plans. Examiners from the state schedule visits to schools to ensure that a school is in compliance with many regulations. Modifications on lesson plans is one thing for which state inspectors often look. The reason for writing modifications, of course, is to ensure that special needs learners are receiving instruction within their abilities from each teacher.

THE LESSON CYCLE

The teacher must remember that teaching is a cycle. As the closure ends a lesson, the teacher has a last chance to assess whether the objectives were met and the lesson was learned (or not). If not, reteaching the content or skills in a different way should be the recourse for the next day's lesson. If the teacher notes success, the next lesson can progress further. Other questions should be asked about how the plan worked. For example, were there strengths and weaknesses in this lesson? If so, a wise teacher notes them on his or her written plans for fine-tuning before this lesson is taught again. Did the materials work well? Are there other resources that could be added? Did children engage in the lesson well? If a small number of children still must have remediation, how will that be accomplished in the coming days? Did the lesson fit well into the time frame that was established? If not, what could be added or taken away? This type of reflection aids teachers in improving their lessons over time and in becoming more aware of the need to know their learners well.

SUMMARY

The purpose of this chapter was multifold. It was written to help teachers: (a) understand the role that goals and objectives play in the world of education, particularly the connection to Texas goals and objectives (TEKS); (b) gain knowledge about the role of long-range goals and plans; (c) understand the intricacies of writing good goals and objectives; (d) consider other areas of the lesson plan that help in providing clear, relevant, age-appropriate, and meaningful instruction; and (e) design lessons in which children explore content in varied ways.

In reviewing the need for designing plans, please do not think that this is another one of those "educational designs" that serves no purpose but to cause work for teachers. Good planning is truly a road map for teachers' yearly and day-to-day professional lives. Effective, experienced teachers may no longer write such elaborate plans as suggested here, but be assured that they have mentally framed plans after years of experience of writing plans. Why do they still need this framework? Plans make sure that children are taught well in the time available and for the sequence needed in knowledge or skill development. Plans help teachers stay focused on set goals rather than being "activity oriented," and they help all stakeholders understand the amount of knowledge or the number of skills and proficiency gained in order to make further curriculum decisions. Planning helps teachers think ahead for the prevention of management problems that may occur as a result of changing strategies or groupings. When a teacher visualizes a lesson ahead of time, she or he can better maintain the flow of a lesson in dealing with the constant interruptions and intrusions that occur in a school setting. Being able to articulate a learning path *for* children (and *to* children) and to the many others interested in education is an important step in becoming a professional. All in all, writing good plans is a worthwhile (and critical) endeavor for children's learning.

GLOSSARY

age-appropriateness   specified skills and tasks (and the quantity to be given) should be able to be accomplished both physically and mentally by a child at a particular age and/or stage of development. The knowledge

to be taught is also judged to be suitable for the age in terms of interest and in terms of topics and presentations seen as suitable for young children.

analysis level   the fourth level of thinking in Bloom's Taxonomy, in which children break apart a complex problem into parts. This is a considered to be a higher level of thinking.

application level   the third level of thinking in Bloom's Taxonomy, in which children must use or apply what they have learned in some manner by solving, constructing, demonstrating, and so forth. The application level is still considered lower-level thinking.

authentic activities/conditions   activities that support real-world connections by attempting to include products and performances that are more "real world" in their applications (writing a letter that will be sent rather than just copying a form, etc.).

closure   at the end of a topic and/or lesson, teachers ask students to sum up or reflect on the important parts of the lesson in some way.

comprehension level   the second level of thinking in Bloom's Taxonomy, in which children demonstrate that they understand by explaining, illustrating, comparing, and so forth. The comprehension level is considered a lower level of thinking.

district/campus goals   many districts and campuses have aims, guidelines, and/or standards for their children that teachers must consider when planning.

evaluation level   the highest level of thinking in Bloom's Taxonomy, in which children make supported judgments of outcomes, decide merits, critique, and so forth.

focus   (sometimes called an "anticipatory set," "hook," "introductory set," or "stage setting") is an event that a teacher plans so as to "entice" children into the lesson in some manner.

goal   a general, broad idea of what the teacher (and others interested in education) want children to learn.

interdisciplinary   integration and planning that makes connections with various subject areas somewhere within each lesson or within integrated thematic units.

knowledge level   the lowest level of thinking in Bloom's Taxonomy, in which children must only recall information or knowledge.

long-range goals   a general map of a teacher's aims for the entire school year in all subjects areas that she or he teaches; normally required to be on file at one's school.

long-range plans   a logical, sequential map of the general knowledge and skills to be taught during units of time (can be for the year, semester, six-weeks, units, etc.). It matches long-range goals.

miniclosure   during the course of a lesson the teacher may pause at different points to sum up and reflect on parts of the lesson that children have just covered.

objective   a specific statement of observable, measurable learning behavior given in terms of who the learner is, what the behavior is, the conditions under which learning will take place (usually the task), and the degree of accomplishment expected.

observable behavior   behaviors for objectives must be able to be seen or heard so that teachers can measure and assess how well an objective and/or a task has been accomplished.

prior knowledge   knowledge about or skill in some area of study that a child already possesses; if teachers tap into this, the chance is greater that children will be able to engage their schema, add to it, and learn more quickly.

rationale   the part of the lesson plan that specifies the reasons for teaching/learning a lesson; telling learners where they will use the knowledge or skills to be taught.

scaffolding   making connections to prior and future learning.

scope   how much or how deeply into a topic instruction will delve.

sponge activity   an activity employed when children enter a room where the lesson will not begin for a moment (all children are not there yet, the teacher needs to take lunch count or attendance, etc.). The teacher may plan for an individual or group activity that can be done independently to help children begin to focus and remain in their seats until the lesson formally begins.

student background   the child's home situation, prior learning, and so forth, that teachers consider when preparing lessons.

student interests   if teachers can tap into what children like/are interested in at a particular grade level and time, students may be more drawn to the information and work in a more motivated manner; part of a good lesson plan.

synthesis level   the next-to-highest level of thinking in Bloom's Taxonomy, in which children put together or apply new concepts in a different setting or create something new.

TAAS   Texas Assessment of Academic Skills; tests the TEKS that are curriculum guidelines set by the state of Texas as basic standards of knowledge and skills.

TAKS   Texas Assessment of Knowledge and Skills; will take the place of the TAAS tests to assess the TEKS (Texas Essential Knowledge and Skills).

teacher input   the part of the lesson plan in which the teacher arranges for children to use new information through guided practice (where the teacher supports children through practicing the use of new knowledge and/or skills) and independent practice (where children attempt new skills and/or knowledge on their own).

TEKS   Texas Essential Knowledge and Skills, which provides a curriculum guide for each grade level tested through the TAAS (Texas Assessment of Academic Skills) or in 2003, the TAKS (Texas Assessment of Knowledge and Skills).

touching on the community   the part of the lesson plan in which a teacher makes connections between new learning and where a child might find that learning in his or her world.

transition   moving from one activity or setting to another.

SUGGESTED ACTIVITIES

1. Obtain the district and/or campus goals for your field placement (or your own district and/or school campus). Observe a planning session and note how those goals are taken into consideration in the planning process.

2. Observe a planning session and note specifically which elements are taken into consideration in terms of long-range planning (through the week, month, and year). Note which elements seem most important (state testing, holidays, seasons, and so forth).

3. After observing a lesson, ask your mentor teacher what his or her goals were in presenting this lesson. Determine in what ways the goal(s) and the actual lesson matched.

4. In your field placement, note if and when teachers give objectives to students (orally or written) during a lesson. Also note how often teachers relate to prior skills and knowledge, relate to the "real world," and consider age-appropriateness during their lesson. What seems to be the effect on children when these are given or not given (or considered or not considered)?

5. Download the TEKS for the grade level in which you are most interested. Follow the progression of one subject or content area. Note the sequencing of the objectives.

6. Observe a grade-level meeting in which the TEKS are used in planning. Find out how these TEKS are aligned with the TAAS (or TAKS) test or other tests in your district or school.

7. Design a lesson plan that includes:

   - goals and objectives that are designed using the criteria in this chapter

   - rationales for the "real world"

   - consideration of student background, prior knowledge, and student interest

   - activities appropriate for the cognitive stages in your desired age group

   - activities using various models of teaching that encourage critical thinking

   - touching upon the community and interests of the student

   - a relevant focus

   - any adaptations to district/campus goals

   - varied resources

   - a strong closure

8. Generate a list of 50 real-world uses for mathematics, language arts, social studies, and so forth.

9. Collect a number of lessons from various Web sites or other sources (some sites are found at the end of this chapter). If their objectives do not match the criteria listed in this chapter (including observable and measurable behaviors and criteria for assessment), change and further develop the objectives so that they do match.

10. Reflect on your own beliefs about the development of children in stages. What will your beliefs mean for children in your classroom? Further reflect upon strategies that will help you plan goals and objectives better for a class with children who are in various stages of development.

11. Think back upon a class that you enjoyed. Reflect upon how that teacher or professor made the class relevant and meaningful. How can you bring that to your own teaching?

12. Reflect upon your beliefs and expectations about the social skills and other types of

knowledge that children bring to school. Further reflect upon why it is worth the addition of these skills into our plans and into our everyday teaching.

13. Occasionally a mentor may say, "I can't believe you have to write that long, detailed lesson plan for your teacher education program." Reflect upon how you might answer as a knowledgeable educator.

PRACTICE QUESTIONS

1. Mrs. Perez teaches second grade in an urban Texas school and enjoys working with other teachers to plan. "It's really easy and fun when everyone is talking and contributing ideas," she noted. In Tuesday's planning session, teachers began to look ahead to the coming month.

   "I think that we really ought to do the unit on butterflies," Ms. McNamara said. "It's getting to be spring and we can work that into science pretty easily. What do you say we look at some activities for that?"

   "Sure, we're happy to go in that direction!" said two other grade-level teachers.

   "I have some great activities on butterflies that the kids just love," Mr. Shaw noted, "They are so much fun to teach! Let me go get my file."

   Mrs. Perez, however, voiced some concern before continuing. The other teachers teased her and said, "You just aren't flexible!" Mrs. Perez was worried that:

   A. A butterfly unit would not be age-appropriate for second graders.

   B. The long-range goals were not consulted.

   C. District and school goals were not consulted.

   D. Both B and C.

2. Jeff Bjorklund showed Ms. Luna, his mentor, an objective that he wrote for the next day's fourth-grade history lesson. "I'm going to be going into all of the reasons that the Texas colonists were angry with Mexico," Jeff told her. The objective stated, "The learner will understand five causes of the Texas Revolu-

tion." Ms. Garcia pointed out that this objective is problematic because it is:

A. Not observable

B. Teacher-centered

C. Too challenging for students in the fourth grade

D. Student-centered

3. Mrs. McAden, principal at Bayside Elementary, was reviewing Mrs. Warner's plans for the coming week. For Wednesday's first-grade reading lesson, Mrs. Warner had written the following:

> Students will read a story about quilts orally in class.

> Students will make paper quilts of their own.

Mrs. McAden wrote a note in the block where this lesson was written. She most probably wrote:

A. "This looks like fun!! Children are going to love this!"

B. "What is your goal here?"

C. "I'm not sure which book you've selected, but "Grandma Bertha's Quilt" is just out and is great for this age group."

D. "I'm glad to see that you are using behavioral objectives now. I appreciate it!"

4. Mr. Farran wanted to include some good objectives at higher levels of thinking in his plans for a fourth-grade unit on the solar system. Which of the following should *not* be included:

A. The learner will tell which planet he/she believes is the most important to us (besides Earth).

B. The learner will select the planet that he/she feels is important to Earth and create a model that depicts that in some way.

C. Students will consider the worth of the amount of money spent so far on space travel and recommend that the space program continue or be discontinued.

D. Students will write a poem about one of the planets of their choice.

5. Ms. Abuhamad teaches fourth grade in an inner-city school where most children are on free lunch. The parents of her students are not well educated for the most part, and many are not readers. Most speak Spanish in the home. She began to teach a unit around a story about a neighborhood setting in which two students live near their grandparents and visits are often made—right across the border in Mexico. In an effort to include some interdisciplinary areas, Ms. Abuhamad decided to integrate some mathematics and social studies questions into the story. After she had taught one story, she asked some of the following types of questions in her discussion: "Let's say," she said, "that you are going to drive from where this story takes place to Wisconsin for a vacation in the lake district "(walking to the map to point out where Wisconsin is)" near where I went to school. How long do you think it will take you to get there by car? If I left here at 8:00 in the morning on a plane, how many hours do you think it would take?" However, this question did not motivate students and several became distracted and inattentive as she tried cuing students to answer correctly. If you were to advise Ms. Abuhamad, you might tell her:

A. Map skills are not an appropriate study for inner-city students.

B. It's important to take into account the background of your students to make instruction relevant.

C. Don't worry about it. You did fine. These kids often don't pay attention.

D. To motivate your class, give one of the disruptive students detention so that you show the class you mean business.

Answers And Discussion

Answer 1: *A* is not correct, because this unit can be developed with skills for any grade level. Even a teacher in high school could develop a unit on butterflies. However, these teachers did not take out their long-range goals chart to check to see whether they were on target (*B*) nor did they check to see where they were in respect to their district goals (*C*).

They might consider other things, too, before jumping into this unit. Indeed, they have made the mistake of falling into the teacher trap of wanting to teach "cute activities" rather than considering many other elements needed for long-range planning. The answer is D.

Answer 2: Objectives should be written so that a teacher can observe a specific behavior from students' performance—and then be able to measure how well students achieved. We cannot look inside children's minds to see whether they understand, so we must devise a way to infer whether they do or not. For example, Jeff might ask students to write or tell reasons so that he can, indeed, determine whether they understand all or a specified number of reasons. The answer is A.

Answer 3: Let's eliminate. Answer D cannot be the answer because we have no information in the scenario on how she was writing objectives before. Answer C is also not a good choice because, although it is useful information, Mrs. Warner no doubt has already selected her book even though she has not included it. It would have been more helpful for her to have given the exact title in her plan so that she could remember it for next year. Answer A is a great pat on the back, but it is more likely that Mrs. McAden asked Mrs. Warner to explain her general purpose(s) in teaching this lesson. The principal would want to know that these were more than "fun activities" and that consideration was given as to why these particular objectives had been developed. The answer is B.

Answer 4: Let's consider how to go about selecting the correct answer. First we could ask, "Are all of these higher-level objectives? Is that what would help us eliminate one of them?" In examining all of them, however, we can see that all four are higher-level objectives, so that is not the criterion for which we are looking. What else, then, would make one of these not suitable? In remembering that one of the indicators for this competency asks beginning teachers to consider age-appropriateness and relevance as a part of planning, we could notice that C would really be above and beyond the age-appropriateness of many fourth graders. A, B, and D would be appropriate for fourth grade, but C would not. Look for multiple ways to eliminate on this test. The answer is C.

Answer 5: Map skills are appropriate for children everywhere, so A cannot be the answer. She was not "doing fine" because children were not paying attention (C). The remedy would not be to become strict (D) but to become relevant. She began with the right idea of a story to which many children in her class could relate, but she jumped into an area that was meaningless and not relevant at that time with her math and social studies questions. She would have done better to ask children about some places that they had visited and use those for her questions. The answer is B.

WEB LINKS

If you type in several of the key words listed at the beginning of this chapter for a search, you will have a long list of sites that offer theory, activities, materials to purchase, and so forth. There may be other search combinations that will help you gain more information. Remember that sites move, can be removed, or may not be found using your server. If a site listed below cannot be located, try typing in other key words to help in your search. You may also try going to the "root" site (normally the first group of letters before a "/" such as seen below in www.gsu.edu).

http://www.gsu.edu/~mstmbs/CrsTools/Magerobj.html

This is an excellent site that clarifies and classifies objectives.

http://faculty.washington.edu/krumme/guides/bloom.html

This site offers a great number of links to other sites dealing with instructional objectives specifically related to Bloom's Taxonomy.

www.adprima.com/objectives.htm

Dr. Bob Kizlik offers a wealth of information on planning and objectives written in a way that is easy to grasp.

www.education-world.com/a_lesson/

This is a resource for many types of lesson plans. Although not all have correctly written goals and objectives, this site should be a bookmark for all beginning teachers.

www.lessonplans.com

This site includes many, many resource suggestions.

www.teach-nology.com

Teach-nology provides an interesting site for many components of teaching, particularly planning and rubrics that help in designing assessment.

www.tea.state.tx.us/teks

This is a gateway to the Texas Essential Knowledge and Skills (TEKS) for various subject areas and grade levels.

http://www.tea.state.tx.us/resources/index.html

Math—

http://www.tenet.edu/teks/math/clarifying/cabygradelevk8.html

Social Studies—

http://www.tea.state.tx.us/ssc/teks_and_taas/teks_and_taas.htm

Technology—

http://www.tcet.unt.edu/START/teks/index.htm

http://www.tcet.unt.edu/START/instruct/lpindex.htm

http://www.galena-park.isd.tenet.edu/links.htm#Lesson

These Web sites provide information and lesson plans that already have links to the TEKS.

http://www.tenet.edu/teks/math/teks/index.html#overview

This site lists questions and answers about the Texas Essential Knowledge and Skills (TEKS).

www.tea.state.tx.us/curriculum/early/prekguide.html

TEKS for Pre-K are found on this site.

http://www.tcta.org/QAteks.htm

This site lists questions and answers about the Texas Essential Knowledge and Skills (TEKS).

REFERENCES

Berliner, D. (1985). *Effective teaching.* Pensacola, FL: Florida Educational Research and Development Council.

Bloom, B. S., Englehart, M. D., Furst, E. J., Hill, W. H., & Krathwohl, D. R. (Eds.), (1956). *Taxonomy of educational objectives: The classification of education goals, handbook I: Cognitive domain.* New York: David McKay.

Brophy, J. (1987). On motivating students. In D. Berliner & B. Rosenshine (Eds.) *Talks to teachers* (pp. 201–245). New York: Random House.

Cabello, B., & Terrell, R. (1994). Making students feel like family: How teachers create warm and caring classroom climates. *Journal of Classroom Interaction, 29*(1), 17–23.

Cangelosi, J. S. (1992). *Systematic teaching strategies.* New York: Longman.

Rosser, R. A., & Nicholson, G. I. (1984). *Educational psychology.* Boston: Little, Brown.

Chapter 4

COMPETENCY 3 – PART 2

Designing Effective Instruction— Considering Other Factors

JANICE L. NATH

University of Houston—Downtown

TERMS TO KNOW

Cooperative learning	Raw score	TEKS
Integrated or thematic approach	Scale score	Thematic unit
Interdisciplinary	Student choice	TLI (Texas Learning Index)
Play	TAAS	
Project learning	TAKS	

Chapter 3 (Competency 3, Part 1) demonstrates how to write effective goals and lesson plans for children. This chapter will assist in understanding other factors necessary for designing effective and coherent instruction. These factors include (a) using state assessment to make decisions about instruction; (b) knowledge of various types of materials and resources (including technological resources and resources outside the school) that may be used to enhance student learning and engagement; (c) providing children with opportunities to explore content from integrated and varied perspectives (e.g., by providing an integrated curriculum, employing play as one learning mode); (d) permitting student choice of activities; (e) involving students in projects; and (f) designing instruction that supports children's growing ability to work cooperatively and to reflect upon other points of view when appropriate. These and other factors will add to the bank of knowledge that teachers need to enhance learning experiences for children.

ANSWERING CHILDREN'S NEEDS

New teachers often ask, "Where should I begin with my instruction? At what level are my children now, and in what areas will they need concentrated help?" Part of designing learning experiences that help children grow in their learning involves diagnosis that will help answer these types of questions. In Texas, the Texas Assessment of Academic Skills **(TAAS)** provides diagnosis of skills. Too often schools focus upon the TAAS (soon to become the Texas Assessment of Knowledge and Skills—**TAKS**) as a summative or "end product" assessment. However, TAAS (or TAKS) scores can provide extensive information to aid in matching instruction to the needs of the

learner. The TAAS (or TAKS) is a standardized test, meaning that the testing process is uniform throughout the state. The testing process should ensure that each child has an equal chance of scoring because the materials, time, directions, and so forth are the same in every classroom on testing days. The TAAS (or TAKS) is also a criterion-referenced test, because a child must correctly answer a certain number of items to show mastery or pass. This is different from a norm-referenced test, where a child's score depends on how it compares with other test-takers (see Competency 10, Chapter 15 for more information on these types of tests). Because the TAAS (or TAKS) test is criterion referenced, it can also report specific objectives that have *not* been mastered. A teacher who knows this type of information can begin to design his or her instruction based on class and individual needs, remembering that children who need remediation on particular objectives are not likely to become excited about becoming lifelong learners if the remediation is constantly presented as drill sheets. The following information will help a beginning teacher better analyze test scores. Scores are reported as follows:

raw score a report of exactly how many items were answered correctly. For example, on a test of 80 items, of which a child answers 75 correctly, 75 is the raw score. A raw score can be converted to a percentage based upon 100 percent (which is the way most schools report grades). This is calculated by dividing the number of items into 100 to receive the exact point value for each item. For example, there are 50 items on a test, and 100 divided by 50 equals 2. Therefore, each item is worth two points. Multiply the point value by the *raw score,* or items answered correctly. If a child correctly answers 40 items as a raw score on a 50-item test, the percentage score is 80 percent ($40 \times 2 = 80$). Another way of doing this is to divide the raw score (or number a student correctly answered) by the number of test items ($40 \div 50 = .80$ or 80 percent). Most teachers have "easy graders" or computer grade books that do this quickly and easily, but they should understand the way that a percentage score is calculated.

scale score A reported statistic that compares a child's score with a minimum passing standard. The question that this particular score answers is, "How does achievement on this test compare with established minimum requirements for passing?" Thus this score specifies how far away from the minimum score a student scored in both directions ("passing," "advanced knowledge/skills," "high or low proficiency," and so forth). The difficulty of each test is taken into account in the computations.

Texas Learning Index (TLI) This index is statistically computed to allow teachers to compare children's performances (and growth) across grade levels or years. The TLI score lists the grade-level achievement, followed by the maximum score possible on a test. For example, Maria, in Ms. Rivera's third-grade class, scored 75 on reading (the minimum passing score is 70). Her TLI score would be 3-75, and in the fourth grade she scores 4-80. By comparing these scores, a teacher can note that Maria is right on a growth achievement course and has actually made a bit more than a year's growth.

Other statistical terms for teachers to remember in working with standardized tests include the mean (average score), the median (the score that is exactly in the middle of the distribution of scores), and the mode (the most frequently occurring score). Standard deviations tell how far from the mean a score falls and the variability of scores (again, see Competency 10, Part 1, Chapter 15, for more information).

A number of different reports are issued as state results on the TAAS (or TAKS). One that is most helpful for diagnosing "trouble spots" for students is the Objective Performance on the campus TAAS (or TAKS) report. There each objective is listed for each TAAS (or TAKS) test, and these are also disaggregated or broken down into levels of difficulty (Beginning, Intermediate, and Advanced). For example, on the reading section, the following objectives may be listed in all three levels: word meaning, supporting ideas, summarization, analyzing, and evaluation. The total number of items tested is shown as the raw score (or exactly how many items were answered correctly) and is given for each child. The child's proficiency rating on the entire test is also given.

If a teacher analyzes this information carefully, he or she can see what areas need emphasis for student growth. TAAS (or TAKS) scores are important in Texas education, though some criticize the use of these scores for purposes other than the instructional design and assessment cycle. For example, the scores are involved with high-stakes school recognition and funding and, consequently, principals' reputations. However, a teacher should always remember that these scores are truly a valuable tool in targeting and designing instruction to help children grow academically each year.

OPPORTUNITIES TO EXPLORE

Competency 3, as a whole, asks teachers to be able to plan a lesson using the components discussed in Part 1 (Chapter 3), but it also addresses the exploration of content from integrated and varied perspectives. The following section of this chapter investigates this aspect further.

Integrated or Interdisciplinary Content

Texas standards tell us that teachers should be able to provide children with opportunities to explore content from an integrated perspective. To accomplish this, teachers often design special **thematic units** in which a number of lesson plans fall under one "umbrella" topic. An **integrated or thematic approach** refers to teaching units in which many subject areas are included under one topic or central idea and where the lines between these subject areas are often blurred. In Competency 3, Part 1, Chapter 3, we noted how to reference other subject areas (at least briefly) within the content of each lesson. As a review, creating integration among subject areas is done for the purpose of increasing relevance and tying subjects together more—as might occur in real life. For example, art and music can tell us much about historical periods, but only exemplary teachers usually make these connections for children. More often, art is done during art time or art period, social studies during its allotted time, and so forth. However, besides making sure that other topics are integrated or touched upon in each lesson, teachers can prepare integrated or **interdisciplinary** units that reach across many subject areas, thus increasing interest and connections for students.

Units can be oriented to more "real-world" problems and situations; thus the need for certain skills or knowledge often emerges naturally and rationally for children. Therefore, rather than learning through memorization, an integrated unit stresses conceptualization or understanding. Thematic units also normally offer opportunities for assessment in more authentic contexts. For example, in a Native American unit (normally found only in social studies), each child can be assessed through the observation of his or her proficiency in understanding volume measurement (a mathematics concept) while measuring ingredients to make his or her own Indian fry bread. Children also detect sets (also a math element) in rhythm as they listen to Native American music and construct pattern sets as they string Native American-style necklaces.

Selecting proper unit topics or themes is very important because units must (a) be able to incorporate a number of **TEKS** in each subject area; (b) be appropriate for the child's interest level; (c) be logical in their connections and sequenced correctly in all subject areas used; (d) be broad enough to include many interdisciplinary topics; (e) be coordinated with other teachers, if classrooms have special teachers or are departmentalized; and (f) be checked with other grade levels to ensure that children do not replicate units every year.

Selecting a topic is the first part of planning a unit. Student interest and age-appropriateness are important considerations. Children enjoy units on such themes as seasons, apples, bats, dinosaurs, bugs, plants or flowers, pumpkins, butterflies, castles, recycling, a particular book, "our town," Texas, a specific country or area, and many, many more. Normally, thematic units can be organized (a) through particular themes as seen above, (b) from literature and/or language, (c) through issues

or problems, (d) through projects, and (e) through subject areas or disciplines. For example, Ms. Brandt, a Pre-K teacher, began to design a unit on apples for her class. Some of the integrated topics she thought to include were mathematics (teaching volume, measurement, etc.), colors (through various shades of apples), sorting, history (Johnny Appleseed), and so forth.

The design of the unit should include many of the components of the lesson plan introduced in Competency 3, Part 1, Chapter 3. Thus, teachers should include (a) unit objectives, (b) subjects to be integrated, (c) a unit rationale, (d) content to be taught within the framework of the unit, (e) time allotted for the unit, (f) overall assessment, and so forth. In unit plans, a list of resources and needed vocabulary is also important. Based upon the unit plan, teachers then turn to designing daily plans and begin to "put the puzzle together." Most importantly, the entire unit should be planned before teaching *any* of the lessons to ensure that all parts of the unit follow proper sequencing for clear learning.

Exploring through Play

Play is also an important part of student exploration. Indeed, research tells us that play is supportive to children in social competence, cognitive development, language development (Fromberg, 2002), and physical development. Brewer (2001) suggests that in a school setting play can be described on a continuum of teacher involvement from *free play* (children have free choice of many materials and how to use them within reasonable bounds) to *guided play* (teachers select materials in order to design the discovery of specified concepts) to *directed play* (the teacher shows learners how to play in a certain manner, using song games, finger plays, and so forth).

Sayre and Gallagher (2001) list three overall categories of play: (a) functional play, (b) symbolic play, and (c) games with rules. *Functional play,* or *practice play,* begins during the very early years of life when a child repeatedly practices an action or schema, although this type of play recurs later when a child needs to master a new skill. In Pre-K, for example, children often play "school," in which they practice beginning writing skills over and over. Children also use this type of play to explore materials thoroughly.

Symbolic play, the second category, can be solitary or cooperative but is extremely important because it requires increasingly sophisticated mental representations to be created for people, objects, and actions, thus advancing cognition (Bornstein et al., 1996). Symbolic play consists of both constructive play and dramatic play. In *constructive play*, a child uses objects or materials to represent or symbolize real things in life (such as when a chair symbolizes the cockpit of a plane for a "pilot"). Teachers who join in play can help stretch a child's imagination and skill while still leaving the child in control. Children who play with others, particularly a teacher who is knowledgeable about this type of play, learn more. *Pretend* or *dramatic play* employs the use of imagination, involving various roles and situations. This type of play normally lasts through middle childhood, and if the play involves others and negotiations of their roles, it is called *sociodramatic* play. Recently two young girls on the playground were pretending to be horses jumping over fences. Another girl wanted to join the group and was allowed, after it was determined that she would come into the play as a groom. This type of play can be characterized as *oral playwriting*, where children serve as the audience, voice, and oral co-editors for one another (Fromberg, 2002).

Games with rules is a third category in which children understand and agree to rules (either those they make up themselves or prearranged rules). To do this, they must already have social skills. Educators have argued that very early youth sports organizations can be frustrating and confusing to children if they are not developmentally ready for the logical thought patterns and social skills needed for this type of play.

The following categories of play have also been identified, based upon the social role of the player: (a) solitary or independent play, (b) onlooker play (c) parallel play, (d) associative play,

(e) rough-and-tumble play, and (f) cooperative play. *Solitary* or *independent play* develops at about age 2 but can be seen all through childhood. Children in solitary play have no interaction with others—either adults or other children—and may be oblivious to those around them. In *onlooker play*, a child who is playing alone may observe others playing and may alter his or her play as a result of what is observed in others. *Parallel play* has also been described, in which children play nearby (or parallel to each other), perhaps even sharing materials, yet no connections are made with the other child. This type of play may still be seen in Pre-K children, yet most often teachers see Pre-K children engaged in *associative play*, in which children play and interact together and may even agree to share some materials in an unstructured manner—but are normally unable to sustain this for long. Also seen in early to middle childhood is *rough-and-tumble play*, in which children, particularly boys, play roughly and often in roles. Aggression, however, is not the goal, and they normally finish with no angry feelings (although anger can appear when unpopular children engage in this type of play). From Pre-K through the remaining elementary years, teachers also see increasingly sustained *cooperative play*, in which children are involved in a particular "game." In the "game" are roles, themes, leaders, and specific rules. These must be negotiated and accepted because rebellion sometimes threatens how the game will go. For example, in a doctor/patient game, if both parties refuse to play unless they can both be the doctor, the play is over.

Play as a learning mode offers definite benefits, many of which are physical and work toward improvement in building muscles and coordination. EC–4 teachers also know that when children are denied recess or physical play, the day can become very long. The release of energy that certain types of play provide works positively for concentration later. Because assuming roles encourages perspective taking and increases verbal and social skills, play also helps maturation in social development. Children may also be able to work out emotional conflicts through play.

Movies and/or television sometimes depict children who are encouraged to act out their feelings, as psychologists observe through play with dolls in some way. This may offer insight into certain events. However, our instructional interests fall into the realm of play as an avenue to exercise cognitive abilities, particularly through the assimilation process discussed in Competency 1, Chapter 1. In play, because anything is possible, children can introduce and incorporate many new creative ideas, situations, objects, and so forth into their schemas of thinking. Pretending can be seen as the beginning of abstract thinking. Wood and Attfield (1996) note that, "Children become world weavers in their play" (p. 51) where novel forms of creativity emerge in fantasy. Children, however, are using considerable logic and reasoning to create the "what ifs" in their roles and games. Quite often this imagination spurs them to problem-solve (Brewer, 2001) and organize. For example, in some types of play, children must first organize their area (the sandbox becomes a bakery, and the edges become counters). When materials are not readily available, children can initiate problem-solving techniques to substitute and pretend for props.

When children play together, opportunities arise for many different viewpoints or perspectives. This, in turn, produces cognitive conflict (disequilibrium), as described by Piaget's theories. When disequilibrium happens, children begin to adapt by assimilating and accommodating information as they see the demand for new knowledge from new sources. In addition, skills can be tried out without risk in play. At heart, most children want to dominate their environment (to be "masters of their universe"), instead of being limited to their abilities and the rules their caregivers and teachers dictate. Play is the self-initiated mechanism that satisfies the need for freedom and independence (Berlyne, 1960). It is joyful and requires no extrinsic rewards.

Play is a natural part of childhood, and when initiated by children, can be taken advantage of by teachers who tap into its benefits by providing structures in which curriculum is embedded. For instance, when teachers provide all of the tools for a kitchen center, children are going to explore measurement in their play; when tools for a science lab center are provided, children are going to experiment; when tools for a store are provided, children will happily explore supply, demand, and exchange; telephone centers involve experimentation with communication, and blocks provide for delving into spatial concepts in building and construction. Each center should be carefully thought through for a match between what the teacher wants children to accomplish in play and the activities that the center offers. Accessories and space for play should be carefully considered. *All* children in Pre-K–4 should have an opportunity to engage in exploration through play. Good teachers furnish many types of exploration possibilities by providing resources and support.

Physical resources are an important part of play. Children will play with whatever is available, but there is also a quality issue in setting the stage. For example,

> ". . . if all that is available is pre-mixed, drippy paints with thick stubby brushes and poor quality paper this [play] will become repetitive and unchallenging. In our experience children benefit from learning to use a variety of brushes and paints as well as a wide range of media in their efforts to become real world artists. They are capable of mixing paints and using thin brushes and benefit from being able to decide consciously which media are appropriate for a task. In learning to use these tools creatively and efficiently, children then go on to play with the media and develop new uses and combinations. . . . A curriculum which denies and constrains children's play in a range of contexts limits their creativity, their ability to experiment, take risks, test out possibilities, reflect on action, and make connections between areas of learning and experience." (Wood & Attfield, 1996, p. 92)

Time is another resource that teachers can provide along with physical resources. There is often a rush for more "formal" lessons—even with younger children. Yet the cognitive development that is enhanced in play is well worth the time spent. For example, as children grow, their socio-dramatic play often takes on different characteristics termed "frame play." In *frame play,* objects become less important, and play is negotiated by establishing rules and roles and story plots, often like a performance (Brostrom, 1995). It is important to note that experimenting with roles is a positive part of character and language development and creativity.

Thus a teacher should decide the curriculum and set the stage for many types of exploration through the resources and support she or he provides. It is important to recall that young children need time to explore materials (and, perhaps, structured experiences) before they are able to employ them in play. When providing materials for play centers, such as blocks, teachers will note that children must first examine each type of block carefully before beginning any construction or play with the block. It should be remembered that children do not choose particular areas or materials for play unless they are somewhat meaningful. Thus, multiculturalism (see Competency 2, Chapter 2) is relevant; young children first need to see resources with which they are familiar. For example, some Anglo teachers of young children along the border of Texas might find that children are not choosing the kitchen center often. However, they may discover that if they include more of the implements, clothing, and recipes typically found in Hispanic kitchens, children will feel more comfortable coming to the center. Other new resources can be introduced later. Furthermore, children must have times when they select their own area of play. However, teachers also have to balance children's experiences so that students do not restrict themselves to "gender-specific" areas. Boys *and* girls (and all ethnicities) need to play in a science center, the blocks area, a hospital or kitchen area, and so forth, and teachers must be seen in all of the centers. A female teacher who never goes to the blocks center or a male teacher who never is seen in the kitchen center send pow-

erful messages to children about "gender places." Parents who are aware of the role of play can often contribute to the process of exploration and growth and can share details that will help teachers understand a child's development.

Teachers have a great influence on play, particularly with roles they assume (stager/director, playmate, assessor, and so forth). We have seen how the design and provision of materials can set the stage or direction for investigation. To gain full benefit from play, teachers must also consider their interaction during play at times. The key is "at times." If the teacher is too hovering or too directive in play with children, children may feel a loss of control and feel manipulated, and they may quickly lose interest. However, teachers can be invited into (or can insert themselves into) a child's play with questions about the resources that are being used, they can model or demonstrate something before and during the play, they can employ think-alouds or adopt or accept a role to join in, they can cue or suggest the next step within the game, and so forth. For play to work toward discovery and experimentation, children need to maintain a degree of independence. If modeling or demonstration occurs during play, it usually must be as "part of the game" rather than "look at me and see how this works now." Remember that part of the joy of play for the child is that *he or she* is manipulating the environment. When a teacher can insert new knowledge that still enhances the child's control, the joy of discovery is maintained and curiosity enhanced; when the teacher is too directive, the delight and motivation can be lost. Teachers should also be aware of age-appropriateness, particularly considering the zone of proximal development, which is a place where children can succeed with support from an adult or capable peer (Vygotsky, 1987) as they provide resources and "a stage" for play. Children who do not yet have the dexterity or other abilities to work with certain items such as small objects (for example, construction of models with small pieces, and so forth) will not be inspired to explore and play, whereas children who are more advanced will be motivated by the intricacies of more details in play. Simply, if the "game" or situation is too far advanced or too elementary for the child, play and exploration will decline rapidly. In addition, teachers should be attentive to children who experiment with roles and language that are negative—for example, asserting power or fear. It is for those reasons that teachers must be vigilant without smothering when intervening in play.

The role of assessor in play is a serious one for teachers. Children should be monitored through observation and assessed using formative, diagnostic, and summative evaluation. Areas such as the following can be tracked through time: oral language development, social development, spatial abilities, chosen activities, gross motor skill development, fine motor skill development, application of prior learning, cooperation, learned skills/concepts, attitudes, concentration/attention, type of play, needed interventions, and so forth (see Competency 10, Chapter 15, on assessment for more details). Anecdotal records over time can capture patterns of advancement or delay. A checklist of skills is also a way to maintain a record of progress over time. Teachers should remember when assessing play that children, when stressed, may respond by reverting to less advanced levels of play.

Motivating through Student Choice

One concept repeated throughout the overall PPR philosophy is that of **"student choice."** Teachers may wonder why student choice is such an important concept and when it is appropriate. Most motivational theories include student choice because of its ability to increase intrinsic motivation (see Competency 4, Part 1, Chapter 5). Certainly a major goal for educators to have is children choose to learn something for the sake and joy of learning—rather than for some external reward. Asking children to set some goals for themselves and to choose activities that help them learn encourages intrinsic motivation. For example, when children set their own goals toward gaining certain knowledge or skills, the focus shifts from pleasing someone else (teachers or parents) to pleasing themselves. It is similar to adults who

select a vacation spot. Often vacationers know little about an area, but having selected the place where they want to travel, they become excited and may spend a great amount of energy learning details about the place they plan to visit by using the Internet, obtaining travel guides, talking with others who have been there, and so forth. This learning may include gaining extensive knowledge about what there is to see in the area, what restaurants they would like to try, and other points of interest. Thus the planning process often becomes an exciting and motivating part of the travel itself. The same is true for children when *they* choose a topic or activity. The fact that they have selected the topic can be so motivating that they want to reach deep inside the subject. Also, when success is obtained, children can attribute it to their own efforts and self-determination. This, in turn, increases intrinsic motivation, self-esteem, the chances of their trying again, and future success. Student choice in projects can, for example, also tap into the intrinsic curiosity and excitement of children. Teachers' lore often tells stories of children who are "really smart but bored." It is often these children who drop out of school later because the confines of traditional classrooms do not hold their motivation. Student choice, however, helps to motivate their interests and energies.

At a famous school in England, children come in each day and the teacher asks, "What do you want to learn today?" The teacher then supports the child in that area. Obviously, when a state curriculum determines knowledge and skills that *must* be taught and learned, total student choice in learning is not an option. However, there are many appropriate times when children can be given choices. For example, when children are problem solving or during questioning, teachers can either impose their solutions on students or support children in working out their own solutions through discussion, conflict resolution, brainstorming for multiple solutions, and so forth. It is still important for the teacher to be a guide in the process of student choice. Children who select from activities that are not developmentally- or age-appropriate can become frustrated or tire quickly, and they may not be able to achieve their goals at all. Thus offering an "either/or" or a "menu" of various opportunities to explore (or requiring teacher preapproval for children's ideas) can help children fit into options where they can gain success. However, a teacher should accept other good suggestions offered by children, if appropriate. Working through learning center projects where choices are available within the center also increases interest and motivation. For example, providing many different books on bugs, along with various materials for researching and creating a "bug of your choice," is much more motivating to children than having them listen to teacher instructions and, as a whole class, color and cut out the same bug. Creativity and interest are tapped in the first instructional example, but following along is the only option in the second. Both can be appropriate at times, but many traditional classrooms never promote the former. Monitoring children as they work through projects can also help them succeed by preventing them from going so deeply that they bog down or from skimming along the surface in such a shallow way that they do not feel self-worth in their efforts. Remember, too, that offering choices in exploring learning is positive for *all* children, not just for higher-level children.

Exploring through Projects (Project Learning)

Everyone has had a time in his or her life when a certain topic was pursued as the focus of in-depth research. With adults and their hobbies, we are probably acquainted with someone who knows all about a sport. For example, an avid golfer knows the many types of golf clubs and the materials from which they are made; the names of famous professional players and the grandest tournaments; the best courses around the state, the country, and the world; and so forth. This learning is extremely exciting and meaningful to that person. The same type of interests occur for young children in various subjects. Thus at times, the most appropriate study is an independent or small-group **project** in

an area of interest. A project should (a) be a long-term study of a particular subject; (b) offer children choices in topics and what they want to know about those topics; (c) have parts of the project that blend with concepts and skills needed in the curriculum; (d) be age-appropriate; (e) require a hands-on culminating presentation shared with the class and include a visual product of some type such as a chart, poster, video, computer presentation, skit, model, diorama, etc.; and (f) require a final written report (or computer presentation) that includes a literary product of some sort, such as a report, pamphlet, journal, short biography, or another appropriate form. The advantages of project learning include intrinsic motivation, expertise learning, and student choice. Wise teachers begin by offering examples and/or menus of projects and some examples of completed projects. Setting timelines, monitoring progress, and providing feedback along the way are necessary for children in helping them maintain continuous forward momentum (rather than having them cram at the end to finish). It also helps reduce the possibility that a parent will do the project the night before it is due. Scoring rubrics that are given *before* the project begins will help children understand the scoring value and expectations for each part of the project.

Planning for Instructional Grouping

A teacher can plan a lesson for children in a variety of settings: individuals working alone at their seats, with partners, in small groups, or the class working as a whole. The way in which a teacher plans instruction for student grouping has many consequences. However, for having children gain varied perspectives (as required by this competency), using cooperative groups is crucial.

At times a fruitful plan involves teaching a lesson or part of a lesson to the class as a whole. For example, *whole-group* or *whole-class instruction* gives a teacher the best opportunity to impart information to all members of the class at one time, to have everyone see a demonstration, or to participate together with all class members in a discussion. However, *small-group instruction* (or **cooperative learning**) allows pairs or small groups of children to interact more with each other, to be more active learners, to gain from the perspectives of others, and to use individual learning styles or preferences. Small group instruction also gives the teacher the opportunity to supervise closely in the role of facilitator. *Independent instruction* allows children to work alone—either on something chosen by the teacher or by student choice of a project or learning center. Other types of independent strategies may include *mastery learning* (in which children master and are tested on one set of skills or concepts before going on to the next level), individual learning centers, and computer-assisted programs. All grouping strategies have a place at various times in the classroom with consideration for different learner goals. Thus at times teachers must deliver information in a more direct manner, while at other times the goal may be to have children think more for themselves or show what they can do individually (such as during an independent practice activity). At still another point, teachers may wish to boost children's social development through small-group instruction. Each day a lesson should contain a variety of strategies and groupings in order to provide motivation and to match the goals and objectives that are a part of lessons. The job of teachers in helping children grow is to *monitor* (constantly gain feedback from children as to how their learning is progressing) and then to make adjustments in instructional strategies and grouping when needed.

Exploring through cooperative learning.
During the past decade, educational researchers have conducted an incredible number of studies on cooperative groupings. Moreover, the results in multiple areas, including academic achievement, have been positive overall. Any teacher who has developed a repertoire of cooperative groupings for children has probably come to the same conclusions that these educational researchers have reached—varying classroom settings with cooperative groups is good for children in a number of

different ways! Remember Vygotsky's theory from Competency 1, Chapter 1. His theory explained that children learn through social interaction in the "context of collaborative dialogues" (Bjorklund, 2000, p. 71) with an adult or a capable peer. Leighton (1999) also explains that "good cooperative learning strategies engage children in sharing how they think, examining it themselves [as they try to explain it to others], gaining insight from the critiques of their peers, and enlarging their conceptual understanding by hearing how others understand the same concept" (p. 272).

In the chapter that examines diversity, Competency 2, Chapter 2, it was shown that some cultural learning styles fit well with cooperative groups, although other cultural groups prefer to work individually (remembering that this could also be a learning style that is an individual preference rather than a cultural style). By varying groupings, teachers find that some children "shine" in one type of grouping. However, children also need to strengthen working in their opposite style. If a teacher does not vary grouping, some children may never work in their preferred style or strengthen their weaker style. Gardner's theory of Multiple Intelligence (1983, 1993) (outlined more thoroughly in Competency 4) supports this premise with his identification of *Interpersonal Intelligence* (the capacity to understand, communicate, and work well with others) and *Intrapersonal Intelligence* (the capacity to understand one's self, be self-directed, independent in learning, reflective, etc.). By working in ways that enhance different types of intelligences, children will flourish in the classroom and in their lives ahead.

There are other good reasons to use cooperative strategies. Cooperative groups provide a place for children to begin leadership skills. In cooperative groups, children are, in turn, responsible for leading a group to obtain a goal. High achievers need group work as much as do other children. They are often the children who wish to work alone (and may not always have the skills to work with others). Yet, lack of these skills can certainly be detrimental later in their schooling and in life, as they seek leadership positions.

Teachers can also be concerned about management problems with young children in groups, yet management is another positive reason for using groups. A goodly number of teachers spend their days attempting to stifle student interaction as children work individually in their seats. In some schools, children are discouraged from talking even at lunch. In traditional classrooms, children are likely to have about three minutes a day to "legally" talk in class—and that is usually as they answer instructional questions for the teacher. Therefore, children do as adults would if asked not to talk more than three minutes a day; that is, they talk illegally, forcing the teacher to take names and give detentions or other punishments. Yet in cooperative groups, teachers *require* children to interact—and with their peers! Now talking with classmates becomes legal and channels pent up energy into instructional goals. In other words, children are going to talk, and teachers can "fight it" all day long or divide it into "my time" and "your time." Children often cooperate much more during teacher time when they know that their time will follow. Establishing rules and assigning roles is good management for group work.

There is also a "synergy" that comes from working in a group. *Synergy* stands for "centered energy," which can mean several things. First, synergy means that there is simply more fun and motivation when talking and working with others. When an activity is fun or pleasant for children, their energy level is higher and they are more involved in learning. More heads are often better than one, so there is energy when many ideas are suggested and discussed. This is supported by researchers such as Johnson and Johnson (1989), who found that children generate many more ideas through high-quality cognitive strategies and metacognitive approaches than they would have generated alone. Bjorklund (2000) tells us that, "Cooperative learning requires that children explain their ideas to one another, persuade, and resolve conflicts. These all require children to examine their own ideas more closely and be able to articulate them so someone else can understand them" (p. 69). Bjorklund continues to discuss

Teasley's (1995) work, noting that, "Children who worked in pairs and talked aloud generated better hypotheses than children who did not talk aloud. This result suggests that collaborative learning leads to improved problem solving not simply because of the collaboration per se," (p. 69) but because children are actively engaged in the language of thinking. Finally, there is energy in teamwork when many are working towards a goal and success is realized for all (rather than one winner and many losers). By directing this type of energy into learning, all students benefit!

In our diversity chapter (Competency 2, Chapter 2), it was noted that more than likely children who are differently-abled will be mainstreamed into many classrooms. This may create some challenges, both for the child and for the teacher, depending on the child's needs. If there is a physical challenge, a child may, for example, not always hear some of what a teacher says, may not have the ability to reach supplies, and so forth. In the case of an LEP (Limited English Proficiency) student, the child may not understand some of what the teacher says. Whatever the instance, groups can provide much support both for the teacher and for a mainstreamed child. If a mainstreamed child has two or three other group members to depend upon, it is certainly better than depending on the teacher alone. Grouping also provides a way for others in the class to see a child with special needs more on a personal basis and to help understand the child's different abilities.

Examining yet another reason for cooperative groups, we find that a teacher can give only so much praise to children, and yet self-worth is often increased by the praise of others. With praise in cooperative activities, children are able to receive not only the satisfaction of contribution to a mutual goal (which increases intrinsic motivation) but can begin to see others and themselves as resources in diverse ways; that is, everyone brings strength to the group! Children are also capable of motivating their peers when a teacher is not.

Yet more reasons exist for using cooperative groups. Even today with integrated classrooms, division between diverse groups exists. Yet Slavin

(1983) found that children chose more friends from other ethnicities when cooperative groups were used, and ethnic relations improved dramatically. Still another reason for using cooperative learning is that it often provides for cooperation rather than continued competition, as in most traditional classrooms. Not that competition should have no place, for it is a part of what has made America a great nation. But there is a price for focusing on competition exclusively. Rugged individualism, as part of America's culture, has historically forced more focus on working alone rather than on cooperation. This long line of rugged individualism comes from times in our country when a person could strike out across America, clear land miles from anyone else, and live self-sufficiently. That is no longer the case. Most Americans now live in neighborhoods where housing is very close together. Much of our work space is crowded, and most Americans work in positions that involve many people or work with the public in some way. It is widely accepted that most people do not lose their jobs because they cannot do the work, but because they cannot get along; hence the need for social skills that are a part of cooperative learning. When children are placed in long-term core groups, more empathy is shown when they begin to know one another better, and less isolation is felt. Many families move often, forcing young children to come into new classrooms. Placing a new student in a group at once provides a sense of belonging. In the wake of student violence in schools in the past few years, the sense of isolationism becomes an important rationale for employing small cooperative grouping practices. "For the common good" also has a particularly poignant ring in the days following the tragedy of Sept. 11, 2001. It is these ideals brought forth in cooperative education that we want to join with individualism to maintain our American way of life. Finally, and perhaps most importantly, cooperative groups improve academic achievement with a vast number of children (Johnson et al., 1981; Slavin, 1983), particularly when group rewards are coupled with individual accountability.

Teaching social skills. One part of successful work with groups is to increase the use of social skills. "…When students move to complex cooperative projects, they need help in learning how to listen to each other, resolve conflicts, set and revise agendas, keep on task, and encourage each other" (Kagan, 1992, p. 4:5). However, these skills do not just appear once children are placed in groups. Some teachers may decide that groups are not worth the bother, but this is often because they fail to include the teaching of social skills as a part of group work. Each social skill that teachers wish to encourage must be taught as a mini-lesson embedded in group instruction and must be reinforced continuously. For example, if "giving praise" were a skill to be taught along with a cooperative lesson, a teacher would announce it as the "Skill of the Day" and ask children, for example, "What does praise sound like?" Children and the teacher together would generate a list of praise words to use that they would then practice delivering to each other in pairs. Also important would be, "What does praise look like?" Now the class focuses on body language such as "thumbs up," "silent cheers," "pats on the back," and so forth, that indicate that a child has done well and should receive recognition. These, too, should be practiced with a partner. To increase incentives to use praise during the time children are working in groups, the teacher can carry a clipboard to note any time that he or she hears children using the "Skill of the Day." Groups that do so receive extra points, a small prize, or other reward. At first, of course, this is very stilted, and children are extrinsically motivated to act in positive ways. However, as children work together, teachers will find that the environment is so appreciated that the practice, in fact, becomes embedded in the classroom. The teacher must always be watching for opportunities to praise a child for acting in a prosocial manner with others, especially when seen using social skills taught in this manner.

Another way of reinforcing social development, skills, and responsibility is to designate roles for children in groups, so that each child has the responsibility of a job. Many of these roles are obvious: secretary, timekeeper, materials manager, taskmaster, quiet captain, direction giver, summarizer, reflector or evaluator, and others that may be needed. Other roles reinforce the use of social skills include: group praiser, cheerleader, encourager, reflector, and so forth. These roles can be written on role cards with a brief job description on the back and set upon children's desks or attached with a string to hang around their necks.

Teachers must be careful to create heterogeneous groups with attention to equalized gender, ethnicity, and, particularly, ability. This prevents teams from being seen as "win/win" groups or, worse, "lose/lose" groups, or from creating other types of strife because of observable differences among groups.

To maintain motivation to stay with a particular group, there must be both group and individual accountability. Assessing both is part of a teacher's job in cooperative education. Many look back on their own experiences in groups and remember times when they did more than their share while others "skated through." Yet the same grade was given to all! Or perhaps someone did not do their part at all, so the whole group received a deduction in grade points. Instances like these make group work distasteful to some students. Therefore a teacher must plan carefully. Teachers who use groups wisely may establish two places for accountability: group points and individual grades. Teachers prepare a rubric that shows clearly how a group can work toward adding points to a group score or extra points on an individual's grade rather than assigning one grade to all group members. Within a group assignment, these teachers also establish an individual assignment on which the student receives a grade to be recorded in the grade book. Mrs. McNamera, for example, was setting up her groups for her reptile lesson. Her third graders were divided into groups of four. Each group was to prepare a poster for presenting information on four reptiles. The poster was to be divided into four blocks, which were to show the name of a reptile, its characteristics, the food it eats, and its habitat, with illustrations in each block (either hand drawn or download a

picture, print it, cut it out, and paste it on). Each child would be responsible for a block that would be graded on an individual basis. If the group finished its poster and all blocks were correct and complete, Mrs. McNamera would offer 15 points to a group score. If a group received at least 100 points from this and other group projects during the week, they could have lunch in the classroom with Mrs. McNamera (with music and games). Three members of the Spy Kids group worked very hard on their poster, but one member did not complete his block. Three members received an *A* in the grade book, and one received a *B* (due to the missing illustration). The group as a whole did not receive extra group points. Thus the teacher was using groups to help students manage and encourage each other to complete a project. When one member did not complete the assignment, however, the rest of the group was not penalized academically. Individual accountability was built into Mrs. McNamera's plan. In the same class, another group helped and encouraged one member to watch his time. When Brandon became frustrated with his drawings and wanted to quit, his group rallied around to help him pull up his reptile on the computer and print it instead. They all received good grades for the grade book and group points toward a reward.

Creating positive interdependence is a definite aim of cooperative groups (Kagan, 1992). When children see that "what is good for one is good for all," they become concerned with the gains of all members of the group—including themselves. Thus creating a team goal with recognition that is based on contributions of all members is one step toward positive interdependence. Structuring tasks, supplies, and the like, so that no one person can do a task alone is another way to create positive interdependence. This is an important skill for young children to learn, because most of the important things in their lives will be centered around positive interdependence; that is, many sports cannot be played when members walk off in a rage; games are rarely for one person and, if they are designed for one, they are often less fun. Earning money normally involves others;

certainly when a child grows up, he or she will find that most businesses operate on this premise.

Various types of cooperative groupings. The preceding text has discussed many reasons for using cooperative learning. Let us look at some of the more popular models that are useful with children:

Twos-to-Fours (Think-Pair-Square) is a cooperative configuration that begins with a group of four. Pairs are formed and then share problem solving or obtaining answers to questions, followed by both pairs checking their answers together. Getting the correct answer as a group is almost guaranteed. All children are thinking—rather than in traditional question-and-answer sessions, in which the teacher asks a question of the whole class and only a few children raise their hands and are called on.

A similar group activity, Numbered Heads, goes a step further toward synergy when reviewing recall or other low-level information. In Numbered Heads, each child in a group of three or four numbers off. The teacher then calls out a question such as, "Who was the ...? Where was the ...? What is the answer to ...? What is the next step ...?" (or any number of questions that can be taken from any subject area). The teacher then quickly calls, "Think time!" (in which students think quietly for a moment about their own answers), followed by "Talk time!" (children discuss their answers and come to a consensus for their whole group on the answer they feel is correct). Now the teacher calls out a group name and a number from that group ("Sharks, Number Two"). If the child who is Number Two can give the correct answer, the entire group (the Sharks) receives a point. The group with the highest number of points, of course, wins for the day. This is an excellent "game" to play because it makes review fun and builds team spirit and interdependence through a bit of competition between groups.

Another cooperative group activity that is good for review/recall/application questions is Inside-Outside Circle. The class is evenly divided.

If there is an odd number, the teacher steps in as a partner. Half the class is asked to make a circle facing outward. The other half joins them, forming a circle facing inward and opposite a person in the Inside Circle. The teacher then calls out a question or problem. All members of the Inside Circle answer. Their Outside Circle partners "check their answer" and praise them, or reinforce their efforts ("Good try," "You are getting there," etc.) should they say the wrong answer. The teacher repeats the correct answer loudly enough for all to hear. The Inside Circle then rotates one person to the right, and another question is called out. The process is repeated until the circle has rotated all the way around. The Outside Circle then becomes the "answerers" and the Inside Circle becomes the "checkers/praisers" until the outside circle has rotated all the way around to the original partner. This is a good review strategy (also good for mental math problems and facts) because all children are involved, all interact with many others in the class, and all are praised. It is a safe review for all, as well, for if a child should happen not to know the answer, he or she can wait until those on either side say it, and then give the answer. Thus the child, although still participating, can avoid some of the embarrassment that comes when put on the spot by the teacher to answer alone.

Round Robin or Round Table makes sure that everyone in a group has an opportunity to speak; time is allotted to each member. A "gatekeeper" in the group makes sure that when time is up for one person, the next person has his or her chance to contribute. Think-Pair-Share or other types of small-group discussion models give children an opportunity to generate their own thoughts as the teacher poses a divergent or open-ended question. Children are given a moment of silence to think about their answer or opinion, and then they are directed to share their interpretations with another person or others in a group. Often children go to evaluative levels of conversation almost immediately.

Flashcard Pairs is played in three rounds. Flashcards with a question or problem on the front and the answer on the back can be made for many subjects. During the first round, one child is designated the tutor, the other the tutee. The tutor holds up the question card for his or her partner. If the correct answer is given, the tutee receives exaggerated praise. If not, many helpful hints, cues, visual images, and so on, are given by the tutor to aid the tutee in getting the answer. However, if the answer still cannot be given, the card is not "won" by the tutee but placed in the bottom of the pile to come around again. When the tutee has won all of the cards, roles are switched. When both players win all cards, round one is complete. In round two, the same rules apply, but only one or two hints are allowed. In round three, no hints are allowed (but praise for right answers or effort is always given). Both partners learn from this game because the tutee is trying to remember answers but the tutor is also thinking quite hard to develop cues to help the tutee think of the answer.

Slavin's (1983) *STAD* (Student Team Achievement Division) is one of the most popular cooperative strategies because it works on rewarding team effort through improvement points. STAD's basic steps are as follows: (a) children are pretested (or a post test from a previous chapter or unit can be used); (b) without telling children, they are ranked in order of their scores or abilities; (c) the teacher then groups so that there are approximately one high, one low, and two middle-level children in each group; (d) the teacher presents the next lesson(s); (e) children do "team practice" or study in groups with the aim of helping each other; (f) children take a quiz or check homework or class work; (g) improvement scores for each group are computed and communicated; and, finally, (h) teams celebrate. There are several ways of calculating improvement points. One way is to give a point for each number amount that a child's score increases (for example, on the first quiz or homework paper, Morgan scored a 93, and on the second she earned a 97, so she brings a positive difference of 4 improvement points to the group). All 100 percent scores earn 10 points unless there are more points in the improvement factor (for example, 87–100 = 13 improvement points). This helps children who continuously do well to try for a score of 100 every time. Also, depending on the class, a teacher may want to factor in decreasing scores (89 on the first quiz to 83 on the second brings a score of –6 to a group). Each time children are tested, the teacher adds all of the groups' scores. Groups should continue together over a set time period for which a number of points can be calculated. Teachers can use this for competition among groups for quizzes, class work, or homework, or they may set a standard point goal for all groups to reach before receiving a reward. This is an excellent way to employ flexible grouping—a student may be a part of one group for mathematics, another for language arts, and so forth.

The most student-centered of all cooperative models is the group investigation process. In *group investigation,* Sharan and Shachar (1988) found that disadvantaged students, as well as nondisadvantaged students, achieved academic gains of more than twice those in whole-class methods. In this model, originally advocated by John Dewey, problem-solving groups are organized to explore a set of inquiries. Acting as a "mini-society," children identify problems, analyze what is needed to solve these problems, and identify and fill the roles needed for solving these problems. Students then complete the project, evaluating their progress toward solutions formatively and summatively. Negotiations used in a real democratic society are extremely important to this process. One result when children work together to actively participate in meaningful learning is that the teacher moves from being a disseminator of information to the roles of learner and facilitator of learning (Brodhagen, 1995). When children are working and learning on their own, the teacher is in the role of facilitator and coach, aiding students only when they need help rather than controlling each part of the learning process. One example of group investigation centered on an elementary school in an urban neighborhood. Children found that the schoolyard was full of trash, creating a negative environment for play. Their investigation centered around clean-up and prevention strategies, including scientific experiments on waste, letters to local residents and the mayor's office, and so forth.

Jigsaw II is another way of grouping students that can lead to higher levels of thinking, although it can be used for lower-level activities as well. Children are placed in an original core (or "home") group, where they number off or receive a designation card. From here each member goes away to become a member of a new "expert" group. For example, Alisia is originally in the Dinosaurs group. Alisia is number one in this group, so when she regroups, she goes to a table where the "Expert Ones" are meeting. At the new expert tables, group members concentrate on only a part of the whole assignment, literally becoming experts on their piece of the "jigsaw puzzle." Their task in the new group is to learn the material and design new ways to help the rest of their group learn and remember the material. They then return to provide their original group with their piece of information or new skill(s). No member of the group can be successful unless all are because no one member of the original core group has all of the pieces. This is interdependence at its best. As you may see, this model *could* be very teacher directed with little high-level thinking. However, teachers can use it at the synthesis and evaluative levels.

Mr. Long decided to use Jigsaw for part of his work on "The Rain Forest" unit. In a classroom of 24 students, 6 core groups of 4 children each were formed. Each table numbered off, and all of the "ones" repositioned to a table together, the "twos" to another table, the "threes" to a third table, and the "fours" to still another area. The new "ones" group at their expert table were given the task of concentrating on learning all about the animals of the rain forest while other expert tables were assigned topics such as the destruction of the rain forest, parts of the rain forest, and the environmental effect of the rain forest. The teacher helped to facilitate this by making sure that each group judged or determined the most valuable main points given in the information, formulated a creative way to teach the information to others, and designed visual or other method(s) to aid in this effort. All "experts" then returned to their original core group, and in an orderly manner, each expert

gave a presentation gained from his or her expert group. The original group then synthesized all of the information on rain forests and created a product (such as an information pamphlet) that included information from each expert.

In another example, Mrs. Silva's fourth-grade students in expert groups were each given a different mystery. Expert groups were to analyze the story for selected elements, synthesize the story so it could be retold well, and isolate what elements made it exciting. However, they were to leave out the very end or "the who done it." Children returned to their group to retell the story briefly and to share with their "home" group the elements required. Each child was then asked to respond to the genre as a whole, select at least one other mystery that they want to read from the reports of their group, tell why, and read the additional story.

Many other grouping configurations are possible in addition to the ones introduced in this chapter, as well as variations of those discussed here. *Cooperative Learning,* by Kagan (1992), is an excellent book for teachers; it lists well over 100 various cooperative groupings. It is organized so that the selection of a cooperative format can be made with a particular purpose or goal in mind (for example, enhancing thinking skills, mastery of skills, communications skills, teambuilding, and so forth). Many other books and Web sites on cooperative learning are available.

SUPPORTING RESOURCES

In planning excellent lessons and experiences for children, many materials, technology, and other resources can be used to support instructional goals and objectives and engage students in meaningful learning. A number of categories of resources can be used to support teacher instruction. Parker (2001) lists and describes resources to help teachers design richer and more exciting lessons. These may include print resources, visual resources, computer-based resources, technology-related resources, media resources, audio resources, human resources, manipulatives, and content-specific resources.

In addition to the various kinds of subject area books that can enhance many lessons, an endless list of other printed materials can be used to enhance particular lessons. These include dictionaries, atlases, magazines, catalogs, timelines, transparencies, advertising material, menus from restaurants, newsletters or reports from various agencies, comic books, catalogs, pamphlets, diaries, journals, flipcharts, newspapers, and telephone books. For example, restaurant menus and toy catalogs are excellent for addition lessons in mathematics. Many of these resources from outside the school strengthen connections to the "real world." Other visual resources that may contribute to lessons are geo-boards, primary artifacts, art work, flannel boards, mobiles, cartoons, charts, collages, posters, transparent coins, graphic organizers, maps, word walls, clocks, and so forth.

Computer-based resources certainly can enrich lessons (see Competency 9, Chapter 14). The list of Web sites that provide information on particular subjects for children is almost endless. There is no doubt a match for almost every topic that a teacher could imagine. The computer can also add elements to lessons for the teacher, increasing the chances that children will remember lessons well. For example, one early elementary class read *Owl Moon* and, during the unit, the teacher accessed owl calls from a Web site, while the class listened in a darkened room. In addition, of course, are the many computer software and CD-ROM packages that increase knowledge and skills in almost every area, particularly with mathematics and reading. There are mastery learning programs (CAI—Computer-Assisted Instruction) in which students can pass through one level at a time, continuing only after each has been mastered. Social studies packages offer simulations, problem-solving, and map skills among other topics. In one fourth-grade class, children, after using *The Oregon Trail* (a program that asks students to make decisions regarding going across America in olden days), built their own "wagon" from boxes to show the exact size of the wagons

used and filled it with modern-day supplies they would take (if they had that same amount of space). In addition to multiple mathematics and social studies skills, this helped children to isolate what was truly important in their lives. Afterward they donated food goods to the Thanksgiving Food Drive.

A teacher can also use technology-based tools suggested by Parker (2001) that may or may not interface with computers: camcorders, printers, slide shows, LCD units, hectograph machines, overhead projectors, calculators, electronic grade books, laser pointers, and digital cameras, to name a few. In this category, for example, an exciting book report can be filmed as a "news flash." Children, as "news anchors," give a short news story about the plot of their book (do not forget parental releases when filming children). These resources often overlap with media resources. Many schools or districts provide a media center or library where VCRs, slide projectors, filmstrip machines, CD players, tape players, digital cameras, software games, and the like can be checked out to enhance lessons. Sometimes media centers have other types of supplies and machines that can help prepare materials easily and protect them for later use (die-cut machines, laminating machines, and so forth). Providing sets of objects for young children to construct, sort, and so on, can be daunting without die-cut machines.

Among many audio resources are sound systems, tape decks, CDs, books on tape, listening kits, and teacher-made tapes. In employing audio resources, music, as well as various sound effects, often enhances lessons. In addition, young readers often benefit greatly from following along with taped books.

Manipulatives are hands-on materials that should be a part of many, if not all, Pre-K–4 lessons and many upper elementary lessons. Teachers most often use them for mathematics, but manipulatives for many subjects fulfill needs for kinesthetic/tactile learners (those who learn best through movement or touch). Many manipulatives are "packaged" and are expensive to buy, but others are common items or can be made by hand. Dried food items (macaroni, beans, and so on) as well as buttons and other inexpensive articles can be used for counters. Folder centers that require manipulation can be made easily from items such as tiles, tongue depressors, and yarn. A manipulative social studies activity, for instance, might employ pictures with a hole on the side, showing the events of the Texas Revolution. Children must "string" the pictures in order of occurrence of events. Other manipulatives may include bingo with map symbols, or in language arts, friendly and business letters on tag board. The letters are cut apart, and children must put the various parts back together in proper order. Teachers' books have many ideas for these types of manipulative centers that can be a part of a lesson to add remediation or enrichment. Specialized art materials might also overlap with manipulatives in this category. Such items as clay, finger-paints, stencils, and other supplies can make many lessons come alive with creativity.

Parents and members of the community can add much to lessons. Often teachers think that human resources mean inviting guest speakers to tell children first-hand about specialized knowledge, but human resources can also contribute items or provide sites for field trips. Such is often the case with zoos, museums, ranches or farms, park centers, discovery centers, plant nurseries, and so forth. Businesses can partner with schools to help provide extra materials, but teachers may also ask businesses to contribute to particular lessons. For example, a local florist may provide ferns with spores for science lessons, or a decorating center may donate old wallpaper samples for lessons on texture. Professionals and older students in a school or district, such as nurses, special area teachers, or high school students who want to work with young children, can also provide more information or help with skills. With human resources, there are some considerations that beginning teachers should understand: (a) check school policy for guest speakers and check with the principal; (b) prepare the speaker by informing him or her about age-appropriate issues (such as attention spans), where the information he/she

will present will fit into other instruction, and how to get to the school and your room through office check-in; (c) prepare students by scaffolding the talk around information in their lessons, reminding them of rules, and having them think about questions they can ask; (d) prepare for late speakers, no-shows, or surprises during the presentation; and (e) follow up by further scaffolding information in future lessons. A final activity should be to send the visitor a thank-you letter from the whole class.

Where can teachers obtain all of the materials that help make lessons excellent learning experiences and their classrooms exciting places to be? Most schools have resource closets and/or areas in a library where materials (games and manipulatives) are kept so that they are accessible to all teachers. Sometimes these items are checked out early in the year and not returned, making it difficult to know what is available. Teachers should inquire about these materials and how they may be obtained in order to enrich lessons later on. They should visit this area early in the year to see whether any items will fit their planning. Also, many schools run out of supplies early; for example, by February there may be no more red construction paper available. New teachers should check with veteran teachers who have taught at this school before to find out about sources and availability of supplies. Many districts have centers where items can be constructed for little or no cost. Regional centers, if located nearby, may have materials to offer. Museums and teachers' stores (and online teachers' supply stores) are good sources of materials. Many games and books can be found at garage sales at bargain prices (but check to see that all game parts are there and pages are not torn out). As noted above, many businesses may contribute free items or offer a teacher discount. It is certainly worth asking. Local restaurants and grocery stores may contribute items as well such as incentive coupons, cartons for sorting, menus, plastic utensils, placemats, and others. Teachers typically spend a great deal of their own money on supplies for their children. It is certainly worth it to ask for contributions and discounts.

Figure 4.1 Active versus Passive Classroom Experiences

The discussion so far addresses the "extra" things that teachers can acquire to make their lessons come alive for children. These and other instructional decisions can make a difference in classroom experiences. As shown in Figure 4.1, these experiences fall along a continuum from (a) active, direct experiences (where children are engaged in real life learning and/or are present in a real-life setting) to (b) simulated experiences to (c) vicarious experiences to (d) experiences where there are visuals to (e) the opposite end of the spectrum, where children only *hear* about information (the teacher lectures or tells about information).

The best kinds of experiences are active and direct, wherein children interact with the real world. What educators should avoid is having children only listen passively. It is the use of resources that provide added experience in every other category.

When making decisions about resources, teachers should keep in mind the following two points. First, there must be a strong link between the lesson topic or skill and the resource. Good instructional design does not entail a teacher showing a film or video clip just to show it nor having students listen to a tape "just because it's nice." It should contribute to interest or understanding of the lesson in some manner. A lesson is like a wrapped package, where the paper and the ribbons all go together, and the gift is all tied together with a big matching bow. Therefore, the correlation between the resource, material, or technology and the lesson topic and skill must be strong or provide for student needs in some way. For example, manipulatives provide for children's developmental needs and tactile needs. Second, when deciding on a resource, the main consideration should be the educational purpose rather than availability. Not all lessons are appropriate for technology, for example. Resources should not be used simply because they are accessible but because the "fit" is right with the lesson. Teachers have so much more available to them in these times than in days gone by. It is well worth the effort to seek out available resources whenever possible and to use them wisely to enhance understanding.

SUMMARY

Both parts of this competency offer information that contributes to good planning and instruction for children. This chapter examined many factors that teachers should take into account when designing plans for young children: using state testing results to guide instruction, knowledge of many resources that enhance instruction, integration of subjects, employing play and cooperative groupings, allowing student choice, project learning, adding meaningful resources, and so forth. Each of these is an important part of designing instruction that is valuable and motivating for children. If teachers plan carefully using these concepts, they will find that young children will respond and learn well. The time spent "up front" in planning with these elements will make a difference to children each and every day. Teachers who "shortchange" the planning process and elements that go into planning often "shortchange" their students. Thinking deeply about planning makes a difference to what children receive in instruction.

GLOSSARY

cooperative learning   instruction that is structured for partners or small groups to work together.

integrated or thematic approach refers to teaching units in which many subject areas are included under one "umbrella" topic or central idea, and where the lines between these subject areas are often blurred.

interdisciplinary integration and planning that make connections with many subject areas somewhere within each lesson or within integrated thematic units.

play voluntary, meaningful action initiated by children where reality is suspended; in play, skills can be practiced, symbolism employed, rules followed in games etc.

project learning the long-term study of a particular subject that involves having learners become a "experts," usually on a topic of their choice.

raw score a report of exactly how many items were answered correctly on a test.

scale score TAAS (TAKS) reports this statistic, which compares a score with a minimum passing standard based upon the difficulty of the test.

student choice allowing children to have choice in how they demonstrate learning.

TAAS Texas Assessment of Academic Skills; an examination that tests the TEKS (curriculum guidelines set by the state of Texas as basic knowledge and skills).

TAKS Texas Assessment of Knowledge and Skills examination, which will replace the TAAS to test the TEKS.

TEKS Texas Essential Knowledge and Skills, which provides a curriculum guide for each grade level tested through the TAAS (Texas Assessment of Academic Skills) or TAKS.

thematic units an organizational method in which a number of lesson plans are designed to fall under one topic (shapes, apples, pumpkins, cause-and-effect, and so forth).

TLI (Texas Learning Index) an index that is statistically figured to allow teachers to compare children's performances across grade levels or years.

SUGGESTED ACTIVITIES

1. Obtain a TAAS (or TAKS) report for a child in your class and evaluate the needs of that child, using reporting information. If in a field placement, ask whether your school will "white out" a child's name and other identifying criteria so that you can work with reported scores.

2. Prepare a lesson in which you carefully document the TEKS to be taught. Align instruc-

tion with those TEKS that you have selected. Note what prior TEKS the learner must have mastered before success can be obtained in this lesson.

3. Observe an early childhood classroom where children are working in "play centers." Document the ways in which the teacher works with children in his or her different roles while children play. Note which roles seem effective and in what situations. Reflect on a teaching situation in an *upper* elementary grade level. How would you modify the roles and instruction to still employ play?

4. Prepare a lesson to teach that includes a cooperative group activity. Include learners' roles and a social skill(s). Have a colleague tape your lesson. As you watch the tape, focus on your role as facilitator. Notice your interactions with each group and your "travel path" around the room. Be sure to include both group and individual accountability in your lesson.

5. Reflect upon your beliefs and expectations about the social skills and other types of knowledge that children bring to school. Further reflect upon why it is worth the addition of these skills in everyday teaching. Interview your mentor for his or her ideas and compare beliefs.

PRACTICE QUESTIONS

1. Ms. Bradford has set up several centers in her Pre-K room. One center is the "Vehicle Center," which consists simply of two chairs with seat covers on them, placed where the driver faces the center of the classroom. Children who come to this center can "go anywhere they would like and in whatever type of vehicle." Ms. Bradford normally waits until a child is seated in the "driver's seat" and is obviously playing, and then she slides into the "passenger's seat." "Wow," she says, "This is a nice vehicle." "M-m-m," says the child, as she continues driving. "What kind of vehicle is this?" "Car," is the reply. "What color?" "Green." "Where are we going?" asks the teacher. "To the store," again comes a short reply. "What will you buy at the store?" inquires the teacher. "New colors. Mine are broken." "I

need to stop at the post office. Do you think you could stop for me? What do you think I need to do there?" "I dunno." "I need to mail a letter." Ms. Bradford should:

A. Not spend so much time with one child because the rest of her class will suffer.

B. Not intrude on this child's play, because she could stifle the imagination of children in this center.

C. Ask another child to sit as the passenger so that both children can pretend that they are driving to the spot of their choice.

D. Continue this format because young children tend to learn more in symbolic play when they are playing with someone else.

2. Mrs. Mays, a fourth-grade teacher, was examining her children's last year's TAAS (TAKS) scores in mathematics. She noted that Dante received a 3-68 on his TLI. What does this tell her about Dante?

A. Dante should be further diagnosed for remediation in various math skills this year, using the Objective Performance on the campus TAAS (TAKS) report.

B. The TLI (Texas Learning Index) allows Mrs. Mays to compare Dante's math scores for on-level growth skills.

C. Dante was not quite on grade-level achievement in mathematics.

D. All of the above.

3. Mrs. Lowrance designed a discovery unit on plants in science for her first graders. The unit was centered on how long it would take a seed to sprout. First she wanted each group to come to consensus on a prediction, then she scheduled groups to measure and mix soil in a heavy Ziplock® bag (just enough so that the seed was surrounded by dirt but could still be seen through the Ziplock® bag). Groups would also carefully measure and add water to their Ziplock® bag. Mrs. Lowrance then planned to hang each Ziplock® bag on her "clothesline" by the windows. Each day groups would examine their Ziplock® bag and draw the results on an experiment sheet. This sounded like a great unit, but when Mrs.

Lowrance began to teach it, she found that children were confused about what they were to do and became argumentative over the tasks. Mrs. Lowrance had been really excited about trying groups and these activities, but now she began to dread each science period as the unit progressed. What could Mrs. Lowrance try to best salvage what is left of these activities?

A. She could stop all group work and have each child do his or her own worksheet.

B. She could teach a social skill of the day and assign roles in the group for each activity.

C. She could set firm management limits so that children would know that no arguing was allowed.

D. She could stop these activities and tell children that because they couldn't act right, they would not get to have enjoyable activities such as these.

4. Mrs. Kilmain, a new kindergarten teacher at Pecan Grove Elementary, was excited to teach an integrated unit on pumpkins. She was going to have children weigh pumpkins and then weigh themselves to compare the two weights. Then she planned for children to measure various sizes of pumpkins, followed by cutting the tops off and having children count the seeds inside. In planning, she should:

A. Check with other grade levels to make sure they don't have a pumpkin unit.

B. Design unit goals and a rationale(s) since she only has activities listed.

C. Add subject areas other than math.

D. All of the above.

5. Ms. Mitchell was planning to teach a lesson on plants to her fourth graders. What would be her best plan for resources?

A. Find pictures of various plants and seeds on the Internet.

B. Talk about it with students and point out the examples in students' science books.

C. Ask parents to send some seeds and plants they have as examples.

D. Ask the neighborhood florist to bring

samples of flowers, fern with spores, etc., and allow students to dissect them as she or he gives a short talk.

ANSWERS AND DISCUSSION

Answer 1: It is true that the Pre-K teachers could not spend a great deal of time in one place with one child without monitoring the rest of their classrooms. However, due to the placement of the center, Mrs. Bradford could see the class as she was seated and could time her conversations so that she could move quickly if needed. *A* is not the *best* answer. The remaining answers focus on knowing that this center was placed in the classroom to encourage symbolic play. Here children construct more knowledge, using mental representation, or symbolism, through play and are more likely to do so when "playing" with someone else. *B* is not the answer. Mrs. Bradford could ask that another child come to the center, but she would be the best person in the classroom to help direct this. Answer *C* can also be eliminated because the center is a vehicle center, so children can decide what type of transportation they would like. Perhaps they would like to be in a construction vehicle that is digging or in a boat or a plane, for example, so they do not necessarily have to be driving. The best answer is *D*.

Answer 2: *A, B,* and *C* are all true. The answer is *D*.

Answer 3: Group work has such good benefits that we would not want to switch over to having children do individual work nor would we want to have children stop this concrete experiment. Mrs. Lowrance could "come down on them" with management threats, but children, at the height of excitement, don't always remember. The best idea is to assign specific roles and responsibilities for each day's activity (for example, one set of roles for three in a group would be: materials manager, measurer, and mixer/planter). She could also teach a "skill-of-the-day" and reward members with group points when she saw them using the

skill. If the "skill-of-the-day" was politeness, she would model for them what politeness might look like in the day's activities ("Oh, Jason, thank you for holding this bag open for me," or "You are so helpful to clean off my desk, too."). Then she would have children practice some phrases before sending them to work. The answer is *B*.

Answer 4: Mrs. Kilmain has begun to jot down a number of activities. As part of an integrated unit she would need to consider all of the above. The answer is *D*.

Answer 5: The teacher should never just talk (*B*) if any other resources are available at all. The Internet may be a good supplemental resource, but the more "real life," the better (*A*). Although parents could send samples (*C*), those samples may not be the kind that would be easy for children to dissect, and because plants that are picked in yards often rapidly deteriorate, a teacher might not know how many samples he or she would have on a specific day. Bringing in an expert guarantees that the samples will all be the same and that they will be easy for children to dissect. In addition, there will be a good human resource from the community. The answer is *D*.

WEB LINKS

If you type in several of the key words listed at the beginning of this chapter for a search, you will have a long list of sites that offer theory, activities, materials to purchase, and so forth. There may be other search combinations that will help you gain more information. Remember that sites move, can be removed, or may not be found using your server. If a site listed below cannot be located, try typing in other key words to help your search.

www.edhelper.com/

www.atozteacherstuff.com/themes/

http://LessonPlanz.com/Lesson_Plans/Thematic_Units/

http://www.esc20.net/curriculum/

Thematic units for an integrated curriculum can be found at all these sites listed above.

www.atozteacherstuff.com/articles/
cooperative.shtml

A huge amount of information is offered here on
using cooperative groups.

http://www.clcrc.com/

This site is designed by Johnson and Johnson, two
pioneers in cooperative learning. Find research
along with practical steps for conflict resolution
(and so forth) at this site.

http://www.jigsaw.org/

This site provides an extension on everything you
might want to know about Jigsaw.

http://sps.k12.mo.us/coop/ecoopmain.html

Here you will find information on teaching with
cooperative groups.

www.iasce.net/resources.htm

This page lists a great number of links to cooperative learning sources.

http://4teachers.org/intech/lessons/

www.esc20.net/etprojects/

The strength of these two sites lies in their ability
to help you design Web-based lessons.

REFERENCES

Berlyne, D. E. (1960). *Conflict, arousal, and curiosity.* New
York: McGraw-Hill.

Bjorklund, D. (2000). *Children's thinking.* 3rd ed. Belmont, CA: Wadsworth.

Bornstein, M., Haynes, O., O'Reilly, A., & Painter, K.
(1996). Solitary and collaborative pretense play in
early childhood: Sources of individual variation in
the development of representational competence.
Child Development, 67, 2910–2029.

Brewer, J. A. (2001). *Introduction to early childhood education: Preschool through primary grades* (4th ed.). Boston:
Allyn and Bacon.

Brodhagen, B. L. (1995). The situation made us special.
In M. W. Apple & J. A. Beane (Eds.) *Democratic
schools* (pp. 83–100). Alexandria, VA: Association for
Supervision and Curriculum Development.

Brostrom, S. (1995). *Frame plays amongst six year old children: Possibilities and limitations.* Paper presented to
the European Conference of Education Research,
Bath, September 1995.

Fromberg, D. (2002). *Play and meaning in early childhood
education.* Boston: Allyn & Bacon.

Johnson, D., & Johnson, R. (1989). *Cooperation and competition: Theory and research.* Edina, MN: Interaction.

Johnson, D., Maruyama, G., Johnson, R., & Skon, L.
(1981). Effects of cooperative, competitive and indi-
vidualistic goal structures on achievement: A meta-
analysis. *Psychological Bulletin, 89,* 47–62.

Kagan, S. (1992). *Cooperative learning.* San Juan Capis-
trano, CA: Resources for Teachers, Inc. (1-800-Wee
Co-op).

Leighton, M. (1999). Cooperative learning. In J. Cooper
(Ed.), *Classroom teaching skills* (pp. 267–307). Boston:
Houghton Mifflin Company.

Parker, M. (2001). Instructional materials and resources.
In C. G. Henry & J. L. Nath (Eds.). *Becoming a teacher
in Texas: A course of study for the Professional Development ExCET* (pp. 215–232). Belmont, CA:
Wadsworth.

Sayre, N., & Gallagher, J. (2001). *The young child and the
environment.* Boston: Allyn and Bacon.

Sharan, S., & Shachar, H. (1988). *Language and learning in
the cooperative classroom.* New York: Springer-Verlag.

Slavin, R. (1983). *Cooperative learning.* New York:
Longman.

Teasley, S. D. (1995). The role of talk in children's peer
collaborations. *Developmental Psychology, 31,*
207–220.

Vygotsky, L. (1987). *Thought and language.* Cambridge,
MA: MIT Press.

Wood, E., & Attfield, J. (1996). *Play, learning, and the early
childhood curriculum.* London: Paul Chapman Publishing Ltd.

Competency 4

The teacher understands learning processes and factors that impact student learning and demonstrates this knowledge by planning effective, engaging instruction and appropriate assessments.

The beginning teacher:

- Understands the role of learning theory in the instructional process and uses instructional strategies and appropriate technologies to facilitate student learning (e.g., connecting new information and ideas to prior knowledge, making learning meaningful and relevant to students).

- Understands that young children think concretely and rely primarily on motor and sensory input and direct experience for development of skills and knowledge, and uses this understanding to plan effective, developmentally appropriate learning experiences and assessments.

- Recognizes how various characteristics of students in early childhood through grade 4 (e.g., attention span, need for physical activity and movement) impact teaching and learning.

- Teaches, models, and monitors organizational skills at an age-appropriate level (e.g., establishing regular places for classroom toys and materials, sorting blocks by shape and size during cleanup).

- Stimulates reflection, critical thinking, and inquiry among students in early childhood through grade 4 (e.g., provides opportunities to manipulate materials and to test ideas and hypotheses, provides repetition for increased conceptual understanding, supports the concept of play as a valid vehicle for learning).

- Analyzes ways in which teacher behaviors (e.g., teacher expectations, student grouping practices, teacher-student interactions) impact student learning, and plans instruction and assessment that minimize the effects of negative factors and enhance all students' learning.

- Analyzes ways in which factors in the home and community (e.g., parent expectations, availability of community resources, community problems) impact student learning, and plans instruction and assessment with awareness of social and cultural factors to enhance all students' learning.

- Understands the importance of self-directed learning and plans instruction and assessment that promote students' motivation and their sense of ownership of and responsibility for their own learning.

- Analyzes ways in which various teacher roles (e.g., facilitator, lecturer) and student roles (e.g., active learner, observer, group participant) impact student learning.

- Incorporates students' different approaches to learning (e.g., auditory, visual, tactile, kinesthetic) into instructional practices.

Chapter 5

Using Learning Theories and Processes

S A N D Y   C M A J D A L K A

University of Houston- Downtown

TERMS TO KNOW

Accommodation

Assimilation

Behaviorism

Chunking

Classical conditioning

Cognitive learning theory

Concept

Conditional knowledge

Constructivism

Contiguity

Declarative knowledge

Defining attributes

Encoding

Information processing

Learning

Long-term memory

Metacognition

Modeling

Negative reinforcement

Nonroutine problem solving

Operant conditioning

Positive reinforcement

Presentation punishment

Procedural knowledge

Punishment

Rehearsal

Removal punishment

Routine problem solving

Schema

Sensory memory

Social learning theory

Transfer

Vicarious learning

Working memory/short–term memory

This chapter addresses learning theory and its relationship to Competency 4. The teacher is responsibile for helping children increase their learning to the greatest extent possible. Although theorists do not all agree on one absolute definition of learning, they do agree that classroom teachers must be aware of the varying dimensions of learning and the theories that support them. This chapter discusses behaviorism, social learning theory, and cognitive views of learning. Also addressed are other critical factors related to learning theory and how they can be applied in the classroom to maximize student achievement.

BEHAVIORISM

Behaviorists define **learning** as a change in observable behavior as a result of experience (Skinner, 1953). Three categories of behavioral learning are usually noted: contiguity, classical conditioning, and operant conditioning. Each of these categories is described below. With regard to **behaviorism,** the focus is on the *observable* (or measurable) behavior that is produced or elicited.

Contiguity

The first and most basic of the three categories of behavioral learning is contiguity. **Contiguity** is the simple pairing of two behaviors enough times so that a person continues to pair the two even when only one is presented. For example, most people are so familiar with "knock, knock" jokes that when someone says, "Knock, knock!" one can't help but automatically respond with (or at least think to oneself), "Who's there?" The two have been paired so many times that they have become associated with each other. This is called simple stimulus and response learning. When a stimulus is presented (knock, knock), the response comes almost automatically. Another example is a ringing telephone. Even if a person is busy, he or she is likely to respond and answer the phone. People who are in the shower will sometimes even answer the phone simply because they have been "conditioned" to respond to the given stimulus because of the number of times the two have been paired. Contiguity can be very useful in the classroom, especially for rote memorization. Although many educators frown on rote memorization, it does have a prominent place in learning. For example, many people learn the multiplication tables using rote memorization. When someone asks, "What is 8 times 10?" most people reply quickly that the product is 80. They don't have to think to themselves that 8 times 10 is actually 8 groups of 10, which is $10 + 10 + 10 + 10 + 10 + 10 + 10 + 10$. If we had to go through this process every time someone asked a simple multiplication question, imagine how long it would take! Luckily, through contiguity, 8 times 10 has been associated with 80 enough times that the answer has become automatic. The drawback to contiguity learning is that some teachers use it to pair a stimulus with a response without ever showing children the true relationship between the two. For example, when asked, "What is 4 times 7?" children may be able to say "28," but they may not know *why* it is 28 or *how* to get the answer. Effective classroom teachers should teach the concept of multiplication in a manner that ensures that all children understand. When everyone has a firm grasp of the concept, the teacher can move to contiguity so that responses are automatic and save time. Teachers should not confuse simple stimulus/response with true understanding. Stimulus/response is simply the automatic pairing of a response to a given stimulus.

Classical Conditioning

Another category of behavioral learning theory is **classical conditioning.** Usually associated with the behaviorist Ivan Pavlov, classical conditioning goes a step further than simple contiguity. Classical conditioning occurs when a conditioned response to a stimulus (that may have been learned through contiguity) is paired with a *second* stimulus enough times that the new stimulus also produces the original response from the first stimulus (Pavlov, 1928). This conditioned response is often an emotional or physiological response. A famous example is Pavlov's experiment with dogs and meat powder. Meat powder (stimulus 1) was placed on the tongue of a dog, and the dog began to salivate (response). These two were paired enough times that whenever meat powder was introduced, the response was always the same—increased salivation. Then Pavlov introduced meat powder on the dog's tongue while ringing a bell at the same time. Now there were two stimuli, meat powder (stimulus 1) and the ringing of the bell (stimulus 2) with still the same response—increased salivation by the dog (actually caused by stimulus 1, not the bell). After enough pairings of the two stimuli (meat powder and bell), Pavlov was ready for the final stage of the experiment. He rang the bell (stimulus 2) but did *not* give the dog meat powder. What happened? The dog still salivated! Pavlov had paired the ringing of the bell with the meat powder enough times so that even when the powder was not presented, the dog salivated. This is classical conditioning.

An example in the classroom would be a child's sweaty hands right before his turn to read in front of the class. Why? He has had experiences in the past being ridiculed by his peers while his teacher did nothing to stop them (stimulus 1). Even though the child might be in a new class and the original ridiculing peers and teacher are not present, he exhibits the original response (sweating when asked to read). He associates the second stimulus (reading in front of others) with the original stimulus (ridicule from peers). These types of responses require that a teacher consider children's background and past learning experiences.

Operant Conditioning

The third category of behavioral learning is **operant conditioning,** and is usually associated with B. F. Skinner. Operant conditioning proposes that learning occurs as the result of reinforcers or punishment (Skinner, 1953). When a behavior occurs, it is either rewarded or punished. Rewarded behaviors will continue to occur and possibly increase, and punished behaviors will stop or decrease. There are two basic types of reinforcement and two basic types of punishment. Each is discussed below.

Reinforcement

Reinforcement means that a behavior will increase or continue and has two basic types: positive and negative (not to be confused with good and bad). With **positive reinforcement,** something such as a sticker, verbal praise, a pat on the back, or a high grade is given to the child to increase the behavior or increase the likelihood that it will occur again. With **negative reinforcement,** something distasteful is removed, such as a disliked chore, in order to increase the behavior or its likelihood of occurring again. For example, children may be told that if they study hard and make good grades on their daily quizzes, they will be excused from taking the big weekly test. In this example, a negative reinforcement is being employed, because the big exam is being taken away as a reward for increasing study habits and daily quiz grades. Keep in mind that both positive and negative reinforcement *increase* behavior. Some cautions for using negative reinforcement in the classroom are discussed in Competency 8, Part 2, Chapter 13.

Reinforcement theory can be a bit tricky for teachers because what they often view as punishment can actually be reinforcement for certain children. Ramon, for example, really dislikes going to music class. Right before music class every day, he begins to act out so badly that Mrs. Martinez, his teacher, sends him to the office. She believes that she is punishing him, but in actuality she is rewarding him because he is now going somewhere other than music class. Time-outs from dreary lessons can be seen in the same light. Teachers should examine the situation carefully to be sure that they are not actually *reinforcing* children in some way if an inappropriate behavior does not *decrease* when a particular "punishment" is introduced.

One common use of reinforcement is seen in behavior contracts in which a child is offered a reward beginning with a small amount of improvement. Each week the amount of improvement must increase to receive a reward—until the bad behavior has been mostly or completely extinguished.

Punishment

Unlike reinforcement, the purpose of **punishment** is to decrease or stop a behavior. Again there are two basic types: presentation punishment and removal punishment. **Presentation punishment** occurs when a child is *presented* or given something to stop a behavior such as a bad grade, a verbal reprimand, extra homework, a spanking, or the old favorite, "the evil eye," from the teacher. On the other hand, **removal punishment** occurs when something pleasurable is taken away from the student to stop the behavior. For example, a student might lose his recess or field trip privileges, have a toy taken away, or not be allowed to eat lunch with the rest of the class. Both types of punishment can be used effectively to stop undesired behaviors in the classroom. This is described in further detail in the discussion on motivation in Competency 8, Part 2, Chapter 13.

SOCIAL LEARNING THEORY

Social learning theory proposes that we learn by observing others in our environment (Ban-

dura, 1977). **Modeling** is the most critical factor for Bandura's theory and is discussed below.

Modeling

Research shows that we imitate behaviors that we see in others. This begins very early in life. A baby may smile back at his mother when she smiles first. When a toddler sees someone pet a dog, he or she tries to pet it, too. We often hope for positive role models for our children—those people whom children admire and who we feel model desired behaviors. The teacher in the early years of school has a tremendous amount of influence. When a teacher is courteous to his or her students, the students are more likely to be courteous to each other. When a teacher models that he or she thinks reading is interesting, for instance, children are more likely to believe that reading (or whatever the subject matter) is interesting.

Modeling does not always have positive results, though. When a teacher sees a storm coming and becomes frightened, she models for her children fearful behavior, and they in turn can become frightened when seeing a storm in the future. Also, students may imitate negative behaviors such as smoking when they see others model it for them. Teachers sometimes wonder why a young child comes to class and says a bad word. Where did he or she learn such behavior? Someone has modeled it. Usually children are more likely to imitate the behaviors of a model important to them (i.e., a parent, teacher, friend, or someone on television or in the movies whom they think is "cool"). Modeling also applies to instructional tasks for students and learning other behaviors. By observing the teacher, children learn to turn the pages of a book from right to left and to point to the words while moving their fingers from left to right. Children also imitate their teacher's voice inflections when reading certain parts of a story and imitate how to physically touch each math manipulative item while counting the total number (one-to-one correspondence). For this reason, classroom teachers need to be conscious of the behaviors they exhibit in front of their children. If children see that a teacher is biased in any way, much of the class can take on this demeanor. Young children tend to watch their teachers and imitate many of their behaviors.

Vicarious Learning

Another important aspect of social learning theory is **vicarious learning.** This goes beyond modeling in that children "learn" by seeing a model's behavior either rewarded or punished. For example, a child may see that a peer who did well on an assignment received praise from the teacher. The child deduces that if she does well too, she might also receive praise. On the other hand, a child might see a classmate come to class without his homework assignment and observe that he has his recess taken away. The child did not have to experience the loss of homework and play time himself in order to learn from the modeled behavior. He learned what the punishment would be vicariously through his classmate's experience. Teachers who choose students who are "sitting up straight with everything put away" to line up first are using vicarious learning to have others get ready, too.

COGNITIVE VIEWS OF LEARNING

Unlike behaviorism, which views learning as a change in *observable* behavior, **cognitive learning theory** proposes that learning takes place when there is a change within a person's internal mental structures or mental processes (Eggen & Kauchak, 2001). Although these changes may not be outwardly observable, they are still considered to be learning. Two commonly discussed views of cognitive learning are information processing and constructivism. In Competency 1, Chapter 1, some terms that are commonly used when discussing cognitive views of learning were introduced. These are reviewed and extended below.

A **concept** is a mental structure that categorizes similar ideas, objects, events, people, or expe-

riences. For example, birds are placed in a certain category in one's mental structure, and everything placed in that category has something in common (i.e., they fly, have feathers, have a beak, have wings). It should be noted that just because someone has developed a concept for "bird," it doesn't necessarily mean that the concept is accurate. For example, not all birds fly. This leads to defining attributes. **Defining attributes,** also referred to as defining characteristics or defining features, are the important criteria one sets in order to determine whether an item fits into the concept category. If a child sees the ability to fly as a defining attribute for birds, his or her concept of "bird" will not include penguins, ostriches, emus, and so forth. Similarly, if one of the child's defining attributes for the concept of "ball" is that it must be round or spherical, a football would not fit into his or her category for "ball." If a child's defining attribute for "ball" is that it is an object that one can either throw or kick to friends, a bowling ball would not fit into that concept of "ball." As children begin to develop their concepts, even though erroneous and incomplete, they may need several experiences to help them redefine the concepts. For example, consider a young child learning the concept of shoes. He may see shoes as only the tennis shoes with laces that are put on his feet. Then one day someone brings him a pair of tennis shoes with Velcro® instead of laces. The child might redefine his concept to show that laces are not a defining characteristic, but looking like a tennis shoe still is. Another day someone brings him a pair of outdoor sandals and calls them "shoes." The child might redefine his concept as anything that goes on his feet for walking. Similarly, if his defining characteristic is that shoes are something that go on his feet, what about socks? What about snorkeling fins or flippers for swimming in the water? Each time the child is presented with these new experiences or new information, he is forced to decide whether he will ignore the information or change his defining attributes for that particular concept. One can see that a teacher must consider definitions and attributes carefully when introducing concepts. In addition, a teacher must consider enriching children's learning with a variety of visual and concrete items to help children form correct concepts.

Figure 5.1 A child's concept of "bird."

A **schema** is one's mental structure for organizing all of the various concepts or behaviors one has developed and their relationships to each other. For example, even though one has a concept for the word "animal," it can be called a schema, because it likely contains an organization of several other concepts (i.e., birds, cats, dogs, etc.)

and their relationship to each other. A young child's schema for "animal" may include these common examples and a few others. However, as children get older and have more experiences, they may add categories such as farm animals and zoo animals. As students get even older, they may include more categories such as birds, fish, mammals, reptiles, amphibians, and so on. A high school student may even have categories such as vertebrates and invertebrates. Furthermore, they may include categories of invertebrates such as echinoderms, annelids, and mollusks. The level of schema development depends on the knowledge and experiences an individual has had. Just as a person's concept can be inaccurate, so can a person's schema. For example, many children would not allow the concept of human beings to be placed in their schema of animals. See Figure 5.2 for an older child's scheme of "animal."

Teachers who understand these theories of developing concepts know that young children are

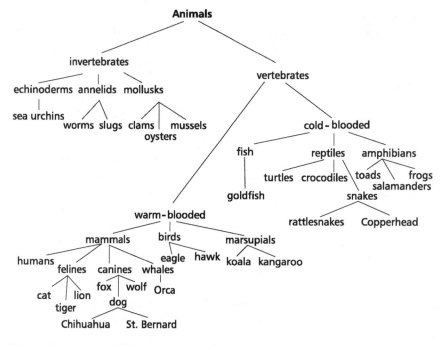

Figure 5.2 An older child's schema of "animal."

learning many new concepts in their classrooms. Teachers are careful to make sure that children's concepts are built soundly and, because of their understanding of common misconceptions about particular concepts and schemas, that they can help children learn more quickly and accurately. Competency 8, Part 1, Chapter 12 discusses how to build instruction around attaining concepts.

INFORMATION PROCESSING

Information processing is a cognitive view of learning that likens the mind to a computer with a place for data input, storage, and retrieval for future use. Figure 5.3 may be of help in conceptualizing the theory of information processing.

According to the theory of information processing, information enters the brain or mind through our senses, whether sight, sound, smell, touch, or taste. This information is stored briefly in **sensory memory,** often for less than a second, and then the information is lost. This is a good thing, too, because if people remembered everything that they saw or smelled, imagine how overloaded their brains would be: everything they saw or smelled (the perfume of a person next to them, the feel of clothes touching one's skin, the sound that breathing makes), imagine how overloaded their brains would be. This does not mean that we are incapable of remembering the information.

On the contrary, we can remember the sensory input longer if we give it something—our attention. If we decide to pay attention to something (i.e., the sound of the seconds ticking away on a clock), we can move that bit of information out of sensory memory and into working memory.

Working Memory

Working memory, also called **short-term memory,** is the place where we store everything to which we are currently paying attention. This memory store can hold information for a longer period of time than can sensory memory. As long as we are paying attention to the information, we can keep it in working memory. If we decide to no longer pay attention to the information, it may stay in working memory for roughly 20 more seconds, but then it is lost. Also, working memory is very limited in its capacity to hold a large amount of information. Think of yourself when you look up a phone number to call. You are paying attention to the number, so it is in your working memory. If you do not dial that number within 20 seconds or so, you may find yourself holding the phone but not remembering the number to dial. So you return to the phone book. If you want the information to stay in working memory longer than 20 seconds, you must continually pay attention to the information. One strategy for doing this is called rehearsal.

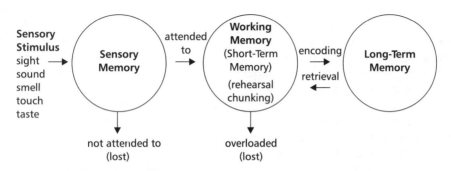

Figure 5.3 A Conception of the Information Processing Theory.

Using the **rehearsal** strategy, one forces him-or herself to pay attention to the information by repeating it over and over. With this strategy, after a person looks up the needed phone number he or she may repeat the number again and again while putting down the phone book, walking over to the phone, picking up the receiver, and starting to dial the number. This can be a very effective strategy—but beware! If someone interrupts before the person dials the number, and if he or she responds, the phone number may be lost. The sequence of going back to the phone book must be repeated. Attention was removed from the phone number—if but briefly. When attention is no longer paid to information, it is quickly lost. When teaching concepts to young children, teachers ask continuously for all children's attention (often waiting until they are sure "all eyes are on them") because they understand this concept. See Competency 8, Part 1, Chapter 12 for more information on attention spans.

Researchers believe that working memory can hold anywhere between five and nine items at a given time (Miller, 1956). Any more than that and one's memory is overloaded and the information is lost. One method to help keep more information in working memory is called chunking. With **chunking** one gathers or groups bits of information into one unit of information to allow for more items to be included in memory. For example, if you were asked to remember the following string of letters, "s, e, y, i, t, h, i, s, t, a, n, s," you might have difficulty remembering them all, even with rehearsal, because there are more items to remember than the usual five-through-nine limit. However, if you "chunk" the information by rearranging the letters into the sentence into "Isn't this easy?" you will have consolidated 12 individual bits of information into three bits of information. Three bits of information are much easier to remember than 12. However, being able to store more information in working memory does not ensure that long-term learning will occur. As a classroom application, think of studying for an exam. Immediately before the exam

you may be repeating certain key concepts, definitions, and "chunks" of information to yourself so that you can write them on the exam. Once the exam is over and you turn it in and walk out the door, much of the information is gone. This is how many students are able to pass an exam without truly learning or internalizing the information. If teachers want their children to internalize information and remember it for a longer period of time, they must find ways to help the children move information from short-term memory into long-term memory.

Long-Term Memory

Long-term memory is the place where information is stored permanently in our minds. Although rehearsal can be used as a strategy to get information into long-term memory, countless repetitions may be needed. For example, you know how to spell your first name and last name by heart. You have heard it or written it so many times that it becomes permanently encoded or written into your memory. **Encoding** is the process of moving information into your long-term memory. Supposedly there is no limit to the amount of information that can be stored there. However, we can't know for sure. Also, it is believed that there is no limit to the length of time that something can stay in long-term memory. You can ask yourself, "Who were all my teachers and teacher aides from kindergarten through high school?" If there is no shortage of long-term memory length, why can't you remember every one of your teachers? The information is likely there in your memory. The problem is retrieving it. The process is similar to overgrown pathways that haven't been used for a while. At one time these pathways were clear, but now they are so overgrown that there is difficulty getting through. Teachers want to be sure to create as many clear pathways to the information as possible so that when one path becomes overgrown and impassable, there are still other routes that can be used to retrieve the information. This is why teachers must approach a subject in many different ways during instruction. What is a clear pathway for one child may not be very clear for another. The more organized information is and the more it is connected to past learning, the more easily it can be recalled. This is the theory of information processing.

CONSTRUCTIVISM

Another cognitive learning theory is constructivism, which also views learning as a change in mental processes. For constructivists, learning need not be *observable,* as required by behaviorists. **Constructivism** focuses on the importance of the child's being able to construct his or her own knowledge schemas rather than the teacher's constructing of knowledge for the student (Brophy, 1992). As noted, a schema is the child's mind map for all his held concepts and the way those concepts are interrelated. A child's concept for "bunny rabbits" may be that they have long ears, are soft and furry, hop, and have twitchy noses. If the child has numerous encounters with rabbits, he may be able to build his concept to include the following: strong hind legs that kick, can be picked up by the scruff of the neck, and don't always like carrots. This change in the child's mind map or structure is what constructivists call "learning." Let us review two concepts introduced in Competency 1, Chapter 1: assimilation and accommodation—mental processes that are discussed in constructivism.

Assimilation occurs as the child encounters new information and does not have a schema or concept already developed for it. Rather than create a new schema or concept, the child places the information wherever it seems to fit best. For example, a child sees a garden hose and doesn't already have a schema or concept for it. He may call it a snake because that is the closest concept he has to it. The object is long, skinny, green, lying in the grass, and so forth. Note that in this case, there is nothing random about the process or the choice of schemas into which the new informa-

tion is placed. The child didn't put the hose in the "chair," "flower," or "people" categories. He simply placed the new information where it made the most sense or "best fit," according to the concept and schema he already had in place from his past experiences. This is called *assimilation.* The other process used is accommodation.

Accommodation occurs when the child has enough experiences with the information (i.e., the garden hose) to figure out that it does not adequately fit where he previously assimilated it. He might see his brother turn on the hose, pick it up, drink water from it, and then spray it in the air or water the lawn. After enough experiences with the water hose, the child will eventually make a new mind map or schema for the information. Furthermore, it will not likely be linked to animals or creatures that crawl on the ground. It might instead be linked to his concept of garden tools or lawn equipment. This type of change in mental processes, in which a new mind map is created or a new category created, is called *accommodation.* Constructivists believe that information constructed by a learner in these ways will be more meaningful than if the child is simply given a definition. Constructivist teachers, therefore, offer many opportunities and examples (and nonexamples), along with the time needed for a learner to build his or her own meaning—with guidance, of course, from the teacher.

COMPLEX COGNITIVE PROCESSES

Metacognition

Metacognition is a complex cognitive process that requires knowledge of and control over one's own mental processes. It is sometimes referred to as "thinking about thinking." Everyone thinks, but not everyone thinks *about* his or her thinking. For example, when you are reading a difficult passage in a textbook and something doesn't make sense, do you notice, or do you just keep on reading? A metacognitive person will say to himself, "Hm-m-m! I didn't quite understand that." If you know that you didn't understand, choices can be made as to what to do next. Will you keep reading and hope it eventually becomes clear, or back up and read the passage again? Will you look for contextual clues to help you understand? Children who have learned to "think" about their mental processes are better equipped to learn in the classroom because they develop strategies or plans of action that work when mental roadblocks arrive. Strategies can also be a part of classroom instruction. Problem solving is discussed in the following subsection. Think of times that you have a problem to solve. Do you just jump in, or do you try to think of a viable strategy first? Another example is studying. When studying for an exam, do you know which study strategies work best for you and which parts of the chapter need the most attention? These are all behaviors related to metacognition—thinking consciously about one's own thinking.

Problem Solving

Two basic types of problem solving are used in the classroom: routine and nonroutine. **Routine problem solving** occurs if is an answer or procedure to follow that makes the answer readily available. For example, "Sally goes to the store to buy some books. One book she wants to buy is $3 and the other is $6. However, Sally has only $10 total to spend. If she wants to buy both books, will she have enough money?" Although this kind of problem can be tough for some young students, it is still classified as routine. The first step is to identify the problem itself: Is $10 enough money to buy a book for $3 and another book for $6? The second step is to pick a strategy for solving the problem. Do I need to subtract 6 from 10 and then 3 from 10? Do I need to subtract 3 from 6 and then 6 from 10? Do I need to add the 3 and the 6 together and then subtract from 10?

When a strategy has been selected, the next step is to represent the problem, whether physically with a picture or symbolically with numbers.

The child might draw a picture of 10 one-dollar bills so that he or she can mark them out while working through the problem. Or a child might draw three one-dollar bills and then another six one-dollar bills to count the total money needed. He or she might, depending upon age, simply write $3 + 6$ and then $10 - 9$. These are all methods of representing the problem. The next step in problem solving is to actually carry out the strategy chosen, such as marking out the dollars as "used," performing the numerical operations, or taking the 10 one-dollar bills and pretending to "pay" for the items one dollar at a time. The last step is to evaluate the strategy and method used to see how well it worked. This particular problem is considered routine in that there are set ways, or algorithms, to solve it. Effective teachers understand the importance of metacognition in teaching children many strategies from which to choose to help them think through problems.

The other type of problem solving is **nonroutine problem solving.** A nonroutine problem is one that is novel (new) to the student and for which there is not an easily identifiable solution available. An example is, "There are 25 students in a classroom but only 24 cookies. What should you do?" This type of problem allows for a discussion of sharing or even of someone giving up his or her cookie to another class member. This type of problem allows for more open-ended thinking, with the idea that there may be multiple solutions to the problem. Although both of these examples fall under the content area of mathematics, problem solving can be used in any of the content areas. For example, in social studies, "Anita has a friend that she knows just told a lie to the teacher. What should she do?" Avenues to investigate might include: Should she tell the teacher about the lie? Should she talk to her friend and ask her why she lied? Should she just ignore the situation and let her friend do what she likes? This is a nonroutine problem in that a correct answer is not readily available to the child. Strategies and rehearsal of strategies strengthen problem solving, so teachers should plan carefully to use both in the classroom often.

TRANSFER OF LEARNING

Classroom teachers certainly do not have enough time to teach everything that they wish to teach. For this reason, making use of **transfer** in learning becomes very important. There are two basic types of transfer: positive and negative. *Positive transfer* occurs as the child learns information in one area and is later able to apply that learning correctly or appropriately to another area. For example, if a child learns from having a classroom hamster that pets need to be given food, water, clean bedding, attention, and so forth, the child might transfer this knowledge to the care of other pets and/or the habitats of other animals. The teacher will probably not have enough space or energy for a pet mouse *and* a pet rat *and* a pet bunny, a pet goldfish and so forth. However, he or she assumes that general learning from the experience or activity will "transfer" to other areas. This is how the teacher makes effective use of learning time when time is limited. Also, when children learn how to be courteous to their peers in the classroom, it is hoped that this learning will transfer to other social situations with peers or adults—next year in school, at the neighborhood playground, at the grocery store, and so forth. However, not all transfer is desirable. *Negative transfer* occurs as a child takes information from one learning situation and inappropriately applies it to another situation. For example, a child who learns that animals in cages are pets and can be touched and handled might see a raccoon in a cage and try to pet it, only to find that the animal tries to bite him. Also, a child who was bitten by a dog might now be afraid of all dogs, believing that all dogs will bite. This is taking information learned in one situation and inappropriately generalizing it to another. Think of the child who has learned that "if it comes out of a box that resembles a cereal box, it must taste good." He or she might open a box of cat food and have a distasteful surprise! Again the child is taking information learned from one experience and incorrectly applying it to another. Teachers must anticipate misconceptions during learning in order to avoid negative transfer. They must also try to encourage positive transfer by connecting knowledge whenever possible.

TYPES OF KNOWLEDGE

Knowledge is typically classified into three basic types: declarative, procedural, and conditional. **Declarative knowledge** refers to basic facts and information. Some people refer to it as "knowing that." Some examples are: I know that 5 times 7 is 35; I know that the cheetah is considered to be the fastest land animal; and I know that there are differences between the Asian elephant and the African elephant. Declarative knowledge is extremely important, but teachers shouldn't let students stop there. **Procedural knowledge** is knowing *how* to do something, such as, "Do you know how to change a flat tire, or do you know how to go about the procedure of multiplying 243 by 6?" **Conditional knowledge** is knowing *when* to use certain knowledge or procedures. For example, I know how to multiply, add, subtract, and divide, but given a problem to solve, can I determine which of the above operations is the correct one to use in that particular situation? Another example is that I know how to change a flat tire, check the oil, and add brake fluid to my car, but do I know *when* these should be done? If the car breaks down on the side of the road, am I able to determine from the sounds and symptoms what should be done? Think of a young child who knows what certain items of clothing are and how to dress him- or herself (that is to physically put clothes on his or her body, or procedural knowledge). But if the child were to feel the temperature and weather conditions outside, would he or she be able to judge the right type of clothing to wear? Should he or she dress warmly? Dress in light clothing? Wear a raincoat? This is conditional knowledge. Teachers should remember that although procedural knowledge is important, it can be incomplete without the appropriate conditional knowledge to go along with it.

APPLICATION TIPS FOR
THE CLASSROOM

The following suggestions apply the theories discussed in this chapter:

- Use divergent thinking and questioning techniques, not only convergent.

- Give children opportunities to draw their own conclusions based on what they have experienced.

- Make use of children's background knowledge to help relate new information to old so that learning isn't isolated. For example, before reading a new story or text to children, ask them to share what they already know or have experienced concerning the proposed topic.

- When teaching new concepts, help children see the connections between new learning and their past learning. They should be able to expand on their existing schemas.

- Provide children with both examples and nonexamples of concepts to help ensure accurate views (see Competency 8, Chapter 12 for the concept attainment model).

- Help children see the connections between various concepts they have of the world and how these concepts relate to each other. Make sure that children are successful at a task at a concrete level before requiring that they perform the task at an abstract level (to avoid memorization without understanding).

- Use multiple methods of teaching content so that learners have more than one "pathway" for reaching the information.

- Provide children with opportunities to investigate nonroutine problem solving in order to improve their thinking skills, creativity, and metacognition.

- Model the use of metacognition for children. When you come to a word you don't know, think it through out loud. When solving a problem, think out loud to show your mental thought processes.

- Use teaching and learning methods that allow children opportunities to construct their own knowledge (i.e., discovery learning, inquiry learning).

- Help your children go beyond declarative knowledge to develop procedural and conditional knowledge.

SUMMARY

Although there is no single, clear, agreed-upon definition of learning, much research has been carried out in the area of learning and learning theory. The ultimate desire is to find out how children learn so that teachers can better align learning activities and teaching procedures to help ensure student success. As teachers study these learning theories, they need not ask themselves whether they are personally aligned most with the behaviorist, cognitivist, or social learning theorists. Teachers should, however, acknowledge that each theory has much to offer in the realm of teaching, learning, and the educational process in general. Texas teachers should realize that certification examinations place a higher emphasis on constructivism than on other learning theories presented in this chapter. Nevertheless, throughout each day in classrooms, teachers use and see examples of all of these theories. Also, teachers should stay current with new findings as more knowledge about brain research and other learning factors become available. As beginning teachers move into classrooms and begin performing teaching duties, they should ask themselves, "Is my activity in line with the way theorists believe learning occurs? Are my lessons and teaching delivery consistent with the way theory says children learn best?" Always keeping these questions at the forefront of teachers' minds will help ensure that they do their best to help students reach their maximum learning potential.

GLOSSARY

accommodation   the process of adjusting existing mental schemes or creating new ones in response to new information from the environment.

assimilation   the process of placing new information from the environment into already existing mental schemes.

behaviorism   a view of learning that emphasizes the role the environment plays on the changing of observable behavior.

chunking   grouping bits of information into one unit of information to allow more items to be included in memory.

classical conditioning   learning as a result of pairing a stimulus with an automatic physiological response.

cognitive learning theory   a theory of learning that emphasizes the change in a person's mental structures as a result of a need to make sense of the world.

concept   a mental structure that categorizes similar ideas, objects, events, people, or experiences.

conditional knowledge   knowing when and why to use declarative and procedural knowledge.

constructivism   a view of learning that emphasizes the role of the learner in building his or her own understanding and making sense of the world.

contiguity   the simple pairing of two behaviors enough times that a person continues to pair the two even when only one is presented.

declarative knowledge   a type of knowledge that is factually based; knowing "that___."

defining attributes   the important criteria set that determines whether an item fits into a concept category——also called defining characteristics or defining features.

encoding   the process of moving information into long-term memory.

information processing   a cognitive view of learning that likens the mind to a computer with a place for data input, storage, and retrieval for future use.

learning   a change in mental processes or observable behavior.

long-term memory   a place where information is permanently stored in the mind.

metacognition   a complex cognitive process that requires knowledge of and control over one's own mental processes.

modeling   a learner changes his or her behavior as a result of having observed a behavior in another person.

negative reinforcement   the removal of something undesirable in order to increase a behavior.

nonroutine problem solving   solving a problem for which there is not an easily identifiable solution available.

operant conditioning   learning as a result of reinforcers or punishment from the environment.

positive reinforcement   the introduction of a valued reward to increase a desired behavior.

presentation punishment   the introduction of something disliked or distasteful to decrease a behavior.

procedural knowledge   knowledge of the steps necessary to complete a task—knowing "how."

punishment   adding or taking away something that results in a decrease in a behavior.

rehearsal   the process of repeating information over and over to oneself to keep it in working memory.

removal punishment   the removal of something pleasurable in order to decrease a behavior.

routine problem solving   solving a problem for which there is a procedure to follow that makes the answer readily available.

schema   the mental structure for organizing all of the various concepts one has developed and their relationships to each other.

sensory memory   a place where information received from the senses is stored for a very brief moment (usually less than 2 seconds).

social learning theory   a theory of learning that emphasizes what we learn through observing the behavior of others in our environment.

transfer   applying the learning of previous information to the learning of new information.

vicarious learning   learning that results from seeing someone else's behavior rewarded or punished.

working memory   a place where information is temporarily stored in our minds (usually for 20 seconds or less)—also called short-term memory.

SUGGESTED ACTIVITIES

1. Make a concept map showing your schema of a topic you know well. Make another concept map showing your schema for a topic that you do not know well. Compare the two maps.

2. Make a list of your own mental processes that you intend to model for your students.

3. What is something that you have learned vicariously through another person's behavior and consequences or reinforcement? What is something that you learned personally (firsthand) that you *wish* you had learned vicariously? Observe a lesson. In what ways did the teacher use vicarious learning? List ways that vicarious learning will be valuable in your classroom.

4. Observe a classroom teacher delivering a lesson to students. Make note of the learning strategies he or she uses. Is one strategy given a heavier emphasis than the others? Which one? Do you think this teacher is typical of other teachers?

5. Write three examples of routine problems and three examples of nonroutine problems. Solve one of the routine problems and one of the nonroutine problems while talking to yourself out loud (to model metacognition). What type of thinking and strategies did you use for each?

PRACTICE QUESTIONS

1. Ms. Carter is a second-grade teacher and is teaching a unit on spiders. She wants to be sure that her students know that a spider is not an insect, because spiders have eight legs and insects have only six. Her best method of ensuring that students remember this information on a long term basis is to:

   A. Have learners write, "Spiders have eight legs, and insects have six legs," 20 times each.

   B. Bring into the classroom examples of spiders and insects (dead, alive, or plastic), and have children count the number of legs of each.

   C. Have children research insects and spiders in books and look at the pictures and diagrams in their books.

   D. Have children watch a video on the differences between spiders and insects.

2. Ms. Schmidt teaches fourth-grade mathematics. She is demonstrating on the board how to solve a particularly difficult word problem. As she works, she talks to herself out loud about the method she thinks she should use and why. As she continues working through the problem, she "explains" to herself the procedures she is using and how they will help her eventually solve the problem. Ms. Schmidt's likely reason for "talking out loud" during the demonstration is:

   A. She wants her students to know that she is competent in the subject matter.

   B. She wants to ensure that students who are primarily auditory learners understand the material.

   C. She understands the importance of modeling metacognitive behaviors and thought processes.

   D. The material is difficult, and talking out loud helps her to think better.

3. Ms. Thompson wants her Pre-K students to understand the concept of "soft" versus "hard." She knows that simply explaining the material is unlikely to be effective because:

   A. Most children are poor listeners.

   B. The concept is too advanced for Pre-K students to grasp.

   C. The method is inconsistent with the way children learn.

   D. Most young children have a limited vocabulary.

4. Mr. Alaniz wants to introduce a unit on friendship to his first-grade students by asking an open-ended question to get them thinking about the topic. To accomplish this goal, which of the following is the best question to ask?

   A. Is friendship important?

   B. Who is your best friend?

   C. What does it mean to be a friend?

   D. Is it important to have friends?

Answers and Discussion

Answer 1: Although repetition is an effective method of keeping information in short-term memory, writing the information 20 times is not likely to be enough repetition to move the information into long-term memory *(A)*. Watching a video *(D)* and researching information in books *(C)* can both be effective learning experiences for students, but to make the information more meaningful and more likely to be remembered, the teacher should have the students actively engaged with concrete material (real or plastic insects and spiders) to experience the information first hand. The answer is *B*.

Answer 2: Although it is important for students to see their teachers as competent, this is not Ms. Schmidt's primary reason for "telling" her thinking out loud *(A)*. Also, although auditory learners may benefit from hearing the teacher talk about the information *(B)*, it may or may not be helpful to the rest of the students. Although it is true that thinking out loud can help when solving a difficult problem *(D)*, the likely reason for her behavior is that she wants to model for her students how to "think about thinking" so that they will be more likely to use metacognitive strategies in the future when solving problems on their own. The answer is *C*.

Answer 3: Although it is true that young children have a limited vocabulary in comparison to adult learners *(D)*, most young children at this grade level have a sufficient vocabulary to comprehend the basic concepts being taught. The concept of "soft" versus "hard" is not too advanced for the students *(B)*, because they experience softness and hardness in their everyday lives, even if indirectly. Although many young children are not primarily auditory learners and may prefer visual, tactile, or kinesthetic modes of learning, that doesn't mean that they are poor listeners *(A)*. The method will be ineffective because young children need to construct their own knowledge through meaningful experiences. This will not happen as a result of simply listening to an explanation. The correct answer is *C*.

Answer 4: Neither question *A* nor *D* is likely to stimulate students' thinking, because each can be answered with a simple "yes" or "no." Although question *B* may prompt a variety of responses from the class as a whole, each child's answer is likely to be limited to one or two names. To have students think more deeply about the subject of friendship, an open-ended question with a variety of possible answers is more effective. The correct answer is *C*.

WEB LINKS

Remember that Web site locations may change. If any of these sites have moved or cannot be located, use terms in the index to search for further information.

www.educationau.edu.au/archives/cp/04.htm

This site provides information on the various learning theories. Included are contiguity, constructivism, information processing, operant conditioning, and multiple intelligences. For each theory, the following are provided: an overview, principles, examples, and applications.

www.ship.edu/~cgboeree/perscontents.html

This Web site provides biographies of Skinner, Bandura, and Piaget as well as an in-depth analysis of the theories of each.

www.bfskinner.org

The B. F. Skinner Foundation provides a summary of operant conditioning as well as a searchable index for other publications by Skinner.

www.hcc.hawaii.edu/intranet/committees/FacDevCom/guidebk/teachtip/teachtip.htm

Teaching Tips Index provides multiple techniques and strategies for teaching in the classroom. Also included are basic assumptions about learning, the ten principles of learning, and a model and discussion of active learning.

REFERENCES

Bandura, A. (1977). *Social learning theory.* Upper Saddle River, NJ: Prentice Hall.

Brophy, J. (1992). Probing the subtleties of subject-matter teaching. *Educational Leadership, 49*(7), 4–8.

Eggen, P., & Kauchak, D. (2001). *Educational psychology: Windows on classrooms.* Upper Saddle River, NJ: Prentice Hall.

Miller, G. A. (1956). The magical number seven, plus or minus two: Some limits on our capacity for processing information. *Psychological Review, 63*, 81–97.

Pavlov, I. (1928). *Lectures on conditioned reflexes.* New York: International Universities Press.

Rief, S. F. (1993). *How to reach and teach ADD/ADHD children: Practical techniques, strategies, and interventions for helping children with attention problems and hyperactivity.* Curriculum Tools. Hoboken, NJ: John Wiley & Sons, Inc.

Skinner, B. F. (1953). *Science and human behavior.* New York: Macmillan.

Woolfolk, A. (2001). *Educational psychology* (8th ed.). Needham Heights, MA: Allyn & Bacon.

Chapter 6

Considering a Range of Factors That Impact Learning

JANICE L. NATH

University of Houston—Downtown

TERMS TO KNOW

Community as a resource
Community stress
Emotional intelligence
Facilitating teaching style

Learning styles
Modalities
Multiple intelligences
Organizational skills

Parenting styles
Stress factors
Student-centered teacher
Teaching styles

Competency 4, as a whole, deals with learning processes and factors that impact student learning. Part 1 of this competency (Chapter 5) focuses upon learning theory, while this chapter centers on other factors that impact children's learning. These factors include organizational skills, home and community factors, learning modalities and styles, and so forth. Because so many factors impact learning, information on some factors required for this competency overlaps with that in other chapters. To avoid covering factors in depth twice, referrals are made to other chapters. Be sure, however, to review all of the factors listed in the indicators for this chapter. If factors appear in more than one competency, you can be sure that they are important for this examination.

ORGANIZATIONAL SKILLS

Organizational skills have a great deal to do with learning in early childhood. Organizing involves grouping related items or behaviors into categories and/or patterns that designate relationships. You may recall Piaget's belief that children learn by acting on objects to test them through a schema (see Competency 1, Chapter 1). For example, a very young child may organize a schema to drop a toy from his or her crib over and over again to test how many times someone will pick it up and put it back. As children grow, they organize and repeat a schema "with variation" on objects so as to provoke new effects (Berk, 2001). This is an important step for children seeking to understand the basic regularities of their physical world, so the child may now begin to test what happens when he or she tosses the toy out farther instead of simply dropping it. Thus the child may begin to test the limits of his or her physical ability and the environment through an organized

pattern of behavior. Educators can generalize this same type of schema to Pre-K learners as children begin, for example, to use finger paints. First children may begin to use one color and their whole hand to cover a page in sweeping motions. As they begin to look at other options available, questions may arise, such as, "I wonder what would happen if . . . ?" Thus, experimenting to test the materials and their physical abilities may begin with additional colors added and blended, a single finger used to draw an image, or a palm to pat a design, and so forth. Older children may do the same as they write. At first a schema for writing a descriptive story may be organized to include a dry description of several sentences. Yet one day the cognitive processes may churn into thoughts such as, "What would this sound like if I added a touch of humor to my description?" or "What would happen if I used our new vocabulary word here? Would my paragraph sound better?" Thus the experimentation begins. Educators should be there to encourage this process of experimental development and introduce new ideas to try.

Organization of materials is important to this process, and sorting into categories (categorization) increases children's readiness for the selection of tools with which to experiment or to act on problems. Young children in a kitchen center, for example, look in a categorized drawer for a proper "tool" with which to measure or stir. Older children search through a mental database organized in a category of adjectives to find the proper one to use in a descriptive sentence. Children also learn to "take out and re-sort"—a preparation for rules on reversibility. These skills, in turn, relate to the growing skills of reasoning by analogy and cause-and-effect relationships. Cognitive theories of learning also remind teachers that through organizational schemes such as presenting advanced organizers (outlines, set-up questions, etc.), information can be made more meaningful. What is meaningful, to learners can be processed into long-term memory much more easily.

How do children grow in these skills? Teachers, Piaget believed, can guide them by providing appropriate materials and conditions to organize. A teacher who is sensitive to young children's growing need to understand, explore, experiment, categorize, and problem-solve provides many opportunities to increase organization in the curriculum and in everyday routines. For example, a teacher labels and provides areas for children's play or work, often with many categories of materials found within. During the introduction of such an area or center, teachers establish where categories of objects are to be found and demonstrate how and where they are to be returned. During the return process, children are first tasked with consistent organizational ways for cleanup (for example, begin stacking all of the large blocks first, then the medium blocks, followed by the small blocks). Later, teachers can change to other, more novel categorizations for return (red blocks first, then the blue, or many other variations). This sets the base for later development in categorization (for example, when the child works concretely with sorting base-ten blocks into categories of ones, tens, and so forth). Remember that very young children may have developmental difficulty concentrating on more than one perceptual attribute at a time in sorting (centration), so early childhood teachers should begin with simple organization of categories in centers and in class. Of course, children should have opportunities to explore on their own as well and to create and sort their own categories. Every effective teacher of young children knows that manipulatives of all kinds and in all subject areas should be a large part of activities each day, but he or she also knows that several minutes should be allowed for children to explore or "play with" manipulatives before instruction begins so that they have an opportunity to see properties of the objects for themselves before the structure of a lesson begins.

Another factor relating to organization skills and learning is that of repetition or rehearsal. Practice and repetition increase the chances that learning will last. When teachers have children form a routine of organization, children repeat the sorting of the categories over and over. Thus there is an emphasis that is reinforcing to the long-term memory (Eggen & Kauchak, 1996). Guided practice and independent practice in a lesson plan provide opportunities for the repetition of knowledge and skills, while classroom routines reinforce other behaviors related to organization. Teachers of young children understand the reason that early childhood classrooms should promote these skills and behaviors and provide the tools for practicing consistent organization in centers and in the general classroom. These teachers find that they are laying excellent groundwork for children's learning.

HOME AND COMMUNITY FACTORS THAT IMPACT LEARNING

Many factors impact student learning, and some of the most influential come from the home and community. Indeed, studies show relationships between intelligence and the home environment for very young children. Kaplan (2000) emphasizes that "such factors as the responsivity of the caregiver, parental involvement with the child, the variety of stimulation available, the organization of the environment, the caregiver's restrictiveness, and the play materials available at an early age predict later cognitive development" (p. 209). Therefore it is not difficult to understand that children who grow up in stimulating environments that parallel much of schooling readiness (and with attentive caregivers) are often "ahead" and may be more successful in school. However, increasing numbers of children are growing up in environments that do not provide elements needed for school readiness and success. Although the school cannot make up for certain factors in the home, teachers of young children can provide as many of these elements as possible to help children achieve success (because the teacher sees the young child for many waking hours). White (as cited in Kaplan, 2000) noted that more successful children's mothers were "designers—that is, they constructed an environment in which children were surrounded with interesting objects to see and explore . . . [they] interacted frequently with their children in interplays of 20–30-second duration . . . and were not overly permissive or overly punishing. They had firm limits, but they were not very concerned about such minor things as mess and bother" (p. 210). These are good guidelines for teachers as well as parents of young children. The presence of a caring adult (such as a teacher) outside the immediate family who offers the child a support system and a coping model can often increase resilience and keep maladjustments from occurring, even when the home is not as supportive of factors that promote school readiness and success (Berk, 2001).

Parental expectations can be understood by young children very early, and these expectations can be related to children's success if they are positive and realistic. However, children's development may actually be hindered by parents who show disappointment and "push" children too hard into unrealistic expectations in the early years. Parenting styles may increase the effect of the expectations set for children. The following four identified **parenting styles** offer much insight for teachers into young children's behaviors: (1) authoritative, (2) authoritarian, (3) permissive, and (4) rejecting-neglecting. Berk (2001) offers teachers a window into children of these various parenting styles. *Authoritative* parents, Berk details, have children who are the most well adapted. This style offers a balance of structure and rationality, so that the child perceives high expectations and demands within reason. These factors are coupled with a sense of belonging, and often, though not always, warmth and affection. Reasonable autonomy is present in an authoritative home—that is, encouragement for children to make their own decisions (within reasonable limits), and children in these homes seem to feel a sense of fairness. Children of authoritative parents

are often well adjusted, happy, persistent, independent, confident, and self-controlled. Conversely, *authoritarian* parents expect conformity "because they say so." These parents often resort to punishment and force, rejecting a child when he or she is unwilling to obey. Quite often these children are anxious, withdrawn, and unhappy and can be hostile in situations when they are frustrated with peers. They may be angry and defiant or may simply retreat from challenging situations. *Permissive* parents are those who place few demands on children, and children are often free to regulate their own behavior and activities. However, young children too often do not have the maturity for decisions such as when to go to bed, when and what to eat, and so forth. These children may appear to be very immature, with difficulty in controlling their impulses. In school they may be disobedient and rebellious when asked to do something that they do not want to do. These children may also be overly demanding and dependent on adults (not self-reliant). *Rejecting-neglecting* parents simply are not there for their children—with neither demands nor structure (Kaplan, 2000). It is these children who may face the worst difficulties in growing up. These parents either expect nothing and neglect their duties or openly reject the child. In later years, these children are often the ones who turn to drugs or gangs to create care or the illusion of care. Learning what parenting styles exist in the home may be one key to understanding a child's behavior. Offering a classroom with an authoritative teaching style can provide an environment that is structured and rational with high expectations and a sense of belonging for many hours of a child's day.

Stress in the home can also impact learning and can originate from many areas: overly high expectations, poverty, neglect, working hours that allow little family interaction, illness of a family member, a family member's substance abuse, divorce and/or single-parent situations, addictions of a family member, and so forth. Children may live with and/or come to school with a caregiver other than their own parent, including step-parents, relatives, friends, appointed court guardians, current girl- or boyfriends of a parent, and others due to a number of different situations. These situations, at the extreme, may include abandonment by or incarceration of a parent. Studies have also investigated young children who have not had an opportunity to form attachments with caregivers (Kaplan, 2000). Some of these children have difficulties in interpersonal relations, have little persistence, show few emotions (either positive or negative), have difficulty later on with popularity with peers, and in extreme cases may even appear retarded. Kaplan also states that when a caregiver is under stress, he or she can be tense, angry, less demonstrative in positive loving behaviors, and more arbitrary and punitive in managing his or her children. In other words, there is little positive responsiveness and/or stimulation provided at home, but *much* inconsistency. These stressful situations often produce children who come to school with a host of attention-seeking, negative behaviors that disrupt learning. Young children such as these may turn their attention to the teacher as a surrogate, in a manner of speaking, and teachers of young children should be aware of their influence in these situations. This speaks to the importance of having a warm, nuturing classroom where children feel welcome and accepted. When a child is behaving badly, it is also a reason for the teacher-as-a-problem-solver to consider home stress. It is also good practice for teachers who are dealing with bad behavior to make it clear that a child is still wanted and belongs in the classroom community, even though a particular behavior must change. Activities that teach what stress is and why it occurs help children understand the symptoms of stress (such as displaced anger) and show them positive ways of diluting it. Such activities can be positive in helping to provide a classroom in which the emotional needs of children are supported.

Children who come from stressful situations may have also missed opportunities for language development because of a lack of stimulation, responsivity, and freedom. Kaplan (2000) indicates that impoverished children often play fewer language games, are asked less often for language, use simpler sentences, and have less variety in vocabulary. Children from low socioeconomic neighborhoods may be able to function very well "on their own turf," but the language needed for success in school and for opening many doors later in their lives may be undeveloped. Currently, readiness programs such as Head Start and other developmental preschools have worked to overcome difficulties that young children face from the stresses of poverty, in hopes that these children can begin school on an equal footing with children from more enriched situations. Hopes for curricula in early programs often include classes for better parenting skills and health provisions, along with development in school readiness for children.

Communities as a whole can provide much support to children through a wide range of resources that provide enriching experiences. Yet some **communities** increase children's levels of **stress.** Communities can be places of fear, where children often experience violence, racism, crime, and negative adult behaviors. Communities can create stress with crowded space, noise, poverty, and pollution. Children may react by withdrawing, reacting with their own anger and violence, or affiliating with gangs for perceived protection—even as young children. Schools and classrooms can provide the warmth and safety that make a difference in a scary world. Schools can also ensure that children experience other opportunities through field trips and through technology. Teachers are important in helping shape children who are resilient—even with the stresses that come from their world—by first providing lessons that consider the needs of children. Instruction that begins "in the child's world" and then moves out reaches many more children than does the teacher who begins instruction "in his/her own world," particularly if those worlds are very, very different. Consideration of preschool readiness factors, resources in the family (both emotional and monetary), and community resources can help a teacher make decisions that are instructionally good for children.

Communities of all kinds and all economic levels *can* also be full of rich **resources** for children for a teacher who seeks connections. These may include (a) guest speakers from the community who can add to many areas in the curriculum; (b) businesses that can provide incentives, supplies, or even partnership monetary support; (c) civic and parental school groups, which are able to provide many types of support, including monetary and human resources (tutors, "big brother/sisters," "adopt-a-grandparent," and so forth); (d) suitable pastimes for children's out-of-school entertainment hours, such as playgrounds, sports facilities, and parks; and (e) cultural extensions [such as museums, etc.] that provide quality entertainment outside school and/or through school field trips. Ponticell (2001) listed the following community groups that can provide resources for a teacher or a school:

- Civic groups (Lions, Kiwanis, Rotary, Jaycees, etc.)

- Cultural groups (in art, music, horticulture, drama, ethnic heritage, etc.)

- Economic groups (chambers of commerce, real estate boards, etc.)

- Fraternal groups (Masons, Knights of Columbus, Elks, etc.)

- Government agencies (park services, law enforcement, health care, etc.)

- Patriotic groups (Daughters of the American Revolution, Veterans of Foreign Wars, American Legion, etc.)

- Political groups (political parties, League of Women Voters, etc.)

- Professional groups (law, medicine, dentistry, engineering, etc.)

- Retired citizens groups (AARP, etc.)

- Welfare agencies (health, recreation, child care, etc.)

- Youth organizations (4-H, Future Farmers of America, Future Teachers of America, Girl or Boy Scouts, Red Cross, etc.)

A teacher who goes an extra step to take advantage of community strengths will be well rewarded because children gain much from these connections. Teachers who live in the neighbor-hood of their school understand their communities well. Those who "drive in" should take the time and effort to search the school neighborhood for keys to understanding the people who live and work there and to make all attempts to use whatever resources possible to strengthen home/community school ties.

Other factors from the community and home are discussed in Competency 2, Chapter 2 (a multicultural view of the community and home) and Competency 11, Chapter 17, (dealing with the home and family in more depth). Teachers do well always to consider investigating the home and the community as part of understanding **stress factors** that impact children's ability to learn because of anxiety and nervousness. Teachers should also remember that their classrooms may become an oasis for children whose lives have stress in their environment outside school. Teachers can provide a great deal of structure and warmth during the many hours they spend with children.

LEARNING AND THINKING STYLES

A great deal of work has been done in the area of learning styles and modalities during the past few decades, as factors that affect children's learning. Basically these areas refer to the how, when, where, with whom, and with what a person learns best (Woolfolk, 1990). Some of the most familiar research focuses on preference of sensory input or modalities such as visual, auditory, tactile, and kinesthetic. Others (Kolb, 1985; Witkins et al., 1977) focus on differences in how people perceive, then process information—that is, some learners use their senses to probe, whereas others analyze their thinking carefully before acting. Sternberg (1992) categorizes thinking styles, and other researchers have examined the effects of environmental preferences for learning (low light, noise, time of day, etc.). More recent work has been done by Gardner (1993) in his Theory of Multiple Intelligences. This section examines research on learning and thinking styles and the effect they can have on teaching and learning.

Everyone has his or her own learning style, or preference for learning in certain ways, but what creates these **learning styles**? According to Keefe and Ferrell (1990), it is a combination of one's neurobiology, personality, and development. When we perceive, interact with, and respond to a learning environment, our neurobiology, personality, and development (personal elements) come into play cognitively, affectively, and physiologically (Hewit & Whittier, 1996; Jacobsen et al., 1993; Keefe, 1982; Schmeck, 1988). All of us know that we have a favorite way to study and learn. If we metacognitively analyze our own preferences, some of us may, for example, find we must study out loud or reorganize our notes to learn. Some of us may curl up in a warm, cozy chair, all alone, with silence, to rehearse our notes, while others may need a desk with a bright light, the radio playing in the background, and consultation on the phone with friends. There are many puzzle pieces to each individual learner's preferred style.

Why is this important in a classroom? Teachers have control over many of the elements concerned with learning styles and modalities (such as presenting visuals for visual learning preferences, providing manipulatives for tactile learners, setting up the physical environment of the classroom, etc.). In addition, teachers employ various teaching styles in their presentation of materials. Therefore it is important to understand these preferences because by matching instruction or environment to children's preferred style(s) or, conversely, by never offering instruction in certain learning styles in the classroom, teachers can enhance or impede children's learning. In the real world, students must eventually work under many conditions, so teachers must balance areas that are not as favored by a child, but they should also offer students opportunities to "shine" in their preferred style. Finally, teachers must understand that children who have a preference for a particular style are sometimes not well served by schools. In contrast, children with styles favored in school settings flourish naturally in traditional settings.

Many inventories or surveys are available to determine children's various learning styles. Some are easily downloaded from the Internet. These inventories will help teachers create learning profiles for individual children and help in reaching and extending learning in many ways. Teachers can vary their instruction daily, using various styles, so that at one time or another, all of their children's preferences are touched and weaknesses in learning and thinking styles can be strengthened. Remember that finding an individual student's style(s) could be one key to reaching a child who is not doing well with a current teaching style. Enjoying learning and being able to succeed are two factors in motivation. Matching learning styles with students can increase the possibilities that these will occur.

Modalities

The way in which a child prefers to receive sensory input is termed *modality preference*. This refers to the **modality** in which a child receives best, despite his or her sensory reception preference. In other words, a child may prefer visual input but actually learn better kinesthetically. Teachers should be alert for both.

Teachers often teach using their own preferred modality. However, a teacher who teaches through a single modality may negatively affect the achievement of children who learn better through modalities not being employed in a classroom. The following modalities have been identified:

visual modality

learns best visually (reading, graphic organizers, seeing on a video or television)

auditory modality

learns best through hearing (orally, through lectures, tapes)

tactile modality

learns best through touching (sandpaper letters, writing in shaving cream, manipulatives) *kinesthetic modality*

learns best by doing and involvement in movement (role play, lab experiments, dressing up, hand or body movements to songs and concepts)

As a teacher, why should one care so much about these modalities? Sandra Rief (1993), noted educator, researched the following information on student retention. She found that students retain:

10% of what they read

20% of what they hear

30% of what they see

50% of what they see and hear

70% of what they say

90% of what they say and do (p. 53).

Teachers who prepare lessons that involve each type of modality will thus have students who learn and retain much, much more.

Cognitive Learning Styles (Field Dependent and Field Independent)

One identified cognitive style differentiates field-dependent thinkers from those who are field-independent. To understand the concept of field-dependent and field-independent styles for your children, think now about how *you* best like to receive and act on information. Do you see the forest or the trees? See Table 6.1.

If you selected the (a) statements on the left, you are a field-dependent learner, but if you felt that you agreed more with the (b) statements on the right, you are a field-independent learner. Neither has advantages over the other; both are valuable ways of learning for different children and different situations. It is easy to see, however, how learning in a classroom would progress if a teacher addresses only one type of learner. An effective teacher offers children opportunities to learn in the style below.

Thinking Styles

Teachers can categorize themselves and their children in other ways in terms of learning preferences and thinking styles. Sternberg (1992) chose to focus on thinking styles in terms of "mental self-governments." See if you can pinpoint your thinking style among the following styles. Implementing and doing appeal to an *executive* mind. Solving problems that are structured, following directions or guidelines, and recalling information are also preferences for executive thinkers. Children who think in this manner do very well in tra-

Table 6.1 How Do You Learn Best?

The forest	or	The trees?
(a) Do you like to have the whole picture, general idea, or overall "feeling" of the materials first? Do you tend to look at the whole in order to figure out how the parts work? Do you tend to form an overall picture as you read, listen, or observe? Do you bog down if faced with a book that begins with many details first? (global orientation)		(b) Do you prefer to have a structured view in which each part is categorized and clustered? Do you tend to look at the individual parts to see how the whole works? Do you create a structure as you read, listen, or observe? Do you find overviews distracting? Do you prefer step-by-step instruction? (local or analytical orientation)
(a) Do you depend on colleagues and feel more motivated working in a group? Do you like having goals already set for you? Are you responsive to praise? Does criticism really affect you? (extrinsically motivated)		(b) Do you like to work alone much better and have a strong sense of direction? Do you like setting goals by yourself? Is praise really not needed? Does criticism not bother you too much? (intrinsically motivated)
(a) Do you seek the social relevance in materials whenever possible? (socially oriented)		(b) Do you seek to focus on the nature of the content or materials? (content oriented)

ditional classrooms. *Legislative* thinkers, however, prefer creating, formulating, imagining, and planning. Creative writing assignments, designing experiments, and imagining different outcomes are all attractive tasks to legislative thinkers. *Judicial* thinkers are those who enjoy tasks that involve judging, evaluating, and comparing. They also prefer critiquing, evaluating solutions and outcomes (rather than creating them), and comparing events, books, characters, and so forth.

Sternberg (1992) also identified four other styles based on "forms of government." Again, think of your own preferences. In a monarchic style of government there is only one central, predominate goal (the king's or queen's). Thus, in a *monarchic* form of thinking, a child prefers to deal mentally with only one task or concept at a time and often remains fixed upon that goal until it is finished. These children are not good "mental jugglers" in terms of learning. Monarchic children who are in whole-language classes may be confused and frustrated because subjects and assignments merge and blend. Hierarchic forms of government, however, have many goals that are set in order. Children who are *hierarchic* learners can set priorities while mentally juggling several assignments at once. Oligarchic governments have equal, multiple goals, all of the same importance. *Oligarchic* learners are good mental multitaskers, but it can be difficult for some of them to set priorities; all goals seem equally important. Oligarchic learners are challenged by juggling many assignments and often do all of them well—or none of them well, because an inability to set priorities can sometime occur. The *anarchic* thinker, like anarchy in government, has no rules or structure. This type of thinker takes a "pot shot" approach to learning that may involve breaking traditional mindsets. Often this child does not do well in traditional classrooms where procedures and guidelines are always to be followed.

A teacher may slant instruction toward his or her own style. However, a mismatch with a student may produce a child who seems uninterested or unwilling to participate in instruction. Sternberg (1992) cautions teachers to remember that children who match a teacher's style appear to be brighter than those who do not. Sternberg also recommends, as do all learning and teaching style researchers, that teachers provide instruction using a variety of learning and teaching styles in order to meet the needs of all students.

Other Preferences That Impact Learning

Dunn and Dunn's (1978) research continues to hold attention. In their Learning Styles Inventory, they group factors that affect learning into five categories: environmental factors, emotional factors, sociological factors, physical factors, and psychological factors. *Environmental factors* include preferences for and reactions to learning in different light intensities, sound, temperature, and even the arrangement of the room and construction of the furniture (design). *Emotional factors* focus on responsibility, motivation, and persistence, along with the need for (or no need for) structure and supervision in learning. *Sociological factors* center on preferences for learning in groups (large or small), alone, with an adult, in a team, or in a varied group. *Physical factors* are related not only to the senses (all of the modalities already mentioned in this chapter) but also to times of day and the need for food intake during learning. *Psychological* factors consider analytic and global thinking as well as reflective and impulsive processing (as described later in this section) and cerebral preferences. Dunn and Dunn have examined a host of factors that can affect classroom learning. In response, teachers should offer a variety of instructional presentations and environmental settings that take these factors into account. This is one reason early childhood rooms may have a variety of furnishings that allow children to work on the carpet at times or read in a bean bag chair, in addition to the traditional desk. A teacher can collect data on children to determine preferences. Monte, for example, works very well while having his snack (food intake), while Teneisha reads for long periods of time in the rocking chair (need for movement) but not at her desk. These are cues that help a teacher understand his or her learners more fully.

Cognitive Perception and Processing Styles

Another way of looking at the way that learners perceive, interact with, and process an event is related to cognitive perception and processing styles, as shown in Table 6.2 (Kolb, 1984).

What do we mean by concrete or abstract perception (how the learner perceives), as shown in the second column? Hewit and Whittier (1996) explain this by asking us to think in terms of people who report an event or accident. Some report by relying heavily on their senses (concrete), whereas others think through and analyze exactly what happened (abstract). For example, here are two different accounts of an accident: "I saw this huge truck coming. I saw the car hit from behind.

I heard this large crash. I jumped back," (concrete) versus, "As the truck approached the car from behind, it was obvious that a crash would occur and that I might be hit" (abstract). Children who perceive abstractly may be able to solve or work through a problem simply by thinking it through symbolically or by using numbers, whereas those who perceive concretely may need to have manipulatives or other concrete items to "see it or feel it."

What about *how* children process information (conceptual tempo), as noted in Table 6.2. Have you also noticed that some learners "jump into" an experience immediately when it is offered (active), while others "step back" and watch for a bit first (reflective)? Reflective learners first tie a new experience to past learning to help make sense of the event, whereas active learners want to experience an opportunity first, then reflect. Teachers would tend to believe that reflective thinkers do better, but at the extreme, they can ponder for so long that they bog down in deci-

Table 6.2 Cognitive Perception and Processing Styles

	Learning Style	Way Learner Perceives	Way Learner Processes (Conceptual Tempo)	Preferences in Learning	Other
Type 1:	Imaginative (or Relational)	Concretely	Reflectively	Watching, sensing, listening, feeling, personal experience, sharing ideas, loves variety, difficulty with auditory and visual	Asks "Why?"; sees from multiple experiences, so has difficulty with decisions
Type 2:	Analytic	Abstractly	Reflectively	Watching, asking why, thinking, devising theories, sequential thinking, being thorough, seeking "expert opinion"	Prefers traditional classrooms; high achiever, often more interested in ideas than people; fears mistakes
Type 3:	Commonsense (Structured or Solution-Oriented)	Abstractly	Actively	Problem-solving, thinking, doing, practical application, systematic	Asks, "How?"; needs structured classroom
Type 4:	Dynamic (Energetic)	Concretely	Actively	Sensing, feeling, doing, trial-and-error, flexibility, risk-taking, hands-on, spontaneous, plunges into experience	Seeks to influence others, manipulative or pushy; dislikes traditional classrooms

sion making. Active learners can be so quick as to be impulsive and error prone at extreme limits. Both types of learners can be taught to become more efficient in each area.

Multiple Intelligences

Howard Gardner's theory of **multiple intelligences** speaks of capacities that reside inside a person. He currently identifies eight intelligences: verbal-linguistic, logical-mathematical, intrapersonal, visual-spatial, musical-rhythmic, bodily kinesthetic, interpersonal, and naturalist. This theory offers us a new look at children as we ask, "How is this child smart?" rather than, "How smart is this child?" Table 6.3 (Campbell, Campbell, & Dickinson, 1996) offers an overview of these intelligences.

Gardner believes that the number of intelligences is not limited and has introduced the idea of yet another intelligence termed "existential." These are people who are easily able to contemplate the questions of existence and who find great meaning in life.

Why is this concept of multiple intelligences important for teachers to understand? By school age, it is believed that a child already begins to show strength or favor in certain areas, although all of these intelligences are believed to be a part of each child. This work is particularly exciting because it offers some fundamental principles to children and teachers. First, it supports the philosophy that "all children can learn" because children respond to learning in different ways. Therefore, if teachers provide situations for learning in each of these areas, more likely than not, children will respond and learn more easily and retain more of what they learned. Next, intelligence can be learned. This is motivating to children as well because they understand that over time they can increase their ability in all of these areas. Thus intelligence is not viewed by Gardner as fixed at birth. There is the capacity to develop all of these intelligences to higher levels. By offering children an opportunity to work in their dominant intelligence, they can excel. Certainly classrooms are more inviting when instruc-

tion and environment are matched to a child's primary intelligence at some point during the day or week. When offered another intelligence in which to work, children have the opportunity to build intelligence in that area.

Emotional Intelligence

Emotional intelligence is another important factor that can influence success. **Emotional intelligence,** as addressed by Daniel Goleman (1995), refers to recognizing, using, understanding, and managing emotions. Evidence shows that those who are emotionally adept are at an advantage in life. Testing for emotional intelligence involves measurement in stress tolerance, motivation, innovation, intuition, empathy, optimism, happiness, self-actualization, flexibility, social skills, and other areas. Children who lack emotional intelligence are often those who are labeled as inappropriate, with behavior management problems (such as bullies or "outcasts"), because they lack the ability to read emotions in others. Success in school and beyond can be affected by the inability of a student to use his or her emotional intelligence, although the child may be intelligent in many other areas. Considerable work is being done to help children in this area. For example, one emotional intelligence problem that some children have is the inability to discern easily the nonverbal emotions of others (*dyssemia*). Thus these children react inappropriately. Early childhood teachers should work on the identification of facial features associated with particular emotions, provide activities that help children understand personal space (including having one's belongings in another's space), help children see that voice level is related to emotions, and so forth. If a teacher recognizes extreme difficulties, he or she should ask for specialized help early on.

One example of a lesson that can increase emotional intelligence begins by asking young children to first think of emotions they have and then pretend that strange creatures from another galaxy have just landed and want to know about how earthlings communicate feelings. Children

Table 6.3 Gardner's Multiple Intelligences

Intelligence	Attributes	Some Successfully Matched Careers
Verbal-linguistic (Smart with Words)	Ability to think in words and use language to express and appreciate complex meaning; learns through listening, reading, writing, and discussing; creates original writing or oral communication	Journalists, poets, authors, speakers, political debaters, lawyers
Logical-mathematical (Smart with Numbers)	Ability to calculate, quantify, consider propositions and hypotheses, and carry out complex mathematics; perceives patterns, relationships, and abstract symbols, and problem-solves by posing and testing hypotheses	Engineers, mathematicians, computer scientists and designers, scientists, accountants
Visual-spatial (Smart with Pictures)	Ability to perceive external and internal imagery, to re-create, transform, or modify images, to navigate oneself and objects through space, and to produce or decode graphic information; learns by seeing and observing (with graphic representation or through visual media); thinks in pictures of mental imagery	Architects, painters, sculptors, pilots, astronauts, designers, sailors, photographers, videographers, art critics, mechanics
Bodily kinesthetic (Smart with the Body)	Ability to manipulate objects and fine-tune physical skills; learns by touching, handling, or manipulating what is to be learned along with concrete experiences such as field trips or role play; needs to move; is able to express ideas and feelings through the body	Athletes, surgeons, dancers, workers of crafts, builders
Musical-rhythmic (Smart with Music)	Possesses a sensitivity to pitch, melody, rhythm, and tone; immediately reacts to music; sensitive to environmental sounds	Musicians, composers, conductors, instrument makers, music teachers, music critics
Interpersonal (Smart with People)	Capacity to understand and interact effectively with others; easily perceives the feelings, thoughts, motivations, behaviors, and lifestyles of others; communicates effectively both verbally and nonverbally; easily adapts to different environments or groups; uncanny ability to "read" people; has "people skills"	Teachers, social workers, actors, politicians, counselors, comics
Intrapersonal (Smart with Self)	Ability to construct an accurate perception of oneself and use such knowledge in planning and directing one's life; works independently; empowers others; uses self-discipline, self-esteem, etc., to function well in situations	Theologians, psychologists, philosophers
Naturalist (Smart with Nature)	Ability to classify patterns in nature and to recognize flora and fauna and weather change patterns	Botanists, forestry careers, zoologists, meteorologists

then draw or act out expressions that represent various feelings. A hula hoop might be employed to show personal space, and children can demonstrate examples and nonexamples of situations in which voices should be loud and shrill or soft. Almost all children who do poorly in school have difficulty in some area of emotional intelligence. Goleman (1995) reports that areas such as confidence, curiosity, intentionality, self-control, relatedness, capacity to communicate, and cooperativeness are all readiness factors for school success that relate to emotional intelligence. Teachers of young children should consider it part of their expanded mission to nurture these areas, for they are developed from birth through the childhood years.

Investigating Students' Styles

Numerous inventories have been constructed for measuring learning styles, intelligences, and modalities. Many teachers survey all of their children to determine learning style preferences in order to better meet individual needs throughout their classrooms. However, when teachers have a child who is having difficulties, they should investigate a learning style mismatch as a possible option. When teachers give children choices, quite often the children select an assignment in their preferred style. Motivation remains higher because children feel more comfortable with the structure of their choice.

One instrument that identifies learning styles was developed by Manzo, Lorton, and Condon (1975) and Manzo and Casale (1981) and is informally administered. A strong point for using this inventory is the awareness teachers gain as to whether a student has a strong dislike for a commonly used mode of presentation.

Teaching Styles

Along with learning styles, much research has examined **teaching styles** (Fisher & Fisher, 1979). A teacher's choice of emphasis, instruction, interactions/ways of communicating, and classroom mannerisms make up a style of teaching. A teaching style is developed through knowledge of education, beliefs, and past experiences—coupled with a teacher's own personality. As is the case with learning styles, these styles can be examined within various frameworks, often overlapping somewhat in labels.

One classification system identifies three types of teaching styles: teacher-centered, content-centered (or subject-centered), and student-centered. A *teacher-centered* style involves the teacher's filter-

ing and processing of information down to children. In this style, all instruction, content, and assessment are decided by the teacher in an autocratic manner. *Content-centered* or *subject-centered* teachers are often "respected experts" in their field(s). Methods of instruction often include lecture and text-driven readings with assignments, and these experts can impart a great deal of knowledge, often being noted as brilliant and/or entertaining lecturers. In essence, however, covering the material is more important to them—often at the cost of the learner. Within the three classifications listed above, the **student-centered teacher** uses the teaching style that Texas would prefer to see its teachers use. In a *student-centered* approach, teachers employ a facilitating manner, constantly focusing on the needs of learners in every respect. Teachers continuously ask whether children are able, ready for, and interested in the instruction that will be implemented. Student decisions about learning are respected and encouraged, and the teacher considers him- or herself a learner in the classroom community as well. Some educators make a more distinctive category of *purely student-centered*. In this pure style, the curiosity of children is followed completely, so the curriculum emerges from whatever they wish to learn. There is no preset curriculum, because teachers cannot know what the children will be interested in each day. However, when the student-centered style is presented on the state exam, Texas is really referring to a more modified student-centered style than a radical student-centered style, as seen in Table 6.4. You may assume that Texas means and wants "student-centered style" for an answer.

Another classification dyad (where two styles of teaching contrast sharply with one another) consists of the traditional teaching style and the facilitating teaching style. In a *traditional teaching style,* teachers are autocratic; that is, they make the decisions and operate in a subject-centered, task-centered, formal, and prescriptive manner. They most often teach in classrooms with desks in rows facing the front. Lessons are, as a rule, lecture type or other teacher-centered type in which teachers do the demonstrations and have children learn in

Table 6.4 Teaching Styles

Teacher-Centered	Learning-/Student-Centered	Purely Student-Centered
Traditional	Facilitating	Completely child-centered
Task-oriented	Student-centered	Laissez-faire
Subject-centered	Equal concern for task, material, and students	Child-directed as to his/her interest (teacher follows in emergent curriculum)
Autocratic	Democratic	
Formal	Cooperative planner (respects and asks for student input)	
Prescriptive		
Top-down instruction		

a deductive manner. The transference of knowledge is from teacher to student in a top down approach. This, at first glance, may sound like a teacher whom children would not enjoy. However, there are times when this can be an appropriate style, and there are children in the room who shine when matched with this style (for example, the executive thinkers described earlier). The difficulty comes when this is the *only* style employed by a teacher.

A **facilitating teaching style,** however, is mostly democratic in style. Some joint learning decisions are made with students. Instead of desks in rows, teachers often have students arranged in small groups or in a circular pattern, demonstrating that this is a student-centered classroom. The instruction is often cooperative and inductive in nature, with many inquiry and problem-solving activities in evidence. Teachers provide the stage for active student learning and aid when needed. Concrete rather than abstract learning is emphasized. Teachers in this type of classroom are seen as fellow learners. Although some learners respond very well to traditional teaching styles, Texas maintains an overall interest in teachers who employ a more facilitative manner.

By using knowledge of teaching and learning styles, a teacher can plan and instruct more effectively. Teachers cannot justify using only one approach or providing only one type of environment for learning. Neither can they accommodate

each learner at every moment. However, the more teachers know about learners and their various learning preferences and intelligences (and the more they know about themselves and their own teaching styles), the better they can design instruction that lets children excel in their areas of preference and dominance while challenging children in areas of nonpreference that may need strengthening. This is one more step toward knowing oneself as a teacher and one's children as individuals to provide the best instruction possible.

OTHER FACTORS THAT HAVE AN EFFECT ON LEARNING

Other indicators and parts of this competency are discussed in depth in other chapters. However, those studying for the PPR should observe the way the indicators are written in this competency as well. Note below in italics the language of Competency 4, for each term and concept discussed in other chapters. Be sure to know each of these terms and concepts well by revisiting these chapters if needed. Because these areas are covered in more than one competency, they are sure to be important to the state examiniation.

See Competencies 1 and 8 for information on various student characteristics that impact teaching and learning (*e.g., attention span, need for physical activity and movement*) in Pre-K–4.

See Competencies 3 and 8 for discussion on stimulating reflection, critical thinking, and inquiry among students in early childhood through grade 4 (*e.g., providing opportunities to manipulate materials and to test ideas and hypotheses, providing repetition for increased conceptual understanding, supporting the concept of play as a valid vehicle for learning*).

Competencies 3, 5, and 7 also offer information for analyzing ways in which teacher behaviors impact student learning (*e.g., teacher expectations, student grouping practices, teacher-student interactions*). In addition, Competency 3 covers instruction and assessment that minimize the effects of negative factors and enhance student learning.

Competency 8 addresses the teacher's understanding of the importance of self-directed learning in planning instruction *and assessment that promotes students' motivation and their sense of ownership of and responsibility for their own learning.*

Competency 8 also analyzes ways in which various teacher roles (*e.g., facilitator, lecturer*) and student roles (*e.g., active learner, observer, group participant*) impact student learning.

SUMMARY

Children and teachers bring to the classroom many factors that affect learning. To be truly effective, a teacher must be cognizant of all of the factors that make up and influence learners. Indeed, the teacher must often problem-solve to discover what type of stressors from outside the classroom are creating difficulties for learners. A teacher must also know many of the positive factors, connections, and resources that he or she can use to enrich his or her classroom and make instruction more meaningful. This chapter has examined some of the *many* factors that influence learning. In particular, organizational skills, home

and community, and learning and teaching styles have been featured. Be sure to note additional factors covered in depth in other chapters.

GLOSSARY

community as a resource   communities can provide many resources that contribute to the education of children, including community members as guests, monetary resources, and enriching facilities such as museums.

community stress   feelings of anxiety that children may have when they come from communities that are impoverished, with high-crime areas that can provide little support for children and can cause them to be nervous and afraid for their safety.

emotional intelligence   refers to recognizing, using, understanding, and managing emotions.

facilitating teaching style   a mostly democratic teaching style (some joint learning decisions with students are made) in which students are arranged in small groups or in a circular pattern (demonstrating that this is a student-centered classroom) and the instruction is often cooperative and inductive in nature, with many inquiry and problem-solving activities in evidence. The teacher is seen as a fellow learner who sets the stage and provides help as needed for students to actively engage in learning.

learning styles   a preference for learning in a certain way (global, local, monarchial, etc.).

modalities   refers to the preference in learning of a particular sensory input such as visual, auditory, tactile (touching), and kinesthetic (movement).

multiple intelligences   Howard Gardner identified areas of intelligence including verbal-linguistic, logical-mathematical, intrapersonal, visual-spatial, musical-rhythmic, bodily kinesthetic, interpersonal, naturalist, and existentialist.

organizational skills   one factor in learning that involves categorizing and repetition by children.

parenting styles   four styles of raising children have been identified: permissive, rejecting-neglecting, authoritarian, and authoritative.

stress factors   children may become anxious and nervous because of situations in their homes or community, and because of this stress may have difficulties in learning.

student-centered teacher   the teaching style that Texas prefers to see its teachers use. Teachers employ a facilitating manner and constantly focus on the needs of the learners in every respect. Teachers continuously ask whether children are able, ready for, and interested in having the instruction implemented. Student decisions about learning are respected and encouraged, and the teacher is a learner in the classroom community.

teaching styles   a teacher's choice of emphasis, instruction, interactions and ways of communicating, and classroom mannerisms.

SUGGESTED ACTIVITIES

1. Think about yourself and the parenting styles in your home and those of some close friends and/or relatives. List the effects this had on performance in school.

2. Identify or ask your mentor to identify a child in your class who has been labeled as an at-risk student because of home or community stress. Using confidentiality, observe this child and chart behavior and learning over several weeks.

3. Determine your own teaching style, using the information given in the chapter or a survey. Using a lesson that you have constructed, analyze it in terms of children who do not match your styles. Reflect on what this means for those children.

4. Observe several lessons in your field placement, if applicable, or examine your teaching plans. Make a chart for each modality. Chart the amount of time during the lesson that each modality was used. Reflect on what this means to learners.

5. Prepare a short unit outline in which all of the multiple intelligences are used.

6. Prepare one lesson in a unit, ensuring that all modalities are employed.

7. Prepare an emotional intelligence lesson.

PRACTICE QUESTIONS

1. Mr. Ramsey is aware that he needs to provide opportunities for his children to excel in a nonthreatening atmosphere, using their different learning styles. Which of the following activities offers the best opportunities to accomplish this goal?

A. Designing a rubric to grade the student's learning logs.

B. Allowing students to retell their big books to check comprehension.

C. Giving students many opportunities, such as creating a play, creating costumes, and learning in independent and cooperative groups.

D. Using cooperative learning strategies instead of whole group lessons.

2. Mrs. Freeman noticed that Brandi was becoming "plain annoying." Ever since the beginning of school, she had clung to Mrs. Freeman, making sure that she was almost in her lap during circle and sometimes even clinging to her skirt. Often Brandi would not work more than one problem without raising her hand for help. Mrs. Freeman should first:

A. Investigate using a behavior contract to gradually create space.

B. Make sure that she calls children up one at a time to the circle area and that she always calls Brandi toward the end so that there are no more places near her.

C. Seek information on home stress and/or parenting styles to understand Brandi's behavior better.

D. Tell the principal about this extreme attachment, and recommend moving her to another room.

3. Brandi's behavior in the scenario above could indicate:

A. Parents who are permissive in their caregiving style

B. Parents who are authoritative

C. Parents who are rejecting-neglecting

D. Parents who are authoritarian

4. Mrs. Wingfield was designing a unit on communications. In her first lesson, she had children watch a video on many types of communications, such as phones and computers. She then read children a story about the Pony Express in her social studies slot. In science, children created their own "string" phones with two cans attached by string and

listened to each other talk. They then wrote an email to a pal. Finally, children role-played a telephone conversation in which they requested information of some kind. Mrs. Wingfield was most attentive to what factors in her instruction?

A. Teaching styles

B. Modalities and multiple intelligences

C. Organizational skills

D. Field-dependent and field-independent factors

Answers and Discussion

Answer 1: Designing a rubric that tells students *exactly* what is expected for an exact grade helps students meet a teacher's expectations (*A*), but it may or may not allow for different learning styles. Answer *B* is a good way to check for comprehension, but there is no variety of learning style offered here. Answer *D* offers students one alternative style of learning but does not talk about a *choice* situation. Answer *C*, however, offers children a variety of activities in which they can "shine." The answer is *C*.

Answer 2: A behavior contract (*A*) might be a good idea, but answers *B* and *D* are not good teaching practice. Mrs. Freeman would be wise to first seek further information on home stresses and/or parenting styles to better understand Brandi's behavior. Then she would be able to plan ways to best go about improving it. The answer is *C*.

Answer 3: Brandi's behavior could indicate parent(s) who use a permissive parenting style. Children of permissive parents are often overly dependent on adults. The answer is *A*.

Answer 4: Mrs. Wingfield designed her unit to include all modalities (seeing, hearing, touching, and movement) along with multiple intelligences in combining different tasks. The answer is *B*.

WEB LINKS

Remember that sites move, can be removed, or may not be found using your server. If a site listed below cannot be located, try typing in other key words to help your search, or go to the root or original part of the URL and navigate from there.

http://ericps.crc.uiuc.edu/

This site provides links to many articles on parenting styles. If it does not work, do a search for the "National Parent Information Network." One particularly good article is also found at:

http://npin.org/library/2001/n00545/n00545.html

http://familyeducation.com

This is a very full site for many areas in education, including multiple intelligences, learning styles, and emotional intelligences. Once you are into the site itself, locate the area called "site search." Then enter the key words for the subject that you want. A few of the links may not work, but keep going—many do.

http://members.aol.com/susans29/lsa.html

A number of sources are listed on how to determine various learning styles and modalities, how to identify ways to work with particular styles, and further theory information. Many, many sites on learning styles are included. Just do a search using "learning+styles."

http://www.mxctc.commnet.edu/clc/survey.htm

This Web page includes the Learning Styles Modality Preference Inventory, where you can determine whether you or your students are primarily visual, auditory, or tactile/kinesthetic learners.

http://www.owecc.net/lad/learningstyles.html

The Teaching and Learning Center of Owensboro Community College provides a summary of the three learning modalities: visual, auditory, and tactile/kinesthetic. Characteristics of each type of learner are given, as well as suggestions for study strategies based on preferred modality. Also included are a learning styles inventory/survey and links to other related Web sites.

Multiple intelligence sites include:

http://www.members.tripod.com/~RheaultK/index.html

http://www.newhorizons.org

http://www.d118.s-cook.k12.il.us/south/curriculum/team6c/Egypt/egypt2.htm

http://www.ldrc.ca/projects/

These sites provide further information about multiple intelligences, testing for intelligences, and how to work with students using all intelligences. The last offers an inventory to investigate your multiple intelligences. Many more sites on this topic are available.

Emotional intelligence sites include:

www.eiconsortium.org

http://www.eq.org

Again, these are but two of the sites for this topic.

REFERENCES

Berk, L. (2001). *Development through the lifespan.* Boston: Allyn and Bacon.

Campbell, L., Campbell, B., & Dickinson, D. (1996*). Teaching and learning through multiple intelligences.* Needham Heights, MA: Allyn & Bacon.

Dunn, K., & Dunn, R. (1978). *Teaching students through their individual learning styles: A practical approach.* Reston, VA: Reston Publishing.

Eggen, P., & Kauchak, D. (1996). *Educational psychology: Windows on classrooms* (5th ed.). Upper Saddle River, NJ: Merrill Prentice Hall.

Fischer, B., & Fischer, L. (1979). Styles in teaching and learning. *Educational Leadership, 36,* 251.

Gardner, H. (1993). *Frames of mind: The theory of multiple intelligences.* New York: Basic Books.

Goleman, D. (1995). *Emotional intelligence: Why it can matter more than IQ.* New York: Bantam.

Hewit, J. S., & Whittier, K. S. (1996). *Teaching methods for today's schools: Collaboration and inclusion.* Boston: Allyn and Bacon.

Jacobsen, D., Eggen, P., & Kauchak, D. (1993). *Methods for teaching: A skills approach* (4th ed.). New York: Merrill.

Kaplan, P. (2000). *A child's odyssey.* Belmont, CA: Wadsworth.

Keefe, J. W. (1982). Assessing student learning styles: An overview. In *Student learning styles and brain behavior: programs, instrumentation, research,* (ed.) (pp. 18–12). Reston, VA: National Association of Secondary School Principals.

Keefe, J. W., & Ferrell, B. G. (1990). Developing a defensible learning style paradigm. *Educational Leadership, 48*(2), 57–61.

Kolb, D. (1985). *The learning style inventory.* Boston: McBer and Co.

Kolb, D. (1984). *Experiential learning: Experience as the source of learning and development.* Englewood Cliffs, NJ: Prentice Hall.

Manzo, A. V., & Casale, U. P. (1981). A multivariate analysis of principle and trace elements in mature reading comprehension. In G. H. McNinch (ed.). *Comprehension: Process and product. First Yearbook of the American Reading Forum* (pp. 76–81).

Manzo, A. V., Lorton, M., & Condon, M. (1975). *Personality characteristics and learning style preferences of adult basic education students.* Research monograph of Center for Resource Development in Adult Education, University of Missouri—Kansas City.

Ponticell, J. (2001). School and community connections. In C. Henry and J. Nath (eds.). *Becoming a teacher in Texas: A course of study for the Professional Development ExCET* (pp. 350–363). Belmont, CA: Wadsworth.

Rief, S. F. (1993). *How to reach and teach ADD/ADHD children: Practical techniques, strategies, and interventions for helping children with attention problems and hyperactivity.* Curriculum Tools. Hoboken, NJ: John Wiley & Sons, Inc.

Schmeck, R. (Ed.). (1988). *Learning strategies and learning styles.* New York: Plenum.

Sternberg, R. (1992). Thinking styles: Keys to understanding student performance. In K. Ryan and J. Cooper (eds.). *Kaleidoscope* (pp. 109–116). Boston: Houghton Mifflin Company.

Witkin, H. A., Moore, C. A., Goodenough, D. R., & Cox, P. W. (1977). Field-dependent and field-independent cognitive styles and their educational implication. *Review of Educational Research, 47*(1), 1–64.

Woolfolk, A. (1990). *Educational psychology* (4th ed.). Englewood Cliffs, NJ: Prentice-Hall.

Domain II

Creating a Positive, Productive Classroom Environment

Competency 5

The teacher knows how to establish a classroom climate that fosters learning, equity, and excellence and uses this knowledge to create a physical and emotional environment that is safe and productive.

The beginning teacher:

- Uses knowledge of the unique characteristics and needs of students in early childhood through grade 4 to establish a positive, productive classroom environment (e.g., encourages cooperation and sharing, teaches children to use language to express their feelings).

- Establishes a classroom climate that emphasizes collaboration and supportive interactions, respect for diversity and individual differences, and active engagement in learning by all students.

- Analyzes ways in which teacher-student interactions and interactions among students impact classroom climate and student learning and development.

- Presents instruction in ways that communicate the teacher's enthusiasm for learning.

- Uses a variety of means to convey high expectations for all students.

- Knows characteristics of physical spaces that are safe and productive for learning, recognizes the benefits and limitations of various arrangements of furniture in the classroom, and applies strategies for organizing the physical environment to ensure physical accessibility and facilitate learning in various instructional contexts.

- Creates a safe, nurturing, and inclusive classroom environment that addresses students' emotional needs and respects students' rights and dignity.

Chapter 7

COMPETENCY 5 – PART 1

The Case for Teacher Enthusiasm and High Expectations

MYRNA D. COHEN

University of Houston—Downtown

TERMS TO KNOW

Affective domain

Classroom climate

Community of learners

Conventional ethics

Explicit communication

Implicit communication

Industry versus inferiority stage

Initiative versus guilt stage

Modeling

Preconventional ethics

Self-efficacy

Self-fulfilling prophecy

Zone of proximal development

Imagine that two second-grade teachers, Ms. Garcia and Mr. Brown, are having lunch together and are discussing their classes. Mr. Brown has noticed that Ms. Garcia's students are much more enthusiastic than his are. He remarks, "My students do not really seem to care much about learning. Even the ones who do their work do it just to get it over with. They are just not the kind of kids who get excited about school. You 'lucked out' this year. You have such an enthusiastic class."

Mr. Brown, in his above comment, reveals that he has not yet learned one of the most important factors about teaching. In all probability, Ms. Garcia did not "luck out." She most likely has implemented important teaching strategies in order to stimulate her children to learn enthusiastically and to work hard. Mr. Brown is mistaken in thinking that it is the children who determine the classroom environment. Professional and effective teachers know that this is not the case. It is the teacher who creates and shapes the **classroom climate** (the way a classroom feels to its members) through the use of expert teaching skills. Communicating enthusiasm and setting high expectations is critical to establishing an environment for learning and excellence. These two skills are discussed at length in this chapter.

ENTHUSIASM

Many of us use the word "enthusiasm" quite often in our daily language and can readily recognize it in the classroom when we see it. Yet it is a difficult concept to define precisely. Enthusiasm connotes keen interest, positive feelings, passion, and inspiration. It is usually contrasted with apathy and lack of emotion and interest. Because it is believed that enthusiasm facilitates learning, understanding how to communicate teacher enthusiasm and instill enthusiasm in students is of utmost importance for teachers.

But how does one encourage enthusiasm? Social cognitive theory and the work of Albert Bandura (1986) help shed some light on how to "teach" enthusiasm to students. According to this theory, we learn from **modeling,** or observing the actions of others. Modeling can involve all three domains of learning: cognitive, psychomotor, and affective. Enthusiasm is most closely aligned with the **affective domain,** the domain of feeling. Quite simply, teachers who display enthusiasm for learning are also teaching enthusiasm.

What does enthusiasm look like in the classroom? Try to make a list of teacher behaviors that you think manifest enthusiasm. Compare your list to the one printed below, which Arends, Winitzky and Tannenbaum (1998) present in their text. The list, compiled by Collins, is entitled "Elements of Enthusiasm." This list describes teacher behaviors thought to indicate enthusiasm in teaching.

Vocal Delivery

Varied, lilting, uplifting intonations, many changes in tone, pitch

Eyes

Shining, frequently opened wide, eyebrows raised, eye contact with total group

Gestures

Frequent movements of body, head, arms, hands and face; sweeping motions; clapping hands; head nodding rapidly

Movements

Makes large body movements, swings around, changes pace, bends body

Facial Expression

Changes denoting surprise, sadness, joy, thoughtfulness, awe, excitement

Word Selection

Highly descriptive, many adjectives, great variety

Acceptance of Ideas and Feelings

Accepts ideas and feelings quickly with vigor and animation; ready to accept, praise, encourage, or clarify in a nonthreatening manner; many variations in responding to pupils

Overall Energy

High degree of spirit throughout lesson

These are possible indicators of an enthusiastic teacher. They probably occur naturally when teachers are *truly* excited about their content and pedagogy. A teacher's enthusiasm must be sincere rather than artificial; it should not be an act. Although all teachers prefer some parts of their curriculum over others and have their more favorite and less favorite topics, they should find value and interest in every topic they teach, whether it be in mathematics, language arts, science, social studies, or the fine arts. Children are adept at detecting and emulating a teacher's apathy or lack of interest, so teachers should not be apathetic about *any* lesson they teach. When teachers are genuinely enthusiastic about their instruction, they are naturally more animated, use varied voice inflections, and are more physically active in the classroom.

One way teachers can foster their own enthusiasm in teaching is to make certain that what they are teaching is purposeful and relevant. As teachers choose the goals, objectives, and activities for lessons (see Competency 3, Chapter 3), they must make sure that they have a sound rationale for their choices. If a teacher does not believe and demonstrate that what he or she is teaching is exciting and important, the students will not either. On the other hand, if a teacher is convinced that his or her lesson is meaningful and fascinating, students will observe and model that attitude. Enthusiasm is "catching." When a teacher is sincerely intrigued by a topic, his or her comments will follow suit. For example, "Open your books

to page 17 and let's read about the voyage of Columbus" does not convey the same interest as "It is amazing how many obstacles Columbus had to overcome to make his voyage. Let's look together at page 17 to see what some of them were and try to imagine how he felt about them." It is clear that the teacher making the second comment is much more intrigued by the topic than the first.

Another way to nurture teacher enthusiasm is to shape an environment in which the teacher is also learning. This is best achieved by creating a **community of learners** in classrooms wherein *everyone* in the community is learning, students and teacher alike. No one has a monopoly on ideas and knowledge, not even the teacher, although the teacher is the community leader. Teacher enthusiasm thrives because the learning process becomes unpredictable and consequently more interesting and exciting.

Emphasizing student-centered strategies rather than teacher-centered strategies is one way to keep enthusiasm for learning high. With teacher-centered strategies, wherein teachers ask many convergent questions, "right," factual answers are already known. Teachers do most of the talking and limit the element of surprise and spontaneity in lessons. However, when teachers ask divergent questions and encourage creative thinking, they are opening the door for themselves to learn from their own students. They enter into an unpredictable and exciting learning experience together with their students. Please refer to Competency 7, Chapter 11 for more information about constructing these types of questions.

Suppose a teacher is doing a fourth-grade social studies unit on immigration 100 years ago. He or she could teach this in a teacher-directed fashion by having students read the related chapter in their textbooks, answer questions at the end of the chapter, outline the main points, and learn the information. The teacher could ask students questions, the answers to which are found in the book. This approach may arouse less enthusiasm in the teacher and, subsequently, in students than would a more student-centered, active-inquiry approach. A student-centered approach creates real-life learning. Thus an authority does not hand down all of the answers, rather one has to search for and construct answers, usually in collaboration with others. Knowledge is dynamic rather than static. Different children studying an identical topic may have very different experiences and ideas. This follows Dewey's (1966) vision of education, in which school learning models real-life learning.

Imagine that Mr. Snow's fourth-grade class is working on the social studies unit described above, immigration 100 years ago. However, he has chosen a student-centered, active-inquiry approach. To begin, he has brainstormed, together with his students, a list of questions about this topic that includes:

Why did people from Europe want to come to the United States at that time?

Why did some people want to come and not others?

How much money did a family need to live in the United States 100 years ago?

What were the jobs that paid the most money 100 years ago in Europe and in the United States?

Could anyone come to the United States then?

What did the immigrants miss about Europe?

How did Americans feel about the new people coming to their country?

Mr. Snow and his children learn about this topic by investigating these and other questions that the students initiate. Children work in groups or in pairs on the questions that interest them the most and answer other questions that come up during their work. They figure out ways, with teacher assistance, to find information. For example, Mr. Snow has identified some "now-adult" children of immigrants from this time period who live in the community, and he provides opportu-

nities for his students to interview them. His children think up questions and construct a questionnaire for this purpose. In addition, some students choose to search the Internet for information. They also use the library for sources that describe conditions in Europe and in America at that time. This supplements the information in their textbook. As students search for answers, Mr. Snow makes suggestions about how to find valuable information and guides his children. After several days, students share their information and draw conclusions based on synthesizing what the class has discovered. Many teachers find that enthusiasm for learning is a natural by-product of engaging in authentic learning experiences with their students, such as in the example just described.

Student-centered lessons also foster more student involvement than do teacher-centered lessons. Involvement is closely associated with enthusiasm. Notice that in the example above, all children are working. Contrast this with a classroom in which the teacher asks students questions one at a time or has one child at a time come to the overhead projector or to the board to work a problem while the remainder of the class waits. Although many teachers can make this an enthusiastic exchange, the slow pace more than likely robs the lesson of enthusiasm. When only one student is performing, the rest are waiting. When students of any age wait too long and, perhaps, even fail to get a turn themselves, enthusiasm wanes.

It can be argued that teachers who have a high sense of **self-efficacy** as professionals show high enthusiasm for teaching. *Self-efficacy* refers to a person's beliefs about his or her success. Those with high self-efficacy believe that they can succeed; those with low self-efficacy do not hold such beliefs (Good and Brophy, 1997). For a teacher, high self-efficacy means confidence that teachers *can* make a difference. Sometimes teachers believe that the home and environment are such powerful determinants of children's success or failure in school that they have little to contribute. This reflects a lack of self-efficacy, and teachers with this attitude can be less passionate about their instruction because they believe that in the end they have little effect. On the other hand, those who feel competent, who feel that they have solid teaching skills, and who feel that despite the often difficult physical and environmental factors that accompany students, teachers can have a positive effect on children, are very enthusiastic. In nurturing enthusiasm for teaching, it serves teachers well to develop a can-do attitude—a strong sense of teacher self-efficacy.

In addition to focusing on teacher enthusiasm, the work of Erik Erikson (Eggen & Kauchak, 2001) also helps one understand how to instill enthusiasm for learning in children. Erikson's psychosocial theory defines eight crises that people need to overcome over the duration of their lifetimes. The successful resolution to a crisis results in positive personality traits, whereas less successful resolutions result in less favorable ones. For teachers of children in Pre-K through fourth grade, two of Erikson's stages are of particular interest: *initiative versus guilt* and *industry versus inferiority.* Understanding how to guide children through these stages so that they arrive at more positive resolutions of their inherent challenges allows for more enthusiastic learning on the part of students.

The **initiative versus guilt stage** influences children of ages 3 through 6. In this stage, children display an explorative and investigative attitude in which they are eager to try things on their own. Teachers should encourage this initiative and nurture their students' sense of competence. For example, if a child takes the initiative to water the classroom plants on his or her own and, in so doing, spills the water, the teacher should still give the child credit and praise for taking that initiative. She may, however, guide the child by explaining that next time the class watering schedule must be followed, or that a watering pitcher should be used rather than a glass without a spout. In other words, the fact that the child was taking initiative, or trying to do a task independently, should be recognized and valued. Children at this age who are not encouraged for their efforts in this way may later be reluctant to take risks or initiate acts. As they become more timid and avoid creativity, their enthusiasm for learning may be diminished. Children who are encouraged for their independent initiatives will be more likely to explore, invent, and take risks. They also are more likely to develop a positive self-concept.

The **industry versus inferiority stage** influences children of ages 6 through 12. Here children are ripe to develop a sense of enjoyment from competence and from mastery of challenging tasks. Teachers can help children in finding activities that are at the appropriate level for success. Assignments that are too difficult will result in frustration rather than a feeling of accomplishment. Likewise, assignments that are too easy will not allow for a sense of satisfaction. Teachers must design challenging learning experiences and set up their students for success. In this way, their children will enjoy success, learn to appreciate the fruits of their efforts, and develop a sense of competence. If they put forth effort and continually fail, they are in danger of developing a sense of inferiority, wherein they see that working hard is futile. Children also may not appreciate working hard if success comes too easily. They may believe that their efforts are not worthy of the end product. Therefore, through an understanding of Erikson's theory, teachers can foster enthusiasm for learning by instilling both *initiative* and *industry* in children.

Expectations

Teachers who expect much from their children usually get it. Likewise, teachers who expect little, get little! This phenomenon has been described as the **"self-fulfilling prophecy"** of expectations. One cannot underestimate the power that teacher expectations have on students in terms of both instruction and management. Imagine being in a class in which the teacher says, "This is a very difficult story. I don't think that you will understand the plot or theme because your potential is limited and your reading level is too low." One probably would feel deflated and might internalize the teacher's beliefs about his or her abilities. Yet children to whom a teacher says, "I know that you will be able to read and understand this material. Even if there are difficult words in the text, they will not bother you because you are bright and you'll be able to figure out the meaning," probably would feel motivated, would work hard, and would make great strides.

Rosenthal and Jacobson (1968) examine the strength of teacher expectations in the classic study *Pygmalion in the Classroom.* This study, replicated many times, shows that students meet teachers' expectations even when teachers are given wrong information about the ability of students. Teachers of low-achieving children were told by researchers that they had accelerated students, while teachers of high-achieving students were told that they had remedial ones. After several weeks, slow students were performing at an accelerated level and the gifted students were performing poorly. In light of the above "turned around" phenomenon, it is apparent that effective teachers believe that their children can learn, and they clearly communicate this belief to learners. Effective teachers set high expectations and don't give up on their students.

Because teacher expectations have such a strong influence on student achievement, it is vital that teachers establish high, yet realistic goals and objectives for their students. An understanding of cognitive development is one tool for teachers to employ to ensure that their expectations are both realistic and rigorous. Piaget's stages of cognitive development (see Competency 1, Chapter 1) are indispensable for this purpose. For example, it may be unreasonable to expect a 4-year-old child to understand that the amount of clay in a ball and that in a pancake shape does not change with the shape. At this stage of development, most children have not yet mastered the concept of conservation. Expecting children at this stage to comprehend this would be unreasonable and frustrating. Likewise, according to Piaget, one should expect 8-year-old children to understand logical problems if they first work through a concrete representation. If teachers do not expect these 8-year-olds to understand abstract concepts at all, they will be guilty of low

expectations. Yet if teachers expect students to do so without any concrete illustration, they will be guilty of unrealistically high expectations. It is the responsibility of the EC–4 teacher to know the stages of cognitive development in order to establish realistic yet high goals and objectives.

Vygotsky (1987) also offers a theory to aid in constructing high, yet realistic, goals and objectives though his **zone of proximal development.** Vygotsky believed that "with assistance, every child can do more than he can by himself—though only within the limits set by the state of his development" (p. 187). Teachers expand students' mental capacities by helping them think on deeper levels. Although initially students reach those same levels only with assistance, they will eventually be able to reach them independently. When this occurs, students' level of independent thinking moves up a notch, and the teacher's assistance brings them to an even higher point (see Figure 7.1). The space where children can expand their thinking with the assistance of the teacher is called the *zone of proximal development.* The level of *actual development* is the point wherein students can function on their own without assistance. The level of *potential development* is the point that the students can reach with the assistance of the teacher. The zone between the actual development and the potential development is the zone of proximal development. In setting high, yet realistic, expectations for our children, teachers should be skilled in determining zones of proximal development. Of course, each child has a different zone, and it is the challenge of the teacher to identify that zone and teach to it. Different children may need different kinds of *scaffolding* (teacher or capable peer assistance) to help them work through their zones. Again, if one miscalculates and determines that the zone of a child is lower than it actually is, there is the danger of establishing low expectations, and fruitful learning will not occur. If one miscalculates and determines that the zone of a child is higher than it actually is, there is the danger of establishing unrealistically high expectations, and frustration (rather than fruitful learning) will occur. One key to establishing high yet realistic expectations

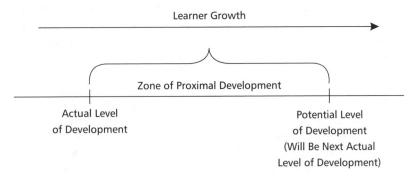

Figure 7.1 Vygotsky's Zone of Proximal Development

for children is to think about goals and objectives in terms of Vygotsky and his zone of proximal development.

As teachers reflect upon how to formulate expectations, they also want to make certain that they do not disadvantage any student. In other words, teachers should examine their expectations to be sure that they are not influenced by any type of stereotype or bias. Stipek (1998) presents evidence demonstrating that teachers may often unknowingly be guilty of such practices. For instance, they may let irrelevant factors such as a child's physical appearance or the performance of his or her siblings factor into their expectations. Research has shown that ethnicity also can affect teacher expectations. African-American males seem to be the most vulnerable for unfounded lowered expectations—even in early grades. Economic status likewise has been found to influence expectations because teachers seem to hold higher expectations for more affluent children. This author once mentored a student teacher who commented, "I was so surprised to see that Janie got a low grade on her test. She looks so smart!" What did Janie look like? She was White, well dressed, and practiced good hygiene. Apparently this student teacher thought that minority children with older clothes and in need of showers and dental care might not "look smart." Teachers need to be aware that these tendencies exist and should engage in deep self-reflection so as to avoid such unjust judgments when setting expectations.

Teachers also need to be cognizant of how expectations may color interpretations of student behavior. Teachers may give the benefit of the doubt to children whom they perceive as having higher ability and deny it to those whom they perceive as having low ability. For instance, if a "smart" child misreads a word, a teacher may justify the error by thinking that this child is tired or perhaps excited about an upcoming holiday. If a "slow" child misreads a word, a teacher may assume that the child is not capable of better reading skills. This practice allows interpretations to confirm beliefs that may be erroneous to begin with. Teachers must be careful not to deny any child the conditions to prove their assumptions wrong.

Awareness of these tendencies becomes particularly important when considering how teacher expectations of students' intellectual abilities affect achievement. It has been argued that the influence of teacher expectations is strongest in the early grades (Good & Brophy, 1997). Children in early grades do not yet have folders and files of academic records that indicate their levels of competence. Because there is little past performance data upon which to determine expectations, perceptions of young children's abilities are more malleable and take on greater significance. Teachers of younger children may also be more influential than teachers of older children. The structure of the early elementary school allows for more teacher impact than in later grades because there is more opportunity for teacher/student interaction. Elementary children generally have one main teacher for the entire school year and interact with that teacher extensively. This differs from later elementary grades, in which teachers are often departmentalized or from intermediate, middle, and high schools where students interact with many teachers daily. Research also indicates that there are larger expectation effects on reading achievement than on math achievement, perhaps because reading is often taught using in-class ability groups (Smith, as cited in Good & Brophy, 1997). Because reading is the major focus of earlier grades, this compounds the powerful influence that EC-4 teachers can have on their children.

Teachers owe it to children to have high expectations of their abilities. When low expectations prevail, the roads to success and achievement are often blocked. One reason for this is that teachers' perceptions of student ability may result in instructional inequities. For example, research has shown that teachers using in-class ability reading groups had more effective strategies with the higher groups and less effective ones with the lower (Allington, as cited in Good & Brophy, 1997). When instructing more advanced readers, teachers gave longer reading assignments, asked more higher-level questions, and allowed for more discussion time of ideas. In contrast, in the lower groups, there was less emphasis on meaning and more on drill and practice. Students in lower groups were interrupted more often for errors and were given phonetic clues to help them figure out words. For children in higher groups, errors were more often overlooked, allowing for uninterrupted concentration on concepts and text messages. If higher-group students received teacher cues, they were of a semantic or syntactic nature that encouraged students to figure out word meaning from the context. This is in contrast to the phonetic cues given to children in lower groups.

Evertson, as cited in Good and Brophy (1997), found similar instructional inequities in high school instruction. EC–4 teachers should heed Evertson's conclusions. High school teachers of lower-achieving classes were found to be less clear about their objectives, to introduce concepts in a more confusing fashion, to make less of an effort to connect lessons to students' lives and interests, to have more inconsistencies in their discipline, and to take student input less seriously. Students in higher classes were found to have more choices for creative projects and assignments, whereas less autonomy, more structure, and activities with less creativity were observed in lower-level classes. Teachers were found to devote more time and energy planning for higher-level classes than lower ones. Communicating low expectations to young children can result in lower achievement, which in turn may subject them to inferior instruction in their later school experiences.

Elementary teachers should be cautious not to follow the above trends that have been detected in the secondary grades. They also should be aware that the expectations they have of their children affect the way the children view themselves and their abilities and that teachers communicate expectations to students daily. Children receive a strong message from various teacher behaviors such as those just described. Children may perceive their teachers as communicating, "You are not that important, and your chances for success are not high. You are not worth my time." If students "hear" these messages repeatedly over the years, they begin to internalize and believe them.

How do children know what teachers expect of them? In addition to communicating this through goals and objectives, teachers convey many expectations through their interactions. As Oakes and Lipton (1999) point out, teachers usually do not **explicitly** convey their expectations to their students, but rather they **implicitly** communicate them. For example, regularly asking higher-level thinking questions of a select group of students communicates high expectations. The teacher believes that they can answer those difficult questions. Repeatedly asking lower-level questions of a select group of students can imply just the opposite: These children can't handle the difficult ones, so give them the easy ones. Sensitive teachers understand how their behaviors may be interpreted by children.

Sometimes good intentions backfire, so teachers must monitor their actions with individual children carefully. For example, a child may attribute his success and failure to either controllable or uncontrollable factors. Ability is an uncontrollable factor; laziness is a controllable one. A child may perceive that his teacher thinks he has low ability when the teacher conveys pity as a reaction to the child's failure. Yet another child may perceive that his teacher thinks that he has high ability when the teacher conveys anger as a reaction to the child's failure (Stipek, 1998). Therefore reacting with anger or pity can carry very different messages and, consequently, different expectations to children. In addition, teachers' helping behaviors may carry important implicit messages about expectations. For example, Mrs. Moss who is monitoring seatwork may see Bea struggling but decide not to help her. Bea may interpret this by thinking, "Mrs. Moss thinks I am smart enough to figure this out by myself." Yet Mrs. Moss may see another struggling child, Jackie, and decide to offer help even though the child did not ask for it. Jackie may think, "Mrs. Moss does not think I can figure this out by myself. She thinks I need her help even though I did not ask for it." Teachers should be aware of how their feedback and behavior may be interpreted by each of their children and should act with sensitivity.

Good and Brophy (1997) compiled a list of teacher behaviors that implicitly communicate teachers' perceptions of high- and low-ability students. Many of their items are of special interest to EC–4 teachers. For instance, these researchers mention that teachers tend to wait less time for low-achieving students to answer before calling on someone else. Teachers rarely try to improve on low achievers' responses by asking probing questions, as they frequently do with higher-achieving children. Teachers also tend to call on low achievers less often, especially when asking more thought-provoking questions. Teachers interact less in their nonverbal communication with low achievers. They maintain less eye contact and less frequently lean forward and nod their heads as they do with high achievers. They also give briefer and less informative feedback to questions of lower achievers. Stipek (1998) mentions other behaviors as well. For example, teachers tend to seat lower achievers farther from themselves. They praise for less demanding work and react with pity rather than anger for poor performance. Teachers should remember that their expectations can "create" high and low achievers.

Teachers formulate and convey not only expectations of achievement, but also expectations of student behavior. The selection of instructional activities is often affected by these expectations. For example, Oakes and Lipton (1999) note that teachers select more student-centered and nontraditional activities when they view their children as having higher learning potential. Teachers also implement active and interactive methods for children for whom they hold high expectations, while worksheets and drill-and-skill activities are employed for students for whom they hold low expectations. Many stimulating and cutting-edge methods and strategies are denied to some children because teachers believe that some students, usually those in lower ability classes or, tragically, those who are culturally different, cannot handle these innovations. Comments such as "Oh, I think cooperative learning is great, and I use it regularly with my gifted children, but it would never work with my lower-level children. They are not capable of working in groups. I can do only worksheets and individual seat work with those children," highlight a sad paradox. Because teachers often have low behavioral expectations of children who are struggling academically, they also refrain from implementing motivating and innovative methods in their instruction. Ironically, it could be that those are the very methods that would motivate these children and, in turn, improve their academic performance. All students, except perhaps those very few who have been diagnosed with certain disabilities, are capable of learning cooperatively. The only obstacle for many of them is that their teachers do not hold high enough expectations for them.

Teacher expectations also impact classroom management. Just as children meet high cognitive expectations, they also meet high behavioral expectations. Determining class rules, for example, should reflect high expectations for behavior, yet ones that are appropriate for the children's developmental level. For example, young children in Pre-K through second grade have short attention spans and need frequent physical activity. Expecting them to sit still and remain attentive for hours at a time would be inappropriate. Likewise, children of this age group may break rules because remembering rules is difficult for them. Effective teachers should not expect young children to remember rules after just one or two explanations. This illustrates a high expectation that is unrealistic and would cause frustration for children and teacher alike.

Kohlberg's theory (Eggen & Kauchak, 2001) of moral reasoning (see Competency 1, Chapter 1) is a useful tool that aids in our understanding of children's moral development and behavior and, consequently, our expectations of them. According to Kohlberg's theory, young children generally follow rules because of external consequences that might befall them if they do not. They are at the **preconventional ethics** level. At this point, they view moral behavior through an egocentric perspective. That is, they are concerned about being caught and punished if they disobey (stage 1) and about the advantages that they will enjoy in return for being obedient (stage 2). Kohlberg asserts that young children are not yet morally developed enough to follow rules, because children at this age are egocentric and have difficulty considering others (stage 3) and young children cannot consider the inherent value of rules to an orderly and just society (stage 4). Stages 3 and 4 comprise the **conventional ethics** levels. Teachers of young children would be foolish to expect children to understand that disobeying a rule might have an adverse effect on society. As we construct and explain our rules, our expectations should be high but realistic. This theory does not encourage us to expect children not to behave well, but rather it helps us understand behavior from a developmental perspective. For example, if a child does not automatically want to share toys, or if he does not see things from another person's perspective, we

understand that this is so because of his moral developmental level. Many parents wonder why young children don't react to the comment, "Eat your peas because many children are starving throughout the world." A better approach, given Kohlberg's theory, would be, "You must eat your peas before you can have dessert." With this in mind, we can design management systems that provide clear consequences, both positive and negative, that allow children to operate within realistic boundaries. Kohlberg helps frame expectations that can be met.

SUMMARY

This chapter examined two elements crucial to establishing an environment for learning and excellence: enthusiasm and expectations. Enthusiasm is best conveyed through teacher modeling. To nurture their own enthusiasm, teachers are advised to consider the relevance of their instruction, the use of authentic learning strategies, and teacher self-efficacy. In addition, we can foster children's enthusiasm for learning by supporting Erikson's concepts of initiative and industry. High expectations for student achievement and behavior are also emphasized. Teachers have to be cognizant of their children's developmental levels in order to establish realistic yet high goals and objectives. Teachers communicate their expectations for students mainly in an implicit fashion. It is important for teachers to be aware of the strong influence that their expectations can have on children. They should also be aware that bias and prejudice can affect expectations and that expectations often impact quality of instruction.

GLOSSARY

affective domain   the part of learning that is associated with feelings and emotions. Other domains of learning are cognitive and psychomotor.

classroom climate   the feelings that the members of a classroom share about the social, emotional, and academic aspects of their environment. A positive elementary classroom climate is one in which children feel safe and successful.

community of learners   learning environments wherein everyone in the group is learning together and from one another in a supportive manner. In a classroom, this means that all children as well as the teacher learn together.

conventional ethics   Kohlberg's stage of moral reasoning (ages 10–20), in which a person's moral decisions are based on concern for other people and the laws of society.

explicit communication   conveying a message in a clear, unambiguous manner, usually in words, so that both the one sending the message and the one receiving the message are aware of the content.

implicit communication   conveying a message in a hidden manner. Implicit messages are often conveyed through body language or behavior.

industry versus inferiority stage   Erikson's stage wherein children in middle childhood (ages 6–12) may or may not develop appreciation for mastery and competence through a sense of accomplishment.

initiative versus guilt stage   Erikson's stage wherein children in early childhood (ages 3–6) may or may not develop a sense of autonomy, curiosity, and risk-taking.

modeling   learning that is a result of observing the behaviors and actions of others.

preconventional ethics   Kohlberg's stage of moral reasoning (until age 10) wherein a child's moral decisions are based on external consequences and personal benefit.

self-efficacy   a person's beliefs about the causes of his or her success. High self-efficacy refers to the belief that the reasons for one's success are in his or her control. Low self-efficacy refers to the belief that the reasons for one's success are not in his or her control.

self-fulfilling prophecy   a phenomenon wherein a mistaken expectation leads to internalization and actions that cause that expectation to become a reality.

zone of proximal development   Vygotsky's term for the level of development at which a person can expand his or her thinking and skills with the help of a more able adult or peer.

SUGGESTED ACTIVITIES

1. Observe a lesson and analyze it in terms of expectations that are communicated in interaction patterns that the teacher employs. For example, does the teacher communicate the same expectations for all children through the use of wait time, the distribution of higher-level questions, feedback to answers, and so forth? You may do this by making a seating chart marked with "B" for boy, "G" for girl, "H" for high achiever, "L" for low achiever, and other student categories. During the lesson, keep a record of the types of questions asked for each student, the number of times each student is called on, the amount of wait time each receives, and other pertinent information. Sharing your findings with your mentor in a professional discussion is one avenue for reflection for both your mentor and you.

2. Obtain weekly lesson plans for a class of children in any grade from Pre-K through 4. Check the lesson goals and objectives for realistic, yet high, expectations, considering the developmental levels of the students. Discuss further your ideas with your mentor. Summarize your discussion in writing.

3. Review the mission statement of several elementary schools for references to the concept of high expectations. Choose a school that includes this concept, and then discuss with the principal how the concept is encouraged on the campus. Write a summary of his or her comments and your impressions.

4. Interview several teachers and ask them to define "enthusiasm" as it relates to their teaching. Ask them to rate their own enthusiasm level and analyze why they chose this rating.

5. Observe children participating in various kinds of classroom activities, including those that are teacher-centered and those that are student-centered. Compare the levels of enthusiasm for each, and hypothesize as to what might constitute the differences that you detect.

6. Videotape a lesson that you teach. Analyze your behavior and that of the students for enthusiasm.

7. Ask the principal and/or assistant principal of the school at which you are doing fieldwork whom they consider to be the most enthusiastic teachers on campus. Arrange to observe in their classrooms. Note which attributes or behaviors they use to create enthusiasm.

PRACTICE QUESTIONS

1. Ms. Parker is mentoring a new first-grade teacher, Ms. Rosa. Ms. Parker recognizes that teacher enthusiasm is a critical component to effective teaching and wants to instill this in Ms. Rosa. Her advice should include all of the following *except*:

   A. Be sure to tell your children every day that you are enthusiastic and that you want them to be enthusiastic, too.

   B. Make sure that you believe that what you are teaching your children is important and relevant.

   C. Try to pay attention to varying your voice inflections and moving around the class as you teach.

   D. Ask questions to which you are curious to hear your students' responses.

2. Ms. Parker also explains that in order for Ms. Rosa to instill enthusiasm in her children she should:

   A. Have them look up a word in the dictionary and discuss its meaning.

   B. Be enthusiastic herself.

   C. Meet with the children's parents and explain to them how enthusiasm facilitates learning.

   D. Give gold stars to the children that are exhibiting the highest levels of enthusiasm.

3. After a month of teaching, Ms. Rosa comes to Ms. Parker for advice. Ms. Rosa explains that she is well aware of the importance of high expectations. With this in mind, she planned to devote 40 minutes with her first graders going over their lines for the upcoming Thanksgiving Day play. Although she had high expectations of them, the children disappointed her. They started to get fidgety after just 15 minutes. Ms. Parker explains that:

   A. High expectations should be used for achievement, not for behavior.

   B. Ms. Rosa was not realistic with her expectations for first graders.

   C. Punishment should be given to those who became fidgety.

   D. First graders should not be expected to participate in a Thanksgiving Day play.

4. Ms. Parker observes Ms. Rosa teaching a lesson on bats. She asks her children what they already know about bats. Then she reads a beautifully illustrated big book about bats. Afterward the children discuss what they have learned from the story and how their feelings about bats may have changed. Ms. Rosa then has the children decorate cut out figures of bats. Susie is not coloring her bat and is staring out the window. Ms. Rosa comes up to Susie and says, "Come on, Susie. Just put some color on the paper!" Susie then takes one crayon and half-heartedly makes some stray marks on her paper. "That is wonderful!" exclaims Ms. Rosa. You are a very talented little girl!" As they confer after the lesson, Ms. Parker suggests to Ms. Rosa that:

   A. Ms. Rosa should immediately call Susie's parents. They need to know about her apathetic behavior.

   B. Ms. Rosa did a good job in motivating Susie by complimenting her.

   C. Ms. Rosa communicated low expectations by praising Susie as she did.

   D. Ms. Rosa did not have realistic expectations of Susie.

Answers and Discussion

Answer 1: Remember that in this question we are looking for advice that is *not* appropriate. In choice *A*, the advice is not sound because it involves an explicit, rather than implicit, approach to instilling enthusiasm in students. Telling children that you are enthusiastic is meaningless. You must model it. The old saying, "You can talk the talk but if you don't walk the walk students will not believe you" is applicable here! Choice *B* is good advice because this would help a teacher develop sincere enthusiasm. Choice *C* is good advice because these characteristics have been identified as indicators of teacher enthusiasm. Choice *D* is good advice because this may also help increase sincere interest and enthusiasm on the part of the teacher. The answer is *A*.

Answer 2: Choice *A* may help develop children's vocabulary and dictionary skills, but knowing the definition of enthusiasm does not mean that they will practice it. Choice *B* is correct because if the teacher models enthusiasm, she is implicitly teaching it. Choice *C* may be an interesting endeavor, but again, this is an academic, explicit approach that would not be effective in getting children to be enthusiastic. Choice *D* is incorrect because using this behavioral approach may encourage a superficial display of behaviors but would not necessarily instill true intrinsic enthusiasm. The answer is *B*.

Answer 3: Choice *A* is not true. High expectations are important for both achievement and behavior. Choice *B* is the correct answer. Ms. Rosa determined unrealistic goals and did not take into account the developmental level of her children. First graders need to be physically active. Asking them to sit still for 40 minutes is not realistic. Furthermore, they do not have long attention spans. Asking them to pay attention to *one* activity for 40 minutes is also unrealistic. Choice *C* is not advisable. The teacher is at fault here for inappropriate planning, and her children should not be punished for it. Choice *D* is incorrect because there is no evidence in this scenario or elsewhere that first graders should not participate in Thanksgiving Day plays. The answer is *B*.

Answer 4: Choice *A* is incorrect. There should be no cause for alarm for this one incident of low interest on Susie's part, especially because Ms. Rosa has not yet tried any interventions. Choice *B* is incorrect because Ms. Rosa's compliments were ineffective. She is not instilling in Susie a sense of industry by complimenting her on work that involved no real effort. Choice *C* is correct. By complimenting Susie on a half-hearted effort (Susie half-heartedly makes stray marks with one crayon), Ms. Rosa is implying that she has low expectations of Susie. The answer is *C*.

WEB LINKS

Remember that Web site locations may change. If any of these sites have moved or cannot be located, use terms in the index to search for further information.

http://www.emory.edu/EDUCATION/mfp/effpage.html

This site has a variety of information about self-efficacy. It presents the latest research and an overview of theories, instruments, photographs, and more. It helps teachers understand the concept of self-efficacy for themselves and for their students.

http://www.pacificnet.net/%7Emandel/

Teachers Helping Teachers

This Web site offers resources for teachers that enhance self-development. Included are lesson plans, ideas for field trips, and ideas for stress reduction. This site helps maintain teacher enthusiasm as teachers share ideas with one another and network.

http://www.coe.uh.edu/~srmehall/theory/social.html

This site provides added information about Vygotsky and applications of his theory to classrooms.

http://snycorva.cortland.edu/~ANDERSMD/KOHL/content.html

This site provides information about Kohlberg's theory of moral development. It includes applications for the classroom and discussion and critique of his ideas.

http://www.yale.edu/ynhti/curriculum/units/1980/1/80.01.04.x.html

This site provides extensive information about each of Erikson's stages of personal and social development.

REFERENCES

Arends, R. I., Winitzky, N. E., & Tannenbaum, M. D. (1998). *Exploring teaching*. USA: McGraw-Hill.

Bandura, A. (1986). *Social foundations of thought and action: A social cognitive theory*. Upper Saddle Hill River, NJ: Prentice Hall.

Dewey, J. (1966). *Democracy and education.* New York: MacMillan.

Eggen, P., & Kauchak, D. (2001). *Educational psychology: Windows on classrooms.* (5th ed.). New York: MacMillan College.

Good, T. L., & Brophy, J. E. (1997). *Looking in classrooms* (7th ed.). New York: Addison-Wesley Educational Publishers Inc.

Oakes, J., & Lipton, M. (1999). *Teaching to change the world.* Boston: McGraw-Hill College.

Rosenthal, R., & Jacobson, L. (1968). *Pygmalion in the classroom: Teacher expectations and pupils' intellectual development.* New York: Holt, Rinehart, & Winston.

Stipek, D. (1998). *Motivation to learn: From theory to practice* (3rd ed.). Needham Heights, MA: Allyn and Bacon.

Vygotsky, L. (1987). *Thought and language.* Cambridge, MA: MIT Press.

Chapter 8

Maintaining a Safe and Productive Physical and Emotional Environment

ANGELA SPAULDING

West Texas A&M University

TERMS TO KNOW

Bullying	Deficiency needs	Perception
Classroom environment	Environmental factors	Self-actualization
Conciliation	Growth needs	Self-esteem
Conciliatory gesture	Individual security	Stereotypes
Conflict	Life position	Transactional analysis
Conflict resolution	Maslow's hierarchy	
Culture	Needs	

Competency 5 addresses establishing a classroom climate that fosters learning, equity, and excellence. The previous chapter discusses how teacher enthusiasm and high expectations contribute to the classroom environment, whereas this chapter discusses how to create a safe, nurturing, and inclusive classroom environment that respects students' emotional needs, rights, and dignity. This chapter also addresses characteristics of physical spaces that are safe and productive for learning and the benefits and limitations of various arrangements of furniture in the classroom. In addition, it describes how to organize the physical environment to ensure physical accessibility and to facilitate learning in various instructional contexts.

To establish a good environment at school, teachers must understand how various external factors (e.g., conflict within students' families, peer relationships, gang- or drug-related community problems, malnutrition, physical arrangements) affect students' lives and their performance in school. Teachers should be able to create a learning environment that takes advantage of positive factors and minimizes negative ones. Signs of stress in students (e.g., clinging, crying, an increase in aggressiveness) should be recognized, and teachers should respond appropriately to help children deal with stress. Teachers should understand factors inside and outside the classroom that influence children's perceptions of their own worth and potential (e.g., grouping practices, classroom arrangement, parent and teacher expectations, prior experiences in school), and recognize the effects of these perceptions on learning. Finally, teachers should plan instruction to enhance all students' self-esteem and to create an environment in which all students feel safe, accepted, competent, and productive.

UNDERSTANDING ENVIRONMENTAL INFLUENCES

Many factors impact the learning that occurs in classrooms. These factors may come from within the classroom (e.g., teaching methods, equipment and supplies, teacher-student interactions) or may be what children bring with them to class (e.g., attitudes, beliefs, experiences, developmental levels). Effective teachers know this and are constantly scanning their classrooms for signs of physical or emotional influences and using this information to better serve their children and to keep them safe. The best way teachers can identify these influences is by knowing their children well. When a teacher knows his or her children, he or she can detect changes in physical or emotional influences that may impact the classroom environment. By understanding environmental influences that affect children, teachers can create a classroom environment that helps counter negative influences that children may have experienced or are presently experiencing. A **classroom environment** can be defined as a setting in which classroom members (i.e., teacher and students) reside for the purpose of learning. This environment includes all of the factors or influences that impact the classroom members and the interactions that all members of the classroom have with one another. This chapter should help teachers become more knowledgeable about creating classroom environments that are supportive, fun, motivating, and full of learning.

PHYSICAL AND EMOTIONAL ENVIRONMENTAL FACTORS THAT IMPACT LEARNING

Perception

Perception is often defined as "how the world is viewed through each individual's eyes." This individual perception is often referred to as selective perception because of the hundreds of different experiences that selectively have brought us to this moment in time. Our culture, stereotypes, life positions, and even our own individual security influence this selectivity. If you watch detective shows on television, you have probably seen that one of the hardest parts of a crime scene is to try to put all of the stories of witnesses together—each may have seen the act from a different angle or perspective. A child's individual perception impacts the learning experience in numerous ways. Teachers must always remember that a student's perception is reality to that student. Children "see through the eyes" of a combination of their historical experience, present needs, and the inherent properties of the scene being perceived (Napier & Gershenfeld, 1999). Because what is seen is always a combination of what is actually occurring and what is happening within us at that moment, it is unlikely that two people will ever perceive the same thing in exactly the same way (Harrison, 1976).

To be an effective teacher, one must understand that each student comes to the classroom with a different set of perceptions and that many of these perceptions can be distorted. According to Napier and Gershenfeld (1999), "even with the most objective task, it is nearly impossible to keep our subjective views from altering our perception of what really exists" (p. 3). Therefore the way children view their teacher, peers, classroom, subject matter, or purpose for learning is impacted greatly not only by what actually happens everyday in the classroom but also by children's experiences and immediate needs. The following discussion examines four areas of perception: culture, stereotypes, life positions, and individual security.

Perception and culture. Cultural experiences affect the way students behave. These experiences affect how they think, how they treat others, and how they treat themselves. Basically culture consists of behaviors absorbed or learned from a group. In education, we often refer to **culture** as children's behaviors learned in their lives outside school. Teachers cannot understand their classrooms without making reference to the cultural and personal backgrounds of all of their children and examining their own cultural baggage as well.

Cultural differences are well documented, as we have seen in Competency 2, Chapter 2. For example, cultural differences in eye gaze and eye contact affect the perceptions of others. In addition, these cultural differences impact classroom communication. When one person greets another, the following sequence generally takes place: gaze—smile—eyebrow lift—quick head nod (Eibl-Eibesfeldt, 1972). This behavior may seem ordinary until you realize that all students do not share the same cultural behaviors. The most distinguishing feature in the cross-cultural use of eye contact is the focus of the listener's eyes (Burgoon, Buller, & Woodall, 1989).

According to Spaulding and O'Hair (2000), Anglos are socialized to gaze directly at the speaker's face when they are listening; as we also saw in Competency 2, Chapter 2, students from other cultures often refuse to look directly into the eyes of an authority figure (such as a teacher). In these cultures, direct eye gaze with an authority figure is considered rude and inappropriate, and not looking up is a sign of respect, especially to a teacher. Japanese Americans, for example, avoid eye contact when listening by focusing on the speaker's neck. Teachers can easily misread children because of their eye contact if they are unaware of cultural differences. A teacher could, for example, perceive that the student was not paying attention or not telling the truth or, if the culture matched the teacher's, could conclude that the child was polite while others in the class are not. This is just one example of how perception and culture can impact the classroom learning environment.

Body language, mannerisms, and deep-rooted beliefs may differ in various cultures. These differences may be based on ethnicity, religion, gender, or even on being raised in a certain area of a country. They may be profoundly related to a student's socioeconomic background. Because students are in various stages of cultural growth, they may exhibit very strong cultural differences or none at all.

Perception and stereotypes. Stereotypes are preconceived notions of how individuals from certain groups think, feel, and act. As classroom members, students rapidly turn for support to other students they believe share their own stereotypes (Kelley, 1951; Napier & Gershenfeld, 1999; Slater, 1955). Stereotypes can have negative consequences for the classroom environment. Even young children may form stereotypes that result in the acceptance or nonacceptance of other students. Class members are then discriminated against because of this acceptance or nonacceptance (Locksley, Ortiz, & Hepburn, 1980). People who have felt unaccepted in a group know how miserable it can be. This issue has been examined as one factor in the Littleton, Colorado, shooting in the spring of 1999. Feeling unaccepted in a classroom may not result in violence, but it often inhibits the learning process. Students who perceive that they are accepted and valued do better in school, so teachers should make sure that all children feel accepted in the classroom environment.

Stereotypes can be based on a variety of differences: family background, race, ethnic background, religion, parental occupation, grades, athleticism, hobbies, economic status, or any number of other factors. Stereotypes are often the result of generalizing one person's behavior to a whole population of people (Quattrone & Jones, 1980). Teachers must be aware of such stereotypes so as to promote a classroom culture that accepts and celebrates differences. When a teacher values each student, the teacher sets a strong example for other students to follow. Teachers must become conscious of any stereotypes that they consciously or unconsciously carry as well as the stereotypes that exist within a classroom. These stereotypes often come with set expectations about another group's abilities or behaviors. For example, some stereotypical myths are: athletes are more brawn than brains; attractive students perform better; middle-class children perform better than lower-class children; White children perform better than African-American children; students with disabilities can't learn; or women with blond hair lack common sense. Some schools have recently promoted uniforms as a way of removing visual stereotypes because children often dress according to their group, either by choice or economics, or they may even try to wear a symbol of their stereotyped group. It is apparent that these myths can create negative learning conditions in a classroom.

Teachers should keep in mind that students are complex, unique individuals—no two are the same! A teacher's job is to enjoy and *celebrate* this uniqueness and to teach students to do the same.

Perception and life position. Our present perceptions are the result of past experiences. The theory of **transactional analysis** (TA) (Berne, 1976; Woollams & Brown, 1978) explains this premise. According to TA, all of one's experiences in life, starting as an infant, have worked together to develop one's own concept of self-worth and assist in formulating a sense of worth of others. Napier and Gershenfeld (1999) describe development of self-worth this way:

> We did this by crystallizing our experiences and making decisions about the kind of life we would have (sad, happy); what parts we would play (strong hero, loner); and how we would act out the parts of our life scripts (adventurously, in fear, slowly, with permission). (p. 6)

For example, if you were continuously praised as a child, you would begin to see yourself as worthy of praise. If you were ridiculed frequently as a child, you might see yourself as unintelligent, with little to offer. It is through these experiences that we form a life script or a **life position.**

As we grow older, we become a self-fulfilling prophecy—continuing to reinforce what we learned about ourselves as a child. Children entering classrooms have already begun to form their life positions, even at an early age. Teachers have some children who, based on the way they have been treated in life, already feel that they are going to fail at school. A teacher's job is to help young students find a way to overcome and redefine that life position. It is clear that life position can impact learning in a classroom. It is also very evident that, as part of the many experiences that children have in a classroom, the teacher can help create perceptions toward school and learning—either positively or negatively.

Perception and individual security. When young children enter a new classroom group, they often experience a lack of **individual security**, which results in anxiety (Bennis & Shepard, 1987). Feelings of anxiety may be mild to extreme, depending upon the student. Holtgraves (1991) defines anxiety as a feeling of uneasiness that is brought about by a conscious or unconscious feeling of danger (not necessarily real) and a readiness to meet that danger. When experiencing anxiety, students feel insecure about themselves. They may feel as if other class members could harm them in some way. Harm may come in physical, emotional, or mental ways. In this state of anxiety, students experience self-doubt about the way others perceive them. As a result, their behavior is based on these feelings. Children can act out in various ways because of this self-doubt. Some students may withdraw; others may become loud and rambunctious; others may lash out (as if cornered). At this point, teachers may see children caught in self-conflict between the wish to interact with others and the need to protect themselves, and between the desire to succeed within the group and their doubts regarding their ability to contribute (Turquet, 1978). It is the teacher's job to help children see a classroom as a welcoming and safe place.

Napier and Gershenfeld (1999) remind us that when individuals join a group, they change. Thus a child's in-group behavior may differ from his or her out-of-group behavior. From this, one can see how group membership or peer pressure can impact children. Think about the number of groups, both large and small, in which children can have membership—everything from their family to a neighborhood play group to a church group to sports groups—and how a child's group behavior differs drastically from group to group. Consider the classroom as a group that children join. As the leader of this group, the teacher must create an environment that makes students want to be members!

Conflict

A natural by-product of human interactions is **conflict.** Effective teachers must understand conflict and its role in the classroom and school. Most people see conflict as purely negative, which is not necessarily true. What is always true, however, is that conflict does not manage itself. Children can bring into a classroom conflict that originated elsewhere. Other times the conflict originates in the classroom. No matter where it originates, it has the potential to impact classroom learning negatively or positively, depending upon the manner in which the teacher deals with it. To deal effectively with conflict and to teach children to do the same, teachers must have skills in managing it. They develop these skills by (1) understanding conflict contaminants, (2) identifying conflict types, and (3) implementing appropriate conflict resolution strategies.

Conflict Contaminants

Conflict contaminants are conditions in which negative conflict grows and thrives. These are conditions that have a negative effect on classroom learning. Several authors (Harvey & Drolet, 1994; Roberts, 1982; Spaulding & O'Hair, 2000) refer to these contaminants as pollutants that clog and choke a classroom climate.

The following are examples of conflict contaminants that can occur in a classroom, with a detrimental impact on learning.

Negativism. Students get into more conflict when negativity is predominant in the classroom (Harvey & Drolet, 1994). Teachers must promote a positive classroom environment with children. They can achieve this easily by being accepting, welcoming, and encouraging to their children. Greeting students every morning is a way that clearly shows them, "I'm glad you are here, and we have the potential for a great day!" In positive classroom environments the teacher has made allowances for different personalities and learning styles and does not play favorites. Furthermore, the actions of the teacher must always represent what is best for children. For example, some teachers see sarcasm as a way of teasing or "fitting in" with kids. However, its use is not in the best interest of students, because sarcasm is often misunderstood by children, resulting in hurt feelings, anger, or vicarious fear that the teacher may turn on them next. Very young children are developmentally unable to understand teasing and sarcasm. It is better left out of the school environment.

Unrealistic expectations. Much has been written about high expectations for students but little about "working up" to those expectations. If a teacher has unrealistic expectations of children academically and behaviorally, the children are likely to experience failure. With failure comes negative conflict that is often created by finger pointing, excuses, and feelings of inadequacy. Children need to experience success in order to achieve more success, and a teacher's job is to help them find it academically, socially, and mentally. Teachers should provide opportunities for each child to succeed at small tasks before moving him or her to more complex tasks. Particularly with young children, teachers must make sure that they build in successful opportunities throughout longer projects to encourage continued working and learning. They should also be very careful to guard against placing an expectation label on a culturally different child (e.g., not expecting a low socioeconomic student to succeed academically because of his or her lack of experiences and

resources). Effective teachers stop and celebrate successes because they know that success breeds success.

Poor communication skills. When poor communication exists between children, between the teacher and the children, or between the teacher and parents or administration, conflict will likely occur. Without effective communication, teachers leave their classrooms open to rumors, incorrect information, and missed information. They also miss opportunities to get to know the students, which means that they won't be able to meet individual needs. By using various types of delivery systems for communication (e.g., written and oral) and seeking student feedback (e.g., oral, written, and nonverbal), teachers can ensure that children have interpreted messages in the way they were intended.

Personal stressors. Personal stressors are personal conditions that teachers and children (and their families) experience, such as health problems, lack of sleep, financial difficulties, improper nutrition, a mom's pregnancy or a new sibling, lack of organizational skills, or lack of social skills. For many children, personal stressors can also be of a social nature, such as number and quality of friendships, perception of student's own physical attractiveness, athletic abilities, and friendships. All of these stressors have the potential to affect student learning and the classroom climate as well as to promote conditions for conflict. Teachers may find themselves limited as to the handling of many of these stressors; however, seeking the help of school administration, community services, or counselors may assist them in getting help for children. The classroom teacher is generally the first person to note and report these stressors because of his or her daily contact with students. Children may present symptoms such as unusual crying, clinging, not wanting to come to school and/or to leave, reverting to behavior of much younger children, or becoming increasingly withdrawn, depressed, or aggressive. Any drop in grades should be investigated.

Neglect or abuse can cause extreme stress for children. The child may show signs listed above as well as physical and other emotional signs. Physical signs of abuse may include bruising, welts, cuts, burns, broken bones (or signs of breaks that haven't healed properly), or other injuries in various stages of healing. Particularly in the warm Texas climate, teachers may notice that children are wearing inappropriate, long-sleeved clothing on hot days, thus hiding injuries. Children may shy away from any physical or close contact. Many times children who are in abused or neglectful situations at home do not want to leave school at the end of the day or change behavior during the time leading up to a holiday. They may also become aggressive in acting out, either with the teacher, with toys, or with other children.

Signs of sexual abuse may include torn or stained underwear, trouble walking or sitting, pain, itching, bruises, bleeding in the genital area, or signs of a sexually transmitted disease. Children may use terms indicating that they know much more than they should at their age and may even act seductively. Sudden weight gains or losses may also indicate a problem, as may running away from home.

Emotionally abused children may develop speech disorders and show signs of delayed physical development. These children also may act more or less mature than is normal for their age, may have difficulty making or keeping friends, and may have extreme and rapid behavioral changes.

Neglected children most often have poor hygiene, delayed physical development, and poor dental and medical attention. They may disclose information about the lack of supervision at home. They may ask for or steal food and appear very tired. Their dress is often inappropriate for the season. They may be the first to arrive at the school grounds and the last to leave and may miss school frequently.

If a teacher should notice any of these symptoms and suspect neglect or abuse, this must, by law, be reported (see Competency 13, Chapter 19). Children's Protective Services in Harris County also advises teachers to be approachable, be good listeners, and be supportive in telling children that they did the right thing by coming to the teacher with such problems. Teachers must not overreact (this may frighten a child) nor talk about a suspected abuser negatively in front of a child. They should evaluate the situation for immediate danger and get medical help right away. Word-for-word information should be written down and reported within 48 hours. A child's life or safety may depend on the teacher.

Savior syndrome. Some teachers have a condition known as the "savior syndrome." These are teachers who, though well meaning, try to fix *every* problem. This can put teachers into conflict situations. "When you try to solve someone else's problems, you do two perilous things. First, you rob the other person of the opportunity to grow. . . . Second, you increase the chances that you will become an actor in the conflict yourself (Harvey & Drolet, 1994, pp. 75–76). Although all teachers should be involved in helping students with serious problems, when children become dependent upon a teacher for help with every problem (without thinking or acting for themselves) conflicts can emerge. Teachers who make choices for children—give them the answers to all of their questions and problems—become accountable for the consequences of those choices. A good rule of thumb to bear in mind is that teachers want children to grow to depend on themselves rather than to maintain dependence upon a teacher. Consider tattling. Certainly, teachers do not want to raise children who think it is wrong to tell, even when there is apparent danger (as some students did in recent violent situations). They also do not want children to expect teachers to solve every social situation in the classroom and on the playground. Talking with children in a Town Meeting situation allows the teacher to help them decide which situations need the teacher's immediate attention. It also helps children bring situations to "the floor," where all can contribute ideas to solving problems. Having a box in which children place written complaints or having a specified time during recess when information is reported can help a child decide whether the tattle is important enough to tell.

Jumping to conclusions. At times students, parents, and teachers alike are guilty of jumping to conclusions before getting all of the necessary information to make a judgment or decision. For example, a teacher may assume that a student who is often in trouble is the cause for all problems that occur in the class. This creates harmful conflict because the facts are not considered. Jumping to conclusions creates unnecessary conflict. A good teacher always gets the facts straight before saying or doing anything. Time and further conflict will be saved in the long run if teachers take the time to get all the details.

Lack of support and trust. Students need to feel supported in the classroom. Those who feel supported show signs of increased creativity, communication, and personal growth. Without support, they are less likely to try new academic challenges for fear of failure and the resulting consequences. Teachers can show children support in many ways. For instance, they can take extra time to watch their students demonstrate the newest playground skills and, at the first opportunity, praise the involved children and acknowledge their efforts. In addition, children can be engaged with teachers in conversations about topics that interest them. Teachers can be available to answer questions when children have them (or during special sharing times), gear classroom teaching to include all learning styles and use a great deal of positive reinforcement and encouragement. These are only a few of the many supportive actions that teachers can use to build trust and support. Think about the kinds of actions that make people feel supported in general. These are likely to be the very same types of actions that are important to students. The more children feel supported by a teacher, the more trust will develop and grow.

Preference protection. Some teachers operate under the condition of preference protection, which is the protection of one's preferred way of doing something. It is often exemplified by the statement, "It is my way or the highway." Teachers must spend more time thinking about where they want children to go academically and less time insisting that there is only one way to get there. Tunnel vision occurs when a teacher feels that his or her way is the only way. This limits student creativity and success. Children operate out of many different learning styles, many of which differ from their teacher's style. The goal is for children to learn—not that they all learn in the same way as the teacher.

Types of Conflict

Teachers must accept the fact that conflict is a necessary and inevitable part of life in the classroom. They must also be able to identify the types of conflict that occur so that they can manage them properly. Conflict doesn't necessarily feel good, but it is necessary for personal and classroom growth. Think about the times in your life when you grew the most—whether personally or professionally. More often than not, those growing situations were full of conflict. By managing the conflict, you have become a stronger person. Whether we want to acknowledge it or not, we all need some conflict to challenge and enrich our lives.

Harvey and Drolet (1994) provide a five-way classification of conflict that is helpful in defining the types of conflict with which teachers deal. The types of conflict are as follows:

Value conflict. Value conflict is the most difficult type of conflict to resolve because it deals with a person's individual beliefs, values, or convictions. These may be deep-seated religious, moral, or other beliefs that a student has carried over time. For example, recent conflicts over prayer at school events led to conflict between students who want to pray and those suing to stop the practice. Certain holiday celebrations can also create conflict for those who wish to celebrate and those who do not (or whose parents do not wish them celebrate).

Tangible conflict. Tangible conflict is conflict over resources that can be measured and may include time, money, supplies, parking spaces, classroom space, and location. For children, these resources can also be the types of toys they own and the clothes they wear (or want to own or wear). When resources decline, tangible conflict increases.

Interpersonal conflict. This is a very common type of conflict in classrooms and schools. It is often seen in the conflict between student "cliques" based on academics, sports, music, or other common interests. Interpersonal conflict results when an individual or group has feelings of dislike toward another individual or group. It is interesting to note that interpersonal conflict is often a secondary conflict resulting from another unresolved type of conflict.

Territorial conflict. Territorial conflict occurs as the result of territorial invasions or the expectation that another will expand his or her present territory or responsibility (Harvey & Drolet, 1994; Spaulding & O'Hair, 2000). Consider a student who is asked to share his supplies or books with another student but feels that his supplies are his private property. In this case, conflict is created through the feeling that another student is invading the first child's property. Or consider the student who is doing a group project and learns that his partner is not holding up his end of the bargain. The first student now feels that he must complete not only his own part of the project but also his partner's. The first child is being forced to expand his responsibility into someone else's in order to get the project finished.

Perceptual conflict. As we discussed earlier in the chapter, people often have distorted images of one another. This is certainly true in the classroom. Children and teachers often jump to conclusions about the motives and goals of others. Most perceptual conflicts occur because the conflicting parties don't have the facts. For example, perceptual conflicts can arise in classes with immi-

grants who have come from countries whose culture is dramatically different from the norm. The students are unsure how to relate to one another. According to Meyer (1987), conflicting parties often have mirror-image perceptions of one another—each attributes the same virtues to themselves and vices to their adversaries. In other words, those on each side of the conflict believe they are taking the most logical and beneficial action possible, while they see their adversaries as taking an illogical and detrimental action. Perceptual conflicts often grow into other types of conflict if not resolved early on. Ruby Payne (1995) describes children who live in poverty as having very limited vocabulary, usually only for casual interactions. These students come across as very rough and, at times, impolite. Conflict may occur in their conversations with others because the receiver of their messages may perceive the message to be inappropriate and offensive. As a result, interpersonal conflict may develop.

Conflict Resolution

After identifying one or more of the five types of conflict mentioned above (value, tangible, interpersonal, territorial, or perceptual), teachers must next know what strategies to use in resolving the conflict. The following **conflict resolution** strategies have been found to be effective (Ball, 1989; Filley, 1975; Harvey & Drolet, 1994; Huse, 1975; Meyer, 1987).

Using conciliatory gestures. It is common for communication between two conflicting children or student groups to come to an impasse. When communication ceases, conflict cannot be resolved. At this point in the conflict, a **conciliatory gesture** can be of tremendous value. A conciliatory gesture can be as simple as a smile or kind word, or it can be as complex as a concession. **Conciliation** is the process whereby one side of the conflict initiates a gesture of good faith in the hope that the other party will reciprocate with a similar type of gesture (Meyer, 1987; Osgood, 1962, 1980). Choosing an adversary as a play partner or member of a team may be the gesture needed to begin solving the conflict. The initial conciliatory gestures put pressure on the opposing side to act. The intent is to move both conflicting parties toward decreased tension and increased communication and eventually to cooperation and conflict resolution.

Avoidance. Avoidance is a conflict resolution strategy that is overused not only by students but also by adults. However, it can be helpful in some situations. For instance, if two students are having real difficulties getting along, teaching them the technique of "just don't go there" or helping them maintain a greater distance may help the overall classroom environment and may help them avoid losing their tempers or initiating an unpleasant situation. At other times, avoidance may make conflict worse. Ignored conflict often mushrooms into deeper conflict or other types of conflict. For example, if the two students mentioned above continued to show signs of increasing conflict, the teacher would not want to ignore those warning signs. A visit with the school counselor would be a good first step in getting help for a potentially volatile situation.

Altering the group structure. In a classroom, altering the group structure may mean changing the physical space to separate two conflicting students, changing a student's schedule, or even changing a teacher's job responsibilities. Like the strategy of avoidance, this strategy sometimes pushes the conflict out of sight temporarily—only to have it return with increased intensity.

Appealing to a higher belief or value. When conflict seems unresolvable, focusing on an overarching value, belief, or goal can help resolve it. For example, two teachers involved in an interpersonal conflict may decide to put their differences aside in order to do what is best for children. Developmental levels have a great deal to do with the effectiveness of this strategy. A very young student may not be able to use it, whereas a teacher may appeal to older children to work for the greater good of all. Some younger students may not see the value of sharing, for example, for the good of all, but some can. Remember that age and developmental level are individual. Teachers often expect too much from older children.

"I Need you and you need me" strategy. This strategy helps individuals to understand how two conflicting students or student groups may have resources that, when shared, help each side to achieve their own goals and interests. Sometimes this strategy is stated as the "I'll scratch your back if you scratch mine" resolution. In the classroom, this strategy helps students to realize the value of others. For instance, a student who is strong in math can help tutor a fellow classmate in return for help with an art project.

Role clarification. When a student or other individual is uncertain about the role he or she is to have in a group or is confused about the role that other individuals are to have, conflict occurs. Different perceptions or expectations about roles also can create conflict. A teacher can use role clarification as a resolution strategy, by having each student define his or her responsibilities in the group and then having them define the responsibilities of others in the group. The group then compares the responses. From this comparative analysis the teacher can see where role confusion is occurring. These roles can then be clarified to resolve the present conflict and prevent future conflict. If a teacher can do this "up front," it often avoids conflict. For children during group work, one strategy is to provide a "job label" to wear around the neck with this responsibility written on the reverse side.

Direct order. A direct order is a conflict resolution strategy that is used frequently by teachers. Actually, it is overused. With a direct order, no input is sought from the conflicting students. We know that without input, most conflicts will not be completely resolved and will reappear. Harvey and Drolet (1994) suggest using the strategy of direct order when resolution is needed immediately (as with a physical fight) and when the person issuing the order is an authority figure accepted by the conflicting children.

Communication. It may sound rather obvious to say that communication is needed to prevent and resolve conflict, yet many conflicts occur because of poor communication. To be effective, a communicated message must be sent in a clear and concise manner. Teachers must determine the best way to communicate their intended messages. They may find that the best way to send a message is not just one way but multiple ways. For example, a teacher may first verbally send a message and then send the same message in a written form or technological form to reinforce the original message. The more reinforcement a message has, the more likely it will be remembered. To determine whether a message has been received and interpreted in the manner intended, feedback is needed from the receiver or receivers of the message. Having the receiver restate the message in either verbal or written form can accomplish this. Many teachers ask students for feedback with the question, "Does everyone understand?" This is an ineffective way of getting helpful feedback because many children feel insecure about acknowledging that they truly don't understand something. In addition, a question such as this does not tell you *what* the students understand. They could easily understand the wrong thing. Many types and levels of communication operate at one time, so it is easy to misunderstand a message. To help prevent conflict, teachers should be continuously monitoring to see that students understand what is being communicated and that they understand what children are communicating in return. Asking children to "repeat back" lets teachers hear exactly the message received. Teachers should also monitor the back-and-forth flow of communication to parents to ensure that both parties are "on the same page."

Seeking additional information. Seeking additional information is a good way to keep from overreacting to misinformation. Misinformation and rumors are everywhere. Many a child has become angry or upset over something that he or she *thought* was said or done. Sometimes the perceived event never occurred, or it occurred under conditions that were acceptable. Many student conflicts can be resolved through this strategy. When teachers hear the "He said–She said" conflict, they should immediately seek the facts.

Ruby Payne (1995), in her research on poverty, explains that the telling of events is different and difficult for children in poverty. Thus teachers must seek additional information from these children in a more structured way. For example, asking a broad question such as, "Tell me about the fight on the playground today," might stop the flow of conversation for children of poverty because often they don't have the skills to express everything they see. Payne suggests that teachers help structure conversation by asking more sequential questions, such as, "Whom did you see on the playground during the fight?" "What was Romero doing?" "What was the first thing you saw that told you a fight was about to occur?" These types of questions allow teachers to seek additional information in a manner to which children can respond effectively.

Outside intervention. Sometimes conflict becomes so intense that an outside perspective is needed. This means involving a third party who can help negotiate, arbitrate, or just offer wise council with regard to the conflict. When a teacher is involved in a conflict or a conflict is occurring in a classroom, a school administrator or counselor may be a good resource to contact. If children trust the teacher, the teacher may also find him- or herself providing a third-party perspective. Outside intervention can be especially helpful in dealing with conflicts that result from sibling rivalry or blended families.

Group dynamics interventions. A group dynamics intervention is a strategy that includes a wide variety of programs and events. These can include multicultural awareness, personality inventories, challenge courses, trust-building exercises, team-building exercises, and cooperative learning experiences. These interventions are designed to help students get to know each other better so that they can resolve misconceptions and build unity and cooperation. Many ideas may be found in Competency 3, Chapter 4, Part 2 for cooperative groupings.

Compromise. Compromise is a strategy that allows both conflicting students and groups of students to meet halfway. In other words, each side gives up part of what he or she wants in order to resolve the issue. In a compromise, it is important that both parties give equally, otherwise resentment and further conflict will result. Teachers may be asked to help discover and mediate what compromises will work. Conflicts requiring compromise can also occur among staff members. This is particularly distrubing if it spills over into the halls or classrooms, and children witness it. Conflicts can range from heated personal disagreements to professional disagreements. For instance, a school may receive special funding to expand its reading program but not have enough money for all teachers to have the materials they want in their classrooms. A compromise might be to set up a literacy closet that houses a variety of reading materials for all teachers rather than having separate sets in each classroom.

Expanding or developing new resources. Conflict often occurs when resources are scarce. Resources can be defined as materials, time, territory, personnel, information, or influence (Ball, 1989). When scarcity occurs, individuals begin to scramble to get their fair share. Young children often perceive that there will not be enough, so conflict begins even before materials are disseminated. When they come up empty handed, conflict occurs. This issue can be resolved by expanding the current resources or by developing new resources. Education systems are often short of resources, so teachers must be creative in developing new resources. One who found her classroom constantly involved in conflict over computer time in the classroom resolved the issue by writing a grant for more computers in her room and allotting more time for students to use them. Assignments may have to be modified, time delegated, or other decisions made to equalize resources.

Democratic vote. A school is planning a fall festival and each class is asked to host an activity in their classroom. To choose an activity, the teachers ask for suggestions and then allow the class to vote on its favorite. This is an example of resolving conflict through democratic vote. Using a democratic vote to resolve conflict is a majority-rules strategy. With this strategy, a vote is taken from all members of the conflict. It can be a written vote, a raised hand vote, or an oral vote. The group with the most votes wins. Although the democratic vote is certainly an option to conflict resolution, it is much better if the conflict can be resolved with a more cooperative type of resolution strategy first so as not to create winners and losers. In certain conditions, a student may perceive that the teacher already knows that he or she is in the minority and that the vote is a "setup" to use peer pressure to vote against him or her.

Other conflict resolution strategies. Our discussion has certainly not covered every type of conflict resolution strategy available. Effective teachers develop additional strategies to deal with each individual in a class. For example, when it is used appropriately, humor can be employed to calm a stressful or highly emotional situation. Teachers should think back to situations of conflict in their own lives. What types of conflict resolution were used? Were they appropriate for the context or environment? Were they effective? The next section reflects further on these types of questions and answers.

Matching Conflict Types with Resolution Strategies

Even if a teacher knows some conflict resolution strategies to use in the classroom, how will he or she know what strategy to use—and when? Actually, this is one of the most difficult tasks in deal-

Table 8.1 Matching Resolution Strategies with Conflict Types

Conflict Resolution Strategies	Value Conflict	Tangible Conflict	Interpersonal Conflict	Territorial Conflict	Perceptual Conflict
Expanding and developing new resources		♥♥♥♥♥		♥♥♥♥♥	
Compromise	↔	↔		↔	
Group dynamics interventions		↔	♥♥♥♥♥	↔	↔
Outside interventions			↔	♥♥♥♥♥	↔
"I need you and you need me" strategy	♥♥♥♥♥		↔	↔	↔
Altering the group structure		♥♥♥♥♥	↔	↔	
Seeking additional information			↔		♥♥♥♥♥
Communication			↔		♥♥♥♥♥
Direct order	↔	↔	♥♥♥♥♥	↔	
Role clarification			↔	♥♥♥♥♥	↔
Appealing to a higher belief or value	♥♥♥♥♥	↔	↔	↔	
Avoidance	↔		↔		
Democratic vote	♥♥♥♥♥	↔			
Using conciliatory gestures	↔	↔	♥♥♥♥♥	↔	
Using humor*		↔	↔	↔	↔

♥♥♥♥♥ Preferred strategy for the conflict type
↔ Possible strategy match for the conflict type

* No preferred strategy match because of the delicate manner in which humor must be used.
From *Building Teams, Building People* by T. Harvey & B. Drolet, 1994, Lancaster, PA: Technomic. Copyright 1994 by Technomic Publishing Company, Inc. Adapted with permission of Scarecrow Press.

ing with conflict. The following questions can help teachers choose the appropriate resolution strategy (Spaulding & O'Hair, 2000).

- What is the source of the conflict? What additional conflicts are likely to arise as a result of this conflict?

- Do the conflicting groups or individuals have the necessary communication or problem-solving skills to work through their differences?

- Do the potential losses outweigh possible gains?

- Who stands to gain—one party or all parties?

- How much time is available for resolving the conflict?

- Is the issue major or minor?

- Is additional research or information needed?

- Are tempers too hot for a productive resolution?

- Will a temporary solution suffice for the present?

- What communication failures are at the base of the conflict?

When resolving conflict, keep in mind that all conflict resolution strategies are situational. Conflict rarely involves just one type; therefore teachers must reflect carefully upon the strategies they use and their potential outcomes. To help teachers select the appropriate strategy, Table 8.1 matches resolution strategies with conflict types.

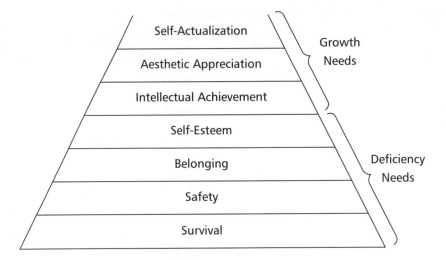

Figure 8.1 Maslow's Hierarchy of Needs.
From "A Theory of Human Motivation," *Psychological Review, 50* (1943), pp. 370–396. Copyright 1943 by the American Psychological Association. Public Domain.

Factors That Impact Learning: Needs

As we continues to study **environmental factors** that affect student learning, we must understand that children's ability to learn is greatly influenced by the degree to which their needs are being meet. A **need** is a requirement for the well-being of an individual. We can best understand these needs by looking at **Maslow's hierarchy** of needs (Maslow, 1954). According to Maslow, individuals pass through certain developmental stages. These stages are represented in Figure 8.1.

As we can see from Figure 8.1, Maslow discusses the needs of all individuals. The way a person acts in a given situation depends upon the developmental level at which he or she is operating. Theoretically students move upward through the hierarchy, meeting each need before being able to move to the next one. The most basic needs, or **deficiency needs,** are at the bottom of the hierarchy. These needs must be answered before human beings can move to growth needs. The following discussion defines each of the needs in the hierarchy.

- **Physiological needs** include such basic survival needs as shelter, food, and clothing. Students who come to school hungry, sleepy, or without the appropriate clothing will probably not be successful learners until these needs are met.

- **Safety needs** are the needs that we all have to feel safe in our environment. Almost every child develops some sort of fear during childhood and these fears can be real or imaginary. Certain fears are more common than others. Four-year-olds commonly have a fear of the dark and monsters. Older children may face social fears and fear of failure. Teachers who develop a safe environment in the classroom can help ease children's fears.

Some children may feel threatened by other students in the school environment. This may be a case of bullying or even more extreme types of school violence such as gang-related crime. When children feel threatened by their teacher in any way, learning cannot be accomplished. Children who fear to leave at the end of the day because of safety issues in their neighborhoods or homes often cannot concentrate on school tasks, especially during the afternoon.

- **Belonging and love needs** are the needs we all have for love and acceptance. Unfortunately, all children do not get the love they need at home. Many students may be, or at least feel, abandoned. As families go through divorces or other wrenching events and one or both parents are no longer there, children almost always experience the confusion of not knowing where they belong as their home as they knew it disintegrates. As a result, they may have a hard time adjusting to social aspects of school. They feel unworthy of acceptance if they have not been accepted in their formative years. As a result, their self-esteem is low, which can enhance feelings of isolation. A child who also does not feel that he or she is a part of the classroom or accepted by the teacher and the school will not be as successful a learner.

Families can also be transient, due to seasonal work, poverty conditions that inspire "apartment hopping" with "move-in specials," or many other reasons. These children may change schools several times a year. A child who is not given a special welcome and assigned a desk separated in a row rather than at a table with other children or at desks grouped together may take a long time to feel as if he or she belongs. One teacher was even overheard to say as the principal arrived with a new student by her side, "Don't give him to me! I got the last new one!" Time and attention often equal love to children, so teachers should set aside time at recess or arrange to eat lunch with children several times a week to hear their stories—at times when they can truly listen. Providing core groups and other cooperative activities can enhance childrens' feelings of belonging.

- **Esteem needs** relate closely to love and belonging needs. **Self-esteem** is a condition in which one has confidence and satisfaction with oneself. In *Lost Boys*, Garbarino (1999) found that violent children have almost always experienced the pain, rage, and shame of rejection. When children are faced with multiple threats to safety, belonging, and self-esteem, the accumulation is often too much for them to bear, and a downward spiral begins. However, a teacher can often provide that one ray of hope for children to create resilience.

Research has shown that slow learners can have low self-esteem (Biehler, 1978). When students perceive that they are less capable than their classmates at activities (e.g., academics, athletics, music), they begin to devalue themselves. This devaluation harms self-esteem needs. Children who have very low self-esteem live with what has been termed "toxic shame," which makes them feel "fundamentally disgraced, intrinsically worthless, and profoundly humiliated in their own skin, just for being themselves" (Garbarino, 1999, p. 58). Teachers must make sure that they show positive feelings toward all children and do not consistently single out the most talented. They may also find themselves in the role of helping students discover their own talents. If a teacher believes in each child and finds something about each that shines, children will have a better chance to believe in themselves. Kohn (1993) found that programs that were artificial and involved catchy slogans ("I like me!") were "nice" but not so valuable, especially to children with very low self-esteem. The only thing that really helps is when a child can attribute success to his or her own efforts rather than to luck or catchy slogans. It is a rare person who feels fulfilled in the areas of love, belonging, and self-esteem. Most individuals with self-esteem needs seek personal recognition and strive to win the approval of others—sometimes positively and sometimes negatively.

- **Growth needs** are those needs that can be answered only after deficiency needs have been met. They include intellectual achievement, aesthetic appreciation, and self-actualization.

- **Self-actualization need** is the need to fully realize one's potential. Many people live their entire lives and never realize their full potential. This is a higher-order need. Self-actualizing people have worked through their own needs and feel accepted and secure, without the need for approval or recognition of others. Although it is unlikely that children will realize this level during their childhood or adolescent years, the teacher's contribution impacts children's ability to meet this future need. Studies on resilience suggest that nurturing early childhood programs play a major role in ensuring that children turn away from violence. The programs improve intellectual development while providing screening for children whose lower needs are not met (Gabarino, 1999). With encouragement and challenge, teachers can help children lay a foundation for self-actualizing. Teachers do truly touch the future!

A major application of Maslow's hierarchy in the classroom is that teachers must make sure that the lower-level needs of children are satisfied so that they are more likely to reach and function at higher levels. Students will be better learners if they are physically comfortable, feel safe, feel as though they belong and are loved, and, as a result, experience self-esteem. Teachers are very important to the development of children's need gratifications because they are responsible for what happens in the classroom.

Based on Maslow's work, Biehler (1978) provided suggestions for meeting student needs. These can be summarized as follows:

1. Do everything possible to satisfy the deficiency needs—physiological, safety, belongingness, and esteem.

- Be aware of the physical condition of your students. (This may involve noticing signs of abuse such as frequent bruises on children and recognizing when they are ill.) Younger children may become frightened when they fall ill or are hurt at school. Teachers can prepare a mini-lesson with a "field trip" to the nurses office to show what will happen in that event, so children are prepared ahead of time.

- Make your room physically and psychologically safe. Daily routines and rules should be well established, and good classroom management should be in place. The teacher should know what children have in their desks and what they bring to school. Age-appropriate furniture and school supplies are important for safety in the classroom; furniture should be arranged so that children can move safely around the room. The teacher should also ensure that no cleaning chemicals or other toxic substances are in the cabinets or in children's reach and that other dangerous materials or equipment are removed from the classroom at once. Parents should be sent a checklist at the beginning of the year to note any foods, scents, and so on, to which their children are allergic.

- Show your students that you take an interest in them and that they "belong" in your classroom. Plan activities that encourage teamwork. Remember, that the teacher as a model can easily cue children that some are accepted and others are not, making it "okay" for some children to ostracize others.

- Arrange learning experiences so that *all* students can gain at least a degree of esteem.

2. Enhance the attractions and minimize the dangers of growth choices. If you establish situations in which students feel pressure, tension, or anxiety, students will choose safety and do their best to remain uninvolved. If you minimize the risks and make learning seem

exciting, even the less secure student will want to join in. Doing this with young children can build positive risk takers and problem solvers.)

3. Direct learning experiences lead to feelings of success to encourage a realistic level of aspiration, an orientation toward achievement, and a positive self-concept.

   ■ Make use of goals and objectives that are challenging but attainable.

   ■ Provide knowledge of results by emphasizing the positive.

   ■ Consider the advantages and disadvantages of symbolic and material rewards.

4. Be alert to the damaging impact of excessive competition.

5. For students who need it, encourage the development of a desire to achieve.

6. Take advantage of natural interests, try to create new ones, and encourage learning for its own sake.

7. When appropriate, permit and encourage students to direct their own learning.

Adapted from *Psychology Applied to Teaching,* (1978), p. 525. Copyright 1978 by Houghton Mifflin Company. Reprinted by permission.

Factors That Impact Learning: Societal Ills

Teachers spend more time with children during waking hours than do some of their parents. One advantage a teacher has in spending time with children is that she or he gets to know them very well, and this puts the teacher on the front line of defense when it comes to recognizing problem symptoms that may be occurring with a child or a group of students. Many societal ills affect children. Among them are school violence, abuse, neglect, broken families, and drugs and alcohol—to name only a few. To help children, teachers must learn to identify the symptoms of these ills.

Student violence. Topping the list of concerns of educators, parents, and students is the increasingly aggressive behavior of students. It seems that every day we hear of more school-related violence

even with young children. Unfortunately, this is a situation for which teachers must be watchful and prepared. Table 8.2. reveals the contents of The National School Safety Center (1998) report that describes the characteristics found in youth who have caused school-associated violent deaths.

Teachers who know and recognize these student characteristics could save lives. If a teacher feels that a child is beginning to exhibit some of these symptoms, he or she should discuss the situation with the school counselor and administrator. Teachers of young children often do not suspect that young students are capable of some of the behaviors discussed in the table, yet statistics show that by age 8 young boys may already be forming destructive patterns

Bullying is not often thought of as violent behavior, but in reality, it certainly can consist of or become a precursor to violent behaviors. Bullying can have negative consequences for the general school climate and the right of students to learn in a safe environment without fear (Banks, 1997). Many boys who later commit violent acts were recognized as bullies very early on, often in grade school (Fried & Fried, 1996). Bullying consists of such behaviors as hitting, threatening, teasing, taunting, spreading rumors, enforcing social isolation, and stealing. Research has found that boys tend to engage in aggressive bullying actions such as hitting and threatening whereas girls tend to utilize more passive strategies such as spreading rumors and enforcing social isolation (Ahmad & Smith, 1994; Smith & Sharp, 1994). Approximately 15 percent of students are either bullied regularly or are the initiators of bullying behavior (Olweus, 1993).

Bullies tend to be students who desire to feel powerful and in control. They often come from homes in which physical punishment is used and parental involvement and warmth are lacking (Banks, 1997). They may even have parents who support aggressive behavior in various ways (Brophy, 1996). Students who are victims of bullying are typically anxious, insecure, cautious, paranoid, and suffer from low self-esteem, rarely defending themselves or retaliating when confronted by stu-

Table 8.2 Characteristics Found in Youth Who Have Caused School-Associated Violent Deaths

The potentially violent youth . . .

1. Has a history of tantrums and uncontrollable angry outbursts.
2. Characteristically resorts to name calling, cursing, abusive language.
3. Habitually makes violent threats when angry.
4. Has previously brought a weapon to school.
5. Has a background of serious disciplinary problems at school and in the community.
6. Has a background of drug, alcohol, or other substance abuse or dependency.
7. Is on the fringe of his/her peer group with few or no close friends.
8. Is preoccupied with weapons, explosives, or other incendiary devices.
9. Has previously been truant, suspended, or expelled from school.
10. Displays cruelty to animals.
11. Has little or no supervision and support from parents or a caring adult.
12. Has witnessed or been a victim of abuse or neglect in the home.
13. Has been bullied and/or bullies or intimidates peers or younger children.
14. Tends to blame others for difficulties and problems s/he causes.
15. Consistently prefers TV shows, movies, or music expressing violent themes.
16. Prefers reading materials dealing with violent themes, rituals, and abuse.
17. Reflects anger, frustration, and the dark side of life in school essays or writing projects.
18. Is involved with a gang or an antisocial group on the fringe of peer acceptance.
19. Is often depressed and/or has significant mood swings.
20. Has threatened or attempted suicide.

From The National School Safety Center. Copyright 1998. Reprinted by permission.

dents who bully them. They also lack social skills and friends, have overprotective parents, and are socially isolated (Banks, 1997). A bully's actions generally occur when adults are not looking, so teachers and parents may not be aware of the problem until it has escalated into a volatile situation. Given this situation, Smith and Sharp (1994) emphasize the need to develop whole-school bullying policies, improve the school ground environment, and empower students through conflict resolution, peer counseling, and assertiveness training. Teachers can work with children to develop class rules against bullying. They should become listening ears for any children who would like to confide in them with regard to acts of bullying. Showing victims how to become stronger by standing up to bullies helps both the bully and the victim. Teachers should be vigilant in watching for symptoms of bullying such as withdrawal, evi-

dence of physical abuse, a drop in grades, torn clothes, or a need for extra money or supplies. Most importantly, teachers should not model bullying behavior by bullying children in their classes—physically or verbally. They should model nonphysical, consistently enforced discipline measures as opposed to ridiculing, yelling at, or ignoring children when they misbehave.

Gang activity. Another factor that impacts student learning and health is that of gang activity. The National School Safety and Security Services (2000) states that students join gangs for power, status, security, friendship, family substitutes, economic profit, and drug and alcohol use. They also make it clear that gang members cross all socioeconomic backgrounds and boundaries regardless of age, sex, race, economic status, and academic achievement. Gang identifiers* may include:

- Graffiti: unusual signs, symbols, or writing on walls, notebooks, etc.

- "Colors": Obvious or subtle colors of clothing, a particular clothing brand, jewelry, or haircuts.

- Tattoos: Symbols (or ink drawings) on arms, chest, or elsewhere on the body.

- "Lit" (gang literature): Gang signs, symbols, poems, prayers, and procedures. These may be in notebooks or other documents.

- Initiations: Suspicious bruises, wounds, or injuries resulting from membership requirements.

- Hand signs: Unusual hand signals or handshakes.

- Behavior: Sudden changes in behavior or secret meetings.

*From The National School Safety and Security Services. Copyright 2000.

Even young children may be at risk in some urban neighborhoods where gang activity is rampant. Because some gangs are "generational," teachers may have students with young parents who are gang members. Most often young children are brought in as "gang runners" because they are not suspected. Children join gangs for protection and belonging. Theory suggests that if schools and classrooms provide a safe place where children can fulfill more of their needs, gang membership is likely to decline.

Factors That Impact Learning: Physical Space

Competency 5 examines the effect of the physical setting on learning. Environmental design has been shown to affect student behavior and attitudes toward school (Ainley, 1987; Gunter et al., 1995). Young children receive messages about their classroom from the choices and arrangement of furniture, materials, and other elements of their room (Brewer, 2001). Designers who work commercially are paid a great deal for arranging spaces and furniture that encourage

particular behavior from people. Why should teachers not reap the benefits of what they know? For example, a "cold" room tells children that obedience and order are the priority here, whereas a "warm" room says, "Participate! Explore!" (Brewer, 2001). This is one reason that so many school districts have invested funds into their office areas—to make them seem more inviting to children and families when they first enter. Teachers also should tell children and their families that their classrooms are safe and welcoming spaces. When empty, classrooms are, by their design, cold institutional spaces. Teachers can create space that is inviting by using colors, textures, personal items, displays of children's work, other furniture besides desks (carpets, rockers, bean bag chairs), and so forth.

The National Association for the Education of Young Children (1991) lists the criteria devised by the National Academy of Early Childhood Programs for evaluating an appropriate physical environment for early childhood programs (reprinted with permission from Accreditation Criteria and Procedures of the National Academy of Early Childhood Programs by the National Association for the Education of Young Children, 1991, Washington, DC: National Association for the Education of Young Children):

Goal: The indoor and outdoor physical environment fosters optimal growth and development through opportunities for exploration and learning.

Rationale: The physical environment affects the behavior and development of the people, both children and adults, who live and work in it. The quality of the physical space and materials provided affects the level of involvement of the children and the quality of interaction between adults and children. The amount, arrangement, and use of space, both indoors and outdoors, are to be evaluated.

G-1. The indoor and outdoor environments are safe, clean, attractive, and

spacious. There is a minimum of 35 square feet of usable playroom floor space indoors per child and a minimum of 75 square feet of play space outdoors per child. Program staff have access to the designated space in sufficient time to prepare the environment before children arrive.

Limited indoor space may be offset by sheltered outdoor space where climate permits reliance on outdoor space for activities often conducted indoors. Limited outdoor space may be offset by a greater amount of indoor space (such as a gym) that permits an equivalent activity program. Space requirements are stated as minimums. More space than the minimum is preferred, although too much space can be a problem if not properly arranged. The key word is usable—space that is used for permanent storage should not be measured when assessing the amount of space. The required amount of outdoor space is indicated by the number of children using the space at one time. Use of outdoor space should be scheduled to allow for enough space and also to prevent competition among age groups. Very young children should have separate time or space outdoors. Observation of interactions between children and involvement of children in activity are good indicators of whether sufficient space is available. When space is shared with other programs or organizations, prior access for staff preparation is critical.

The environment should be attractive, colorful, and have children's work and other pictures displayed at children's eye level.

G-2. Activity areas are defined clearly by spatial arrangement. Space is arranged so that children can work individually, together in small groups, or in a large group. Space is arranged to provide clear pathways for children to move from one area to another and to minimize distractions.

The arrangement of space is as important as the amount. Children should be able to move freely from one activity to another without unduly disturbing others. Activity areas should be divided so that children in one area are not distracted by those in other areas. Well-organized space invites desired behaviors and facilitates positive interaction between people and active involvement with materials.

G-3. The space for toddlers and preschool children is arranged to facilitate a variety of small group and/or individual activities, including block building, sociodramatic play, art, music, science, math, manipulatives, and quiet book reading. Other activities such as sand/water play and woodworking also are available on occasion. Carpeted space as well as hard surfaces such as wood floors and ample crawling/toddling areas are provided for infants and nonwalkers. Sturdy furniture is provided so nonwalkers can pull themselves up or balance themselves while walking. School-age children are provided separate space arranged to facilitate a variety of age-appropriate activities and permit sustained work on projects.

This criterion refers to activities rather than areas of the room. For example, science and math are activities; they are not limited to parts of the room, although the room should be arranged so that they do occur. Block building, sociodramatic play, and book reading are facilitated by separate areas. Art and cooking projects that are messy should be near a source of water. School-age children must have a separate space.

G-4. Age-appropriate materials and equipment of sufficient quantity, vari-

ety, and durability are readily accessible to children and arranged on low, open shelves to promote independent use by children. Materials are rotated and adapted to maintain children's interest.

Materials and equipment are evaluated on several levels. A variety of equipment is needed as well as appropriate kinds. All age groups need active play equipment, materials that stimulate the senses, construction materials, manipulative toys, dramatic play equipment, art materials, and books and records. . . . Children are more likely to use materials constructively and creatively if materials are accessible to them, organized to promote independent use, and periodically changed to provide variety.

G-5. Individual spaces for children to hang their clothing and store their personal belongings are provided.

Personal storage space may be provided in a variety of ways, but children and adults should have individual spaces for storing personal belongings that are easily identified.

G-6. Private areas are available indoors and outdoors for children to have solitude.

Children who spend long periods of time in group settings need opportunities for privacy and solitude. Such provision can be made by environmental arrangement and planning, both indoors and outdoors. These areas should be easily supervised by adults. Privacy can be provided by using equipment such as tunnels and playhouses, or small enclosed spaces in room arrangements.

G-7. The environment includes soft elements such as rugs, cushions, or rocking chairs.

Softness can be provided in many ways— cozy furniture such as rockers and pillows; carpeting; grass outdoors; adults who cuddle

children on their laps; and soft materials such as play dough, water, sand, and finger paints.

G-8. Sound-absorbing materials are used to cut down on excessive noise.

Noise is to be expected and even desired in environments for children. The purpose of this criterion is not to eliminate noise. Acoustical building materials, strategically placed carpets, and other similar sound-absorbing materials can be very effective in minimizing excessive noise and enhancing the quality of the living environment for both children and adults. Excessive environmental noise can be fatiguing and cause stress.

G-9. The outdoor area includes a variety of surfaces, such as soil, sand, grass, hills, flat sections, and hard areas for wheel toys. The outdoor area includes shade; open space; digging space; and a variety of equipment for riding, climbing, balancing, and individual play. The outdoor area is protected by fences or natural barriers from access to streets or other dangers.

Outdoor areas will vary depending on geographic location. This criterion emphasizes that a variety of types of surface and equipment be provided. While hills and shade are not always available, the environment can sometimes be supplemented with other materials such as awnings, inclines, or ramps. The outdoor area must be fenced or protected by natural barriers from streets and other dangerous areas. The criterion implies that an outdoor play space must be provided or arranged, such as pre-arranged use of a neighboring community or school playground." (pp. 43–46)

Every teacher is limited by the physical dimensions of his or her room. However, teachers should never be limited by their imaginations on how to manipulate that space so that children want to be there.

SUMMARY

Teachers should be aware of environmental factors that affect children. Why? Because whatever is affecting them will have consequences for learning in the classroom. As the social ills of today increase, both in number and intensity, all children must deal with much more than did the generation before them. Far too many children must deal with the harsh realities of abandonment, broken families, abuse, and poverty. Others may be impacted by peer pressure, distorted perceptions, learning disabilities, or low self-esteem. Whatever impacts children will find its way into the classroom and more than likely into a teacher's heart. When it does, the teacher can fulfill the most important role in teaching—that of truly making a positive impact and lifelong difference in the life of a child. The following student plea should ring constantly in every teacher's ears: "Don't tell me how much you know until you show me how much you care."

GLOSSARY

bullying   behavior that may consist of hitting, threatening, teasing, taunting, spreading rumors, enforcing social isolation, and stealing. May have negative consequences for the general school climate.

classroom environment   a setting in which classroom members (i.e., teacher and students) reside for the purpose of learning; can be positive or negative.

conciliation   the process whereby one side of the conflict initiates a gesture of good faith in hopes that the other party will reciprocate with a similar gesture.

conciliatory gesture   a gesture of good faith that one party offers in hopes that it may be returned.

conflict   a natural by-product of human interactions.

conflict resolution   strategies and ways to resolve conflict.

culture   students' learned behaviors in their lives outside of school.

deficiency needs   basic needs, according to Maslow, that must be met prior to growth needs. Deficiency needs include physiological needs, safety needs, belonging and love needs, and esteem needs.

environmental factors   factors that exist inside or outside of the classroom and affect student learning.

growth needs   needs, according to Maslow, that can be answered only after deficiency needs have been met. Growth needs include intellectual achievement, aesthetic appreciation, and self-actualization.

individual security: security about oneself. Students may feel a lack of it when entering a new classroom.

life position   a sense of self, based on the sum of the person's previous experiences.

Maslow's hierarchy   the developmental stages that Maslow believed an individual experience.

needs   a requirement for the well-being of an individual.

perception   the way the world is seen through each individual's eyes.

self-actualization   the ability to realize one's own potential.

self-esteem   a sense of confidence and satisfaction with oneself.

stereotypes   preconceived notions of how individuals from certain groups think, feel, and act.

transactional analysis   a theory that all experiences in life, beginning in infancy, develop people's concept of self-worth as well as assist them in formulating a sense of the worth of others.

SUGGESTED ACTIVITIES

1. Observe a preschool classroom and then a fourth-grade classroom. Identify as many conflict contaminants as are evident. Reflect on how these contaminants could create unwanted conflict.

2. Interview several teachers to discover what they feel are the most common environmental factors that impact learning in the classroom.

3. Devise a checklist for a safe preschool and elementary classroom. Take it to an observation school and see how well the rooms match your list.

4. Practice your conflict management skills. Choose a conflict situation in which you are currently involved. Decide which type of con-

flict it is and which resolution strategy(ies) you will use. Implement the strategies and reflect on what you have learned.

5. Interview students from four differing cultures (ethnic, religious, economic, or with close ties to another country, for example). Find out how the students differ and how they are the same with regard to the way they view school, engage in communication, and deal with conflict.

6. Ask your mentor to help identify a student in the school who may have bullying tendencies. Shadow the student, if possible, and note his or her interactions with others. Also note the reactions of others carefully.

7. Ask your mentor to help identify a student who is new. Shadow the student, noting his or her behaviors carefully.

8. Interview your mentor to see if he or she has ever discovered a case of abuse, and, if so, what were the circumstances that led to the discovery.

9. Think about a new group you joined. How did you feel when you joined that group? Compare your feelings to those that students may have when joining a new classroom. What can you learn from the comparison that will make you a better teacher? What were the things that made you feel welcome or not welcome? Prepare a list of activites and materials with which to welcome a new student to your classroom.

10. Think about the classroom environment that most positively impacted you during your "student" years. List the characteristics of the classroom and the teacher that contributed to that positive impact. What can you learn from this that will help you as a classroom teacher?

11. Reflect on Maslow's hierarchy of needs. Think of one classroom example that applies to each of the four basic needs. Examples may be from your own classroom experience as a student or from observing classrooms as part of your pre-service teaching requirements.

PRACTICE QUESTIONS

1. Mr. Cogwell has early childhood students who are having difficulty getting along. He has witnessed several near altercations on the playground this week. He has also noted that the conflict is impacting other children by the way they are beginning to take sides. What should Mr. Cogwell do?

   A. Ignore the conflict because it will go away.

   B. Determine what course of action the conflicting students should take and tell them to do it or else.

   C. Decide on a conflict resolution measure such as one discussed in this chapter.

   D. Get the facts by talking to each conflicting child to determine the type and intensity of the conflict before determining the conflict resolution strategy to use.

2. Last week, a new student, Toby, was placed in Mrs. Estrada's early childhood classroom. The new child is extremely shy and seems to have difficulty in socializing with the other students. Mrs. Estrada knows that in order for this child to do well academically in her class, he must feel successful and accepted in the classroom group. Which of the following should Mrs. Estrada do?

   A. Realize that the way Toby is reacting to his peers and the classroom environment is impacted greatly by his perceptions. As a result, she should visit with Toby to find out what his perceptions are.

   B. Find out all she can about his past experiences in school and at home to determine whether these experiences are affecting his present behavior.

   C. Determine Toby's cultural background to determine whether his behavior is related to cultural differences.

   D. All of the above.

3. Which of the following statements is false?

   A. If you were continuously ridiculed as a child, you would likely see yourself in your school years as a person worthy of praise.

B. The students who enter your classroom will already have life positions established.

C. When students enter a new classroom or group of any kind, they are likely to experience anxiety.

D. Students often act out in disciplinary ways when they feel self-doubt.

4. Mrs. Brown has noticed that one of her fourth-grade students, Carlos, is becoming very withdrawn and unresponsive. He avoids any social contact with the other children in her class, and this has resulted in negative consequences for Carlos. The other students have begun to taunt him at times, and most refuse to work with him during group activities. Mrs. Brown does not want this situation to get out of control. What should she do?

A. Children often know what is going on long before teachers do. Mrs. Brown should ask the other students in her class to help her discover what is bothering Carlos before he becomes violent or completely unresponsive.

B. She should accept the fact that Carlos is from a cultural background that does not always encourage total acceptance of traditional values and priorities. Carlos will eventually come around if left alone.

C. Mrs. Brown should set the example by making Carlos feel accepted and valued in her classroom. She should let him know that he is a valued member of her class and that in her classroom, everyone can feel safe and protected.

D. She should have Carlos transferred to another class with students who have similar needs as his own.

Answers and Discussion

Answer 1: Choice *A* is not helpful, because this conflict is unlikely to go away. Choice *B* is unproductive for several reasons. First, without student input, Mr. Cogwell will not gain cooperation and the conflict will not end. Also, by resolving the conflict for the students, he robs them of the opportunity to grow, and he becomes responsible for the consequences that result from the solution. Choice *C*, deciding on a conflict resolution strategy, is not a bad idea, but it is not what you would do first. Answer *D* is the *first* action to be taken (fact finding) so that he can identify the type of conflict occurring and match it to the appropriate resolution strategy. The answer is *D*.

Answer 2: All of the answers are correct actions that Mrs. Estrada could take to begin to understand why her new student is having difficulties adjusting to her classroom. The answer is *D*.

Answer 3: If you were ridiculed continuously as a child, you would likely experience feelings of lack of self-worth as you got older. Statements *B, C,* and *D* are all correct and are discussed in this chapter. The answer is *A*.

Answer 4: The other children in the class are already reacting negatively to Carlos' behavior shift. If they are asked to "spy" upon him (*A*), Mrs. Brown will have reinforced their suspicions that he is truly an outcast and cannot be trusted at this time. It is true that culture can affect students' interactions in certain circumstances (*B*). However, Carlos demonstrated a *shift* in behavior from when he entered Mrs. Brown's classroom. Answer *B* also would show that the teacher is brushing off this shift in behavior as a stereotyping explanation rather trying to search for individual concerns. Transferring a student (*D*) who is experiencing difficulties in one teacher's classroom to another is simply another way of avoiding a problem. Teachers have a responsibility to all children in their charge. If they begin eliminating children from their classes just because they pose potential problems, they might soon find themselves without any students to teach! Carlos may be experiencing some emotional influences, either at home or at school, that are affecting the way he behaves in class. A teacher must establish an environment that is supportive, enjoyable, motivating, and full of learning, and must pursue ways to help. The answer is *C*.

WEB LINKS

Remember that Web site locations may change. If any of these sites have moved or cannot be located, use the key terms in this chapter to search for further information.

General Education Web Sites

www.education-world.com

This is a large education site with everything from information about lessons plans and curriculum to current issues facing teachers.

www.teachers.net

This site is called the ultimate teacher resource. Considering its size, it just may be!

www.earlychildhood.com

This is a vast resource of activities and curriculum ideas, sharing boards, craft ideas, and articles about issues in early childhood.

http://www.factsinaction.org

This Web site contains information for parents and teachers on the following subjects: Major Issues in Early Education; Making it Count: Measuring Program Outcomes; In Brief: Summaries of Recent Research; In the Classroom: Putting Research into Practice; and National Policy News: Federal Policy Updates.

http://teacher.scholastic.com

This Web site has separate sites for teachers, children, and parents. The teacher page has lesson plans and reproducible, professional resources; authors and books; online activities; news; research tools; and reading programs.

http://www.atozteacherstuff.com

This site provides more themes, lessons, tips, articles, a store, a discussion board, and links.

Conflict Resolution

www.stark.k12.oh.us/docs/units/conflict

This site provides an example of how to integrate the teaching of conflict resolution into various subject areas.

School Psychology

http://mail.bcpl.lib.md.us/~sandyste/school_psych.html

This site includes research on learning disabilities, ADHD, functional behavioral assessment, autism, adolescence, parenting, psychological assessment, special education, mental retardation, mental health, and more.

Societal Issues

www.nida.nih.gov/Prevention/Prevopen.html

This is a great research-based guide by the National Institute on Drug Abuse entitled "Preventing Drug Use Among Children and Adolescents."

www.schoolsecurity.org

Facts and questions about school safety and gangs are found here.

REFERENCES

Ahmad, Y., & Smith, P. K. (1994). Bullying in schools and the issue of sex differences. In J. Archer, (Ed.) *Male violence* (p. 123). London: Routledge.

Ainley, J. G. (1987). Equipment and materials. In M. J. Dunkin, (Eds.), *The international encyclopedia of teaching and teacher education.* New York: Pergamon.

Ball, S. (1989). Micro-politics versus management. Towards a sociology of school organization. In S. Walker & L. Barton, (Eds.). *Politics and the processes of schooling* (pp. 218–241). Philadelphia: Open University Press.

Banks, R. (March, 1997). *Bullying in schools.* Champaign, IL: University of Illinois at Urbana-Champaign Children's Research Center. EDO-PS-97-17.

Bennis, W. G., and Shepard, H. A. (1987). *A theory of group development.* In G. S. Gibbard, J. J. Hartman, & R. D. Mann, (Eds.) *Analysis of groups* (pp. 56–67). San Francisco: Jossey-Bass.

Berne, E. (1976). *Beyond games and scripts.* New York: Grove Press.

Biehler, R. F. (1978). *Psychology applied to teaching.* New York: Houghton Mifflin.

Brewer, J. A. (2001). *Introduction of early childhood education: Preschool through primary grades.* 4th ed. Boston: Allyn and Bacon.

Brophy, J. (1996). *Teaching problem students.* New York: Guilford.

Burgoon, J. K., Buller, D. B., & Woodall, W. G. (1989). *Nonverbal communication: The unspoken dialogue.* New York: Harper & Row.

Eibl-Eibesfeldt, I. (1972). Similarities and differences between cultures in expressive movements. In R. A. Hinde, (Eds.), *Nonverbal communication* (pp. 297–314). Cambridge, England: Cambridge University Press.

Filley, A. (1975). *Interpersonal conflict resolution.* Glenview, IL: Scott Foresman.

Fried, P., & Fried, S. (1996). *Bullies and victims: Helping your child through the schoolyard battlefield.* New York: M. Evans.

Garbarino, J. (1999). *Lost boys: Why our sons turn violent and how we can save them.* New York: The Free Press.

Gunter, P., Shores, R., Jack, S., Rasmussen, S., & Flowers, J. (1995). On the move: Using teacher/student proximity to improve students' behavior. *Teaching Exceptional Children, 28*(1), 12–14.

Harrison, A. A. (1976). *Individuals and groups.* Monterey, CA: Brooks/Cole.

Harvey, T. & Drolet, B. (1994). *Building teams, building people: Expanding the fifth resource.* Lancaster, PA: Technomic.

Holtgraves, T. (1991). Interpreting questions and replies: Effects of face-threat, question form, and gender. *Social Psychology Quarterly, 54*(1), 15–24.

Huse, E. (1975). *Organizational development and change.* New York: West.

Kelley, H. H. (1951). Communication in experimentally created hierarchies. *Human Relations, 4,* 39–56.

Kohn, A. (1993). *Punished by rewards.* Boston: Houghton Mifflin.

Locksley, A., Ortiz, V., & Hepburn, C. (1980). Social categorization and discriminatory behavior: Extinguishing the minimal intergroup discrimination effect. *Journal of Personality and Social Psychology, 39,* 773–783.

Maslow, A. (1954). *Motivation and personality.* New York: Harper and Row.

Meyer, D. G. (1987). *Social psychology.* New York: McGraw Hill.

Napier, R. W., & Gershenfeld, M. K. (1999). *Groups: Theory and experience.* New York: Houghton Mifflin Co.

National Association for the Education of Young Children. (1991). *Accreditation criteria and procedures of the National Academy of Early Childhood Programs.* (pp. 43–46). Washington, DC.

National School Safety Center. (1998). Checklist of characteristics of youth who have caused school-associated violent deaths. [online]. www.nssc1.org/reporter/checklist.htm.

National School Safety and Security Services. (2000). What do school officials and other interested individuals want to know about school security and gangs. [online]. www. schoolsecurity.org/faq/schools.html.

Olweus, D. (1993). *Bullying at school: What we know and what we can do.* Cambridge, MA: Blackwell.

Osgood, C. E. (1962). *An alternative to war or surrender.* Urbana: University of Illinois Press.

Osgood, C. E. (1980). *GRIT: A strategy for survival in mankind's nuclear age?* Paper presented at the Pugwash conference on New Directions in Disarmament, Racine, WI.

Payne, R. (1995). *Poverty: A framework for understanding and working with students and adults from poverty.* Baytown, TX: RFT Publishing.

Quattrone, G., & Jones, E. (1980). The perception of variability within in-groups and out-groups: Implications for the law of small numbers. *Journal of Personality and Social Psychology, 38,* 141–152.

Roberts, M. (1982). *Managing conflict from the inside out.* San Diego: Learning Concepts.

Slater, P. (1955). Role differentiation in small groups. *American Sociological Review, 20,* 300–310.

Smith, P. K., & Sharp, S. (1994). *School bullying: Insights and perspectives.* London: Routledge.

Spaulding, A., & O'Hair, M. J. (2000). Public relations in a communication context: Listening, nonverbal, and conflict-resolution skills. In T. J. Kowalski (Eds.), *Public relations in schools.* 2nd ed. (pp. 137–161). Prospect Heights, IL: Longman.

Turquet, P. M. (1978). Leadership: The individual and the group. In G. S. Gibbard, J. J. Hartman, & R. D. Mann, (Eds.), *Analysis of groups* (pp. 86–112). San Francisco: Jossey-Bass.

Woollams, S., & Brown, M. (1978). *Transactional analysis.* Dexter, MI: Huron Valley Institute Press.

Competency 6

The teacher understands the strategies for creating an organized and productive learning environment and for managing student behavior.

The beginning teacher:

- Analyzes the effects of classroom routines and procedures on student learning, and knows how to establish and implement routines and procedures to promote an organized and productive learning environment.

- Demonstrates an understanding of how young children function in groups and designs group activities that reflect a realistic understanding of the extent of young children's ability to collaborate with others.

- Recognizes the importance of creating a schedule for young children that balances restful and active movement activities and that provides large blocks of time for play, projects, and learning centers.

- Schedules activities and manages time in ways that maximize student learning, including using effective procedures to manage transitions; to manage materials, supplies, and technology; and to coordinate the performance of noninstructional duties (e.g., taking attendance) with instructional activities.

- Uses technological tools to perform administrative tasks such as taking attendance, main-taining grade books, and facilitating communication.

- Works with volunteers and paraprofessionals to enhance and enrich instruction and applies procedures for monitoring the performance of volunteers and paraprofessionals in the classroom.

- Applies theories and techniques related to managing and monitoring student behavior.

- Demonstrates awareness of appropriate behavior standards and expectations for students at various developmental levels.

- Applies effective procedures for managing student behavior and for promoting appropriate behavior and ethical work habits (e.g., academic integrity) in the classroom (e.g., communicating high and realistic behavior expectations, involving students in developing rules and procedures, establishing clear consequences for inappropriate behavior, enforcing behavior standards consistently, encouraging students to monitor their own behavior and to use conflict resolution skills, responding appropriately to various types of behavior).

Chapter 9

Managing Classroom Routines

DIANE MULLINS CLAY

University of St. Thomas—Houston

TERMS TO KNOW

Cambourne's conditions of
   learning

Compensatory education
   programs

Flexible groups

Glasser's basic needs

Grand conversations

Independent learners

Nurturing environment

Paraprofessionals

Routines

Sponge activity

Tactile and kinesthetic learners

Transition

The State Board for Teacher Certification (SBEC) has identified pedagogy and professional responsibility standards for teachers of early childhood through fourth grade. They have also described specific knowledge and skills teachers should possess to create effective classroom management procedures ensuring that student learning occurs. Beginning teachers should know and understand how classroom routines and procedures affect student learning and achievement, how young children function in groups, and how to organize student groups to facilitate cooperation and productivity. They must also understand the importance of time management for effective classroom functioning, procedures for managing transitions from one activity or lesson to another, and routines and procedures for managing and using materials, supplies, and technology. Noninstructional duties and procedures for performing these duties effectively should also be a part of their knowledge, as should understanding the classroom roles of paraprofessionals, volunteers, and other professionals (including substitute teachers) in accordance with district policies and procedures. This chapter provides suggestions for the implementation of these concepts.

CLASSROOM ROUTINES AND PROCEDURES

Even the most knowledgeable teachers will find their teaching efforts futile if they have not first established effective routines and procedures for the classroom. Successful learning depends on the development of an environment in which children easily **transition** (or move from one activity to another), understand routines, and know their responsibilities and the teacher's expectations in the classroom and on the school grounds. Effec-

tive classroom management is multifaceted. It encompasses much more than creating a schedule and keeping children on task. Teachers of young children must also ensure that students work in a classroom environment that nurtures and ensures successful learning experiences. This requires classrooms that are communities of self-disciplined learners who take responsibility for their learning, celebrate each other's achievements, and expect that learning will occur for all members. Achieving a successful and nurturing learning community requires that teachers make these areas their first priority in the school year. After this supportive environment is established, an effective learning routine becomes possible.

The importance of establishing effective classroom routines and procedures cannot be overemphasized. Learning does not occur in a chaotic and disorganized classroom. Cummings cites 1994 research by Wang, Haertel, and Walberg suggesting that "classroom management has the greatest effect on student learning, as compared with other factors including cognitive process, home environment and parental support, school culture, curriculum design, and school demographics" (2000, p. 1). Although establishing effective classroom management necessitates more than creating and implementing schedules and routines, these elements are an important consideration as teachers think about a holistic management plan. Although they must teach children the necessary behaviors to follow routines and procedures, they must also focus on establishing an accepting and nurturing environment (Cummings, 2000).

Teachers attempting to enforce rules of behavior on students without first creating an accepting and **nurturing environment** (a classroom where children's emotional, social, and psychological needs are met, as well as their intellectual needs), soon realize how frustrating and difficult that decision can be. Understanding children's developmental needs is a large part of creating a nurturing learning environment. Before planning schedules and routines, teachers must understand children's needs as they grow and learn. For example, younger children need frequent periods of rest. With their short attention spans, they also find it both physically and mentally difficult to sit or be still for long stretches of time and need varied periods of activity within sequences of scheduled times. Structure, for young children, is important. Any mother can tell new teachers that children who are off their schedules or routines can create chaos in the home. A structured routine provides a sense of security for young children. Teachers are wise to establish a schedule and follow it as carefully as possible. Of course, they cannot control school schedules that often vary with assemblies and other interruptions and must be flexible in going with the flow in that respect. However, the younger the child, the more structure is needed.

Glasser (1986) emphasizes the importance, for both teachers and children, of finding the environment, routines, and classroom activities satisfying. He theorizes that children will work if they find school satisfying. For this to occur, teachers must be aware of students' needs so that they can create a nurturing learning environment and provide effective instruction. Human beings are born with five **basic needs** built into their genetic structure, according to Glasser (1992), and if what children are asked to do in schools does not satisfy one or more of these needs (or if children do not care for the teacher), they will do the work poorly or not at all. Children will also seek to satisfy these needs in *any* way possible, including disrupting the class. These five needs are survival, love, power, fun, and freedom. These are examined more closely below:

- **Survival.** Survival for EC–4 students means comprehending what is expected of them in the classroom and having the understanding, ability, and resources to fulfill those expectations. Smith (1985) writes that even young

children form "theories of the world" (p. 73) to make sense of their world and learn from it. Their "theories of the world" form the basis of all of their perceptions and understandings, including experiences they are likely to encounter with both written and spoken language. The effectiveness of our theories of the world is illustrated by Smith's assertion that very young children seldom appear confused by experiences in their environment. He suggests that "the first time many children run into a situation they cannot possibly relate to anything they know already… is when they arrive at school" (p. 75). However, teachers of EC–4 students can create warm environments that meet their children's need for survival by ensuring that expectations are developmentally appropriate (see Competency 1, Chapter 1) and by providing successful experiences daily for each child.

- **Love.** All human beings respond to love and nurturing. EC–4 children flourish when teachers make them feel lovable and capable. Part of creating a nurturing environment includes affirming all children and celebrating their successes and contributions to the classroom community. Each child should feel that the classroom is his or hers as well as the teacher's. Remember, too, that children may try to seek love and attention in other than appropriate ways. By providing a nurturing environment and redirecting inappropriate behavior, teachers increase the likelihood that children's needs will be met.

- **Power.** One of the goals of all teaching should be the development of **independent learners** (children who can initiate their own projects and topics of study without the teacher's direct and constant supervision). Children should come to see themselves as empowered to learn and take responsibility for their actions. Even the youngest learners can assume age-appropriate responsibilities and make choices for their learning and behavior in the classroom. When children are stifled by oppressive management that allows no choice or input, they either become passively resigned to the situation or aggressively rebellious to gain some power for themselves. Too often teachers become embroiled in power struggles with children unconsciously. They begin to withdraw privileges from children who act out for fear that these children can't be trusted to handle any responsibility. The more the teacher takes away, the more the child seeks some way of gaining power. Using positive reinforcement methods and giving power seekers opportunities to take power in the classroom as leaders can help move these children in positive directions. Cowley (1994) writes, "When we give children authority we don't get chaos, we get art. We get children alive to education" (p. 54). Including children in the process of management and establishment of rules gives them ownership and power.

- **Fun.** Ben and Jerry, the ice cream entrepreneurs, printed a bumper sticker that should appear in all classrooms. It reads, "If it's not fun, why do it?" This philosophy is diametrically opposed to the old-fashioned idea that "School is not supposed to be fun. It's for learning!" When young children get excited about learning and teachers realize that learning is a social process, classrooms become dynamic, exciting places. If not, students will often create their own entertainment (often at the teacher's expense).

- **Freedom.** Children need the freedom to make some choices regarding their learning. Of course, teachers are always in charge of the classroom and curriculum planning, but even very young children can be given the freedom to make choices each day. All children can choose books for silent reading, topics for drawing or writing in journals, and learning centers to visit. Older students can suggest topics for thematic study, work with other students to construct representations of their learning, choose pieces to include in

their portfolios, and participate in **grand conversations** (student-initiated and student-led discussions about a book read by a group of children) after reading self-selected books. Allowing children the freedom to choose some of their learning activities increases motivation and enthusiasm and encourages active learning.

Learning is affected by the emotional climate of the classroom and the extent to which activities and routines support young learners. Tompkins and McGee (1993) suggest that learning is increased if **Cambourne's seven conditions of learning** exist. They are immersion, demonstration, expectations, responsibility, employment, approximation, and engagement. Following is a discussion of each.

- **Immersion.** Children are surrounded with or immersed in a variety of developmentally appropriate and stimulating learning materials.

- **Demonstration.** Teachers clearly model and explain behaviors and procedures expected of students.

- **Expectations.** Students, parents, and teachers believe that successful learning experiences and appropriate behavior will occur. Students are supported and encouraged by these positive expectations.

- **Responsibility.** The ultimate responsibility of learning falls on the learner. Moffett and Wagner (1992) stress the importance of student ownership in the learning environment when they say, "As soon as others want the results of learning more than the learner, the game is over" (p. 22). In the same way, children should understand that a well-managed classroom has more to offer them, and that the responsibility for maintaining the order and organization of the classroom belongs to everyone.

- **Employment.** Students must have time to participate in effective learning activities. The importance of time on task is well known. Teaching children effective routines and procedures increases the amount of time available for teachers and students to spend on learning.

- **Approximation.** Learning increases when teachers create risk-free environments and encourage risk-taking and experimentation rather than expecting perfection and exactness from young learners.

- **Engagement.** Children are encouraged to be active learners who are highly involved in learning decisions and activities rather than students who passively complete teacher-directed assignments. It is almost impossible for students who do not have a vested interest in the learning or who are not engaged with the materials to learn.

Understanding children's basic needs and the conditions that enhance learning enables teachers to create effective and nurturing classrooms. Hayes and Creange (2001) maintain that "establishing consistent and predictable classroom routines is the best way to make children feel confident and secure. **Routines** (constant procedures that occur in the classroom over and over again in the course of a day or during the week) are a child's and a teacher's best friend" (p. 17). Examples of typical classroom routines include taking attendance; determining the lunch count; getting ready to go the lunchroom; going to the restroom; leaving the classroom for ancillary subjects such as art, music, or library; taking up or returning work; making the transition from one subject to another; and getting ready to go home at the end of the day.

Children welcome the predictability and security of consistent routines and procedures. Knowing what the teacher expects and how to fulfill those expectations gives children the power, survival (safety and security), and freedom noted in Glasser's (1992) list of basic human needs. After routines and procedures are established, teachers can devote more class time to instructional activities and less to repeating directions for daily activities.

Teachers can most effectively teach students routines and procedures by first carefully thinking through how a routine will work in their classroom with its particular design (for example, where students should place work, where and how supplies should be obtained, etc.). Teachers should walk through these routines before the children arrive in order to locate trouble spots. Next they should model the routines to be established and have children practice the desired behaviors. Teachers should continue to model the desired behaviors and routines and have children practice routines until all children understand their expectations. Most importantly, teachers should allow enough time for all children to learn the expected routines. Many teachers of young children fail to realize how much time is needed at the beginning of the year to teach procedures and routines. Veteran teachers know that little else occurs during the first 2 weeks of school, especially in the younger grades. Yet this is time well spent, for it facilitates learning for the remainder of the year.

Mrs. Garcia wanted to establish a routine for taking the lunch count each day. She showed children laminated apple shapes, each with a picture of a child along with his or her name. A pocket chart had one of the following pictures on each row: a lunch box and a sack, a milk carton, an ice cream cup, and a lunch tray. Mrs. Garcia explained the importance of giving the cafeteria a correct count each day and told the children that they could help her with this very important task. "Every morning when you come in, stop at the pocket chart, find the apple with your picture on it, and place it on the correct line." She reinforced the routine in several ways. First she took her apple and demonstrated where it would go if she wanted a plate lunch or just wanted to buy milk. After going through all of the choices with her apple, she invited the children to come one at a time and place their apple on a designated line. To reinforce the routine, she redistributed the pictures and asked her children to decide what particular children were ordering, according the their pictures on the pocket chart. Knowing that the children would need a reminder for a while, she greeted each one the next morning with "What are you having for lunch today?" Until the routine became established, she used a few minutes of early morning circle time to bring the children's attention to the chart and discuss what each child was getting for lunch. Children who had forgotten to place their apple could do it at this time. It also provided a check for each child to make sure that he or she had placed his or her apple by the correct picture.

Throughout the year, teachers should continue to remind children about expectations. ("*Quietly*, wait at your desk until . . .""On our way to lunch, I *expect to see* boys and girls following the rule about . . ." "*Raise your hand* if you can tell me . . ."). By saying the rule first, teachers remind children before the action. If children do not remember, teachers should remind them in a kindly way and wait for the expected behavior. Teachers should avoid becoming frustrated when having to repeat instructions or having children practice the desired behavior again. Young children need much reminding delivered in a kind and loving, but structured manner.

Organizing Groups

Creating a caring, supportive environment requires that teachers understand how young children function in groups and how to organize student groups to facilitate cooperation and productivity. Working with children in groups or allowing them to play and work in independent group activities increases social interaction among children and lessens incidences of isolation they might experience. Observing children as they work in groups affords teachers opportunities to observe closely, assess, and make instructional decisions about students.

Children cannot work together in groups until the class as a whole has jelled into a supportive community, where all learners understand what is expected of them and feel invited to participate in learning. Harwayne (1992) maintains that even brilliant lessons have no value unless

children value learning, each other, and the learning community. As is the case with all activities, routines, and procedures, children have to be taught how to work effectively in groups (see Competency 3, Part 2, Chapter 4 for cooperative learning models).

"It had been estimated," according to Elkind (2001) "that some 85% of children have been in out-of-home placements before entering kindergarten" (p. 66). Imagine the myriad of experiences that one classroom of children may have already had in working with others. This points out how important is is for teachers to know exactly what they expect of children and to teach them explicitly how they are to work together.

Because teachers can organize groups in many ways, they should consider what works best for them and their children. Some teachers organize participation in learning centers by assigning children to work together in specific centers on a rotation cycle. Sometimes children are required to visit all or a specified number of centers. Other teachers allow children to choose any center that has fewer than the designated maximum number of participants. Other classrooms are organized so that children may always work in the center or centers of their choosing. Whatever the preference, exact plans and procedures for sharing materials and working in centers should be clear to children through modeling and practice.

Teachers also have a range of grouping options available when planning instruction. Groups can be organized around the following criteria:

■ **Instructional need.** When attempting to meet children's individual learning needs, teachers group children according to specific skills or strategies that need teaching or reteaching. For example, a group of kindergarten students may need to practice identifying beginning consonants. More advanced children may be grouped to work on fix-up strategies for identifying vocabulary in context. These **flexible groups** (students grouped for a *short* period to learn or practice a specific skill or strategy) change as different skills are addressed so that children do not become bored with material they already know or frustrated with material that is too difficult.

■ **Interest.** Students who identify similar interests may work together to gather information and learn more about the topic. These are also flexible groups and change as students become interested in pursuing other topics.

■ **Ability.** Students can be grouped according to their ability. Teachers of young children often group them by ability for reading and math. Advocates of ability grouping point out that it allows teachers to target more specific skills for each group, and children's needs can be met more easily. However, many experts have found that when grouping by ability, the groups become inflexible and do not change throughout the year. This inflexibility is detrimental to children's progress. Tompkins & McGee (1993) assert that students who are placed in low-ability groups "receive different kinds of instruction than students in high-ability groups, stay in low groups throughout their school lives, and are at much greater risk for failing and dropping out of school" (p. 332). In fact, in *Becoming a Nation of Readers,* Anderson et al. (1985) state that nothing determines a child's future success in school more that the reading group into which he is placed in first grade. It behooves all educators always to consider what is best for children *now and in the long run* when making grouping decisions.

■ **Mixed ability.** Many times grouping children of different abilities is appropriate and effective. Children working on cooperative learning assignments should have different levels of ability and achievement. Often students who do not excel academically make invaluable contributions to group projects through practical, logical, or creative thinking. Children come to see that they can all learn from each other and that everyone can make worthwhile contributions to the group's work enhancing self-worth. Also by pairing students of mixed ability, learners on a higher level have the opportunity to learn more by teaching or tutoring someone else while lower achievers benefit from extra practice and peer modeling.

EFFECTIVE SCHEDULING

Teachers cannot expect successful learning and self-discipline by students to occur unless careful thought has gone into creating a schedule that ensures effective time management of the school day. Having a schedule allows teachers to plan activities effectively and efficiently. Children welcome the order that a consistent schedule gives to the school routine. Several factors must be considered when creating schedules.

■ Glasser is not the only advocate of the importance of fun in the learning environment. Effective teachers understand that periods of play and opportunities to work on projects or in learning centers contribute to children's learning. The teacher's challenge is to balance periods of play with restful times so that children do not become too tired or too fidgety from long periods of stillness. In its *Standards for Quality Programs for Young Children,* the National Association of Elementary School Principals (1990) asserts that play should be respected as an appropriate way of learning.

■ Experienced teachers know and common sense should tell us that hungry children do not learn as well as those whose nutritional needs are being met. Most schools provide breakfast (as well as lunch) for children whose families qualify. The connection between nutrition and learning is so great that all programs for young children should offer nutritious snacks (Rothlein, 1991). Not only are the children's physical needs met, but they also develop healthy habits.

- The needs and abilities of students should determine the timing and length of the activities in which students will participate. Younger children have shorter attention spans than older ones and therefore need opportunities to change activities more frequently (see Competency 8, Part 1, Chapter 12). A reading lesson for first graders may last 50 minutes and include six activities—listening to the teacher read a story, participating in group discussion that compares the story to a previous one, creating a Venn diagram comparing the main characters, reading a readers theater script for one of the stories, rereading the class newsletter, and looking for words with short *a* vowel sounds in the newsletter—while a group of fourth graders may spend a 50-minute class writing in their literature journals and participating in grand conversations**.** Both lessons lasted 50 minutes. The older students changed activities once during that period and each activity lasted approximately 25 minutes. The first graders changed activities five times, and none of them lasted longer than 10 minutes. Younger children need to switch activities more often than older ones in order to maintain interest, attention, and enthusiasm.

- Children need a balance between restful and active movement activities. Teachers should alternate these activities so that children do not become tired or lethargic. Active movement activities are suited to times during the day when children have the most energy. Restful activities work well when students are quieter or demonstrate that they are ready to settle down a bit. Movement within the lessons should vary for **tactile** and **kinesthetic learners** (students who learn best by handling or manipulating materials and moving about during a lesson). Effective teachers observe their children closely, monitor learners' needs carefully, and know when it is time to take a break. If children are particularly lethargic, teachers can move the class into some exercises while listening to upbeat children's music. When children are too active, they can put their heads down and listen to some restful music or to a soothing story.

- Teaches should take special classes into consideration when planning the schedule. These special classes normally consist of library, art, music, resource, and **compensatory education programs** (programs that provide supplementary services for academic assistance and are designed to meet the needs of at-risk students). Classroom teachers must cooperate with other professionals and programs when planning a consistant and effective schedule for their classroom.

- Flexibility is crucial. Unplanned moments come into every teacher's well-planned schedule. Lessons sometimes take much longer than planned or end much sooner than expected. If children are enthralled with a lesson or activity, a teacher need not abruptly stop if he or she can extend it without interfering with other teachers' schedules. Likewise, a teacher should be prepared with short activities or quick games that children enjoy when they are needed to fill time before the next activity is scheduled. Elementary teachers often need to fill small pockets of time when an assembly does not begin as scheduled, a bus is late, the cafeteria is backed up, and so forth. Short activities can utilize brief periods of time for learning and practicing critical thinking skills. They also ensure that children remain attentive and help prevent management difficulties.

MANAGING TRANSITIONS

Effective teachers understand that time lost during the day results in learning lost for their students. They maximize time spent on teaching and learning while minimizing time spent on transitions and routine procedures (activities that occur daily in the classroom but are not of an instructional nature). Think about how much time is lost during each week if a teacher loses 5 minutes a day at the beginning and the end of five subjects. He or she will have lost almost an hour of instructional time each day—more than 4 hours by the end of the week. Imagine how that will add up over the course of a school year.

Efficient teachers do not assume that young children understand how to move quickly from one activity to another transition or the efficacy of following daily routines. Teachers must first identify for themselves the particular procedures and routines that they want children to implement and then model and explain them to the children. Then children must be allowed to practice the procedures and routines until it is evident that they understand what is expected. Jones and Jones (2001) state that not only does this practice offer safety and comfort to students, but it also helps children learn how to monitor transitions for themselves, thus encouraging the development of independent learners. The following suggestions should provide practical advice for beginning teachers.

- Post a daily schedule in the classroom, even if the children cannot yet read. Teachers can make children aware of the order of the day's tasks by referring to the schedule each morning and again in the afternoon. The children will soon remember that one activity follows another each day. The schedule also provides a sense of order and predictability for the learners.

- Create a routine for beginning the day so that children know what to do each morning. Decide where children will store backpacks and lunches. If teachers want papers returned first thing in the morning, they should have well-marked boxes or trays available for students. If children are aware that the same activity will occur every day (for example, a **sponge activity** that is always waiting on the board in the morning), learners can begin to

settle down and work independently as soon as they arrive and put their things away. As mentioned this allows teachers a few moments to attend to the lunch count and other early morning responsibilities before beginning the first lesson of the day.

- Some activities might occur several times a day. These include lining up, turning in completed work, going to the restroom or water fountain, moving to centers, and moving from center to center. Teach children how to perform these tasks quietly and efficiently so that learning is not disrupted or learning time wasted.

- Determine a signal that lets the children know that their undivided attention is needed. Some teachers raise their hand and wait for the children to raise their hands as they become aware of the signal. Others say a phrase for children to repeat or follow, such as, "Clap three times if you hear my voice." The important point to remember is that teachers should never give instructions or begin transitioning from one activity to another until they have every child's attention. It is futile to expect children to follow directions that they have not heard or do not understand.

- Ensure that all instructions and directions are clearly understood by children before insisting that they be carried out. Asking children to repeat instructions is a good way to check for understanding. For young children, this might involve giving very simple and specific instructions rather than complex ones. Putting directions and page numbers on the board (or, for children who do not read yet, felt pictures of glue, scissors, etc. in order on a felt board) helps clarity in directions.

- Arrange furniture, centers, and materials so that they are accessible to students and contribute to efficient working and moving within the classroom. The room arrangement should facilitate transitions and ease of movement. It should also facilitate the teacher's movement to all children for both monitoring instruction and behavior. The teacher's proximity also increases the likelihood that children will stay on task and ensures that the teacher will be able to answer questions, clarify instructions when needed, catch children's mistakes before much repetition is practiced, and redirect children's attention. All of these actions contribute to the quality of learning in the classroom.

- Always have instructional materials ready for children. Teachers should gather everything they will need the day before or early in the morning before children arrive. Have board work or overheads already up when children come in each day, rather than using those first minutes of the day to write on the board. Have any computer presentations booted up, tapes cued to the correct place, or other technology set for beginning a lesson. This kind of preparedness increases the amount of instruction time and decreases children's opportunities to become bored or restless. It also leaves the teacher free to observe and assist students who need additional help or monitoring.

- All children enjoy being noticed and praised for their accomplishments. Teachers should be sure to notice students who follow routines and should praise them for helping their learning day go well. Not only is the teacher rewarding their behavior, but also others are learning vicariously. The teacher is also reinforcing the concept that children are ultimately responsible for their own learning.

- Get to know the effective teachers in the school. Notice their routines and procedures for beginning the day and making transitions. Ask other teachers for suggestions. Most teachers are delighted to help a beginning teacher. Make use of the wealth of knowledge and experience available to you.

MANAGING AND USING MATERIALS, SUPPLIES, AND TECHNOLOGY

Organization and order are hallmarks of well-managed classrooms. "A place for everything and everything in its place" may sound trite, but it is excellent advice for setting up a classroom. Management difficulties often occur when a teacher or students are distracted by trying to locate supplies. This is another area in which the teacher can benefit from the advice of experienced teachers. Observe the way other teachers organize their classrooms. Look for professional magazine articles that offer hints on organization. Again, teaching children routines and procedures for managing and using materials and supplies requires modeling on the teacher's part and practice on the children's part. The following suggestions should help with this very important task.

- Decide which materials will be stored in cabinets or on shelves (to be passed out to students as needed), and which supplies children will keep in their desks.

- When children sit at tables in small groups, much time is saved each day by placing baskets stocked with pencils, crayons, scissors, and glue in the center of the tables. Children then do not have to search through desks every time they need one of these supplies. If a teacher does not wish to have baskets on the tables all day, he or she can stack them nearby. The teacher can easily put them on group tables and pick them up at the end of an activity.

- Have clearly identified places for all supplies and materials. Label storage areas in case children forget.

- Provide easily accessible, labeled trays for papers returned from home, homework assignments, class work students have to turn in, and any other papers that children will handle on a regular basis. At the beginning of the year, teachers may have to remind children often where they should put their papers. However, the students will begin to learn where to put papers and assignments. Soon time spent teaching children where to put things can be used for instructional activities.

- Set aside one time during the day for sharpening pencils. Keep a jar of sharpened pencils on your desk just in case students need one. It takes much less time to exchange pencils with a student than it does to stop instruction while one or more students go to the pencil sharpener. Any veteran teacher can testify that one child needing to go to the pencil sharpener quickly sets off a chain reaction of dull pencils needing attention.

- A similar way to facilitate getting lessons started quickly and optimize learning time is to have all materials children need for activities close at hand. Keep extra paper and supplies for students who do not bring them to school or who run out. Delaying the beginning of a lesson because one or two children need supplies disrupts the learning for everyone in the classroom. If the teacher has prepared a folder of "Reminder Notes," the teacher or the child can quickly fill in the name of the school supply needed the child can take home that day.

- Remember that some young children may have little experience using and caring for the many kinds of materials found in most classrooms. They may never have seen or used many of the items available to them there. Do not assume that young students will know how they are expected to use or care for supplies and materials. Model the correct procedures for using and caring for classroom materials. Teachers must establish clear rules and remind children of those rules each time materials or equipment are used. Allow children to discuss the importance of caring for items in the classroom and the consequences of not caring for them properly. Set consequences for the

misuse of materials and supplies, and be consistent in enforcing them when children fail to follow the rules. When children understand that the misuse of materials will result in their not being able to use them, they will comply with the rules. Young children may learn from dictating a story about using and caring for classroom materials and supplies. They can illustrate the pages and bind them into a book that can be read and discussed as needed. Older children may do math problems to understand the cost involved in not properly caring for and using materials and supplies.

- Young children often have egocentric behavior (see Competency 1, Chapter 1). Working together in groups may prove difficult for them, yet learning to work and play together must be part of the EC curriculum. Teachers who encourage children to work together must make certain that children begin to understand how to share and why it is important. This matter can be discussed at group time. Children will also enjoy listening to books about sharing. They can role-play sharing situations and dictate or write stories about the importance of sharing and the consequences when children forget to share. As with all desired behaviors and skills, learning to work in groups takes time and practice.

- The routines and procedures for using and sharing materials and resources in the classroom—modeling, guided practice, discussions about proper use, creating classroom "how-to" books—also apply to the use of technology. However, teachers may need to teach small groups or even pairs how to select and operate programs rather than relying on whole-group instruction. Even young children can tutor a classmate after they become proficient on the computer. Allow children to share their expertise. It is crucial to monitor children's behavior and use of technology—particularly if no screening devices are set up for Internet use (see Competency 9, Chapter 14).

These are just a few of the routine procedures repeated daily in EC–4 classrooms. Each teacher should analyze the day-to-day routines that contribute to learning if carried out efficiently, plan for all anticipated procedures, and quickly adapt routines when the unanticipated occurs. And it will!

NONINSTRUCTIONAL DUTIES

Beginning teachers are often surprised at the amount of time consumed daily by noninstructional yet highly essential activities. Creating effective routines for important but noninstructional duties allows more time for teacher-student interaction and instruction. The following suggestions should help the beginning teacher.

- One of the first tasks of the day is usually determining the lunch count. Decide on a way for children to specify their lunch plans quickly as they come into the room.

  This can also help the teacher with attendance, as he or she can quickly glance at the chart to see who is not there. Children should then know to either go to a center, begin a sponge activity, or begin another routine established by the teacher.

- List *all* of the times during the day that children move on a regular basis (circle time, reading groups, going and returning from lunch, breaks, center time, share time, recess, library, and so forth). Decide how each will occur and try to visualize problems that could happen in the process.

- Another important task teachers face every day is making certain that children get home in the correct manner. Teachers must know exactly how each child is getting home every day. The younger the child, the more important this task becomes. The end of the day is often hectic, and children can

easily be misdirected. Because the school is responsible for children until they arrive home, classroom teachers must have effective procedures in place for getting each child home safely. Consider creating a grid on a bulletin board that has a row for every option for getting home: walkers, day-care pickup, parent pickup, bus riders, and so forth. Have children place their photographs on the row that identifies how they will get home. If a parent sends a note explaining a change in the regular routine, attach the note to the picture of the child so that it can be easily found at the end of the day.

- Communicating with parents and keeping them informed about their child's progress is crucial and definitely worth the time and effort needed. In fact, most schools require that teachers document communication between school and home. Many schools have a specific day to send home folders containing graded work for the week. Teachers should consider keeping a chart inside the folder in which they record all grades in each subject for that grading period, including a section for teacher-parent communication. This routinely gives the teacher the opportunity to keep parents informed about their child's progress, and affords parents the chance to ask questions or request a conference.

THE ROLES OF PARAPROFESSIONALS, VOLUNTEERS, AND OTHER PROFESSIONALS

Policies and procedures vary from district to district and from school to school regarding the roles of **paraprofessionals** (trained assistants who perform duties at the direction of a teacher or administrator) and volunteers in the classroom. A new teacher may be paired with an experienced paraprofessional who can provide a great deal of information about the school's policies and procedures.

Children benefit from the smaller adult-to-students ratios that exist when other adults help in the classroom. Some of the tasks and activities that others can perform include preparing materials for teaching activities, working on specific skills with small groups of children, tutoring, reading with individual children, typing the weekly newsletter, supervising centers, and putting papers in take-home folders. Although having other adults help in the classroom is beneficial for both the teacher and children, it requires that the teacher determine exactly what is needed for the paraprofessional or volunteers to do—and that the teacher monitor their interactions with children. Communication is key to a positive relationship with another adult in the classroom. Feedback is also essential for an aide to understand his or her responsibilities, and praise lets a paraprofessional know that his or her efforts are appreciated. A paraprofessional may be assigned to a classroom or a specific child from another school area (special education, for example). If that is the case, the paraprofessional may have responsibilities assigned that will not allow him or her to take on extra classroom duties from the classroom teacher. Teachers should always remember that even when volunteers and paraprofessionals work in the classroom, the teacher of record is ultimately responsible for the children's learning and the work planned for them.

Other professionals such as special education or compensatory teachers, counselors, and diagnosticians may observe in the classroom or assist in some way. The principal and assistant principal often come into the classroom for many reasons—particularly to help with teacher assessment. Their feedback is invaluable in the first few years of teaching. The teacher should become familiar with the help and services he or she can expect and should take advantage of the resources available in the school.

All children appreciate the stability and predictability of a well-organized classroom. Often a teacher's absence results in a day of learning lost for children. Ensuring that the classroom runs well when the teacher has to be absent requires that he or she plan ahead. Experienced substitute teachers can often read lesson plans for the week and continue with the activities planned for the students. However, this is not always the case. Teachers must take the time to prepare a folder that can be set aside for emergencies, with work for at least an entire day. They should choose activities for each subject that can be understood easily by a substitute and with which the students are familiar. They should also include the daily schedule, attendance sheet, seating chart, special routines for individual students, directions for finding needed materials and equipment, and any other information that contributes to a well-run day. Teachers might want to leave the name or names of children who would be good helpers for the substitute and the names of nearby teachers who can be called upon for help. Teachers who suspect they are becoming ill or know they will be gone should prepare their lessons for the days they believe they may be out. The short-form lesson plans in small boxes in planning books are often not enough to allow a substitute to provide a good learning day. The more a teacher can lay out for a substitute, the more learning will occur while the teacher is away.

SUMMARY

Learning is maximized when teachers establish routines and procedures that enable students to make effective transitions from one activity to another. Creating such a classroom is a multifaceted endeavor. It includes: (a) creating a nurturing and caring learning environment; (b) making decisions about storing, using, and distributing materials and supplies; (c) effective use of time management that increases time on task; (d) implementation of noninstructional duties; (e) grouping children for instruction and cooperative groups; and (f) effectively organizing for volunteers, paraprofessionals, and substitute teachers. Although many of these activities appear to be noninstructional, effective teaching and learning cannot occur until they have been introduced, modeled by the teacher, practiced by students, and have become an integral part of the classroom routine.

GLOSSARY

Cambourne's conditions of learning   if the following seven conditions are met, learning increases: immersion, demonstration, expectations, responsibility, employment, approximation, and engagement.

compensatory education programs   programs designed to meet the needs of at-risk students that provide supplementary services for academic assistance. Additional funding, normally from the federal level, is provided for these programs.

flexible groups   students grouped for a short period to learn or practice a specific skill or strategy.

Glasser's basic needs   if the following five needs are satisfied, children will most likely learn: survival, love, power, fun, and freedom.

grand conversations   student-initiated and student-led discussions about a book read by the children.

independent learners   active learners who can initiate their own projects and topics of study. They can work alone or with a group, without the teacher's direct and constant supervision.

nurturing environment   a classroom where children's emotional, social, and psychological needs are met as well as their intellectual needs.

paraprofessionals   trained assistants who perform duties at the direction of a teacher or administrator.

routines   activities that occur in the same manner daily in the classroom but are not of an instructional nature such as taking up papers and lining up.

sponge activity   a short activity used to immerse children in independent work while the teacher takes care of classroom business such as attendance, lunch count, and so forth.

tactile/kinesthetic learners   students who learn best by handling or manipulating materials or moving about during a lesson.

transition   to move from one activity to another.

SUGGESTED ACTIVITIES

1. Visit at least two classrooms. Observe the environment and interactions among children and between the teacher and the children. Make note of the presence or absence of the following:

   - Evidence of a schedule posted in the classroom
   - Children's awareness of and ability to complete routines and procedures
   - The ease with which transition from one activity to another occurs
   - The degree to which children appear to be responsible and self-directed learners
   - Factors suggesting that children are invited to learn

2. Create an ABC book or prepare a PowerPoint presentation of factors teachers should keep in mind when planning and organizing schedules and classroom routines for EC–4 learners.

3. Role-play examples of teacher behaviors that encourage and discourage the development of caring and supportive learning communities within the classroom.

4. Work in groups of three to research a topic or area discussed in the chapter.

5. Use several annotated bibliographies of children's books to identify those that discuss the topic of sharing.

6. Find at least three sample classroom schedules in professional books and magazines. Compare the ways that authors plan active and quiet activities throughout the day.

PRACTICE QUESTIONS

1. Ms. Navarro eagerly looks forward to her first year of teaching. She has just been employed as a first-grade teacher. Her training for the EC–4 classroom prepared her to be an effective teacher. As she works in her classroom the week before school begins, she reflects on the importance of using routines and procedures as an effective class management strategy. She recognizes the importance of having a good beginning for the year and is determined to do all she can to plan (*before* children arrive) for a smooth and effective first few

weeks of school. Reflecting on factors that contribute to managing a classroom and the instructional program, several issues come to her mind. The most important consideration in establishing the routine of having children respond to a "signal" to support good time management is:

A. The teacher should have the children's full attention before giving directions, and a signal can facilitate that need.

B. To provide ownership, the children select the signal that is their favorite by voting among several options the teacher identifies.

C. The signal used by the teacher should be changed every few weeks to train the students to be flexible.

D. The signal the teacher chooses should be approved by the principal in advance of its implementation.

2. In planning for the physical arrangement of the classroom, Ms. Navarro should:

A. Choose an arrangement that best supports her educational philosophy and planned instructional practices.

B. Provide for student safety as the primary focus, such as keeping the desks in straight rows to facilitate student movement.

C. Place an equal number of boys and girls at each table grouping to promote equity.

D Visit other first-grade classrooms during the first week of school and make a final arrangement of her room during the second week.

3. Allowing for student choice in the selection of learning centers will likely result in all of the benefits listed below *except*:

A. Promotes active learning

B. Increases student performance on standardized tests

C. Helps students become independent learners

D. Increases student motivation

4. In creating groups for instructional purposes, Ms. Navarro should consider:

A. Students' scores on standardized or state tests administered the prior year

B. Information from the previous year's teachers, explaining how children were grouped based on performance last year

C. Forming and finalizing groups by the end of the first 6 weeks

D. Keeping group membership flexible by grouping children according to instructional needs or interests

5. The most effective way for Ms. Navarro to teach routines is to:

A. Establish the consequences for noncompliance before introducing the routine.

B. Reinforce the desired student compliance by pointing out students who follow the routine and those who do not.

C. Follow the steps of explanation, modeling, practicing, and reinforcing.

D. Achieve mastery of the routine by all students by practicing the routine until all children are successful.

Answers and Discussion

Answer 1: It is futile to give directions or instructions to children if they are not listening. You will end up repeating directions several times, and children will quickly learn that you do not really expect them to give prompt and complete attention. It *is* important for children to experience ownership in the classroom and for teachers to be flexible in planning and decision making, but these answers are not the best considerations when establishing a signal for getting students' attention. The answer is *A*.

Answer 2: Room arrangement should facilitate instruction and the activities that the teacher plans for children. If teachers plan to implement centers and small-group work, the room arrangement will be crucial to the success of their plans. All of the distracters are true in part. Student safety considerations do not necessitate putting desks or tables in rows, however. Attention to diversity issues is of supreme importance. Yet, many times there will not be an equal number of boys and girls in the class. Learning from experienced teachers is invaluable, but the organization of your classroom must facilitate *your* educational philosophy and teaching activities. The answer is *A*.

Answer 3: Implementing centers does not guarantee high standardized test scores. Centers are used in classrooms to encourage children to make decisions, allow them to work independently or with a small group, and to increase their enjoyment and motivation while learning. The answer is *B*.

Answer 4: Flexibly grouping children by instructional requirements or by interests ensures that their needs will be met. The other answers leave no room for improvement or change in the children's ability or level of learning. Groups should not be formed based on one or two tests administered the previous year. Even if another teacher had the exact class last year, grouping decisions should be made based on current observations and the students' performance this year. Group membership should never be final. Even if you use ability grouping, group membership should change as children's needs change. The answer is *D*.

Answer 5: Although students should understand consequences for noncompliance of rules for routines and procedures, do not begin teaching a concept on such a negative note. *B* and *D* are good ideas to remember but are not the *best* answer. The most effective practice for teaching routines and procedures includes explanation and modeling by the teacher, practice by the students, and reinforcement of the desired behavior by the teacher. The answer is *C*.

WEB LINKS

Remember that Web site locations may change. If any of these sites have moved or cannot be located, use terms in the index to search for further information.

http://www.atozteacherstuff.com

A to Z Teacher Stuff: PreK–12 Network

This site includes themes, lesson plans, worksheets, tips, articles, a teacher chat room, and links to other education sites. The tips section includes many topics for organizing the day, including attendance and lunch count, classroom jobs, learning centers, managing papers, organization, and parent involvement.

http://www.bigchalk.com

bigchalk: The Education Network

This is another excellent Web site for lesson plans and teaching ideas. Place the word "scheduling" in the search window, select "K–5" for grade level, and find a great site for creating an effective learning environment.

http://www.birdnest.org/robertsona2

The Early Childhood Connection

This site is an excellent resource for teachers of ages 2–8. It includes finger play and action verses, lesson plans and thematic units, science brain-teasers, reading/book/author study, and general early childhood links that include classroom management.

http://www.ericeece.org

ERIC Clearinghouse on Elementary & Early Childhood Education

This site includes a wealth of information on any topic related to EC–4 education. Click on "AskERIC" to find published work on a myriad of topics.

http://perpetualpreschool.com

The Perpetual Preschool

In addition to many ideas for thematic teaching, "Teaching Tips" includes behavior management, parent participation, and transitions.

REFERENCES

Anderson, R., Hiebert, E., Scott, J., and Wilkinson, I. (1985). *Becoming a nation of readers*. Washington, D.C.: The National Academy of Education.

Cowley, J. (1994). *Whole learning: Whole child*. Bothell, WA: The Wright Group.

Cummings, C. (2000). *Winning strategies for classroom management.* Alexandria, VA: Association for Supervision and Curriculum Development.

Elkind, D. (2001). *The hurried child: Growing up too fast too soon.* Cambridge, MA: Perseus Publishing.

Glasser, W. (1986). *Control theory in the classroom.* New York: Harper and Row.

Glasser, W. (1992). *The quality school: Managing students without coercion.* New York: HarperCollins.

Harwayne, S. (1992). *Lasting impressions.* Portsmouth, NH: Heinemann.

Hayes, K., & Creange, R. (2001). *Classroom routines that really work for pre-k and kindergarten.* New York: Scholastic Professional Books.

Jones, V., & Jones, L. (2001). *Comprehensive classroom management: Creating communities of support and solving problems.* Boston: Allyn and Bacon.

Moffett, J., & Wagner, B. (1992). *Student-centered language arts, K–12.* Portsmouth, NH: Heinemann.

National Association of Elementary School Principals. (1990). *Standards for quality programs for young children.* Alexandria, VA.

Rothlein, L. (1991, September). Nutrition tips revisited: On a daily basis, do we implement what we know? *Young Children, 46(6),* 30–36.

Smith, F. (1985). *Reading without nonsense.* New York: Teachers College Press.

Tompkins, G., & McGee, L. (1993). *Teaching reading with literature: Case studies to action plans.* New York; Merrill.

Chapter 10

COMPETENCY 6 – PART 2

Managing Student Behavior

TERRY BRANDT

University of St. Thomas—Houston

TERMS TO KNOW

Alternative education program

Code of ethics

Consequences

Discipline

Individual Education Program (IEP)

Management plan

Placement Review Committee

Proximity

Rules

Student code of conduct

This chapter addresses Competency 6 of the Pedagogy and Professional Responsibilities test in Texas and focuses on various methods that teachers may employ to manage student behavior effectively. Beginning teachers should know and understand theories and techniques relating to managing and monitoring student behavior. They should know appropriate behavior standards and expectations for students at various developmental levels and be able to communicate high and realistic expectations for children's behavior. Teachers should be able to ensure that children understand behavior expectations and **consequences** (results) of misbehavior. Beginning teachers should also understand the significance of district policies and procedures for managing student behavior and ensuring ethical behavior in the classroom. They should be able to consistently enforce standards and expectations for student behavior and ethical work habits. They should know how to encourage students to maintain ethical work standards and monitor their own behavior. Beginning teachers should know and understand appropriate responses to a variety of student behaviors and misbehaviors and be able to use effective methods and procedures for monitoring and responding to positive and negative student behaviors.

DEVELOPING A PLAN

A primary issue of concern among teachers is that of managing disruptive behaviors in children. This issue becomes more difficult when a child's behavior is seen in a group setting and/or when the teacher is challenged to respond to behavior concerns of more than one student. One of the most common errors made by teachers of young children is attempting to impose authority on a classroom rather than encouraging students to manage themselves.

All children display undesirable behavior at some time. The ability to guide young children's behavior in a positive manner is often challenging and complex; however, effective guidance requires patient and nurturing teachers who understand the tasks of children at various ages; are aware that normal children are naturally curious, active, and impulsive; and recognize that the main goals of positive classroom management are to assist children in developing skills to control themselves and in taking responsibility for their own behavior (Ruffin, 2000).

In developing a **management plan**, teachers must decide whether they want their students to do only as they are told or learn to ask themselves what is appropriate for them to do. Do teachers want the children in their classrooms to behave only because the teachers are around or to develop the skills to control their own behavior in any setting? Acquiring skills needed to manage young students positively often requires that teachers make some important shifts in their thinking about managing children.

DEVELOPMENTAL STAGES OF CHILDREN'S SOCIAL DEVELOPMENT

Understanding children's development and providing careful guidance for behavior can lead students toward developing self-management, self-confidence, and problem-solving skills. Only then is classroom **discipline** an effective life guide. Developmentally, children below the age of 10 normally view rules as fixed, permanent, and externally enforced by authority figures. At this stage, children don't fully understand rules set down by others and may make ethical decisions based on their chances of getting caught and being punished. They may reason that if they were caught, the act was wrong; if not, the act was right. For very young students, the consequences of their acts determine whether they see themselves as good or bad, and they make decisions without considering the needs or feelings of others. It is difficult for them to take the perspective of others (empathy) because of egocentrism or being able to take other perspectives (see Competency 1, Chapter 1). For older students in the lower elementary grades, obeying **rules** and exchanging favors are judged in terms of the benefit to the individual. Kohlberg describes this stage as *market exchange* (Ruffin, 2000). Children obey because of what it might bring them ("If I scratch your back, you will scratch mine!"), and they may see fairness as "an eye for an eye." A class of elementary students may also contain children who have reached the stage at which they do the right thing so as to please others and to be seen as a "good" boy or girl. Effective classroom managers know the developmental variations that may be present in the classroom. The following are some guidelines suggested by Ruffin (2000) to assist teachers in determining an array of effective approaches.

Mid-Threes to Five—Major Task: Learning an Identity

The student: is bold, quarrelsome, contrary, full of energy and zest for life; goes from independence to clinging; uses "naughty" words; tells bold stories that may sound like lies; has difficulty sharing or playing cooperatively; learns many new skills and abilities.

The teacher should: give affection and respect; have understanding and patience; provide outlets and opportunities for all the energy and developing intelligence; continue firm, consistent rules and expectations; accept the testing of limits with a sense of humor; be a model of cooperative behavior; begin to use reason and logic with the child, which is more possible as a child nears age 5.

Mid-Fours to Sixes—Major Task: Learning an Identity

The student: becomes more cooperative with age; shows lots of energy, wiggling, and giggling; loves to talk about self; can do many things and loves to show them off; has many new fears; still tells tales; may try out taking things that belong to others; tattles and is a poor loser; shows interest in numbers and letters; begins to play cooperatively with others, but disagreements can easily occur.

The teacher should: give affection, clear directions, and expectations; encourage children to try new things; provide a variety of activities that allow children to learn by doing; let children participate in planning activities and in doing small, helpful chores; provide opportunities to show off skills.

Mid-Fives to Nine—Major Task: Learning to Be Productive and Successful

The student: is fair minded; shows off; insists on following rules fairly, often to an extreme; begins to prefer friends of the same sex; frequently finds and loses best friends; likes special projects that feel useful, productive, and grown-up; tests limits with determination; finds enjoyment in mastery and competence through success and recognition of accomplishments.

The teacher should: give affection, flexibility, respect, and moments of undivided attention; specify clear and reasonable limits, with opportunities for negotiations; assign simple classroom duties with reminders; be fair and reasonable; allow children to participate in planning activities; set challenges that are neither too difficult nor too easy in their attainment and that convey to the child a sense of accomplishment.

Students should be taught what constitutes appropriate behavior, what the school and classroom rules are, and how to follow them. Obviously this will be approached differently, depending upon the age and grade level of the learners. Children below the fourth grade require a great deal of instruction and practice in classroom rules and procedures. Brophy (1983) notes that effective management, especially in the early grades, is more an instructional than a disciplinary enterprise. Effective managers socialize their children to the student role through instruction, modeling, and much practice. It is important that teachers be consistent in articulating demands and monitoring compliance, but most important is to make sure that children know what to do in the first place.

Teaching children to be responsible, self-controlled, and self-managed cannot be accomplished only as a start-of-the-year unit. It must be taught through the way teachers handle everyday situations. The behaviors of teachers, the processes of the classroom, and the curriculum should all work together. Management plans should include opportunities for children to learn social skills through taking responsibility (see Competency 3, Part 2, Chapter 4), involvement in age-appropriate activities, and talking about feelings that are related to each other, their teachers, and their required activities.

ESTABLISHING STANDARDS OF BEHAVIOR

Even though establishing standards of behavior and maintaining discipline are not instructional activities, productive learning does not occur until they are in place. Many of the instructional practices of effective teachers reinforce good behavior, while maintaining discipline in the classroom enhances learning. Both work in concert to enhance effective classrooms. Wong and Wong (1998) believe that student achievement is directly related to the degree to which the teacher establishes good control of the classroom procedures in the very first week of the school year. Preservice teachers often hear the admonition not to smile until Thanksgiving. Although that advice may be a bit extreme, it is imperative that children know what is expected of them and what is acceptable and unacceptable in the classroom. Research focused on the beginning-of-the-year behavior of teachers has shown that effective management

practices produce much more positive outcomes when they are enacted from the very first day of school. Research further indicates that teachers who are ineffective managers at the beginning of the year find it very difficult to establish and maintain control in their classrooms later on (Emmer, 1982; Emmer, Evertson & Anderson, 1980).

Ultimately, the goal is for students to exercise self-discipline. However, teachers cannot assume that students know what constitutes proper behavior, and children do not automatically understand what teachers expect of them. Every teacher has different expectations for his or her learners. Although consistency is enhanced when entire schools follow a particular set of rules, children quickly learn which behaviors are acceptable to various teachers. Children may find that the expectations of their music teacher are different from those of their PE teacher, which are different still from those of their computer teacher. These all may differ from the expectations of their homeroom teacher. Students need to understand specific expectations, classroom rules, and the rewards and consequences that accompany them. Experienced teachers decide ahead of time which rules must be established, and they must learn to give clear and specific directions to children regarding expected behavior. One way to accomplish this is to say, "*Quietly* put your supplies in the center basket," or "*Wait for my signal* to walk *quietly* back to your desk from the circle," or "When I call your name, line up *quietly*." Teachers then wait for children to comply and call on those who do so first. This rewards good behavior. Sometimes children are good only long enough to get their reward—for example, being first in line but become disruptive once there. A smart teacher will send them to the end of the line, back to their seats, or even reverse the line, leading children from the rear instead of the front. The following suggestions can serve as guidelines as teachers begin the important task of establishing and maintaining standards of behavior (Clay & Brandt, 2001):

■ **Young students need a warm, safe, supporting, inviting environment.** The importance of the teacher in creating such an environment cannot be overstated. Children are much more likely to respond appropriately when they feel that the teacher respects them as individuals and truly cares about their well-being.

- **"Rules imposed by external constraint remain external to the child's spirit.** Rules due to mutual respect and cooperation take root inside the child's mind" (Piaget in Lickona, 1991, p. 112). Many students walk into classrooms on the first day of school and find the rules for classroom behavior already posted. In contrast, teachers who agree with Piaget's philosophy immediately begin building a sense of community by allowing students to participate in establishing behavior guidelines for the class. Giving children the opportunity to discuss and choose the rules for the classroom is another way to allow them a measure of power and freedom in the classroom. The teacher, however, is a significant member of that community and should play his or her part in establishing rules rather than simply asking students to decide. Ideas to consider when developing rules and expectations with students include stating rules in a positive format, limiting rules to five or fewer, and guiding students' thinking and decision making so that they select broad categories for rules. For example, "Move safely through the school," covers many behaviors, including don't run in the hall, don't push, stay in line, and don't bump into others. Discuss and explain rules and expectations during the first class. Consistently enforce all rules and expectations.

- **Discussing rules and procedures with the students is important but it may not be sufficient to obtain the desired behavior.** Be certain that students understand exactly what is expected of them. Explain the desired behavior and model what is expected. Then have the children practice the behavior until it is apparent that they all understand. Send management details home to be signed by parents or caregivers so they can be of informed support. Spend as much time as necessary ensuring that each child understands what is expected of him or her. Occasionally it might be necessary to reinforce or reteach a desired behavior. Never think that the time spent developing an awareness of what is expected is wasted or can be put to better use.

- **When a system of rewards and consequences has been established and the students understand them, the teacher must enforce them consistently and impartially.** Young children have a strong sense of what is fair and unfair. Teachers who appear inconsistent and capricious in dealing with rewards and consequences do not command the respect of children. It becomes impossible to build and maintain a strong sense of community in such an environment.

- **Encourage students to practice self-discipline.** Allowing children choice and input in the establishment of rules is one way to help students develop self-discipline. Another way is to teach the life skills necessary for children to succeed in this area (Elias et al., 1997). Goleman (1997) contends that children need to be taught emotional awareness lessons to succeed in school and later in life. Among the areas included in emotional awareness are learning to control impulses, recognizing one's feelings, monitoring what children and those around them are feeling, and recognizing hostility in others (see Competency 4, Part 2, Chapter 6, for more on emotional intelligence).

- **Remember that the best way to maintain discipline is to maintain interest.** Children who are actively involved in learning activities seldom become discipline problems. Many discipline problems can be avoided with careful planning and preparation. When students come into the classroom and find interesting and motivating assignments ready, and when the routine and procedures are familiar to them, they are much more likely to begin and continue working.

- **Be organized and plan wisely.** When children are not involved and there is nothing to do, they find something with which to occupy themselves—usually inappropriate activities. A good lesson plan is the first, best line of defense in management.

- **Students who experience success in the classroom are less disruptive.** Knowing students' strengths, interests, and needs enables teachers to plan instruction and activities that invite success, provide positive reinforcement, and validate students' worth as individuals (Elias et al., 1997).

- **Maintain a safe, inviting learning environment that encourages risk-taking.** Oftentimes the classroom is the only place in children's lives where they experience a sense of acceptance and self-worth. An important concept found in this book emphasizes that a child should always feel that he or she *belongs* in the class and should never feel the equivalent of wanting to run away because no one in the classroom cares, or, worse, no one likes him or her. Corrections of behavior should be seen as mature steps in growth. When a child needs discipline, be certain that the child understands that it is the behavior that is unacceptable, not him or her.

- **Be proactive rather than reactive in your system of discipline.** In addition to planning and preparation, observe the behavior of the students carefully. Walk about the room so that students are aware of your physical presence and realize that you are noticing theirs. Oftentimes your physical presence or **proximity** to a student who is disruptive or off task will be enough to redirect his or her behavior. At other times, a mild desist lets a child know that the teacher has seen his or her misbehavior. An example

could be simply calling a child's name or repeating the assignment as in, "Jeffery, we are on page 15." Be proactive in spotting difficulties with the physical environment of the room and school ahead of time. Ask yourself questions such as, "Do children crash against each other or into desks when moving to the trash can?" or "Is there a game I can make into a routine to help keep students quiet who are waiting at the restroom and water fountain?"

- **Learn to distinguish between minor distractions and truly disruptive behavior.** Problem situations are those that (1) interfere more than casually with class work and progress, (2) have a strong potential for impeding work or damaging feelings, or (3) involve *intentional* violation of class agreements or rules. Calling attention to minor disruptions can draw attention to a child and away from the learning environment. Although some children are embarrassed by this focus, many who are seeking attention and power are getting it from the teacher in this manner. The lesson stops, and all eyes turn toward the child and his or her behavior. A good technique when discovering this ploy is to create an "invisible child," which allows the teacher to ignore a minor behavior that is annoying. Quite often the behavior will go away if not reinforced by the teacher's constant attention. There is a careful balance to be made, however. The "ripple effect" occurs when a teacher does not stop an inappropriate activity for one or more children. When others in the class notice that this seems to be acceptable behavior to the teacher because it was not stopped, the class suddenly seems to take it up. A teacher must really know children well to maintain correct judgments in these areas. However, overtly disruptive or dangerous behavior requires immediate attention

- **Reinforce desired behaviors.** All of us want to be successful and accepted by others.

Children are no exception. By acknowledging and praising positive behaviors, teachers reinforce them and increase the chance that students will repeat them.

PREVENTING CLASSROOM DISCIPLINE PROBLEMS

Teachers who are regarded as effective managers are those whose classrooms are orderly, have a minimum of student misbehavior, and have high levels of time on task. Teachers who are ineffective managers are those whose classrooms lack these qualities. Although this appears relatively self-evident, Kounin (1970) suggests that effective and ineffective teachers do not differ greatly in their methods for dealing with disruption. Instead, effective managers are found to be much more skilled at *preventing* disruptions from occurring in the first place. Research conducted during the past 20 years has yielded the following list of behaviors that comprise effective classroom managers (Cotton, 1997).

- **Holding and communicating high expectations for student learning and behavior.** Effective managers, through personal warmth and encouragement, make sure that children know they are expected to learn well and behave appropriately.

- **Establishing and clearly teaching classroom rules and procedures.** Effective managers teach behavioral rules and classroom routines in much the same way as they teach instructional content, and they review these frequently at the beginning of the school year and periodically thereafter.

- **Specifying consequences and their relation to student behavior.** Effective managers are careful to explain the connection between children's misbehavior and teacher-imposed sanctions. This cause-and-effect connection, too, is taught and reviewed as needed.

- **Enforcing classroom rules promptly, consistently, and equitably.** Effective managers respond quickly to misbehavior, respond in the same way at different times, and impose consistent sanctions regardless of the gender, race, or other personal characteristics of misbehaving students. Children who see the teacher as biased against them in any way or perceive that the teacher is unfair immediately become rebellious and unwilling to work.

- **Sharing with students the responsibility for classroom management.** Effective managers work to instill in children a sense of belonging and self-discipline. One technique for this is to offer children choices when discipline is needed ("Jessica, you may work with your group nicely or you may work alone in the 'time out' area"). Another part of sharing this responsibility is teaching children to search for reasons and alternatives. For example, if Gerardo threw a block and hit Juan, the teacher could, after taking care of Juan, seek the reason for the act. Was Gerardo trying to hurt Juan, or was he exploring the property of the materials? The teacher would talk with Gerardo to problem solve for alternatives. Although some punishment may be in order if the intention was to harm, the child has a clear model of different ways to behave for next time.

- **Maintaining a brisk pace for instruction and making smooth transitions between activities.** Effective managers keep things moving in their classrooms, which increases learning as well as reducing the likelihood of misbehavior.

- **Monitoring classroom activities and providing feedback and reinforcement.** Effective managers observe and comment on student behavior, and they reinforce appropriate behavior whenever they can.

In addition to this general, strongly supported list of practices associated with well-disciplined classrooms, other effective approaches for establishing and maintaining positive, orderly classroom environments have been identified. For example, engaging in misbehavior is sometimes a response to academic failure, and improvements in classroom order can be made when marginal children are provided opportunities to experience academic and social success. Many children simply do not perceive a connection between their level of effort and the academic or behavioral outcomes they experience. These children have what psychologists call an "external locus of control" and do not believe in their own ability to influence events (see Competency 8, Part 2, Chapter 13). Often, they do not have the skills to identify inappropriate behavior and to move from inappropriate to appropriate behavior. Improvements in behavior may occur when children are taught to attribute their success or failure to their personal effort; learn to check their own behavior and judge its appropriateness; talk themselves through a task, using detailed, step-by-step instructions; and learn and apply problem-solving steps when confronting classroom issues.

It is important for teachers to realize that they have a responsibility for preventing behavioral problems through their management decisions. For example, many behavioral problems with young children occur over sharing, but many young children are developmentally unable to manage this concept well. Therefore thinking clearly through routines for supplies will help prevent disruptions. Children may also have discipline problems because of movement transitions. Teachers should plan a classroom that is well designed for both the children's and the teacher's movement. Centers should have clear routines for visitation and should be visible by the teacher from all parts of the classroom.

SPECIFIC DISCIPLINE PROGRAMS

Many educational program developers have responded to the prevalence of school discipline problems by preparing and marketing packaged programs that purport to bring about reductions in misconduct and consequent increases in school order (Charles, 2000). Although these programs are widely applied, research on their effectiveness is generally inconclusive, though all provide food for thought.

Reality Therapy (RT). Glasser's Reality Therapy involves teachers helping students make positive choices by making clear the connection between student behavior and consequences. Class meetings, clearly communicated rules, and the use of plans and contracts are featured.

A Positive Approach to Discipline (PAD). PAD is based on Glasser's Reality Therapy and is grounded in teachers' respect for students and instilling in them a sense of responsibility. Program components include developing and sharing clear rules, providing daily opportunities for success, and in-school suspension for noncompliant students.

Teacher Effectiveness Training (TET). The TET philosophy differentiates between teacher-owned and student-owned problems and proposes various strategies for dealing with them. Students are taught problem solving and negotiation techniques.

Transactional Analysis (TA). Within the context of counseling programs, students with behavior problems use terminology and exercises from Transactional Analysis to identify issues and make changes. The notion that each person's psyche includes child, adult, and parent components is basic to the TA philosophy.

Assertive Discipline (AD). Developed by Lee Canter, Assertive Discipline is a well-respected and widely used program. AD focuses on the right of the teacher to define and enforce standards for student behavior. Clear expectations followed by a set of consistently followed consequences are major features. Rewards for the achievement of good behavior are established ahead of time and are also consistently applied.

Adlerian approaches. Named for psychiatrist Alfred Adler, "Adlerian approaches" is an umbrella term for a variety of methods that emphasize understanding the individual's reasons for maladaptive behavior and helping misbehaving students to alter their behavior, while at the same time finding ways to get their needs met.

Boys Town Education Model (BTEM). The BTEM is a teaching philosophy that integrates a socials skills curriculum, a crisis intervention process, and a motivation system.

Consistency Management & Cooperative Discipline (CMCD). Developed by H. J. Freiberg, CMCD is a program that builds on shared responsibility for learning and classroom organization between teachers and students. It emphasizes prevention rather than intervention, shared responsibility between teacher and student, and value-based discipline.

No one program appears to be the answer to every school discipline issue, but all of those previously listed include components that have been validated as effective. As Wayson et al., (1982) point out in their summary of the discipline practices of effective schools, these schools generally do not use packaged programs; instead, they either develop their own programs or modify commercially available programs to meet the needs of their particular situation. It is essential, however, that all teachers incorporate into their classroom management plans whatever program is being implemented in their school. Young children do not respond well to perceived inconsistencies in discipline practices among teachers.

With elementary age children, the best results are obtained through vigilantly reminding students about the rules and procedures of the school and classroom and monitoring their compliance with them (Brophy, 1983; Doyle, 1989). The developmental level of young children is such that they tend to regard all punishment as unfair and unde-

served. Older students generally do regard punishment for misbehavior as fair and acceptable, provided that the punishment "fits the crime." Judicious discipline requires that the teacher decide (perhaps in discussion with children in certain situations) on logical consequences rather than a set of pre-established punishments. For example, if children mark on the desks, they must clean the desks during "their" time. If they throw trash, they must clean the room. The rationale for this method is that the teacher knows his or her children well and understands that certain sets of punishments may not be a deterrent to certain children. More affluent parents may, for example, simply send money to replace items damaged by their children; thus no impact is made on the child. The child who is made to "work damage off," however, will perhaps have a better understanding of the value of a damaged item the next time.

Occasionally, teachers are confronted with children whose behaviors are beyond the remedies of even the best-managed classrooms. When this occurs, teachers should not hesitate to hold a conference with caregivers and to make use of the available counseling services to seek the cause of the misconduct. Using multiple human resources may assist students in developing needed skills to behave appropriately. In severe or chronic cases, in-school suspension programs often include guidance, support, and plans for change and skill building. Teachers in schools where children are sent to in-school suspension should always provide work to do there.

POLICIES AND PROCEDURES

The policies and procedures that govern classroom management and school discipline are derived from a combination of federal and state laws, local district policies, and individual campus procedures. Teachers should become familiar with the information provided to them in board policies and in faculty and student/parent handbooks and align their management plans to all applicable policies and procedures.

Code of Ethics

The Code of Ethics and Standard Practices for Texas Educators (Texas Administrative Code of 2000) states that teachers should strive to create an atmosphere that will nurture to fulfillment the potential of each student. To accomplish that goal, teachers should measure success by the progress of each student toward realization of his or her potential as an effective citizen, deal considerately and justly with each student, and seek to resolve problems including discipline according to law and school board policy. The **code of ethics** also requires that teachers not intentionally expose a child to disparagement and that they make every reasonable effort to protect children from conditions detrimental to learning, physical health, mental health, or safety. Teachers should hold every child in their care in the highest regard and serve as a model for respect and consideration in dealing with the rich diversity that is present in today's classroom.

Student Code of Conduct

Texas state law requires that the board of trustees of each independent school district, with the advice of a district-level committee, adopt a **student code of conduct** for the district (Texas Education Code of 2000). The student code of conduct must be posted and prominently displayed at each school campus. The student code of conduct must:

- Specify the circumstances under which a student may be removed from a classroom, campus, or alternative education program.
- Specify conditions that authorize or require that a principal or other appropriate administrator transfer a student to an alternative education program.
- Outline conditions under which a student may be suspended.

A teacher who knows that a child has violated the student code of conduct must file with the school principal or the other appropriate administrator a written report, not to exceed one page, documenting the violation. The principal or the other appropriate administrator must send a copy of the report to the child's parents or guardians no later than 24 hours after receipt of a report from a teacher,

Removal by Teacher

A teacher may send a student to the principal's office to maintain effective discipline in the classroom. The principal is required to respond by employing appropriate discipline management techniques consistent with the student code of conduct. A teacher may remove from class a student:

- Who has been documented by the teacher to repeatedly interfere with the teacher's ability to communicate effectively with the children in the class or with the ability of the child's classmates to learn.
- Whose behavior the teacher determines is so unruly, disruptive, or abusive that it seriously interferes with the teacher's ability to communicate effectively with the children in the class or with the ability of the child's classmates to learn.

If a teacher removes a student from class, the principal may place the student in another appropriate classroom, in-school suspension, or an **alternative education program.** The principal may not return the student to that teacher's class without the teacher's consent unless the school's three-member **placement review committee** determines that such placement is the best or only alternative available.

A teacher must remove from class (and send to the principal for placement in an alternative education program or for expulsion, as appropriate), a student who:

- Engages in conduct punishable as a felony.
- Engages in conduct that contains elements of assault or a terrorist threat.
- Sells, gives, or delivers to another person or possesses or uses or is under the influence of

marijuana, a dangerous drug, or other controlled substances.

- Sells, gives, or delivers to another person an alcoholic beverage, commits a serious act or offense while under the influence of alcohol, or possesses, uses, or is under the influence of an alcoholic beverage.

- Engages in conduct that contains the elements of an offense relating to abusable glue or aerosol paint.

- Engages in conduct that contains elements of public lewdness or indecent exposure.

- Engages in conduct that contains elements of retaliation against any school employee.

In addition, the teacher may remove from class any child whose continued presence threatens the safety of other children or the teacher or is detrimental to the educational process. Most districts have specific, written policies and procedures regarding the type of documentation required to substantiate the removal of a student from the classroom. In the wake of school violence in the past years, teachers of young children should be vigilant for behaviors that could lead to violence later. Helping a child to receive needed support and counseling early on may help prevent maladjustment later.

Removal of Students with Disabilities

Only a duly constituted Admission, Review, and Dismissal (ARD) committee may permanently remove from a classroom a child with a disability who receives special education services. However, the teacher may request that the disruptive child be removed from the classroom for up to 10 days (Gorn, 1999). A child with a disability who receives special education services may not be removed from class if the behavior demonstrated in the classroom is a manifestation of the disability as addressed in the student's **Individual Education Program (IEP).** However, if the behavior of the child is not related to the disability, the district standards of conduct for all children apply. It is best for the teacher to consult with the special

education coordinator and school counselor regarding the extraordinary behavior of any child.

A local board of trustees in a district may add to the state requirements for a student code of conduct as long as the additional requirements are not in violation of other state or federal laws.

WE MAKE THE RULES AND CHILDREN BREAK THEM

Any teacher who has ever given a gold star or a sticker to a child who followed the rules knows that rewards are great motivators—but not for very long. No matter how rewarding the teacher makes it to "be good," children still need help in following rules. Getting children to follow the rules can be hard work, especially if teachers don't follow the rules themselves! For example, if teachers don't allow talking in line, they should not gossip with colleagues as they wait. *Early Childhood Educator* (Johnson, 2001) recommends the following four smart ways to make rules that children can and want to follow:

- Tell them what you want them to do, not just what *not* to do. For example, "Walk inside, keep your hands to yourself, and use respectful voices," is more positive than "Don't run, don't hit, and don't yell."

- Get students' help in making the rules, and then help them remember what they said. For instance, have a discussion about what would be some good rules and write down their answers. Make this list into a usable poster for all to see.

- Choose a few good, positive rules that really matter—not a bunch of little ones. For example, choose the big, important rules that matter the most to everyone; rules that address the need for respect for self, others, and property, and rules for safety ("Respect others' property and space.")

- Create rules that you are willing to enforce, teach, and model yourself. Know the purposes of the rules and how to teach the lessons. Children will sense whether you are confident about enforcing the rules and why.

Ineffective Disciplinary Practices

Teachers should be aware of the strategies that have been shown to be *ineffective,* in part because this knowledge can assist them in planning local programs, and in part because, unfortunately, some of these practices continue to be widely used. Ineffective practices include:

- Vague or unenforceable rules. The importance of clear rules becomes obvious when observing, as researchers have, the ineffectiveness of "rules" such as, "Be in the right place at the right time."

- Teachers ignoring misconduct. Both student behavior and attitudes are adversely affected when teachers ignore violations of school or classroom rules (unless a teacher is targeting a specific child to extinguish attention-getting behavior by creating an "invisible child").

- Ambiguous or inconsistent teacher responses to misbehavior. When teachers are inconsistent in their enforcement of rules, or when they react in inappropriate ways (such as lowering students' grades in response to misbehavior or "blowing up" and jumping to harsh consequences), classroom discipline is generally poor.

- Punishment that is excessive or that is delivered without support or encouragement for improving behavior. Among the kinds of punishment that produce particularly negative student attitudes are public punishment and corporal punishment.

Consequences for Misbehavior

Teachers have a responsibility to let their children know clearly what acceptable and unacceptable behavior in the classroom are. Young children must learn that inappropriate behavior carries with it very real consequences. When disruptive behavior occurs, the teacher must be prepared to deal with it calmly and quickly. A progressive series of consequences that students receive, should they choose to disregard the classroom rules, should be in place to guide the teacher's response. Canter and Canter (1992) recommend that teachers follow these guidelines when choosing consequences for their classroom discipline plan.

- Consequences must be something that children do not like, but these must never be physically or psychologically harmful.

- Consequences must be presented to students as a choice, a logical result of the misbehavior. Teachers want young children to enjoy the writing process, for example. Yet a traditional punishment is to have children "write lines." The logic of this doesn't quite fit, because teachers have now created an association between writing and punishment. The most effective punishments are those in which children are excluded, because of their behavior, from exciting activities in which they want to participate. However, too often the lesson may not be exciting, so time-out can, in fact, be a reward.

- Consequences do not have to be severe to be effective.

- Consequences for Assertive Discipline should be organized into a hierarchy that clearly spells out what will happen from the first time a child breaks a rule to the fifth time the same child breaks a rule the same day. Many teachers who use Assertive Discipline have visual charts that show children where their behavior stands (though some educators argue against posting names). If a child misbehaves, he or she is required to move a marker of some type further along a continuum of increasingly unpleasant consequences (miss recess, call home, and so forth). These consequences are paired with rewards for good behavior. This program works very well for some children, although others may need more individual treatment, or they may arrive at the most unpleasant consequence 30 minutes after the morning bell. Collecting many ideas for management will benefit the teacher and his or her class.

Whatever consequences the teacher chooses, they should be developmentally appropriate for the children, and the teacher must feel comfortable using them. They should be easy to implement and should be ones to which children will respond. Effective consequences are always the result of a good match between the personalities and abilities of the teacher and his or her students.

RESPONDING TO MISBEHAVIOR

Several common-sense strategies exist for effectively guiding young students when they misbehave:

- **Always focus on the behavior.** It is not children that we want to change—it is the inappropriate behavior. We want to support appropriate behavior. When good behavior is noticed, teachers should always compliment children to let them know that they have matched expectations.

- **Be consistent.** Clearly state the expectations and consequences of your students' behavior. Set guidelines and limits, and stick to them.

- **Concentrate on shaping positive behavior.** Let your students know that you expect positive behavior. Use gentle reminders about expectations for classroom conduct.

- **Structure the environment to support appropriate behavior.** Children are naturally curious. Arrange the classroom in a way that allows young students to explore without "getting into trouble." As mentioned in other chapters, provide consistent routines to help them know what is expected of them. Station yourself where your eyes can sweep the room easily, no matter where you are. Then peripheral vision will catch children's actions. This is one way that teachers gain "eyes in the back of their heads" or "withitness."

- **Allow your students to make acceptable choices.** Give them responsibility for their behavior whenever possible. Ask children, "What do you think would make this right?"

- **Allow your students to experience logical consequences.** Remind children of limits and consequences in positive ways. When misbehavior occurs, deal with the behavior in a firm, assertive manner and in such a way that the punishment "fits" the crime (i.e., if a child runs down the hall, he or she has to go back and walk; if children are pushing in line, the teacher has the line turn around and go back and begin again, even though they may arrive late).

- **Help children work it out themselves whenever possible.** The more you coach, and the less you referee, the more children will learn.

- **Ignore misbehavior when appropriate.** Try to focus the child's attention elsewhere. Do not focus all of your attention on the student, because some children misbehave to get attention. If the misbehavior is not hindering other students, try to create an "invisible child." However, be sure to give attention *immediately* to positive behavior if and when the child complies.

- **Interrupt or stop behavior that is harmful or unfair.** Use assertive intervention to stop harmful behavior immediately to protect the student, other students, or the environment.

Treat your students with unconditional positive regard. They deserve your respect, even when they misbehave. Controlling behavior is a learning process for young students. Teachers can teach children appropriate behavior by modeling effective responses and interactions

Techniques That Backfire

Albert (1996) surveyed teachers regarding methods they had employed that backfired on them. The list tends to make almost all teachers uncomfortable because they recognize some very often repeated "sins" of classroom management:

Raising your voice, yelling, or "losing it"

Saying, "Because I said so."

Using degrading put-downs

Attacking the student's character

Using physical force

Insisting that you are right

Making assumptions

Pleading or bribing

Making unsubstantiated accusations

Making comparisons with other students

Using tense body language

Using sarcasm

Acting superior

Having a double standard

Preaching

"Backing the student into a corner"

Bringing up unrelated events

Mimicking the student

Commanding or demanding

All of the above are teachers' attempts to control rather than guide the behavior of their students. They are usually the result of ineffective or absent management plans and a lack of understanding of the nature and needs of students.

GUIDING STUDENTS TOWARD SELF-MANAGEMENT

The goal of an effective classroom management plan is to assist students in becoming self-managed. The teacher seeks to help children make good decisions and interact with others without adult assistance. A good first step is to change the focus from discipline to guidance. Rather than focusing on the role of the teacher as the disciplinarian, place the emphasis on helping and assisting children in their behavioral growth and development. One very important aspect of guidance is the process of helping young students strengthen their feelings of self-worth. Children should be given opportunities to develop a sense of competence, the belief that they can accomplish tasks and achieve goals independent of adults. They also need to feel that they can, to some degree, influence and control the events around them. Through an expanding sense of control and competence, young children learn to like and value themselves. They begin to develop a feeling of worth. The result is positive self-esteem.

Cummings (2000) states that a child who loves his or her teacher is more likely to perform than one who feels disconnected from the classroom. When teachers take time to ask *why* a misbehavior occurred, they will have their class working with them, not against them. Cummings suggests that Covey's (1989) habit of "Seeking first to understand, then to be understood" should be the guiding principle in dealing with misbehavior. Children should be assisted in identifying and overcoming the challenges they face in the everyday classroom. The bottom line is that if teachers want good behavior, they must teach the skills for good behavior. Albert (1996) suggests a series of guidelines:

- **Establish a positive classroom environment.** The teacher should strive to connect with students by building relationships. The classroom should be pleasantly arranged, decorated, and maintained as an inviting but not *too* stimulating place for young children to spend the day.

- **Use democratic procedures and policies.** Students should be invited to contribute in meaningful ways in the development and implementation of the policies that govern everyday life in the classroom. Asking children how to problem solve in management issues increases critical thinking, too.

- **Implement cooperative learning strategies.** Continuous competition can be eliminated from the classroom with the use of learning groups. Cooperative learning helps children to develop a sense of personal and communal responsibility as they work together to achieve specific academic goals (see Competency 3, Part 2, Chapter 4). Assigning roles such as a taskmaster, quiet captain, and so forth, also can help children be more responsible for their behavior and the behavior of others in their learning community.

- **Conduct classroom guidance activities.** Such activities focus on helping students understand themselves and others and on teaching students to solve interpersonal problems peaceably by using conflict-resolution skills.

- **Choose appropriate curriculum methods and materials.** Boredom and frustration with learning are likely candidates for misbehavior. Activities should be selected at the level of engaging challenge (zone of proximal development); see Competency 1, Chapter 1, and Competency 5, Chapter 7.

Guiding the behavior of young students involves establishing mutual respect and expecting cooperation. Effective discipline is positive and child focused. It encourages self-control and appropriate behavior. Through effective classroom management, students can learn to make positive choices, learn problem-solving skills, and learn values of respect and responsibility.

SUMMARY

Competency 6 emphasizes communicating high and realistic expectations for students' behavior, ensuring that children understand behavior expectations and the consequences of misbehavior. To accomplish these tasks, teachers must know the stages of their children's social development and apply the appropriate levels of guidance.

Teachers should familiarize themselves with a number of classroom management programs so that they are able to make suitable adaptations to their own, unique campus and classrooms situations. In addition, behavioral management plans must align closely with both state laws and district policies regarding student conduct. The goal of all classroom management strategies should be guiding students toward self-management. To attain this, teachers must be fair in their responses to both positive and negative student behaviors, firm in their encouragement of students to maintain ethical work standards, and consistent in their enforcement of standards and expectations.

GLOSSARY

alternative education program   a campus or district-level placement for disruptive students or students who have violated school policies or state laws. This is an alternative to suspension from school, and is normally housed in a separate facility in a district, although it may be "in school."

code of ethics   required standards for the professional conduct of educators. It is a set of behavioral principles that guide interactions.

consequences   the results of breaking rules. When written into a management plan, these are usually responses that match the level of misbehavior or the number of repeats of inappropriate behavior.

discipline   a set or system of behavioral rules and the related corrections for misbehavior. The instruction and activities are designed to encourage proper conduct and prosocial actions on the part of students.

Individual Education Program (IEP)   a comprehensive statement of the educational needs of a disabled child and the specially designed instruction and related services to be employed to meet those needs. Often behavioral objects are included.

management plan   a set of rules and consequences as well as the related instruction in proper conduct that supports learning.

Placement Review Committee   a campus committee required under the Texas Education Code to review the placement of a student after removal by the teacher.

proximity   a technique wherein the teacher moves closer to the student to prevent or stop the student from misbehaving.

rules a set of behavioral guidelines that are most effective when few in number and stated in the affirmative. For example: "Children will respect each other's space." or "Students will respect each other's property."

student code of conduct a required set of behavioral expectations and consequences including conditions for suspension, placement in an alternative education program, and expulsion.

SUGGESTED ACTIVITIES

To reinforce and expand on the information presented in this chapter, the teacher may consider the following activities:

1. Visit at least two classrooms. Observe the environment and interactions among the children and between the teacher and the students. Make note of the presence or absence of classroom management practices. Discuss with teachers their philosophies of classroom management. Compare theirs with your own views.

2. With a group of fellow-students, research various classroom management programs. Compare the differences among those that emphasize high and low teacher involvement, those that emphasize teacher-directed behavioral controls, and those that focus on student self-guidance.

3. Obtain copies of student codes of conduct from two or more districts. Compare the similarities and differences.

4. Explore the Web sites listed in this chapter. Search for other Web sites that address related topics. Build a folder of the ideas that you want to implement.

5. Interview a successful teacher. Ask the teacher to identify specific methods that he or she believes are necessary to establish and maintain good student behavior.

6. Attend teacher-training workshops on classroom management provided by local school districts and regional education service centers.

7. Read books on the range of behaviors that should be anticipated among children of the age you plan to teach. An excellent series has been created by Louise Bates Ames of the Gessell Institute of Human Development. The series is available through Dell Publishing.

8. Interview a campus-based special education coordinator. Ask what resources are available to the regular education teacher in order to best serve a special education student with respect to behavior. Ask what the classroom teacher's role is in preparing and implementing an Individual Education Program.

PRACTICE QUESTIONS

1. Ms. Soweto has a number of students who become so deeply involved in what they are doing that they strongly resist when she announces that it is time to clean up. Occasionally some of them respond by destroying whatever they are working on and acting out. Ms. Soweto's best initial strategy for addressing these children's needs would be to:

   A. Involve them mainly in activities that can be completed in relatively short amounts of time.

   B. Permit them to continue working as the other students clean up.

   C. Warn them several minutes beforehand that it is almost clean-up time.

   D. Ask other students to help them at clean-up time.

2. Margaret arrives at school one morning very agitated. Her mother tells the teacher, "She's been 'hyper' all morning. I barely managed to get her here." Which of the following strategies would likely be the most effective for the teacher to use to calm Margaret down?

   A. Ask her to sit quietly in the time-out chair for a few minutes.

   B. Help her get started on an activity that is likely to channel her energy productively.

   C. Remind her of the behavior rules the class has established.

   D. Talk privately with her to try to discover the cause of the behavior.

3. Of the following, a primary school teacher's best strategy for helping students listen attentively at class meeting time is:

   A. Give a weekly "good listener" sticker to the child who listens best each week.

   B. Establish a routine that signals that it is time to listen, and follow that routine before every meeting.

   C. Permit the students who listen most attentively during class meetings to speak first.

   D. Establish clear guidelines about the consequences for not listening, and follow the guidelines consistently.

4. The children in Mr. Alvarez's class have been complaining about sharing because there are not enough "good markers" for everyone. Mr. Alvarez asked the children to explain what they meant by "good markers." After listening to their explanations that markers had "mixed colors, gone dry," and so forth, he encouraged the children to suggest solutions to the problem. His approach in this situation was designed to promote the students' autonomy primarily by:

   A. Encouraging children to think of themselves as capable of solving problems

   B. Guiding children to reach consensus on an issue of importance to them

   C. Helping children recognize that there are strategies they can use to resolve conflicts with their peers

   D. Putting children in a situation in which they are faced with a question that they must settle

5. For the first few weeks of school, Carl has been very uncooperative when it comes time to clean up the classroom. As soon as cleanup is announced, he tries to escape from his responsibilities by hiding, acting out, or bothering his classmates as they try to clean up. Which of the following would be the teacher's best initial response to his behavior?

   A. Speak to Carl in private immediately after he engages in this type of behavior.

   B. Let Carl be first in line for the next activity whenever he voluntarily participates in cleanup.

   C. Stand near Carl at clean-up time to make it easier to monitor and redirect his behavior if necessary.

   D. Point out Carl's behavior to the rest of the class when he is not helping.

Answers and Discussion

Answer 1: Young students require advanced warning when changes are to take place. They are more comfortable when they can anticipate a change rather than confront it immediately. Teachers should help children in their time management. Using a kitchen timer to signal when half the time is gone for an activity helps children understand the passing of time. Set it again for a few minutes before the activity is to end. When used as a routine, children normally react automatically and begin to clean up. The answer is *C*.

Answer 2: Students who are upset often benefit by redirection, especially if the new activity is something the child finds pleasing and personally interesting. The answer is *B*.

Answer 3: Students respond best to routines that have been thoughtfully developed and practiced. They also respond best when they understand expectations and feel comfortable in meeting those expectations. The answer is *B*.

Answer 4: One of the principle steps in establishing autonomy in students is to help them develop a sense of capability. Learning to solve their own problems rather than always relying on the teacher is essential. The answer is *A*.

Answer 5: The teacher's goal is to help the student feel comfortable in the task. By remaining close to the student, the teacher not only reinforces the importance of performing the task, but also is readily available to lend assistance or guidance if it is needed. The answer is *C*.

WEB LINKS

Remember that Web site locations may change. If any of these sites have moved or cannot be located, use the Terms to Know in this chapter to search for further information.

http://www.edpsych.com

This is the site of the *Early Childhood Educator*. It provides constantly updated articles on helpful hints for parents and teachers.

http://ericeece.org

This site is the ERIC Clearinghouse on Elementary and Early Childhood Education. It is a terrific source for the latest publications in management and discipline practices.

http://www.educationworld.com

This is the site of Education World, which is an outstanding source of books, materials, articles, and sources.

http://www.aft.org/lessons/two/elements.html

Lessons for Life: Responsibility, Respect, Results is one of several classroom management and ethical development sites of the American Federation of Teachers.

http://www.nwrel.org/scpd/sirs/5/cu9.html

This is the site of research reviews by the Northwest Regional Educational Laboratory. It is a very good place to begin further exploration into research on classroom management and discipline.

http://education.indiana.edu/cas/tt/v1i2/what.html

Go to this site for a self-evaluation checklist on your classroom management effectiveness.

www.suelebeau.com

Ms. LeBeau's Home Page is a wonderful set of links to all things helpful in instruction and management.

REFERENCES

Albert, L. (1996). *A teacher's guide to cooperative discipline.* Circle Pines, MN: American Guidance Service.

Brophy, J. E. (1983). Classroom organization and management. *The Elementary School Journal 83*(4), 265–285.

Canter, L., & Canter, M. (1992). *Assertive discipline: Positive behavior management for today's classroom.* Santa Monica, CA: Lee Canter & Associates.

Charles, C. M. (2000). *The synergetic classroom.* New York: Longman.

Clay, D., & Brandt, T. (2001). Managing the classroom environment. In C. G. Henry & J. L. Nath, (Eds.), *Becoming a teacher in Texas* (pp. 258–282). Belmont, CA: Wadsworth.

Cotton, K. (1997). *Schoolwide and classroom discipline.* Portland, OR: Northwest Regional Educational Laboratory.

Covey, S. (1989). *The seven habits of highly effective people: Restoring the character ethic.* New York: Simon & Schuster.

Cummings, C. (2000). *Winning strategies for classroom management.* Alexandria, VA: Association for Supervision and Curriculum Development.

Doyle, W. (1989). Classroom management techniques. In O. C. Moles, (Ed.), *Strategies to reduce student misbehavior,* (pp. 11–31). Washington, DC: Office of Educational Research and Improvement. (ED 311 608)

Elias, M., Zins, J., Weissberg, T., Frey, K., Greenberg, M., Haynes, N., Kesler, R., Schwab-Stone, M., & Shriver, T. (1997). *Promoting social and emotional learning: Guidelines for educators.* Alexandria, VA: Association for Supervision and Curriculum Development.

Emmer, E. T. (1982). *Management strategies in elementary school classrooms.* Austin, TX: Research and Development Center for Teacher Education. (ED 251 432)

Emmer, E. T., Evertson, C. M., & Anderson, L. M. (1980). Effective classroom management at the beginning of the school year. *The Elementary School Journal 80*(5), 219–231.

Goleman, D. (1997). *Emotional intelligence.* New York: Bantam Books.

Gorn, S. (1999). *What do I do when . . . The answer book on discipline.* Horsham, PA: LRP Publications.

Johnson, I., (Ed.). (2001). *Early childhood educator.* Alamosa, CO: Paideia Press.

Kounin, J. S. (1970). *Discipline and group management in classrooms.* New York: Holt, Rinehart and Winston, Inc.

Lickona, T. (1991). *Educating for character: How our schools can teach respect and responsibility.* New York: Bantam Books.

Ruffin, N. (2000). *Developing responsibility and self-management in young children: Goals of behavior management.* Petersburg, VA: Virginia Cooperative Extension.

Texas Administrative Code of 2000. Title 19. Education. Part 7. State Board for Educator Certification. Chapter 247. Educators' Code of Ethics. Rule §247.2. Code of Ethics and Standard Practices for Texas Educators. *Texas school law bulletin.* Austin, TX: Texas Education Agency.

Texas Education Code of 2000. Title 2. Public Education. Subtitle G. Safe Schools. Subchapter A. Alter native Settings for Behavior Management. Section 37.001. *Texas school law bulletin.* Austin, Texas: Texas Education Agency.

Wayson, W. W., DeVoss, G. G., Kaeser, S. C., Lasley, T., Pinnell, G. S., & the Phi Delta Kappa Commission on Discipline. (1982). *Handbook for developing schools with good discipline.* Bloomington, IN: Phi Delta Kappa.

Wong, H., & Wong, M. (1998). *How to be an effective teacher: The first days of school.* Mountain View, CA: Harry K. Wong Publications.

Domain III

Implementing Effective, Responsive Instruction and Assessment

Competency 7

The teacher understands and applies principles and strategies for communicating effectively in varied teaching and learning contexts.

The beginning teacher:

- Demonstrates clear, accurate communication in the teaching and learning process and uses language that is appropriate to students' ages, interest, and backgrounds.

- Engages in skilled questioning and leads effective student discussions, including using questioning and discussion to engage all students in exploring content; extends students' knowledge; and fosters active student inquiry, higher-order thinking, problem solving, and productive, supportive interactions, including appropriate wait time.

- Communicates directions, explanations, and procedures effectively and uses strategies for adjusting communication to enhance student understanding (e.g., by providing examples, simplifying complex ideas, using appropriate communication tools).

- Practices effective communication techniques and interpersonal skills (including both verbal and nonverbal skills and electronic communication) for meeting specified goals in various contexts.

Chapter 11

COMPETENCY 7

Communicating Effectively

MYRNA D. COHEN

University of Houston—Downtown

TERMS TO KNOW

Advance organizer

Analogy

Convergent question

Divergent question

Group processing

Leading question

Modeling

Nonverbal message

Probing question

Run-on question

Wait time

Competency 7 supports the notion that one pillar of good teaching is good communication. To be a master teacher, one needs to be a master communicator. In the discussion that follows, we examine what teachers can do to excel in communication. Four aspects of communication are explored: clear, accurate and appropriate communication; questioning skills; communicating directions, explanations, and procedures; and interpersonal skills.

CLEAR, ACCURATE, AND APPROPRIATE COMMUNICATION

Effective teachers are those who communicate with clarity and accuracy and with consideration for their children's developmental levels and interests. When teacher explanations are clear, logically sequenced, and connected to something with which the children are familiar, the chances for understanding are high. Conversely, when teacher explanations are vague, haphazardly put together, and foreign to students' experiences, the chances for understanding are greatly diminished. Explaining ideas in a classroom setting is more challenging and complex than explaining ideas in everyday conversation. It is a skill that requires attention and practice (MacDonald & Healy, 1999). Suggestions regarding classroom communication are presented in this section.

First of all, a teacher's choice of words and phrases is important. Precise, clear terms and words should be used in instruction rather than vague and ambiguous ones such as "sort of," "perhaps," or "somehow." Negative intensifiers such as "not much," or "not very," detract from clarity as do expressions such as "I guess," "you know," or "basically." Making a conscious effort to rid oral instruction of these terms improves clarity. Compare the following two sentences for clarity, and note that the second sentence is more effective.

1. This lesson, boys and girls, might help some of us learn a few more rules that can maybe help us with our spelling of most plurals.
2. In today's lesson we will learn three rules to help us spell plurals.

In addition, supporting verbal language with nonverbal communication aids comprehension. **Modeling** how a task is done is one powerful support. For example, a kindergarten teacher may say clearly, "OK, boys and girls, glue your orange circle inside the box on your paper," but unless the teacher simultaneously models this action as he or she speaks, the instructions might be confusing to children. Nonverbal support can also include written language, visuals, and concrete objects. A teacher who says, "Today we are going to learn about the equator" while pointing to it on a globe or map is using such support. A teacher who writes a new vocabulary word on the board or shows it on a sentence strip as he or she gives a definition also enhances clarity. A teacher who has each child hold a stuffed bear as she or he reads *Goldilocks and the Three Bears* creates a concrete support system.

Clear instruction also requires logical sequencing and precise objectives. Communicating the lesson objectives to children and using an **advance organizer,** a type of road map for the lesson, enhances clarity and helps children follow the sequence of concepts. For example, a teacher may begin a social studies lesson with, "Today we are going to discuss five ways that Native Americans used the buffalo in their lives. We will explore how the buffalo was used for food, shelter, clothing, tools, and amusement. Those uses are listed for us here on this chart" (shows chart). Children now know what to anticipate for the upcoming lesson and how the ideas are related to one another. To present concepts in a logical order and to avoid irrelevant or disjointed topics from interfering with that progression, the teacher should think about how the ideas of the lesson fit together. Preparing thoughtful lesson plans gives teachers the opportunity to consider how to put concepts together so that they build upon one another effectively.

Moreover, it is vital to signal conceptual transitions during instruction so that children understand, for example, that one idea is ending and another one is beginning. A teacher may say, "We have seen how different parts of the buffalo were used for clothing. Now, let's turn our attention to ways that the Native Americans depended on the buffalo for shelter." This comment signals to children that the discussion of one idea has ended and another one is about to begin. In addition, signals can be used to convey to students which concepts are the most important. This can be accomplished by giving vocal emphasis to chosen ideas or by repeating them (Eggen & Kauchak, 2001).

Clarity is also enhanced when teachers elaborate concepts with varied examples and/or analogies. It is difficult to think up examples and **analogies** on the spot, so teachers should prepare a list and include it in the lesson plan. Concrete examples, such as pictures, are worth a thousand words. They may take some time to find, but the clarity they provide will greatly enhance communication. For instance, when discussing the concept of camouflage, the teacher could elaborate by showing examples of jungle animals such as tigers and zebras, or colorful birds and butterflies in the tropics, or local insects such as grasshoppers or walking sticks in a more familiar environment. Examples could also include army uniforms and other military equipment. If a concept is foreign to children, using an analogy, wherein it is compared to something familiar, is very beneficial. For example, animals adapting to their environment could be analogous to people putting on coats in winter or waterproof raingear in wet weather. It is crucial for the teacher to choose examples and

analogies with which the children are familiar in order for instruction to be effective. To do this well, teachers must be knowledgeable about the developmental levels of their children (see Competency 1, Chapter 1), their cultures, and their interests (see Competency 2, Chapter 2).

Teachers can assess the effectiveness of their communication while the lesson is in progress. Asking students to paraphrase or summarize ideas from time to time is a good indicator of comprehension. Also, children's facial expressions and questions help teachers know when and how to adjust their presentations. Videotaping or audiotaping lessons to analyze them for clarity is an excellent tool for teachers.

SKILLED QUESTIONING

The content and construction of questions used in the classroom are covered in Competency 8. This competency, however, focuses on the ways in which the teacher communicates questions to children. Different ways of communicating questions determine different results. Teachers are expected to understand the intricacies of this process and to use questions wisely. Even the best question can fall flat on its face if it is not communicated effectively. There are many subtle and some not-so- subtle techniques to take into account as teachers consider how they will use questions in their classrooms. Look over the following ways that teachers describe their classrooms.

1. Every one of my children participates when we ask and answer questions in our class discussions.

2. My children think deeply about our questions in class. They give them serious thought.

3. My children are animated and involved in our discussions. They are motivated and excited!

4. My children listen intently to one another during class discussions.

Are these descriptions too good to be true? Most teachers would love to be able to say these things about their children, and some honestly can. The good news is that these descriptions are not to be found only in utopia. They are not far-fetched and do not depend on a magical potion. In fact, research has found specific ways to bring about these kinds of results with students; any teacher can one day honestly make similar remarks about his or her classroom. Let us look at each claim in detail and examine how each might be accomplished.

1. Every one of my children participates when we ask and answer questions in our class discussions.

We have all been in classrooms where a few dynamic students monopolize the discussions while the others inconspicuously fade into the background. One wonders whether the quiet students have ideas of their own and whether they are even paying attention to the lesson. Do they have interesting thoughts, but are they too shy to express them? Or are they thinking about what they will eat for lunch that day? Most teachers and children would rate classes with more student involvement as the more successful ones, but whose responsibility is it if only a fraction of the students are active? Most educators would agree that it is the teacher who determines the level of student participation. For those who value complete student participation, there are a number of points upon which to ponder.

First of all, teachers have to consider whether they are really giving all of their children equal opportunity to participate in class. Teachers often scoff at this question, but, in truth, sometimes they are not aware that they are being partial. Favoritism can be operationalized by their use of nonverbal language to encourage selected students to participate: using more eye contact, closer proximity, or encouraging facial expressions. More obviously, teachers may simply call on some students more than others. One type of bias is logistic orientation, which means that teachers may pay more attention to the students sitting in the front of the room, or on the left or right side. Gender and cul-

ture are important to consider as well, and teachers unwittingly may give hidden messages through the patterns of interaction that they direct. Imagine the hidden message of a teacher who calls only on boys for higher-level thinking questions and only on girls, minority students, or lower socio-economic status (SES) children for lower-level ones. Implicitly, these teachers are saying that they have higher intellectual expectations of boys than of girls, minority children, or less affluent children. Indeed, research has found that teachers often allow more time for boys to answer (wait time) than they do for girls, implying that they believe less in girls' abilities (Sadker & Sadker, 1994a). These tacit messages deter the children in question from participating because they are meeting the teachers' expectations as they internalize the implicit prejudice.

What can a teacher do to overcome these behaviors that result in unequal class participation? Fortunately, it is easy for a teacher to investigate whether he or she has biased tendencies by doing audiotape or videotape analyses of lessons or by asking a colleague to observe the class. Being aware of a bias is the first step in overcoming it. In addition, a teacher can employ a number of techniques to get all students to respond and to overcome unintended inequities. One way is to call on students in a pattern that is hidden from them. For example, the teacher may decide to call on children from every other table from front to back. They should change their patterns frequently so that children will not anticipate their turns. Using the class roll or seating plan can be helpful, too. In addition, moving around during the course of a lesson helps teachers be more equitable if they tend to call on children nearest to them. Some elementary school teachers put the names of their children on tongue depressors and randomly pull out a stick to call on students. The important point is that teachers should be aware of what they want. If choosing only volunteers is in order, that is fine at times. However, if teachers want all children to participate, they must be aware of possible personal biases and their effect on groups of children and should employ methods whereby equity of participation is assured. Teachers can train themselves to be equitable questioners.

Another way of getting all children involved is to have them commit individually to an answer by demanding a total-class response. A popular technique is the "thumbs up, thumbs down" method. For example, a teacher may say, "Do you think that these two bottles hold the same amount of liquid? All those who think yes, thumbs up, all those who think no, thumbs down." Everyone in the class responds within a few seconds, and the teacher can instantly get an idea about the thoughts of all children. Some teachers of young children elaborate on this technique further by using props. For example, during a phonics lesson a teacher may pass out pictures of objects pasted to a stick. He or she then may say, "Listen to the following paragraph. When you hear the 'l' sound, hold up your lollipop pictures, and when you hear the 'm' sound hold up your monkey pictures." Another way to accomplish total participation is to ask students to write a response. For example, the teacher may say, "Who do you think was the luckiest character in this story? Write your choice on a piece of paper and be ready to explain it." The teacher then can walk around the room, glance at responses, and make comments about the ideas. The important point here is that each student has committed to a more thoughtful answer. This technique can also flow easily into a Think-Pair-Share activity, which is discussed in detail in Competency 3, Part 2, Chapter 4.

Asking clear questions is an important skill that also impacts participation. Students need to feel safe about expressing ideas, and if they are unsure of what the teacher is asking, they may be reluctant to step forward. Questions that are vague and ambiguous, such as, "What about the space race in the 1950s?" lead children to wonder what you are getting at rather than to think about the topic. **Run-on questions** have the same effect. When children hear questions such as, "Could conditions on Mars support life, and would you want to live there?" they are left wondering which part of the question is the real one (Kindsvatter, Wilen, & Ishler, 1996). **Leading questions** are

ineffective in that they inhibit students' thoughts. Asking "Why was Davy Crockett important to Texas?" is more confining than "Do you think that Davy Crockett was important to Texas?" In the former leading question, the teacher infers that she believes Davy Crockett to be important to Texas and assumes that children agree. In this situation, students may avoid considering other opinions or may be reluctant to disagree with the teacher. Furthermore, negative questions are less favorable than positive ones. A negative question such as, "Who doesn't think that Davy Crockett was important to Texas?" would be intimidating, as would "Who doesn't know about Davy Crockett's life?" Out of embarrassment, children may not respond, in which case the question serves no purpose.

As these examples indicate, constructing well-phrased questions impacts the level of student participation. Because it is difficult to compose quality questions on the spot in the midst of a lesson, it is advisable to write well-thought-out questions into the lesson plans. The teacher may or may not be able to get to ask them as planned. However, even if the teacher does not implement them exactly as anticipated, the mental act of writing them out beforehand will have increased the likelihood of coming up with well-phrased questions during instruction. It is also important to be sensitive to children's feedback when engaged in discussions. Confused looks or unrelated children's responses are cues that the questions were not clear. In these instances, rephrasing or simplifying questions is in order.

2. My children think deeply about our questions in class. They give them serious thought.

The teacher also determines the quality of answers offered by children. Different questions are asked for different purposes. If a teacher asks a lower-level, **convergent question,** for which all answers should converge, or be the same, he or she should anticipate a simple recall response. An example is, "In which hemispheres is the United States located?" There is a right or a wrong answer that children either know or don't know. These recall questions are beneficial and should be used appropriately. However, they should be taken for what they are—questions that do not require creative or higher-level thinking. There is no problem with using recall or convergent questions. The only problem comes with using them too often and at the expense of **divergent questions,** questions with many possible answers. Bloom's taxonomy (see Competency 3, Part 1, Chapter 3) offers a stepladder for teachers to follow, not only for creating objectives but also for constructing questions on various levels.

Teachers who ask good, thought-provoking, divergent questions should anticipate a thoughtful response, assuming that they have asked the question skillfully. For example, a teacher should not undermine his or her own question by expecting children to answer quickly. Children need time to think about the question. A teacher who calls on a child a split second after asking a question is essentially telling the class that the question does not require much reflection, that it can be answered on the spot. However, by waiting after posing the question, the teacher communicates the opposite, that the question is complex and cannot be answered quickly. The time between asking a question and calling on a student to answer it is termed **wait time.** Research shows that if a teacher extends wait time, more children will have answers and more will attain a deeper level of thought. Sometimes teachers find it difficult to refrain from calling on children who eagerly wave their hands and beg to be called on immediately. But the teacher is in control and if the students see that he or she insists on reflection time, they will change their behavior to meet the teacher's expectations. Some teachers have devised gimmicks to condition themselves to allow for wait time. Counting silently to 10 or walking across the room before calling on a student may be helpful. It is difficult to fight the impulse that most of us have to "fill the silence" and shorten wait time. However, it is worth the effort because it encourages more and deeper thinking.

Another way to encourage reflection is by using **probing questions.** Rather than just accepting students' initial responses as the best that they can do, teachers can probe students so that they will refine and sharpen their thinking. For example, if a child responds that cats are his favorite pets, the teacher can ask him what differences he sees between cats and dogs as pets, or between cats and birds or fish, and why he chose one over the other. These questions stretch students to deeper levels of thinking as they ponder aspects that they might not have considered on their own. A teacher who uses no probes conveys to the students that they are not capable of more than their initial response.

Not all questions need to be higher-order ones. There is a time and a place for all kinds of questions. Often there is good reason to ask a convergent, lower-level question. Yet is important to note that effective teachers make informed decisions about the questions posed and are cognizant of the purposes and effects of those questions. Whether or not students think on deep levels is not happenstance. It is determined to a large degree by the type of questions teachers ask and by the manner in which they are asked. Teachers should know whether they want students simply to recall information or to think creatively, and they should ask accordingly. If divergent questions are used, wait time and probes will encourage student reflection.

3. My children are animated and involved in our discussions. They are motivated and excited!

Again, student motivation is not an uncontrollable mystery; teachers have great influence over it. One consideration is that students of all ages thrive on the approval of their teachers. The ways that a teacher responds to students' comments can either motivate them to participate or discourage them altogether. But what is motivating to children? This is a complicated question because different children prefer different rewards. For example, one child may thrive on public praise from the teacher, but a more inhibited child may be embarrassed by the same public praise. Experienced and sensitive teachers can adjust their feedback accordingly when they know their children. In general, however, teachers should make all children feel positive about participating in order to increase their motivation.

Feedback given for convergent questions has to convey whether or not the answer is correct. Some teachers may feel reluctant to tell children that they are "wrong" for fear of harming their self-esteem. Although this kind of sensitivity is admirable, it is truly doing the children a disservice to let mistakes go undetected. For example, if in a third-grade class a child remarks that there are mountains in Houston and Mr. Wiley does not correct her because he is reluctant to hurt her feelings, this is obviously poor judgment on the teacher's part. The comment must be corrected lest the whole class be misguided. Furthermore, children deserve to know that they made a mistake, why they have made the mistake, and what they need to do to improve (Kindsvatter, Wilen, & Ishler, 1996). In this case, the teacher could find out on what basis the student made her comment. Does she not understand what a mountain is? Does she think that since she has not seen all of Houston, there also may be mountainous parts of the city? Did she say it just because she wanted to participate and feel part of the class? After the reason for the error is determined, the teacher can help the child improve in a supportive and kind way.

As for harming egos, research has indicated that the manner in which the feedback is given is more powerful than the feedback itself. **Nonverbal messages** take precedence over verbal messages (Sadker & Sadker, 1994b). If a teacher says, "Sue, this was one of the best fables written by a student that I have ever read," but says it with a frown and in a harsh tone, the student will probably give more credence to the negative body language than to the positive verbal message and will interpret that as negative feedback. Thus even if a child stands to be corrected, the manner in which the correction is made determines the child's feelings about it. Furthermore, the teacher should be evaluating the idea, rather than the child. This

makes corrections less threatening. For instance, the comment "You are illogical" is much more damaging to a student than the comment "Your idea is illogical." Furthermore, students should feel appreciated for participating, even if their answers are "wrong." Giving feedback for *divergent* questions is another matter because there are no right or wrong answers. Here teachers should be open to original thinking on the part of their students. By no means should teachers limit their praise to ideas that conform to their own. Children should be given credit for contributing creative answers, even if they are so creative that they challenge the teacher's beliefs.

Kindsvatter, Wilen, and Ishler (1996), in their discussion on praise, point out that criticism seems to be more prevalent in classrooms than praise, even though praise is motivating and criticism is discouraging. They also point out that the most effective praise is specific rather than generic. A child will be more rewarded with a comment like "Good, Sue! That shows you have been thinking about the characteristics of mammals that we discussed last week" than a comment like "Good, Sue! Interesting point." The former shows that the teacher listened to the answer and the appreciation is credible. Giving specific praise prevents teachers from overusing reinforcement words, a practice that detracts from motivation. Expressions that are overused and general, such as "good, "right," and "okay," become empty and nonmotivating in the students' eyes. Teachers should be cautious not to overuse certain words and to be as specific as possible. One effective technique is to ask each child to select a favorite word or phrase to be used for praise. Children can even write their chosen words on decorated index cards to be placed on their desks. With this technique, not only are the words reinforcing, but the classroom environment becomes a warm, supportive place with small signs of "terrific," "right on," "good thinking," and so forth displayed throughout the room. Another technique is to post a chart with original praise words on a wall that is easily visible to the teacher. When the teacher cannot think of an original word, glancing at the chart can solve the problem. This technique can be expanded so that the list includes new vocabulary words for the children or even foreign words to enrich the children's knowledge and to spice up the day.

Another way to motivate students is to incorporate their answers and comments into the class discussion. Their ideas can be applied to new concepts, compared to similar examples, or used in the closure of the lesson. For example, a teacher may implement closure on a lesson on bats by saying, "Today we discussed some characteristics of bats. Maria pointed out that bats often live in caves, and Joey mentioned that they sleep upside down." The teacher can also paraphrase a student's idea for the class to better understand children's intent. These practices are considered effective for increasing motivation (Kindsvatter, Wilen, & Ishler, 1996).

Asking divergent, thought-provoking questions in and of itself motivates children to participate. It is much more exciting to think about questions that do not have clear-cut answers than to address those that have only one correct answer. If teachers ask questions to which they already know the answers, the questions are not authentic ones. It is no secret that the teacher is primarily interested in finding out whether children have learned the material rather than in finding an answer to the question. These questions are artificial and are unique to classrooms and learning contexts. Yet when teachers ask questions to which there can be new answers, learning becomes more dynamic for everyone. Consider the teacher who asks, "Are animals in our neighborhood well cared for? What happens to stray animals that are near our school? How can we be sure that animals are treated well?" These are authentic questions that the teacher and students can ponder together. Children understand that the teacher is learning along with them and that he or she is genuinely interested to hear the responses. Learning becomes authentic and exhilarating. Thinking and problem solving, which are inherently enjoyable and stimulating, permeate the classroom.

4. My children listen intently to one another during class discussions.

Teachers also impact how intently their students listen to one another. First of all, the teacher imparts this through his or her actions, or modeling. Sokolove, Sadker, and Sadker (1994) maintain that, "Students consciously and unconsciously imitate their teachers' styles of behavior, and often accept the attitudes and values projected by their teachers as their own" (p. 191). Johnson and Johnson (1994) concur. "Because there is evidence that students are most likely to imitate the person with the greatest power and control over the distribution of rewards, the teacher's behavior will have a powerful influence on student behavior" (p. 189). Therefore, when the teacher listens with respect to children's ideas and gives each student contribution thoughtful consideration, that teacher is conveying the value of children's ideas in the learning process. It also follows that children's creative thoughts should never be ridiculed or censured by the teacher. Children, in turn, will listen to each other respectfully and not ridicule each other. When it is clear that the teacher believes that children's answers are important for learning and that children as well as the teacher express important thoughts, the children will value each others' responses and listen to each other as they imitate their teacher.

The seating arrangement of a classroom can encourage or discourage children from listening to one another. A classroom that is set up so that all desks are in rows facing the front of the room sends the message that students will communicate with the teacher but not with each other. Indeed, it may be physically difficult for children to hear one another when seated in this fashion. If, on the other hand, the desks are arranged in a semicircle or with one half of the students facing the other half, the implicit message is that students will converse with each other and exchange ideas. Seating children in groups conveys a similar message. In these arrangements, children see each other's faces rather than the backs of their heads. Naturally, this is conducive to student-to-student communication.

Another technique to encourage students to listen to one another is for teachers to diminish their own presence in class discussions. The teacher can refrain from commenting on a child's idea and ask another child to react instead. Consider this example:

Teacher: Why would a young man in the 1400s have wanted to go on a voyage to explore the world?

Joey: Maybe to have some adventures and because he wanted to leave home?

Teacher: Sharon, what do you think of Joey's idea?

To answer the question, Sharon had to have listened carefully to Joey. The teacher did not repeat Joey's idea but assumed that all of the children listened to him. In a class discussion, it is common for all responses to filter through the teacher. However, there are alternatives. Discussions can proceed with children commenting on other children's ideas and the teacher's remarks only occasionally dispersed among the children's interactions. Teachers who implement this kind of exchange encourage children to value each other's ideas and to listen intently.

In addition to modeling and to the indirect techniques mentioned above, teachers can teach listening skills directly as part of their classroom curriculum. In fact, productive communication skills should be taught, especially in classrooms that rely on good student-to-student interaction and in classrooms that use group work and discussion extensively. Teachers should not take it for granted that children will instinctively acquire these skills. Listening to others without interrupting, checking for understanding, treating others with respect, understanding how others feel, and controlling emotions are often addressed directly (Aronson & Patnoe, 1997), as are building and maintaining trust, providing leadership, and managing conflicts (Johnson & Johnson, 1994).

Johnson and Johnson (1994) point out that such skills are vital to the learning process in order to engage in effective cooperative learning. They are also valuable in and of themselves for future workplace and social interactions. Teachers implementing cooperative learning often work on team building and interpersonal skills before they even begin to teach the academic subject matter. Johnson and Johnson recommend an eight-step approach for the direct teaching of these skills.

1. Ask the students what skills they think they will need in order to cooperate (compete, work individually) successfully.

2. Help the students get a clear understanding of what the skill is, conceptually and behaviorally.

3. Set up practice situations.

4. Ensure that each student receives feedback on how well he or she is performing the skill.

5. Encourage students to persevere in practicing the skill.

6. Set up situations in which the skills can be used successfully.

7. Require that the skills be used often enough to become integrated into the students' behavioral repertoires.

8. Set classroom norms to support the use of the skills. (pp. 188–190)

Another technique that builds expertise in interactive skills is for children to engage in self-evaluation of those skills. This type of activity heightens students' awareness of their behavior and helps them identify skills on which they need to work for improvement. **Group processing** (Johnson & Johnson, 1994) is a popular way to accomplish this. Here students discuss their strengths and weaknesses as a group and determine goals for working together more effectively in the future. The processing can be accomplished in numerous ways. For instance, children can assess individually or in groups, and orally or in writing. They may complete a reflective assessment form on themselves and on each group member. The form may include questions concerning the quality of children's work, how much the child contributed to the group learning, how dependable the student was about completing assigned tasks, or whether or not the child asked for help when necessary. Young children whose reading and writing skills are not yet developed can respond by circling a smiley face or a frowny face as the teacher reads contributing factors. Group members can compare their ratings and discuss discrepancies. Through self-assessment and reflection, the students become less dependent on their teacher for evaluation and more empowered in understanding what to do in order to work together productively.

COMMUNICATING DIRECTIONS, EXPLANATIONS, AND PROCEDURES

Another important skill for communication in the classroom is clarity in giving directions. In addition to explaining concepts and ideas relating to the subject area, teachers must communicate well when it comes to explaining classroom procedures. If teachers give clear, understandable instructions, children will be able to meet these expectations. But ambiguous directions can result in nightmares for teacher and students alike. Imagine being a student of a teacher who says, "When your group finishes the project, answer questions 1 through 5 on page 53." On the surface this sounds clear enough, yet as the children proceed they may wonder whether they are to continue to work as a group or an individual, whether they should write the answers or prepare them orally, or whether it is permissible to talk about the answers with fellow classmates. Children generally want to please their teachers, but teachers sometimes unwittingly make it difficult for the students to do so by not communicating well.

When teachers prepare important yet complicated directions, for example, for a new activity, they should visualize the children going through each stage of the activity so that they do not overlook any detail. As they communicate the directions, they should do so orally as well as in writing. In this way, they are accommodating different learning preferences, and children can refer to the written instructions if they do not recall some of the details. Always writing the page number of the text being used on a specific area of the board can avoid confusion. If appropriate, graphic representation might also be of value. If children cannot yet read, the teacher can use pictures or symbols to represent the instructions. For example, using a felt board, a teacher can visually reinforce directions for a cut-and-paste project by placing cutout felt scissors by number one, a glue bottle by number two, crayons by number three, and so forth. For a group activity, the directions should be explained in whole-class format before the students divide into groups because if clarification is in order, it is easier when the class is still in whole-group format. Asking children to repeat directions is also a good way to ensure that directions have been communicated well. Reiteration of important steps is also advisable. Remember that clear directions add to a positive class climate because they make children feel safe. Children can concentrate on the task at hand rather than expend energy wondering what they are supposed to do. They are able to please the teacher when they understand what is expected of them.

INTERPERSONAL SKILLS

In addition to knowing how to communicate when teaching, effective teachers also know how to communicate with their children in other contexts, such as in noninstructional situations. Children appreciate teachers who make them feel valued, respected, and comfortable. Teachers who can develop positive relationships with their students are often those to whom students turn in times of confusion. Those teachers are the ones who frequently become role models and mentors. Because of the positive interpersonal groundwork built by these teachers, children often look to them for guidance and support. They are the ones of whom students will often say in later years, "She (or he) changed my life." Effective interpersonal communication also influences learning because rich learning is generally tied to good feelings and to strong emotional bonds with those involved. Following is a selection of concepts teachers should consider as they reflect upon developing effective teacher-to-student communication.

Active Listening

Of course, communication is a two-way process. Just as teachers have to be aware of what they are saying to children (with both words and body language), conversely, they also must be sure that they understand what children are saying to them. Sokolove, Sadker, and Sadker (1994) explore this skill in detail, as do Johnson and Johnson (1994). Some of their most important points are discussed in the following paragraphs.

Think about all of the nonverbal actions that say that someone is really listening to and interested in what the other person is relaying. With young children, bending, kneeling, or sitting down so that both adult and child are on the same level is important. Direct eye contact, a relaxed posture, leaning forward, and being physically close are all signs that you are intently listening to the other. Of course, the opposite is also true. We would not feel compelled to share our thoughts and feelings with someone who would not look at us, or who would stand as far away from us as possible with arms folded on the chest. Most of us would tend to end the conversation, given this kind of response. Orally, we can encourage the other to continue talking by being quiet. Our silence tells the other person that we want him or her to talk. In addition, occasionally summarizing or paraphrasing what the other person has said keeps both participants on track. If a summary is inaccurate, it provides an opportunity to clear up misunderstandings and improve communication. These summaries should be nonevaluative and noninferential. They should reflect the speaker's message without our opinion attached. For example, saying "So, with your mom's new job she is not at home when you leave for school in the morning. You're saying that mornings are more difficult for you now," is better than, "So, it is really sad that your mom isn't home in the mornings. How could she have taken a job with those hours? How can she expect you to get to school on your own? How irresponsible of her."

As teachers listen, they should also pay attention to nonverbal messages. These messages can be reflected back to the speaker to give him or her more knowledge (to determine whether there are discrepancies between the verbal and nonverbal messages). For example, a teacher helping a child who is having difficulty with a mathematics concept may say, "When I ask you to do a set of problems, you say they are easy, but then you take a long time fiddling through your supplies before you get started." As noted, nonverbal messages are usually more genuine than verbal. Teachers can share their observations and interpretations carefully with the speaker to see whether their reading of the message is accurate. One might say, "When we begin a writing assignment, you take a long time to begin the first sentence. That makes me think that you might find this work difficult. Sometimes when we put things off it is because we are uncomfortable with them. Is there something we can do together that would help you feel more comfortable with the writing process?"

If a teacher practices the techniques of active listening, the chances that children will share ideas and concerns increase. Teachers who wish to have close interpersonal relationships with children outside the academic environment should consider practicing these skills. Active listening encourages children to confide in the teacher.

Realness

This quality, defined by Rogers (Rogers & Freiberg, 1994), relates to the way that the students perceive the teacher. Rogers believes that children should be able to see their teacher as a real person, with all strengths and weaknesses, rather than as an unapproachable, perfect authority figure. When children view their teacher as a real human being, they can identify with him or her more. They may think, "Even the teacher has good days and bad days. It's okay for me to have a bad day once in a while, too!" Teachers who are excited at times and sad at others seem more real. When a teacher is willing to admit to imperfection, there is more honesty in the classroom environment. A teacher who insists on being viewed as a flawless authority gives students a false impression about human nature and is less approachable than a "real" teacher. Students should learn from their teachers that, just as we all have special talents, we all also have faults that we need to recognize. Teachers can also share and model the way in which they deal with faults that plague them. For example, teachers may reveal that they, too, sometimes fall into the trap of procrastinating and not managing their time wisely. They may admit that they, too, must sometimes work late into the night when they have put off a project and now must meet a deadline, although they wish that they could eliminate this tendency. Teachers are not people playing interchangeable roles, but are genuine and unique human beings, and students should recognize them as such. Moreover, by communicating their feelings appropriately, teachers also model how to express feelings to others.

Acceptance

Rogers (Rogers & Freiberg, 1994) maintains that by accepting students, teachers create a strong feeling of trust in their classrooms. Teachers who "accept" children have a basic belief in the goodness and well-meaning intentions of children even though some of their behaviors may find disfavor in the teacher's eyes. There is also a distinction between the children and their behaviors, so that the teacher may disapprove of the child's actions but never of the child him- or herself. A child whose teacher displays "acceptance" knows that the teacher trusts and believes in him or her and that even foolish actions will not shake that trust. This quality is reflected in the comment, "Maria, your constant chattering during class is annoying," which is quite different from the comment,

"Maria, *you* are annoying." The former comment communicates rejection of the behavior but not the child; the latter does not differentiate between child and behavior and implies a personal rejection. When teachers exhibit acceptance, students still have to suffer the consequences for their poor behavior, but deep down, their teacher's belief in them as good and worthy human beings will not be damaged. Children whose teachers "accept" them in this fashion gain a strong sense of security, which facilitates learning.

Empathic Understanding

According to Rogers (Rogers & Freiberg, 1994) empathic understanding adds to a student's feeling of well-being in the school environment. Teachers who exhibit this quality are able to see through their children's eyes. They recognize that their children experience the world through perspectives different from their own and can glimpse what those perspectives are. This ability makes children feel that someone understands them, a feeling that increases security and improves their learning environment. Teachers with empathic understanding try to get a deeper understanding of how their children perceive reality and react accordingly. The opposite of empathic understanding is egocentrism, which is "embeddedness in one's own viewpoint to the extent that one is unaware of other points of view and the limitation of one's perspective" (Johnson & Johnson, 1994, p. 66). As classrooms become more diverse, practicing empathic understanding becomes more crucial.

Cultural Sensitivity

The best teacher communicators understand that they have to take the cultural norms of their children into account in their teacher-student interactions. The diversity in our schools is great, and it is constantly growing. The probability of a teacher's instructing students from cultures different from his or her own is very high. It is probably impossible for a teacher to be an expert on the communicative norms of every single culture represented by the students in our schools. Yet the teacher, at minimum, should acknowledge that cultural differences exist and that it is his or her responsibility to try to understand students better in order to communicate better with them.

Researchers have investigated many multicultural aspects of education upon which teachers should reflect. For example, children may be comfortable with different cultural norms than those of the teacher and of the school culture. Norms are defined as behaviors and habits that permeate an environment. These are often so taken for granted that members of the culture may not even be conscious of them. Just as fish may not know that water exists until they are taken out of it, many people are not aware of their cultural norms until they are immersed in a different culture. It is the responsibility of teachers to heighten their own awareness of cultural norms so that they do not impair communication with their students.

Many examples of nonmainstream cultural norms can be found in educational writings. Not acknowledging them can lead to harmful misunderstandings. For example, as mentioned previously, the use of eye contact is one norm that could interfere with communication. Some cultures use indirect rather than direct eye contact as a sign of respect. Conversely, in our North American culture, direct eye contact is a sign of respect, although if it is too direct, it may be seen as defiant. If a culturally insensitive teacher converses with a student who will not look teachers directly in the eye, that teacher may unjustly come to the conclusion that the student is acting disrespectfully. A wiser teacher would consider that there may be a cultural misunderstanding at play and would be less likely to misjudge the student. Similarly, the distance that people place between themselves and others is also culturally bound. North Americans prefer a greater distance than South Americans do, for instance, and children prefer less distance than adults do. In addition, some cultures are comfortable with physical touch and others are not. In some cultures, conversations between students and teachers about personal subjects are accepted, and in others they are not. Questioning authority is valued in some cultures, whereas in others it is disfavored.

Master teacher communicators are aware that these cultural discrepancies exist, even though they may not know about each of them specifically. Such teachers are not quick to judge students; rather they explore the possibility of cultural misunderstandings before jumping to conclusions. When a teacher is feeling negative about a student, one of the first questions that he or she needs to ask is if there is a cultural difference at play and whether it is affecting the relationship with that student. For example, suppose that a student did not participate at all in a class activity wherein feelings about family were discussed. A sensitive teacher would consider numerous possibilities for this behavior. Maybe the student was being obstinate to attract attention, or maybe the student was just shy, or maybe there was a cultural element at play. Perhaps it was against the cultural norms of the student to talk publicly about something so personal. Sensitive teachers include culture as a variable to consider in the analysis of student behavior. In this instance, the lack of participation could have been due to any of the possibilities considered. The crucial point is that the teacher included culture as a variable to consider.

In addition to impacting student-teacher communication, cultural norms can also impact student achievement. When there is a difference between communication patterns used in school and those used at home, learning may suffer, especially with young children. Consider, for example, the asking of questions. In White cultural interaction patterns, parents often ask children questions to which they clearly already know the answer. They may ask, "What animal is this?" or "What color is the balloon?" In Black culture, this kind of questioning may not be customary. These questions would not be asked because it is clear that the adult knows the answer. Because patterns like the former are used in school, children who are accustomed to this mode of questioning have a high comfort level; they understand what is expected of them. Yet these kinds of questions might be unfamiliar and confusing to children who are not used to such patterns (Heath, 1990). Other varied communication patterns that could lead to misunderstanding in the school environment include the use of praise, corrections, clarification, and the ways of calling on students (McGroarty, 1990). Effective teachers must be aware of these cultural norms as well and not discriminate against children who need to be acculturated into the world of school.

Respect

A positive classroom environment presupposes mutual respect between teacher and children. But what does it really mean for a teacher to respect students? One point is that the teacher has responsibilities toward the students just as the students have responsibilities toward the teacher. For example, teachers expect their students to come to class prepared, with assignments completed and materials ready. Teachers should likewise come to class with well-prepared lessons, assignments graded within a reasonable time frame, and so on. Teachers who value their children's time are also showing respect. Assigning busywork with little instructional value indicates a level of disrespect on the part of the teacher. Fairness toward children is another aspect of respect. Children deserve rules that are well explained, with consequences that are consistently carried out. Examinations should not be constructed to trick children but should be valid evaluation instruments.

Perhaps most important, respectful teachers do not make fun of their children. A child may resent a teacher for a lifetime if that student is humiliated in class. Making a joke at the expense of a child is inexcusable. Teachers who sincerely respect their children do not belittle them outside the classroom either, not even in the teachers' lounge. Likewise, teachers who manage their classes by intimidation techniques are abusing their power. Children who behave for fear of erratic outbursts and degradation harbor resentment for their teacher, not respect. Teachers should avoid using sarcasm with children, even if it is well intentioned, because it can be easily misconstrued and become hurtful. For example, a teacher may joke with a gifted child who usually gets excellent grades by saying, "Sharon must have studied very hard for this spelling test. Even she got all of the words right!" Children may not grasp the intended playful sarcasm in this remark. Sharon might think that the teacher believes she is weak in spelling and has to work very hard to do well. Moreover, other children in the class, upon hearing the comment, may likewise get this impression because they comprehend the remark at face value. They may also begin to fear that the teacher will turn on them next. For these reasons, although humor is appreciated, sarcasm should be avoided with children. Classrooms that emanate mutual respect are safe places for students; classrooms without it are frightening places that impede learning.

SUMMARY

This chapter explored ways in which teachers can improve their communication skills. The importance of communicating clearly was addressed in terms of using precise vocabulary, stating lesson objectives, drawing attention to the transition from concept to concept, and employing relevant and appropriate examples and analogies. Developing expertise in questioning was also emphasized. Skilled questioning results in fair and equal student participation, thoughtful responses, student involvement, and positive student-to-student interactions. Paying careful attention to clarity when giving directions and explaining classroom procedures was also stressed. Finally, several aspects of effective interpersonal skills such as active listening, acceptance, and cultural sensitivity were highlighted.

GLOSSARY

advance organizer   a technique usually used at the beginning of the lesson, wherein the teacher provides students with the structure, overview, and nature of content of the upcoming learning experience.

analogy a comparison wherein one describes similarities between ideas that are generally considered dissimilar.

convergent question a question for which there is one correct answer.

divergent question a question for which there are many possible answers.

group processing an activity wherein members of a group reflect and evaluate their functioning as a group.

leading question a nonobjective question in which the opinion of the one asking the question can be inferred from the way in which the question is asked.

modeling teacher demonstrations of tasks; learning that is a result of observing the behaviors and actions of others.

nonverbal message a communication expressed with body language, gestures, tone of voice, expression, and so forth.

probing question a follow-up question used to encourage deeper thinking through elaboration, clarification, justification, and so forth.

run-on questions more than one question asked at one time.

wait time the time between asking a question and calling on a student for a response.

SUGGESTED ACTIVITIES

1. Observe a classroom for a number of lessons. Evaluate the classroom for each of the following components and analyze the teacher's actions that you believe contribute to each component.

   - Clarity of teacher explanations
   - Quality of student participation
   - Quality of student answers
   - Student-student interaction
   - Types of teacher feedback

2. List and discuss any instances of cultural misunderstandings or cultural sensitivities that you have seen at your school observations.

3. Develop an activity that may help your future students become more sensitive to cultures other than their own.

4. Do you see effective interpersonal communication skills among teachers and students at your school? Explain your answer by giving specific details.

5. Use metacognition to analyze whether or not you were a good listener in a conversation. What impedes being a good listener in the classroom? How can you overcome obstacles?

PRACTICE QUESTIONS

1. Ms. Chips is reviewing her lesson plan for tomorrow's topic on fables. She plans to read three fables with her children. She wants to instill higher-level thinking and tries to list some divergent questions. Which of the following questions would be *least* helpful for Ms. Chips?

   A. What are some things that these three fables have in common?

   B. Which of the three morals do you think is most important to your life?

   C. Why do you think so many people like to read fables?

   D. Who wrote and illustrated each of the fables that we read today?

2. Mr. Moreno wants to discuss the concept of rules with his inner-city first graders. He wants them to understand how important it is to have rules and to follow them and he wants to enhance this concept with examples and analogies. Which of the following statements would be the most effective for Mr. Moreno?

   A. Rules are really important. Think about how important it is to follow directions when you want to mail in a rebate for a refund.

   B. Think about playing hide and seek. What if you were playing with friends who did not follow the rules? What would happen to the game?

   C. Think about playing the game Trivial Pursuit. What would happen if you were playing with friends who did not follow the rules?

D. What would happen if your parents did not follow the rules when they filed for their income tax?

3. Ms. Davies notices that Rosa, one of her second-grade students, seems troubled and distracted in class. Ms. Davies would like Rosa to talk about what is troubling her. One afternoon Rosa begins to tell Ms. Davies what is on her mind. To encourage Rosa to continue talking, Ms. Davies might

A. Sit down so that she is on the same level as Rosa, maintain eye contact, and listen without interruption.

B. Respond in the middle of Rosa's story to tell Rosa about her own experiences.

C. Immediately give Rosa some advice in order to save time.

D. Stand up so that Rosa must glance upwards to Ms. Davies. In this way, she will realize that Ms. Davies is an authority figure.

4. Mr. Arlens has car pool duty and sees that Kathy has been misbehaving. Kathy opened another student's backpack, took out a box of crayons, and threw it on the ground, making that child cry. She also pushed and shoved some students smaller than she. Which of the following is the most effective verbal response that Mr. Arlens could give to Kathy's actions?

A. Kathy, your behavior today is very bad.

B. Kathy, you are a bad girl today.

C. Kathy, you are an inconsiderate person. Who would want to be your friend?

D. Kathy, I am going to tell your parents what a rude girl you are.

Answers and Discussion

Answer 1: Note that we are looking for the *least* helpful question for higher-level thinking. Choice *D* is a convergent question for which there is a right answer. Students must locate the correct names of authors and illustrators in order to answer this question. Choices *A*, *B*, and *C* are all divergent questions, which can have multiple answers. For choice *A*, numerous commonalties exist among the three fables that children may think of, although fables share some standard characteristics. For choice *B* there is certainly no right answer, because this question involves personal judgment. Choice *C* also has numerous possible answers that involve the children's opinions. The answer is *D*.

Answer 2: Remember that examples and analogies must be age appropriate and relevant to children's lives. Choice *B* is relevant and appropriate because first-grade children who are not very affluent probably play hide and seek. It is not an expensive game that must be purchased. Choices *A*, *C*, and *D* are not age appropriate. Although children may see adults carrying out these activities, they are not as relevant, and therefore not as effective, as choice *B*. The answer is *B*.

Answer 3: Choice *A* includes behaviors that facilitate communication: being on the same physical level, maintaining eye contact, and quiet listening. Choice *B* is incorrect because by telling about her own experiences, Ms. Davies communicates to Rosa that she does not want to listen, but that she would rather talk. Choice *C* is inappropriate for two reasons: Giving quick advice stymies communication because it is judgmental. Also, time should not be an issue when encouraging someone to open up and communicate. Choice *D* is inappropriate because this body language emphasizes the distance between teacher and child, rather than closeness. The answer is *A*.

Answer 4: Choice *A* incorporates effective interpersonal skills because it separates the child from the behavior. It is the behavior that is bad, not Kathy. The child perceives that the teacher dislikes her behavior but not that the teacher dislikes her. This is the essence of "acceptance." Choices *B*, *C*, and *D* all imply that the child herself is bad or rude or inconsiderate. The emphasis is on the dislike of the child, rather than the dislike of the behavior. The answer is *A*.

WEB LINKS

Remember that Web site locations may change. If any of these sites have moved or cannot be located, use terms in the index to search for further information.

http://www.infed.org/thinkers/et-rogers.htm

This site offers information about Carl Rogers and his theories.

http://sps.k12.mo.us/coop/ecoopmain.html

This Web site offers cooperative learning lessons for all grade levels (K–5) and various content areas.

http://ericir.syr.edu/Virtual/Lessons/new2.shtml

This site offers a collection of lesson plans. There are plans for all levels including grades Pre-K–4. These plans provide an excellent source of ideas for student-centered activities and divergent questions.

http://www.splcenter.org/teachingtolerance/tt-index.html

This site is for teaching tolerance. It helps teachers foster equity, respect, and understanding in the classroom.

http://www.ascd.org/frameedlead.html

This site offers articles from *Educational Leadership* many of which relate to ideas in this competency.

http://www.pdkintl.org/kappan/kappan.htm

This site offers access to current issues of the *Phi Delta Kappan* journal. Selected articles can be viewed in their entirety online.

REFERENCES

Aronson, E., & Patnoe, S. (1997). *The jigsaw classroom.* New York: Addison Wesley Longman.

Eggen, P., & Kauchak, D. (2001). *Educational psychology: Windows on classroom* (5th ed). New York: MacMillan College.

Heath, S. B. (1990). Sociocultural contexts of language development. In Bilingual Education Office, California State Department of Education, ed., *Beyond language: Social and cultural factors in schooling language minority students* (pp. 143–186). Los Angeles: Evaluation, Dissemination and Assessment Center.

Johnson, D. W., & Johnson, R. T. (1994). *Learning together and alone.* Boston: Allyn & Bacon.

Kindsvatter, R., Wilen, W., & Ishler, M. (1996). *Dynamics of effective teaching.* White Plains, NY: Longman.

MacDonald, R. E., & Healy, S. D. (1999). *A handbook for beginning teachers.* New York: Addison Wesley Longman.

McGroarty, M. (1990). Educators' responses to sociocultural diversity: Implications for practice. In Bilingual Education Office, California State Department of Education, ed., *Beyond language: Social and cultural factors in schooling language minority students* (pp. 299–334). Los Angeles: Evaluation, Dissemination and Assessment Center.

Rogers, R., & Freiberg, J. H. (1994). *Freedom to learn.* New York: MacMillan College.

Sadker, M., & Sadker, D. (1994a). *Failing at fairness.* New York: Touchstone.

Sadker, M., & Sadker, D. (1994b). Questioning skills. In J. Cooper, (Ed.), *Classroom teaching skills* (pp. 115–152). Boston: D. C. Heath.

Sokolove, S., Sadker, M., & Sadker, D. (1994). Interpersonal communication skills. In Cooper, J., ed., *Classroom teaching skills* (pp. 189–231). Boston: D. C. Heath.

Competency 8

The teacher provides appropriate instruction that actively engages students in the learning process.

The beginning teacher:

- Employs various instructional techniques (e.g., discussion, inquiry) and varies teacher and student roles in the instructional process, and provides instruction that promotes intellectual involvement and active student engagement and learning.

- Applies various strategies to promote student engagement and learning (e.g., by structuring lessons effectively, using flexible instructional groupings, pacing lessons flexibly in response to student needs, including wait time).

- Presents content to students in ways that are relevant and meaningful and that link with students' prior knowledge and experience.

- Applies criteria for evaluating the appropriateness of instructional activities, materials, resources, and technologies for students with varied characteristics and needs.

- Engages in continuous monitoring of instructional effectiveness.

- Applies knowledge of different types of motivation (i.e., internal, external) and factors affecting student motivation.

- Employs effective motivational strategies and encourages students' self-motivation.

Chapter 12

COMPETENCY 8 – PART 1

Actively Engaging Children in Learning

JANICE L. NATH

University of Houston—Downtown

TERMS TO KNOW

Attention span
Classroom Discussion Model
Convergent questions
Deductive strategy
Discovery learning
Divergent questions
Halt time
Inductive strategy

Instructional strategy
Learner-centered (or student-centered)
Model of teaching
Monitoring
Pacing
Risk-free environment
Role-play

Selective attention
Simulations
Teacher-as-an-audience/observer
Teacher-as-a-coach
Teacher-as-a-guide
Teacher-as-a-facilitator
Teacher-centered
Wait time

Competency 8 centers on the development of appropriate instruction that actively engages children in the learning process. Included in this chapter are: (1) variations of teacher and student roles, (2) instruction and variations of strategies that promote intellectual involvement and active student engagement, (3) presentation of relevant and meaningful content, and (4) monitoring of instructional effectiveness. The second part of this competency (Chapter 13) describes motivational issues associated with developing and implementing instruction that fully engages students.

TEACHER ROLES

Competency 8 is about instruction that *actively* engages children in learning. But what does that really mean? Aren't children engaged in learning all of the time when they are at school? Sadly, the answer is, "No." What is it, then, that makes learning active and engaging? It is very simple, in a manner of speaking—it is when the teacher has designed instruction so that *children* are doing most of the work of learning and thinking during lessons, rather than the teacher. Does this happen when teachers spend their day telling or giving children information then asking them simply to recall it? Does it happen when children are asked continuously to use only lower-level thinking or provide lower-level answers on worksheets? Again, the answer is, "No!" Children become more engaged when higher-level teaching strategies and techniques are implemented, instruction is exciting, and the roles of teachers and children change throughout the days and weeks of the school year.

When investigating strategies for children in creative thinking areas, researchers find that exciting teachers ask children to take on the roles of

(or "become") explorers, authors, designers, teachers, and performers so that learners *produce* knowledge rather than passively listen or *consume* knowledge. This requires that teachers change their role from that of a traditional instructor or a "banking role," where teachers "deposit" knowledge into children (Freire, 1993), to roles that make children active learners. When teachers take on the roles of facilitator, coach, learner, and audience, children become more engaged in learning.

The role of **teacher-as-a-facilitator** is evident when teachers set up opportunities for children to collaborate, design, and create in a more independent but supported manner. Facilitating teachers provide a rich learning environment and structure for learning, then help when there are questions or stumbling blocks. Facilitators "ease the way" by instructing through supporting, rather than directing or telling. They often engage children in exploratory or inductive approaches in which children make decisions in their own learning (Fradd & Lee, 1999). In addition, educators Ryan and Cooper (1998) advise that for technology to be truly integrated into the classroom, teachers must move from whole-class instruction to small-group instruction where the teacher serves as a **facilitator** and/or coach. Sometimes rather than have children turn in a paper, teachers move into the role of the **teacher-as-an-audience** (or **observer**) when a student product is completed, then demonstrated, explained, or performed by children. Creating a weather channel "report" in groups to explain a weather phenomenon, for example, then recording it on videotape for viewing by the class is a higher-level synthesis activity. A teacher *facilitates* during the writing process and then later participates as an *audience* member, as the class watches and critiques the weather reports. In another example, the teacher-as-an-audience role can be illustrated as a teacher watches skits that small groups have prepared on the progression of blood through the circulatory system (rather than giving a short lecture on the process). We also see this trend during a lesson on why geometry works in bracing construction. In this type of lesson, children are given materials such as straws and tape to see which group can create the highest structure that will stand on its own. Groups or individuals are *facilitated* during the construction process, then watched (*audience* role) as they explain their structures and rationales for their buildings to the class. The **teacher-as-a-guide's** role comes in mediating and adjusting to help students obtain information on their own (such as in Suchman's Inquiry, introduced later in this chapter). In this role, it is important for the teacher to scaffold, model, and provide direction, although students should still be the "active seekers" of information. Essential to all of these roles is the **teacher-as-a-coach,** where immediate feedback and encouragement is given to children as new skills are attempted. This involves closely monitoring children at each step of learning so that immediate corrections and encouragement can be offered, because children who practice mistakes retain those misconceptions. It is very difficult to go back and change learning when rehearsal and repetition have occurred over a period of time. Because the roles that teachers assume have such a direct impact upon children, teachers should continuously reflect upon all roles they assume in the classroom. If a teacher always maintains the position of traditional "sage-upon-the-stage," children will tend to be passive receivers of education, rather than active seekers.

The roles discussed above are the major categories of teacher roles, but there are many other types of roles for which teachers wear "different hats" during their school year. For example, a teacher must sometimes wear the hat of a psychologist, a communications specialist, a human relations specialist, and many others. In Competency 3, Chapters 3 and 4, other teacher roles are discussed. As a reminder of these roles in play, teachers set the stage (*stager/director/planner*) in order for play to be of educational value. Thus they provide suitable materials for play to take place and facilitate it by providing specified areas that promote play. In this role, teachers clearly label areas or centers so that children understand the purpose of play there, they provide physical areas that are set apart for particular purposes (such as larger areas for cooperative play and smaller areas for quiet listening or individual reflective play), and they design areas in which others do not wander through, interrupting building construction or other play projects. The role of *playmate,* or *active participant,* is where teachers model and elaborate in play. As a participant, the teacher can also become a *co-explorer* (Elgas & Lynch, 1998), as she or he asks children questions or participates in play as a problem solver. As co-explorers, teachers can participate through parallel play, in which the teacher plays alongside of children, not with them (but children are viewing what the teacher is doing). As a co-player of any type, the teacher must let the child lead in play. In yet another role, the teacher may become an active *observer* in order to evaluate and support students' play. As an *evaluator,* the teacher must be able to diagnose difficulties, reflect upon students' successes in development and learning through play, and communicate growth to others. See Competency 3, Part 2, Chapter 4, for more details.

HOW TO USE VARIOUS ACTIVITIES

Variation in activities is critical for children's interest and motivation. Everyone becomes bored after a time with the same methods of instruction—no matter what type of instruction might be used. Indicators for this competency maintain that beginning teachers should be able to employ a variety of engaging activities. A most effective way to bring variety into the classroom is through changing instructional strategies often and engaging children in *models of teaching.* Employing an **instructional strategy** means to select a way of instruction that will meet the needs, goals, and objectives of learners. Thus after teachers decide what must be taught, the choice of instructional strategies answers the questions of, "Now, how will I teach that?" and "What will my strategy be to have children learn this in the best ways possible?" In making choices for "how," teachers must always keep in mind the reasons behind their choices, asking questions such as (a) why should I teach content or skills that way; (b) what are the strengths of the strategy I am considering; (c) what is the fit to the content; and, particularly, (d) for whom am I making these choices?

Strategies can be viewed within several different frameworks. For example, there are **teacher-centered** strategies and **learner-centered** strategies. In *direct instruction,* for example, teachers traditionally provide and/or explain information, model skills and expectations, and finally give students an opportunity to practice with feedback followed by evaluation. The learner's role is more as a "receiver" of knowledge. The teacher has a very *visible* role in teacher-centered strategies. On the other hand, by using a cooperative learning strategy, children are more active and interactive in their learning, as the teacher moves into the background in the role of facilitator, described earlier. However, both can be appropriate, depending on the circumstances. Each is a part of instruction that creates variety.

Strategies can also be defined as deductive or inductive. A **deductive strategy** begins with "knowns" and moves to conclude with "unknowns," such as in a lecture-type lesson or in a "direct teach" described above, wherein a teacher provides definitions or steps for skills, and children follow with guided and independent practice. However, an **inductive strategy,** such as an inquiry or a discovery lesson, begins with curious events, scenarios, "unknowns," or interesting questions and moves to "knowns," or to finding answers. This is a more student-centered approach, in which the child actively searches for knowledge. Again, the teacher serves as a facilitator or guide in an inductive approach. Many teacher education students are confused by the inductive and deductive approaches. Perhaps they have seen or read of the famous

Sherlock Holmes telling his friend, Dr. Watson, "Deductive, my dear fellow, deductive!" Teacher candidates assume that crime solving is deductive. That is not the case. When he said, "Deductive!" Sherlock was systematically instructing, or lecturing Watson on how the facts of the case came together to determine "who done it." The process by which Holmes searched for important evidence and put many pieces of evidence together to find the answer or solve the crime was strictly *inductive*.

Models of Teaching

Models of teaching offer us a clear plan for instruction that can help us reach the goals that we select. But what is a **model of teaching?** Think of a model simply as an empty building. A building can be filled with many different types of things, as can a model of teaching. Perhaps the best known models of teaching are those classified under the heading of cooperative grouping, such as Jigsaw II, STAD, Numbered Heads, and so forth (see Competency 3, Part 2, Chapter 4). Just as a building can be filled with apartments, offices, or storage rooms, a teacher knows that a cooperative grouping model can "be filled" with language arts, science, social studies, mathematics, and other subject areas. Besides cooperative models there are other models of teaching that are "empty buildings," waiting for subjects to be put inside—many of them offering opportunities for children to work at higher levels of thinking. Each model comes with instructions for the teacher and rules for children to follow during the learning process. A crucial part of each of these models is that, as learners complete the model, teachers ask for reflection on children's thinking processes or ask children to use their metacognitive skills to look back on what happened during the learning process. As an example, a teacher may ask what led individuals or groups to come up with answers quickly, what led them astray, or how their learning process or strategies could be better refined next time. Such models and processes are often at the evaluative level of thinking.

Inductive models of teaching. The terms "deductive" and "inductive" were introduced earlier. Under both strategies, models of teaching can be found that can help children gain information and engage in the thinking process. In deductive lessons, teachers give children background knowledge and information, and conclusions are brought together at the end. In deductive-type instruction, the teacher is the most active player, while children listen and receive information. After receiving information, students normally apply it in some way toward the end of the presentation. A traditional example is a teacher who gives children a short talk on a topic, conducts a question-answer session, and then asks the children to practice the skills introduced. In inductive models, however, children are given pieces of information, and they must actively form conclusions on their own—or "build their own learning." This is a very *constructivist* notion (children construct their own learning through interaction with the environment); the teacher acts as a guide and/or facilitator. A deductive model, such as lecture-type introduction, often sets the stage for information gaining, whereas inductive models take students to much higher levels of thinking. These approaches can often be combined in one lesson plan or varied from day to day. Thus a teacher may begin with an inductive model as a focus activity and continue with a deductive model to introduce further information, or vice versa. Both deductive and inductive strategies have an important place in teaching and in creating a learning environment with variety, although in too many classrooms we only find deductive teaching strategies.

Some areas of inductive strategies must be considered to make sure that they are being used correctly. First a teacher must be sure that induction is proper for the goal he or she has set. For example, if students have no background knowledge or "tools" on the subject or skills with which to think, they will be frustrated as they try to determine what teachers are asking in induction. Thus student level and background are important to remember in the designing of inductive strategies. As a warning, in inductive teaching some

teachers may blend into the background, refusing to help students at all, even during mental roadblocks encountered by children. This leaves children lost or completely off track, wasting valuable learning time. Teachers *must* participate, stepping in to help just when needed. The following sections are overviews of some popular models of teaching that help children construct their own thinking, often at higher levels.

Concept Attainment. Concept Attainment is an inductive model that is very simple to use and offers children a "gamelike" atmosphere to determine a concept. It can be employed as a wonderful *focus* activity that draws children into the subject matter of the day. It can be used with Pre-K through fourth grade, depending on how you "fill" the model. As a note, teachers normally give children the objective of the lesson early on. In the Concept Attainment model, however, the objective should be stated *after* playing so that the concept is not given away (as children must guess the concept through the "game").

In the Concept Attainment model, the teacher presents, one at a time, examples and nonexamples of the concept in writing, in pictures, or with concrete items. An important rule is to be sure that children do *not* call out an answer that is the actual concept during the process of the game. That is left for the end of "the game." Instead, during the beginning of the game, children "test their hypothesis" by suggesting an item as an example or a nonexample, which the teacher then confirms by placing it in the correct category area. Children compare and contrast each of these examples or nonexamples in an effort to determine the essential attributes that make it belong to the hidden concept. To show children this process, teachers can present a simple practice game with a simple concept, listing each word one at a time:

Examples	Nonexamples
apple	carrot
pear	rock
orange	
peach (and so forth)	

When asked to contribute examples or nonexamples, children may offer grapes, bananas, and so forth as examples and corn and peas as nonexamples. The teacher confirms by writing the words under the correct column (or for younger children, placing tangibles or pictures in a correct "ring," which is usually made of yarn and laid out in the center during circle time). If the teacher uses pictures, he or she can place them on one side of a board (example) or the other (nonexample). Teachers also can use technology to create programs by scanning in pictures as examples or nonexamples. When most of the class has a good hypothesis of what the concept is, the teacher switches modes to Stage 2, showing or giving examples and nonexamples and asking children to tell in which category they should be placed. At this point, the teacher may ask, "Is a potato an example or a nonexample?" Again the teacher either writes or places a concrete item, picture, or word in the correct category. When it is obvious that most children have a clear idea of the concept, the teacher asks someone to name it (in the example above it is, of course, *fruit*). If the correct answer is given, the teacher should ask for even more examples until all the possibilities that children know are exhausted. Of course, the teacher may also contribute examples to help expand whole-class knowledge. The class then discusses the attributes that make up the concept and sets rules for that concept. Finally, the class discusses strategies that helped them identify the concept. Concept Attainment has not only been shown to help students develop clearer concepts but has also helped with retention of information. Most importantly, teachers will find their children very actively involved in thought! Teachers will gain insight into the entire body of knowledge that the class has on this concept—valuable information for a teacher! Teachers can then continue with a lesson with confidence, rather than wondering about what children know (and which child knows what) and without covering material students have already learned.

Let us look at an example of a Concept Attainment game. There are four stages to the game: (1) the teacher presents examples and nonexamples and asks students to do so; (2) students categorize when given examples and nonexamples; (3) students brainstorm, after confirming the concept, for all known examples; and (4) students reflect on strategies. A quick "game" at the lower elementary level can use either concrete items or pictures rather than words (although words can be used if they are age appropriate). First the teacher presents several examples and nonexamples. A good rule to start with is two examples and one nonexample, one at a time, separating them from each other. In this game, plastic toys, words, or pictures of each item can be used.

Examples	Nonexamples
a horse and buggy	a basket
a dog sled	a telephone
a person on ice skates	a bowl
a hang-glider	a table
a tank	

The teacher must remember that children are *not* allowed to guess or tell the concept at this time, but they can test their hypothesis by offering an example or a nonexample. The teacher should begin at this point to say, "Raise your hand if you can give me another example." Marissa, when called on, offers, "A boat." The teacher immediately adds a boat to the area where examples are being placed. If she says, "A glass," the teacher immediately places a glass (if the teacher has one, or just confirms her answer) on the nonexample side. If it is unclear, the teacher leaves it in the middle and comes back after the game is over to discuss why it was placed in the middle. Employing the group process at times is valuable. When children appear to be having difficulties "getting" the concept, the teacher can have them engage in a few minutes of small-group discussion to share thoughts and generate ideas.

After several contributions, children may now have a "good guess" as to what the concept is (often evidenced by their excitement). Yet at this point, they are *still* not allowed to have it confirmed by the teacher. Though some may be so excited that they shout out the answer, children should be told that this is not the time for the answer to be revealed. They are to wait to make sure that what they are thinking is correct, so requests such, "Let's see if you can confirm your hypothesis by offering another example or a nonexample," should be made. Next, the teacher should switch to the mode of holding up an item or picture and having children tell whether it is an example or a nonexample. Then, the teacher places it correctly under examples or nonexamples.

Teacher holds up:	Students categorize it as:
a picture of an airplane (or a plastic one)	an example
a picture of a book (or a real one)	a nonexample

After several items have been shown or words/concepts given and children have categorized them correctly, the teacher should ask one child or the class as a whole to announce the concept. If the answer is given correctly (*transportation*, in this case), the teacher asks students to (1) generate any other examples they know; (2) give attributes of the concept; and (3) give a good, clear definition. Finally, the teacher has children analyze their thinking strategies to determine what helped them arrive at the concept. Young children may not have the vocabulary to give the concept's name but may be able to state a fair definition. This is perfectly fine. The teacher should ask whether any class members know the exact word(s) for the concept. If not, now is the time to introduce the new vocabulary, praising children for their efforts in understanding the definition.

This example game was designed for young children, but it is easy to see that the same process could be modified for all elementary students and for many concepts in mathematics, language arts, science, or social studies—in fact, for every subject area. For example, concepts such as metaphors, similes, adjectives, adverbs, and proper nouns could be used in language arts. In science, concepts such as reptiles, things that can be attracted to a magnet, or a particular planet in the solar system are appropriate. Even or odd numbers, numbers that all add up to a particular sum, particular shapes, and so on, are all excellent for mathematics concepts. Using pictures can be particularly valuable with certain concepts. For example, if the concept is a landform (rivers, for instance), teachers may collect and show pictures of rivers that are used for recreation, that have cut

out canyons, that are huge and raging, that almost dry up in hot desert areas in summer, that are so calm and navigable that large cities have been built up on their banks, that are broken by huge waterfalls that prevent navigation, and so forth on the example side. Children will certainly understand more about the concept of a river and its implications for social studies than they would if the teacher had them write a definition from the board, view the geography text with one example picture, and then note the feature on a map.

When there are concepts to be learned, the Concept Attainment "game" is a way to involve students actively. How much more thinking is done by the children in this game format than if the teacher were to give them a concept definition, followed by a few stated examples? Older elementary children (individually and in small groups) love to design and be in charge of their own Concept Attainment games. Teachers should guide them in the construction to make sure that their examples and nonexamples are clear.

Discovery lessons. Another effective inductive model is **discovery learning.** Education texts may use several terms that refer to discovery, such as *inquiry, inductive learning, discovery lesson,* or *problem solving.* All of these mean that teachers do not give conclusions to the children in an explicit way, but instead, children must generate conclusions for themselves through active involvement in learning experiences of some type. A discovery lesson in science, for example, may begin when the teacher reads a story about a lake. Near this lake, people live and use the lake for recreation. Each child has been given an item or substance that represents a use of the lake. As the teacher reads about the lake and each child hears his or her item mentioned, he or she brings up and contributes items (old fishnets, detergents, etc.) to a huge jar of clear water. In the end the jar is dirty and filled with trash, and children discover that people living near a lake must think ahead or the beautiful, clear lake will be no more. In another example, children are taken outside, where the teacher has previously scattered on the grass an equal number of short strands of yellow, brown, and green yarn. In "bird" teams, children are given a short, timed period to pick up as many strands of yarn as they can. Teams then count and categorize their strands by color, discovering soon that the "caterpillars" (the short yarn strings) that are camouflaged green are the least likely to be seen and taken from the grass in large quantities. The teacher can have children repeat this process on other surfaces, if desired.

The indicators behind this competency also suggest that teachers can maximize children's thinking by prompting them to examine discrepancies between their observations and their expectations. Discovery lessons are excellent places for this to occur. These lessons often begin with children being asked to predict. After predictions are made, the children observe an interesting phenomenon or discover information in other ways. Then the teacher guides them in examining discrepancies between what learners may have originally thought or observed and the knowledge gained in the lesson.

The following lesson plan demonstrates a teacher's use of discovery techniques.

TEKS: Science 3.2/3.3

Integrated Subjects: Science, History, Language Arts

Objectives: In groups, students will (A) predict orally and (B) discover:

- how much weight it takes to sink a vessel through an experiment involving tanks of water in which they place weights in a vessel until it sinks, and
- how dispersing weight can affect the vessel in "rough seas" (by moving the weights around in the vessel and then stirring the water).

Each student will write the results of the experiments in four complete sentences. Students will listen to a historical story.

Focus or Set Induction: Students will participate in predicting "formulas" for the experiments.
Connecting Prior Learning: Students will be reminded of the cause–and–effect

paragraphs they wrote last week in language arts. They will be asked to try to determine how this experiment might relate to cause-and-effect. Through questioning, they will also be reminded of the filmstrip they watched yesterday in science about the scientific expedition that discovered the Titanic below the ocean. The class will discuss what they already know about weight (sinking/floating) and about boat design.

Touch on Community & Student Interest and Rationale: Remind students that Texas has some major ports in the United States where ships of many kinds bring goods to us from around the world. Both Houston and Corpus Christi are large port cities. There are even large cruise ships, though not as large as the Titanic, that sometimes sail from Galveston. There are many jobs in Texas that employ people both on land and on the sea with regard to these ports and ships. Some jobs are related to ship/boat safety (Coast Guard or flood relief, for example) and other people work in ship design. Most students will go out on some type of boat or ship. Science helps us to know about ship safety. It is important to know about this concept in order to protect yourself in a small boat.

Materials: Teacher: water tanks, play boats, weights, the experiment form, group role cards
Students: paper and pencil
Activities:
Teacher Input/Guided Instruction:
Teacher will ask students to predict the results of experiments.
Teacher will divide the class into groups of four and assign roles (reorder, materials manager, clean up, and turbulence director). Teacher will give experiment rules and demonstrate.
Teacher will do one example together with students and fill out one area of experimental form together, then assign groups to experiment with a number of weights to see if their boat sinks or floats.

They will place weights in boats until they sink. Teacher will direct students to repeat the experiment while one student causes water turbulence (direct how much!).

Students will disperse weights in various ways to test dispersion properties.

Teacher will read a story about the Titanic survivors.

Independent Practice: Groups will complete their experiments and experiment form.

Children will individually complete a short paragraph on the results of their experiment in at least four complete sentences.

What will students do who finish early? Students will go to the class library and take a book on the Titanic.

Evaluation: Participation: Students must participate in their group by fulfilling their job that comes with their role (group points). Group: Groups must complete their experiment form together as a group and each sign it (group points).

Individual: Each student must complete a short paragraph of at least four sentences stating the results of their experiment.

A = Student has at least four sentences that are complete and states results correctly.

B = Student has three sentences with results or four sentences with slightly less clear results.

C = Student has two sentences with results or three to four sentences with unclear results.

D = Student makes an attempt.

F = Student makes no attempt.

Closure: The teacher will ask questions that determine how well students were able to understand the material.

Examples: How much did each small weight actually weigh? How many did it take to sink your boat?

What was the least safe way to arrange your weights in "rough seas"? Why?

Why is this concept important?

What kinds of work do people do using this concept?

Who are people whose lives may depend on this concept?

What important cause-and-effect relationship have you discovered today that relates to some boating disasters?

Inquiry lessons. An inquiry model is a very easy and quick way to bring students into higher levels of thinking through guided discovery. Many of us remember the game of "Twenty Questions" because it was so mentally stimulating. One similar inquiry model, developed by Richard Suchman (1962), has the teacher select a puzzling situation. Again, because this is an instructional model of teaching, it can be used for any subject area or grade level. This model teaches problem solving through discovery and questioning. Teachers may want to use it in many ways: as a focus activity to draw students into the concept of the day, as an activity that may take a good portion of the class period, or as a closure to apply the concept of the day to a real situation or bridge into the next session.

After presenting a situation or an experimental phenomenon in an inquiry, children gather information about the answer by asking questions that can be answered by the inquiry leader with only a *yes* or *no*. The burden is on the child to formulate questions that will gain information leading to the answer. This is a fine time to teach children how to ask "umbrella" questions that help them quickly narrow to the answer rather than taking "pot-shot" guesses (putting forth one guess or hypothesis after another). Look at the difference in thought processes if we were playing, "I'm thinking of a vegetable" in the following sequences of questions.

Pot Shot Questions	Umbrella Questions
Is it a potato?	Does the part we eat grow above the ground?
Is it an onion?	
Is it a carrot?	Is it round?
Is it a beet?	Is it green?
Is it beans?	Do we eat it only cooked?

Umbrella questions indicate a much higher level of thinking than do the "pot shots." As the process goes along, the teacher is allowed to "feed" whatever information is necessary to have children stay with the game or complete it in the time planned. In addition, children may ask (or be directed) to caucus, or talk together in small groups about what they know or need to know, before returning to the inquiry. After they develop and test their hypothesis through the question-answer inquiry, they can develop rules that explain the theory. Finally, they may analyze the process and evaluate the results of participation.

For young children, an inquiry may be very simple, such as the examples just shown, or inquiry can make use of a *mystery box*. This box can be a simple box (or even a sack) containing an item that is held by the teacher during the process of inquiry. Children are asked to guess what is inside (after again being taught about "umbrella" questions). There are other ways to use this concept of mystery "guessing." In the case of a *feelie box,* a hole is cut in both ends of the box and tube socks (with the toes cut out) are attached, one to each end. The top of the box is held down with a jumbo rubber band. Students put their hands through the tube socks so that they can feel (but not see) a concrete item inside. This adds a tactile sensory input. For example, a teacher may begin a unit on birds. In each of several boxes, the teacher places an item that is connected with birds (a feather, a small nest, an egg). Boxes are then rotated among children's tables and students ask yes-or-no questions for a focus discovery on the topic of the day. For older children, the inquiry may still use a box (for example, to deal with metaphors on textures or for the introduction of various rocks, such as those with glassy surfaces, large crystals, sandy surfaces and so forth).

In science classes, inquiry is most often seen when we show the class an experiment that seems amazing in some way to the particular age of student. Making clouds or rain or collapsing a can after heating/cooling are typical examples in elementary schools. Showing an example such as this as a focus activity triggers the curiosity of children, increasing the chances that they will engage in finding out "why" through their own yes-or-no questions and later experimentation.

Inquiry can be more complicated, involve much more information, and use a step-built-upon-step process. For example, the teacher may introduce the interaction of engineering and science for older elementary children through a questioning inquiry dealing with difficulties of extracting oil. "In one rich oil field in the North Sea," the teacher may begin while showing pictures of a place where, "the weather is so harsh that lives are often lost and the environment is often damaged with conventional oil rigs. Scientists and engineers began to try to solve this problem. What kind of rig do you think they designed and built to solve this problem?" Thus begins the inquiry, with questions that can be answered only with *yes* and *no*. Children must ascertain what the structure was (a solid structure the size of the Empire State Building that was build in a fjord and towed out to the oil field and "sunk"). However, inventions by children that come from this process are usually wonderfully creative (submarine-type rigs, balloon rigs, barge-type structures that leave with the bad weather and return in good weather, and so forth). Other questions could be: When would this type of rig be beneficial in Texas (during hurricane season)? Why would this be a good idea (to avoid oil spills on our Texas coast)? Why would this construction be difficult in Texas (we wouldn't have a place to build such a tall structure)? Would this type of construction still be possible for Texas coastlines (perhaps because our coastline is very shallow in many places, the construction would not need to be so tall)?

History is rich with ideas for discovery and inquiry, too. For example, a teacher may want to introduce a unit on Egypt with an interesting focus inquiry such as the following, asking children to become archeologists.

A city in Egypt was besieged by Persians. Although the city had enough water and food to last for a long time, the people threw open the city gates and surrendered. Why would they have done that?

(Egyptians, who believed cats were gods, could not stand the fact that the Persians, who believed cats were just cats, were lobbing cats over the city walls.)

Again, the inquiry would begin with questions that could be answered only with *yes* or *no*. Beginning questions might be, "Were the people ill?" "Were they tricked into opening the gates somehow?" The teacher should ensure that children's ideas are supported by making statements such as, "That is a good thought because history shows that in a siege that is often the case," or other encouraging remarks. When appropriate he or she should ask, "How do you think an archeologist might know or discover this?" When children need more help, they can be directed to "use your groups" to see what has already been discovered and to generate more questions. After a few minutes, children return to the whole-class format. This may be done several times during the process, depending on the desired length of the activity. As a guide, the teacher can "feed" as much or as little information to children as needed to maintain pacing and interest. Also, teachers should remember to ask children to rephrase questions that cannot be answered by a *yes* or *no*. Following the inquiry focus activity, a teacher would continue with the remainder of the lesson plan.

An artifact (either real or a picture) might also be introduced for an inquiry: "To whom do you think this shoe (pen, book, tool, or whatever) belonged?" "How would we know?" "Why would it be important?" "What would it tell us about a particular person, author, time, or group of people?"

Mathematics, reading, and health also are rich in areas that can offer puzzling situations. Inquiring minds want to know! What could be more exciting than watching a scientific experiment with a puzzling outcome or being presented with an age-old question about an archeological mystery? Rather than being *told* all about it, children unravel what is known in the scientific exploratory tradition. At times, there is no known answer to a real-world problem or situation, so

children have the opportunity to hypothesize with current knowledge as to the "latest theories." This entire process is one in which children shift from extrinsic to intrinsic rewards of learning (Gunter, Estes, & Schwab, 1995). It is the same concept that has kept the television series "Unsolved Mysteries" in reruns for many years—people are caught up in wanting to know, and they love the process of trying to guess the answer or solve the mystery. It is a higher-level thinking process that provides variety to instruction.

When they select any one of the models discussed above as a part of a lesson, teachers can ensure that children are thinking at upper levels. Incorporating a variety of instructional models into a lesson also increases motivation. Many other instructional models of teaching involve higher levels of thinking: Concept Development, other submodels of cooperative groupings, conflict resolution models, Synectics, the Classroom Discussion Models, and so forth. Two texts that explain these very well are *Models of Teaching* (Joyce & Weil, 1996) and *Instruction: A Models Approach* (Gunter, Estes, & Schwab, 1995). If a local university offers a course in models of teaching or a similar "strategies" course, in which many models are included, teachers should take advantage of this excellent professional development activity. Most teachers who have taken such courses feel that these types of courses are extremely valuable to their teaching in that the models boost variety and higher-level thinking.

Simulation and role-play. Simulation and role-play are also exciting ways to provide children with creative avenues to engage in problem-based learning. A **simulation** is a type of scenario that involves abstractions of the real world, where roles are often established and skills are used to work through a process to a goal. This is related to, although not exactly like, **role-play** situations, in which children "become" specific people and act through a scenario (such as advisor to Colonel Travis at the Alamo). There is no script—the child acts according to his or her own thoughts as to what would have happened. In role-play, children are asked to "pretend" to be in a given situation, where they will explore various ways of handling their reactions. The DARE program, for example, actively engages children in refusing drugs by capitalizing on role-play to help children generate ways of "just saying no" when approached by peers or others to take drugs. Joyce and Weil (1996) have suggested several steps for successful role-play. In the warm-up stage, the scene or problem is introduced in detail. Roles are then analyzed and selected, followed by the setting of the stage for action. The observers (or audience) are then prepared for participation in the form of watching for alternative solutions, describing feelings, and so forth. The situation is then enacted, followed by review, discussion, and evaluation. Students then reenact the situation with the alternatives, followed again by discussion and evaluation. This phase can be repeated as many times as needed, and the role-play concluded by an overall period of description of experiences and generalization, in which children relate the situation to their own lives and/or current situations or problems.

A simulation is often more complex, structured, and lifelike than a role-play, with problems to overcome and a goal to reach. Young children who are discovering the concept of why communities and cities developed in certain locations in the settling of America might simulate a situation in which the teacher lays a "highway" (a length of adding machine tape) across the classroom. Children are told that this highway is a 4-hour stretch of road, and that they should think of when they have been in a car that long and what they felt was needed along the road as far as stopping points. The teacher distributes materials for the quick construction of drawings as children are designated to "become an owner" of a business or other facility. Drawings are then placed at the "midpoint" of the highway (at the 2-hour interval, if this is a good place) and perhaps labeled with specific names if there are multiple overlaps for certain businesses (McDonald's, Wendy's, etc.). Normally children come up with fast-food restaurants and gas stations at this stage. The teacher then asks where the people who

own and work at these places will live, because they surely wouldn't want to drive two hours to work there. At this point, some children can be assigned to work on homes for business owners and workers. The simulation of building a town continues as children are asked where the people will buy groceries, where their children will go to school, and how they can receive mail, as buildings are added to the town. The simulation can take other twists and turns (perhaps as to what happens when too many of one type of business are established or a bypass is put around the town), or a teacher may redo the highway as a wagon trail and think in terms of the needs of travelers in the past. Another historical simulation may place children on: (1) East and West Coast rail construction teams who will work to meet in the middle, (2) a construction team that originates from each "major city" to connect East to West, or (3) a team who designs their own plan. Each team appoints roles and workers, and all teams go outside to see which team will be the fastest and most accurate as they "build their coast-to-coast railroad" using Popsicle® sticks. Much of the rationale behind simulation is that children make decisions and can see the results of their decision played out. After the simulation, it is extremely important to "debrief" so that children can reflect well on what connections were made. A number of simulation packages are available for the computer (see Competency 9, Chapter 14), with exciting scenarios and excellent graphics, but teachers can create other exciting simulations for their classes (with or without technology) with some imagination and/or research. Simulations and role-play are exciting and engaging ways for children to learn. Drama can also contribute to variety in the classroom when scripts are provided for children to read in a character's role.

Discussions. Teachers, through their educational process, have spent a great deal of time in various types of discussions led by professors and, before that, by their own teachers. Depending on how classroom discussions throughout the educational process were structured, these experiences could have been either extremely thought provoking and engaging or dismal, with a few students (often the same ones each time) engaged with the teacher as others drifted off into their own thoughts and activities. Too often this ineffective pattern is repeated when teachers arrive in their own classes. However, discussions can offer educational situations in which children learn a great deal as they listen to other students who are formulating ideas and questions. In turn, learners create their own ideas and knowledge. Yet this happens only when the teacher has planned a discussion well and when all children are engaged.

Discussions can be planned for either a whole class or small groups, where even more participation can be encouraged. The teacher must prepare for the discussion as carefully as she or he prepares for a whole lesson. Good discussions don't simply happen! Astute teachers decide on goals and objectives for the discussion and prepare an opening focus activity to lead into it. They connect the discussion to prior or future learning. They also prepare a list of questions in advance that are crucial to the topic, questions that transition to other dimensions of the topic if the discussion begins to lag, and questions that make children think even more deeply. The teacher should also ensure that each student has an equal opportunity to add something to the discussion. Rules should be established or reviewed to encourage contributions, listening, waiting for a turn, and not veering from the subject (this often happens with younger children). When ending the discussion, they summarize all that was said in the discussion. Teachers are encouraged to end the discussion when it seems right, rather than at the exact time allotted in a plan. Interest in a discussion dies when teachers try to stretch it to fit a period of time, so there should always be extra activities ready in case a discussion ends early. Good planning and good structure contribute to good learning.

Classroom Discussion Model. Models of teaching help structure learning to ensure that more children are active. The Classroom Discussion Model provides this type of a framework.

First children are taught how to construct various types of questions at three levels of thinking: factual (the answers can be found in the material), interpretive (an opinion), and evaluative (a judgment or critique). As children read, listen, or watch a video, each class member makes up a question at each level and includes the answer. If children are old enough to be writing, they should write their questions as they read, listen, or watch. Children then come to a circle with their questions and the teacher directs a child to begin asking his or her factual question to the group. The teacher may use a technique such as a "hot potato" for children to toss in selecting someone to answer (with the idea that one cannot receive the hot potato more than a set number of times and must receive it at least once during the discussion). After all of the factual questions are asked and answered by children, the round turns next to the interpretive questions (What do you think?). From this level on, children should ask other children to support their reasons in answering. When they have finished asking and answering these questions, the final round turns to evaluative questions, in the same manner. Often at the interpretive and evaluative levels, many want to contribute, and this should be encouraged as long as the time is available. Children may also have designed some of the same questions. It is a good review for them to be asked again, but if many have designed the same question, the teacher should ask whether children can think of others on the spot. If not, they can pass on that round but be among the first in the next round. Older elementary children can increase the numbers of questions they are asked to formulate before the discussion, so that they will have a question or so on which to fall back if another classmate has already asked their question. The final step is to have students reread or watch the video again. This "sets" the information they have read about or seen.

Why is this discussion model superior to those in which teachers ask questions from the teacher's edition or those that she or he has designed? There is ownership in making up these questions, so children see the questions as "theirs," and thus important to them. Children are also the ones who hold the answers. This is more empowering to them because they are stepping into the role of the teacher much more in this model. It also is engaging because children know that everyone will be included and that their opinions and judgments will be tapped. Finally, they will have turned the reading or listening information over and over in so many ways that they can remember the material well. As a note, reading materials or videos must allow for multiple questions at three levels. The teacher should read ahead or watch and formulate his or her own questions for a check before using the model. During the discussion, the teacher should reread and formulate other questions along with the children to model the importance of reading and participating as a co-learner.

For meaningful discussions. For classroom discussions in general, teachers should remember several ideas to help make them more meaningful. When a guest speaker is coming or children are going on a field trip, most teachers go to considerable trouble to "set the class up" for the experience, with the idea that children will be able to learn more and discuss more afterward. A wise teacher cues children ahead of time to listen and watch carefully for certain elements in the experience. Yet rarely do teachers go through this process when children are going to read (or be read to) or see a relevant video or other informational presentations in the day-to-day class. However, teachers who "set the class up well" for a discussion find it makes a vast difference as to how the discussion develops after the presentation of information. Children must have some tools and/or knowledge to discuss, so unless they *attend* to a reading or other presentation, they will not be able to participate well later. Teachers often have better attention and have children who make more contributions when interest and attention is generated in the beginning. For example, a teacher may show children a book cover and ask them to (a) predict what they think the book

might be about, (b) remember whether they have heard or read books by the same author, (c) tell whether they have seen the characters in other books, (d) predict whether this book might be similar to others they have read, and (e) listen for a particular situation (or whatever questions are appropriate for a particular type of presentation). Other advanced organizers can help children attend so that they will be able to participate well in discussion later on. Stating the objectives of a discussion before the presentation is also important. A teacher might state, for example, "Today we are going to see a video on the early explorers in Texas. During the video, I want you to write one question and its answer because afterward we will be discussing this video. For tomorrow, I will select 10 of your questions for our quiz."

Physical space is also an important part of a successful discussion. Children seated in desks facing the teacher subliminally receive the message that they are to formulate questions and answers only for the teacher—not for their classmates. A discussion involves more than a back-and-forth volley from child-to-teacher-to-child-to-teacher. One purpose of a discussion is to increase social skills and communication among peers. It is difficult for that to happen when all interactions must go through the teacher. Therefore putting children in a circle or "U" conveys the appropriate message that it is important to talk *and* listen closely to others rather than just to the teacher.

Going off track can cause a classroom discussion to fizzle or to lose so much direction that it becomes meaningless. Young children often have their own egocentric views or stories that they wish to share—often at inappropriate times. Effective teachers know that this will happen and are proactive in stating discussion rules ahead. Rules should be set such as, "Boys and girls, during this period we will be talking about the information you saw on the video (or the story or article you read). I know there are other things that we want to share sometimes. I will leave 5 minutes at the end to talk about other things, but if you bring up another topic during our discussion, I will ask you to hold on to it until your time at the end (an example of "my time/your time"). That will help us make sure that we will have the time to hear from everyone on this topic right now."

Effective discussion leaders also often provide visuals or graphic organizers of some sort as the discussion progresses. Classification organizers, concept webs, time lines, and so forth, can be of major help to children who need organization skills and/or visuals. These leaders also learn how to paraphrase respectfully so that all children hear an answer that a soft voice may have given or the reorganized contribution of a child who had difficulty presenting his thoughts. Consult Competency 10, Part 2, Chapter 16, for important feedback techniques that encourage more conversation rather than closing down a discussion.

Teachers as discussion leaders should also think of the logic of a discussion. A discussion should have a sequential flow (from simple questions and ideas to complex or from recall to evaluation level). It should also allow time for reflection as children think back over what made the discussion go well and the most important things they learned.

MAXIMIZING CHILDREN'S THINKING

We have seen several modes of instruction that help to increase higher-level thinking and active involvement for children. Questioning is another way to help maximize students' thinking skills. Unfortunately, research shows that most teachers ask a great percentage of knowledge-level and comprehension-level questions—lower-level thinking. Why? Three reasons are that (1) teachers have difficulty thinking of higher-level questions when they are in "the heat of the moment" in the middle of class; (2) teachers do not plan for these questions or write them ahead, along with their lesson plans; and (3) these questions take a bit more time for children to answer, causing teachers to become impatient. Knowledge, preparation, patience, and skill are required for this area of teaching.

Some educators classify questioning into two categories: **convergent** and **divergent questions** (discussed in Competency 7, Chapter 11). These terms are easy to remember when considering what *converge* and *diverge* mean. Converge means that all answers must come together—in other words, there is only one response or one type of response, and this very "narrow" response can be anticipated (and is known or owned by the teacher). This one-true-and-correct-answer can be memorized and recalled. "What is the capital of Texas?" for example, can be answered only with, "Austin!" *Diverge,* however, means to go away from or push apart, so the responses in divergent questions can take many different directions or broader paths; these answers are open-ended. Among the latter type of responses are opinions, hypotheses, and evaluations—all higher-level thinking. "What is the best thing we do to help clean up Gulf Coast beaches?" can have many answers and many opinions. With divergent questioning, a child's answer cannot be anticipated, because the student takes factual information and makes it his or her own in some manner. Another type of question is divergent in nature—the *productive* question (Moore, 1998). These questions have unpredictable answers that students create or produce imaginatively. In other words, students synthesize their own unique answers. Scaffolding and sequencing have much to do with a plan for questioning. If we lay a solid foundation of convergent, knowledge-level questions, then the child is better able to move into divergent questioning. If a teacher is able to move from a lower-level Bloom's (1956) taxonomy knowledge level through several levels to evaluation (see Competency 3, Part 1, Chapter 3), the child will have an easier time answering those questions at higher levels because the language and tools needed for application will be in place.

How should teachers prepare for higher-order questions? First, preparing these types of questions in advance is a must. Writing them into lesson plans will guarantee that they have been thoughtfully worded. Teachers must be sure to note whether questions match lesson objectives.

In a more constructivist manner, they should plan to have children help create some of their own questions at different levels—particularly at interpretative (opinion) and evaluative (judgment) levels—for classroom discussion.

Questioning at higher levels can be used in various sections of the lesson plan. For part of a focus, for example, an engaging higher-level question can draw children into the lesson to come. For instance, "What do you think might happen if we don't stop some of the destruction of the rainforest?" might open a health or science class (lose medicines, gain polluted air, etc.), or a prediction of "What do you think will happen when I put this balloon over heat and this one over ice?" could open another science class. For a closure, the teacher might ask children a higher-level question to generate dialogue about the lesson or connect today's lesson to tomorrow's in an exciting way.

A RISK-FREE ENVIRONMENT FOR CRITICAL THINKING

Have you ever offered a "far out," creative idea in a group or class and had it scoffed at, or have you intuitively known that a teacher thought your idea was really "weird?" How many additional responses did you offer in that situation? The answer is probably, "None!" The importance of an open environment is crucial for critical thinking. The teacher—the most visible person in the room, the one who controls the rewards in the classroom, and the person who is seen as the learned person—is a model for acceptance of divergent thinking.

"Learning is enhanced by challenge and inhibited by threat," emphasize Gunter, Estes, & Schwab (1995, p. 9), explaining that challenge can always be seen as a risk to one's self-esteem or success. With new learning, mistakes usually occur. Teachers can set the stage for a learner to "take a chance" or not. In what ways? First, teachers should model respect for the answers of *all* students unless, of course, the answers are inappro-priate in language or subject matter, or are manipulative ways to create management problems. Children are able to understand intuitively whether the **environment** is **risk-free** and open, or whether teachers will threaten them in some way for their responses. A *risk-free environment* is one in which all children feel that their opinions, contributions, and thinking are valued. The tone of voice or the way a question is "pressured" on children can intimidate them, especially in critical thinking. No one wants to look or feel less than bright in front of peers—children are no exception! Encouraging students' questions (not just their answers) in an open manner also increases the atmosphere of openness for thinking. Formative support should be given often during the process of critical thinking, along with formative grades. Credit for effort during the process also helps demonstrate to children that teachers are interested in the learning and thinking process. Using encouragement for improvement rather than only rewarding a correct answer or giving a high grade also helps to promote cooperation (rather than competition) and can encourage students to take chances in learning. An open environment is one in which asking questions, particularly higher-level questions, is never used to embarrass or manipulate a child. Before expecting children to answer certain knowledge-based questions, teachers should be sure that they have taught the material. **Wait time** and really listening to children's answers also have much to do with an accepting environment

Using teachable moments also indicates respect for students' thoughts. A *teachable moment* occurs when a student veers from the lesson plan with a thought or question that, although not directly on the topic, is truly valuable for all students—so the teacher follows the child's lead. The lesson plan is left for a time, and the teacher directs the lesson to the thought introduced by the child, returning to the plan when appropriate. Many times it is in teachable moments that higher-level thinking is generated because the information is of so much interest to children—they brought it up.

Also important in higher-level thinking is reacting to students' responses. Teachers' reactions show value for children's thoughts. By repeating the main points of a student's answer, teachers let children know that they are listening well. Unfortunately, because most children are trained early to expect that teachers want a quick answer, it may take time for teachers to train themselves and their children to react to longer, higher-level questions and answers. Children of all ages sense when teachers are trying to rush through a questioning session. Nonverbal teacher behavior is important in critical thinking questions; children may know when teachers are impatient for them to finish so the discussion can move on. "Impatient" body language tells a child clearly to "hurry up and think, and then finish." Children also sense when teachers consider their opinions much more important than their students', and when teachers are not really interested in what they have to say but are manipulating them into the "correct" answer. For example, particularly in divergent questioning, teachers may have a tendency to say, "Yes, but . . ." This tends to stop further divergence.

Authentically rewarding students for thoughtful answers increases the chances that they will try again. Praise words such as "Good!" or "Great answer!" may not spur children on. Yet phrases such as, "Your answer was so thoughtful. It really has added another dimension to this topic," "I'm impressed with the depth of your answer," or "Wow! Look how this relates to what Raul answered earlier—you are really making some great connections here," are much more meaningful. Critique is also important in helping students reach higher levels. Studies show that teachers do not give enough effective critiques of children's answers. Specific feedback allows children to reach a teacher's expectations much more closely. For example, a teacher might say or write to a child, "If you go back and look at your second argument more closely, I think your answer will really improve," or "You have done some exceptional thinking in this paragraph. Your ideas are crystal clear!" This is much more specific than,

"Good" or, worse still, just putting a grade on a paper with no feedback. Rewarding children for higher-level thinking is critically important. They are rarely spurred to think when there is no challenge or encouragement for their ideas.

Probing is another way to increase levels of questioning. This can be seen as a reward for many children because the teacher is "staying with" their ideas. Probing questions follow a student's response by asking a child to think more deeply and thoroughly about what he or she just said. Teachers should be careful to do this with *all* of their children, though, rather than just one or two of the "smarter" ones. If a teacher continually interacts orally with only a few, the rest of the class loses interest.

Even management sets the stage for higher-level thinking in several ways. First, if teachers are model listeners and require that the class be quiet to hear an answer, children will vicariously see that their answers are important, too. Teachers should ensure that children are quiet so that learners with soft voices are heard when they answer, particularly if it is a longer, higher-level answer. However, teachers must recognize that talking all at once in group work is often part of the process in divergent situations, and management techniques must change. They should ask children to talk in 6-inch voices (rather than 12-inch voices) so that neighboring classes are not disturbed—*but students should talk!* With children whose home language is not English, it is important to remember that they may gain much more during this process by speaking in their native language.

Modeling a think-aloud process for students is also an effective strategy for cueing students on divergent thinking. For example, many times teachers can give a simple knowledge answer to children's questions. "Why is there so much air pollution here, teacher?" asks Keisha. A teacher could answer with a quick, "Because it's expensive to have antipollution equipment," but a teacher interested in modeling deeper intellectual thinking might show his or her thought processes. "I've often thought of that same question, Keisha, when I'm driving downtown. It seems like I can almost taste pollution in the air. I ask myself what all of these people are doing on this freeway in their own cars. They are all going to work at different places, and each car is using gas and putting emissions into the air—which means that we need lots of refineries. Sometimes I see those refineries that provide us with gas and oil for our cars putting smoke into the air, too. Why don't they fix this? Well, one of the answers is a mass transit system . . . oh, but what would be the cost of having trains or monorails all though the city? Very high . . . and the same for installing pollution prevention on factories . . . very expensive. Installing better pollution devices on cars causes them to be more expensive, too. People will always need to work to make money, and cities offer jobs for so many people, so I suppose that the answer to part of your question is expense. Can you think of other reasons?"

Equity issues associated with Competency 2 can also be linked with higher-level questioning. Teacher behaviors associated with the questioning of low-achieving children have been identified. These behaviors consist of asking low achievers lower-level questions most of the time or exclusively, giving them less wait time and eye contact when asked, assessing their answers and work differently, and overall, interacting with them less. Langer et al. (1990) found that cultural minorities often lost confidence in the fast-paced, convergent question-and-answer sessions that teachers often employ, while divergent, open-ended questions encouraged confidence. However, a teacher must be careful to provide children with enough support for them to be able to understand the question or engage in a strategy and to answer (Fradd & Lee, 1999). In other words, building up to these types of questions and strategies is a necessity. For all children, divergent questions are much more likely to captivate interest for participation. It has also been found that teachers often ask boys, rather than girls, questions that call for more complex, abstract, higher-level thinking, and boys' responses most often receive teachers' active attention. In addition, teachers may engage only a few of their top students academically in higher levels of activity. A teacher may have to go so far as to keep a note card, marking a name when a child answers a high-level question, to ensure equity. Another strategy is to have a mental grid of the classroom and direct high-level questions to seat numbers to make sure that all students are covered (through establishing a pattern that seems random, such as calling on every fourth student rather than going down a row).

Teachers' expectations about children's responses are critical. If the teacher sets expectations for careful, thoughtful answers for *all* students, the likelihood of that result increases. *Failing at Fairness* (Sadker & Sadker, 1994) addresses many of these issues in depth. If a teacher expects all students to be able to deal with higher levels of thinking and uses strategies for making sure that the entire class participates in questioning at higher levels, the whole class will become engaged. Thus setting an environment in which high expectations are the norm will most likely produce high achievement in thinking.

LINKING HIGHER-LEVEL THINKING TO ASSESSMENT

Higher-level thinking can also touch on assessment. Teachers can design assessment instruments to be at thoughtful, higher levels or simply at the recall/knowledge level. Tests that offer only knowledge- or application-level, fill-in-the-blank, short answer, true-or-false, or lower-level matching questions do not stretch children into deeper thinking. Although essay questions are time-consuming to grade, they do offer children an opportunity to think at higher levels. Careful construction of multiple-choice items can provide higher levels of thought as well, and student portfolios offer a chance for children to engage in evaluative thinking as they critically judge which works they will select for their portfolio, and why. In terms of observation, rubrics for grading can include areas noted for higher levels of student thinking. In authentic assessment, children simulate a more real-world scenario, and they can be assessed for using more logic and creativity. Employing higher-level strategies with lower-level assessment is not an effective or fair measurement for students' abilities. Teachers should try to make this connection during lesson planning. Competency 10, Part 1, Chapter 15, discusses assessment in more detail.

THE LANGUAGE OF THINKING

Using the language of thinking is also an important part of setting the stage for critical thinking. "Just as the colors on an artist's palette influence the painting that emerges, the words we have available to us influence the way we think about the world, including the inner world of our own mental life," state Tishman and Perkins (1997, p. 371). If metacognition is "thinking about thinking," the vocabulary of *thinking words* is the tool that guides, assesses, and evaluates the process. This language, according to Tishman and Perkins, creates a disposition or an invitation for thinking in a certain way. Many teachers ask children generic-type "thinking" questions but do not use specific terminology to help children process more. Yet by using the language of thinking, teachers can extend and guide the thought processes and theory building of children. For example, a teacher could ask, "Do you think that the Old 300 (the first Texans from the U.S. to come to Mexico) really intended to keep the contract they made with Mexico for their land grants?" One child might answer, "No," while the teacher continues with, "Hm-m-m-m. How about you, Keisha?" attempting to raise more discussion. However, if teachers use the language of thinking, the thought process for children deepens, as shown in the following example.

"Does anyone have a *theory* about why the early Texans did not follow the agreement they made with Mexico for their land grants?"

Jason might offer, "I think that they weren't so used to life as it was in Mexico in those days."

"What *reasons* do you have for thinking that? Is there some *evidence* to support that?" the teacher follows up.

"Well, I think that these guys were Americans and that they were used to voting on things and stuff like that," Jason might note.

"Hm-m-m. Can you add any other *evidence* to that *theory*?" the teacher might continue.

"Well, I know that Austin went down to Mexico City to ask the Mexican government for some things for the colony, like some representation, and the Mexican government put him in jail for a long time. It really made the people back in Texas mad."

"Wow! That's an interesting *hypothesis*. Would it make you angry, for example, if we had a discussion about ways to make our school better, and we sent Jamie (the class president) down to the office to ask Mrs. Gleason, our principal, to listen to those ideas—and Mrs. Gleason gave Jamie in-school suspension? How angry would you be if you were a Texas colonist at the time for Austin to be put in jail? What would be some things that you would have done? Does anyone else have other evidence for that *hypothesis?*"

Note again that the use of the language of thinking increases the likelihood that children will go deeper in their thought processes.

ALLOCATING TIME

Learning takes more than input. It also takes time. Time is needed to gather thoughts for a deeper answer, time is needed for activities that deeply involve learning, and time is needed to reflect on the lesson as a whole. Aspects concerning the time in which children are actually engaged in learning, or *academic learning time,* are embedded in the indicators for this competency.

Giving children time to organize their thoughts into deeper answers through wait time has much to do with the learning environment. Giving 3 to 5 seconds of silence (**wait time**) after a question is asked increases the chances that more children will volunteer and that the same students will not always answer. Answers will also be more deliberative and pensive in nature. If teachers find it difficult to have that much silence between asking a question and calling on someone for an answer, they may ask a question and then walk to another spot in the classroom before calling on a child. If a teacher has the class in a circle, he or she should scan the circle and mentally say the names of at least five children with their hands up before calling on one. This also helps cue the teacher as to which students have their hands up consistently, so that they can tap children other than those. Teachers who wait a few seconds to respond after a child has answered show that careful consideration is being given to the answer. **Halt time** is another important strategy—that is, stopping the forward motion of the lesson completely to give children time to digest material (Moore, 1998). This period of silence follows a time when children have been heavily engaged in complex material. Teachers simply pause for a short time so that the class has a moment to collect and reflect on the materials without pushing forward. This might be compared to an intense physical workout during which one pauses for a moment to "shake it out." Children sometimes need the time to mentally "shake it out" when the concepts are difficult and at higher levels.

Pacing is yet another time-related issue that affects engaged learning. *Pacing* refers to the movement in time (or momentum) of the lesson. A teacher can sometimes set the pace or timing of a lesson too fast for children to catch all of the information or practice skills needed to gain confidence. A teacher's presentation of information can also drag with the result that many children become bored and involved in their own activities rather than in learning. The lesson can feel jerky, meaning that changes between activities, or *transitions,* are not smooth and thinking is interrupted. This can also occur when something superfluous to the lesson interrupts or when children ask teachers to "go back" (or the teacher realizes that he or she must go back) because the presentation of directions or knowledge was not given clearly. No teacher can predict when an announcement from the office or other school interruptions will break student (and teacher) timing and concentration, but good sequential planning (including plans for transitions) and preparation, with materials ready and placed where they can be found easily, increase the likelihood that teachers will not have to break the flow of instruction. Other issues can also affect pacing—both negatively and positively. Classroom management issues cause pacing to be broken and narrow the time that teachers have for learning. On a positive note, sometimes teachable moments break pacing, when the teacher notes something of such interest to children that the class veers off from the regular plans for a time to investigate. These teachable moments often involve higher-level thinking because children are interested in finding deeper information on a topic. For best results in a classroom, teachers set pacing such that the lesson always seems to be moving slightly forward. Thus just as children are finishing one activity, another is beginning. Established routines for putting away supplies, moving into small groups, passing in papers, and other activities also aid in pacing so that needless time is not spent in organizing children for learning.

Other time considerations must be made for children of different ages. The attention spans or concentration levels of children are just beginning to develop during early childhood. Teachers find that Pre-K children, with their shorter **attention spans** (the amount of time that a child can spend on a given task), are unable to sustain attention for long periods of time. Therefore, the key to maintaining attention is to plan material that can be presented in small segments with simple, clear directions. Teachers should be attentive to children at all grade levels and be ready to change activities when they notice that children are losing engagement. **Monitoring,** as was first introduced in Competency 3, Part 2, Chapter 4 (also an indicator for this competency), is a key factor in gauging attention spans. Earlier, monitoring was introduced as a means of gaining constant feedback from children as to how their learning is progressing, then making adjustments or changes in instructional strategies and grouping, as needed, to help students grow. Monitoring is crucial for keeping students engaged because it provides teachers with signals for changing activities as needed. This can occur for several reasons. Children may have remained on one activity too long, or the difficulty or ease of the material may have caused them to become uninterested or bored. Effective teachers monitor and respond to children's needs immediately—for motivation, learning, and management.

Teachers can affect the attention spans of their children in other ways. In Competency 4, Part 1, Chapter 5, the information processing theory tells much about gaining and holding the attention of learners. First, it suggests that teachers must stimulate the senses to gain students' attention. This is the first step in getting information into long-term memory. One way to gain and hold attention is to employ all learning modalities (visual, auditory, tactile, and kinesthetic) in lessons and to increase variety in instruction. However, there is a balance factor. The senses of young children can become overwhelmed by too much information and/or sensory overload at one time; thus attention becomes too sporadic to gain long-term memory placement. Many parents experience this at birthdays or other gift-giving times, when children have so many gifts that they cannot pay attention to one thing for any length of time. Curiosity also can stimulate interest; therefore discovery can create and hold interest, as can active involvement, which is heavily discussed in this chapter. When experiences are satisfying, attention is maintained longer.

The time of day can also be a factor in maintaining attention. Most young children are more alert in the morning hours; thus young childhood teachers often try to schedule math and reading (subjects that require more concentration) before lunch. Most young childhood teachers also know that they should keep a regular schedule and must limit distractions and interruptions as much as possible to help maintain attention. Teachers should help parents understand that their arrival during the middle of a class can disrupt attention. This awareness will help the teacher set up appropriate times for conferences. Young childhood teachers also know that distraction and waning attention in the days right before holidays and special events mean that these are not the times to plan for "heavy" subjects. Activities that require a shift in attention can also be difficult for younger children. Teachers who wait until "all eyes are on me" have more success in giving directions and information because more children refocus their attention. Having children repeat directions also gains attention. Practicing routines to recapture attention quickly can work to a teacher's advantage.

Knowing about **selective attention,** or the ability to focus on one stimulus while ignoring other stimuli (particularly if the stimuli are superfluous), is also an important concept to remember for young children. When older elementary children are presented with various stimuli of color, movement, sound, and novelty, they are likely to "tune out" that which is not so important, so they are not as likely to be distracted. However, a Pre-K child's attention is often caught by these incidental stimuli. For example, computer games or videos often have a great deal of color, decoration, or loud sounds. Guest speakers sometimes are dressed as a favorite animal or character, and the attention of young children may focus on the other stimuli rather than the information the "character" or the program is offering. Remembering this, teachers should focus young children's attention directly where it is needed and reduce as much extraneous stimuli as possible when assigning important tasks.

Millions of children are identified as having attention deficit disorder (*ADD*) and attention deficit hyperactivity disorder (*ADHD*), which adversely affect their ability to pay attention. Most of these children are identified in the early childhood years. If modifications are not made, they can become "at risk" for failure both in school and in society. However, teachers often label young children who are a bit difficult to manage or who have short attention spans as having ADD or ADHD. A full diagnosis by experts is needed because a short attention span may be due to a number of other conditions, including individual development, environmental stressors, or other physical disorders. The diagnosis of ADD or ADHD can often be *automatically* accompanied by a course of controversial drugs. Teachers should always begin to document children whom they see as demonstrating very short attention spans, extreme distractibility, noticeable difficulty remaining still, impulsive activity, and seemingly reckless behavior or difficulty remaining in control. When identified, children can be helped through various behavior modifications and, perhaps, though prescriptive medication if it is appropriate. If a child is taking a drug such as Ritalin for ADD or ADHD, the teacher has an important responsibility to communicate with parents and help monitor (though not administer) the correct dosage so that the child gets maximum benefit of the drug without becoming dazed or lethargic.

LEARNER-CENTERED AND TEACHER-CENTERED INSTRUCTION

To gain more perspective on how Texas would like its teachers to go about their work, it may be helpful to think of strategies and teacher roles in terms of their teacher-centeredness or learner-centeredness. Teacher roles were introduced ear-

lier, but because they are an important concept for this competency, they are extended here. Teacher-centeredness means that the focus of the classroom is on the teacher and what she or he is delivering. This is normally a traditional lecture approach. This may be appropriate for some college classrooms, but even in college lectures one finds students who disengage when asked to simply listen and take notes. Learner-centeredness, however, places the focus of instruction directly on the needs of the learner or the child and creates active learners. The lesson plan given in Competency 3, Part 1, Chapter 3, stresses areas that help teachers begin to work towards learner-centeredness. These areas include age-appropriateness, relevance, student interest, student needs, and so forth. This chapter includes strategies that help supplement that process to a much greater extent.

If a continuum were constructed such as the following, in Figure 12-1, where would the teacher's role of facilitator be placed and where would that of a coach's role be placed? Where would one place behaviorism and constructivist learning theories given in Competency 4, Part 1, Chapter 5? Would lecture or "telling" be closer to the teacher or the student as the center of action? What about cooperative groups? These continuums may help teachers see better how teacher-centered or student-centered a model, strategy, or activity may be.

Of course, there are no clear-cut points in the placement of these concepts on such a continuum. However, most educators would place the learning theories and the teacher roles as shown in Figure 12-2.

The placement of teaching strategies on such a continuum is more difficult because most models can be modified—thus changing their posi-

Teacher-Centered   Student-Centered

Figure 12-1 Continuum along which methods, learning theories, and teacher roles can be placed.

tions on the continuum. For example, although most educators would agree that lecture fits best on the teacher-centered side of the continuum, some lectures are more student-centered, such as interactive lecture, and others are definitely more teacher-centered, such as the "talking-head" model. Likewise, inquiry can be open (more student-centered) or guided (more teacher-centered). Other models have many submodels. Cooperative learning (as described in Competency 3, Part 2, Chapter 4) in general is more student-centered. Inside-Outside Circle (partners face each other, answer questions given by the teacher, and then rotate to the next partner) is much more teacher-centered than is Group Investigation. Any model can be implemented in

a more teacher-centered or more student-centered way. Taking that into account, one way to place the models is in the fashion illustrated in Figure 12-3. Consider whether or not you agree with this arrangement. As teachers continue to design instruction, they should think carefully about the place on the continuum where their choices fall.

The importance of understanding this concept for this exam is that Texas believes that learning should be mainly student-centered and constructivist. Thus children should be active learners rather than simply passive listeners most of the time in our classrooms. Knowing which models fall toward the student-centered side will aid in that quest.

Figure 12-2 Placement of learning theories and teacher roles on a continuum.

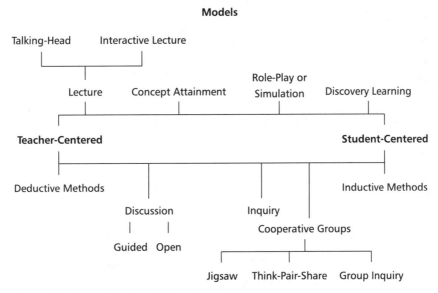

Figure 12-3 Placement of models on the continuum.

CRITERIA FOR EVALUATING APPROPRIATENESS OF MATERIALS, RESOURCES, TECHNOLOGY, AND INSTRUCTIONAL ACTIVITIES

Teachers must think carefully about the materials, resources, technologies, and instructional activities that they select to compliment and enhance a lesson. These materials can be seen as meaningful parts of the lesson that add interest, understanding, and deeper thinking when properly selected. Each choice should be made deliberately, based on children's varied characteristics and needs. Instructional activities (such as those discussed in this chapter), materials, resources, and technologies should:

- Be seen as relevant and "in the flow" of the lesson rather than seen as a separate "stand alone" (i.e., they should coincide with the goals and objectives of the lesson).

- Be age-appropriate and at the developmental level of children (as well as containing on-level vocabulary, if applicable) and adaptable to several levels of children.

- Be up-to-date and contain accurate information (if applicable).

- Be motivating in some way (visually attractive, inducing curiosity, challenging, etc.).

- Be long enough or contain enough depth to involve learning (rather than a short exposure).

- Be free from bias.

- Have directions and procedures that are easy for both teacher and children to follow.

- Be of quality rather than quantity.

- Work up through various levels of thinking.

- Be seen as matching students rather than as students matching materials (for example,

some teachers work straight through a textbook rather than considering students' needs closely).

- Be accurate.

- Be at the reading level of children (if print is included).

- Be free from confusing, superfluous information.

- Should encourage deeper understanding.

SUMMARY

This chapter has looked carefully at the emphasis on higher-level thinking skills and a variety of ways to incorporate those into teaching. Educational researchers (Eggen & Kauchak, 1996) continue to recommend that practicing cognitive thinking skills is extremely important for internalization. Rather than being considered a separate skill ("It's time for critical thinking now, class!"), these skills should be integrated into the curriculum often. That way, children are practicing with all subject areas and they are deepening their knowledge of each of the subject areas at the same time. They are also more active and engaged in learning.

Competency 8 also reminds teachers to vary their roles in the classroom while monitoring and adjusting instruction to children's needs. This chapter has examined several areas that will help teachers become more adept at using higher-level thinking: the selection of various strategies and models of instruction in the lesson plan, direct questioning techniques, and the creation of an accepting environment for taking risks in learning.

One reason that teaching is such an engaging profession is that teachers are involved in higher-level thinking each day, too, as they design creative lessons, solve problems, participate in discussions, and evaluate many areas of their practice. Our children deserve the same stimulating situations.

GLOSSARY

attention span   the time period that a child can spend on a given task.

Classroom Discussion Model   as children read or listen, they design questions of their own at three levels of thinking to ask in a discussion group.

convergent questions   questions that have only one answer, usually recalled from facts.

deductive strategy   a lesson plan begins with the teacher giving students information followed by students applying the concepts in guided practice and independent practice (such as in a "direct teach" or lecture-type lesson).

discovery learning   information is not given in an explicit way to children—students must discover it themselves through inquiry (or an inductive approach).

divergent questions   open-ended questions that can have many answers (opinions, hypotheses, and evaluations that are higher-level thinking).

halt time   stopping the forward motion of the lesson completely to give children time to digest material.

inductive strategy   instruction begins with curious events, scenarios, "unknowns," or questions, then moves to "knowns," or finding the answers (such as in a discovery or inquiry lesson). It is a more student-centered approach, in which the child actively searches for knowledge.

instructional strategy   selecting a way of instructing that will meet the needs, goals, and objectives of learners—the "how will I teach particular information to children?" component.

learner-centered (or student-centered)   a teaching approach that places the focus of instruction directly on the needs of the learner (rather than on the teacher or the subject discipline) and creates active learners.

model of teaching   an instructional strategy created for a particular purpose (such as cooperative grouping, inquiry model, etc.) in which any subject area can be employed within the framework.

monitoring   the teacher constantly gains feedback from students as to how their learning is progressing.

pacing   the "feel" of the movement in time (or momentum) of the lesson.

risk-free environment   a classroom in which all children feel that their opinions and contributions are valued.

role-play   children "become" specific people and act through a scenario without a written script.

selective attention   the ability to focus on one stimulus while ignoring others that are superfluous.

simulation   a type of scenario that involves abstractions from the real world, where roles are often established and skills are used to work through a process to a goal.

teacher-as-an audience   a role in which the teacher is an observer when a student product is completed, then demonstrated, explained, or performed.

teacher-as-a-coach   a role in which teachers give immediate feedback and encouragement to children as new skills are attempted.

teacher-as-a-facilitator   a role in which teachers provide a structure for learning, then help when there are questions or stumbling blocks in a rich learning environment.

teacher-as-a-guide   a role in which the teacher mediates and adjusts to help students obtain information on their own.

teacher-centered   lessons in which the teacher imparts information and learners are passive receivers of knowledge rather than active learners.

wait time   the time a teacher waits between asking a question and calling on a child; the longer the wait time, the more children raise their hands, and the more thoughtful the answers.

SUGGESTED ACTIVITIES

1. Collect lesson plans and methods that have various higher-level activities embedded within them.

2. Collect various concepts that could be employed in a Concept Attainment game.

3. Collect information or events that could be used in an inquiry for your grade level.

4. Find an Internet site that focuses on higher-level skills.

5. For your preferred grade level, collect readings with which a Classroom Discussion Model could be used. Discuss the above findings with your mentor.

6. Shadow at least three children of different grade levels in your field placement. Keep a chart by marking the time when their attention span is lost. Average the time for each student. Consider why their attention may have waned.

7. In your observation classroom, observe several lessons. Create a chart that divides lower-level

questions from higher-level ones. Record when each is asked and the wait time given. Note probing techniques and body language of the teacher during both types of questions.

8. Focus upon a child in your field placement. As you teach a lesson, use various techniques to increase the attention span of the selected child.

9. Tape a lesson that you teach, and note the number of higher-level questions you ask. Note the frequency of those who answer, in terms of the level of achievement, gender, and various ethnicities in the class.

10. Plan and conduct a formal discussion, using the guidelines listed in this chapter.

11. Select a model of teaching and plan a lesson that is appropriate for your grade level.

12. Examine carefully your beliefs on some of the main issues of this chapter (attention span, teacher-centeredness, learner-centeredness, higher-level activities, etc.). Does the way in which you teach now match the recommendations for young children? If not, reflect upon strategies that you will use to help align your practice more with current beliefs.

13. Reflect upon your experiences as a student in elementary school, middle school, high school, and college. How often were student-centered activities used in classrooms? Compare and contrast your college classes that were student-centered with those that were teacher-centered. What differences did you experience?

14. Reflect on strategies you plan to use to increase the amount of higher-level questions that you will ask.

PRACTICE QUESTIONS

1. Mrs. Huff was teaching a problem-solving lesson in third-grade mathematics. She noticed that her children had been working very hard to understand and to "stay with her." "Stop just a moment," she asked the class. "I want you to 'shake it out' for a second. Put your head back, then forward, then on your left shoulder, and now your right. Now roll your head all the way around. All right, now, let's think quietly for just a moment about the problem-solving strategies that you have learned so far that work best for you. Without working the next problem, just think through our list of strategies right now. Remember, just think quietly." Children sat in their seats for about a minute, silently, with their eyes shut. What would be the best thing Mrs. Huff could say or ask next?

A. "Now, who can tell me again a strategy that works well for them?"

B. "Let's all turn in our book and look at the next problem together."

C. "I am so happy with what you have done so far, but we have a ways to go yet today."

D. "Thank you so much for keeping your eyes shut and for sitting quietly."

2. Mr. Faseler integrated reading and science by first introducing a story about a family that was shipwrecked on an island. In the story, some supplies had washed ashore, and the family wanted to see whether they could use these to create a means to make electricity. Later in science class, Mr. Faseler had children discover concepts about electrical current by presenting them with the same supplies as the family in the story had. He did very little talking and had groups work through the project on their own in discovery, as he walked around, smoothing out a few small problems here and there. His main role in this lesson as a teacher was:

A. Instructor

B. Facilitator

C. Coach

D. Audience/observer

3. Mrs. de la Garza, a new teacher, had her kindergarten class ready in the circle when their guest speaker arrived. To introduce her unit on spring, Mrs. de la Garza had asked that Mr. Chang from the local nursery bring in a variety of plants and talk with children about them for about 30 minutes. When he arrived, he set out his samples and began to talk to the children about them. Mrs. de la Garza was distressed to find that Mr. Chang continued

beyond the agreed time period, and children started to interrupt with questions, move around, and talk to their neighbors. She was embarrassed by their behavior, especially because she had specifically prepared them for a guest. She should:

A. Interrupt Mr. Chang for a moment and remind her class of the rules she had given them for having a guest speaker.

B. Let Mr. Chang know very nicely that the class schedule must move on.

C. Wait for Mr. Chang to leave and talk seriously about their behavior, threatening never to invite a guest again.

D. Ask Mr. Chang some questions that would engage children more than the ones they were asking.

4. Mr. Marshall teaches fourth grade in a school that is characterized as "at-risk." Many of the students are impacted by poverty and have limited experiences with the world and with text. His fourth-grade social studies class is beginning a unit of study on the Texas Revolution. As an introduction to the study, Mr. Marshall read to the class the first chapter of a diary-like book about a child during the Texas fight for independence. He used "think-alouds" throughout the shared reading, asking students to predict at appropriate times and to help make his thinking explicit to students. He engaged the class in a discussion of the chapter and encouraged them to make links to their personal lives. Each student had a paperback copy of the book.

"Think-alouds" support children's thinking about their ongoing understanding in powerful ways because:

A. This particular class cannot do the higher-order thinking necessary for this unit of study.

B. Students need auditory feedback as they follow along in their own novels.

C. The "think-alouds" explicitly demonstrate metacognitive operations that support strategic reading and writing.

D. This strategy gives concrete examples to the students to increase their vocabulary.

Answers and Discussion

Answer 1: *B* asks students to delve right back into the work too abruptly. *C* and *D* are both excellent reinforcements for students and would be nice to hear, but *A* acts as a mini-closure to review and reinforce what students have just been thinking of metacognitively. To reinforce that orally will be very fruitful. The answer is *A*.

Answer 2: The teacher uses a variety of instructional strategies and roles to facilitate learning and to help children become independent thinkers and problem solvers who use higher-order thinking in the classroom and the real world. He is not giving out content information or teaching skills, so he is not in an instructor's role, and he is not watching (in the role of audience) as students present. He may be doing some encouraging and giving feedback as a coach, but mainly he has set up a situation for children to discover. He is facilitating that purpose. The answer is *B*.

Answer 3: Every teacher will be in this situation at one point in his or her career: a guest overstays the time allotment and children become restless. It can be very embarrassing. Our first inclination would be *A, C,* or *D* to salvage the situation. However, the children's attention spans at this age are not going to last much longer, whatever she does, and we do not know how much longer Mr. Chang might continue to talk. It would be best to let Mr. Chang know that the class schedule must move on—in a very nice way. Mrs. de la Garza's first mistake was asking a guest to speak with children in the circle for such a long period of time. Attention span for a lecture at this age is not long. Having children in one activity for too long can breed management difficulties. It can also cause students to lose information toward the end, from inattention. The answer is *B*.

Answer 4: Answer *A* is certainly not correct, because intelligence is not related to economic level. Answer *B*, auditory feedback, is a good idea for other learning styles, but not the best answer. Answer *D*, "think-alouds," may make all kinds of connections—not *all* concrete, though. Answer *C* is correct because this technique supports children in monitoring their own ongoing understanding. As the teacher tells children his thoughts while he reads, children check their own thoughts and understanding against his. Metacognitive thinking is literally "thinking about thinking"—a very active part of "think-alouds." The answer is *C*.

WEB LINKS

If you enter critical+thinking+teaching, or other key words in this chapter, you will have a long list of sites that offer theory, activities, materials to purchase, and so forth. You may also want to try *inquiry+teaching*. Other search combinations may also help you gain more information. Remember that sites move, can be removed, or may not be found using your server. If a site listed below cannot be located, try entering other key words to help in your search.

http://omega.cc.umb.edu/~cct/theses/elemindx.html

This very helpful site offers some critical thinking, articles, and other pathways to help understanding in this area.

www.gsu.edu/~dschjb/wwwcrit.html

This site provides further definitions of critical thinking from a master teaching program, along with information on cooperative groups (with a few activities for critical thinking in the classroom).

http://www.criticalthinking.org/K12/k12class/trc.html

The National Council for Excellence in Critical Thinking provides a list of its principles and pedagogical implications for critical thinking, along with some links to lessons.

http://ublib.buffalo.edu/libraries/projects/tlr/thinking.html

Here you will find articles and links for critical thinking.

REFERENCES

Bloom, B. S., Englehart, M. D., Furst, E. J., Hill, W. H., & Krathwohl, D. R., (Eds.). (1956). *Taxonomy of educational objectives: The classification of education goals, handbook I: Cognitive domain.* New York: David McKay.

Eggen, P., & Kauchak, D. (1996). *Educational psychology: Windows on classroom.* (5th ed.). Upper Saddle River, NJ: Merrill Prentice Hall.

Elgas, P., & Lynch, E. (1998). In L. Johnson, M. LaMontagne, P. Elgas, & A. Bauer (Eds.), *Early childhood education: Blending theory, blending practice* (pp. 111–132). Baltimore: Paul H. Brookes Publishing Company

Fradd, S., & Lee, O. (1999). Teachers' roles in promoting science inquiry with students from diverse language backgrounds. *Educational Researcher, 28*(6), 14–20.

Freire, P. (1993). *Pedagogy of the oppressed.* New York: Continuum.

Gunter, M. A., Estes, T., & Schwab, J. (1995). *Instruction: A models approach.* (2nd ed.). Boston: Allyn and Bacon.

Joyce, B., & Weil, M., with Showers, B. (1996). *Models of teaching.* (5th ed.). Boston: Allyn and Bacon.

Langer, J., Bartolome, L., Vasquez, O., and Lucas, T. (1990). Meaning construction in school literacy tasks: A study of bilingual students. *American Educational Research Journal, 27,* 427–471.

Moore, K. D. (1998). *Middle and secondary school instructional method.* (2nd ed.). Boston: McGraw-Hill College.

Ryan, K., & Cooper, J. (1998). *Those who can, teach.* (8th ed.). Boston: Houghton Mifflin Company.

Sadker, M., & Sadker, D. (1994). *Failing at fairness: How our schools cheat girls.* New York: Simon and Schuster.

Suchman, J. R. (1962). The elementary school training program in scientific inquiry. Report to the U.S. Office of Education, Project Title VII. Urbana: University of Illinois Press.

Tishman, S., & Perkins, D. (1997). The language of thinking. *Phi Delta Kappan, 78*(5), 368–374.

Chapter 13

COMPETENCY 8 – PART 2

Motivating Learners

SANDY CMAJDALKA

University of Houston—Downtown

TERMS TO KNOW

Attribution theory
Behavioral approach
Cognitive approach
Deficiency need
Disequilibrium
Equilibrium
External locus of control
Extrinsic motivation
Growth needs

Humanistic approach
Internal locus of control
Intrinsic motivation
Learned helplessness
Learning goals/mastery goals
Maslow's hierarchy of needs
Negative reinforcement
Performance goals
Positive reinforcement

Presentation punishment
Punishment
Reinforcement
Removal punishment
Risk-free environment
Self-concept
Self-efficacy
Self-esteem
Stability

Motivation can be defined as "a force that energizes, sustains, and directs behavior toward a goal" (Baron, 1992, 1996; Pintrich & Schunk). Woolfolk (2001) defines motivation as "an inner state that arouses, directs, and maintains a person's behavior" (p. G-7). Although there are varying definitions of motivation, research is clear that motivation is strongly correlated with achievement (Wang, Haertel, & Walberg, 1993; Weinstein, 1998). For this reason, it becomes increasingly necessary for teachers to pay attention to motivation and its role in the classroom and in the learning process. As Slavin (1987) says, "Students who are academically unmotivated to learn do not learn (p. 316). Motivated students have positive attitudes toward school, describe school as satisfying, persist on difficult tasks, cause few management problems, process information in depth, and excel in classroom learning experiences (Stipek, 1996). Researchers contend that children are naturally motivated to learn but that many lose this motivation as they progress through the primary grades (Carlton & Winsler, 1998; Hauser-Cram, 1998). This chapter addresses critical issues in motivation and how teachers can help establish and maintain motivation in the EC–4 classroom.

EXTRINSIC AND INTRINSIC MOTIVATION

Motivation is generally classified into two basic categories: extrinsic and intrinsic. **Extrinsic motivation** occurs when children are motivated to perform a certain behavior by an environmental factor—something outside themselves. Examples are studying only in order to earn good grades, turning in a lost item only for the reward money, or going to work only to receive a paycheck. Think of reasons for studying for this certification examination. If studying to receive a passing grade and to be certified as a teacher in the state of Texas is the only reason for learning this information, this is an example of extrinsic motivation. However, if one also wants to learn so as to become an effective teacher, this is intrinsic motivation. One can think of extrinsic and intrinsic motivation as opposite ends of a motivation continuum. Thus, **intrinsic motivation** occurs when the desire to perform or behave comes from within oneself. An individual may go swimming because it is pleasurable, or may paint a picture because he or she simply enjoys the activity. Many behaviors can stem from both extrinsic and intrinsic motivation, depending on the person and/or the situation. An example is reading a book. Some children might be motivated to read a book because it was assigned reading from class and they know that they will be tested on the material (extrinsic motivation), or they may be motivated to read a book because the topic is of interest to them or they find it an enjoyable pastime (intrinsic motivation). Some children read a book for both extrinsic *and* intrinsic reasons. Both types of motivation can work together. Another example is exercising. Many people exercise because they know they need to get in shape, they want to look better in a swimsuit, or a doctor said it was necessary for good health (extrinsic motivation). Others exercise simply because it makes them feel good (intrinsic motivation).

Many teachers use various forms of extrinsic motivation in their classrooms, such as giving stickers or prizes for desired behavior. This technique can certainly be effective. However, the ultimate goal is to help children develop intrinsic motivation, or the love of learning for its own sake. When children are intrinsically motivated to learn, they will learn without prodding or pushing from the teacher and will develop into lifelong learners. Although both types of motivation can be used successfully in the classroom, it is important to be mindful of when and how teachers use them. For example, if an activity is already intrinsically motivating to children, providing external rewards can sometimes decrease the students' motivation to perform the activity on their own. Children may internalize that the activity must be difficult or boring if the teacher is offering them rewards for doing it. When extrinsic rewards are overused, children may begin to ask what is in it for them before they perform a task with questions such as "Do we get candy?" This is counterproductive to promoting intrinsic motivation. However, some tasks do call for extrinsic rewards, especially those that children perceive to be negative or distasteful. In these cases, it may be appropriate to use external rewards initially to get the children to perform the desired behavior and then gradually try to increase students' interest in the activity, moving them toward more internal rewards. Remember that a person's motivation for a particular behavior does not have to be strictly extrinsic or intrinsic. It can be a combination of both. For example, a teacher may pursue a bilingual certificate to receive an additional stipend (extrinsic motivation) but this same teacher may also have a personal desire for working with second language learners (intrinsic motivation).

GENERAL APPROACHES TO MOTIVATION

Although there are several approaches to motivation, this chapter focuses on the following three general approaches: behavioral approach, cognitive approach, and humanistic approach, each of which is related to theories discussed in Competency 4, Part 1, Chapter 5, of this book.

Behavioral Approach

The **behavioral approach** to motivation is based on behavioral theory. It proposes that learners are essentially motivated by reinforcement or punishment received from their environment. A **reinforcement** is the introduction of something that results in the *increase* of a behavior, and a **punishment** is the introduction of something that results in the *decrease* of a behavior. Reinforcement is classified as being either *positive* or *negative,* and punishment is classified as being either *presentation* or *removal* (see Competency 4). Keep in mind that with the behavioral approach to motivation, the reinforcement or punishment is administered *after* the behavior has already occurred. Therefore the individual behaves in anticipation of the reinforcement or punishment.

Reinforcement. For this section of the chapter, remember that the end result of reinforcement is an increase in behavior.

Positive reinforcement consists of introducing something that increases a behavior. For example, many teachers give stickers, tokens, coupons, or other tangible rewards to students after they have exhibited a desired behavior. However, a reward does not have to be tangible to be classified as a positive reinforcer. A teacher may reinforce a desired behavior by "giving" a student a smile, a pat on the back, or verbal praise. Each of these is considered a positive reinforcement because it results in an increase in the desired behavior and it is something that was "given" to or "received" by the student. Another example of positive reinforcement is good grades. In studying for this examination for certification, for instance, some candidates are motivated by the thought of earning a high grade on this exam.

Although the use of positive reinforcement is an excellent tool for promoting motivation, there are also some criticisms associated with it. First, if a child receives too many rewards (e.g., stickers, candy, etc.) for a behavior, he or she can become *satiated* (or "full") and no longer have a need or desire for that reward. When this occurs, a new reward or reinforcer must be found. Also, teachers must remember that a reward must be valuable to the *child*. If not, the reward will not cause a change in behavior. Many teachers of young children must work hard to provide rewards that are initially valuable and retain their value to children. Second, tangibles can become expensive for EC–4 teachers, so teachers should try to find free reinforcers that have some educational or social value when possible (coupons for extra computer time, listening to taped books or music, lunch with the teacher, etc.). Other rewards can be simple—being allowed to work on the floor, taking one's shoes off, wearing a sticker, and so forth. Finally, using rewards continuously to increase behavior can imply to the child that there is no inherent value in the task itself and that the only reason to continue the behavior is to receive the reward. This can be counterproductive if teachers want their children to be motivated to learn for the sake of learning.

As noted in Competency 4, Part 1, Chapter 5, **negative reinforcement** consists of taking something away to increase the desired behavior. The seat belt buzzer when one turns the key in his or her car ignition is one example of this concept. This noise is very annoying. If one puts on the seat belt, the annoying buzzing sound stops. This is an example of negative reinforcement, because something was removed or taken away (the annoying sound) for the purpose of increasing the desired behavior (putting on the seatbelt). An example with children might be telling a child that he or she does not have to do household chores for one week if an *A* on a report card is produced. The child is being rewarded by the removal of something (chores), and the result is an increase in the desired behavior (getting good grades). If a teacher rewards children by taking away their homework assignments, however, he or she is implying to learners that homework is unpleasant and not something they should normally want to do. Even if the teacher is successful in increasing student motivation to perform the desired behavior, student motivation to do homework (or whatever task was removed) will decrease in the future. For this reason, teachers must

be vigilant with the use of negative reinforcement in the classroom as it can be counterproductive in overall motivation for children.

It is also important to note that the word "negative" in negative reinforcement should not be associated with words like "bad." It is negative because something is being taken away, just as in positive reinforcement, something is being given. It is like addition and subtraction. Although positive and negative reinforcement differ in whether something is being given or taken away, they are both types of reinforcement, which means that the end result is an increase in desired behavior.

Punishment. The opposite of reinforcement is punishment. The purpose of punishment is to *decrease* or stop an undesirable behavior. There are two basic types of punishment: presentation and removal.

Presentation punishment occurs when the student is given (or presented with) something that will decrease a behavior. Examples include bad grades, verbal reprimands, or having to stay late after school. When a teacher uses presentation punishment, children perceive the item presented to be unpleasant. Logically, if teachers want children to enjoy writing, they should not assign "lines," or have children write one hundred times "I will not . . . ," as punishment. Similarly, if teachers want their students to enjoy reading, they should not assign extra reading assignments as punishment. This gives students the message that the teacher considers writing and extra reading unpleasant, disagreeable tasks.

With **removal punishment,** something perceived as pleasurable is taken away from the student to decrease the behavior. Examples of removal punishment might be time out from an exciting activity, not allowing the student to work with peers during group time, or loss of free time, computer time, or recess. A popular though questionable use of this strategy is to take away field trip or party privileges from students who exhibit undesirable behaviors. It is questionable because the teacher may believe these activities are valuable enough to the child to make a change in behavior. Quite often they are not, and the children who most need the experiences are isolated or left behind. The intent of punishment is to decrease or stop the undesirable behavior. It is extremely important to remember that a teacher might, in fact, be giving a *reinforcer* to children who act up in an activity that they dislike and are removed. It is likely that those children will act up next time to get out of the activity again (an increase in behavior rather than a decrease). Furthermore, children who love attention often "inspire" the teacher to give them attention (children don't necessarily care what kind of attention) in the form of verbal reprimands, stopping the class, or another focus on the child. What the teacher sees as negative attention, or punishment, the child sees as positive.

Cognitive Approach

Another approach to motivation is the **cognitive approach.** This approach emphasizes the learner's internal desire to learn, stemming from innate curiosity and a natural desire to make sense of the world. Cognitivists propose that all babies are born with inquisitive minds and the natural desire to learn (Piaget, 1952). It is only after negative experiences that children become unmotivated to learn. Remember that, according to Piaget, people have a natural drive or need for **equilibrium,** which is the balance between our understanding of the world and our experiences. According to cognitive theory, learning occurs only after a student's state of equilibrium has been disrupted, resulting in a state of **disequilibrium.** According to the theory, students are motivated to learn new information to resolve the imbalance and return to a state of equilibrium. For example, a child believes that he knows what a bird is and is in a state of equilibrium with his schema. However, when the teacher tells the child that a bat is not a bird, the child is placed in a state of disequilibrium and is motivated to learn (or resolve the imbalance) and return to a state of equilibrium. Similarly, a child may believe that a tomato is a vegetable. However, when he or she is told or reads on the Internet that a tomato is actually classified as a fruit, disequilibrium occurs, resulting in the student's desire to learn in order to resolve the imbalance. Under this theory, it becomes the teacher's job to continually "keep students off balance" intellectually (if just a little at a time) to motivate them to learn or search for equilibrium.

Humanistic Approach

The behavioral approach to motivation stresses the importance of rewards and/or consequences of behavior, and the cognitive approach stresses a person's innate need or desire to make sense of the world. The **humanistic approach** stresses that people are motivated by a natural desire or need to reach their maximum potential. Under this approach, teachers must appeal to the child's sense of competence, personal choice, self-determination, and desire to improve him- or herself and be the best that he or she can be. This approach focuses on the needs of the whole child and how meeting or not meeting those needs affects motivation. An important theorist under this approach is Maslow. His proposed hierarchy of needs follows.

MASLOW'S HIERARCHY OF NEEDS

Maslow proposes that a person has a variety of needs and attends to those needs in a certain order. He classifies these needs into two basic categories: **deficiency needs** (lower-level needs) and **growth needs** (higher-level needs). Deficiency needs are subcategorized into physiological needs (such as food, water, and air), safety needs (such as shelter and freedom from harm), belongingness and love needs (such as acceptance and affection), and esteem needs (such as self-respect and self-worth). According to Maslow, children whose deficiency needs have not yet been met are not able to attend to the higher growth needs of self-actualization (or maximizing one's potential to the fullest). Although a teacher's job is to further a child's intellectual achievement, this may not be possible if the child has other basic needs that have not yet been met. It becomes crucial, then, for the teacher to identify unmet needs and to help the child meet those needs whenever possible. It is for this reason that many government programs now offer schools free and reduced lunch programs. A child who is hungry cannot attend to the task of learning. His or her attention is focused on physical hunger. Similarly, a child who is fearful for his or her safety or lacks adequate self-esteem cannot attend to higher-order learning, because his or her attention is placed elsewhere. Little learning occurs in a classroom in which the teacher creates a negative environment and the children fear the teacher. Basically, if a child's lower-level needs are not met, he or she will not be motivated to learn nor to reach the higher-level needs of self-improvement and self-actualization.

SELF-PERCEPTION AND MOTIVATION

Various terms are associated with the realm of self-perception. This chapter will focus on three such terms: self-concept, self-esteem, and self-efficacy.

Self-Concept

Self-concept refers to the way people see themselves. For example, a child may see himself or herself as an excellent student in mathematics, an average student in reading, a poor runner, a good friend, and a poor artist. These views may be accurate or inaccurate, but they stem from the *child's* perception of him- or herself. The child might actually be a poor student in math and an excellent student in reading, but the self-concept is

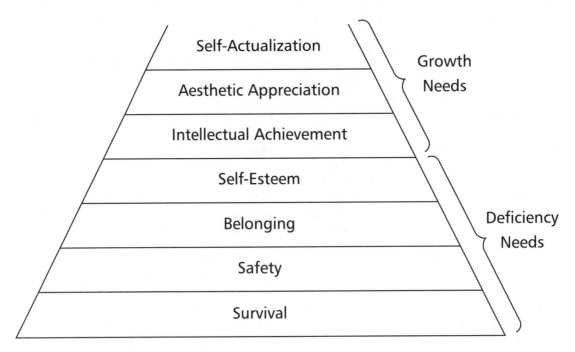

Figure 13-1 Maslow's hierarchy of needs.

based strictly on how the child views him- or her-self—accurate or not. Self-concept itself is not associated with any affective feelings (neither good nor bad). It is simply the way one perceives oneself, and children may have different self-concepts for different academic content areas and other areas of their lives.

SELF-ESTEEM

Self-esteem, on the other hand, is how a child *feels* about his self-concept. It has to do with values. If being a fast runner is not important to the child, his- or her self-esteem will not be lowered by that lack of ability. However, if the child perceives running ability as being very important, his or her self-esteem may be lowered by the inability to run fast. This applies to any area of skill or knowledge in schools.

Research shows a high correlation between student self-esteem in a particular content area and achievement in that area. For this reason, it becomes increasingly important for teachers to work on raising the academic self-esteem of their students. Many teachers try hard to raise children's self-esteem, but it is important to keep in mind that the only ways to do this are to help them change their self-concepts or help learners raise their abilities. A teacher cannot simply tell a child that she should feel good about her reading ability or mathematics ability. To change self-esteem, the teacher must change the child's perception of self or self-concept. For example, Ms. Martinez tried telling Bonnie that she is, indeed, a good reader, but Bonnie needs evidence to be convinced. Ms. Martinez must provide her with numerous opportunities to be successful in reading and other related activities. When Bonnie has had repeated successes, she is more likely to see herself as competent and to have positive self-esteem in that area. It is important to note that positive self-esteem in one area in no way guarantees positive self-esteem in another. Children need to believe that they are competent in math, reading, social skills, and so forth.

Self-Efficacy

Self-efficacy is a person's belief that he or she is a capable human being who can reach his or her goals. A learner who has healthy self-esteem based on his or her self-concept develops a sense of self-efficacy. Children who have reached a high level of self-efficacy are motivated to set goals for themselves and to continue achievement at a higher level. These goals are discussed in the next section.

GOALS AND MOTIVATION

Students who are able to set effective goals are more motivated to achieve those goals. If the goal is too easy to achieve, then the student will not see the success as having any significance. If the goal is too difficult to achieve, the student will not be able to reach the goal, and frustration may set in. For this reason, the goals students set for themselves must be challenging, yet realistic and achievable. A child should also be able to set both long-term and short-term goals. Examples of long-term goals are learning to read, mastering the multiplication tables, and being able to write a paragraph by the end of the school year. Examples of short-term goals are learning the letter *s* and the sound it makes, learning the 3s times-table, and being able to write two or three sentences at a time. If the child sets only long-term goals, it may be a very long time before success is reached, and motivation may diminish. Setting short-term goals allows the child to achieve multiple successes along the way while still pursuing a longer-term goal. This helps the student maintain motivation.

Goals, whether long-term or short-term, are classified into two types: performance goals and learning goals. **Performance goals** focus on how well a child performs on a particular task at a particular time. Examples of performance goals are a grade on a weekly spelling test or a score on the outlining of a science text chapter. On the other hand, **learning goals** (also referred to as **mastery goals**) focus on the degree to which a child eventually learns or masters the material in the end, regardless of the length of time it may take. For example, even if a child earns a score of 85 percent on the weekly spelling test, a learning goal would focus on the correct spelling of 100 percent of the words (even if it's not until 3 weeks later). Similarly, if a child earns a low score on his outlining of a chapter in his science textbook, a learning goal would focus on whether or not the child eventually did understand the necessary material and how it was organized, even if this did not occur at the initial time of reading. Teachers find that when they focus on performance goals in the classroom, their children are motivated by the grades they hope to receive. However, if the focus is on learning goals, they are more likely to be motivated by the desire to obtain mastery of the material.

ATTRIBUTION THEORY

Attribution theory deals with a child's idea as to the source of his or her failures and successes. In other words, if a child succeeds, what does he or she believe is the reason for that success? If the child fails, what does he or she believe is the reason for that failure?

Locus of Control

Locus of control is where a child believes control over events lies (i.e. the location of the control). Locus of control is usually categorized as being either external or internal. An **external locus of control** means that a child attributes his or her success or failure to an environmental factor—a factor that is *outside* his or her control. For example, a child who performs poorly on an exam and has an external locus of control may say that the exam was unfair in some way, the teacher did a poor job of teaching the material, or the teacher did not like him. Similarly, a child who performs well on the exam but still has an external locus of control is likely to say that the exam was easy, the material was easy, the teacher liked her, or that she

had just plain good luck. On the other hand, an **internal locus of control** means that a child attributes his or her success or failure to an *internal* factor—a factor involving control over herself in some way. If this child performs poorly on an exam, she may attribute her failure to a lack of ability or not enough time spent studying. If she has an internal locus of control and she does well on the exam, she may attribute it to her high ability or hard work in class and studying. Children with an external locus of control believe that they cannot control their success or failure; those with an internal locus of control believe that they are the main reason for their success or failure.

Children with an internal locus of control generally have high motivation because they believe that effort makes a difference. Those with an external locus of control generally have low motivation because they believe that hard work is irrelevant to success. Teachers should be sensitive to children who are developing an external locus of control, for whatever reason, and should try to help them develop a more internal perception of success and failure. Teachers can promote this concept by dividing learning tasks into small units, which facilitate early and quick success. This helps children believe that "they can do it." This theory tells teachers that success often breeds more success.

Stability

Stability refers to the child's perception of a situation as changeable or not. When a child regards a situation as stable, there is less motivation because he or she thinks that it will always be that way, no matter what. Conversely, when a situation is regarded as unstable, there is stronger motivation—for it may change for the better. For example, if a child thinks that a teacher is "out to get him or her" and always gives the child a bad grade, the situation is seen as stable (i.e., the child can do nothing to make the teacher like him or her nor can he or she change the way the teacher grades). This results in poor motivation to work. He or she believes that no matter what is tried, the situation is not likely to change. However, if a child does poorly on a paper and attributes it to the fact that he did not take much time or effort, that is something that is unstable and can be changed. Such children can be motivated to work harder in the future because they believe they can change the outcome the next time.

Perception of ability may be stable or unstable. The belief that one's ability is fixed, that it may even be genetic, connects it to stability. However, the belief that one's ability can change through hard work and perseverance connects it to instability. Viewing ability as unstable enhances motivation, whereas the stable view can stunt motivation, particularly if a child views his inborn ability as low.

Learned Helplessness

Learned helplessness is created when a learner has failed numerous times and believes that the reason is beyond his or her control (whether internal or external) and beyond his or her ability to change. For example, children who fail repeatedly at a task and believe that the reason is their inherent lack of ability (stable and beyond their control) will eventually "learn" that no matter how hard they try to understand the material, they will fail anyway. If they believe that the teacher dislikes them (external) and they fail repeatedly, they eventually "learn" that no matter how hard they try, the teacher will fail them anyway. This serves as a major obstacle in the area of motivation. Such children are not motivated to make an effort, because they have come to believe that no matter what they do, they will not succeed. Therefore they stop trying. Teachers who go to the aid of children too quickly and too often can create learned helplessness. Children begin to rely on the teacher, and they internalize that the teacher also believes them incapable. For this reason, teachers who are monitoring children should be careful not to go too quickly to help them or to stay too long with a particular child. They should avoid setting up a dependent relationship.

ANXIETY AND MOTIVATION

Research shows that children who are anxious do not learn as well as those who are not anxious. Similar to Maslow's hierarchy of needs, any attention devoted to anxiety is attention taken away from the learning task at hand. Many factors can cause anxiety in children: instability at home or school, trouble with friendships, fear of failure, and so on. Teachers can help children overcome some of these factors. Others are beyond their control. Even if a teacher is not able to control all of the anxieties of children, he or she needs at least to be aware of the effect of anxiety on motivation to learn. Children need to be provided with a learning environment that is as emotionally and physically safe and predictable as possible in order to minimize unnecessary anxiety.

EFFECTIVE VERSUS INEFFECTIVE PRAISE

One way to increase motivation is to provide students with praise for their successes and for their *efforts* toward success. Praise falls under the category of positive reinforcement and is the behavioral approach to motivation. Although praise can be a useful tool in promoting motivation in children, teachers should be careful to use it effectively. Effective praise is specific and genuine. Children know it when their teachers lavish them with praise that is not genuine or deserved. They learn to mistrust the teacher's praise, even if it is genuine in the future. Also, when teachers are too general with their praise, such as saying "Good," or "Nice job," the child is left unsure as to what they did, specifically, that was worthy of the praise. It is more effective to be specific with praise- "I like your choice of adjectives in this sentence," or "I appreciate the way you waited patiently for your turn to stir the cookie dough." This lets children know more clearly which behaviors the teacher would like them to repeat in the future. The following guidelines are helpful to teachers interested in increasing the effectiveness of their praise in the classroom.

Effective Praise

According to Brophy (1981), praise when used effectively:

- Is delivered contingently
- Specifies the particulars of the accomplishment
- Shows spontaneity, variety, and other signs of credibility; suggests clear attention to the student's accomplishment
- Rewards attainment of specified performance criteria (which can include effort criteria)
- Provides information to students about their competence or the value of their accomplishments
- Orients students toward better appreciation of their own task-related behavior and thoughts about problem solving
- Uses students' own prior accomplishments as the context for describing present accomplishments
- Is given in recognition of noteworthy effort or success at tasks that are difficult
- Attributes success to effort and ability, implying that similar successes can be expected in the future
- Leads students to expend effort on the task because they enjoy the task and/or want to develop task-relevant skills
- Focuses students' attention on their own task-relevant behavior
- Fosters appreciation of and desirable attributions about task-relevant behavior after the process is completed (p. 396).

Ineffective Praise

According to Brophy (1981), praise when used ineffectively:

- Is delivered randomly or unsystematically
- Is restricted to global positive reactions
- Shows a bland uniformity, which suggests a conditional response made with minimal attention
- Rewards mere participation, without consideration of performance process or outcomes
- Provides no information at all or gives students information about their status
- Orients students toward comparing themselves with others and thinking about competing
- Uses the accomplishments of peers as the context for describing students' present accomplishments
- Is given without regard to the effort expended or the meaning of the accomplishment
- Attributes success to ability alone or to external factors such as luck or easy tasks
- Leads students to expend effort on the task for external reasons—to please the teacher, win a competition or reward, and so on
- Focuses students' attention on the teacher as an external authority figure who is manipulating them
- Intrudes into the ongoing process; distracts attention from task-relevant behavior (p. 396).

PRACTICAL APPLICATIONS FOR THE CLASSROOM

Teacher Characteristics

Teachers can exhibit many characteristics as they help promote motivation in their classrooms. First, teachers should show that they are warm and compassionate and that they really do care about each of their children's needs, feelings, and learning outcomes. Many children see themselves through the eyes of their teachers. If they believe that their teacher cares about their learning, they will come to believe in the importance of learning and be motivated to learn. Second, teachers are powerful models when showing their own enthusiasm for subjects and motivation to learn. When children see that their teacher is enthusiastic about a lesson or topic, they perceive the topic as interesting and exciting. This helps promote intrinsic motivation. Similarly, when students see that their teacher loves to learn, they are more likely to become self-motivated, lifelong learners as well. Finally, it is important for teachers to have high expectations of their children. Studies show that teachers who hold high expectations get better results than do those who have lower expectations. Studies have also shown that when a teacher believes that the class consists of high achievers, he or she holds higher expectations for the students who, in turn, perform well. In contrast, a teacher who believes that his or her class consists of low achievers is likely to have lower expectations for the students, who, in turn, perform poorly relative to other students. This is a well-researched, self-fulfilling prophecy. Many nonverbal behaviors send messages to learners implying either, "I know you can do this," or "I doubt that you can do this." For the most part, children rise to the expectations that their teachers place on them.

Classroom Environment

The classroom teacher has control over much of the classroom environment for learners. The teacher can create a place where students feel safe and secure and are not afraid to try new and challenging tasks. This is referred to as a **risk-free environment.** In a classroom in which performance is emphasized and failures ridiculed, students learn not to risk failure and attempt only tasks that are easy and at which they are likely to succeed. However, true learning occurs when students are willing to risk failure by trying new methods and are willing to learn from their mis-

takes. Only a child who has a low fear of failure will be able to accomplish this. Teachers should be sure that *effort to learn* is rewarded along with performance. If children know that failure is an acceptable and necessary part of learning, they will be more motivated to try tasks that are challenging.

Teachers should make sure that the tasks required of students are challenging enough to catch their motivation and interest but not so difficult that success is unobtainable. Remember, however, when the tasks are *too* easy, teachers convey to the students that they do not believe the students are capable of doing more. This can reduce students' motivation to try more challenging tasks.

Another aspect of the classroom environment is competition, which can be a healthy motivator when a child is part of a group and not all alone. When students are left to compete on their own, only the highest achievers have an opportunity to win. This sets up a situation for learned helplessness for lower achieving students and even for average students. Teachers must ensure that all of their children have an opportunity to be successful. It cannot be said enough times to teachers that success at a task leads to further motivation for future tasks and future success.

An important part of classroom environment is choice. Children need to be given choices concerning their learning and the topics they will be studying. Although it is the teacher's duty to make sure that children learn important skills, the topic chosen to reach that goal can be negotiable. Children who are given choices in their learning and control over their learning experiences are more likely to be motivated to learn the overarching objectives.

Lesson Plans and Delivery

Lesson plans, discussed in Competency 3, Part 1, Chapter 3, can play an important role in students' motivation to learn. To increase motivation, it is important that teachers present an introduction that is motivating and captures children's attention for each lesson or learning activity. Some call this the "anticipatory set," "focus," or "motivational set." Children cannot learn when they are not paying attention, so this is a priority. Teachers must also give children a reason for learning the material. Simply stating, "You will need to know this for the next grade level," is not sufficiently motivating for students. They need to know why they need the learning *today* and how it is relevant to their lives *today*. Teachers must be sure to connect the new learning to students' own experiences, interests, cultural backgrounds, and so forth. Usually, finding a way to motivate children intrinsically produces the greatest results in achievement. Freiberg and Driscoll (2000) describe an effective motivational set as one that "... arouses curiosity, poses interesting questions, uses dramatic appeal, and creates a need or interest. It induces an affective or emotional response from the learners" (p. 76).

In addition, teachers should be sure that their objectives do not focus primarily on the lower levels of Bloom's taxonomy (knowledge, comprehension, and application). Although these are important, teachers should also capitalize on the higher-order objectives of analysis, synthesis, and evaluation. Furthermore, Bloom's taxonomy only addresses the cognitive domain. To keep motivation high, teachers also must include objectives in their lessons from the affective domain (receiving, responding, valuing, organizing, and internalizing) and the psychomotor domain (moving, manipulating, communicating, and creating) (Freiberg & Driscoll, 2000). This attention to the development of the whole child leads to more variety in lessons and learning activities and an increase in learner motivation.

Teachers should be sure to use a variety of authentic learning tasks that are meaningful and relevant to students' lives, experiences, and interests. This helps increase students' intrinsic motivation to learn or to participate in the learning experience. Again, teachers should plan to give children choices in their learning. Although it is ultimately up to the teacher to ascertain that the appropriate objectives from the curriculum are met, he or she should use student input to help decide how to reach those objectives. Giving children reasonable choices (from a menu, for example) increases their motivation and also shows that the teacher has confidence in children's abilities to make competent decisions.

Another effective method for motivating students in the classroom is to use good questioning techniques. Teachers who ask only knowledge-based, closed-ended questions imply to the learners that there is only one right answer and that knowing the right answer is what should be valued. The use of open-ended questions such as, "What does it mean to be a friend?" or "Tell me how this picture makes you feel," communicates to children that several answers can be of value and that the teacher is interested in their ideas. Children who feel free to express their opinions and differences of views are more likely to participate in discussions and, therefore, more likely to learn from the experience. Teachers should be sure that they allow all children time to *think* about their answers before they call on someone to share. And teachers should not call on only the students who have their hands raised!

Another technique for motivating children is for teachers to offer numerous opportunities for active learning and participation. A child does not have to be physically moving in order for an activity to be classified as *active* participation. The student could be participating covertly, for instance, as he or she ponders the following questions: "Think quietly to yourself about a time in your life when you were very afraid. What were you afraid of? Was it a person, or a thing, or an event? What made it so frightening for you?" Active learning isn't just "hands on." It is also "minds on," where children are engaged in thinking.

Finally, teachers should be sure that their lessons have a closure that motivates children to make use of a newly acquired skill or to learn more about it. It is not enough to just say, "Tomorrow we will . . ." A closure should be some kind of a "hook" that peaks the students' curiosity and makes them want it to be tomorrow *today*. If teachers do this successfully, when they begin the introduction for the continuing lesson, motivation will already be established.

Teaching Strategies

Although direct instruction and other teacher-centered activities can be excellent tools in reaching curriculum goals, it is also important to include a variety of student-centered activities, such as discovery learning, role-playing, inquiry, and simulations. These and other teaching strategies are described in further detail in the previous chapter. The key is for teachers to use a variety of teaching strategies to keep interests and motivation levels high.

Additional Tips for Teachers

- Learning should be meaningful, interesting, and relevant to children's lives, backgrounds, and experiences.

- Use cooperative learning often instead of only competition.

- Create an environment in which children feel safe and valued.

- Be sure to arouse children's natural curiosity and interest.

- Be sure that all children have an opportunity to succeed and *do* succeed.

- Provide a risk-free environment with a low level of anxiety.

- Set high expectations for *all* of your children.

- Model that you are motivated and interested in learning.

- Use student input for planning—allow them to have choices and control over their learning experiences.

- Use assessment as an opportunity to congratulate children on their achievements and successes, not simply as a task for assigning grades.

- Encourage students always to put forth their best efforts.

- Use effective praise that is specific and genuine.

- Focus students' attention before beginning a lesson.

- Enlist active participation: hands-on and minds-on.

- Help children improve self-esteem by focusing on changing their self-concepts.

- Help children develop intrinsic motivation.

- Help children develop an internal locus of control.

- Accept and treasure the diversity of your children.

- Remember that "variety is the spice of life." Use a variety of teaching strategies and activities every day within your lessons.

- Make use of field trips, videos, guest speakers, and so on.

- Make use of art, music, drama, and so on, in your lessons.

- Make use of creative food experiences to add to your lessons.

- Plan for movement in your activities when children have been still for a long period of time. The attention span of young children interferes with motivation when children must be quiet and still too long.

- Provide children with an opportunity for creativity.

- Make learning challenging for your children—not too hard or too easy.

- Help children meet their lower-level basic needs whenever possible.

- Help children not to fear failure—to accept that it is a necessary path to learning.

- Make use of learning or mastery goals whenever possible.

- Focus on developing the whole child through the cognitive, affective, and psychomotor domains.

- Make use of higher-order objectives.

- Encourage higher-order thinking.

- Ask open-ended, divergent questions.

- Make effective use of group dynamics.

- Make use of all five senses in learning, not simply seeing and hearing.
- Leave children motivated at the end of a lesson.

SUMMARY

Although a teacher's job is not primarily to motivate students, motivation is a critical issue for educators. Even if a teacher believes that his or her job is strictly to advance children's intellectual achievement and development, theory suggests this may not be possible without the necessary motivation. The subtitle of a popular teacher's book on motivation, *Before You Can Teach Them You Have to Reach Them* (McCarty & Siccone, 2001) puts this into perspective. A student who is not motivated to pay attention cannot focus on the learning at hand. A student who has unmet basic lower-level needs cannot spend time focusing on the higher academic needs. Also, teachers want to ensure that when children leave the classroom, they leave as lifelong learners rather than just children who study something to pass a test. Finally, a child who does not see the value in learning certain material is unwilling to devote time and effort to learn it effectively. It doesn't matter how much talent a child has if he or she is unmotivated to use it. The classroom teacher is the one who can make the difference for students.

GLOSSARY

attribution theory   a description of how beliefs about the causes of people's successes and/or failures influence their motivation.

behavioral approach   an approach to motivation that emphasizes the role of rewards and punishment.

cognitive approach   an approach to motivation that emphasizes the desire to make sense of the world.

deficiency needs   the four lower-level needs of Maslow's hierarchy (survival, safety, belonging, and self-esteem).

disequilibrium   a mental imbalance between one's cognitive schemes and information from the environment.

equilibrium   a mental balance between one's cognitive schemes and information from the environment.

external locus of control   the belief that one's successes and failures are caused by environmental factors that are outside his or her control.

extrinsic motivation   motivation stemming from the introduction of environmental factors (i.e., rewards and punishment).

growth needs   the three higher-level needs of Maslow's hierarchy (intellectual achievement, aesthetic appreciation, and self-actualization).

humanistic approach   an approach to motivation that emphasizes a person's desire to improve him- or herself.

internal locus of control   the belief that one's successes and failures are caused by one's own ability or effort.

intrinsic motivation   motivation stemming from activities that are their own reward.

learned helplessness   the expectation, based on previous experiences, that all efforts to succeed will fail.

learning goals   goals based on improving abilities and learning with the focus on mastery rather than the time it may take—also called *mastery goals*.

Maslow's hierarchy of needs   a model of motivation based on seven levels of human needs, ranging from basic deficiency needs (survival, safety, belonging, and self-esteem) to the growth needs (intellectual achievement, aesthetic appreciation, and self-actualization).

negative reinforcement   removing something that is disliked or distasteful to increase a desired behavior.

performance goals   goals based on doing well at one particular task in a particular time frame.

positive reinforcement   giving something that is valued (such as a reward) to increase a desired behavior.

presentation punishment   introducing something disliked or distasteful to decrease an undesirable behavior.

punishment   the introduction of something that results in a decrease in an undesirable behavior.

reinforcement   a reward that results in an increase in a desired behavior.

removal punishment   taking away something pleasurable or desired to decrease an undesirable behavior.

risk-free environment   a place or situation in which one feels secure enough to take chances.

self-concept   one's perception of himself or herself.

self-efficacy   the belief that one is capable of accomplishing something.

self-esteem   how one feels about his or her perception of self.

stability   the degree to which something is believed to be changeable or not.

SUGGESTED ACTIVITIES

1. Make a list of activities that you normally perform during the day. In what activities do you engage because they are *intrinsically* motivating for you? In what activities do you engage because they are *extrinsically* motivating? For each extrinsically motivated activity listed, name the reinforcer that drives you to do the activity (e.g., money, respect from peers, grades, verbal praise).

2. Write a lesson plan for any of the content areas, and check it for motivation. Will your introduction capture students' attention and interests or peak their curiosity? Do your objectives focus on higher-order thinking skills, not just knowledge and comprehension? Do you ask divergent questions as well as convergent questions? Will students be able to succeed at the task they have been given? Are you taking learners one step higher than they were before? At the conclusion of the lesson, will they be curious and interested in what they will be learning next? Is there any choice given to students for a learning activity or product?

3. Write a paragraph describing the classroom environment of your ideal classroom. What will you do to ensure that all students feel safe and secure? How will you ensure that all students feel successful and free to express their individual ideas? How will you address self-concept and self-esteem issues?

4. Make a list of five learning activities that will help students improve their self-concepts and self-esteem.

5. Make a list of all of your positive characteristics that will help you be a motivating teacher in the classroom (e.g., warm, caring, smiling often). Include only characteristics that you actually have. Then make a list of all of your negative characteristics that might hinder classroom motivation (e.g., dislike for mathematics as a subject, a tendency to lose patience easily, not enough smiling early in the morning). What can you do to help change some of these characteristics while you are teaching?

6. Make a list of the reinforcers that you are likely to use in the classroom to motivate children. Then classify each as a positive or negative reinforcer. Make a list of the punishments that you will likely use in your classroom. Specify which are presentation punishment and which are removal punishment.

7. Make a list of positive and negative events that have occurred to you personally in your life. For each, determine whether you believe you were the cause of the event (internal locus of control) or whether an environmental factor was the cause (external locus of control).

8. Observe a teacher in a classroom for 30 minutes. Keep track of the verbal praise that he or she gives to the students. Identify each example of praise as either motivating or nonmotivating. What are the teacher's strengths? Discuss ways in which the teacher could improve.

9. Look at Maslow's hierarchy of needs. Which needs do you expect most of your children to have met before they come to your classroom? Make a list of what you can do to help learners who have not had those needs met. How do you plan on helping all of your students reach a level of self-efficacy?

PRACTICE QUESTIONS

1. Mr. Trevor teaches fourth-grade social studies, and he wants to be sure that all of his students learn the content of the day's lesson. However, he notices that Susan is having difficulty paying attention and seems to be nodding off to sleep frequently. Mr. Trevor's best course of action would be to:

A. Punish Susan for sleeping in class.

B. Talk to Susan privately to find out whether she is having a problem getting enough sleep, and if so, how he can help.

C. Ignore Susan's behavior and decide it's not her fault that she can't stay awake.

D. Tell Susan that if she can pay attention for the rest of the class period, he will reward her with extra free time.

2. Ms. Mendez is a first-grade teacher and is teaching a unit on insects. After the first three days of the unit, she realizes that her students do not seem to be motivated to learn the material. Her best course of action at this point would be to:

A. Tell the students that they can go on a field trip to see insects at a science museum if they all promise to participate enthusiastically for the rest of the unit.

B. Show the students a color video about various types of bugs, where they live, what they eat, and so on.

C. Evaluate the unit as a whole, as well as her teaching strategies, to determine how she can make the unit more interesting and relevant to the students' lives.

D. Have the students look up "bug facts" on the Internet to increase their motivation.

3. Tommy is a student in Ms. Jackson's second-grade class. He continually fails his weekly spelling tests. To motivate Tommy to study harder and improve his performance on future spelling tests, Ms. Jackson should:

A. Hold a spelling bee in which the winner receives a coupon for a free pizza.

B. Grade Tommy initially on the basis of improvement.

C. Tell Tommy she knows that he can do better because he is a smart student.

D. Tell Tommy that if his grades don't improve, she will post them on the board for the rest of the class to see.

4. Mr. Salinas is teaching a unit on zoo animals to his kindergarten class. One of the activities

he has planned is for the children to move to music while imitating the movements of their favorite zoo animals. During the activity, Mr. Salinas notices that Benito is not participating. When asked why, Benito responds, "I like the zebra, but I don't know how to move like a zebra. I just know I'll do it all wrong." In response to Benito's concerns, Mr. Salinas should:

A. Tell Benito that it is all right to sit out the activity if he wants to.

B. Tell Benito that participation in the activity is a requirement for the unit and that all students must participate.

C. Tell Benito that there is no right or wrong way to move like a zebra and that he is already doing an excellent job, because one thing that zebras sometimes do is stand still. Then he should encourage Benito to try other movements, such as walking and running.

D. Suggest to Benito that he ask his parents to take him to the zoo so that he can watch the way a zebra moves. Afterward he can show the class what he has learned from observation.

Answers and Discussion

Answer 1: Punishing Susan may make her try harder to stay awake, but it will not solve her problem of being sleepy and having difficulty paying attention (*A*). Similarly, offering to reward Susan for paying attention may make her "wake up" for that particular lesson, but it may not have any effect on future lessons (*D*). Simply ignoring Susan's behavior is likely to result in her continuing to not pay attention and, therefore, not learning the necessary content of the lesson (*C*). Mr. Trevor's best course of action is to speak to Susan privately to determine the cause of the behavior. When the cause has been identified, they can discuss solutions to the problem. If this issue is solved, Susan's problems with sleeping in class and lack of attention will also be solved. The answer is *B*.

Answer 2: Promising children a field trip to the science museum may make them excited about the trip itself, but it is unlikely to change their motivation toward learning the general subject matter (*A*). Showing the students a video (*B*) and looking up information on the internet (*D*) are both good activities for increasing the students' knowledge and interest in that particular lesson; however, this is not likely to produce long-term effects for the unit as a whole. Ms. Mendez's best course of action is to evaluate not only her instructional techniques, but also how she can make the topic of insects exciting for her students and relevant to their lives. The answer is *C*.

Answer 3: Holding a spelling bee, with the prize of a free pizza to the winner, is not likely to motivate Tommy to study harder, because he "knows" he probably won't win anyway (*A*). Telling Tommy that she knows he is smart and can do it is also not likely to motivate him. He needs to believe that he can do it, and that comes from having some successes. When he has achieved a certain level of success, he will know that he can do it (*C*). Threatening to post his grade on the board will only reinforce to Tommy that he is a failure. It is also likely to produce anxiety and other negative feelings in Tommy toward spelling and school in general (*D*). Ms. Jackson's best course of action is to grade Tommy initially on the basis of improvement. If his goal is to improve on the next test (even if just a little), he is much more likely to be successful. As Tommy improves a little more on each test, he will have even more successes. Remember that success breeds success. Eventually Tommy will be able to raise his performance to an acceptable level. The answer is *B*.

Answer 4: Telling Benito that he must participate in the activity does not address the child's concern that he doesn't know how to imitate a zebra's movements. It is also likely to increase his level of anxiety by forcing him to do something he is uncomfortable doing (*B*). Letting Benito sit out from the activity results in his not being included as part of the class. It also doesn't allow him the opportunity to experience an important learning activity (*A*). Suggesting that Benito ask his parents to take him to the zoo and then perform the movements reinforces the idea that there is a "right" way to move like a zebra and that Mr. Salinas expects him to "do it right." Furthermore, this option does not result in Benito's participation in the activity with the rest of the class (*D*). Letting Benito know that, in this particular case, there isn't a right or wrong way to move because it is an imaginary activity is likely to lower his anxiety level. Also, letting him know that he is already successfully imitating a zebra will further decrease his level of anxiety and fear of failure or "doing it all wrong." The answer is *C*.

WEB LINKS

Remember that Web site locations may change. If any of these sites have moved or cannot be located, use terms in the index to search for further information.

www.bfskinner.org

The B. F. Skinner Foundation provides a summary of operant conditioning as well as a searchable index for other publications by Skinner.

www.connect.net/georgen/maslow.htm

This Web site provides a brief summary of Maslow's work, including a discussion concerning his proposed hierarchy of needs. Practical applications for the classroom are also included.

www.hcc.hawaii.edu/intranet/committees/FacDevCom/guidebk/teachtip/teachtip.htm

The Teaching Tips Index provides a summary of general principles for motivating students as well as an extensive list of strategies to help develop and maintain motivation in the classroom. Also included are guidelines for the use of effective questioning techniques along with examples from each level of Bloom's Taxonomy.

www.uga.berkeley.edu/sled/bgd/motivate.html

Tools for Teaching provides tips on how to encourage students to become self-motivated, independent learners. An extensive list of motivational strategies is also included.

www.cyberparent.com/esteem/

This Web site contains useful tips on how to raise self-esteem for children, including the use of effective praise and positive statements.

REFERENCES

Baron, R. (1992). *Psychology.* (2nd ed.). Needham Heights, MA: Allyn & Bacon.

Brophy, J. E. (1981). Teacher praise: A functional analysis. *Review of Educational Research, 51*(1), 5–32.

Carlton, M. P., & Winsler, A. (1998). Fostering intrinsic motivation in early childhood classrooms. *Early Childhood Education Journal, 25,* 159–166.

Freiberg, H. J., & Driscoll, A. (2000). *Universal teaching strategies* (3rd ed.). Needham Heights, MA: Allyn & Bacon.

Hauser-Cram, P. (1998). Research in review. I think I can, I think I can: Understanding and encouraging mastery motivation in young children. *Young Children, 53*(4), 67–71.

McCarty, H., & Siccone, F. (2001). *Motivating your students: Before you can teach them you have to reach them.* Boston: Allyn & Bacon.

Piaget, J. (1952). *The origins of intelligence in children.* New York: International Universities Press.

Pintrich, P., & Schunk, D. (1996). *Motivation in education: Theory, research, and applications.* Upper Saddle River, NJ: Prentice Hall.

Slavin, R. E. (1987). Ability grouping and student achievement in elementary schools: A best-evidence synthesis. *Review of Educational Research, 57,* 293–336.

Stipek, D. (1996). *Motivation to learn.* (3rd ed.). Needham Heights, MA: Allyn & Bacon.

Wang, M., Haertel, G., & Walberg, H. (1993). Toward a knowledge base for school learning. *Review of Educational Research, 63*(3), 249–294.

Weinstein, R. (1998). Promoting positive expectations in schooling. In N. Lambert & B. McCombs, eds. *How students learn: Reforming schools through learner-centered education* (pp. 81–111). Washington, DC: American Psychological Association.

Woolfolk, A. (2001). *Educational psychology* (8th ed.). Needham Heights, MA: Allyn & Bacon.

Competency 9

The teacher incorporates the effective use of technology to plan, organize, deliver, and evaluate instruction for all students.

The beginning teacher:

- Demonstrates knowledge of basic terms and concepts of current technology (e.g., hardware, software applications and functions, input/output devices, networks).

- Understands issues related to the appropriate use of technology in society and follows guidelines for the legal and ethical use of technology and digital information (e.g., privacy guidelines, copyright laws, acceptable use policies).

- Applies procedures for acquiring, analyzing, and evaluating electronic information (e.g., locating information on networks, accessing and manipulating information from secondary storage and remote devices, using online help and other documentation, evaluating electronic information for accuracy and validity).

- Knows how to use task-appropriate tools and procedures to synthesize knowledge, create and modify solutions, and evaluate results to support the work of individuals and groups in problem-solving situations and project-based learning activities (e.g., planning, creating, and editing word processing documents, spreadsheet documents, and

databases; using graphic tools; participating in electronic communities as learner, initiator, and contributor; sharing information through online communication).

- Knows how to use productivity tools to communicate information in various formats (e.g., slide show, multimedia presentation, newsletter) and applies procedures for publishing information in various ways (e.g., printed copy, monitor display, Internet document, video).

- Knows how to incorporate effective use of current technology; use technology applications in problem-solving and decision-making situations; implement activities that emphasize collaboration and teamwork; and use developmentally appropriate instructional practices, activities, and materials to integrate the Technology Application TEKS into the curriculum.

- Knows how to evaluate students' technologically produced products and projects using established criteria related to design, content delivery, audience, and relevance to assignment.

- Identifies and addresses equity issues related to the use of technology.

Chapter 14

Using Technology in the EC–4 Classroom

MARY E. PARKER

West Texas A&M University

JANICE L. NATH

University of Houston—Downtown

TERMS TO KNOW

The following is a partial listing of the terms a teacher must know about technology and early childhood. So many terms are a part of a technologist's vocabulary that not all terms are bolded in the chapter; however, they are defined in the Glossary.

Assistive technology
CD-ROM
Computer Assisted Instruction (CAI)
Database
Desktop publishing
Digital camera
Digital Versatile Disc (DVD)
Distance education
Distributed course delivery
Dragon Dictate
Drill and practice
Fair use
FAQ (frequently asked questions)
Filtering software
Firewall
Font attributes
Graphics
Hardware
Home page
HTTP

Hyperlink
Input devices
Intellectual property
Intellitalk
Interactive multimedia
Internet
Intranet
Keyboarding
Keypal
Language skill
Laser pointer
Liquid crystal display (LCD)
Monitor
Network
Online
Online help
Output device
Password
Personal digital assistant
PowerPoint
Presentation tool
Real time

Remote equipment/device
Risso machine
Search engine
Secondary storage device
Simulation
Slide show
Software
Spreadsheet
Talk Back
Teach timers
Telecommunication tool
Touch screen
Tutorial
Uniform Resource Locator (URL)
Virtual reality
Voice mail
Wireless laptop
Word processor
Zip drive

This competency involves the greatest changes within the professional development knowledge base that an aspiring teacher is required to know. Further, technology continues to change rapidly, requiring that teachers keep up or be left behind (in some cases by their children, who can be very technology savvy). It is interesting to note that this competency refers to "technology" in a fairly narrow way: computers. Throughout the competencies for EC–4 teachers and the TEKS (Texas Essential Knowledge and Skills) for children, we find technology infused everywhere. Texas obviously wants its teachers and children to advance through all stages of technological maturity, as seen below (Ryan & Cooper, 1998):

Stage 1: Technology is applied to things teachers already do (skill-and-drill, for example).

Stage 2: Technology is used to improve upon teachers' and students' tasks (diagnostic programs, increased motivation in games, and so forth).

Stage 3: Technology is used to do things that were not possible before (teachers and children design their own games and presentations, investigate and synthesize information, and so forth).

The challenges of technology for early childhood teachers are great. The first challenge is to obtain the basic equipment needed to meet the demands of objectives inherent in the state standards so that their children are able to demonstrate:

- knowledge of technology foundations
- acquisition of information
- problem-solving abilities
- appropriate communications through technology

The second challenge for teachers is to gain hands-on experience with technological equipment and knowledge of the legal aspects of technology use. Finally, they must be knowledgeable about readiness and grade-appropriate computer use for early childhood.

Two challenges, basic equipment and a teacher's hands-on experience with technological equipment, are relative to (1) the school district with which a teacher negotiates a contract and (2) the depth and focus of technology in one's pre-service education program. The third challenge, that of *application* to instruction of young children, is connected to the quality and scope of technology in a preservice teacher education program. Even without a strong technology focus in an early childhood program, many resources exist that will help in gaining knowledge about developmental readiness and grade appropriateness for early childhood. This chapter will assist teachers in finding those resources.

The following information may be helpful to new teachers attempting to create a technologically savvy classroom. The first concern is establishing the classroom with the needed equipment. If a new teacher "inherits" a room, there may be technology already available. A scan of the physical environment will reveal possible computer access as well as the age and condition of computers, if they are available. The presence of a computer(s) might be part of a standard room at a school, or computers might be found in a computer lab with designated access for teachers. If computers are in the classroom, computer station(s) become an important consideration when designing the physical aspects of the room. Checking for the availability of classroom technology is a good interview question for a new teacher because it shows that he or she is aware of the necessity for children and teachers to be involved with technology.

OBTAINING EQUIPMENT

Every new teacher soon discovers that materials and resources neither miraculously appear nor do they pay for themselves! By the year 2002, most school districts should have a district technology plan. New teachers should ask about the stage of development of such a plan, focusing on the expectations for early childhood. They should then be prepared to take their places as leaders in the technology movement of their schools.

Sometimes grant funds for equipment are available, but these resources are seldom available immediately (i.e., they often must be applied for a year in advance). It is unadvisable for a teacher to "go to the community" to secure funding for projects without prior approval by the school principal. Asking first ensures that all school and district policies are followed. If there is a program in which teachers and classes would like to participate (for example, "Apples for Students," sponsored by a food chain), approval must be secured from a principal before proceeding. This is especially true if teachers intend to use children's help in this time-consuming, lengthy project. There are other ways to obtain **hardware,** including some programs that transfer used government equipment to schools. New schools ordinarily have money set aside for teachers to use when they order equipment, so again, relevant questions should be asked during the interview process. Whatever approach to equipping a classroom is taken, the teacher of the twenty-first century has to become a knowledgeable and competent technologist.

THE PHYSICAL ENVIRONMENT

Teachers of young children know that they must plan carefully for a good technological environment. To provide a good learning environment where children can learn easily with technology and to ensure that expensive equipment is used properly, teachers must structure the classroom (physical environment) in such a way that it is both safe and organized. Teachers who are using

computer centers or other classroom placements should be mindful of:

- Placing computers strategically so that the **monitors** are facing the teacher at all times to ensure that children stay on task, and to be sure that they are not visiting inappropriate Web sites

- Checking glare on screens at different times of the day

- Not allowing or requiring young children to be at the computer too long each day without physical exercise

- Making sure that wires are secured for safety

- Working toward a computer ratio of one computer for no more than five children

- Making sure that children are sitting at least 2 feet from the monitor

- Establishing technology rules that are consistently enforced

- Teaching young children the value of computers so that they work carefully with and around them to avoid damage

Teachers should also arrange for young children to work with computers in a social situation (partners or small groups) as much as possible. This increases language development and social skills. Of course, the instruction must be carefully structured to allow for this setting as well.

When using technology for a teacher's whole class presentation or students' presentations, the following suggestions should be followed:

- Check to see whether the lighting allows projection to be seen (or whether the room needs to be darkened ahead of time).

- Turn on and cue up all files, slide shows, and so on, that are needed, and have each ready so that the only thing needed for a presentation to begin is for the teacher to push one button.

- Check other multimedia (sound, if applicable, for the correct level, and so forth).

- If no projection system exists for whole-class viewing, redesign the lesson so that children come to the computer in small groups. (Trying to show information to the whole class on one screen can create many management concerns.)

Young learners are unlikely to wait for long periods of time while the teacher is "fooling around" with a presentation. As noted in Competency 6, Part 1, Chapter 9, one can prevent discipline problems by having teaching materials ready. This is especially true with technology, for if presentations are not ready, pacing may be completely lost. Young children are particularly vulnerable to off-task behavior during teacher distractions of this nature.

THE TEACHER TECHNOLOGIST

If this is indeed the age of technology and teachers are part of it, they must be a competent part. Competency 9 states that "The teacher incorporates the effective use of technology to plan, organize, deliver, and evaluate instruction for all students." This statement summarily commands that today's teachers be knowledgeable and competent technologists. However, being a knowledgeable and competent technologist means much more than knowing how to use a word processor. Teachers who master Competency 9 will know the differences between the "science of teaching" and the "art of teaching" and will understand that quality technology can be used to integrate the two. A teacher's competence with technological resources will have much to do with how much children learn in the classroom of the future.

Epstein (1993) has identified four essential knowledge and skill components that a classroom teacher should possess (the subtopics are Parker's suggestions rather than Epstein's):

1. Knowledge of developmentally appropriate software

   • Ask for demonstrations by salesmen.

   • Ask the principal to make copies of articles and distribute them to faculty.

2. Knowledge of learning objectives

   • Know what is in a district's curriculum guides.

   • Ask colleagues how they integrate learning objectives.

3. Participation in workshops that combine learning theory and technology

   • Ask the principal to set up campus workshops.

   • Ask the district technology representative to set up workshops.

   • Ask for money to attend a technology conference.

   • Scan a service center's catalog for workshops.

4. Acquisition of a mentor (who is a good teacher technologist)

SHARING INFORMATION

One use of technology that a teacher must know, according to this competency, is how to disseminate information, particularly publishing information, in various ways. A traditional way to provide information to children in the classroom and to other educators and parents is printed copies (newsletters, notes, behavior contracts, weekly folder information, worksheets, etc.). Word processors can help teachers immensely with this task because they provide spelling and grammar checks as well as quick editing. In addition, a copy is easily "saved" for future use. Monitor displays also help teachers provide information to others. Teachers may want to use monitors for video (live television, VCR or **DVD** programs, or teacher-made videos). They may also use the computer monitors to show teacher-made or packaged slide shows (such as PowerPoint), show information from the Internet, or run a CD-ROM program. **CD-ROMs** have become one of the most popular types of programs. CD-ROMs are storage discs that contain a wealth of digital information (print, pictures, sound, and so forth). Many of the newest computers have the capacity to store or "burn" information onto CD-ROMs as they do with floppy disks. Technology programs are used mainly to present information in a classroom setting, but programs can be very useful for open houses and teacher meetings. Other information can be provided by teachers through a class Web page that can be accessed by others on the Internet. What kinds of information can be conveyed? The list includes homework assignments, background information about the class or school, lunch menus, calls for volunteers, ideas for caretakers to use in helping their children at home, calls for help with materials, times for conferences, posted student work (making sure that permission is obtained first), and so forth. As an equity issue, teachers must remember that all caregivers may not have access to electronic information, so teachers should provide other means of communication for those without computers at home or work.

ACQUIRING INFORMATION

Another requirement of this competency is that teachers understand procedures for acquiring information—not only from the Internet but also from remote devices in activities such as distance learning and teleconferencing. *File Transfer Protocol (FTP)* allows teachers to download or transfer files from a remote computer to one's own computer. The possibilities are endless from museums, special interest groups, and many other resources that allow children to see pictures, visit a virtual exhibit, gain text, and so forth. Streaming audio and/or video, allows children to "be there" in **real time** (or talking, listening, and/or watching as an event or conversation is actually happening).

Distance learning can be of use to teachers in instruction but may mainly become a source of professional development. For example, many colleges of education currently offer college credit online. These courses may involve coursework through the Internet, email, and/or situations in which an instructor may be at one location on a television monitor while students are at a different location in real time or taped situations. Broadcasts can be either one-way or two-way situations. In the many Texas locations that are far from universities, the opportunity to continue to grow professionally has increased greatly because of technology.

Never before have teachers and schools had the means to communicate so well. Email functions as a communication system between teachers and the office for sharing ideas, information, documents, and so forth, with the goal of reducing paperwork and the need for time-consuming meetings. Information through districts is also important, because teachers can be given instantaneous announcements. As noted, it can also link parents and teachers for gaining information. Electronic discussion groups can work to enhance professional development. Databases provide instant information on resources for teachers, and the World Wide Web gives teachers in any setting (rural or urban) connections to professional information and organizations.

Legal and Ethical Issues

Every classroom teacher should be concerned about the legal issues surrounding computers. Traditionally, teachers have taken great liberty with duplicating copyrighted materials—so long as it has been for classroom use. The rules of **fair use** with computers, however, will change those old notions! For early childhood, the most pressing of issues probably include what constitutes public domain (there for the use of the public) and what does not. When children do desktop publishing, they may want to use easily recognized logos such as Disney characters or Coca Cola logos. Can they do that? The answer to this question is, unfortunately, "No." Many may think that if no money is involved in copying, no harm is done, but from the creator's perspective, some commercial value of the property is lost. Also, there exists the possibility that others might see a logo and popular company name or slogan and assume that it was "the real thing." If something was created after April 1989, even if no copyright is listed, it is most likely protected. If created prior to that, it is still best to check. Combining music with some multimedia presentations (for older elementary students) is subject to all fair use laws as well. If the music is in the public domain, for example, "Twinkle, Twinkle, Little Star," the child may use it. If the music is newer than 50 years old, it is probably not in the public domain. The best rule regarding the integration of music is to check the copyright on the recording itself. Pictures in magazines are also protected—scanning in pictures from magazines for Internet posting is not allowed. Just because it is posted on the Internet does not mean that it is public domain, or there for the use of anyone who wants it. Also, copying others' work in its entirety is almost never considered fair use. Normally, fair use gives a person the right to copy just enough to make a point, such as in a parody, critique, research, proving a point, and reporting news. Derivative stories or other works, except with parody, are also not allowed. An example might be the creation of Harry Potter stories or stories using computer game characters.

Teachers should teach ethics about sharing software as well. Authors and companies make their livings by selling software. Whenever software is shared without paying for it, it "steals" money out of the pockets of people who spent effort creating a product. Paying the price of software keeps authors working and companies in business publishing new games, new packages, and so forth. The Web site www.templetons.com/brad/copymyths.html provides information in layman's terms about the rules teachers need to know. By doing a Web search of Internet+legal issues+early childhood, you will find thousands of references—but most of them are written by lawyers in highly legalistic terms. Templeton's Web site provides links to other sites that educate you about fair use.

Although the Internet is a vast source of information, there are related ethical concerns. There is no control on what people can put on the Web, so children may have access to incorrect or inappropriate materials of a sexual or violent nature.

Filtering software may prevent some types of information from being received, but First Amendment rights have been a concern. Teachers should always be vigilant with information which children access.

Another ethical concern involves sources. Even in elementary school, teachers should teach children to check sources. In addition, young children should be taught about plagiarism. Because the Internet offers so much material for research ideas, it is becoming a practice for older students to download whole term papers for high school and college classes. Children should learn early the difference between *referencing* information and *creating* information.

For teachers of young children, modeling ethical standards should be a concern. FBI teams would not raid a teacher's room to arrest children working on Harry Potter adventures on a word processor. However, if that story should go outside the classroom as representing these copyrighted ideas, that is problematic for the creator and publisher. Copyrighting and fair use deal with civil damage lawsuits and monetary damages. Children who grow up learning about copyrighting and plagiarism issues will be more likely to be careful to attend to this important topic. Teaching children to cite others' work and not allowing them to copy certain works can reinforce ethical standards.

Computers are communication devices, and children should have the opportunity to learn the skills that society expects in electronic communication. When people are not face-to-face or are anonymous, communication difficulties can occur. The Netiquette Web site (http://www.albion.com/netiquette/) advises users to remember that there are "real people out there." Children should learn early to, as Netiquette advises, "Ask yourself, 'Would I say this to the person's face?'" If the answer is, "No," rewrite and reread. Repeat the process until you feel sure that you would feel as comfortable saying these words to the live person, or about people, as you do sending them through cyberspace. Because receivers cannot know meaning through one's voice or facial features, expression should be used when appropriate (<sneer>, <ha, ha>, or through use of punctuation symbols— ☺). Other expectations for older children include **flaming** (expressing strong feelings), along with copying information to everyone in their address book and excluding adult language use (which should be done only when there is a need). Email communications by children normally are backed up and are deleted from the computer only after several functions are performed. If a teacher suspects predators or unethical use, it is normally easy to locate those communications to see what has occurred.

One reason to use the computer as a communicator is to ensure quick communication in order to save everyone's time. However, certain types of communication take up time. *Spam,* the term for email junk mail, should not be forwarded, and chain letters should never be continued. One excellent concept that can be integrated with technology is summarization skills for quick communication. Also, correct mail addressing should be taught as a time and politeness issue (using a salutation and a closing signature identifying oneself). Forwarding others' emails without permission can be considered a breech of privacy. Emails are seen by many as copyrighted, so permission to forward should be sought. Passing viruses and predators should also be discussed, and children should be taught never to give their full names, phone numbers, or addresses, and to report "strangers" to adults if anyone asks for that kind of information. Teachers who put children's work on a Web site must obtain students' and their parents' permission. For safety, their names should still not be given. Because electronic communication is relatively new, these expectations and others have developed in the past few years. In the past, teachers taught children how to have a good telephone conversation. The computer as a communication and information-gathering device has opened up a whole new realm of expectations that must find a similar place in the curriculum.

Readiness and Grade Appropriateness

During the planning phase of every lesson, teachers should consider whether any technology or technological materials would be useful and appropriate for the lesson and for the age and, if so, which materials would be best. This consideration leads us to consider what knowledge is necessary for grade and age appropriateness.

Teachers must understand the developmental stages of their early childhood students and know that children need structured and unstructured time allotments. Teachers of young children model positive behavior for children while helping them to have positive experiences. How does a young childhood teacher blend readiness and the modeling of positive behavior through technology? The teacher must remember that in early childhood, children seem to learn more when they initiate activity. That fact should be kept in mind when planning direct instruction with the computer. Research shows that teachers who use technology in traditional ways (direct instruction, drill-and-practice) are, unfortunately, in the majority, and that knowledge flies in the face of what we know about early childhood learning (Clements, 1994). A worksheet is a worksheet, be it on paper or the computer. Repetition is needed for remembering skills and knowledge, but too much of this method can lead to emotional stress and subsequent negative effects on young children. Creative writing and pictures for this age seem to be a much better use. Technology seems to increase children's confidence in writing and creative initiative in art and music, if software is available.

It is generally believed that by the age of 3 or 4, children are ready to begin exploring computers. Children this young are amazed by the timing of pushing a button and seeing a response upon the screen and discovering other capabilities offered by the computer. By the time these children reach kindergarten or first grade (and when they have had adequate access earlier), they are ready to begin matching learning objectives with the computer. At this time, and supported by a teacher, they are ready to begin searching for information, writing a letter to a friend, or using a template for **desktop publishing** (creating documents).

Teachers may want to maintain a checklist of the activities and features that they are most likely to use: email, electronic discussion groups, **databases** including library access, World Wide Web, file transfers, and district networks. When teachers categorize these functions of the computer, they can easily decide which learning objectives can best be met through technology. Constructivist teachers will come to see technology and its applications as facilitative tools that are actively manipulated. The applications listed above can, of course, be used as tools that let children use the computer as "an alternative pencil and paper" or as a true "cognitive tool" to engage and enhance thinking. These applications "manage information in ways that allow users to think more clearly, creatively, and critically [allowing] users to organize information in new ways, evaluate it, and construct personally meaningful representations of it" (Ryan & Cooper, 1998, p. 202). Some examples given by Ryan and Cooper include teaching children (with age-appropriate information) to use spreadsheets as a tool for forecasting and predicting trends; using databases to create more personal categories for class, school, or home collections; and using a word processor to revise personal work. One online resource that helps teach about the Internet is an index of sites listed under the following address: http://www.rnc.ro/teaching/mainteach.html

Equal Opportunity and Computers

The "digital divide" refers to a gap between those who have access to technology tools and those who do not. Research has shown that four groups do not enjoy equity regarding computer and technology use and, thus, in time may not reap the benefits of a technology-based economy: children from low-income homes and schools, minority children, children with special needs, and girls (Roblyer & Edwards, 2000). The result of not having equal access can be far-reaching for all of these groups. For instance, those who are not able to grow up playing and learning with computers can be less comfortable using them and may develop feelings of helplessness or negative beliefs about technology. Many fields in the sciences and mathematics rely on computers or other technology, so when children reach upper levels in high school, they may not be comfortable enough to take courses that employ abundant technology. This early reluctance, in turn, blocks access to similar classes in college and in the job market later. Cost may be one issue for some groups, including smaller school districts that cannot afford adaptive or **assistive technology** for special-needs children. Gender bias, however, like the literature of the past, may be evident when motivating software excludes girls in its programs. Stereotyping may send a message that women use computers for clerical jobs. A fifth group, lower achievers, *may* have allocated computer time—but mainly of the skill-and-drill type. The main focus at this age and stage of development is on equal treatment by the teacher, whether from a multicultural perspective, a special needs perspective, or tolerance and bias. Vigilant teachers ensure that traditional biases and inequities that have been evident in our education system do not infiltrate their classrooms nor the realm of educational technology. Teachers should not create unequal situations in their classroom by, for example, assigning homework related to computer work that would create unequal grading situations for students who do not have access. The most important thing is to ensure that all children have equal work time, higher-level activities, and "play time" on the computers.

Teacher Checklist for Readiness

Teachers might use a checklist such as the one below to determine a child's readiness for certain activities. The use of an informal checklist such as the one on page 288 will indicate to teachers where they should begin with their students and technology.

READINESS CHECKLIST

Characteristic	Yes	No
Is the student already reading? (If so, at what level?)		
Is the student already using computer terminology?		
Has the student already used the computer for email or file transfer?		
Has the student used a database to carry out a topical search?		
Is the student motivated to learn about computers?		
Has the student used the computer to produce graphics? PowerPoint?		
Has the student demonstrated an ability to solve technical problems? (spelling checks, grammar checks)		
Is the student easily frustrated?		
Does the student demonstrate an ability to evaluate information found on the Internet?		

Figure 14-1   A checklist for technology readiness.

EVALUATION

Instructional Software Evaluation

Part of teaching with technology involves providing appropriate technology for children. What are some considerations? Roblyer and Edwards (2000) have contributed some ideas for a teacher preview evaluation of software (starred statements also indicate evaluation use for Web sites):

- The teaching strategy to be used is one that is based on sound teaching theory (for example, does it use concrete ideas for young children?).

- The program moves along in a logical fashion (from simple to more difficult, etc.).

- The presentation on screen contains nothing that is confusing or has misleading (or even wrong) information.★

- There is no sarcasm or there are no remarks that could be insulting.★

- The level of reading is correct for the age group.★

- If sound is included, it is not distracting and voices are clear and understandable.

- Graphics and screen layout pull interest in rather than become distracting for children.★

- Grammar and spelling are correct within programs.★

- The content is up-to-date.★

- There is no ethnic, racial, or gender bias.★

- Programs do not contain unnecessary violence or other ethical social concerns.★

- Programs load without problems and do not freeze up when children enter anything.

- Programs provide navigation as stated and have ease of movement within the program.

- Programs are easy for children to use and directions are clear for children.

- There is some degree of control over presentation speed, and displays provide quick responses without noticeable delays.

- Programs foster the intent for which they were designed (remediation, creativity, etc.).

- Testing (at the end of skills practice) matches the stated skills of the program and provides good measure of the skills stated to be taught.

- Programs provide feedback for student performance (and record keeping, if important to the teacher).

- The material integrates well with material covered in class.★

There are also criteria that help to evaluate a Web site for use with children (Roblyer & Edwards, 2000). Teaching children how to evaluate technology such as CD-ROM programs and Web sites is of utmost concern, particularly in establishing accuracy of information. In addition to the criteria starred (★) above, one should add the following to the list for evaluating Web sites:

- Information is accurate and authentic, and the latest update is posted.

- The author(s) can be found easily and has "credentials." The site includes a way to contact an author(s) through email.

- Information is complete but not redundant, and references are provided when necessary.

- The design is consistent, with easily read print and an attractive (not busy) layout.

- Navigation is easy, and pages load quickly; the beginning page provides organization and links; and the links are easy to identify and go to the correct site. Each page provides a way to go forward, backward, or home, and icons clearly represent the link.

- Branching into the site should not be more than three clicks away from home.

- Requests for private information are secure.

- Pages that are probably going to be printed are short and contain few graphics so as to allow quick printing.

- The domain is a reliable one (government, educational, nonprofit) rather than a more personal or commercial site, and there is no discernible bias.

These are several of the suggestions that can help teachers decide whether a site is a good one to use in presentation or instruction with children. Teachers should always bookmark interesting sites on classroom computers so that they and the children can easily access them.

In addition to previewing technology, a teacher can assess the value of a software program or Web site by feedback through (a) pre- and posttesting children on a program, (b) small group try-out, (c) direct observation while children are working through a program, (d) talking with children directly about the program, (e) peer review or peer observation, and (f) reflection or thinking back over a lesson or situation in which the program was used (Newby et al., 2000).

Not only must teachers evaluate the technology that they wish to use with children, but Texas teachers should be planning for children to produce their own products, which will also need evaluation. In addition, the TEKS prescribe skills and technology knowledge that must be assessed by teachers. For the latter, teachers of young children will use mainly observation, but they may also employ interviews, computer tests, projects, and so forth. Other checklists or rubrics can be formulated to help teachers evaluate technology products. For example, the areas shown in Figure 14-2 might be considered with a fourth-grade team project to create a simple slide show on plants.

Of course, when creating a rubric for technology, teachers must consider many factors. Among those factors should be children's ages and experience with technology and the type of technology use demanded. If a teacher is working with word processing only, an assessment instrument or rubric would look very different indeed. Competency 9 stresses four areas that teachers should note in technology evaluation of student products: criteria related to design, content delivery, audience, and relevance to assignment. Note those areas in Figure 14.2.

	3	2	1
Content delivery	All information is correct	Some information is incorrect	Much information is incorrect
Organization of content	Logical and clear	Some information is out of order or unclear	Much information is out of order and unclear
Alignment with curriculum (relevance to assignment)	Solid connection to project title	Some information is connected to project title	Much information is unconnected to project title
Originality	Copied little	Some information is copied directly	Much information is copied directly
Grammar and spelling	Correct	Four mistakes	More than four mistakes
Screen design	Navigation is easy for viewer and screen is uncluttered	Navigation can be done through some screens and screen is fairly uncluttered	Navigation is difficult and/or screen is cluttered
Graphics	Are included and appropriate	Some are included and/or are appropriate	Too many or few are included and/or are inappropriate
Teamwork	All members contributed	Half the members contributed	One person did the majority of the work
Enhancements	Extra points for use		
Audience	Presentation addresses audience at correct level and interest	Presentation and interest are somewhat difficult or somewhat easy for audience	Presentation and interest are extremely difficult or too easy for audience

Figure 14-2   Rubric for Slide Show on Plants Project

LEARNING CENTERS

Learning centers (LCs), like library carrels and resource rooms, are small spaces the teacher creates within the classroom. These small spaces contain specific materials and/or resources that may be designated as basic skills, units of study, and thematic lessons. Learning centers are designed to accommodate a variety of learning styles. Often teachers set up permanent learning centers around the walls of the classroom and designate the centers to meet the learning needs of the class. Centers might be named "library or reading centers," "writing/journal centers," "science centers,"

"social studies centers," "computer centers," "creative thinking centers," "puzzle centers," or "home centers." Each center contains activities that require a review of skills or enrichment activities that nurture a child's creativity, and each may contain a computer for technology activities, if available. Centers can be set up to teach an entire lesson cycle with students working in groups, as each group starts at a different center and rotates through all centers during the lesson. The computer can play a vital role in all of these types of centers, particularly when paired with the opportunity for inquiry-based learning. Computers can also be considered as part of play, depending upon the software or the use of the computer in a pretend situation or game. The value of play was discussed in Competency 3, Part 2, Chapter 4.

ELECTRONIC COMMUNITIES

Clearly, Texas expects a teacher to be both a learner and a contributor to education and an encourager for children to do so, too. No area helps so much as technology in this endeavor. *Virtual learning communities* span distances to create groups joined by interest and expertise. What tools do teachers use for their own learning and to help create virtual communities for children? Mailing lists, or *listservers,* provide a way to send a particular group the same information or the same email message at the same time. Teachers and children can ask to be put on mailing lists for information for special topics and/or can create their own. For example, if a class is involved in a special project of interest to the entire school, a mailing list could communicate progress to all classrooms in the school. *Newsgroups* are another way to become involved in special interests. Rather than being sent information, a reader enters the site whenever he or she wishes to read messages or information that has been posted. Members are often allowed to post messages or articles as well. *Chat rooms* also provide a format for an electronic community. In a chat room, members communicate in real time, so they are typing and reading conversations simultaneously. These can be very exciting for children in remote locations or for younger children paired with older children or adults (high school or grandparent partners, for example), but teachers should always remember to monitor conversations. The use of these communication tools encourages teachers and children to see technology as a meaningful resource.

PROBLEM SOLVING

Competency 9 recognizes that technology should be a facilitating tool. Computer skills that are taught in context of what children are learning are always more meaningful to the learning process. Therefore this competency asks teachers to incorporate technology in problem-solving and decision-making situations. Two views exist on problem solving with technology (Roblyer & Edwards, 2000): (1) teaching of problem solving as a higher-level skill, through which children learn through direct teaching of strategies and practice, and (2) placing children in highly motivating situations where, with some guidance and help, children can develop their own strategies. Teachers can locate software packages that address both of these views through games, simulations, puzzles, and so forth, or by descriptors such as critical thinking, higher-order outcomes, decision making, problem solving, and thinking skills. Of course, they must review software to ensure that the key words listed on a package really match the skill(s) in which they are interested, that it is a match with the curriculum, that is it age-appropriate, and the like. Roblyer and Edwards 2000 provide several steps for helping to integrate problem-solving courseware:

1. Allow students sufficient time to explore and interact with the software, but provide some structure in the form of directions, goals, a work schedule, and organized times for sharing and discussing results.

2. Vary the amount of direction and assistance, depending on each student's needs.

3. Promote a reflective learning environment; let students talk about their work and the methods they use.

4. Stress thinking processes rather than correct answers.

5. Point out the relationship of courseware skills and activities to other kinds of problem solving.

6. Let students work together in pairs or small groups.

7. For assessments, use alternatives to traditional paper-and-pencil tests. (pp. 98–99)

Teachers can also encourage problem solving and exploration when children have computer dilemmas. For example, they can "come to the rescue" whenever a child asks for help in finding tools or manipulating the computer in some way, *or* they can encourage children to search for themselves, experiment a bit, and/or use the internal computer or online help. However, teachers should remember that young children can become frustrated more easily than adults and should be monitored carefully.

The philosophy of the PPR examination directs teachers to assume a restructured technology setting with problem-solving described by Grabe and Grabe (2000), in which children create personal knowledge by acting on content provided by teachers, media resources, and personal experiences, and where: (a) the teacher functions as a facilitator, guide, and learner, (b) children work cooperatively, (c) assessment of knowledge is through application, and (d) technology is used as a source of information for interpretation and original knowledge creation.

PROJECT LEARNING WITH TECHNOLOGY

In addition to using technology in problem solving, Competency 9 asks teachers to incorporate project learning. In Competency 8, Part 1, Chapter 12, project learning is discussed; the guidelines for general projects also apply to technology projects. What sorts of projects might a teacher employ with technology? Grabe and Grabe (2000) suggest interpersonal exchange projects, such as keypals (unstructured exchanges to "get to know" others in remote locations), global classrooms (classrooms in different locales that work on the same projects and exchange information), electronic appearances (chat sessions or email with a "guest speaker," electronic mentoring, and impersonation [someone responds to email in character]. They also recommend information collections that collaborative groups undertake, such as information exchanges

(database or other accumulation of information), group publishing, tele-field trips (sharing information of observations), and pooled data analysis (collecting information from multiple sites). Finally, they recommend problem-solving projects such as (a) information searches (students collaborate using cues and resources); (b) electronic process writing (written work is posted for help and critique); (c) parallel problem-solving (groups at different sites solve the problem, then exchange methods and conclusions); (d) sequential creations (various groups work, in turn, to add components, such as more verses to a poem); and (e) social action projects (children work on authentic problems and share results). These, of course, must be tailored to the specific age group of the class. It is important for teachers to consider the type of technology needed for each type of project and whether it is available before beginning. Children can learn much about technology as a tool in projects such as researching a class pet. Grabe and Grabe (2000) relate the following project:

> Mrs. Knudson wanted to buy a new pet for the classroom and needed help in selection of the best one. Ahead of time, she bookmarked a choice of several potential pets on Internet sites. Children were to click on and read about each and use guidelines such as: (1) it must not be a mammal because of allergies, (2) there would be a maximum cost of $30, (3) it must be able to live in a small area and have inexpensive food, and so forth. In groups, children investigated various aspects of the problem. For example, one group investigated food while the next took costs and so forth. The information was then combined and analyzed, yielding the following recommendation: "We recommend the Budgie because it costs 10 dollar to 20 dollar. They eat green vegetables. And they eat 2–3 teespons of seeds a day. The budgie is in the bird family. (p. 112)

Programs or activities that allow children to investigate, explore, and make decisions create considerable motivation.

THE STATE STANDARDS

The following section highlights and summarizes information directly from the state standards. To ensure a knowledgeable workforce, the State of Texas has devoted Chapter 126 of the TEKS to technology applications. It is appropriate to discuss the TEKS at this point, for they are so specific that teachers will have little difficulty matching them to the standards listed below. The "Introduction" to Chapter 126: Texas Essential Knowledge and Skills for Technology Applications outlines the organization of the TEKS to follow:

TECHNOLOGY APPLICATIONS STANDARDS FOR ALL BEGINNING TEACHERS (EC–12)

Standard I. All teachers use technology-related terms, concepts, data input strategies, and ethical practices to make informed decisions about current technologies and their applications.

Standard II. All teachers identify task requirements, apply search strategies, and use current technology to efficiently acquire, analyze, and evaluate a variety of electronic information.

Standard III. All teachers use task-appropriate tools to synthesize knowledge, create and modify solutions, and evaluate results in a way that supports the work of individuals and groups in problem-solving situations.

Standard IV. All teachers communicate information in different formats and for diverse audiences.

Standard V. All teachers know how to plan, organize, deliver, and evaluate instruction for all students that incorporates the effective use of current technology for teaching and integrating the Technology Applications Texas Essential Knowledge and Skills (TEKS) into the curriculum

Chapter 126. Texas Essential Knowledge and Skills for Technology Applications.

At this time, the technology applications curriculum has four strands: foundations, information acquisition, solving problems, and communication.

As the name implies, "foundations" for early childhood outlines basic computer skills that K–4 students should be able to begin and accomplish with some success. The following summarized listing suggests the nature of the foundational information desired.

(1) Foundations. Appropriate instruction in the foundations of technology will allow students to apply critical thinking skills in the following ways:

- Students learn to make informed technology decisions through the study of technology-related terms, concepts, and data input strategies.
- By quickly and efficiently locating appropriate information, students can move on to analyze and evaluate the acquired information.
- Furthermore, technology is a tool that supports the work of individuals and groups in solving problems.
- Students communicate information in different formats and to diverse audiences.

K–2nd grade children should be able to:
- utilize technology vocabulary listed at the beginning of this chapter and those additions in the glossary. Applications will have to be demonstrated to children along with the appropriate terminology;
- start and exit programs as well as create, name, and save files; use networking terminology such as **online, network,** or **password** and access; and
- use **remote equipment** on a network such as a printer.

3rd–4th grade children should be able to:
- utilize technology vocabulary at a higher level/standard;

- increase efficiency of usage;
- save and delete files, use menu options and commands, and work with multiple software applications;
- identify and describe the characteristics of digital input, processing, and output;
- use proper **keyboarding** techniques such as correct hand and body positions and smooth, rhythmic keystroke patterns;
- utilize correct keyboarding techniques;
- produce and edit documents;
- follow acceptable use practices.

Accomplishing the foundations requirements depends upon the use of computers as well as a basic word-processing program. Teachers should become familiar with correct keyboarding techniques and utilize appropriate software programs. One enhancement to regular classroom teaching occurred as the result of a districtwide project to teach desktop publishing to third through fifth graders. As a result of this program, students produced newsletters for their schools.

Development of one's own technology skills also enables teachers to find resources. Thousands of Web sites exist that tell teachers how to teach every subject and provide detailed lesson plans.

(2) Information Acquisition. Basic computer literacy involving operations and vocabulary set the stage for more advanced literacy in later grades. Under the strand "information acquisition" the teacher sees that K–4 children should understand that the use of technology resources provide a great deal of information—some good, some bad; therefore, students should—with appropriate instruction—learn how to acquire that information and how to evaluate it once acquired. By this age, children are beginning to communicate well and want to acquire information. They also begin to compare. Teachers teach to this readiness by asking lots of open-ended questions. One resource that can help young children learn about the computer is Logo programming.

Information acquisition will require directed supervision to be sure that students access appropriate Web sites. A school may have a filtering device such as Network Nanny in place. If not, teachers should research possible filters. One resource prepared for parents is http://www.ed.gov/pubs/parents/Internet/index.html. Once there, click on "Tips for Safe Traveling" to access beneficial information.

K–2nd grade children should learn:
how to access and evaluate information discovered online.

3rd–4th grade students should:
employ appropriate electronic search strategies to acquire information including keywords and Boolean search strategies;

navigate local area networks (LANs) and wide area networks (WANs), including the Internet and intranet, for research and resource sharing;

apply critical analysis in cases of information conflicts;

determine usefulness of information.

Evaluating Web Sites

Children should learn to evaluate technology too. Smaller children will be able to evaluate Web sites according to:
(1) reading level, or more likely,
(2) graphics appeal.
Teachers may provide children with a basic set of statements of indicators like this (wording will change appropriately with age).

1. I think this Web site is:
   a. easy to access/leave
   b. hard to access/leave
2. I think this Web site is:
   a. easy to navigate
   b. hard to navigate
3. I think this Web site:
   a. has good color and design
   b. does not have good color and design

4. I think this Web site:

 a. has good information/pictures

 b. does not have good information/pictures

Teachers might also want to include items such as font size style as well or visual appeal in this list. If adding "information gained" was "helpful" or "not so helpful," teachers can add critical thinking to the student's choice by following up with, "Why?" This research skill must be developed gradually with cognitive-level consideration.

(3) Solving Problems. Problem solving has long been a mainstay of standard teaching. However, when the technology element is introduced, the child must apply "what is known" to "what is unknown" within the context of technology. This very sophisticated approach to problem solving requires much planning and practice on the part of the teacher. On the other hand, young children are so busy asking questions and making discoveries that the teacher's role involves "setting up" the environment so that children will be successful in solving all kinds of problems.

K–2nd grade teachers should teach children to use research skills and electronic communication:

 • to increase knowledge of a topic.

3rd–4th grade children should:

 • use **software** programs with audio, video, and **graphics** to enhance learning experiences;

 • use appropriate software to express ideas and solve problems including the use of word processing, graphics, databases, spreadsheets, simulations, and multimedia, and use a variety of data types including text, graphics, digital audio, and video;

 • use communication tools to participate in group projects;

 • use interactive technology environments;

 • participate with electronic communities;

 • utilize online help;

 • use software features, such as slide show previews to evaluate final product.

Fortunately, many Web sites cater to problem solving for young children. Also, many software programs devoted to reading and writing skills focus heavily upon problem-solving strategies. One of the best Web sites for problem solving begins at http://edweb.sdsu.edu/webQuest. This inquiry-based program encourages critical thinking. (they can download the template)

(4) Communication. Within the "communication" strand, students learn multiple ways to communicate through technology. By nature young children are very verbal, and although they are not yet proficient with language rules and skills, they are delightfully ready to share information through email. Too much concentration on correctness of communication can inhibit communication, so teachers should monitor carefully according to age/stage of development.

K–2nd grade children should be able to:

 • format digital information for effective communication including using appropriate fonts, color, white space, and graphics;

 • publish through printed copy or monitor display;

 • publish through stored files or video.

Two of the most utilized desktop publishing programs are Pagemaker and Ventura.

3rd–4th grade children should:

 • publish information in a variety of media including print, monitor display, Internet, and video;

 • use presentation software to communicate;

- select representative products to be collected and stored in an electronic program;
- evaluate the product for relevance to the assignment or task;
- create technology assessment tools to monitor progress of projects such as checklists, timelines, or rubrics.

When children discover e-pals within their own classrooms, schools, or districts, they will be "hooked" into using the computer for communication. Because peer interest is usually so high, children will learn from each other. Teachers might also infuse lessons here to control the environment about "safe" e-pals versus predatory e-pals. Again, a good resource for this information is located at http://www.ed.gov/pubs/parents/internet/index.html.

PowerPoint

Students in early childhood are quite capable of preparing a slide show using PowerPoint. This introduction to communication and presentation is easily learned when the teacher provides a model. The template shown below might be used.

By simplifying this template even further (for example, with pictures or clip art of pets, zoo animals, or other categories) the student will not have to write at all. The teacher can increase the level of expectation by increasing the number of frames and adding a research requirement for other graphics sources. Students should present work in a whole class presentation or through a center.

As you can see from the discussion, the four strands of the technology applications—foundations, information acquisition, solving problems, and communication—are quite content specific. As early childhood teachers move toward competency in the technology area, they will build a repertoire of "what works" and "what does not work."

The following discussion provides some additional listings of technological materials and resources, grouped for easy reference.

Online Print Resources

Print resources provide the bases for most instruction, whether from a book or on a photocopied handout or a computer-generated copy. The following list adds print resources via technology that might be used in a classroom to expand materials and resource ideas. Using a scanner, the teacher and/or children can bring these resources into a technology format. Outside the classroom, print resources are housed in school libraries, city and county libraries, and college or university libraries. Although most of these hard-copy resources are readily available, the research and

My PowerPoint Presentation

Title Page Include your name The Title of Your Presentation	What is the first thing you want to write about? the second? the third? Write those points here: 1. 2. 3.	Point 1 Do you want to include a graphic with your presentation?
Point 2 Do you need another graphic?	Point 3 Do you need another graphic?	Summary Write a short summary of the three points you wanted to make. 1. 2. 3.

Figure 14-3   A Power Point Template.

communication capabilities of the Internet are nothing short of phenomenal.

textbooks
books
e-pals
dictionaries/thesauri
advance organizers
pamphlets
interactive atlases
electronic encyclopedia
restaurant menus
periodicals
organizational newsletters
abstracts
postcards
flyers/informational circulars
student journals
thematic booklets
government reports
advertising
trade bulletins
calendars
*newspapers/youth pages
graphs/charts
educational comic books
online newspapers
timelines
microfiche
telephone books
transparencies
Web sites
children's magazines

*Newspapers in Education (NIE) is an international program that most major newspapers support. This program is directed primarily toward contributing in a tangible way to the literacy of the population. Teachers can find newspapers online from all over the world; many of the international papers are in their own language. Access a favorite newspaper and browse to see whether it supports NIE. Teachers can usually download free lesson plans in almost every subject. Many colleges, universities, and regional service centers also have courses or continuing education in the use of newspapers in the classroom. Syndicated pages such as the Mini Page (or other youth pages) have ready-built activities that teachers might employ on a weekly basis in the classroom or in a learning center.

Online Visual Materials and Resources

Teachers create the classroom environment initially through visual means, and students' first impressions of a teacher come through that environment. Visual and print materials overlap in that most visual materials gain attention through color appeal and secondary messages that may be printed. Teachers and schools recognize that many students are visual learners and respect the need to diversify lessons by adding a strong visual impact to the classroom and to the lessons themselves. The Internet provides the ultimate in visual appeal through these highly visual resources:

art works
virtual museums
collages
clocks
plays
cartoons
paintings
posters
graphic organizers
scrapbooks
cartoons
charts
electronic bulletin boards

Computer Hardware-Dependent Resources

The following list deals with more sophisticated computer systems. If your school district is fortunate enough to have access, you may be required to participate in some capacity. Again, caution must be taken to consider age-appropriate instruction where these resources are concerned.

Internet

satellite classes

virtual museums

email

chat rooms

video conferencing

browsing libraries

take-home laptops

Hyper Studio

digital cameras

CAI★

virtual library

software

TENET (TX ed network)

★Perhaps one of the first terms with which new teachers should become acquainted is **Computer-Assisted Instruction (CAI).** These mastery learning programs are divided into two distinct parts: **drill and practice,** and instruction (tutorials). A good example of CAI is the Accelerated Reader Series. Students are often pretested, diagnosed, and placed within a CAI at their level—all on the computer. Then they complete lesson sets, one at a time, at their own rate. Normally a test must be completed at the end of each lesson, before going on. A third use of the computer for instruction is the rapidly growing online instruction (**distance education**), but it has not yet reached most public schools, particularly at lower grade levels.

Other Technology Resources

When one thinks of school resources today, it is very common to think first of computers. Children and teachers alike may erroneously categorize all of technology as "computer resources," but for clarity it should be noted that computer resources do not include all technology available to teachers.

The next category of technology-related resources is quite large. Some of the items mentioned are very discipline-specific, yet they are noted here to illustrate the enormity of resource possibilities for the teacher.

neon and digital signs

hectograph machines

microscopes and scales

camcorders

overhead projectors

telescopes

laser writers and printers

reaction plates (athletes)

slide shows

student broadcasts

laser pointers

teach timers

on-screen touch devices

automated grade book software

Automated grade book software.★ Teachers should be aware that the traditional gradebook is on its way out. Some school systems have automated everything from electronic absentee submission, to lesson plans file transfers, to grading. New teachers should ask appropriate questions about the district privacy policy (FERPA) and about the specific system of reporting that a particular district is using. Be aware of whether or not your district is using an electronic homework system, whereby students can contact their teachers at home via email. Other electronic teacher productivity tools listed by Ryan and Cooper (1998) include:

test generators

worksheet and puzzle generators

question banks

portfolio assessment management tools

IEP software management

concept-mapping tools

poster and banner utilities

time management tools (calendar software, etc.)

certificate or award software

lesson-planning software

grant-writing software

Media Resources

Both the technology resource and human resource come together in the form of one of the most valuable school resources: the media center director—formerly the librarian. The domain of the *library* is now often the *media center.* This person's title focuses on the importance of technology within the school. Teachers should see the media center director for a prepared list of resources for their particular school and district. They should secure a copy of that information.

The media center director can make available VCRs and televisions in the classroom, assist with graphics and research via the Internet, copy certain broadcasts, and provide CD players, tape players, and assorted filmstrips and recordings.

Very often the media center director will assist children with filmmaking by providing instruction in the use of cameras, editing processes, and copying videos. Perhaps a **digital camera** (a camera that loads its images into the computer) will be available to make "photos" of each student or to integrate photos or movie clips into class work.

Teachers may check out overhead projectors from this center as well as secure materials for making overhead transparencies. They can, if a computer and color printer are available, also make color transparencies.

On the more practical side, media centers also have die cuts (Ellison Cutter) for making letters, symbols, pictures, and borders for bulletin boards; provide lamination for projects the teacher wants to keep; and provide wonderful rolls of wide, colored paper for bulletin boards and projects.

With the appropriate software, computers can also create banners.

Audio-Visual (AV) Equipment

The traditional audio-visual (AV) equipment of yesteryear is still around, but with the proliferation of technology, some specialized kinds of equipment have found their way into the classroom. The following audio equipment is listed apart from the visual equipment because some of these may not be available in the typical school media center.

microphone

books on tape

players and recorders

mixer

interactive music education (computer based)

speakers

amplifier

instruments (rhythm/piano/guitar)

sound systems

books *with* tapes

teacher-made tapes

filmstrips

kits

films

One source for ordering recorded books is at www.recordedbooks.com

Manipulatives

Research clearly shows that many children who are kinesthetic learners prefer hands-on learning. The lists of manipulatives and hands-on materials is quite extensive, but the premier manipulative is the computer itself! The computer can produce game boards, sentence strips, graphics to enhance graphic organizers, and templates. The computer can generate 3-D models as well. Touch screens for young children provide even more of a manipulative situation than does the keyboard.

SUMMARY

Fortunately, the State of Texas has done a thorough job of precisely aligning teachers' responsibilities with student standards and the subsequent discussion of the TEKS. Notice that the standards for this competency are broad and encompassing, but current college students probably comprise part of the first generation of students who have been raised in the computer age (a cartoon depicting the father asking his very young child to "make the blinking go away" on the VCR comes to mind!). Most will not be daunted by the expectations. Those coming to teaching from another career or from raising a family will find that today's computers can make a teacher's life easier and instruction richer—so it is time to learn! Teachers may be a little intimidated by all of the technological advances of the twenty-first century, but intimidated or not, they must participate in this revolution; otherwise entry into the classroom through this exam will be difficult.

GLOSSARY

The following Web site also offers a quick online dictionary of terms: www.matisse.net/files/glossary.html

assistive technology   technology for specially challenged populations that assists in many areas of their daily lives (adaptive keyboard, "bionics," motorized chairs, voice-input devices, etc.). A wide range of innovative technology allows children with learning and physical disabilities to learn and participate. ARD committees must consider assistive technology as part of an IEP (see Competency 13 Chapter 19 for more on laws regulating differently abled children).

CD-ROM (Compact Disc Read Only Memory) technology that allows information to be "burned" or placed on a disc for storage.

Computer Assisted Instruction (CAI)   a self-learning, technique, mastery involving interaction of the student with technological programmed instructional materials.

database   holds records information in a way that allows users to sort easily, based on criteria needed; can

be used to create and maintain student information files, lists of materials, lesson plans, and so forth.

desktop publishing   the design or layout and production of publications or written documents, using personal computers; can include both text and graphics (important for school newsletters).

digital camera   a camera that stores images digitally rather than recording them on film. After a picture has been taken, it can be downloaded to a computer system and then manipulated.

Digital Versatile Disc (DVD), formerly **Digital Video Disc**   an optical storage medium with improved capacity and bandwidth over the compact disc. Initially marketed for entertainment because it can "hold" an entire movie.

distance education   students and instruction in various locations can be linked through various technology (audio, video, etc.).

distributed course delivery   an instructional model that allows the instructor, students, and content to be located in different, noncentralized locations so that instruction and learning occur independent of time and place.

Dragon Dictate   a voice recognition software program that enables people to control their computers by voice. It replaces the mouse and keyboard as tools for accessing information.

drill and practice   a method of teaching that involves low-level recall and repetition of skills or knowledge.

fair use   legal issues regarding what constitutes public domain and what is copyrighted.

FAQ (Frequently Asked Questions)   on a Web site's home page, a list of questions that have been asked many times, often followed by the answers or by links to answers.

filtering software   applications that limit an Internet user from gaining access to certain inappropriate sites.

fire wall   a filtering system that stops navigation on particular Internet locations and can stop spam or other unwanted solicitations from coming through; can also protect district servers from being accessed from outside and/or from being damaged.

font attributes   the size, italics, bolding, underlining, and style for the type used in producing a document. Some fonts are particularly appropriate for children's use.

graphics   pictures, charts, graphs, drawings, signs, photographic representations, clip art, and symbols that can be used to enhance a product.

hardware   the physical, touchable, material parts of a computer or other system. The term is used to distinguish these fixed parts of a system from the more changeable software or data components, which it executes, stores, or carries. Computer hardware typically consists chiefly of electronic devices (CPU, memory, display) with some electromechanical parts (keyboard, printer, disk drives, tape drives, speakers) for input, output, and storage, although completely nonelectronic (mechanical, electromechanical, hydraulic, biological) computers have also been conceived of and built.

Home page   the first page of a Web site.

HTTP (Hypertext Transfer Protocol)   a set of instructions for communicating across the Internet. Requires an HTTP client program on one end and an HTTP server program on the other end.

hyperlink   a connection or link between two Web pages.

input devices   mouse, keyboard, disk drive, modem, voice/sound recorder, scanner, digital video, CD-ROM, and touch screen.

intellectual property   a product of the intellect that has commercial value, including copyrighted property, such as literary or artistic works, and ideational property, such as patents, appellations of origin, business methods, and industrial processes.

Intellitalk   a talking word processor ideal for young children, people with learning or visual disabilities, and those who speak English as a second language.

interactive multimedia   software packages that include a range of information (text, film clips, photos, recordings, 3-D presentations, and so forth) that can be manipulated easily by users.

Internet   a network that allows people to communicate worldwide by sending for and receiving information through smaller networks, all of which have the same protocols or sets of operating processes.

intranet   similar to the Internet, but allows only filtered information to reach students.

keyboarding   using with fluency the alphabetic, numeric, punctuation, and symbol keys.

keypal   the electronic mail equivalent of a pen pal — someone with whom to exchange electronic mail for the simple joy of communicating.

language skills   capitalization, punctuation, spelling, word division, and use of numbers and symbols, all important in teaching keyboard skills.

laser pointer   an ultrabright LED (Light Emitting Device) light pen, especially desirable as a pointing tool for illustration.

liquid crystal display (LCD)   an electro-optical device used to display digits, characters, or images, commonly used in digital watches, calculators, and portable computers.

monitor   a device that accepts video signals from a computer and displays information (i.e., the "TV screen").

network   a system of computers interconnected by telephone wires or other means.

online   under the control of a central computer, as in a manufacturing process or an experiment; accessible via a computer or computer network.

online help   information that can be accessed through the computer to help with functions or finding information. Help balloons pop up when the cursor is placed over an icon or term. One can find information by entering key words.

output devices   electronic or electromechanical equipment connected to a computer and used to transfer data out of the computer in the form of text, images, sounds, or other media to a display screen, printer, speaker, or storage device. Most modern storage devices such as disk drives and magnetic tape drives act as both input and output devices; others such as CD-ROM are input only.

password   the sequence of characters that one must enter to gain access to a computer or a file.

personal digital assistants   small hand-held minicomputers that provide word processors and check email.

PowerPoint (PPT)   the successor of the overhead projector. This software program can produce text, artwork, pictures, animation, and organization that are then projected onto a screen (overhead projector screen) with the use of a computer and projector; slide show format.

presentation tool   a program that allows an author to create an electronic (perhaps multimedia) presentation of information (PowerPoint, Kid Pix, HyperStudio, Digital Chisel, ClarisWorks, Persuasion).

real time   talking, listening, and/or watching as an event or conversation is actually happening.

remote equipment/devices   the control of an activity, process, or machine from a distance, such as by radioed instructions or coded signals.

Risso machine   a copier that can print material at a superfast rate.

search engine   a database program that allows keyword searches for information on the Internet. There are several types of search engines; the search may cover titles of documents, URLs, headers, or the full text.

secondary storage devices   any nonvolatile storage medium that is not directly accessible to the processor. Memory directly accessible to the processor includes main memory, cache, and the CPU registers. Secondary storage includes hard drives, magnetic tape, CD-ROM, DVD drives, floppy disks, punch cards, and paper tape.

simulation   a program that creates a "real-life" situation in which the user makes decisions either first or in reaction to situations presented by the program, and the computer gives feedback about the consequences of those decisions.

slide show   a presentation of print information, still pictures, or images in a program such as PowerPoint; can include multimedia effects such as audio, video, hypermedia links, and so forth.

software   programs, procedures, and related documentation associated with a computer. Major packages include databases, database management, and spreadsheets; multimedia presentation capability such as video, graphics, audio additions, and text; telecommunications such as email, information retrieval from the Internet, and information publishing.

spreadsheet   a tool that presents mainly numerical data in an organized format such as might be organized by an accountant, although most spreadsheet programs can convert numerical data to graphs and other spatial representations; can be used for maintaining electronic grade books, recording skills, tracking financial records of a teacher's class or school organizations, entering science experiment information, and so forth.

Talk Back   a device used to provide learning in two ways: auditory and visual. It fits over a student's face and ears. The device allows the student to read aloud and hear closely what he or she has read.

teach timers   clock timers that are placed on the overhead so that they are visible to students. Students can keep track of their time when taking a timed test.

telecommunication tools   tools that allow users to access electronic information outside the classroom (Internet and World Wide Web, email, Telnet, videoconferencing, etc.).

touch screens   a computer-based input device that utilizes the monitor for input and does not require a keyboard; used for computerized tests.

tutorials   programs designed to be "teachers" to individual learners; students learn new information from the program in small chunks, and the program assesses how well a student is doing throughout the program and gives a final evaluation.

Uniform Resource Locator (URL)   the draft standard for specifying the Internet location of an object such as a file or newsgroup.

virtual reality   a computer-generated environment that is three-dimensional and involves the user in real-time, multisensory interactions.

voice mail   a system for sending, storing, and retrieving audio messages, such as a telephone answering machine.

wireless laptops   similar to typical laptop computers, but with infrared interface that allows their use throughout the school. Students can check the Internet while looking at a book in the library.

word processor   a basic typewriting tool but with the ability to revise.

Zip drive   a device or built-in device that accommodates a Zip diskette, which can hold 100MB of information.

SUGGESTED ACTIVITIES

1. Specify how you plan to have students use computers in your classes in the following ways:

    a. To collect information

    b. To organize and store information

    c. To communicate

    d. To create visual representations of information

    e. To create visuals for presentations

    f. To create art products

    g. To calculate and interpret numerical data

    h. To use in the writing process

    i. To remediate

    j. To enrich for gifted students

    k. To support a child who is differently abled

    l. Other(s)

2. Research software programs that you might use for each of the following subjects: math, reading, science, history, and writing. Be sure to describe how you would use the program and under what circumstance you would use it.

3. Review computer filtering programs such as Cyber Patrol or Content Barrier. Does your school district employ such a device? Why would parents be likely to support blocking and filtering systems? Why not?

4. What are some of the limitations to using computer resources in your classroom? What laws might be involved?

5. Write a paragraph connecting constructivist theory to using computer resources in the classroom. You may also choose to include discovery learning and/or hands-on activities in the discussion.

6. Design your "dream" classroom that integrates at least a half dozen computers. Be realistic about measurements so that you represent empty space (what is left over after desks and chairs have been considered) accurately. Do not forget about egress and movement, safety with electric cords, screen glare, and placement so that the teacher can easily monitor at all times.

7. Reflect on your computer skills. If they are not as up-to-date as they should be, design a plan for your own instruction (most districts, universities, and service centers publish lists of miniclasses for help in specific areas).

PRACTICE QUESTIONS

1. Miss Perry is a first-year teacher with a great deal of computer experience—she was lucky enough to have used a personal computer all the way through her education training program. In the first month of school, however, she discovers that none of her first graders have much experience with computers other than to "play" along with tutorial software programs such as Jump Start and Reader Rabbit. Because she has little experience teaching early childhood with computers, where should Miss Perry begin with her first graders to meet the technology standards?

   A. She should begin by writing vocabulary words on sentence strips created by the computer.

   B. She should begin by giving students "free time" to explore computers on their own.

   C. She should model accurate usage for basic computer functions and terminologies.

D. She should model usage and then monitor students' usage (while providing appropriate feedback).

2. Mr. Dominguez teaches fourth-grade science. He knows that his children have been working on a computerized version of Accelerated Reader in grades 1, 2, and 3. He also knows that they have shown a very high interest in learning more about desktop publishing, and he has six new computers in his classroom. How can Mr. Dominguez combine the Technology Application for student standards with his science class?

   A. He can locate several science Web sites for research.

   B. He can ask students to do some scientific research at home and bring hard copies of their findings to class.

   C. He can group his students, assign a scientific experiment, and require a "write-up" of the results of the work, using a graphic organizer he has created.

   D. He can involve the local university science professors to help him lecture about writing up scientific results.

3. The most recent trend toward technology in instructional resources is caused by:

   A. Teachers who are just out of college and demanding more computers.

   B. The impact of technology on education at all levels, mainly influenced by the work force.

   C. Most teachers over age 40, who avoid learning about computers. There is a need for those teachers to retire.

   D. Constructivist theory, because most students learn this way.

4. Mrs. Hoya begins a technology-integrated research lesson on dinosaurs in her fourth-grade elementary class. She begins her lesson by asking her children what they want to know about dinosaurs. Emily says she wants to know "*when* dinosaurs lived,"; Franklin wants to know "*where* they lived." Molly asked two questions: "How many kinds of dinosaurs were there?" and "Where did they live?" Mrs. Hoya

made a list of questions, which she wrote on the blackboard for the students, and then told her children that they would use the computer to get the answers to these (and other) questions. How should Mrs. Hoya proceed?

A. She should bookmark Web sites for her students to research.

B. She should demonstrate how to use a search engine.

C. She should hand out copies of research articles so that students can identify key words before going to the computer.

D. She should write Web sites on the board so that students can find information by themselves.

5. A small group of third-grade children were working on a social studies technology project. They called Mr. Baker over to ask for his help in deleting a slide for their slide show. Mr. Baker:

A. Showed them how to do it.

B. Told them how to do it.

C. Told them to try online help first.

D. Told them not to worry about it because they would come to that function just a little bit later on.

Answers and Discussion

Answer 1: The teacher should take every opportunity to model usage and monitor students' usage as they are learning new terminologies (D). Just giving them free time (B) will not encourage them to move forward to new learning tasks. Answer A is teacher use of the computer rather than student use. Simply modeling does not ensure that children will follow accurate usage (C). However, modeling accompanied by monitoring and feedback allows children the guided practice that leads them to independent use. The answer is D.

Answer 2: Getting research ahead of time as homework and having a human resource (such as a professor) speak on the topic are very good ideas.

However, assignments using technology at home are always questionable, because many students may not have access, and asking professors to come is not as relevant or hands-on as having children engaged. The answer is C.

Answer 3: It is true that educated technology experts are in high demand as workers. Realizing the need for quality workers, the educational community has responded by ensuring a quality technologically advanced workforce for the future. The answer is B.

Answer 4: Mrs. Hoya has "research" as one of her objectives; therefore, she should teach (model for) students how to find information through search engines. Simply bookmarking sites will not help them learn how to research, nor will handing them a piece of paper. The answer is B.

Answer 5: Mr. Baker could show or tell them how to do it, but he should begin to build in self-sufficiency by having them try to use online help first (C). Online help appears in different ways for different systems, but teachers and children should learn to find the "help" button and/or "balloons" in which help appears. They should also begin to learn the concise terms, or key words, help to ask the program to find the needed procedures. For example, in this instance, Mr. Baker might have asked that the team go to help, then think of only two words to ask help (*delete slide*). Sometimes the online help procedures can be long and confusing to younger children, so the teacher should be there as a facilitator when needed. The answer is C.

WEB LINKS

One of the greatest resources for teachers integrating technology in the classroom is the World Wide Web. Following is a list that provides a "sampling" of the Web sites children can access for information on materials and resources. When accessing these Web sites, a teacher might find lesson plans, information on technology, graphic organizers, freebies, black line masters, glossaries, and most importantly, ideas. Remember that Web sites change constantly and that the teacher should access sites before using them in the classroom.

http://www.cln.org/int_email.html

Many, useful links for teachers and technology are provided through this site. Information on lessons, technology use in classrooms, places to find keypals for children, and much more are found here.

www.cost.org

A not-for-profit organization that uses technology to expand opportunities for all people.

www.dictionary.com

This site is a primary resource for defining terms.

www.sitesforteachers.com

This Web site contains helpful resources for all ages of students and in all subjects. Each subject has several options: lesson plans, strategies, resources, geography, multimedia, ancient worlds, museums, and organizations. You can even tour the White House on this site.

www.teachnet.org

This Web site stresses that teachers know that technology is a useful learning tool, but it is not an end in itself. It correctly defines technology to include video and audio recording and playback devices, fax machines, copiers, printers, cameras, scanners, and projection devices.

www.teachnet.org

This site provides many links to educational resources: lesson plans, classroom activities, teacher experience stories, special interests, and so on.

www.teachers.net

This site provides opportunities for "teacher chat" in addition to lesson plans and resources listings.

www.pitsco.com

This site links to a collection of some of the best educational resources on the Web. It includes grants and funding resources.

www.execpc.com/~dboals/boals.html

This page is useful in locating and using Internet resources in the classroom. Its purpose is to

encourage the use of the World Wide Web as a tool for learning and teaching.

www.loc.gov

This site has a large collection of text, photographs, sound recordings, movies, and maps of historic events (with lesson plans). This information occurs in the American Memory Collection.

www.nationalgeographic.com

This Web site is interactive and provides material suitable for downloading. Click on "education."

www.pbs.org/teachersource

The main purpose of the Public Broadcasting Service (PBS) is to provide information on using video as a tool for learning in the classroom.

www.si.edu

The Smithsonian Institution site includes a huge photography database that can download photos. Classroom activities and active-learning lesson plans are provided.

www.esc16.net

This site refers to the Region 16 Service Center. Just substitute your own regional service center to see lots of information.

http://askeric.org

ASKERIC. The Educational Resources Information Center (ERIC) is a federally funded national information system that provides, through its 16 subject-specific clearinghouses, a broad range of education-related issues.

www.scholastic.com

This site provides excellent classroom activities and games, curriculum programs and materials, software, and film and video information. You may also access reproducibles, articles, and lesson plans.

www.sdcoe.k12.ca.us/score/actbank/torganiz.htm

This site provides 12 examples of graphic organizers that may be used in the classroom. Click on Graphic Organizers.

www.tea.state.tx.us

Every Texas teacher should "bookmark" this site because it is the Texas Education Agency site. At this site, you can research TEKS, service center resources, and much more.

www.csu.edu.au/education/library.html

This site for Charles Stuart University provides a plethora of information, including a resources link.

www.eskimo.com/~user/kids.html

This Web site offers help with gifted and talented students.

www.enchantedlearning.com

This excellent Web site is committed to early childhood. It contains a learning dictionary, studies on dinosaurs and sharks, connect-a-dot puzzles, and many more high-interest programs with exciting graphics. It is a "must see."

http://www.pbs.org/digitaldivide/links.html#fp

This site provides technology links for girls.

REFERENCES

Clements, D. H. (1994). The uniqueness of the computer as a learning tool: Insights from research and practice. In J. L. Wright & D. D. Shade, (Eds.). *Young children: Active learners in a technological age* (pp. 205–206). Washington, DC: NAEYC.

Epstein, A. S. (1993). *Training for quality.* Ypsilanti, MI: High/Scope Press.

Grabe, M., & Grabe, C. (2000). *Integrating the Internet for meaningful learning.* Boston: Houghton Mifflin.

Newby, T., Stepich, D., Lehman, J., & Russell, J. (2000). *Instructional technology for teaching and learning.* (2nd ed.). Upper Saddle River, NJ: Merrill, Prentice Hall.

Roblyer, M., & Edwards, J. (2000). *Integrating educational technology into teaching.* (2nd ed.). Upper Saddle River, NJ: Merrill.

Ryan, K., & Cooper, J. (1998). *Those who can, teach.* (8th ed.). Boston: Houghton Mifflin Company.

Competency 10

The teacher monitors student performance and achievement; provides students with timely, high-quality feedback; and responds flexibly to promote learning for all students.

The beginning teacher:

- Demonstrates knowledge of the characteristics, uses, advantages, and limitations of various assessment methods and strategies, including technological methods and methods that reflect real-world applications.

- Creates assessments that are congruent with instructional goals and objectives and communicates assessment criteria and standards to students based on high expectations for learning.

- Uses appropriate language and formats to provide students with timely, effective feedback that is accurate, constructive, substantive, and specific.

- Knows how to promote students' ability to use feedback and self-assessment to guide and enhance their own learning.

- Responds flexibly to various situations (e.g., lack of student engagement in an activity, the occurrence of an unanticipated learning opportunity) and adjusts instructional approaches based on ongoing assessment of student performance.

Chapter 15

COMPETENCY 10 – PART 1

Using a Variety of Appropriate Assessment Techniques to Provide Feedback and Monitor Student Progress

PAM LINDSEY

Tarleton State University

TERMS TO KNOW

Academic learning time (ALT)
Age-equivalent scores
Assessment
Authentic assessment
Criterion referenced
Curriculum-based assessment
Domain
Evaluation
Formal assessment

Formative assessment data
Grade-equivalent scores
Informal assessment
Norm referenced
Observation
Observational data
Percentile rank
Performance-based assessment
Play-based assessment

Portfolio
Reliability
Self-assessment
Standard score
Standardized test
Summative data
Teacher-made test
Test bias
Validity

TESTING, ASSESSMENT, AND EVALUATION: WHAT'S THE DIFFERENCE?

In defining assessment, Wiggins and McTighe (1998) call it an "umbrella term we use to mean the deliberate use of many methods to gather evidence to indicate that students are meeting standards. . . . we are referring to information gathered through a variety of formal and informal assessments . . . including observations, dialogues, traditional quizzes and tests, performance tasks and projects as well as student self-assessment gathered over time (p.4)." Current standards and competencies for the EC–4 Professional Certification in Texas emphasize the teacher's understanding and use of a variety of developmentally appropriate techniques to monitor student progress and plan effective instruction. These standards describe both what the beginning teacher should know and understand about assessment and what he or she is able to do with this understanding in order to plan for measuring how much children learn in the classroom. For teachers of young children, the process should include a variety of informal techniques such as observations, interviews with parents, and artifacts of the young child's work over the course of the school year. For teachers of elementary-aged students, both formal and informal data must be gathered, demonstrating the student's skills related to the TEKS (Texas Essential Knowledge and Skills) and the examinations that assess the curriculum presented in the TEKS— the TAAS (Texas Assessment of Academic Skills) to be replaced by the TAKS (Texas Assessment of Knowledge and Skills).

The word *assessment* is often used as a synonym for test or evaluation. However, **assessment** of student achievement or progress involves *much more* than testing but is *less* encompassing than an overall evaluation of students' level of mastery for a specific grade or course. Specifically, a test may measure a small amount of knowledge in a very specific way, such as a unit test or end-of-course exam, whereas an evaluation process typically means the formal methods schools use to measure *overall* student progress. In Texas schools and universities this is often done through comprehensive tests such as the TAAS or TAKS, ITBS, PPR, or TExES as well as with formal observation and other means.

Competency 10 suggests that assessment means any measurement for which the appraisal process is ongoing, developmentally appropriate, and dynamic. Assessment involves the measurement of students' skill acquisition, fluency, maintenance, and generalization on a specific set of objectives or lessons. An assessment process also acts as an evaluation, or critique, of a teacher's instructional techniques—that is, it provides a feedback loop for teachers to see how effective their lessons were in promoting student achievement.

Assessment should involve collection of data from several sources, both formal and informal. Therefore to represent a true picture of how a student has progressed, it includes tests, observations, student conferences, work samples, and projects that allow students to demonstrate how far they have progressed toward the set objectives. In addition, an appropriate assessment process is continuous and ongoing; that is, effective teachers collect assessment data daily, weekly, and sometimes hourly to constantly monitor their students' understanding and progress.

The purpose of an active assessment procedure is to ensure that curricular, program, and placement decisions are based on hard evidence, rather than serendipitous speculation (Choate et al., 1995), and to provide information to students, parents, and teachers concerning students' progress and the effectiveness of the teacher's instruction. The assessment process also provides information for sorting students based on their skill level and evaluating teachers in terms of accountability for student progress (Slavin, 1997). Thus, **evaluation** typically refers to all means used in schools to formally measure performance *and* to make judgments and decisions about this data. "The results of measurements are useful only if educators do something with the information; therefore, evaluation includes assessment but extends into judgments about the quality or worth of an educational program or procedure being implemented." In education teachers may use measurement when evaluating individuals or programs" (Ward & Murray-Ward, 1999, p. 60). Evaluation thus includes formal, informal, and observational data collected before, during, and after instruction. As noted, evaluation data are generally used to make curricular and program decisions. An individual student evaluation is used most often for referral for special education or gifted education assessment.

This chapter offers preservice teachers an explanation of the assessment process, specific definitions of important assessment terms, and descriptions of various types of assessment data sources. It also defines the characteristics of valid and reliable age-appropriate assessment instruments and processes. In addition, a discussion of teacher-made tests based on Bloom's taxonomy should help new teachers at the early elementary grade level construct tests and other assessment processes that are developmentally appropriate to evaluate their children's higher-level thinking skills. For early childhood educators, this chapter describes informal and alternative assessment techniques developmentally appropriate for young children.

THE ASSESSMENT PROCESS

The assessment process involves two main data sources: **formal assessment** (norm-, or criterion-referenced, standardized tests) and **informal assessment** (interviews, observations, alternative assessments, curriculum-based assessment). Accurate (valid), dependable (reliable), and sufficient formal and informal data collection allows teachers to make appropriate instructional and program decisions about their students (Sattler, 1992).

For informal data (such as interviews), validity refers to the truthfulness of the information. In the case of a test, **validity** means that the test measures what it purports to measure. For example, for a teacher-made test to have validity, it must cover the skill or content of the teacher's instruction; thus it must be directly tied to the content objectives (Arends, 1998; Sattler, 1992). If more than half the class fails a test, the teacher should analyze the validity of the test rather than the lack of intelligence of his or her students. Although this outcome could be linked to lack of student preparation for the test, it is more likely a result of an inappropriate format and/or the contents of the test itself. Specifically, the exam was most likely not aligned with the classroom instruction. The same can occur in everyday lessons. For example, the objective of a third-grade mathematics lesson is for children to add and subtract dimes, quarters, nickels, and pennies for totals less than $1.00. During the instructional delivery, the teacher reads a poem about money, talks about the value, shape, and size of the coins, and provides children with coin replicas to manipulate and compare. To assess children's mastery of the lesson objective, the teacher uses an independent practice activity in which children are given a worksheet to solve addition and subtraction word problems using their coins. What is the problem? The teacher did not provide children with the content to be successful on the assessment. Although the poem and the discussion were certainly appropriate topics for review or to focus children's attention, problem solving with money was not addressed during the direct instruction. The grade on this worksheet would be an invalid measure. One way to improve validity includes *ensuring balance* in the number of items (or observations) over the entire area to be assessed rather than a concentration on one particular part. In the example above, for instance, a teacher would have difficulty with validity if an independent practice or a test included *only* the size of the coins. The teacher would also want to assess a young child for developing areas in a balanced and wide range of contexts. Another way to investigate validity is to *compare* children who did well with those who didn't and try to determine the reason for the difference. With young children, the difference between success and failure in a particular task can too often be due to physical skills rather than knowledge. For example, several of Shelly Johnson's Pre-K students did not do well on their math assignment, in which she had them glue beans in a row to show addition. She noticed during monitoring that those who did not do well were the same children who were a bit delayed in fine motor skills. When she questioned these children, she found that they did know the answers but had become frustrated with the task. Yet another way to improve validity is to *know the limitations of each method* and *offer a wide range of methods* of assessment, or many "windows of opportunity," for children to demonstrate what they know and can do.

Reliability relates to the dependability of information. For either a standardized assessment instrument or a teacher-made test, reliability refers to the consistency of results over time. In other words, a reliable test is one that yields similar results time after time when administered to the same group or level of students and under the same conditions (Arends, 1998; Sattler, 1992). For example, a student who scored 95 on Friday of one week will likely score close to 95 on the same test the next week if the test has reliability. Thus a class of similar children under similar instructional and environmental conditions would have the same range of scores on the same test. In the case of informal data, reliability involves concerns such as *teacher bias, disrupting events, student motivation,* and *appropriateness of an assignment* to demonstrate the skill or content assigned. For example, if a fire drill occurred in the middle of a mathematics test in second grade, the results of the test might not show correct learning results (e.g., for children with attention or learning problems who have

trouble refocusing, or for those who may be upset by the interruption).

In addition to reliability and validity factors, assessment data must be as free from bias as possible. **Test bias** refers to the fairness of the test or, specifically, the test design that makes it somehow unfair to a group of students. Because assessment data, especially test data, have become increasingly important and widely used to make important decisions about students, it is critical that teachers and other professionals be aware of the bias of tests toward certain individuals or groups of students. For example, Torres's (1991) study suggests that approximately 5 million students in the United States each year are inappropriately judged using standardized test data such as the TAAS. This study and others suggest that children are often mismatched with an assessment that is culturally or linguistically biased against them. In addition, studies have suggested that age- or grade-based data are often misinterpreted by teachers or parents and that misinterpreted data results in inappropriate placements and/or programs for students (Torres, 1991; Ward & Murray-Ward, 1999). Many would argue that tests such as the TAAS may have a cultural bias (Lawton, 1997). An example of cultural bias is the translating of an American-normed test into Spanish for an immigrant student from Mexico. Many items on a typical intelligence scale can be American culture specific (the colors in the American flag, America's first president, and so forth). Consequently, the immigrant student would be as unlikely to know the correct answer in Spanish as in English. In addition, there can be items that ask for information typical of the region in which the test was developed and that are not typical in another region of the United States. Examples that might influence scores for Texas-tested children might be references to sleds, silos, toboggans, and snowsuits. A teacher candidate originally from Jamaica recently shared her own experiences with testing bias. When she arrived in Texas and was being tested, it was recommended that she be held back, even though she had been a bright student in Jamaica. Because this was so traumatic, she remembers some of the items for which she had no clue, such as, "How does metal feel outside on a winter day?" In Jamaica all experiences would lead to the answer "hot," yet questions like this are used to place children based on their "intelligence."

If the test taker has had adequate opportunity and instruction to be successful on the test, the criteria for an instructional cycle have been met. It is when students have limited opportunities to learn the test information and the test results are used to make educational decisions that test bias becomes a serious problem (e.g., in special education referrals and/or placements, retention, and so forth). Other types of test bias typically discussed in assessment literature are predictive bias, inflammatory bias, true or statistical bias, and inherent bias (including teacher bias).

Predictive bias refers to the ability of a test to predict future performance. For example, SAT (Scholastic Aptitude Test), ACT (American College Testing), and GRE (Graduate Record Examination) ratings are often used as predictors of an individual's college grade point average (GPA) or success in an undergraduate or graduate program. However, Wilder and Powell's (1989) study indicated that a female student's mathematics SAT score may significantly *underpredict* her college GPA and success in college-level math classes. In fact, recent data suggests that the best predictor of college success is a student's high school GPA, not his or her SAT or ACT scores (Arends, 1998). Therefore universities that use high cut-off scores as the only criteria for acceptance are guilty of predictive bias. It is important for schools to use a variety of measures to determine placement and program decisions for students.

Inflammatory bias occurs when items on the test stereotype certain individuals or groups. For example, an item that references an Asian person running a laundry or a blonde female being forgetful or unorganized has inflammatory bias, because it is offensive to certain groups or individuals.

True or statistical bias occurs when variations of scores on certain test items are not related to the knowledge required to answer the item correctly. For example, this could occur if items on a math-

ematics test were related to the scoring of a specific kind of sport (such as calculating baseball batting averages to solve the problem). The item would have true bias because anyone unfamiliar with the sport would be unable to answer the questions, regardless of his or her fluency with mathematical computations (Ward & Murray-Ward, 1999).

Inherent bias usually is found when using interview or teacher-made test data (Arends, 1998; Sattler, 1992). Interview data, as explained later in this chapter, provide important information to the teacher. The inherent bias in interviews pertains to the validity and reliability of the information provided (i.e., the trustworthiness of the information, especially second-hand information). Because people tend to interpret behavior in relationship to their own perceptions rather than what is factual, interview data must be considered informal and interpreted with caution. In addition, teacher bias in grading must be carefully analyzed as a source of inherent bias. Specifically, teachers often allow their personal feelings or a student's past performance to influence the grading of a subjective assignment such as an essay question on a test, written work, or project. This type of bias is often called the "halo effect." Teachers must be careful not to assume that "Patty Perfect's" work is automatically superior based on her *halo* of being an angelic student and past performance. Conversely, teachers must be careful not to assume that "Terrible Theresa's" work is a manifestation of her inappropriate classroom behavior and past performance and, therefore, inferior. Research suggests that teachers inadvertently judge children's academic work based on their classroom behavior, cultural background, and/or special education labels (Christiansen & Vogel, 1998). Ways to prevent this type of grading bias are discussed later in this chapter in the section describing the construction of teacher-made tests.

In summary, a dynamic assessment process provides purposeful, timely information that can be used for several instructional and evaluative purposes. Because assessment data are used to formulate hypotheses and plan instruction, to evaluate students' skill acquisition and progress, and to judge the effectiveness of teachers' instruction, it is important that teachers understand the types of assessment data they need to gather and the purposes for each type.

FORMATIVE AND SUMMATIVE DATA

The two main types of assessment information gathered by teachers in classrooms are formative and summative data. Both may be gathered through formal or informal means. Formative assessment provides teachers with feedback about the students' progress in pre-planning and during the process of instruction or intervention. **Formative assessment data** are collected before or "along the way" and can be used for planning further instructional goals and objectives and/or adaptations as instruction needs emerge. One use of such data is to plan modifications for children with special needs or those who are struggling with traditional grade-level material. Formative data are also used to diagnose students' strengths and weaknesses. Before instruction for elementary-aged children, data sources could include pretests, observations, student and/or parent interviews, past report card grades and TAAS (or TAKS) scores, learning style inventories, student **self-assessment,** and/or class discussions. Formative data may also include discussions with a child's previous teacher. However, the reliability of these type of data must be carefully considered.

Formative data gathered *during* instruction for elementary-aged students is usually found in quizzes, observations, class discussions, oral questioning, and guided and independent practice activities. During instruction, formative assessment data should be gathered frequently, and feedback should be immediate. Formative evaluation should be part of each day's lesson plan and considered an evaluation of children's prior knowledge and skills related to the class or lesson content. It should not be used to make major placement judgements (Arends, 1998; Slavin,

1997). In other words, it should be considered a work in progress.

Formative data for early childhood or kindergarten-aged students, are usually gathered through observations of their play and social and communication interactions. Teachers of young children must be keen observers and should keep anecdotal journals about each child's language and play patterns. In addition, early childhood teachers should communicate frequently with children's parents about their children's behavior at home and in the community. Reliable **observational data** must be collected frequently and in many settings to ensure that the assessment data reflects the truest picture of the whole child. Because young children's play behaviors are typically the most reliable sources of data about their social and cognitive development, **play-based assessment** data are often collected by teachers through structured and unstructured observations, videotaped play sessions, and interviews with parents.

In an elementary classroom, formative data can be collected at the closure of the lesson by asking each student, using a round-robin technique, to identify the most important point he or she had learned during a specific lesson. The teacher records each child's responses and later reviews children's statements to ascertain whether their learning reflects the objectives of the lesson. This information can be used in several ways: for planning, reteaching, or remedial lessons; modifying lessons or extending or expanding concepts of lessons; and/or planning summative (overall) judgments of the children's learning. Teachers should be collecting formative data as they proceed through a course or unit to formulate a plan for instruction. When they report formative data to a student or, in the case of young children, to the child and his or her parents, all can work together to plan activities that will help the child master the instructional goals of the class.

Summative assessments can be formal and/or informal and are intended to help make judgements about students' progress as they complete the curriculum or instructional activities. The purpose of summative evaluation is to summarize how well a student or a group of students has mastered a specified set of learning objectives and to evaluate the success of the teacher's instructional methods. **Summative data** are gathered after instruction and, for elementary-aged children, may include such things as unit or chapter tests, curriculum- or criterion-based tests, cooperative or individual learning projects, products such as PowerPoint presentations or videos, and other activities that answer the question, "In the end, how well did you learn?" Summative data typically compare children's progress with the objectives and learning criteria rather than comparing children with each other. The TAAS, soon to be the TAKS, for elementary grades, and the Texas Primary Reading Inventory (TPRI), for kindergarten, are summative evaluation tools because each measures a student's progress against a specific curricular standard. In addition, TAAS (or TAKS) and TPRI scores give teachers diagnostic information to help them plan instruction. Summative data are usually not gathered as frequently as are formative data. However, both should be closely tied to the course or curriculum objectives and have sound reliability and validity (Arends, 1998; Slavin, 1997).

For early childhood educators, summative data may also include portfolios of children's work containing samples of their artwork or other classwork, photographs, videos, or other artifacts that demonstrate their progress over the grading period. A culminating product of the summative data could be narrative reports to parents, describing their child's improvement in social interaction skills and/or communication skills, development of higher-level play skills, and/or work behaviors (such as following directions, time on task, and so forth).

FORMAL ASSESSMENT

Formal assessments are typically standardized and either norm or criterion referenced. A **standardized test** is usually commercially generated and given to particular groups or individual students.

It comes with a set of instructions so that every test taker should have, as much as possible, an identical test-taking environment. For example, when a student is referred for special education assessment, formal data are gathered through precise diagnostic instruments. *Diagnostic* assessment or instruments help point out specific areas where problems exist for a child and can be formal or informal, formative or summative. Often these are intelligence and academic achievement tests. Standardized assessment instruments must meet rigorous statistical standards for reliability and validity.

Norm-Referenced Tests

One type of formal assessment is a norm-referenced test. A **norm-referenced** test is one that has been standardized on a clearly defined group called a *norm group*. These scores are reported in **standard scores** or **percentile ranks** that compare an individual child's performance with that of his or her norm group (Choate et al., 1995; Sattler, 1992). For example, the WISC-III is a norm-referenced intelligence test. A child's score compares his or her performance with others in the same norm sample or age group and reflects his or her rank within the norm group. Because the mean or average score for the WISC-III is 100, a score of 100 indicates average intelligence within a particular age group or norm sample. This score could also be reported as in the 50th percentile, which means that the individual scored as well as or better than 50 percent of the norm sample. Standard scores express the individual's distance from the average or mean in terms of the standard deviation of the norming sample (see Figure 15-1).

A good way to remember the elements of a norm-referenced test is to think of it as a test that seeks to identify how close to a theoretical *normal* test taker an individual scores, or the normal score for a large number of test-takers. Or, how does a specific individual compare to a large group of his or her same-age peers? Scores are related to the theoretical score distribution, or bell curve (see

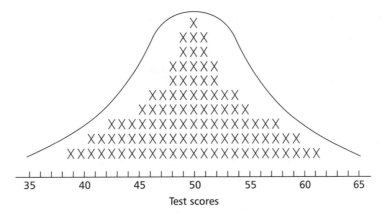

Figure 15-1   Frequency of scores forming a normal bell curve. If 100 people take a test and the score for each is marked by an x on a graph, the result could suggest a normal curve. In a normal distribution, most scores are at or near the mean (in this case, 50) and the number of scores further from the mean progressively decreases.

Figure 15-1), where the majority of test takers (about 68 percent) score at or close to the mean or average score and the others score at some distance from the mean. An individual's score is reported in standard deviations from the mean (or the average) and as positive (+) or negative (-), depending on the direction from the mean. Using our previous example of an IQ of 100 as the mean (or average score), a child whose score was 115 would be reported as scoring one standard deviation above (+) the mean, and a student with an IQ of 85 would be reported as scoring one standard deviation below (-) the mean. This implies that most children score within one standard deviation (within 15 points plus or minus) of 100, with a smaller number scoring significantly above or below 100. The bell curve allows for only four standard deviations (+ or -) on either side of the mean. The further away from the mean or average an individual scores, the fewer other individuals will be in that population. For example, very few individuals score above 145 (three deviations) or below 60 (three deviations) on a traditional IQ test. Individuals scoring in those ranges are extremely gifted or children with mental challenges. Varied tests refer to these

scores in different ways (z-scores, t-scores, etc.) but the concept of deviations remains the same.

Test scores distribution, like the bell curve, are an important tool for the classroom teacher to help him or her to determine the validity of a teacher-made test. For example, if a teacher gives a test and every student in the class scores 97 percent or better, the teacher could reach one of two conclusions: (1) that he or she was a fantastic teacher who reached all of his or her children, or (2) the test was not challenging enough to differentiate between students who had and had not mastered the content.

Other ways to report norm-referenced test data are by **age-** or **grade-equivalent scores.** One often sees these scores reported by grade level and gain. This type of reporting is often misleading and should be avoided as much as possible. Because age- and grade-equivalent scores are based on developmental norms, reporting such scores assumes that all children of certain ages have developed a specific level of academic or social skills and/or that all children in certain grades have received uniform instruction. For example, a child in fourth grade who obtains a grade-equivalent score of 6.9 in mathematics cannot be assumed to have mastered all arithmetic processes taught in sixth grade. Rather, the score was more likely determined by superior performance on fourth-grade arithmetic problems or the fact that there were one or two sixth-grade-level problems on the test that were answered correctly.

Norm-referenced tests are typically used to categorize students for special or gifted education placements. Norm-referenced scores are important because they provide information about a student's performance compared to that of his or her same-aged peers as well as information about the student's developmental, academic, physical, or social changes. A norm-referenced test, however, provides little information about how students learn or the success or failure of instruction. Therefore other types of assessment sources must supplement norm-referenced data (Choate et al., 1995; Sattler, 1992).

Criterion-Referenced Tests

Criterion-referenced tests are also standardized formal measures and are used to provide information about a child's mastery level for specific skills or content. A child's scores reflect mastered skills such as arithmetic operations, mathematical reasoning, written language, reading comprehension, and word decoding. Criterion-referenced tests use absolute standards to answer specific questions about student achievement (e.g., Does Angelina read beginning third-grade material with 70 percent accuracy?). Many criterion-referenced tests are used for "high-stakes" entry- and exit-level decisions for children who will be in gifted or special education classes. Criterion-referenced scores also provide information useful in formulating instructional objectives, thereby helping teachers determine where to start and how to sequence classroom instruction. The PPR and TAAS (or TAKS) are examples of criterion-referenced tests and are scored in percentages of 100. To pass or be considered at the appropriate level of mastery, students must receive a predetermined percentage out of 100. For the PPR

and TAAS (or TAKS), that percentage is currently 70 but may be raised in the future.

CURRICULUM-BASED ASSESSMENT (CBA)

Curriculum-based assessment (CBA) is defined as a direct measure of a child's progress through the classroom curriculum. CBA provides teachers with information about how each child is moving ahead with specific curricular objectives created by the teachers for their lessons (Overton, 2000) or with district- or state-driven curriculum. Curriculum-based assessment may be formal or informal in design and collected before, during, or after instruction so that it can be used as a source of both formative and/or summative assessment. Regardless of the method, CBA is generally criterion-referenced, with a standard designated within a set of objectives to an indicated mastery (Choate et al., 1995). In other words, a curriculum-based assessment process is designed by a teacher to assess a child's mastery of the content and is based on a percentage or passing score. Typically, and unfortunately, the standard percentage for mastery is 70 percent and is normally given as the child's grade in the course or content area. This arbitrary percentage, of course, does not make sense for some functional skills (telling time, counting money, and so forth). Some skills need 100 percent accuracy to be functional, but the teacher cannot require 100 percent mastery if the school's or test's criteria for "passing" is set at 70 percent.

Curriculum-based assessment is most helpful to teachers making decisions about the type, pace, and effectiveness of instructional strategies. When an effective CBA process is in place, both the learner and the teacher are well informed about the student's progress and the efficacy of instruction. Although posttests are most common, curriculum-based assessment may include teacher-made tests, chapter tests, unit tests, portfolios, authentic projects, performance assessment, quizzes, and/or work samples. CBA can be accomplished through traditional assessment procedures (e.g., teacher-made tests) or alternative assessment measures (e.g., portfolios) as long as the measure is a valid standard for evaluating a student's progress.

Just as CBA may use a number of data sources, it may be accomplished in several ways. It may be achieved by setting course objectives, testing the objectives, teaching, and retesting. This method would obviously involve a pretest to determine the child's current skill level and a posttest to determine whether his or her skill had improved (Blankenship, 1985). Another type of CBA uses observational data related to the child's **academic learning time** (ALT), the time when children are actually *understanding* and *succeeding* at the task (Gickling & Thompson, 1985). This method is appropriate for teachers of young children and is another example of play-based assessment. Two other terms that describe time issues with regard to instruction are *allocated time* (time that a teacher sets aside and plans for learning) and *engaged time* (time on task or time when children are actively involved, whether understanding is present or not).

Curriculum-based assessment has many advantages over the use of standardized or group achievement tests. Curriculum-based assessments help teachers determine what to teach by providing information about the exact skills in the curriculum that children have or have not mastered. They are popular with school personnel who want to make sure that children have mastered TAAS (or TAKS) skills. Teachers may teach a unit or skill and then give a posttest designed in the TAAS (or TAKS) format. Children who do not achieve a passing score typically receive special support through remediation and/or reteaching of the nonmastered skill. This process is very effective in teaching both the academic and test-taking skills necessary for success on the TAAS (or TAKS).

Curriculum-based assessment is also effective because teachers may use several data sources, including daily student improvement charts, to illustrate children's progress toward mastery and completion of short-term instructional objectives. CBA facilitates the evaluation of student progress and program effectiveness, and it is also useful in conducting educational research. CBA reports are easy for parents to understand because students' progress may be graphed or charted daily or weekly, thereby demonstrating even very small increments of improvement. Unlike standardized and annual group achievement tests, CBA allows teachers to evaluate the effectiveness of a specific instructional strategy by providing precise, timely information. In addition, curriculum-based assessment is both valid and reliable, because (a) it uses material from the student's own classroom; (b) it is brief; and (c) its performance samplings are repeated frequently. Further, curriculum-based assessment has been shown to increase student achievement because it matches the assessment process to classroom instruction.

Obviously, when what is taught relates exactly to what is being assessed, student achievement increases. Because CBA data are collected frequently, these data help teachers make decisions about the severity of a particular child's skill deficits. For classroom teachers initiating special education referrals based on a child's lack of progress, CBA data are particularly useful. To identify a student who may have specific learning problems, the classroom teacher must have precise information about the target student's skill level, rate of progress, and intervention teaching. This type of documentation gives a clear indication of the nature and severity of a student's educational need for specialized services.

Finally, CBA complies with the requirements of the Individuals with Disabilities Education Act (IDEA) because it specifies the student's present skill levels or competencies within the curriculum. Because the latest revisions of IDEA strongly suggest that children with disabilities be included in or be progressing toward the regular curriculum goals, compliance with the law is important to both classroom teachers and special education teachers. Curriculum-based assessments allow both kinds of teachers to evaluate the degree to which a special needs child's Individual Education Plan (IEP) instructional objectives are being met (Choate et al., 1995).

Teacher-Made Tests

One type of CBA is a **teacher-made test.** Teacher-made tests are probably the most common way used to assess older elementary-aged children's progress in a specific content area. These tests, like all other assessment data sources, must be reliable and valid. The construction of a reliable, valid teacher-made test is a laborious process that involves thoughtful planning. The test must relate directly to the course objectives and classroom instruction. Most instructional objectives cover a range of behaviors and knowledge such as important facts, major concepts, and vocabulary about a topic, as well as critical and analytical thinking and problem solving about course content. Therefore when planning a test, a teacher must first decide how much of the test will be devoted to each **domain** (or related area), what weight will be given to each section, and which information will be included in the test. Obviously, a 6-week test cannot include every bit of information covered during that time period. A table of specifications (see Figure 15-2) is often useful for organizing the planning process. Tables of specifications allow teachers to predetermine the content of tests (Arends, 1998; Slavin, 1997).

For teachers of young children, a table of specifications for other skills might include such things as the number of colors or letters the child can identify or name.

After the teacher has decided which topics and behaviors to test, the second step is to decide the format of the test. Specifically, will the test be objective, essay, or a combination? All three formats have advantages and disadvantages.

An *objective* test (e.g., multiple-choice, true-false, fill-in-the-blank) can be scored objectively (i.e., relatively free from bias), because there is typically only one correct answer. In addition, a great deal of content can be covered. One disadvantage of this type of test is that it is difficult to write objective items that assess the student's higher cognitive functions and problem-solving skills. Another disadvantage is that a valid, reliable, objective test is very time-consuming to construct. The placement of blanks, cueing words such as "a" or "an," and/or true-false questions that are not *completely* true or false are also problems inherent in constructing a valid objective test. In addition, teachers must consider the element of guessing, especially with true-or-false items. Finally, objective tests can measure only a limited range of understanding and skills (Arends, 1998; Slavin, 1997).

Essay tests are best for assessing children's higher-level thought processes and creativity. In addition, essay items take less time to construct. However, good clear questions take some thought and planning, and teachers must prepare sample answers and grading criteria. Criticisms of essay tests include teacher bias in grading and limited coverage of content. Both of these criticisms may

Unit covered: Prehistoric times

Three-week topic: Dinosaurs

Anticipated time to take the test: 20 minutes

Student behaviors and cognitive processes

Topic/Content	Recall Questions	Higher-Level Thinking Questions
Physical characteristics	3	1
Names	5	1
Extinction	2	3
Total Number	10	5

Figure 15-2   Example of a Table of specifications.

Domain	Number of Points
Grammar, spelling, and mechanics; uses complete sentences.	20
Content: Describes the dinosaurs using adjective words such as *color* and *size*.	40
Accuracy: Descriptions are accurate in detail; habitat is accurately described; food is accurately reported.	40

Figure 15-3   Example of a Scoring Rubric.

be addressed through the careful construction of questions, use of sample questions and answers, and designation of specific grading criteria through scoring rubrics. A *scoring rubric* is a tool that helps eliminate teacher bias in scoring essay answers and/or other writing projects (See Figure 15-3). Scoring rubrics provide children with an outline of the expected content and number of points each domain is worth. In this way, children have a clear understanding of the teacher's expectations of an acceptable answer. Rubrics should be designed and provided with *any* assigment where subjectivity, or teacher opinion, is of concern. Teachers may also use a holistic scoring procedure to reduce bias in grading. *Holistic scoring* involves skimming through all of the essays and selecting samples that can be judged as poor, average, and outstanding. These samples then become the model for judging other papers (Arends, 1998; Slavin, 1997).

Rubrics can be broken down to describe a grade even more fully, if desired. For example, a teacher may design the content domain as: learner gives at least two description sentences of four dinosaurs (40 points); learner gives at least two descriptions of three dinosaurs (30 points); and so forth. Deciding these criteria *ahead* of time will give a much more objective grade and help children understand the expectations. Grades with rubrics are also much easier to defend to parents and administrators if questions arise.

Another consideration when planning a teacher-made test is the actual administration. Teachers in learner-centered classrooms must consider several things as they plan when and how

the test will be administered. For example, the students' level of text anxiety must be considered. Although test anxiety is a normal part of the testing situation, high anxiety is neither healthy nor productive. When test takers have high levels of stress or anxiety, their ability to think constructively and recall learned information is significantly diminished (Jensen, 1998). Teachers must find ways to lessen test anxiety by making sure that children know what is expected of them. Using humor before the test and giving children a few minutes before the test to simply take a deep breath are good ways to create a more relaxed testing environment. The best way to eliminate test anxiety is to make sure that the classroom instruction is adequate and appropriate so that children are prepared and have confidence in their ability to be successful on a test.

Teachers must also organize the learning environment so that it is conducive to test taking. For example, children should have ample room to work, minimizing opportunities to share their work. Other considerations include sufficient time, appropriate support for children with special needs, environmental considerations such as lighting and temperature, and specific test-taking routines and instructions. One common error made by beginning teachers is the failure to develop classroom test-taking routines and clear instructions. A good routine to follow includes (a) passing out the tests face down and asking students to wait until everyone has a test to turn them face up; (b) instructing students not to begin until they are told; (c) reviewing instructions for each section of the test; and (d) providing the children with guidelines about how long to spend on each part. If a new test format is being introduced, the teacher should explain the procedures and expectations of the format. In addition, preparing and scoring a "freebie" question in each section often lessens test anxiety and promotes student success. Because children often rush past the written instructions when they perceive that they know the test format, teachers should not only read the directions aloud, but also provide time for children to ask questions before beginning the test (Arends, 1998).

Grading the test is the final step in the process. Teachers may grade on a curve or grade to criteria. Grading on a curve is typical for secondary and university classes. Using this method, teachers follow a formula that gives 10 percent of the students a grade of A, 20 percent B, 40 percent C, 20 percent D, and 10 percent F. With this grading system, even children with a high degree of mastery may fall into the lower grading areas, and vice versa. This method fosters a competitive classroom environment.

Grading to criteria or mastery may be used by teachers at all levels. The approach defines precisely the skills and objectives for the class and then measures student performance against those criteria. This approach enhances an effective instruction cycle: instruct, assess, reflect, redesign, and return to instruction. Typically predetermined, a percentage of correct items determines a child's grade. For example, a spelling test could be graded so that a child must score 90 percent to 100 percent correct to earn an *A* (Arends, 1998; Slavin, 1997). In theory, all students taking the test could earn an A.

As a review, guidelines for effective teacher-made testing procedures include providing clear instructions to children about the content and format of the test. It is also important to test frequently so that children have an opportunity to be successful, and the teacher has the opportunity to reteach. Finally, it is essential that teachers be specific and explicit about their grading procedures. When children understand the expectations of the teacher and see the fairness in the grading system, they are more likely to accept judgments made about their work (Arends, 1998).

For teachers of young children, teacher-made tests consist of pictorial items assessing preacademic skills such as reading readiness, counting, and/or matching. Kindergarten teachers also use individualized oral-testing procedures that track each child's progress through the kindergarten curriculum. In addition, computer software is often used in kindergarten classrooms as an indicator of children's skill level. Software packages such as Sticky Bear may have a short test component at the end of the lesson. These testing units are often in a game-like format. It is important for teachers of young children to remember that children process information most efficiently through sensory input. Specifically, most Pre-K and kindergarten children are primarily kinesthetic and tactile learners who need movement, color, and/or music to enhance their cognitive processes. Therefore any testing materials developed by teachers for these children should focus on a "hands-on" and/or game-like format (Dunn & Dunn, 1999; Jensen, 1998).

CONSTRUCTING A TEACHER-MADE TEST

As mentioned previously, an objective test has advantages and disadvantages, but it is probably one of the most-used data sources in elementary classrooms. To construct a reliable and valid objective test takes planning. Each item must be clear and must assess the information and/or skills provided by classroom instruction. In addition, clear, concise instructions for completing each section of the test should precede each group of test items.

Multiple-choice items are probably the most effective type of objective item and the most difficult to construct, especially if the teacher wishes to tap higher-level thinking skills such as analysis, application, and/or synthesis (Slavin, 1997).

A good multiple-choice item has a stem with enough contextual information so that the test-taker completely understands the problem or question being posed. The stem should be straightforward and specific. The item must also be written so that the correct answer is not easily revealed, (i.e., all distracters must be plausible yet clearly recognizable as wrong by students who really know the content). Distracters should also be grammatically consistent with the stem (i.e., verb cues should not be identifiable by *a* or *an,* and so forth) and of approximately the same length, (Arends, 1998; Slavin, 1997).

Consider this example:

1. ___A dinosaur was a prehistoric animal that

   (a) ate only plants and seeds.

   (b) had wings, fangs, and claws.

   (c) laid eggs and became extinct.

The above is an example of a well-constructed multiple choice item. In contrast, the following is a poor example of an item.

1. A dinosaur:

   (a) prehistoric animal that ate only plants and seeds

   (b) wings, fangs, and claws

   (c) became extinct

In this example, the distracters are of unequal length and are not grammatically consistent with the stem. An added hint for ease in grading is to put all blanks on the left side so that a key can be placed alongside the answers for quick checking.

To test students' higher-level cognition, multiple-choice items must be carefully thought out and worded. The PPR has many application-based multiple-choice items (see the Practice Questions at the end of this chapter). Typically, this type of item sets up a situation or scenario and poses multiple-choice questions based on the situation.

True-false items are useful if the content of a lesson requires that students compare alternatives, learn definitions, or distinguish fact from fiction. They are also a good alternative to multiple-choice items if the instructional objective does not lend itself to several distracters. True-false items must be written so that the choice is clear.

For example, "Prehistoric means before written history," is a clear item. "Prehistoric animals lived in ancient times" is ambiguous because the word *ancient* means old—but not before written history. The use of words like *always* and *never* is also confusing. They are giveaways in true-false items. The obvious drawback to using true-false items is that children have a 50 percent chance of guessing the correct answer. Therefore this type of item should be used sparingly (Slavin, 1997). In addition, it is a good idea to have the students write out the words *true* and *false* or have *true* and *false* printed beside each item for the students to circle. This prevents the argument over whether the letter is a T or F, based on the child's or the teacher's perception of handwriting skills.

Matching items are helpful in measuring large amounts of factual information. In a matching item, children are provided with two lists and asked to select which items closely match. Experts caution against using lists that are too long; most agree that a list of six to eight items is preferable, and there should be approximately two extra items to avoid the process of elimination (Arends, 1998; Slavin, 1997). In addition, the columns of matching items should be on one page so that children do not have to flip back and forth to find the answers. Matching items assess basic factual recall. Like true and false items, matching items have a guess or process-of-elimination factor that can adversely affect their reliability, so providing more items in the matching answers column helps to weaken this effect. Drawn lines for matching can become a grading nightmare when children erase or do not make their lines straight.

Fill-in-the-blank items are very popular with classroom teachers because they are easy to write and do a good job of measuring children's recall of facts. The element of guessing is virtually removed with this format unless a bank of answers is provided for the children. Like other test items, fill-in-the-blank items must be clearly written, avoid ambiguous wording, and have only one correct answer (Arends, 1998; Slavin, 1997). For example, "Dinosaurs lived in _____" is a poor item because there is more than one correct answer. Students could answer "prehistoric times," "jungles," "swamps," and so forth. A better format is, "Dinosaurs lived in _____ times, or before written history." For this item there is clearly only one correct response. It is helpful to also position a blank at the left of a question for quick grading, although this format alone can often be difficult for students with reading disabilities. Because these students often use context clues and sequencing to ascertain the correct response, they need to have the sentence sequenced, with the blank appearing in the natural flow of written language.

Constructing Essay Questions

As previously stated, teachers often like to write essay tests because they consider them easy to create. Essay items allow children to express in their own words, often creatively, the concepts they have learned. Short-answer items often require that children synthesize and apply information, evaluate concepts, or think at a higher level more so than do typical objective test items. The difficulty with essay items has to do mainly with fairness or lack of bias in grading and the amount of time needed to grade each essay accurately and objectively.

An essay item, like an objective item, should be clear in purpose. It is important for children to know precisely what is expected (Arends, 1998; Slavin, 1997). Essay items should also approximate the amount of detail needed to answer the question and have an expected length of the response. Essay responses can range from several sentences to a page, depending on grade and ability levels. As previously mentioned, a scoring rubric is helpful in making the teacher's expectations clear. Further, essay items should be tied directly to instructional objectives and classroom instruction. For example, "Discuss dinosaurs" is a poor essay question because it has no parameters or any indication of what is to be discussed. A better item would be "Describe three dinosaurs, and tell where they lived and what they ate. Write one paragraph that includes at least five sentences for each dinosaur." This item gives chil-

dren a clear notion of what they should discuss and the amount of discussion required to answer the question. Essay items are considered reliable and valid if the teacher can answer three critical questions:

1. Does the item measure the content required in an instructional objective?

2. Can the student answer the question well during the testing time?

3. Is the language specific enough that the student can understand what he or she is being asked to write about?

To answer the first question, the teacher must refer to the course objectives that he or she envisioned and wrote before instruction began. For the second question, a good method is for the teacher to practice writing a response before the test is given. He or she can then estimate how much time it will take children to complete the assignment (Arends, 1998). Slavin (1997) suggests that children take about four times longer to answer an essay question than does the teacher who constructed the item. Young children may take even more. Finally, specific, descriptive language is essential for a good essay item. It is better to use words such as *compare, contrast,* or *define* rather than generic, global words such as *discuss, tell all you know,* and *give your opinion.*

The use of a scoring rubric for essay questions minimizes teacher bias in grading and helps students understand the expectations of the grading system. Using the rubric, teachers provide a standard for themselves and one for students (Arends, 1998; Slavin, 1997). In addition, giving the rubric to children helps them adhere to expectations. Rubrics are also appropriate for grading projects, written papers such as stories, posters, and so forth. (See Figure 15-3).

Another way to minimize teacher grading bias is to have children write their names on the back of the papers so that the teacher is unaware of their identity until after grading the essays. However, many elementary teachers know children's handwriting on sight.

INFORMAL ASSESSMENT

Informal assessment includes work samples, portfolios, and projects, as well as other traditional and nontraditional ways of measuring students' understanding and progress. Informal assessment is the critical element for planning, modifying, and pacing instruction, as well as a key factor in determining students' progress in both early childhood and elementary classrooms. Informal data may be formative or summative in nature, with an ultimate purpose of evaluating the appropriateness of a teacher's instructional techniques and the accuracy of a student's performance or the depth of his or her understanding. For example, informal assessment in a mathematics class could include work samples, student interviews, error analysis, demonstration, and cooperative learning projects.

Many assessment experts suggest that informal data should be organized and individualized using assessment planning checksheets or informal inventory worksheets (e.g., Choate et al., 1995; Taylor, 2000; Ward & Murray-Ward, 1999). These organizing tools help teachers and children assess strengths, weaknesses, patterns of errors, and appropriate instructional strategies. For example, a teacher might create a checklist of the academic or behavioral skills that must be mastered by each student and update it weekly or at the end of a unit. Teacher-made checklists may be constructed for individual students, using error analysis data. *Error analysis data* are used to discover specific patterns of errors in a student's work. For example, an error analysis might show that a child misses subtraction problems that have zeroes in the 10's place or cannot identify the differences between the letters *b, d, p,* and *q.* Work sample collections are also helpful for tracking student progress (Overton, 2000).

Student Interviews As Informal Assessment Data Sources

Student interviews or conferences provide teachers with invaluable information about children's perceptions about their learning. Individual conferences with students should be an integral part of any classroom assessment process. These interviews or conferences should focus on students' understanding of the class's curricular objectives and their learning styles and preferences. Because an interview is an exchange of information, teachers must be willing to listen creatively and empathetically (Sattler, 1992). In addition, interviews must be nonthreatening, ungraded situations that allow children to "speak their minds" in an appropriate manner about their progress through the curriculum. Although an interview should be informal, the teacher must have a clear purpose for the appointment and a tentative set of questions or topics about which he or she wants information. It is critically important, too, that children be told before the interview session that the purpose of an interview is for assessment, not conversation. This should be restated at the beginning of the interview time.

Student interviews allow children time to reflect on their learning. Being interviewed also gives them a sense that the class is a reciprocal, respectful learning environment. Even very young children are able to talk about what they have learned about colors, numbers, letters, and so forth.

Some tips to remember when interviewing students are:

Avoid yes-no questions.

Ask direct questions.

Avoid long, multiple-answer questions.

Give children ample time to answer and elaborate (Sattler, 1992).

An example scenario might be:

Teacher: Thanks for coming in today, Josh. I want you to help me by discussing your experiences with your Texas History class this past 6 weeks.

Josh: Okay.

Teacher: I'd like you to tell me the three most relevant or interesting points you have learned about Texas history since we began studying the Texas Revolution.

Josh: Well, I learned more about the Alamo. I always thought Sam Houston was there as the commander, but it was Travis. Sam Houston was later, at San Jacinto. I also learned something about how brave those guys were to stay when they knew they were going to die. I think the reason why the Texans beat Santa Anna in the end is because they were so mad about the Alamo—and Goliad, too! That's what the Texans kept yelling at the Battle of San Jacinto—"Remember the Alamo! Remember Goliad!" I never thought about that before.

Teacher: I'm glad you thought about that part. Do you remember what happened at Goliad?

Teacher Observations As Informal Assessment Data Sources

Effective teachers are accurate observers of children's academic and social behavior; they are good "kid watchers." This is especially true for teachers of young children. **Observation** is defined as the careful watching and recording of events or behavior for later reflection and analysis. Because events happen very rapidly in a classroom, it is often difficult for a new teacher to be a reliable observer (Arends, 1998; Sattler, 1992). Although observational data are very important in a learner-centered assessment system, the reliability and validity of such data should always be highly suspect. Observational data should never be used as the sole source for making decisions about children or instructional techniques because such data often have a high degree of bias.

Being a good observer takes practice and self-knowledge. A reflective observer understands his or her own values, attitudes, and prejudices. For example, if a teacher has negative feelings about including children with disabilities in his or her classroom, accurate observations of these children may be adversely affected by the teacher's negative views. In addition, it is always good to have

someone else, such as a colleague or administrator, observe the situation. Paired observations often help to validate accurate or inaccurate assessments of a situation. If a paired observation is used, the observer must be sure to focus his or her observation on the behavior that is of concern and attend *only* to the targeted behavior(s). A common mistake of observers involves the interpretation of motives behind the behavior rather than the occurrence of the behavior. For example, an observer may tally the number of sound insertions or deletions a child makes in reading a passage aloud but should not make judgements or assumptions about why the child made these (e.g., the student was bored with the passage, he was nervous about reading aloud, etc.) (Sattler, 1992). Specifically, behavioral observations must be as objective as possible. That is why it is a good idea to have more than one person watch and compare what they observe.

ALTERNATIVE ASSESSMENT PROCEDURES AS INFORMAL DATA SOURCES

Alternative assessment procedures have gained in popularity over the past decade. Alternative assessments include portfolios and performance-based assessment. **Performance-based assessment** is often referred to as **authentic assessment** because the student's skills are evaluated by having him or her demonstrate a specific skill by constructing a product or solving a problem that could be generated from a real-life situation (Arends, 1998; Choate et al., 1995). However, some experts would disagree with using the two terms synonymously (Slavin, 1997). Performance assessment is defined by Slavin as student demonstration of a skill such as playing a song or painting a picture, whereas authentic assessment requires that the child perform the skill in a real-life setting. For example, writing a letter to a pen pal and writing a story to read to a younger group of children are examples of authentic assessments.

For young children, an authentic assessment could be performing in a play or concert or creating a piece of artwork that is displayed in the school library or gallery. Authentic assessment results may be interpreted according to the thinking patterns of the student (i.e., how he or she chose to solve the problem) as well as the correctness of his or her solution (Choate et al., 1995). In the following discussion, the terms *authentic* and *performance assessment* are used synonymously to mean assessment requiring that the student demonstrate his or her skill level by producing a product or performance that mirrors a situation found in real life, as much as possible (Choate et al., 1995).

Because performance-based assessment allows students to demonstrate their skills, talents, and problem-solving abilities through creating unique products, it may be individually tailored to a student's particular learning style or strength and is appropriate for students in early childhood and elementary classrooms (Choate et al., 1995). Specifically, performance-based assessment strategies fit well with the theories of multiple intelligences (Armstrong, 1994; Gardner, 1983) and learning styles (Dunn & Dunn, 1999). Both theories suggest that students have specific ways of learning that are often ignored in the traditional classroom setting. Both theories also assume that a learner-centered classroom is one that is sensitive to the diverse ways children learn and that sensitivity manifests itself in instructional strategies geared toward individual success rather than group comparisons.

Gardner's (1983) model proposes that there are many ways of "being smart" (musical, mathematical, linguistic, visual-spatial, naturalistic, interpersonal, intrapersonal, and kinesthetic). He suggests that when students are allowed to express their knowledge through their preferred intelligence, learning is significantly enhanced (see Competency 4, Part 2, Chapter 6, for more information). For example, instead of a multiple-choice test on dinosaurs, a musically smart student might write a song incorporating the important concepts about dinosaurs, and the visual-spatial student might paint a mural or draw illustrations

for the linguistic student's storybook. All of these activities would be considered authentic or performance-based assessment products. The emphasis, then, of performance assessment is testing procedural rather than declarative knowledge (Slavin, 1997). This means that the evaluation of the product or performance must take into account the creativity and interpretation of the child, not simply a correct test response.

Another example of performance-based assessment can be found in the learning styles research of Dunn and Dunn (1999). This well-researched instructional model suggests that students have environmental needs that enhance the learning process: lighting, temperature, intake, movement, and teacher involvement. In addition, the Dunn and Dunn model describes students in terms of cognitive styles and perceptual strengths that should be accommodated in the learning environment. Research on learning styles indicates that when students are taught and assessed through their learning styles or preference, significant gains are made in academic achievement. For example, one instructional strategy created by the learning styles research is the Contract Activity Package (CAP). The CAP is designed to allow students a choice or menu of activities that they may use to demonstrate their knowledge about class content. The CAP is set up to allow children to make choices, create a product, and demonstrate this creation to a friend, a group of peers, a parent, or a teacher (Dunn & Dunn, 1999). CAPs may be created using PowerPoint presentations so that children create their products on a computer. Even very young children are now computer literate and can create beautiful PowerPoint and Web page presentations using color, sound, and music.

In theory, performance assessment (PA) is superior to standardized or traditional assessment procedures because it allows children to demonstrate a broader and deeper understanding of the subject matter. Because of this, many states now include PA items on their state assessment programs (e.g., Vermont, Kentucky, Maryland). In addition, performance-based assessment strategies provide all children with opportunities to demonstrate what they know in a variety of contexts and allow them to engage in a continual process of self-reflection (Armstrong, 1994). Although these measures are still very controversial, they have merit in preparing students for life after school. After all, how many of us take many multiple-choice tests in our day-to-day lives?

The difficulties in using performance-based assessment items are the time involved in developing valid, reliable items and, for standardized tests, the expense of administering and scoring them. Most experts agree, however, that the expense is well worth it in terms of improving the teaching-learning process (Shepard, 1995; Slavin, 1997).

Portfolios are another informal alternative assessment tool. Portfolios have long been used as an assessment and summative presentation of a body of work for such disciplines as the visual arts, architecture, and photography. It has been just during the past decade that portfolios have been used by public schools and colleges of education as a summative evaluation of students' performance. Portfolios are closely related to performance assessment techniques in that they show student progress through specific examples or products. A *portfolio* is defined as a selection and evaluation of samples of student work over an extended period of time (Slavin, 1997). It tells a story of the student's effort, progress, or achievement for a certain time period (Arter & Spandel, 1992). A portfolio, then, is not simply a notebook containing random collections of a student's work, but rather a structured selection of that student's work, demonstrating progress in some way. Some schools (e.g., in Illinois and Kansas) use student portfolios to assess and report student achievement. In these schools, portfolios encompass sample artifacts and reflections that demonstrate what the students have done or can do across all subject areas (Arends, 1998). For example, a portfolio may be structured around a set of questions that the student answers in a variety of ways including essays, video- or audiotapes, visual illustrations, computer discs, and/or reflective journal entries. Typically, in schools that use port-

folios as a major portion of their summative assessment, the portfolio is kept and passed on from grade to grade so that the child and his or her parents can compare such things as writing ability and depth of knowledge from year to year. In addition, the portfolio is refined every year, with some items being discarded and others added. The purposes of portfolios are (a) for a child to reflect on his or her learning and (b) for teachers to assess student improvement over time and in many different contexts (Overton, 2000).

For a portfolio to be considered a valid and reliable assessment tool, the teacher must structure it so that it is a true reflection of student progress, not simply a collection of student work. Obviously, advanced planning by the teacher is a required element. Experts agree that the creation of a purposeful portfolio system entails several steps. Initially the teacher must define his or her purpose for the portfolio. For example, a portfolio may be used as a showcase for a child's best work, a documentation of progress, or an evaluation tool. It is possible for a portfolio to have more than one purpose; however, if this is the case, it should be divided into sections that document each purpose (Ward & Murray-Ward, 1999).

The second step in designing a portfolio is to determine the skills and content to be assessed. Like other curriculum-based measures, portfolio artifacts must be closely tied to the instructional objectives of the course content. Therefore teachers and students must be careful to choose items that reflect progress toward mastery of specified objectives. These items can include teacher-made tests, student reflections, and/or projects or assignments that reflect the student's depth of knowledge about a specific instructional objective.

The third step is to determine who will assess and how to assess the contents of the portfolio. For schools that use portfolios as an assessment tool, it is imperative that they also determine at what grade levels the assessment will take place. Typically, the assessment process uses a rubric design so that objectivity in grading is maintained.

When structural decisions have been made, it is critical to determine how children will be involved in the process. One of the major strengths of a portfolio system is the high degree of student involvement. A child should be involved in decisions about the content and organization of his or her individual portfolio. In addition, a student journal and self-reflections should be required items. For the child to participate in a meaningful way, however, he or she must be trained and have time to select the work and reflect on it. One criticism of using a portfolio system is the time required to organize and evaluate it, although most users agree that the benefits of an effective portfolio are extensive.

Finally, a process by which assessment results are communicated to parents and students must be designed. The very nature of a portfolio lends itself to conferences rather than traditional letter-grade interpretations. However, when assessment results are tied to retention and/or graduation requirements, a specific process must be in place for conferences and standardized results. For these reasons, the use of portfolios as a major component of a school's assessment program is very controversial. Although a few schools use the process exclusively, it is more common for a particular classroom or school district to use portfolios as one piece of their formative and summative assessment process (Cheong & Shively, 1991; Mumme, 1990; Nitko, 1996; Ward & Murray-Ward, 1999).

Electronic portfolios are becoming increasingly popular. This type of portfolio is generally created as a student Web page. Even very young children have created complex Web pages that demonstrated a classroom skill or concept.

SUMMARY

To design an effective classroom-based assessment process takes teacher planning and creativity. The process must incorporate and be closely tied to the instructional objectives of the course content as well as the needs and strengths of a particular student population (and, in Texas, to the state curriculum guides—the TEKS). As Competency 10

suggests, teachers should be aware of and use many different assessment techniques to ensure that all children have the opportunity to demonstrate their understanding and progress. In addition, teachers must collect assessment data frequently to evaluate the effectiveness of their instructional strategies and the depth and breadth of their children's understanding.

GLOSSARY

academic learning time (ALT) the time when children are actually understanding and succeeding at the learning task.

age-equivalent scores based on developmental norms. Reporting such scores assumes that all children of certain ages have developed specific levels of academic or social skills.

assessment a measurement appraisal process that is on-going, developmentally appropriate, and dynamic.

authentic assessment demonstrating a specific skill by constructing a product or solving a problem that could be generated from a real-life situation.

criterion-referenced tests use absolute standards (criteria) to answer specific questions about student achievement or mastery (PPR, TAAS). Passing requires answering a predetermined percentage of items correctly.

curriculum-based assessment the process that weaves curriculum to assessment and determines a student's instructional needs within the classroom curriculum (teacher-made tests).

domain an umbrella term that describes an area of the curriculum, such as basic math skills.

evaluation typically refers to all means used in schools to formally measure student performance or behavior and to make judgments based on the results of the programs or procedures being implemented.

formal assessment includes standardized or norm-referenced tests such as intelligence tests.

formative assessment data assessment data that show a student's progress or lack of progress toward curricular objectives during the process of instruction.

grade-equivalent scores based on developmental norms, reporting such scores assumes that all children or all children in certain grades have received uniform instruction.

informal assessment includes such items as work samples, portfolios, and projects, or oral questioning as well as other traditional and nontraditional ways of measuring students' understanding and progress.

norm-referenced tests   a test taker's performance is reported in relationship to other test takers in the same age or grade sample. Results are reported in standards scores, percentile ranks, or *t* or *z* scores.

observation   the careful watching and recording of events or behavior for later reflection and analysis.

observational data   data collected by the teacher through careful watching and charting of specific student behaviors.

percentile rank   standardized scores that compare an individual with other test takers and report that he/she scored as well as or better than a certain percentage of the norm sample.

performance-based assessment   an alternative assessment method based on a student's performance of a skill based on a real-life situation.

play-based assessment   an observational method for collecting assessment data about young children's social, motor, and cognitive skills.

portfolio   an authentic assessment tool used to assess student progress; consists of a collection of the student's work.

reliability   the consistency of test results over time. A reliable test is one that yields similar results time after time when administered to the same type or level of students and under the same conditions.

self-assessment   a process in which students reflect on their achievement and progress; student interviews and portfolios are often used as student self-assessments.

standard score   a statistical score based on the theoretical normal curve, with a mean and standard deviation; used to report standardized test information.

standardized test   a formal assessment measure in which an individual's performance is compared with others in the test norming sample.

summative data   assessment data collected after instruction to evaluate a student's mastery of the curriculum objectives and a teacher's effectiveness at delivering instruction.

teacher-made tests   informal measures of student progress based on the objectives of the curriculum and classroom instruction.

test bias   the fairness of the test.

validity   the truthfulness of the assessment information; does the score report really measure what it purports to measure?

SUGGESTED ACTIVITIES

1. Collect data about the assessment process used by your mentor, specifically: (a) the types of formative and summative assessment data are used and why; (b) frequency of assessment of children's understanding; (c) self-assessment of effectiveness at delivering instruction; (d) exisence of a formal, planned process; and (e) performance-based or authentic measures used.

2. Collect articles describing alternative assessment measures for elementary-aged or early childhood children. Plan how you could incorporate them in your future classroom.

3. Design a brochure for parents describing the relationship between TAAS (TAKS) or TPRI objectives and your classroom-based assessment program. Be sure that the brochure gives parents an indication of the difference between formal and informal assessment practices and the purpose of each.

4. Design a teacher-made test on the content of this chapter. Include one set of matching items, five true-false items, five multiple-choice items that assess application or analysis skills, and three essay questions that assess higher-level cognitive skills. Design a scoring rubric for your essay items.

5. Design a multi-level assessment process for your future classroom. Specify the types of formative and summative data you will collect, how you will accommodate student diversity in learning, and a schedule for data collection. Describe how you will use the information to improve instruction as well as evaluate student progress.

6. Make a collage of the types of assessment practices used to evaluate student progress. Your collage should demonstrate the definition and use of each assessment practice. Present your collage to three of your classmates and see whether they can interpret the point you are trying to illustrate.

7. Gather a collection of teacher-made tests (including one of your own). Evaluate them for test bias.

8. Find Internet resources for students in early childhood and/or elementary grades to create Web pages as electronic portfolios.

9. Reflect on your personal experiences with assessment practices in school. What kinds of activities did you like best or feel were a true reflection of your understanding and knowledge? Which ones made you feel threatened or less competent? Write your thoughts as a reflective journal entry or letter to the editor of an educational publication.

10. Make an audio- or videotape of your reactions to such assessment practices as portfolios, standardized tests, teacher-made tests, and/or grades. Share your tape with a peer and ask for his or her reactions.

11. Design a survey for your classmates, requesting input about their experiences with assessment processes in school. Collect the data and analyze the results to share with the class.

12. Think back on a test or other assessment techniques you felt were unfair. Try to determine from your current knowledge the reason for your feelings.

13. Visit an early childhood or kindergarten classroom, or interview a teacher of young children about the ways he or she collects assessment data for grading young children.

PRACTICE QUESTIONS

1. Ms. Jenkins teaches fourth-grade Language Arts. Each year she has her children keep a notebook of their work. Ms. Jenkins has specific questions tied to the course objectives that each child must answer by incorporating work samples in his or her notebook. She has weekly conferences with each child to determine whether he or she is keeping up with the notebook and choosing appropriate artifacts to include. At the end of each grading period, Ms. Jenkins collects the notebooks and evaluates each child's mastery of the objectives she covered during the 6 weeks. The child's grade is determined solely by the workbook collection. Ms. Jenkins is using the students' workbooks as:

A. Formative and summative evaluation data

B. Traditional and criterion-referenced evaluation data

C. Standardized and curriculum-based assessment data

D. Formal and curriculum-based assessment data

2. In Ms. Yuan's pre-kindergarten class, she uses comprehension questions about children's favorite books as a measure of their listening comprehension and sequencing skills (both are prereading skills). After reading the book to the class, she interviews each student individually and asks the same set of questions. She uses the interview information to determine specific skills to reteach. Ms. Yuan's assessment process could best be described as:

A. Standardized

B. Summative

C. Informal

D. Formal

3. Ms. Simpson constructed a 6-week test for her third-grade students on their social studies unit on dinosaurs. Her class is 30 minutes long and children were required to complete the test within the 30-minute period to receive full credit. Of her 25 students, only 8 were able to complete the test, and 60 percent of the class failed the test. To compensate, Ms. Simpson simply raised the highest grade of 80 by 10 points and adjusted all the rest of the children's test grades accordingly. After doing so, her final distribution of grades was acceptable: three students made As, eight made Bs, ten made Cs, three made Ds, and one made an F. Ms. Simpson's test would be described as:

A. Reliable and valid

B. Reliable, but not valid

C. Valid, but not reliable

D. Neither reliable nor valid

4. Mr. Seranos, a fourth-grade teacher, referred a student for special education assessment. The diagnostician discussed the types of assessment data required. She listed intelligence testing,

academic achievement testing, information from parents and teachers, and TAAS results. The intelligence test is all of the following *except*:

A. A norm-referenced test

B. A standardized test

C. An informal assessment

D. A formal assessment

Answers and Discussion

Answer 1: Because Ms. Jenkins meets her students individually on a regular basis to discuss their progress, she is gathering *formative* data that directs her teaching and the students' learning. In addition, she uses the notebooks as a *summative evaluation* of the students' progress during a specific grading period; that is, she uses the notebook to determine each student's 6-week grade. The answer is *A*.

Answer 2: Student interviews would be considered *informal* data. In this case, they are also *formative* because Ms. Yuan uses the data to make instructional decisions for individual children. The correct answer is *C*.

Answer 3: If the majority of the students can neither finish nor pass the test, Ms. Simpson should consider the test as *invalid* and *unreliable*. Either the test was not closely related to the instructional content of the course or the wording of the items was not precise enough for the students to interpret it correctly. In addition, the test was obviously too long for the students to complete in the time allotted. The answer is *D*.

Answer 4: An intelligence test is always *formal* and *standardized*, and it is usually *norm-referenced* because it yields standard scores based on the theoretical normal curve. The student or test taker is compared with others in his or her age group or the norm sample. The correct answer is *C*.

WEB LINKS

If sites are no longer operational, use key words from this chapter.

http://www.tea.state.tx.us/student.assessment

This site provides information about TAAS (TAKS) and TPRI objectives and other information regarding the assessment of Texas students. It also provides information about assessment topics relevant to teachers and students in Texas.

http.ericae.net

Click on resources for best practice in assessment. This site provides articles about assessment practices in U.S. classrooms.

http://www.indiana.edu/%7Eteaching/sfcats.htm

This site has practical suggestions for classroom-based assessment procedures. It also explains why classroom-based assessment is important for teachers and students. In addition, it has some really good suggestions for collecting formative assessment data that are quick, easy, and valid.

http://www.indiana.edu/%7Eteaching/formsum.html

This site has very good definitions of summative and formative evaluation. It is a one-page summary with examples.

http://www.lgu.ac.uk/deliberations/assessment

This site provides an excellent discussion of the purposes of assessment and why it should be a positive, helpful experience for students and teachers.

http://www.ncrel.org/sdrs/areas/rpl_esys/assess.htm

Provides up-to-date information about multidimensional and innovative classroom assessment strategies.

REFERENCES

Arends, R. I. (1998). *Learning to teach*. (4th ed.). Boston: McGraw Hill.

Armstrong, T. (1994). *Multiple intelligences in the classroom*. Alexandria, VA: The Association for Supervision and Curriculum Development.

Arter, J. A., & Spandel, V. (1992). Using portfolios of student work in instruction and assessment. *Educational Measurements: Issues and Practice, 11*(1), 36–44.

Blankenship, C. S. (1985). Using curriculum based assessment data to make instructional decisions. *Exceptional Children, 52,* 233–238.

Brown, S., Race, P., & Smith, B. (1996) *An assessment manifesto.* http://www.lgu.ac.uk/deliberations/assessment/manifes.html.

Cheong, J. I., & Shively, A. H. (1991). *Issues and reflections on implementing portfolio assessment systems, K–12.* Paper presented at the annual meeting of the California Education Research Association at Santa Barbara, CA.

Choate, J. S., Enright, B. E., Lamoine, J. M., Poteet, J. A., & Rakes, T. A. (1995). *Curriculum-based assessment and programming.* (3rd ed.). Boston: Allyn & Bacon.

Christiansen, J., & Vogel, J. R. (1998). A decision model for grading students with disabilities. *Teaching Exceptional Children,* November-December, 30–35.

Dunn, R., & Dunn, K. (1999). *The complete guide to the learning styles inservice system.* Boston: Allyn & Bacon.

Gardner, H. (1983). *Frames of mind: The theory of multiple intelligences.* New York: Basic Books.

Gickling, E. E., & Thompson, V. P. (1985). A personal view of curriculum based assessment. *Exceptional Children, 52*(1), 205–218.

Jensen, E. (1998). *Teaching with the brain in mind.* Alexandria, VA: ASCD.

Lawton, M. (1997). Discrimination claimed in Texas exit exam lawsuit. *Education Week 17,* http://www.edweek.org/ew/1997/08taas.h17

Mumme, J. (1990). *Portfolio assessment in mathematics.* Santa Barbara: University of California at Santa Barbara.

Nitko, A. J. (1996). *Education assessment of students.* Englewood Cliffs, NJ: Merrill.

Overton, T. (2000). *Assessment in special education.* Columbus, OH: Merrill.

Sattler, J. M. (1992). *Assessment of children: Revised and updated.* 3rd ed. San Diego: Sattler.

Shepard, L. A. (1995). Using assessment to improve student learning. *Phi Delta Kappa, 52*(5), 38–43.

Slavin, R. E. (1997). *Educational psychology: Theory and practice.* 5th ed. Boston: Allyn & Bacon.

Taylor, R. (2000). *Assessment of exceptional students: Educational and psychological procedures.* (5th ed.). Boston: Allyn & Bacon.

Torres, J. (1991). Equity in education and language minority students. *Forum, 14*(4), 1–3.

Ward. A. W., & Murray-Ward, M. (1999). *Assessment in the classroom.* Belmont, CA: Wadsworth.

Wiggins, G., & McTighe, J. (1998). *Understanding by design.* Alexandria, VA: ASCD.

Wilder, G. Z., & Powell, K. (1989). *Sex differences in test performance: A survey of the literature.* (College Board Rep. No. 89-3). New York: College Entrance Examination Board.

Chapter 16

COMPETENCY 10 – PART 2

Flexibility, Responsiveness, and Effective Feedback

VERÓNICA LÓPEZ ESTRADA

ISELA ALMAGUER

The University of Texas—Pan American

TERMS TO KNOW

Conference	K-W-L chart	Story maps
Context	Language Experience Approach	Writing process
Feedback	Reciprocal teaching	
Flexibility	Responsiveness	

THE EFFECTIVE TEACHER

As young children, we've all seen her, admired her, and wanted to be her—that elementary teacher who inspired us to follow in her footsteps. What was so special about her? What moved us to try to emulate her? Or maybe it was not a she, but a he. How were we able to recognize, even at a very young age, that this was an effective teacher? Was it knowledge of the subject matter? Was it a way of making children feel competent and special? Was it the manner in which she or he spoke to us as individual children and collectively as a whole class? Or, was it the way learning was made interesting and fun?

Even very young children are able to recognize a good teacher. Indeed, many teachers share the experience of being inspired by a teacher in their childhood whom they wish to emulate when they begin teaching in their own classrooms. Among the most common questions that future teachers have as they enter the profession are those that pertain to effectiveness in the classroom. But what makes an effective teacher effective? This chapter discusses the flexibility, responsiveness, and expertise of effective teachers.

Borich (2000) identifies five key teacher behaviors that are considered essential for effective teaching. These behaviors, consistently supported by research, include lesson clarity, instructional variety, teacher task orientation, engagement in the learning process, and student success rate. These key behaviors show that teachers must demonstrate **flexibility** and **responsiveness** in their teaching to provide optimal learning conditions in a classroom. For a teacher to be considered flexible and responsive, he or she must be aware of how learning is progressing during instruction and must react quickly to student needs by changing or modifying instruction appropriately.

For instance, if we take the first of Borich's (2000) teacher behaviors, *lesson clarity*, we may assume that this means that effective teachers are able to make their points understandable to children, keeping in mind their age and their cognitive and developmental levels; that they explain concepts clearly so that their students are able to follow in a logical and step-by-step order; and that they have an oral delivery that is clear, audible, and free of distracting mannerisms. Insofar as teachers prepare to teach lessons with clarity, it is imperative that they always leave room for flexibility and responsiveness in their plans because children do not always engage in their lessons or learning activities in exactly the way that was anticipated. Sometimes teachers find that one or more of their children do not want to participate, for whatever reasons (e.g., the subject is difficult, unfamiliar, or outside their worldview; they are excited or anxious about something else; they didn't get enough sleep the night before and so forth).

Also, when children just "don't get it," teachers must be ready to reteach on the spot, or teach the information in a new and different way. When children "get it" so quickly that it is redundant and unchallenging to have them continue with the plan, teachers must be flexible enough to jump ahead with them to maintain a forward learning pace. Perhaps a question, discovery, or other event is so exciting that the energy of the whole class is focused on it. The teacher should then use flexibility by leaving his or her original plan to use this teachable moment to engage students. In this case, the teacher's intrinsic motivation, as well as that of children, is high in learning for the sake of learning. Teachers must adjust and modify instruction to motivate children to participate in well-planned lessons. Being flexible and responsive in teaching means that teachers should be able to promote student learning by

(a) providing responsive instruction that makes use of effective communication techniques, (b) providing instructional strategies that actively engage children in the learning process, and (c) providing timely, high-quality feedback.

It is notable that the eminent scholar-philosopher of education of our time, John Dewey (1998), stated that education is essentially a social process and that effective educators must begin to teach by getting to know students, being responsive to their needs, and allowing for flexibility in lesson planning. Dewey's insights regarding flexibility and responsiveness in teaching were first published more than 60 years ago and continue to be relevant in our classrooms today.

RESPONSIVE INSTRUCTION MAKES USE OF COMMUNICATION TECHNIQUES

In the **context** of a classroom, effective communication between teachers and students is crucial to the teaching and learning process. It allows shared meaning to occur so that all members of the class (including the teacher) are on the same page. *Meaning negotiation* occurs in whole-class discussions, small-group activities, one-on-one talks between the teacher and student, and peer interactions. As a note, feedback should be seen as a two-way street. The teacher uses feedback from children to view windows on their past knowledge, new learning, and so forth, and then, in turn, gives feedback on that information. This continues until there is shared meaning or understanding. These patterns can occur quickly or over a long period of time in the classroom. Being responsive and allowing for flexibility in meaning negotiation should be modeled by teachers who act more as guides or facilitators of knowledge than dictators or dispensers of knowledge. Consider the following classroom discussion as a good example of a teacher who is demonstrating flexibility and responsiveness in her discussion with kindergartners about sea life. Note her effective questioning techniques and willingness to allow her children to share their prior knowledge and experiences with one another.

> **Mrs. Palomo:** Good morning boys and girls! Today we will begin a new unit on sea life. We are going to learn a lot of new and interesting facts about sea life. First we will create a **K–W–L chart** where we will write everything we *already know* about sea life. Then, we will write everything *we want to know* about sea life. Finally, after we finish studying sea life, we will go back to our K-W-L chart and write down everything *we learned* about sea life. Let's begin by writing down *what we know* about sea life. Who would like to share what they know? Raise your hand if you would like to share so that everyone can hear well.

> **Kendra** (raising her hand): There are lots of sea animals that swim in the sea. It's their home!

> **Sara** (interjecting excitedly): I went to the beach and saw a jellyfish in the water! My daddy said they are dangerous!

> **Mrs. Palomo:** You are both right! Let's write down that we know the sea is the home of many sea animals. Thanks for raising your hand, Kendra! Also, jellyfish are sea animals that can be dangerous. What else do we know about sea life that we can add to the chart? Joe, your hand was up.

> **Joe** (raising his hand): My daddy told me that sea turtles are extrincted because there are very few of them still alive. I hope more sea turtles are born.

> **Mrs. Palomo:** I agree! Let's write that sea turtles are becoming extinct. I hope that more sea turtles are born, too, Joe. Perhaps we can look in books or on the Internet to find out how many sea turtles are left. Maybe we could give people ideas or suggestions that will help to keep sea turtles from dying out or becoming extinct.

Joe: I think sea turtles are beautiful!

Mrs. Palomo: I think sea turtles are beautiful, too.

Larry (interjecting): I have a fish at home in my fish tank. His name is Fred, and he is blue. Well, kinda gray, but sorta blue. Maybe Fred wants to be in the sea with his brothers and sisters and his friends. Should I take him to the sea?

Mrs. Palomo: Good point, Larry! We can also have fish at home. Some fish live in salt water and others live in fresh water like the water in rivers and lakes, and some even live at home in a fish tank. What kind of water does Fred live in?

Larry: Well, when we clean out the tank, we put water from the faucet. It is not salty water. So I know that not all fish live in the sea because some live in water that is not salty, like Fred.

Mrs. Palomo: That's a very good observation, Larry! Let's add that to the chart. Not all fish are sea fish because some live in fresh water. I'm sure that Fred is happy in his fish tank because that is his freshwater home. What else can we add to the chart under K for things we know about sea life?

Maggie (raising her hand): Fish have different colors and shapes.

Mrs. Palomo: Maggie, yes! Thank you, too, for raising your hand. Let's add that to the chart. What are some of the colors that you've seen in fish, boys and girls?

Raul (raising his hand): ¡Maestra, yo sé que unos peces son azules, otros son verdes, y amarillos, y otros son morados!

Mrs. Palomo: ¡Muy bien, Raul! Vamos a agregar que peces vienen en muchos colores, por ejemplo, azul, verde, amarillo, y morado. Did some of you understand that, boys and girls? Raul said that fish come in blue, green, yellow, and purple. Let's add that to the chart. Let's find out

which fish come in many colors, like blue/azul, green/verde, yellow/amarillo, and purple/morado!

In this scenario, Mrs. Palomo shows her ability to be flexible and responsive in a discussion with her kindergartners, who responded excitedly to her questions. The children at times interject or interrupt one another's responses (as Sara does to Kendra, who raises her hand before responding, and Larry does to Joe in his discussion with Mrs. Palomo about sea turtles). Mrs. Palomo listens closely to her children's contributions and writes them down. Note that Mrs. Palomo does not say, "Sara, you've interrupted Kendra. Wait your turn!" or "Larry, Joe is talking now! You have to raise your hand to be recognized." Instead, she (a) considers the developmental stage of her children; (b) rewards those who follow her requests by acknowledging their raised hands; (c) gives oral feedback that is supportive and that leads to conclusions in some cases (certain fish need fresh water); and (d) encourages children to take risks. Also notice that Raul, an English Language Learner, is motivated to participate in this activity because, although he clearly comprehends this whole group discussion in English, his teacher allows him to speak in his native language, Spanish. Understanding that some English Language Learners are reluctant to try speaking in the language of instruction, Mrs. Palomo responds in an affirming and supportive manner that will encourage Raul to take risks in future classroom activities involving oral communication in English. Even if a teacher does not speak Spanish, a few words of praise can be easily learned in an ESL child's first language to confirm their participation with feedback ("muy bien," "bueno," etc.).

PROVIDING HIGH-QUALITY, TIMELY FEEDBACK

Feedback generally comes in three forms or types: (1) everyday oral feedback during class, (2) written feedback, and (3) grade reports. Reporting grades and achievement scores is an extrinsic motivator for students. By this we mean that grades and achievement scores motivate students to engage in an activity for extrinsic purposes or only because they want a good grade or don't want to fail—as opposed to doing it for the sake of learning something. However, giving thoughtful and timely attention to grades is a traditional part of a teacher's job. One of the biggest challenges of teachers is to inspire children to become intrinsically motivated to learn and, eventually, to be life-long learners. Effective teachers routinely provide feedback in oral and written forms to assess and evaluate student performance in their classrooms as well as to motivate their students to learn for intrinsic purposes. Teachers who consistently provide their children with timely, high-quality feedback enable them to use it to guide and enhance their learning.

For low-achieving students, feedback should focus on the encouragement of persistence in developing and on their accomplishment during the process of the particular learning event (e.g., "Look at you! You are already halfway through without a single error!" or "Oh, wow! I see that you are getting the first problem without my help!"). If teachers give low achievers the answers, sympathize, or praise them too much for obviously easy work instead of giving helpful cues and constructive feedback, these children begin to perceive that the teacher believes they are not capable. Teachers should offer feedback throughout the learning process for *every* learner. Knowing and understanding the characteristics of effective feedback for students, the role of timely feedback in the learning process, and how to use constructive feedback to guide each child's learning are key components of effective teaching.

Characteristics of Effective Feedback

Have you ever had a written paper returned with only a grade and no comments? Weren't you curious about what you did well or not so well? How you could do better next time? If you've done poorly, it is difficult to improve unless you know what to work on the next time. It is also hard to feel good about receiving a high mark without understanding what was exceptional so that those elements could become part of your repertoire of skills. Teachers must use appropriate language and formats to provide students with timely feedback that is substantive and specific rather than skimpy and vague.

Questioning is one way to gain information and give feedback. Burns, Roe, and Smith (2002) identify seven types of useful questions that guide reading and tap different types of comprehension and factors related to comprehension. Pay close attention to the language and format that these questions use to elicit specific responses from students, thus enabling and encouraging the teacher to provide high-quality feedback that pushes students to think.

1. *Main idea questions* help children to become aware of the relationship among details. "What is a sentence that explains what this selection is about?"

2. *Detail questions* ask for bits of information covered by the material. "Who was coming to play with Jack?" or "What was Lucas bringing to him?"

3. *Vocabulary questions* check children's understanding of word meanings as used in a particular selection. "What does the word *scale* mean in this sentence?"

4. *Sequence questions* check the child's knowledge of the order in which events occurred in the story. "What three things did Suzy and Sam do in order when they came home from school?"

5. *Inference questions* ask for information that is implied but not directly stated in the material, and they require that students read between the lines. "Do you think that Chato's intentions toward the family of mice were completely innocent throughout the story? Why or why not?"

6. *Evaluation questions* require students to make judgments about the material, and they depend on more than the information implied or stated by the text. The children must have enough experience related to the situations involved to establish standards for comparison. "Was Leon's decision to run away from home the best one he could have made? Why or why not?"

7. *Creative response questions* ask children to go beyond the material and create new ideas based on those they have read. These questions are recommended for class discussions but not for testing comprehension, because almost any response could be considered correct. "Had Jesse not turned in the money to its rightful owner, what do you think might have happened?" and "If you had special powers to change any one event in the story, what would it be, and why?" (adapted from Burns, Roe, & Smith, 2002).

A creative forum for developing and responding to these types of questions is the literature circle, which should be usable in most subject areas. Literature circles are groups that give students opportunities to read and respond to good literature, engage in high-level thinking about books, and do extensive and intensive reading (Burns, Roe, & Smith, 2002). In literature circles, also called "literacy circles," the teacher chooses several books of which multiple copies are available. She introduces each one and lets the children choose the one they want to read. Next she presents the books to the children. They read, or if they are unable to read them independently, she reads and then has children hold discussions about the books. The teacher may participate as a member in a group discussion if she so desires. Then the students respond in response journals or literature logs and help decide about ways to share the experience of the books.

Reading response journals and literature logs allow for the collection of reactions to the reading throughout the reading process—not just at the end—and can be the basis for small-group discussions for children in middle childhood, usually from second to fourth grades. When writing in their response journals or literature logs, children record personal interpretations, strategies for constructing meaning, questions that arise, and issues they want to discuss with others. When responding, either orally or in writing, teachers should offer supportive comments and encouraging suggestions that are motivating to students who find it difficult to finish a book. Oral and written feedback that validates students' thoughts and ideas frees students to take risks in responding to literature. Moreover, written entries provide important information about students' literacy development and become a source of informal assessment.

The following is a list of characteristics of effective feedback that applies to all types of writing assignments for children from early to middle childhood, or EC–4 grades (Soderman, Gregory, & O'Neill, 1999).

- Respond to children's writing thoughtfully and seriously, rather than in a typically "teacherly" way. Center on examples of what was good in the assignment and/or what needed improvement. Give helpful criticism both ways. For example, "I like the way you introduce the idea of acting responsibly as a citizen based on a personal experience" rather than "Good intro," or "Nice beginning paragraph," or "Needs more work."

- Teach by modeling correct usage, rather than correcting the child's mechanics, organization, spelling, or grammar. For example, if a child misspells a word, include the correct version of the word in your response. However, if you have established in a rubric that spelling is part of the grading criteria, be sure to correct the spelling above the word so that children can see their mistake quickly and easily.

- Keep your responses sensitive to the child's current level of understanding and functioning—very brief for kindergartners and first graders, and then expanded as the children's abilities expand.

- Vary the use of punctuation and word use.

- Respond with complete sentences and correct usage rather than informal phrases that could have the tendency to teach or support incorrect usage. At the same time, promote an interactive exchange that is more like a conversation between pen pals than teacher and student.

- If children write about personal problems within their family, respond seriously and thoughtfully with a possible strategy that can be used by the child, but do not take over the problem or try to manage it.

- Keep the focus on the child's agenda rather than on yours in order to keep "teacherness" out of the exchange or on an educational focus. You want to get children writing about *their* interests.

- When providing prompts for children, be sure they are open-ended and require more than simple answers for a response.

- Respond to children's writing with further questions or comments to extend their thinking processes rather than writing continuous questions. The return dialogue method in journaling is a wonderful way not only to reinforce the idea that writing conveys a message, but also to promote higher-level thinking skills. Simply asking children to clarify their written message for the reader or to expand on their idea does just that!

The Role of Timely Feedback in the Learning Process

A key element of behaviorism links faster and more thorough learning with immediate feedback. Psychologists, teachers, even those who work with training animals have used this theory for decades. Frequent and specific feedback usually results in greater learning (May & Rizzardi, 2002). *Frequent* and *timely* are key concepts. There are many ways to provide timely, frequent, and specific feedback in the classroom. Children who receive graded work some time after a concept has been covered do not make the same connections in learning as do children whose work is returned almost immediately. The sooner that feedback is delivered, the better the chance that children will reaffirm that what they were doing was correct, or make corrective changes. Practicing misconceptions or mistakes in skills makes it more difficult for a child to "unlearn and relearn." This is one reason that teachers ask children to check their classwork or homework "right then" rather than have the teacher take it home to grade. Note that it is no longer proper to have children check each other's papers. Children can be embarrassed by a "bad paper," but more importantly for feedback, the child needs to see what he or she did correctly or incorrectly as soon as possible. Of course, a teacher must correct any work to be recorded on report cards.

Teachers often use games for teaching or practicing essential sight words. Games such as Word Toss, Words in a Circle, See the Same, Word Point, and Stepword give students immediate and specific feedback that helps them remember content because it is grounded in an authentic, purposeful activity. Examples of feedback in game situations include: "You are correct! The word is *belief.* Advance two spaces." or "Sorry, the word is *belief,* not *believe.* Go back two spaces." Around-the-World is a competitive game that children particularly love. It provides immediate feedback and vicarious learning, and it can be played in any subject, in class, or in line. In class, a child stands behind a challenger. Any quick question, problem, or large flash card that can be seen by the whole class is presented (for example, a card with a triangle or a rectangle, to be identified as a particular shape). The first child to say the correct answer advances to the next challenger in line or in seating order. All children in the class hear a number of question, with the correct answers given immediately and reinforced by the teacher. The winner is the first child to make it "Around-the-World" to his or her own seat or space. This game should be played in many subject areas so that children with talent in different subject areas can win.

Of course, games are only one way to provide immediate, specific feedback to students. Many instructional strategies and practices facilitate discussions between teachers and students and open opportunities for teachers to provide timely feedback in the learning process. As mentioned in the previous section, teachers often offer timely, high-quality feedback to their students in teaching strategies and activities that include literature circles and interactive journal activities such as response journals and literature logs. Many other effective strategies encourage teachers to give timely, high-quality feedback to their students in EC–4 classrooms. The following are but a few examples: read-alouds, **Language Experience Approach** (LEA), discussion webs, semantic mapping, K-W-L, Directed Reading-Thinking Activity (DRTA), **story maps, reciprocal teaching,** the **writing process** (prewriting, drafting, revising, editing, publishing), and teacher and peer conferences. Some of these strategies are defined in the glossary of this chapter.

Using Constructive Feedback to Guide Students' Learning

One of the most important functions of using constructive feedback is to guide children's learning. The purpose of giving constructive feedback is to build or create understanding. Children do not need traditional criticism; they need constructive feedback that requires modeling on the part of their teachers and practice on the part of students (May & Rizzardi, 2002). Teachers of young children often feel that correcting a child in any manner through feedback is cruel or embarrassing, especially in front of a class—and it can be, if done in a demeaning manner! However, when teachers do not correct student errors, they leave children believing that their wrong answer was correct. Therefore, teachers must always let children know, within a supportive environment, whether or not their answers or thinking are correct. Children need to be confident that their risking an answer will result in kind feedback that is also constructive. Such statements as "You're

almost there," "Look back at step 2 for a second," or "You're on the right track" are more supportive than, "You're wrong," "Think harder," or "You're way off."

A typical teaching event that calls for teachers to offer constructive feedback is the writing process. In recent years, five steps have become standard in teaching the writing process: prewriting, drafting, revising, editing, and publishing. Every stage in the writing process opens opportunities for constructive feedback. For example, a teacher may start a writing unit by asking students to brainstorm topics about which they are interested in writing. She or he might begin by listing them on the chalkboard or on an overhead transparency. As students offer suggestions such as "What I Did During My Summer Vacation," "The Perfect Birthday Gift," "My Favorite Movie," "What I Want to Be When I Grow Up," and so on, teachers can offer constructive feedback as they "think aloud" about some of the processes of this prewriting activity. Reflect on the following scenario in a third-grade classroom.

> **Mr. Irwin:** Class, today I'm going to model the first step in the writing process by using one of the topics in our brainstorm activity. "What I Did During My Summer Vacation" seems like a good topic. What would I include if I were to write an essay on what I did during my summer vacation?

> **John:** How about places I visited—like Houston. My whole family went to see my cousins in Houston.

> **Mr. Irwin:** Wonderful idea! Places you visited, such as Houston, and people you saw. Let's create a word web that begins with a circle around the word "vacation." We'll extend a line and draw another circle with the word "places" and another extended from the word "places" that says—what?

> **John:** Houston!

> **Mr. Irwin:** Right. Now we'll extend another line from the word "vacation"

that says "people." What would come after that?

Margaret: Cousins?

Mr. Irwin: That's right, Margaret. To really develop this essay, I think we'll need more than just two ideas to build on, however. What else could we write about regarding summer vacation? Does someone have a suggestion?

Leslie: Some of us took lessons at the Boys and Girls Club. Like I took swimming lessons and volleyball. Can we write about that?

Mr. Irwin: Of course! What do you think we should do at this point in our word web, Leslie?

Leslie: Draw a line extending from "vacation" and draw another circle and write the word "lessons" in it?

Mr. Irwin: Yes. Can you come up to the board and do that? Okay, are you ready to organize your own now? What questions are there?

Class Members (responding simultaneously): I get it! I'm ready.

Krista: I have a question. I mean, do we have to write about places and people and lessons? I didn't go anywhere special this summer, and I didn't take any lessons.

Mr. Irwin: Good question, Krista. No, you do not have to write about places and people and lessons. Remember that this is just a sample word web to get us started. Now that we've got a sample on the board on this topic, I want all of you to create a word web on the topic of *your* choice on your own, and I will monitor if you get stuck or have any questions.

Krista: Any topic? Like I wanted to write about my brother going away to college and how I miss him so much. Is that okay?

Mr. Irwin: Absolutely, Krista. Why don't you get started on a word web in your

academic journal, and we'll go from there. Okay?

Krista: Okay!

Mr. Irwin does a good job of using constructive feedback to guide his children's understanding of how to construct a word web, organizing thoughts during the prewriting stage of the writing process. Notice how he responds to Krista in this scenario. Sometimes teachers should provide feedback that requires only a brief correction, as is the case with Krista, whereas other times a complete reteach is necessary because major misunderstandings are found. Mr. Irwin offers constructive feedback to all of his children in this scenario and models his metacognitive skills by thinking aloud during the process. After students finish their word webs and begin drafting, he plans to confer with his children to go over each of their drafts. Student/teacher **conferences** initiate opportunities to give constructive feedback that is personal, specific, and most importantly, supportive of students' learning. During conferences teachers are able to listen carefully to children and give individualized feedback on a specific paper, project, or other product in a formative manner. Teachers can often ask questions that clear up misconceptions. Walking the room (*monitoring*) during practice also allows teachers to gain feedback on misconceptions. Teachers who are constantly looking over children's shoulders catch mistakes immediately and can give almost instant, corrective feedback. A teacher who attends to other business when children are working or practicing skills, or spends too long with one or two students, loses this opportunity. "Be there, be quick, and be gone," is a good motto for teachers who wish to give feedback to a class and also be sure that children do not depend on feedback to continue working. Visuals that show strategies, steps, or other important information also offer quick, supportive ways to give feedback to children. "You have Step 1 done correctly, but take a look at Step 2 on our poster," or "Tell me where you are now . . . so what comes next if you look up at the overhead graphic organizer?" or "Look up on the board at what we brainstormed today," or "Look up at the color chart for blue and pick a good $10 adjective . . . azure? Yes!" are all good ways to encourage children to seek their own feedback when needed.

Reporting Progress

Parents and caregivers want and need to know about the progress of their children. Most often, feedback is given through report cards, progress reports (at the midpoint of a grading period), conferences, and other, less formal reports, such as phone calls or emails. Most early childhood programs begin with checklist reports and move into traditional grades in the later elementary years. Reporting progress can sometimes be a wrenching process, but it can be made easier with the following suggestions, including some from McAfee & Leong (2002):

- Make a plan for grading at the beginning of each grading period. First, investigate the number of grades required by the school for each subject area. Then, looking through your long-range plans, decide which assignments will be counted (class work, writing assignments, tests, etc.). Then decide whether certain assignments will count more than others (projects, tests, etc.). Plan to make copies for caregivers of work that illustrates key examples of learning. This plan can certainly be modified as the grading period continues, but it will avoid a rush right before a grading period to collect enough grades for a report card. You may find it important to show the plan to parents or administrators who have questions about a student's grade. Set up a traditional and/or an electronic grade book with this plan in mind, and maintain it faithfully.

- Distinguish between formative and summative progress, and record only summative work. In other words, allow children to make mistakes when they are first learning without

fear that it will count against them on a report card.

- Use a rubric or other such method to specify grades ahead of time. Children can often match expectations if they understand them. Parents, too, can more easily understand a grade when a rubric is presented. The use of a rubric or checklist can also keep teachers from comparing children against each other for a grade or grading on a curve. The comparison method is not a fair one when reporting to caregivers what a child has and should have accomplished.

- Teachers often want to report behavior as part of a grade, but a grade in a subject area should represent only skills and learning. Use the category dealing with social skills or the comments section to indicate behavior assessment. Remember also that caregivers may be confused if they perceive that students can receive a higher (or lower) grade because of their effort. A subject area grade is to be reported as academic achievement only.

- Teachers should remember that this report is part of a permanent record that will follow a child throughout his or her school years. Therefore each entry should be made objectively and with the utmost seriousness.

Schools normally have at least two required conferences a year in which teachers sit down with caregivers and explain progress. Ideally teachers have many other opportunities to share reports of progress. When conducting conferences, teachers should begin and end with successes rather than shortcomings. They should have selective examples of student work that demonstrate achievement (or lack of achievement), with examples that clearly illustrate basic expectations for the student's grade level. Rubrics and student examples (although examples should not be children's work from this particular class or have names attached) can be helpful. Teachers should explain specifically, without educational jargon, the child's successes or difficulties. Vague generalities such as, "He's having some problems with math" should be avoided. When writing or orally giving anecdotal comments, teachers should give caregivers some direction ("Sharon could profit by practicing more place-value problems.")

If teachers are not straightforward with all of their reports, caregivers may feel shocked at the end of a reporting session or at the end of the year. Kindly and with sensitivity, but with honesty, give your professional assessment of academic achievement so that all can work together to continue to help the child. Put together a plan for the future, including realistic suggestions of how caregivers can help. If a child is included in the reporting conference, ask him or her to explain some of the achievement of which he or she is proud and some areas for improvement.

Above all, remember that caregivers have questions about the achievement of their children. The more teachers can plan ahead of time to answer those questions and defend their rationale in reporting, the more comfortable and fruitful the conference will be. Parents have a right to see their child's records (although not in comparison to other children's), and there is a process for parents who wish to contest grades or written comments that they feel are not fair. To maintain understanding, always put yourself in a parent's place during reporting. If you, as a parent, would like to know exact details about the academic learning of your child (in a professional manner), follow that format. If you would like to read certain helpful comments about your child, write in that manner. By reporting in an objective and professional manner, teachers find that caregivers often become strong partners in helping children achieve. For more information on holding conferences, see Competency 11, Chapter 17.

SUMMARY

Teachers are most effective in the classroom when they present their lessons to students at the appropriate level of understanding, while also making room for flexibility and responsiveness. Because children do not always engage in learning activities in the way that teachers wish, instruction must be adjusted in order to motivate children to participate in well-planned lessons. Being flexible and responsive in teaching means that teachers should promote learning by providing responsive instruction that makes use of effective communication techniques and by providing timely, high-quality feedback.

GLOSSARY

conferences   interactions that take place to discuss assignments, events, creations, or progress in any academic area; may be teacher-student conferences or peer-peer conferences in addition to teacher-caregiver conferences.

context   the whole situation or background relevant to a certain event or creation.

feedback   the response given after an action has taken place; in the context of the classroom, there is student and teacher feedback.

flexibility   referring to a teacher, this means being open and willing to accept changes and modifications while teaching.

K-W-L   an instructional activity for expository texts; stands for "what I know, what I want to know, and what I learned." Other versions consist of: K-W-L Plus, K-W-W-L, and K-W-L with focus questions.

Language Experience Approach   the approach whereby a common experience is shared among students who dictate the experience to a teacher who acts as a scribe, writing down the personal experience to form a coherent and informative narrative.

reciprocal teaching   a strategy for teaching comprehension and self-monitoring skills, this technique requires that teachers and students take turns predicting, generating questions, clarifying, and summarizing ideas based on text.

responsiveness   referring to a teacher, this means acknowledging differences in students' experiences and prior knowledge, and using these differences to respond with understanding.

story maps   a graphic representation that aids students in their development and use of a sense of story; used by the teacher to list major events and ideas that make up the story and to generate questions for the guided reading of any narrative.

writing process the process consisting of prewriting strategies, drafting, revising, editing, and publishing. It is used to help students become better writers as they receive timely feedback from the teacher.

SUGGESTED ACTIVITIES

1. Role-play a scenario in which a teacher shows flexibility and responsiveness in response to a child who says, "Robert always answers your questions. He must be smarter than me."

2. Observe a certified teacher in a local public school. Write a journal entry in which you note the teacher's use of constructive feedback to the students. Indicate the extent to which the teacher's use of constructive feedback was effective in guiding student comprehension of content-area material.

3. Write a comment that you would include on a report card for the following situations:

   a. A child is academically advanced but has bad behavior.

   b. A child is academically advanced but does not do assigned work.

   c. A child is not as academically advanced but does all work—incorrectly.

4. Review report cards and progress reports that your mentor has prepared for students. Discuss with your mentor the criteria used to arrive at those assessments.

5. Videotape a lesson that you teach. Note the following interactions:

   a. Letting a child know his answer was correct or incorrect.

   b. Correcting wrong answers suppportively.

   c. Use of redundant terms ("Good!") versus use of more meaningful feedback.

PRACTICE QUESTIONS

Mrs. Cobos has been teaching fourth grade for many years. Her class of 24 students is made up of 13 boys and 11 girls. They are a diverse group, eth-nically and academically. Mrs. Cobos believes in creating an environment that respects students. When assigning roles and responsibilities, she is careful to deal ethically and fairly with all students. Her philosophy is "Every child can learn and be successful." She expects this, and her children know it. Parents like Mrs. Cobos, and they want their children in her classroom because children do well there.

Mrs. Cobos has planned a thematic unit on the environment. On an outside tour of the school, the students work in pairs collecting trash and dumping it into one large bag. "Look at all the trash," says Tom. "Yes," says Robert, "it makes our school look bad." Martha wants to know whether everyone has that much trash. Students begin to voice dismay about how much people throw away. "Is there going to be room for us with all this trash in the world?" asks Jay. Mrs. Cobos responds to the whole class, "What do you think about Jay's concern?" A lively discussion follows. Justin suggests, "I know what we can do to help get rid of the trash." "What?" Rodney asks. "We can recycle," says Justin. Robert asks, "Do you mean at school?" Several students agree, "Yes, that's a great idea!" Mrs. Cobos says, "What will you recycle?" After further discussion, the class decides to collect newspapers and aluminum cans for recycling. Natalia proposes that they involve the entire school, and the rest of the class agrees. Mrs. Cobos comments, "You have done lots of good thinking today, boys and girls. This will be a fine project for our class."

1. Mrs. Cobos's question to the whole class, "What do you think about Jay's concerns?" is an example of:

   A. Using a student's contribution to make a point

   B. Modifying a student's contribution by putting it into different words to make it more understandable to the rest of the class

   C. Using a student's contribution as an example

   D. Acknowledging a child's contribution by using it to stimulate additional discussion

2. The discourse orchestrated by Mrs. Cobos among the students and with herself *best* illustrates which of the following?

   A. Children demonstrate a connection of their learning to other disciplines.

   B. Children consistently take reasonable risks in responding to the teacher or peers.

   C. Children are consistently engaged in appropriate self-management.

   D. Student assessment is aligned with real-life applications.

3. Mrs. Cobos realizes that she needs to know what children understand about recycling. To obtain this information, all of the following would be appropriate *EXCEPT:*

   A. Evaluation questions

   B. Semantic mapping

   C. Webbing

   D. Whole-class discussion

4. Mrs. Cobos knows that reporting grades is an important skill for teachers. She reflects on ways to ensure that she gives effective feedback about her children's progress. She should adhere to all of the following suggestions *EXCEPT:*

   A. Academic grades should be separate from behavior grades.

   B. Both formative and summative work should be graded and recorded.

   C. Rubrics should be used to avoid subjectivity and should be shared with parents and children.

   D. Make sure to know how many grades per period the school requires, and adhere to those guidelines.

Answers and Discussion

Answer 1: Eliminate *A* and *C* because Mrs. Cobos is not making a point with Jay's concern nor is she using it as an example; she is merely calling attention to it. Eliminate *B* because Mrs. Cobos did not modify Jay's contribution. Mrs. Cobos uses Jay's contribution as a springboard for further class discussion. The answer is *D*.

Answer 2: The discourse in a classroom is an integral part of active learning. Effective teachers know how to create a climate of trust, respect, support, and inquiry in which students consistently take reasonable risks in responding to the teacher or peers. The answer is *B*.

Answer 3: Mrs. Cobos recognizes that teachers should be proactive in ensuring that prior learning for new learning is in place. She is likely to understand that this can be accomplished through informal assessments. She might use an advance organizer such as semantic mapping (eliminate *B*) or webbing (eliminate *C*) that helps students see the structure of key concepts and topics, or she might choose to have a whole-class discussion (eliminate *D*). Because evaluation questions involve students' judging or valuing, they would be inappropriate as a means to determine prior knowledge. The answer is *A*.

Answer 4: In this question we are looking for the choice that contradicts best practice. Choice *A* is advisable because teachers should report progress in skills without confounding those accomplishments with behavioral assessments. It is for this reason that report cards often list behavior grades as a separate category. Choice *C* is advisable so that teachers, children, and caregivers are all clear as to the expected standards involved in a grade. Choice *D* is imperative because a teacher is a member of the school community and must adhere to all school policies. Choice *B* is ill advised because children need to be able to take risks and make mistakes as they learn. Their formative assessments can help them understand their strengths and weaknesses as they are learning new skills, but they should not be recorded or counted in their final grades. The answer is *B*.

WEB LINKS

Remember that Web site locations may change. If any of these sites have moved or cannot be located, use the Terms to Know in this chapter to search for further information.

http://www.ri.net/RIDE/prodevelopment/
webstandards.html

This site provides an overview for professional development, reflecting an emphasis on high standards, effective instruction, and quality assessment for learners.

http://www.crede.ucsc.edu/standards/
standards.html

This site includes CREDE standards for effective pedagogy and has helpful tips for fostering critical thinking while being responsive to student contributions.

http://goal.ncrel.org/litweb/index.html

This site contains content such as self-assessment checklists for demonstrating flexible grouping, effective management, and being responsive to student needs in teaching.

http://www.ciera.org/library/archive/index.html

This site provides the latest research in effective teaching practices and helps demonstrate new forms of instruction and assessment.

http://naaee.org/npeee/initialprep/guidelines.html

This site helps teachers design flexible and responsive instruction and make assessment and evaluation an integral part of the teaching process.

REFERENCES

Borich, G. S. (2000). *Effective teaching methods* (4th ed.). Upper Saddle River, NJ: Merrill/Prentice Hall, Inc.

Burns, P., Roe, B., & Smith, E. (2002). *Teaching reading in today's elementary schools* (8th ed.). Boston, MA: Houghton Mifflin Company.

Dewey, J. (1998). *Experience and education: The 60th anniversary edition.* Kappa Delta Pi, an International Honor Society in Education. West Lafayette, IN: Kappa Delta Pi Publications.

May, F. B., & Rizzardi, L. (2002). *Reading as communication.* (6th ed.). Upper Saddle River, NJ: Merrill/Prentice Hall, Inc.

McAfee, O., & Leong, D. (2002). *Assessing and guiding young children's development and learning.* Boston: Allyn and Bacon.

Soderman, A. L., Gregory, K. M., & O'Neill, L. T. (1999). *Scaffolding emergent literacy: A child-centered approach for preschool through grade 5.* Needham Heights, MA: Allyn & Bacon.

Domain IV

Fulfilling Professional Roles and Responsibilities

Competency 11

The teacher understands the importance of family involvement in children's education and knows how to interact and communicate effectively with families.

The beginning teacher:

- Applies knowledge of appropriate ways (including electronic communication) to work and communicate effectively with families in various situations.

- Engages families, parents, guardians, and other legal caregivers in various aspects of the educational program.

- Interacts appropriately with all families, including those that have diverse characteristics, backgrounds, and needs.

- Communicates effectively with families on a regular basis (e.g., to share information about students' progress) and responds to their concerns.

- Conducts effective conferences with parents, guardians, and other legal caregivers.

- Effectively uses family support resources (e.g., community, interagency) to enhance family involvement in student learning.

Chapter 17

Interacting and Communicating with Families

JENNIFER L. MARTIN
JO ANN ENGELBRECHT
LILLIAN CHENOWETH
Texas Woman's University

TERMS TO KNOW

Family diversity

Parent

Family involvement

Types of involvement

Beginning teachers may wonder why encouraging family involvement with schools is considered one of the most important competencies needed by Texas EC–4 teachers. Although the teacher's most immediate and pressing focus may be planning and actual classroom instruction, the impact of family involvement cannot be ignored. "Despite real progress in many states, districts, and schools over the past few years, there are still too many schools in which educators do not understand the families of their students; in which families do not understand their children's schools; and in which communities do not understand or assist the schools, families, or students" (Epstein, 1995, p. 711). **Family involvement** encompasses all interactions between school and home that support student achievement. Similar terms are "family-school partnerships" and "home-school relationships." Classroom teachers have a major effect on family involvement; in turn, this involvement has been shown by an increasing body of research to have major benefits for children, parents, teachers, and schools. No longer can collaboration with the families of students be considered simply a "nice enhancement" to teachers' primary responsibilities. Building strong home-school relationships is one of a teacher's chief tasks.

Federal, state, and local policies have supported the effort to involve families through legislation, mandates, and guidelines (Epstein, 1995). For example, the eighth goal of the National Education Goals, as set out in the Goals 2000: Educate America Act, states: "Every school will promote partnerships that will increase parental involvement and participation in promoting the social, emotional, and academic growth of children" (U.S. Department of Education, 1994). Similarly, in the Texas Education Agency's 1995 publication, *Learner-Centered Schools for Texas: A Vision of Texas Educators*,

proficiencies outlining the skills and attitudes educators should possess to be successful in the coming century were described. Throughout the proficiencies, the importance and necessity of family-school involvement are stressed. Despite clear guidance on the importance of family involvement, limited attention to preparing teachers for this role has been given in teacher education programs (Powell, 2000). As schools increasingly involve families in their children's education, teachers must be prepared for the role of facilitating home-school relationships. Instead of viewing this expanded role as a burden, teachers must recognize the benefits of family-school involvement in helping them achieve their primary goal—the educational success of all students.

Many reform efforts have attempted to improve school performance without complete success; as a result, research continues to focus on a number of variables related to students, schools, and teachers. Recommendations from the National Association for the Education of Young Children (NAEYC, 1996) and research over the last decade have underlined the extent to which families are involved in the educational process as a major key to student success (Kellaghan et al., 1993). The family and the school are major influences on a child, and successful learning cannot be attributed to either one alone but to their joint efforts (Robinson & Fine, 1994; Seeley, 1982). Both families and schools are highly invested in assuring student success, and collaborating toward that common goal can be good for everyone involved.

Benefits of family involvement for students include:

- Improved grades
- Improved test scores
- Improved attitudes

- Improved behavior

- More completed homework

- More engagement in classroom learning activities

- Higher attendance rates

- Reduced suspension rates

- Lower dropout rates (Christenson & Cleary, 1990; Comer, 1984; Jones & White, 2000; National Center for Education Statistics, 1992)

In summarizing research about benefits for students, Epstein (1990) suggested that students at all levels do better academically and have better attitudes about school when parents are "aware, knowledgeable, and encouraging about school" (p. 105).

Families benefit when they collaborate in their children's education. Some of the benefits include:

- Increased parental interactions with children at home

- Better feelings about their ability to help their students

- More positive ratings of teachers

- More understanding of how schools operate

- Better communication with their children, particularly about schoolwork

- Increased level of communication with educators (Christenson & Cleary, 1990; Epstein, 1984; Epstein & Becker, 1982; Epstein & Dauber, 1991)

Teachers, too, experience benefits as they collaborate with families. Examples include:

- More positive feelings about teaching and their school

- More positive ratings of teaching ability and interpersonal skills by parents and principals

- More teacher self-confidence

- Willingness to continue and expand practices to involve families

- Heightened expectations of and appreciation for families as educational partners

- Greater job satisfaction

- Fewer transfers requested (Christenson & Cleary, 1990; Epstein, 1985; Epstein, 1992; Epstein & Dauber, 1991; Hoover-Dempsey, Bassler, & Brissie, 1987; Leitch & Tangri, 1988)

This chapter examines the importance of building strong relationships between schools and the diverse families of today's children. In addition, methods for encouraging and bringing about strong home-school partnerships will be explored. Specific topics include interacting with diverse families, communicating with families, conducting effective parent/teacher conferences, and engaging families in children's education.

INTERACTING WITH PARENTS OF VERY YOUNG CHILDREN

As children grow, many parents have a tendency to become less involved in their schooling on a day-to-day basis. However, parents of very young children often need to feel reassured of their child's well-being at school and with a teacher. Teachers who introduce themselves to families before the beginning of school through a short letter, postcard, telephone call, or email (when possible) are making a positive move that welcomes families into their rooms. For families with a firstborn child, Pre-K, kindergarten, or even first grade may be the first time a child has been to school and out of the care of a parent or other close family member. Welcoming "parties" during the first few days of school can sometimes make this break less difficult. Showing caregivers that the teacher understands their emotions can also make a difference in the way they see the environment of their child's classroom.

Being there to greet children and their caregivers each morning shows teacher interest and caring as well. Teachers should be ready to assure parents calmly that they will help their child become interested in the classroom quickly. Teachers should be ready to comfort children but also have motivating and enjoyable activities ready to draw them in at the beginning of the day. If a parent does not want to leave and the teacher feels that it will not create an even greater problem, he or she can ask the parent to check in with the office and then come back to help read to a group or volunteer in some way. If it is felt that a caregiver's presence is problematic, the teacher should calmly and comfortingly let him or her know that duties must begin; children need to begin to work; and that they should check back during the teacher's planning period, lunch, or recess. It is difficult to manage a class in which a caregiver is attempting to have a conference during class time. Caregivers should be told that the teacher has an obligation to monitor all children just then, but that conference periods are set just for the purpose of being able to give full attention to their concerns.

Teachers should also realize that those who teach at the early childhood levels are often glorified to parents. Parents can seem resentful when their child reports the same strong feelings of love and care about their teacher that he or she once had *only* for the parents.

As the first or second teacher a child has, the Pre-K or kindergarten teacher is often the first to see developmental or other types of difficulties and/or strengths. It is particularly important to communicate early on any thoughts about the needs of young children and to welcome caregivers to the school. Pre-K and kindergarten teachers set the stage for all parental involvement that follows in schools. It is a great responsibility that teachers in the later grades will appreciate.

INTERACTING WITH DIVERSE FAMILIES

A relationship is "a connection; the state or condition that exists between people or groups that deal with one another" (Barnhart & Barnhart, 1983). Forming positive relationships with the primary caregivers—birth parents, adoptive parents, stepparents, foster parents, extended and fictive (nonrelatives considered to be family) family members, and guardians—is foundational to home/school collaboration. For the purposes of this chapter, the word **parent** refers to anyone who carries out the responsibility of caregiver for a child. Recognizing the importance of family involvement, teachers are challenged to create opportunities to build relationships. Positive relationships are built over time and are based on a common interest and familiarity. The central common interest between parents and teachers is the well-being and success of the child.

Some schools attempt to build familiarity with an open-door policy that invites family members to visit the school at any time. Although this is a positive policy, it does not reach out to all families because it is not a specific opportunity and may involve some risk-taking for those unfamiliar with or uncomfortable in a school setting (Nielsen & Finkelstein, 1993). Familiarity is best facilitated by personal contact during which the parent and teacher share information about their lives and interests, as well as their goals and concerns for the child. Teachers are encouraged to maximize informal opportunities that may occur when younger children are dropped off or picked up (Berger, 1996) or during a chance meeting at the grocery store or shopping center, but specific opportunities for relationship building should be created throughout the year. It is a common practice for schools to conduct conferences at which teachers primarily listen and parents share early in the school year (Nielsen & Finkelstein, 1993), and some teachers conduct home visits before the beginning of the school year. These are excellent examples of relationship-building opportunities. Recognizing that these practices cannot occur in all situations, schools and teachers can still facilitate the contact and sharing that build relationships through phone calls, interest surveys, interactive homework, "back and forth" folders, email messages, voice mail systems, and more traditional strategies such as open houses and newsletters. The specific vehicles used to develop relationships are less important than the overall understanding of the value of building and maintaining a positive alliance with families. Three beliefs facilitate a full and equal partnership between families and schools: (1) that both family and school bring something meaningful and valuable to the relationship, (2) that both share a commonality—the child's welfare, and (3) that both share a responsibility around common goals (Workman & Gage, 1997).

To understand children, teachers must understand families. Children bring their family experiences and background with them to school so the context of a family's culture, characteristics, and circumstances must be taken into account. Understanding families is an important prerequisite to creating partnerships between families and schools (Diffily, 2001). Only after understanding and appreciating the diversity in families can we create successful strategies for involvement and partnership.

The typical American family today differs from that of a generation ago or from our perception of what is "typical." **Family diversity** today includes: (a) diversity of cultural background, (b) differences in family characteristics and structure, and (c) circumstances or situational differences. These differences result in diverse languages, economic situations, customs, attitudes, behaviors, and values.

Students today come from a wide range of backgrounds and milieus that may be quite different from those of their teachers. It is imperative for teachers to become aware of similarities and differences in families in order to reach out and respond in sensitive and appropriate ways. For example, parents may be very young and single. Some parents are even incarcerated, and their children live with relatives or friends. Children may live in stepfamilies or families with same-sex parents. Parents may be homeless, living with their children in shelters. They may be extremely wealthy, providing their children with many more experiences than the teacher has had.

Most parents, whatever their background, want their children to succeed. However, they may possess attitudes that are barriers to involvement in schools. Family members may see teachers as authorities or experts who are not to be questioned. They may feel that the only reason teachers want to talk to them is that their child is in trouble or is having problems. Teachers have to be careful not to assume that the way in which they were raised is the only right way. Remember, too, that children cannot choose their families.

Teachers may find that families have a deeply engrained culture. If they are recent immigrants, they may be tied to the customs and traditions of their native land. If *you* were to move to another country, would you want (and want your family) to give up the holidays and cultural and religious traditions of your native land, or would you adopt new holidays and new practices easily? Would you still prefer to gather with other Americans for "a traditional" Thanksgiving or July 4th? Sometimes it is difficult to give up or trade the old for new ways. Culturally sensitive approaches must be developed for families served by each school to take this diversity into account.

Differences in family characteristics and structure are also important to understand. There have been dramatic demographic changes in families and family configurations. The reality is that the mythical all-American family consisting of an employed dad and a stay-at-home mom with children is a very small percentage of all families today. Married couples with children are less than 30 percent of all United States households (U.S. Census Bureau, 2001). Approximately one in four Texas families with children is headed by a single parent (Annie E. Casey Foundation, 2001). According to the U.S. Census Bureau, the majority of children who live with a single parent live with their mother. About 40 percent of these children live with mothers who have never been married. Most of these households have no other adults present; indeed, 6 percent of all United States children under age 18 live in the household of their grandparents, and many of these children have no parent present (Lugaila, 1999). Teachers must be aware and accepting of the impact on children of various situations, such as different roles of fathers, including noncustodial fathers; grandparents or other family members; single parents; cohabiting partners; and stepfamilies. Efforts must be made to keep as many caregivers as possible informed, particularly noncustodial parents. This may take more time but may enhance the parent–child relationship. Although a few noncustodial parents do not care about their children, most do care deeply; and teachers may be certain that *children* care that both parents receive information—especially if the news is positive.

Family circumstances or situational differences must also be considered in planning partnerships. One example of such a difference is the amount of spendable income available to a family. This difference significantly affects the quality of life and the ability of a family to meet the needs of the children. The amount of income makes both obvious and subtle differences. Income influences diet, health care, housing, and child care, as well as other resources available—clothes, school supplies, equipment, time, telephone, computer access, at-home books, educational toys, and choices. Money may influence family stress, safety, conflict, and feelings of despair or hopelessness.

Approximately one in four children in Texas lives in poverty (Annie E. Casey Foundation, 2001). Because many families move into and out of poverty, almost 40 percent of all children will experience poverty at some point in their lives (Kacapyr, 1998). About 10 percent of all Texas children live in *extreme* poverty. Thus, incomes only reach halfway to the *poverty* level (Annie E. Casey Foundation, 2001).

Families have changed, but many stereotypes have not. Teachers may have to change their understanding of what a family is and maybe even what a family does. Because teachers may have unrealistic expectations, it is important for them to examine any personal prejudices and preconceived ideas about families. Acknowledging differences rather than deficits is a crucial step toward accepting diversity.

A successful model for working with families must acknowledge that (a) all families have some strengths; (b) different family forms exist and are legitimate to the children involved; and (c) the job of teachers is to reach out and respond to children from all types of families. The model should be a culturally sensitive one that does not attribute the causes of family problems to personal deficiencies. This orientation attempts to help families express their needs and goals, and then collaborate to help children achieve success. Teachers are challenged to build on family strengths rather than just remediate deficits.

Cultural competence includes the critical elements of self-awareness, knowledge specific to unique cultures, and skills to engage in successful interactions. In developing cultural competence, teachers must first become aware of their own values and assumptions, as well as their own heritage and roots.

To learn about other cultures, contexts, communication styles, and values, it is helpful for all teachers to expose themselves to literature, music, art, movies, and foods representative of other backgrounds. Creating opportunities to interact with people different from themselves will help teachers be more comfortable in interactions. If possible, they should challenge themselves to move outside the familiar and participate in the daily life and language of a different culture or situation. Certainly, if teachers live outside the community in which they teach, they should make an effort to become familiar with the neighborhood of their students and the opportunities and stresses that are a part of children's lives there. Instead of viewing behavior or beliefs as negative or deficient because they do not conform to certain expectations, teachers must be open to accept what other cultures offer. Teachers must be careful not to impose their particular values and beliefs on others. A teacher cannot demand, for example, that a vegetarian student eat the whole cafeteria meal (including meat) because the teacher "feels" that it is healthier to do so, nor can a teacher encourage a child whose religion forbids birthday or holiday celebrations and who they may feel is missing out to stay at the class party and enjoy a treat.

Teachers can identify the characteristics and circumstances of families that make a difference in communication and design unique strategies for family collaboration (Powell, 1998). For example, Asian parents, in general, value punctuality and formality. They may perceive the teacher as rude if they arrive on time for a conference and the teacher is not ready to begin. Some cultures address situations more aggressively than others. This can put one party in a defensive mode. Parents with particular religious beliefs have a constitutional right to withdraw their children from certain activities, such as standing for the Pledge of Allegiance, singing patriotic songs, or eating specific foods. They are likely to approach the teacher with firmness, and their wishes must be honored. Acknowledging unique differences is always valuable.

COMMUNICATING WITH FAMILIES

Teachers have numerous opportunities to devise effective forms of communication with parents. A major task is to design effective school-to-home and home-to-school communication opportunities (Epstein, 1995). An imperative of effective communication is that it not be one-way; rather communication should be redefined to include "two-way, three-way, and many-way channels of communication that connect schools, families, students, and the community" (Epstein, 1995, p. 706). Whenever possible, communication should be in the home language of the families. These communications can take many forms, such as:

- Teacher conferences
- Folders of student work sent home for review and comments
- Availability of translators for families who do not speak English or have limited English proficiency
- Caregiver/student report card pickup, with teachers present for informal conferences
- Phone calls, if possible, both positive and negative in content

- Newsletters
- Effective information on choosing schools, classes, programs of study, and so on
- Clear information on school policies and changes
- Voicemail homework hotlines
- Teacher and school email
- Web sites with updated information on school activities and opportunities

The Importance of Communication

Communication with families has benefits for students, parents, and teachers. Students experience the following positive effects:

- An awareness of their progress and the actions needed to maintain or improve their grades
- An understanding of school policies on behavior, attendance, and student conduct
- Resources to make informed decisions about school programs, courses, and activities
- An awareness of their own role in building home-school relationships, that of courier and communicator

At the same time, parents receive these advantages:

- A more complete understanding of school programs and policies
- An opportunity to monitor and stay aware of children's progress
- Information that helps them respond effectively to children's problems
- Interactions with their students' teachers
- Ease of communication with teachers and schools

Teachers also experience positive outcomes when home-school communications are promoted. Included are:

- Encouragement for increased diversity of types of communications with families

- An awareness of their personal abilities to communicate clearly

- Appreciation for and use of family networks for communication

- An increased ability to invite and understand family views on children's programs and progress (paraphrased from Epstein, 1995)

Factors That Facilitate Communication

Because parents are more involved when schools encourage involvement (Christenson & Cleary, 1990), it is important for teachers to provide many opportunities for home-school and school-home communication. By using many channels of communication—notes, memos, Web sites, email, newsletters, voicemail, phone calls, and so on—teachers maximize their ability to reach the families of their students. Calling immediately in the child's presence for both positive and negative messages can be of benefit.

In all communications, consideration must be given to the language, literacy level, and special needs of families. For example, translators may be needed for conferences, a native-language or lower-literacy-level edition of memos and newsletters may be necessary, or large print may be required. The readability, clarity, and form of all communications should be assessed. Technical jargon and the use of terms and acronyms unfamiliar to those outside the education profession should be avoided. The quality of communication, which may be an important feature in attracting the attention of families, should also be evaluated. Teachers should be sure to keep a card on each caregiver, including the current last name. This name may not match the name of the child; addressing the caregiver by a former name may, in some cases, begin an interaction negatively.

Families are more likely to communicate when the school encourages it. Convenient times should be provided for family communication.

This may involve occasional evening or weekend opportunities for employed parents. Equal attention should be given to both positive and negative communications. For example, when a child has exhibited cooperative behavior over a period of time or academics have improved, a positive note or phone call to the family is likely to be highly appreciated. The child, too, is often motivated by these positive announcements.

Barriers to Communication

Despite the overwhelming evidence of the benefits of school-home relationships, effective interaction is hindered by many barriers. Kieff and Wellhousen (2000) suggest that "developing barrier-free family involvement strategies is important to school effectiveness and children's success in school" (p. 22). Obstacles include (a) parent characteristics, attitudes, and life situations; (b) educational traditions; (c) educational environments; and (d) teacher characteristics, attitudes, and responsibilities.

Parental characteristics, attitudes, and life situations. Parents who stay away from schools often include racial and ethnic minorities, those with lower incomes, those with limited English-speaking abilities, and those who had bad personal experiences in school (Moles, 1996). Teachers may forget that not everyone remembers his or her school experience fondly, and the "baggage" from less-than-positive experiences may increase the chances that a parent either will not come to school or will approach school interactions in an adversarial manner.

The quality of early partnership experiences establishes patterns and relationships that encourage or discourage family involvement in later years. Parents are sometimes intimidated by school personnel and feel that they do not possess knowledge and skills to help their children (Riley, 1994).

Some families are difficult to reach because of physical, social, or psychological distance; age of parent; parental background; family structure; and family personal problems (Epstein, 1992). In some cases, job and family demands leave little free time for family involvement (Moles, 1996; Shartrand et al., 1997).

Educational environments and traditions. Some schools have traditional histories that continue to resist parental involvement (Cibulka, 1996). Schools may be unwilling to share information with parents or may fear that parents will be troublemakers who might make decisions that school leaders oppose (Heckman, 1996). Very informed parents may demand documentation of school decisions; therefore, both administrators and teachers need to be knowledgeable of legal requirements and issues.

Some educational environments deter school-home relationships. Swap (1987) identifies barriers that have an effect on these relationships: (a) limited time for communication, (b) ritualized parent-school contacts, and (c) frequency of communication during crises. Less information is given to parents in schools that serve educationally and economically disadvantaged students (MacIver & Epstein, 1990). According to Epstein (1992), "Families who may need the most information in useful forms are presently receiving the least" (p. 1144).

Teacher characteristics, attitudes, and responsibilities. Just like those of parents, teachers' personal responsibilities may limit their availability to meet with families outside school hours (Swap, 1990). Because of increasing ethnic diversity, teachers and families are likely to come from different cultural and economic backgrounds, which can lead to contrasting values and beliefs (Murphy, 1991). As noted earlier, teachers (and administrators) may not understand families with different backgrounds, experiences, and needs (Epstein, 1992). In environments in which teachers believe their attitudes differ from those of others at the school, family involvement programs are weaker. Stronger programs are reported when teachers feel that they are similar to administrators, other teachers, and parents (Epstein & Dauber, 1991).

Some teachers may lack the confidence to work with families and may hold negative attitudes toward family involvement (Shartrand et al., 1997), including beliefs that parents are not qualified or interested in children's education (New Futures Institute, 1989). Many beginning teachers have low expectations about parental commitments to help children with schoolwork (Moles, 1982). Epstein (1991) found that many teachers had reservations about whether they could motivate parents to be involved. Teachers want more parent involvement but may be frustrated and discouraged by the expectation that they should be the initiator of activities to solve students' motivation and achievement problems (Pryor, 1995). Some teachers do not systematically encourage family involvement. Parents do not always participate, even when encouraged (Shartrand et al., 1997). Although there are some teachers whose attitudes block home-school collaboration, many more work toward making positive differences. Despite the barriers that may be in place to discourage teachers from working to gain parental involvement, effective teachers know that when parents work with them the benefits multiply. Teachers who reach out make a difference.

CONDUCTING EFFECTIVE PARENT/TEACHER CONFERENCES

Parent-teacher conferences are the most common means of family-school communication and can offer a building block for teacher-parent partnerships. However, the hearts of many parents and teachers are filled with anxiety and apprehension when it is time to schedule conferences (Gestwicki, 1996).

Conferences are usually scheduled to share a developmental overview or focus on a particular issue. In either case, careful attention to all aspects of the conference—preparing, planning, conducting, and evaluating—is critical to building a positive home-school relationship and to reducing any anxieties that may occur.

Preparing

The teacher's preparation begins long before the actual conference is scheduled. Long-term preparation involves awareness of personal attitudes toward cultures and varied family situations and roles. This self-awareness is necessary before educators can communicate with families different from themselves (Jordan et al., 1998). Developing basic relationships and interpersonal skills is also critical to effective conferences. Basic relationship skills include reflective listening, building rapport, communicating, genuine caring, and empathizing (Perl, 1995). If a teacher anticipates a problematic conference for any reason, a colleague or administrator should be present or available. Teachers should not be alone in these situations.

Planning

Every school requires some type of parental conferences. Careful planning reduces anxiety and maximizes the time spent in parent-teacher conferences. Planning involves scheduling, preparing materials and documentation, arranging for a translator if needed, and preparing a comfortable location.

Scheduling. Whether invitations for conferences are made by phone, emailed, written, or extended in person, they should be friendly, provide information about the purpose of the conference, and reflect an awareness of parents' busy lives. For example, when a scheduling sheet is posted either physically or electronically or sent home, it should include abundant choices of days and times, allowing for differing schedules as well as the expected length of the conference. Parents are more likely to respond if teachers make it clear that they are eager to be as flexible as possible in accommodating the needs of parents (Gestwicki, 1996).

Preparing materials and documentation. Depending on the purpose of the conference, a list of discussion questions or topics can be sent home for parents to facilitate dialogue. For example, questions might include: (a) How does your child view school? (b) What is your child's activity schedule away from school? or (c) How does your child solve problems at home? (Hoerr, 1997). Teachers should accumulate and organize the necessary documentation and resources to guide the conference discussion. If the primary goal is a developmental overview, an array of writing and art samples, as well as developmental assessments and photographs taken over a period of time, can assist parents in understanding the level of the child's physical, social, emotional, and/or cognitive development. If the conference is to focus on one academic area, such as mathematics or a behavioral issue, the teacher may have work samples, anecdotal records, and related materials that illustrate concretely the topic or issue to be addressed. Planning in advance to assemble *meaningful* examples of work or to document behavior, rather than collecting handy materials, will help families recognize professional commitment. Objective, observable information should be collected for classroom management issues (for example, "In one week, Lisa pushed another student an average of five times a day," rather than "Lisa is causing problems because she is aggressive.")

A brief outline of topics to be discussed helps organize the conference and keep it on track. The outline can be shared with parents at the opening of the conference, along with an inquiry as to additions they would like to make. Whether written or oral, the outline should include a clear opportunity for parental input and questions.

Arranging for a translator. If the primary language of the parent(s) is not the same as the teacher's, it is the teacher's responsibility to make arrangements for a translator. It is not an acceptable practice to have the student serve as the translator (Trejo, 1999). At the least, student translators are in an awkward and vulnerable position serving as go-betweens for some of the most powerful and important people in their lives. The conference can be a moral dilemma for a young child acting as a translator, especially if it involves negative consequences. There is a high probability of misunderstanding and frustration as well as the possibility for student translators to purposefully mislead or misinform the parent, the teacher, or both.

Preparing a comfortable physical location. Conferences can be carried out almost anyplace if the following are available: two or three comfortable, adult-sized chairs; a table on which to spread papers, materials, and beverages; and a door that can be closed and perhaps posted with a sign indicating that "conferences are in progress" (Gestwicki, 1996). Small chairs found in classrooms for preschool and elementary children are uncomfortable for adults and should be avoided if at all possible. Parents and teachers should be at eye level and sitting side-by-side, without a physical barrier such as a desk or wide table separating them. The closed door with a sign indicating conferences in progress conveys a firm impression that the conference is private and confidential.

For schools serving families with limited resources, teachers should prepare for young children who may accompany families to conferences. If child care cannot be provided, a corner where young children can play quietly may have to be prepared. It is helpful to furnish the corner with preschool play materials and books. Extra chairs should be included so that families can feel comfortable bringing to the conference other adults significant in the child's life.

Conducting the Conference

Careful planning and a comfortable setting help put anxious parents and nervous teachers at ease. Opening the conference with casual conversation and an offer of refreshments helps create social comfort. A conference can be structured in a variety of ways but should always begin and end on a positive note. Duffy (1997) offered three parts of a conference that can be adapted to various situations and ages of student. Part one involves listening and sharing stories. It is important for teachers to give parents an opportunity to talk about their child, sharing their love, joy, and concerns. Parents are reassured that the teacher does know their child when the teacher responds with a story or anecdote that reflects knowledge and understanding of their student. For example, parents in areas of generational poverty often see teachers who "get right to the point" as cold and aloof (Payne, 1995). Adding 5 minutes to the beginning of the conference period for casual conversation and stories can improve home-school relationships for some parents.

The second part of the conference addresses the student's performance level in the educational setting. For regular conferences, the teacher may provide a developmental overview documented with materials collected before the conference. Teachers should be ready to explain standardized or other important test scores. For conferences focused on student behavior or special needs, clear examples should be given as objectively as possible, and teacher emotionalism should be avoided. Taking notes on information that parents give about the child helps teachers remember and reflect upon it later.

The final part of the conference prepares for the future by summarizing what has occurred during the conference and developing a plan. This applies especially if the conference was called because of a particular problem. This step may involve setting goals, scheduling another conference, or developing an action plan (perhaps jointly) to address developmental or behavioral issues.

Documentation of a conference is a wise, often required practice that can take several forms. One simple strategy is to take notes, develop goals, and note any recommendations or agreements. The parents can take a copy, and the teacher retains a file copy. In some schools, a standard parent-conference form may be required to provide a format for information such as parent's name, teacher, student's name and age, background information, programs and services discussed, report card explanation, comments, recommendations, and follow-up agreements. In some districts, it is required that both teacher and parent sign conference documentation and that both retain a copy.

Teachers must remember that when they communicate something "bad" about a young child, many parents are likely to consider the communication as reflecting negatively on them or even as a personal attack. Most parents care a great deal for their children. If teachers put themselves in the place of the parents and communicate effectively, even conferences on negative issues should prove to be successful.

Evaluating and Following Up

After a conference, teachers can enhance their own professional development and build a strong foundation for future parent conferences by reflecting on questions such as: (a) How well did I listen? (b) Did I offer enough specifics? and (c) Was I positive in beginning and ending the conference? (Gestwicki, 1996). Within a week after the conference, the teacher should evaluate it and follow up with parents.

Follow-up strategies include sending a note home, emailing, or phoning the parents to thank them for their participation. Depending on the purpose of the conference, the follow-up letter may include goals of the conference, information presented, information gained, student improvement or decline noted since the meeting, and any agreements made. A telephone call is a particularly helpful follow-up strategy when the family needs another conference or referral for other services (Rockwell, Andre, & Hawley, 1996).

Pitfalls to Avoid for Successful Conferences

Many identified pitfalls must be avoided if successful parent-teacher conferences are to take place. These include: (a) using technical jargon or acronyms—"teacher talk," (b) playing the role of an "expert," (c) using negative or destructive eval-

uations about a child's capabilities, (d) conversing unprofessionally about others by being too personal or taking sides, (e) giving advice—either unasked for or asked for, and (f) trying to solve all problems on the spot or trying to force agreement (Gestwicki, 1996). A quick review of these common pitfalls associated with parent conferences can be instructive during the planning and implementation phases and also can assist in evaluating the conference.

Consider the following elementary school conference. Mrs. Chen, a second-grade teacher conducted a conference with the parents of Maria Garcia, who had been exhibiting disruptive behavior over the last 3 weeks. Mrs. Chen called Maria's parents on Monday afternoon and told them to attend a conference on Tuesday after school. As Mr. and Mrs. Garcia entered the classroom, Mrs. Chen invited them to sit in student chairs that she pulled up in a small circle. As she balanced paperwork in her lap, Mrs. Chen launched into a monologue describing the effects of Maria's behavior on herself and her class. She concluded her diatribe with the remarks that "Maria is driving everyone crazy, and I think the best thing for her is psychological help." The parents appeared shocked and asked for examples of Maria's disruptive behavior. Mrs. Chen replied, "Everything she does is disruptive!"

As you can surmise, Mrs. Chen made several strategic errors. She was not sensitive to family scheduling when she demanded that the family meet after school the next day. Mrs. Chen did not adequately prepare the physical environment or materials that provided specific objective examples of Maria's disruptive behaviors. Her emotional reactions to the situation did not help the parents understand what Maria had done to disrupt the classroom. The teacher used emotionally charged language and made a diagnosis that she was not qualified to make.

Let us examine a positive alternative for the same conference. In preparation for asking the parents to come for a conference, Mrs. Chen kept an objective log of Maria's behaviors over the

3-week period, along with a record of school attempts to modify the behavior. She called the parents and inquired whether they could come for a conference at a convenient time in the next week. When they arrived for the conference, Mrs. Chen asked them to sit around a small table in adult chairs. She began the conference by asking the parents to share information about Maria and telling them how much she enjoys teaching and how glad she is to have Maria in her class. Next she expressed her concern about the change in Maria's behavior and its effect on Maria's progress and the classroom environment. Mrs. Chen shared specific examples of disruptive situations over the last 3 weeks and answered the Garcias' specific questions in an objective and caring manner. She suggested that the counselor join them for the remainder of the conference to devise an action plan for decreasing Maria's disruptive behaviors. After the counselor joined them and the plan was made, Mrs. Chen again expressed support for Maria by offering to phone the Garcias in a week to report on how the plan was working and to find out about their questions and experiences at home. The Garcias expressed appreciation to Mrs. Chen and the counselor as they left. This scenario is likely to have a much more positive outcome than the first conference described.

Special Conferences

Teachers of young children are often the first to notice that a child may need special help of some type. These conferences can be especially difficult for parents. It is always helpful to remember that other professionals may assist in helping you explain certain screening or testing procedures. However, many professionals in a room with one parent can sometimes be overwhelming to the parent if each is not truly empathetic and warm. It is of special benefit to try to orchestrate the environment to ensure that the best decisions are made for the child. Legal issues for testing and placing children in special programs must be followed to the letter of the law, including ARD (Admission, Review, and Dismissal) conferences, which are discussed more thoroughly in Competency 13, Chapter 19.

ENGAGING FAMILIES IN CHILDREN'S EDUCATION

Collaboration is a voluntary relationship based upon mutual goals, shared responsibilities for decision making, and an opportunity for both families and schools to share their expertise and strengths. Collaboration empowers parents to contribute to the academic success of their child (Bempechat, 1992). Success does not come from either the home or school alone but from the combination of the two influences (Seeley, 1982). Collaboration is an ongoing process rather than a program of activities; it requires vision, commitment, and continuous effort.

Teachers must see working with families as a crucial part of their job and must broaden their focus to extend beyond the classroom into the home. The Texas State Legislature has stated that the mission for education in Texas is "grounded on the conviction that a successful public education system is directly related to a strong, dedicated, and supportive family and that parental involvement in the school is essential for the maximum educational achievement of a child" (Vornberg, 1998, p. 98).

Involvement is conceptualized as more than PTA meetings or homeroom parent activities. Occasionally families are passive participants, receiving information from teachers, while at other times they are more actively involved. All types of involvement are valuable; parents do not have to be present at a meeting inside the school building for the family to be actively involved or interested in a partnership with the teacher. Involvement is viewed as multidimensional (Grolnick & Slowiaczek, 1994).

Epstein (1992) developed a framework of six **types of involvement.** Consideration of all six types helps a school expand its focus to an integrated view of involvement. Epstein's six types are described in the following section.

Type 1: Basic Obligations of Parenting

Schools can help families establish home environments that support children and enable them to be better students. Workshops given by the school and/or district on guidance and discipline, parent education courses, or family support relative to health and nutrition issues are examples of school-supported or sponsored initiatives in this category.

Type 2: Communications

Schools can facilitate effective two-way communication between families and schools. Communication features listening to parents as often as "telling" parents. Involvement might include focus groups, surveys, and phone calls, as well as voice-mail systems for information or questions and personalized notes to parents. Teachers can facilitate numerous opportunities for family feedback.

Type 3: Volunteering

Volunteering includes supporting school goals and children's learning at any place, at any time. Families can participate in assemblies or functions as well as provide classroom or school assistance. As is the case with the other categories of involvement, families may need specific training on their role as volunteers and the expectations of the teachers. Individuals are more likely to be involved if they are certain about what they are supposed to do.

If teachers are lucky enough to have parents who want to volunteer, they can encourage the relationship by preparing a place for parents to work and to put their belongings. Parents will feel more at ease if teachers specifically outline what can be done to help that day, with materials set aside if applicable. Thanking volunteers often and praising them in front of others when given the opportunity almost guarantee that a teacher will

have help again. Frequent, positive notes thanking volunteers (and notes that recognize all types of family involvement) make a difference.

Type 4: Learning Activities at Home

Families can be provided information and ideas to encourage interaction through motivating, encouraging, monitoring, and taking an active interest in school-related activities. They can be involved in curriculum decisions or participate in interactive homework assignments. Families might be involved in workshops featuring information on appropriate age-level expectations, successful techniques to encourage academic achievement, or subject matter refresher courses to help families assist with homework. One school invited parents to meet in small neighborhood groups, alternating among children's homes, to share information on how to read with their children. A teacher liaison brought suitable books and other materials that could be checked out on that day.

Type 5: Decision Making and Advocacy

Families are included in school decisions through activities such as committees, site-based management teams, or district task forces. Parents are informed about issues and elections and are helped to develop leadership skills.

Type 6: Community Collaboration

Resources and services from the community are identified to strengthen the school program, family practices, and student growth. Families can be provided information on health, cultural, recreational, and other support programs, as well as opportunities for service to the community.

Personal contact from teachers increases family involvement in all categories. Teachers should demonstrate the belief that families share their goals for successful children. An open, inviting attitude should be integrated into all phases of the school's program.

The overall atmosphere of the school must be assessed to determine how welcoming it is for families. Clearly marked exterior signs indicating where to park and where to enter, easily followed maps, and welcome displays or exhibits help schools create trust and willingness to be involved.

An effective strategy is to include opportunities for interaction between teachers and families outside the classroom or school building. As noted some family members may have less-than-fond memories of their own school experiences and may be somewhat intimidated by the school. Although home visits by teachers may be beneficial, some school districts do not allow such visits. Teachers should always check with the principal before making a home visit. In some areas, home visits can be made only in teams. Sometimes neighborhood meetings can be held in community centers, parks, libraries, or churches to overcome these obstacles and offer neutral ground for all participants. Schools can sponsor neighborhood coffees or potluck dinners in comfortable, convenient locations.

Involvement also increases when there is a family or parent liaison at the school, someone whose specific job it is to help families or to focus on creating collaboration. This person can personalize invitations to functions, reach out to families, and coordinate school efforts. A family liaison can also be responsible for training teachers to create partnerships with families. Families may feel more comfortable communicating with the liaison rather than with an administrator or teacher and may appreciate the school's overt effort to increase involvement. Some schools have set aside a meeting room or special lounge for parents or volunteers. Such a place may be more comfortable than a classroom or teacher's lounge and often may become a neighborhood gathering place for mothers with young children. This provides an opportunity for the school to disseminate information and enlist volunteers.

Families may be more open to involvement during certain "reachable moments." These times include transition periods, such as when a child is entering Pre-K or kindergarten or progressing from elementary to middle school. Another reachable moment might be during school programs such as athletic events, musical concerts, school fairs or carnivals, and so forth—times when families may already be coming to the building or have scheduled time for an activity. Almost all parents of young children will come to see their child perform in some way. Teachers who present small programs at the end of the school day or Parent-Teacher Organizations (PTO) that rotate grade-level performances often generate opportunities to meet with parents. A calendar of activities for the semester, with reminder notes and/or phone calls, enables families to plan for participation. Conferences or informal teacher meetings can often be planned in conjunction with such nonthreatening social activities. Teachers and/or administrators can have regular monthly lunches or breakfasts for interaction or an informal exchange of ideas. Some schools feature events such as "pancakes with the principal" to encourage participation.

Food is always an important part of family events. For example, one school increased its attendance at PTO meetings by beginning with a spaghetti dinner, where neighbors could meet other families. Many schools encourage parents and caregivers of young children to come for lunch, which provides an opportunity for interaction among children, parents, and teachers. Special invitations may increase involvement.

Another useful strategy for creating collaboration is to remember the benefits of rewarding families who are partners with the school. Teachers and administrators should routinely recognize and acknowledge the contributions of parents. A teacher can say "thank you" to families in many ways.

SUMMARY

Family involvement is a crucial element in the educational success of students because of the many positive benefits to students, parents, teachers, and schools. Key practices that support strong home-school relationships include honoring and respecting the diversity and uniqueness of families, affirming and building on the strengths of children and families, using positive communication skills, and providing a welcoming school-home partnership. Working with families is not an optional enhancement to a teacher's job description; it is a critical function that must be considered a primary responsibility for all educators.

GLOSSARY

family diversity   diversity of cultural background, differences in family characteristics and structure, and circumstances or situational differences, resulting in diverse languages, economic situations, customs, attitudes, behaviors, and values.

family involvement   encompasses all interactions between school and home that support student achievement. Similar terms are "family-school partnerships" and "home-school relationships."

parent   anyone who carries out the responsibility of caregiver for a child.

types of involvement   parents may participate in school involvement at one of six levels: basic obligations of parenting, communications, volunteering, learning activities at home, decision making and advocacy, and community collaboration.

SUGGESTED ACTIVITIES

1. Secure a school's site-based management plan, parent handbook, and mission statement. Evaluate the effectiveness of these communications with families.

2. Interview teachers at early childhood and elementary levels to determine their perceptions of the benefits of and barriers to family involvement.

3. Interview several parents concerning their experiences in conferences about their children. Explore whether the guidelines for effective conferences were used.

4. Draw a model of each of the following, based on this chapter's content:
   a. A family-friendly school
   b. A school-friendly family

5. With a partner, role-play a poor parent-teacher conference. Role-play the same conference in an effective manner.

6. Compare the demographics of your classroom with those of school children in Texas. How are they similar and different?

7. Interview a school counselor about stresses on families in your school. Ask about the effects of these stresses on the school's students.

8. Write effective letters to parents for the following purposes:
   a. Welcome letter for a new school year
   b. Letter about a student's behavior problem
   c. Letter praising a student
   d. Letter of invitation to a conference

9. Attend a parent-teacher organization meeting at your school. Critique the meeting for its appeal and usefulness to families.

10. Visit a school. Prepare lists of what made you feel welcome and what intimidated you. Generalize those feelings to those you would have if you had a child at this school.

11. Interview a principal, a teacher, and a parent about the types of family involvement they have experienced. Compare their experiences with the types of involvement outlined in this chapter.

12. Design an interactive homework assignment that involves families in their children's school work.

PRACTICE QUESTIONS

Ms. Obasi, a first-year teacher in a large urban elementary school, is preparing to hold conferences with each of her students' parents.

1. Another first-year teacher tells Ms. Obasi that he just does not have time to communicate with parents. In convincing her fellow teacher of the importance of home-school relationships, which of the following reasons is *most essential* for Ms. Obasi to mention?

A. Parents and families can cause problems for teachers if they do not receive communication from teachers.

B. Federal, state, and local policies have supported the effort to involve families in their children's education.

C. The extent to which families are involved in the educational process has been shown to be an accurate indicator of student success.

D. Collaboration with families allows teachers to carry less of the burden of educating students.

2. Ms. Obasi is considering several options for arranging conference times with parents. Which of the following strategies is likely to be *most successful* in setting up effective parent conferences?

A. Sending home an assigned time with each student for the conference

B. Sending home a note asking parents to indicate several times they would be available for a conference, developing a list of conference times from the parental input, and then sending home a list confirming a conference time

C. Sending home a communication indicating times that she will be available for conferences on a first-come, first-serve basis

D. Spending her preparation period calling parents to set up conference times

3. The school in which Ms. Obasi teaches has great student diversity. Which of the following is *least* important for Ms. Obasi to consider as she interacts with students and parents?

A. Most parents of all backgrounds and characteristics want their children to succeed educationally.

B. Culturally sensitive approaches must be developed for the particular families served by a school.

C. The teacher's job is to reach out and respond to children from all types of families.

D. A primary focus of teachers is to remediate deficits arising from students' family and cultural backgrounds.

4. In preparing for a conference with parents who have limited English proficiency, Ms. Obasi should do each of the following *except:*

A. Arrange to have written information translated and sent to the parents.

B. Plan extra time for the conference to allow adequate opportunity for translation.

C. Have the student serve as a translator for the conference because the parent will feel most comfortable with this arrangement.

D. Arrange the furniture so that she can sit beside the student's parents at a table.

Answers and Discussion

Answer 1: Parents and families are sometimes viewed negatively by teachers, but the main motivation for involving families in children's education is not avoidance of problems with families. Federal, state, and local policies have supported family involvement in schools, and collaboration with families allows families and schools to work together toward a common goal of academic success for students. However, the primary reason for teachers to focus on home-school relationships is that such relationships are primary keys to student academic success. The answer is *C*.

Answer 2: Arranging effective parental conferences involves consideration of the needs of parents. In contrast to assigning conference times, strategies that recognize the responsibilities and busy lives of students' families are likely to be most successful. Many parents are not available during working hours, and drop-in conferences may not provide opportunity for ample preparation and meeting time. Strategy *B* takes into consideration the needs of parents and is, therefore, most likely to result in successful and effective conferences. This is also the least time-consuming for the teacher. The answer is *B*.

Answer 3: Remember that the question is asking for the *least* important consideration. A positive view of children and their families aids teachers in working successfully with both. Most parents wish for their children to succeed educationally. It is the teacher's job to become culturally aware of his or her children and their families in order to best respond to them. All families have strengths, and teachers should focus on student and family strengths rather than deficits. The answer is *D*.

Answer 4: To be sure that families who have limited English proficiency are aware of and prepared for conference opportunities, written translated materials must be made available to them. The teacher should plan for a translator other than the student so that the child is not burdened by being inappropriately placed in an adult role. Extra conference time may be needed for adequate translation, and physical arrangements should be made so that no barriers are present between the teacher and the parents. Ms. Obasi should do everything except *C*. The answer is *C*.

WEB LINKS

Remember that Web site locations may change. If any of these sites have moved or cannot be located, use the key terms in this chapter to search for further information.

http://www.aecf.org

The Annie E. Casey Foundation is an outstanding source for current national and state statistics on children. The "Kids Count" data is in understandable form and updated annually. Other information on the status of children is also available.

http://www.childrensdefense.org

"Children in the States 2000" is just one example of the outstanding data and current information available at this Children's Defense Fund site.

http://www.cpirc.org

The Colorado Parent Information and Resource Center presents articles on parent involvement, current research, and excellent links.

http://www.partnersineducation.org

The National Association of Partners in Education is dedicated to providing leadership in developing

partnerships. Resources include how-to manuals, recognition ideas, and many other products.

http://www.nccic.org

This National Child Care Information Center site, part of ERIC, offers information on a variety of topics and links to numerous other agencies and organizations.

http://www.ncpie.org

The National Coalition for Parent Involvement in Education is committed to strengthening family-school partnerships. The Web site has ideas for schools, special activities, a database, and a good resource list.

http://www.tnpc.com

This National Parenting Center site has articles on issues of concern to today's families, book reviews, product ratings, and a chat room.

http://www.pta.org

This Parent Teachers Association (PTA) site is excellent. It has guides for parents and teachers on collaboration and a very good list of resources. Articles, such as teachers' best ideas for involving parents, are short and to-the-point. Information on diversity is also accessible through the site.

http://pfie.ed.gov

The site for the U.S. Department of Education's Partnership for Family Involvement in Education demonstrates the federal government's priority in creating partnerships. Excellent online handbooks, examples of successful programs, teacher training materials, and summer home learning ideas are found here.

REFERENCES

The Annie E. Casey Foundation. (2001). *Kids count*. Available: http: www.aecf.org/cgi-bin/kconline.cgi

Barnhart, C. L., & Barnhart, R. K., (Eds.). (1983). *The world book dictionary* (Vol. 2). Chicago: World Book, Inc.

Bempechat, J. (1992). The role of parent involvement in children's academic achievement. *The School Community Journal, 2*(2), 31–41.

Berger, E. H. (1996). Working with families: Don't leave them standing on the sidewalk. *Early Childhood Education Journal, 24*(2), 131–133.

Christenson, S. L., & Cleary, M. (1990). Consultation and parent-educator partnership: A perspective. *Journal of Educational and Psychological Consultation, 1*(3), 219–241.

Cibulka, J. G. (1996). Conclusion: Toward an interpretation of school, family, and community connections: Policy changes. In J. G. Cibulka & W. J. Kritek (Eds.), *Coordination among schools, families and communities: Prospects for educational reform* (pp. 403–435). Albany: State University of New York Press. (ED 395 718)

Comer, J. (1984). Home-school relationships as they affect the academic success of children. *Urban Society, 16*, 323–337.

Diffily, D. (2001). Family meetings: Teachers and families build relationships. *Dimensions of Early Childhood, 29*(3), 5–10.

Duffy, R. (1997, July-August). Parents' perspectives on conferencing. *Child Care Information Exchange,* 41–43.

Epstein, J. L. (1984). School policy and parent involvement: Research results. *Educational Horizons, 62*(2), 70–72.

Epstein, J. L. (1985). A question of merit: Principals and parents' evaluations of teachers. *Educational Researcher, 14*(7), 3–10.

Epstein, J. (1990). School and family connections: Theory, research, and implications for integrating sociologies of education and family. In D. Unger & M. Sussman, (Eds.) *Families in community settings: Interdisciplinary perspectives* (pp. 99–126). NY: Haworth.

Epstein, J. L. (1991). Effects on student achievement of teachers' practices of parent involvement. *Advances in Reading/Language Research, 5,* 261–276.

Epstein, J. L. (1992). School and family partnerships. In M. Alkin (Ed.) *Encyclopedia of educational research.* 6th ed. pp. 1139–1151.

Epstein, J. L. (1995). School/family/community partnerships. *Phi Delta Kappan, 76*(9), 701–712.

Epstein, J. L., & Becker, H. J. (1982). Parent involvement: A survey of teacher practices. *The Elementary School Journal, 83*(2), 85–102.

Epstein, J. L., & Dauber, S. L. (1991). School programs and teacher practices of parent involvement in inner-city elementary and middle schools. *The Elementary School Journal, 91*(3), 289–305.

Gestwicki, C. (1996). *Home, school, and community relations.* (3rd ed.). Albany, NY: Delmar Publishers.

Grolnick, W. S., & Slowiaczek, M. L. (1994). Parents' involvement in children's schooling: A multidimensional conceptualization and motivational model. *Child Development, 65*, 237–252.

Heckman, P. E. (1996). *The courage to change: Stories from successful school reform.* Thousand Oaks, CA: Corwin Press.

Hoerr, T. R. (1997). When teachers listen to parents. *Principal, 77*(2), 40–42.

Hoover-Dempsey, K. V., Bassler, O. C., & Brissie, J. S. (1987). Parent involvement: Contributions of teacher efficacy, school socioeconomic status, and other school characteristics. *American Educational Research Journal, 24*(3), 417–435.

Jones, I., & White, S. (2000). Family composition, parental involvement and young children's academic achievement. *Early Child Development and Care, 161,* 71–82.

Jordan, L., Reyes-Blanes, M. E., Peel, B. B., Peel, H. A., & Lane, H. B. (1998). Developing teacher-parent partnerships across cultures: Effective parent conferences. *Intervention in School and Clinic, 3*(3), 141–147.

Kacapyr, E. (1998). How hard are hard times? *American Demographics.* Available: http://www.demographics.com/publications/ad/98

Kellaghan, T., Sloane, K., Alvarez, B., & Bloom, B. (1993). Changes in society and the family. *The home environment and school learning.* San Francisco: Jossey-Bass.

Kieff, J., & Wellhousen, K. (2000). Planning family involvement in early childhood programs. *Young Children, 55*(3), 18–25.

Leitch, M. L., & Tangri, S. S. (1988). Barriers to home-school collaboration. *Educational Horizons, 66,* 70–74.

Lugaila, T. A. (1999). Marital status and living arrangements: March 1998 (Update). U. S. Department of Commerce. Available: http://www.census.gov/press-release/www/1999/cb99-03.

MacIver, D. J., & Epstein, J. L. (1990). *How equal are opportunities for learning in the middle grades in disadvantaged and advantaged schools?* (CDS Report). Baltimore: Johns Hopkins University Center for Research on Effective Schooling for Disadvantaged Students.

Moles, O. (1982, November). Synthesis of research on parent participation in children's education. *Educational Leadership,* 44–47.

Moles, O., ed. (1996, August). *Reaching all families: Creating family-friendly schools.* Washington, DC: U. S. Department of Education Office of Educational Research and Improvement.

Murphy, J. (1991). *Restructuring schools: Capturing and assessing the phenomenon.* New York: Teachers College Press.

National Association for the Education of Young Children. (1996). *Guidelines for preparation of early childhood professionals.* Washington, DC: NAEYC.

National Center for Education Statistics. (1992). *A profile of American eighth-grade mathematics and science instruction.* (Technical Report No. NCES 92–486). Washington, DC: Government Printing Office.

New Futures Institute. (1989). *Resource guide series: Vol. 1. Parent involvement in new futures.* Waltham, MA: Brandeis University, Center for Human Resources.

Nielsen, L. E., & Finkelstein, J. M. (1993). A new approach to parent conferences. *Teaching K–8, 24*(1), 90–92.

Payne, R. (1995). *Poverty: A framework for understanding and working with students and adults from poverty.* Baytown, TX: RFT Publishing.

Perl, J. (1995). Improving relationship skills for parent conferences. *Teaching Exceptional Children, 28*(1), 28–31.

Powell, D. R. (1998). Reweaving parents into the fabric of early childhood programs. *Young Children, 53*(5), 60–67.

Powell, D. R. (2000). Preparing early childhood professionals to work with families. In National Institute on Early Childhood Development and Education, *New teachers for a new century: The future of early childhood professional preparation* (pp. 59–86). Washington, DC: U.S. Department of Education.

Pryor, C. (1995). Youth, parent and teacher views of parent involvement in schools. *Education, 115*(3), 410–419.

Riley, R. (1994, February 15). Prepared remarks for presentation at Georgetown University, Washington, D.C. Washington, DC: U.S. Department of Education.

Robinson, E. L., & Fine, M. J. (1994). Developing collaborative home-school relationships. *Preventing School Failure, 39*(1), 9–15.

Rockwell, R. E., Andre, L. C., & Hawley, M. R. (1996). *Parents and teachers as partners: Issues and challenges.* Fort Worth, TX: Harcourt Brace College Publishers.

Seeley, D. (1982, November). Education through partnership. *Educational Leadership,* 42–43.

Shartrand, A. M., Weiss, H. B., Kreider, H. M., & Lopez, M. E. (1997). *New skills for new schools: Preparing teachers in family involvement.* Cambridge, MA: Harvard Family Research Project, Harvard Graduate School of Education.

Swap, S. M. (1987). *Enhancing parent involvement in schools.* New York: Teachers College Press.

Swap, S. M. (1990). *Parent involvement and success for all children: What we know now.* Boston: Institute for Responsive Education.

Texas Education Agency. (1995). *Learner-centered schools for Texas: A vision of Texas educators.* Austin, TX: Author.

Trejo, F. (1999, May 23). Lost in translation: Kids who must interpret for parents miss part of childhood, experts say. *Dallas Morning News,* pp. 1A, 16A–17A.

U.S. Census Bureau. (2001). Washington, DC. Available: http://www.census.gov

U.S. Department of Education. (1994). *Strong families, strong schools: Building community partnerships for learning.* Washington, DC: Author.

Vornberg, J. A., ed. (1998). *Texas public school organization and administration: 1998* (6th ed.). Dubuque, IA: Kendall Hunt.

Workman, S. H., & Gage, J. A. (1997). Family-school partnerships: A family strengths approach. *Young Children, 52*(4), 10–14.

Competency 12

The teacher enhances professional knowledge and skills by effectively interacting with members of the educational community and participating in various types of professional activities.

The beginning teacher:

- Interacts appropriately with other professionals in the school community (e.g., vertical teaming, horizontal teaming, team teaching, mentoring).

- Maintains supportive, cooperative relationships with professional colleagues and collaborates to support students' learning and to achieve campus and district goals.

- Knows the roles and responsibilities of specialists and other professionals at the building and district levels (e.g., department chairperson, principal, board of trustees, curriculum coordinator, technology coordinator, special education professional).

- Understands the value of participating in school activities and contributes to school and district (e.g., by participating in decision making and problem solving, sharing ideas and expertise, serving on committees, volunteering to participate in events and projects).

- Uses resources and support systems effectively (e.g., mentors, service centers, state initiatives, universities) to address professional development needs.

- Recognizes characteristics, goals, and procedures associated with teacher appraisal and uses appraisal results to improve teaching skills.

- Works productively with supervisors, mentors, and other colleagues to address issues and to enhance professional knowledge and skills.

- Understands and uses professional development resources (e.g., mentors and other support systems, conferences, online resources, workshops, journals, professional associations, coursework) to enhance knowledge, pedagogical skills, and technological expertise.

- Engages in reflection and self-assessment to identify strengths, challenges, and potential problems; improve teaching performance; and achieve professional goals.

Chapter 18

Interacting and Communicating with Other Educators and Contributing to the School and District

DONNA CUNNINGHAM
LIN MOORE

Texas Woman's University

TERMS TO KNOW

Action research

Administrator

Campus Improvement Plan

Collaboration

Continuing Professional
    Education

Domain

Family liaison

Horizontal teaming

Mentor

Nonverbal communication

Novice

Parent educator

Professional development

Professional Development
    Appraisal System (PDAS)

Protégé

Reflection

Reflective practitioner

Reflective teaching

Reflective thinking

School community

Self-assessment

Self-efficacy

Site-based decision making

Specialist

Summative

Support system

Teacher appraisal system

Teacher Self-Report Form

Team teaching

Verbal communication

Vertical team

To interact and communicate with other educators and make a positive contribution to the school and district, teachers must understand the importance of working in tandem with the school community. The **school community** includes individuals and organizations that form a partnership to provide meaningful learning experiences and support services for children. It is critical that all of the school community join forces, work together, and *create* together the processes for achieving common goals. Professional knowledge and skills are enhanced when teachers develop and refine their interpersonal skills of:

- Reflection and interaction
- Collaboration
- Participation
- Evaluation
- Professional development

This chapter offers a brief introduction to reflection and the reflective practitioner and then proceeds to answer several questions: What is reflection? How does reflection impact the teacher's professional relationships? What are the opportunities for teacher participation in professional activities? What resources and support systems are available to teachers? How can teachers profit from self-assessment? How are teachers in Texas evaluated? And finally, how are teachers able to identify needs, resources, and ways to participate in continuing professional development?

The concept web shown in Figure 18-1 provides a visual image, or mental picture, of the concepts included in this chapter.

REFLECTION AND INTERACTION

The term **"reflection,"** used in an educational context, means to think carefully about, to recall, and to focus on the specifics of the numerous events, concerns, and dilemmas that are relevant to teaching and learning. Simply put, when educators think seriously about or question the various issues, themes, or circumstances that relate to their professional roles and responsibilities, they are performing "reflective thinking" (Dewey, 1933).

Reflective Thinking

Reflective thinking necessitates that teachers ask *who, what, when, where, why,* and *how* in terms of their teaching. As they refine their reflective thinking skills, teachers are able to answer questions, solve problems, and resolve conflicts.

Reflective Teaching

Reflective thinking propels teachers into **reflective teaching,** which is a positive outcome of examining and evaluating the way teachers teach. Teachers who practice reflective teaching attempt to avoid mistakes by probing, inspecting, and studying what they do. They constantly seek to improve the way they teach.

Because of the immediate demands of the classroom, it is not always possible for teachers to reflect upon events as they are teaching. Reflection-*on*-action occurs when teachers think, question, and review events, actions, or conversations after these things have occurred. When teachers are able to teach and reflect at the same time, they are performing reflection-*in*-action, or thinking about what they are doing even while they are doing it (Schon, 1983).

Reflection need not be limited to events of the past and present. Reflection is a process that also includes thinking about the future (Dougherty, 1997). In fact, teachers may become stagnant when they do not reflect about the future and anticipate what might happen. As they reflect about the future, teachers concentrate on predicting what

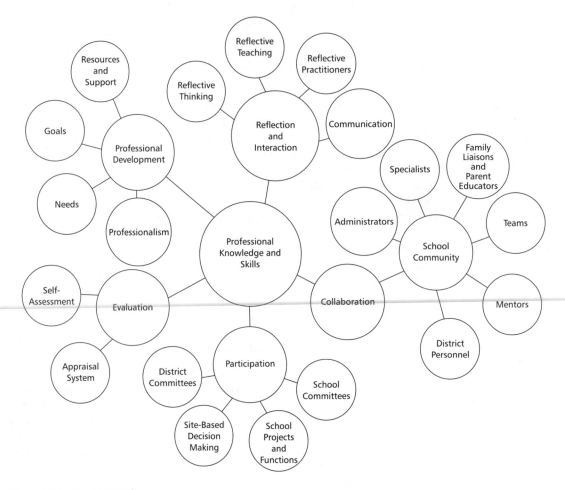

Figure 18-1   Concept Web

might be the results of their behavior, actions, or responses to situations. Unless teachers reflect about what they "... hope to do, [their] future actions will remain somewhat unguided and ineffectual" (Ogden & Claus, 1997, p. 72).

It is crucial for *all* teachers—both experienced teachers and preservice teachers—to acquire and improve their skills of reflection. Teachers who engage in reflection are more likely to improve their teaching skills, connect theory and practice, and deal with real life circumstances and conditions. In addition, professional educators concur that reflection helps teachers increase their:

- insight about and proficiency in their teaching ability

- decision-making and problem-solving skills (Collier, 1997)

- ongoing personal and professional change and growth (Ayers, 1989)

- response to continuous change

- feelings of self-sufficiency, self-reliance, and self-control

- ability to identify, assess, and accommodate student needs

Reflective Practitioners

Because it is considered such a vital component of teacher and student success, reflection and reflection-related activities are included in the majority of preservice teacher professional development education programs (Borko et al., 1997; Dieker & Monda-Amaya, 1995; Galvez-Martin, Bowman, & Morrison, 1998; Kruse, 1997; Pultorak, 1993). Through field experiences, case studies, journal writing, portfolio development, oral debriefing, peer coaching, and critiques, teachers learn to be reflective practitioners. Story writing, solving ethical dilemmas, and sketch journals are also activities that assist teachers in becoming **reflective practitioners,** or teachers who practice reflection, reflective thinking, and reflective teaching.

Shulman (1987) refers to reflective practitioners as ". . . those who review, reconstruct, reenact, and critically analyze their own and their students' performances, and who formulate explanations with evidence" (p. 15). In addition, reflective practitioners are considered to be those who constantly revise, increase, and enrich their knowledge base about teaching methods and procedures, expand their reservoir of classroom strategies, and look for relationships between their own behavior and children's accomplishments. These reflective practitioners are lifelong learners who possess an internal motivation to excel in their teaching. They are constantly searching for new ideas, new possibilities, new opportunities, and new sources of information.

Communication

It is natural for reflective practitioners to become more interactive and communicative with their colleagues. Teachers who practice reflection, reflective thinking, and reflective teaching experience an increase in positive self-esteem and self-confidence. When teachers gain an understanding of what they are doing and become more focused, their professional self-image improves. These teachers become more secure about what they are doing in the classroom, why they are doing it, and how they are doing it. This newfound confidence increases teachers' desire to talk with, or convey their thoughts and insights to, others through **verbal communication.** This sense of security allows teachers to expand "their worlds."

Moving from a more introverted, introspective perspective, teachers begin to think reflectively about other issues related to their professional roles and responsibilities. Teachers who appear self-assured, competent, and knowledgeable about their work elicit respect from their colleagues. As a result, others are inspired to view these teachers as more credible and professional.

Teachers' **nonverbal communication** to their colleagues is observable in their behavior, attitude, and the way they present themselves. Their body language says, "I believe I am capable and competent and can make a positive contribution to teaching and learning and this school."

As a result, teachers' "extended worlds" begin to include others in the school community who are also striving to provide quality learning experiences for their children. As teachers begin to interact and communicate in a positive manner with other educational professionals, they become aware that viewpoints other than their own must be considered and other ideas should be tapped. As teachers acknowledge, reflect, and respect the contributions of other professionals, they can contribute, as equals, in the collaborative process of teaching.

Children observe the communication that occurs between teachers and other teachers, administrators, parents, and staff. Even at a very young age, students are able to decipher the meaning of verbal as well as nonverbal communication that they hear and see in their classrooms, lunchroom, playground, and hallways. They may not understand the exact words of this communication, but young students can "read" facial expressions, tone of voice, and voice level.

Teachers must be aware that all verbal and nonverbal communication should embody the standards of appropriate and acceptable behavior expected of professionals. These standards include

(a) making a distinction between what is and is not suitable for children to overhear, (b) exercising good judgment in expressing dissatisfaction and disagreement, (c) exemplifying tact and diplomacy, (d) accepting unsolicited advice and direction, (e) receiving and responding to criticism, and (f) respecting—even while not agreeing with—authority.

Too often children are subjected to heated discussions, unnecessary gossip, idle talk, back-biting comments, and other unproductive exchanges among school personnel. Such dialogues confuse children, who may assume that the disagreements are about them or because of them. Teachers, administrators, and staff are their "school parents," and the lack of agreement between these "parents" may affect their feelings of safety and protection.

Teachers have numerous opportunities to interact productively as individuals and as members of groups. They are expected to work side-by-side with other teachers in their building and district to promote student achievement. With increasing focus on decentralized education and more local control, even new teachers are expected to become members of many committees.

COLLABORATION

The ability to create together, to work side-by-side, and to cooperate with one another is characteristic of collaboration. Becoming teammates and co-workers in the instructional process is a key component of successful interaction and communication.

Establishing cooperative working relationships accelerates the process of developing quality teaching and supports enhanced learning experiences for children. Cooperation focuses on the positive contributions of each individual as campus and district administrators, teachers, staff, students, and parents work together. **Collaboration** is a more dynamic process, based on partnerships that share a common vision (Christiansen et al., 1997). Stakeholders—people who have a vested interest in the particular outcomes—must join to contribute as equal partners in exploring issues, considering strategies, making decisions, determining action plans, implementing procedures, and then evaluating results. Accountability, therefore, lies with problem solvers who have carefully considered the school and community context, the resources available, and the feasibility of their actions. Through collaborative approaches based on mutual trust and commitment, teachers are both empowered and supported in their actions to improve the educational process.

School Community

The concept of schools as communities emphasizes the value of relationships and the interdependency of members within a well-defined social system. Teachers, administrators, specialists, office and clerical staff, custodial staff, cafeteria and food service workers, children, and their families are all valued members with unique roles and responsibilities.

The idea of a "school community" is not limited to the school building in which teachers are assigned, however. The school community includes all of the faculty, staff, and administrators who are associated with all schools in a district. It is necessary to contribute not only to the activities at the school site, but also to those at the district level.

Within the school community are various individuals who work together to create a positive teaching and learning environment and who can offer counsel and advice to teachers. These professionals include administrators, specialists, family liaisons, parent educators, researchers, and mentors. Some personnel may be assigned at the local campus and others in district offices.

Administrators. Each school is led by professional **administrators** such as principals, assistant principals, instructional specialists, grade-level chairpersons, and supervisors, who are essential to providing support for the personal and academic needs of students. These building personnel supervise the quality of classroom instruction, ensure a safe school environment, oversee the day-to-day school activities of the school, facilitate communication, and assist teachers, parents, and community members.

Principals are the instructional leaders of the school. They are trained to manage the school's classroom and building environment, funds, staff, faculty, and students. Principals establish school goals and objectives, develop budgets, and maintain discipline at the campus. They also approve all teacher and staff appointments and may assign, evaluate, promote, or recommend the termination or suspension of their school employees. Meetings with parents, community groups and agencies, parent-teacher organizations, school board members, and volunteers are also a part of a school principal's assignment. In essence, principals are liaisons between the school and the community and are responsible for the public image of the school. Teachers should keep the principal abreast of what they are doing in the classroom, significant interactions that they have with specific children and parents, and any changes in curriculum content or procedures they wish to make.

Specialists. Numerous other professionals in the school provide emergency and ongoing support for children. Nurses, special educators, school psychologists, resource teachers, librarians, and counselors are specialists to whom teachers can go for information and assistance. **Specialists** can address concerns of teachers as well as the issues and concerns of individual children and groups of children and/or their parents. Teachers rely on the specialists' training in their specific fields and their abilities to be more objective about the abilities, strengths, and limitations of individual students.

Specialists are also available for teacher referrals of students who need additional support or attention. There may be occasions when teachers need help with children who have medical or learning problems, who are exhibiting signs of child abuse and neglect, or who have home issues that are affecting their school performance. School professionals are there to assist with stu-

dent assessments and to link the school with outside community resources that can address children's individual personal issues.

Special education teachers, speech therapists, and diagnosticians are particularly helpful as they support teachers in their classrooms. For example, teachers with concerns about a particular student may invite a diagnostician to observe the child during class time, schedule appropriate testing and evaluation, and interpret results that may lead to the identification of a learning disorder or developmental delay. In addition, these specialists assist the school personnel and children's families in (a) promoting a smooth working environment, (b) ensuring that the best interests of children are being met, (c) modifying classroom activities to meet special needs of children, (d) providing equal educational opportunities and student success, and (e) maintaining open communication between the school, the students, and their families.

Family liaisons and parent educators. Many districts employ **family liaisons, parent educators,** and social workers to link the school directly with community and families. These professionals and paraprofessionals may be housed at each early childhood and elementary school campus or shared among several campuses. Their responsibilities often include coordinating parent meetings, conducting home visits, offering parenting education sessions, organizing family outings and events, and assisting teachers in forming mutually supportive school-family relationships. Teachers may not realize that social workers have strict confidentiality guidelines about some home issues. In working together, each must respect the other's role.

Teachers realize that children's personal needs must be met before they can reach their full potentials (Maslow, 1954). Often children need clothing, food, glasses, medical and dental attention, shelter, and supervision. Although teachers cannot usually provide these services, they can identify children whose needs are not being met and get in touch with school experts who can. Special district personnel are available to answer teachers' questions relating to children's medical and psychological needs, family issues, and social support services.

Teams. All members of the school community work together to support each other and their children. It is common for teachers to work with other teachers in their department or with professionals in different departments. Together they offer and receive help, support, and constructive criticism. Teachers realize that by working together to address children's needs and interests, they will be able to contribute to a positive school climate and increase student achievement. Teaming, or joining others to accomplish instructional objectives, provides teachers flexibility and allows them to utilize their individual strengths.

Teachers may work in teams, splitting lessons or classes, teaching the same lesson to each group separately, or teaching together in the same classroom. Many educators believe that, by teaming, "... individuals across all levels of an organization are given an opportunity to come together on a regular basis to discuss their values and visions (Cunningham & Gresso, 1993, p. 42).

Vertical teaming. With **vertical teaming,** the idea is to gain knowledge from all levels of an organization. In a district, members representing all levels of district employees meet to learn about the entire district, not only their own school. For instance, a vertical team might comprise principals, teachers, students, parents, school secretaries, representatives from the central administration and transportation offices, and a school board member. Another form of a vertical team might include "feeder patterns" where early childhood, elementary, middle, and high school teachers work together to make transitioning easier and learning more logical as students move through their schooling. In a school building, a vertical team often consists of one representative from each grade level.

Members of a vertical team develop a sense of trust and support, gain new perspectives, and are "equals" in decision-making and problem-solving processes. Vertical teaming enhances school effectiveness as it allows individuals at various levels or "planes" to interact and "... express a clear commitment to work together and support school improvement" (Cunningham & Gresso, 1993, p. 54). Proponents of the vertical team approach believe that the interdependency created by vertical teams greatly improves education "... by simply strengthening the connections among people who work at all levels within the organization" (p. 53).

Within a campus, vertical teams are created to ensure consistency while avoiding redundancy in the curriculum. Prekindergarten, kindergarten, and first-grade teachers plan transitions for children as they move from grade to grade. By discussing plans and projects, comparing curriculum objectives, and reviewing student work samples, teachers in first and second grades can better understand their contributions to the successes of children in the third and fourth grades.

Horizontal teaming. In contrast to vertical teams, whose members are at various levels in the school community, **horizontal teams** are composed of members who are at the *same* levels. For example, all same-level music or art teachers in a district may meet for training and curriculum development. These teams of teachers naturally bond with and support each other as they are normally "all in the same boat." Thus horizontal team members tend to form cohesive groups.

Some principals arrange for horizontal teams of teachers at the same grade level to have common planning periods. This facilitates the sharing of ideas and concerns, as well as promoting improved teaching strategies as team members focus on shared goals.

Team teaching. Early childhood educators are more likely than teachers at other levels to be involved in team teaching. **Team teaching** refers to a number of different structures that involve two or more teachers and/or assistants working together in classrooms. Children often benefit from the combined expertise of teachers when classes are joined.

Prekindergarten programs typically hire para-professional teaching assistants to work alongside the Pre-K teacher in classrooms with 3- and 4-year-old children. Similarly, special education teachers often oversee the work of teachers' aides, who supplement the care and education of children with special needs. Although the school principal is legally the supervisor of all educational personnel, classroom teachers are most often the leaders of instructional teams on a daily basis. For children to benefit, team members require clearly defined roles and the ability to communicate effectively (Morgan & Ashbaker, 2001).

Early childhood practices of mixed-age grouping result in teaching teams that work with children whose ages range at least a year apart (Katz, Evangelou, & Hartman, 1990). For example, typical age groupings might include combinations such as K–first (5- and 6-year-olds), first–second (6- and 7-year-olds), second–third (7- and 8-year-olds), or first–second–third (6- through 8-year-olds). Children of various ages, abilities, and interests are purposefully combined in ungraded heterogeneous classrooms to better meet individual needs (Gayfer, 1991). Differences in children's developmental levels are respected, and accommodations are made for a wide range of skills and competencies (Moore & Brown, 1995). In addition, teachers of mixed-age classrooms form adult learning communities within schools by planning together and exchanging ideas, sharing materials, visiting each other's classrooms, and providing mutual support (Moore & Brown, 1996).

Mentors. A new teacher should be assigned or matched with a **mentor,** who serves as friend, advisor, and more knowledgeable guide for the **novice,** or beginning teacher. A mentoring approach acknowledges that it takes time and support mechanisms for teachers to acquire new skills and to apply them appropriately in classroom settings (Lieberman, 1995; Sparks & Loucks-Horsley, 1989). Mentors are not evaluators who determine rehiring, so the risk of appearing incompetent is diminished for the novice, or **protégé.** The mentor's primary role is to build a trusting, professional relationship with the beginning teacher, based on mutual respect and a genuine understanding of the demands placed on novices. Mentors may be asked by the principal or by new teachers to observe in classrooms, offering helpful hints. Another set of eyes in beginners' classrooms can often generate suggestions that can help make the whole year easier.

In Texas, a mentor should be appointed for each novice. However, a mentor/mentee relationship may not always work out well. One reason may be the absence of a common meeting time. Beginners must initiate the search for an experienced teacher who is willing to create a true mentor/protégé relationship. In some schools, a principal, assistant principal, grade-level chairperson, or early childhood specialist will adopt the role of mentor for new teachers. A mentor guides the novice or protégé through the maze of school policies and procedures, explaining calendars of events and routines, demonstrating effective communications with colleagues, and encouraging problem solving (Lakein, 1999).

It is not unusual for beginning teachers to need some assistance with curriculum, instructional strategies, lesson planning, student assessment, classroom management, educational resources, and relating positively with parents and the community. Mentors serve as role models and promote reflective practice by scheduling classroom visits and offering constructive feedback. With thoughtful guidance from supportive mentors, novice teachers learn to make informed teaching decisions, gain professional knowledge and skills, and move progressively toward becoming self-reliant practitioners (Gordon & Maxey, 2000; Portner, 1998).

It is important for beginning teachers to be receptive to constructive criticism and suggestions from both mentors and supervisors. Many mentors volunteer their time or are paid minimally for the extra effort required to help a newcomer. Every teacher's style is different, so it is not expected that novices will incorporate every idea or mannerism of their mentors. However, respect for mentors' experience is appreciated.

District personnel. It is the intent of school district personnel to keep abreast of current educational trends, issues, practices, theory, and advances in learning and instruction. Their expertise is then shared with administrators and teachers. They are particularly attentive to state and national policies, laws, and legal procedures related to individual student needs, assessment, and instruction. Teachers may ask these individuals for support in their own professional development needs, such as curriculum development, program development, and skill-building activities.

District-level personnel, such as the *curriculum coordinator, technology coordinator, special education director, psychologists,* and *diagnosticians,* are typically not located at individual school sites. These professionals coordinate efforts to ensure that the district maintains uniform standards and provides quality, developmentally-appropriate instruction for all students.

The *curriculum coordinator,* who is focused on the scope and sequence of curriculum, assists the district by (a) identifying curriculum needs; (b) providing leadership in making curriculum changes or improvements; (c) collaborating with textbook publishers and their representatives; (d) remaining up-to-date about instructional methods, materials, and equipment; (e) providing workshops and faculty development training; (f) maintaining textbooks and curriculum guides; and (g) organizing and leading committees related to textbook adoption.

The main responsibility of the *district technology coordinator* is to work with faculty and staff to (a) identify technology needs, resources, and funding; (b) train teachers; (c) address issues related to ethical, legal, gender, copyright, and student access; (d) select appropriate software and hardware; (e) design school media labs and centers; (f) oversee equipment maintenance and repair; and (g) evaluate technology programs and projects.

Special education directors work diligently to ensure that children with learning differences are able to participate in appropriate classroom learning environments. These directors collaborate with professionals and paraprofessionals to identify children who need specialized services. Upon identifying children who qualify for additional services, special education personnel design intervention strategies for the students and their families. Teachers can ask the special education director for suggestions about modification of classroom assignments and activities, adaptive technology, classroom aids and resources, behavior management, access, legal and ethical provisions, and outside organizations that offer additional support.

School psychologists and *diagnosticians* test and evaluate children's abilities. An array of comprehensive tests of intelligence, hearing, vision, and general health accompany other indications of a student's capabilities. Records of academic achievement and performance, learning style inventories, classroom observations, and information from the child's family enable a team of these professionals to provide services to all students.

School board. Each district has a school board or board of trustees that contributes to the governance and management of the school district. The people who live within the district boundaries elect the members of the local board. It is the school board's task to:

- Establish overall district policies

- Oversee the district budget, instruction, and salaries

- Approve the hiring of new district employees

- Ensure teacher competency

- Monitor extracurricular activities

- Set school calendars and schedules

- Listen to and address concerns from students, parents, teachers, and the community

- Communicate the district goals, policies, and procedures to the general public

- Examine student achievement, absenteeism, truancy, and the dropout rate

- Participate in the general administration of the district

- Function as public relations officers

- Approve district and campus performance objectives

- Levy and collect taxes

- Issue bonds

PARTICIPATION

Teacher interaction and communication include participation in various school and district activities. New teachers may be unaware of and uncertain about their roles and responsibilities in the school and district. Even though they do not have as much experience as some of the other teachers, they should not hesitate to share their ideas and suggestions with their colleagues. Beginning teachers often have an energy force that is refreshing to teachers who have taught for a longer period of time. New teachers are also fresh from universities and other preparation entities, where they have been exposed to the latest research and methodologies. Teachers with some experience often see new opportunities that have been overlooked, and they become more eager to try out new strategies and techniques. Thus the relationships are the basis for a "mutual admiration society," where each learns from the other.

It is extremely important for teachers to initiate and maintain supportive, cooperative relationships with their professional colleagues. One way to remain a respected member of a team or faculty is to perform all assigned duties, such as attending faculty and committee meetings, and being on time for bus duty, recess duty, and so forth. Professional colleagues are more receptive to building relationships with teachers who are willing to assist other teachers when they ask for help and who reciprocate.

Avoiding gossip, maintaining a professional demeanor in front of students and parents, and striving to uphold community values help form a good foundation for a successful teaching career.

School Committees

Participating as a member of school and district committees ensures that teachers have input in the decisions that closely affect them, their teaching, and their children. A well-run school and district depend on the contribution of time, energy, efforts, and support of its administrators, teachers, faculty, and staff.

Depending on the size of the school and district, teachers may have a wide selection of opportunities to participate in school events and projects. Some committees are happy to accept volunteers, whereas others are based on membership that is elected or appointed.

Developing reciprocal teacher support requires active listening, acceptance, and respect for the diverse ideas and contributions that each teacher offers. As teachers share mutual concerns, seek information, exchange ideas and techniques, and ask questions, they are both sources of strength to others and recipients of support from others. Building this support system requires that teachers (a) be flexible about routines and procedures, (b) agree to compromise, (c) show support for other teachers' projects, (d) be willing to learn new ways of doing things, and (e) volunteer their help with school activities.

School Projects and Functions

School projects and functions create openings for teachers to work with their professional colleagues. Becoming members of the committees at the school campus benefits both teachers and students. Teachers who work together on committees are able to problem solve for themselves and for their students. Some committee work occurs during the school day, but many extracurricular activities or events require teacher participation outside the normal school hours. The number and variety of committees available to teachers (a) keep them involved in school activities, (b) increase their own professional development opportunities, and (c) benefit others as they share their individual expertise and special interests.

Traditionally teachers meet on a regular basis at staff meetings, parent-teacher organization meetings, and departmental meetings. Other committees depend on teachers to help make decisions about school rules and student disciplinary action on their campus and to offer their input and expertise. Teachers may find themselves on committees that provide leadership for holiday programs, plays, musicals, hospitality, talent shows, awards, field trips, guest performances, intramural events, recitals, choir performances, carnivals, fundraising, athletic events, rehearsals, and book fairs. Teachers may also prefer or be asked to join committees whose agendas focus on areas such as crisis and safety management, drug or gang awareness and prevention, child abuse prevention, multicultural awareness, discipline, leadership, tutoring, mentoring of new teachers, technology, school spirit, and admission, review, and dismissal (ARD) for special populations.

Whether teachers volunteer in the school cafeteria or on the playground, help answer phone calls, file in the office, supervise garage sales, or clean up after school functions, their visibility is influential. Involved teachers become role models for their children, who are observing their teacher-teacher, teacher-student, teacher-administrator, and teacher-parent interactions.

Site-Based Decision Making (SBDM)

Reflective teachers are proactive, energetic, and eager to participate in making decisions that impact them, their children, their school, and their community. These teachers realize the personal and professional benefits of working together.

When teachers, parents, community leaders, administrators, and other staff work together as a decision-making body at the school level, they are participating in **site-based decision making (SBDM).** SBDM is also known as school-based management, collaborative decision making, shared governance, shared-decision making, or decentralization.

As part of the SBDM structure, many of the decisions related to educational procedures and processes are made at individual school sites, rather than at the district or more centralized administrative level. Such decisions may include staff development, budgeting, curriculum planning, school organization, selection of new teachers and administrators, school schedules, reorganization, and new programs and procedures. When decisions are made at the campus level, all participants can experience a feeling of ownership and responsibility. The primary purpose of the SBDM, however, is to improve student achievement (Texas Education Agency, 1992, pp. 11–15), particularly through the Campus Improvement Plan. Each school campus in every district has a **Campus Improvement Plan (CIP),** which is the product of the campus-level planning and decision-making process. The CIP supports district goals and objectives and focuses on improving all students' performance. Campus-level committees offer teachers experience in making decisions related to their own school planning, budgeting, curriculum, staffing, staff development, and school organization.

Each Campus Improvement Plan must include (a) student assessments, (b) goals, (c) performance objectives and a plan to achieve these objectives, (d) descriptions of staff and resources needed to attain the goals and objectives, (e) timelines for achieving goals, (f) supervision and measurement of progress toward goals, (g) prevention and intervention plans against school violence, and (h) programs that involve parents in school activities. Campus Improvement Plans are reviewed and revised annually by representatives of the school leadership team. Many schools require participation by all faculty members.

District Committees

Membership in district-level committees expands teachers' choices in making decisions that affect them personally. Committees are formed to celebrate special events such as El Cinco de Mayo, Martin Luther King Day, Cesar Chavez Day, and multicultural fairs. Individual programs (bilingual/ESL, gifted and talented, etc.) and academics (mathematics, literacy, spelling, etc.) frequently have committees to further understanding and communication across the district. In addition, teachers from the various grade levels work together on committees to develop consistency and quality of instruction as children progress from the elementary grades to middle school, and finally to high school.

Teacher assistance with textbook adoption, curriculum design, and site-based decision-making committees at all levels is essential. Committees are needed to (a) design district faculty development training, (b) conduct needs assessments at individual campus sites, (c) approve and purchase technology equipment, (d) examine district resources available and those needed, and (e) identify additional teaching materials. Frequently teacher committees arrange for sessions that develop teachers' knowledge, enhance existing knowledge, and concentrate on individual content area training.

Whether teachers decide to participate on committees at the individual school building or on committees at the district level, they focus their efforts on what is important to children, parents, and the school district as a whole. Through active participation on committees and task forces, teachers facilitate communication and coordination between the schools and the community.

District Improvement Plan

Teachers work cooperatively to support student learning by identifying, achieving, and evaluating their District Improvement Plan. The purpose of this plan is to assist district and campus staff in their attempts to improve performance for all groups of students (Texas Education Agency, 1992).

Teachers can participate in their district's planning and decision-making committees. The District Improvement Plan allows teachers to have significant input about a district's (a) needs, (b) objectives, (c) strategies to improve student achievement, (d) strategies for underachieving students, (d) special programs, (e) dropout prevention and intervention, (f) technology integration, (g) discipline management, (h) staff development, (i) career education, and (j) counseling.

EVALUATION

Teacher Appraisal System

Part of being a professional is assuming the roles and responsibilities associated with that profession. Reflective practitioners are afraid neither to evaluate themselves nor to be evaluated by others. In fact, they seek opinions of experienced educators to guide their own improvement. Trained administrators conduct annual evaluations, with appraisals of each teacher's performance. During the course of the school year, administrators observe each teacher and follow established criteria to identify acceptable performance levels.

The **Professional Development Appraisal System (PDAS)** is the current appraisal system used by the majority of Texas school districts. However, a district may apply for approval to use an alternative system. The PDAS framework was developed in 1995 as a result of the provisions of Senate Bill 1. Professional associations, teachers, principals, superintendents, personnel directors, and service center training personnel participated in the development and field trial of the PDAS. It is the intent of the PDAS to influence student achievement by:

- Increasing the level of professional practice

- Being more sensitive to the needs of teachers and administrators

- Supporting ongoing quality professional development

- Addressing individual student learning needs and instruction

- Enhancing teamwork

- Augmenting school improvement

- Acknowledging good teaching practices (Texas Education Agency, 1997)

The PDAS is designed to (a) link the proficiencies identified in *Learner-Centered Schools for Texas: A Vision of Texas Educators* (Texas Education Agency, 1995), TAAS (TAKS) objectives, student performance, and district and individual campus goals; (b) make connections among learners, curriculum, activities and assessment; and (c) focus on the learner and the learning environment. This professional development appraisal system concentrates on the following eight **domains,** or areas:

1. Active successful student participation in the learning process

2. Learner-centered instruction

3. Evaluation and feedback on student progress

4. Management of student discipline, instructional strategies, time, and materials

5. Professional communication

6. Professional development

7. Compliance with policies, operating procedures, and requirements

8. Improvement of academic performance of all students on the campus

Teachers are evaluated on each of these eight domains. Each domain is scored independently, and the final evaluation includes data gathered from observations of the teacher and a written summary of each observation. Other documentation includes (a) the teacher's completed Teacher Self-Report Form, (b) a written summative annual appraisal report that is shared with the teacher, and (c) a summative annual conference.

The focus of the evaluation is threefold. First, the PDAS describes how teachers contribute to increasing their students' achievement. Second, the evaluation identifies how teachers are making the entire school site safe and orderly. Finally, the PDAS determines how teachers are creating a stimulating learning environment for their students (Texas Education Agency, 1997).

The quality and quantity levels of the teacher's performance are identified in the following four categories of evaluation in each domain. They are:

1. Exceeds expectations (90 percent–100 percent)

2. Proficient (80 percent–89 percent)

3. Below expectations (50 percent–79 percent)

4. Unsatisfactory (0 percent–49 percent)

Self-Assessment

One requirement of the PDAS is the **Teacher Self-Report Form,** which encourages teachers to look within themselves and examine closely their personal convictions. This report becomes a personal, introspective, and informal evaluation, or **self-assessment.** Reflection provides teachers a chance to assess, analyze, and examine their own responses to educational issues and practices. Teachers chart goals for improvement in their practice at the beginning of the year and examine to what extent their goals were attained at the year's end. Evaluation is then an "... evaluation of the teacher by the teacher and for the teacher" (Airasian & Gullickson, 1997, p. 2).

Self-appraisal is absolutely necessary for teachers to become better teachers. By thinking through their own assumptions or by examining "... their underlying beliefs and taken-for-granted assumptions and theories" (Moallem, 1997, p. 149), teachers can identify areas of personal strength, personal challenge, and potential problems.

Within the first few weeks of school, teachers identify and submit their professional goals. Personal self-assessments by teachers will assist them as they complete their written Teacher Self-Report Form, which is a part of the Professional Development and Appraisal System (PDAS). Teachers must complete and present this form to the principal at least 2 weeks before their annual **summative,** or final, conference, which is scheduled for spring.

In the self-report form, teachers identify target areas for their continued professional growth and discuss specific contributions they have made to the improvement of academic performance of their students. Teachers are required to specifically describe how they:

- Made adjustments in their instruction, based on their students' needs

- Monitored classroom performance

- Addressed their students' attendance problems

- Worked with students who were failing or at risk of failing

- Related their professional development activities to campus and district goals

- Applied their professional development activities to their classroom instruction

PROFESSIONAL DEVELOPMENT

The process of self-assessment leads teachers to reflect about their basic ideas and assumptions. Initially they should clarify their beliefs about what it means to be a professional educator. Next they will find it essential to identify their individual needs and goals. Finally, as teachers identify their specific needs and goals, they should determine what resources and support they will need to expedite their professional development. At the same time, administrators are assessing needs for individual teachers and the campus faculty as a whole to determine necessary support for professional growth.

Professionalism

Professionalism is defined primarily by how teachers see themselves as members of the teaching profession. In addition, professionalism involves the images that teachers project, or how others see them as they behave in a professional manner and interact with colleagues, children and their families, and members of the surrounding community. It is a big responsibility. Gone are the days when teachers were given a long list of behaviors deemed "unacceptable" by the community. However, good judgment is required at all times, because teachers represent their schools, their school districts, and the profession whenever they appear in public. Those who uphold professional standards and ethical behavior receive the support of their communities, which approve bond measures, and state legislators, who approve salary increases.

Becoming a teacher in Texas represents a major life transition that affects not only job tasks and work hours but also the teacher's personal identity and status in the community. Most undergraduate prospective teachers progress from their primary roles as university students to those as "student teachers" with limited classroom responsibilities, and finally to positions as full-time teachers, who assume all of the roles and responsibilities of the profession. Those who have chosen teaching after having pursued other career choices are redefining their personal goals and are adding the defining qualities of teaching to their current repertoires.

Needs

One of the first steps teachers must take is to clearly identify their current needs in relation to improving their own professional knowledge and skills. This process will help determine a pathway for **professional development.** Administrators, other teachers, specialists, and district personnel are available to help provide guidance and resources. Professional development is often viewed only as workshops provided by the district or region, but there are many activities that contribute to growth in teaching. As teachers reflect on their needs, they become analytical and diagnostic because they know that they will be laying the foundation for their future growth (Ayers, 1989). Reflective teachers can predict and anticipate their growth needs in particular areas of interest or in light of state initiatives. The growth of reflective teachers never ends. The curiosity and dedication to the profession characteristic of reflective practitioners inspires them to look behind at what they have accomplished and forward to the adventures that lie ahead.

Teachers' interests and needs change, as do their experiences. Individual schools and districts are able to provide for many of these needs. **Support systems** within each school can alleviate teachers' concerns that revolve around the day-to-day classroom. Local, district, or regional personnel are also available to introduce teachers to new trends and issues in their content area, the integration of other subjects into their own content area, behavior intervention assistance, school policies and procedures, and the completion of required paperwork.

Texas districts are divided into 20 Regional Education Service Centers (ESCs), which provide training and technical assistance in teaching, implementing special programs, and complying with state laws and federal regulations. Workshops and other resources are also readily available to teachers.

Goals

Based on their needs, self-assessments, results of the PDAS, recommendations from their principal or campus supervisor, and suggestions from mentors and peers, teachers select some short-term and long-term goals for self-improvement or professional development. While doing so, they must identify appropriate resources and then create a workable plan of action with reasonable time frames.

Teachers realize that self-motivation, time-management skills, stamina, specific planning, and perseverance are required to overcome the obstacles they may face in achieving their goals. Personal effort, endurance, and devotion to becoming all they can become contribute to teachers' abilities to realize their goals. Teachers need not feel alone as they seek to improve. Grants for continuing education, other professional development workshops and activities, and scholarships are available to help them as they continue to grow, both professionally and personally.

To identify, plan for, and achieve their goals, teachers may require support from their principal and coworkers. For example, in order to attend regional, state, and national conferences or specific training sessions, they may need supplemental travel funds, a substitute teacher to cover their classes, and release time to be away from the school campus. Such support is more likely to be forthcoming if teachers offer to share their newly acquired skills with colleagues in team planning meetings or other faculty-sponsored events. Teachers must carefully document their attendance at and participation in all professional development activities and maintain these records for future use, particularly the professional development hours required by the district and/or state. Certificates and other evidence of participation or presentation should become a part of their professional portfolios.

Continuing Professional Education Requirements

Teacher education does not end with university graduation or state certification; it is an ongoing process for which teachers must assume lifelong responsibility. Recent changes in the state certification process underscore the necessity of continuing professional development. Teacher licensure in Texas was previously awarded for a lifetime, but current licensure is based on 5-year renewable increments.

The State Board for Educator Certification (SBEC) adopted a new policy on September 1, 1999, that currently mandates 150 hours of **Continuing Professional Education** (CPE). These hours must be validated as a condition of certificate renewal. CPE emphasizes that teachers are responsible for updating their knowledge and skills in content areas, best practices, research, and technology that support improved student achievement (State Board for Educator Certification, 2001a). The following have been identified by SBEC as acceptable CPE activities:

- Participating in institutes, workshops, seminars, conferences, or in service or staff development that relate to or enhance the professional knowledge and skills of the educator

- Completing undergraduate or graduate courses, or training programs through an accredited institution of higher education in the content area knowledge and skills related to the certificate being renewed

- Participating in interactive distance learning, video conferences, and online activities or conferences

- Accomplishing independent study, which may include self-study of relevant professional materials (books, journals, periodicals, video- and audiotapes, computer software, and online information) or writing a published work

- Developing curriculum or CPE training materials

- Serving as an assessor for the principal assessment process

- Teaching or presenting a CPE activity

- Providing professional guidance as a mentor educator

Whatever their goals may be, Texas teachers can choose from a wide selection of activities and programs that will help them develop into better professionals.

Resources and Support

Although most teachers begin their careers with anticipation, enthusiasm, and a strong sense of commitment to making a difference for students, the reality of everyday teaching can be overwhelming in the first few months on the job (Moir, 1999). Survival becomes the major goal of beginning teachers, who need to be accepted as professionals by students, parents, colleagues, and supervisors. New teachers may be frustrated by doubts and limited **self-efficacy** (Baptiste & Sheerer, 1997; Katz, 1972). When teachers experience limited self-efficacy, they believe that they lack the power to be effective and the ability to accomplish what they intend to do.

The imperfect behavior of students, the unexpected demands of paperwork and extra duties, and the sense of isolation that comes from teaching behind closed doors often lead new teachers to struggle on their own. Novices may suffer from fatigue or a sense of failure or depression, or may find themselves becoming more authoritarian and

dominating in their treatment of students (Gordon & Maxey, 2000). Admitting that they do not know how to manage their classrooms, how best to organize curriculum, or how to grade assignments equitably risks appearing incompetent and "not worthy" of being a teacher (North Carolina Department of Public Instruction, 2000). Disillusionment may follow, as beginning teachers question their career choices (Gordon & Maxey, 2000; Olebe, 2001; Young & Crain, 1993).

Without adequate support for both emotional and practical needs, an alarming proportion of new teachers leave the field within 2 to 5 years (Gordon & Maxey, 2000; Halford, 1999; Katz, 1977). In an effort to retain and fully assist teachers, school districts are recognizing the importance of providing support for new teachers in negotiating the challenges of their first years of teaching. School districts also realize that teacher support and development must ". . . be sustained, on-going, intensive, and supported by modeling, coaching, and the collective solving of specific problems of practice" (Darling-Hammond & McLaughlin, 1995, p. 598).

Teachers can access numerous resources for support, information, and training. Resources may exist in the school community. Campus- and district-level teacher training includes inservice sessions, special programs, groups, and research. Universities, Regional Education Service Centers, and professional organizations offer support for teachers' professional growth and development.

When teachers seek opportunities for professional growth, they will no doubt look first to their own campus and district to discover faculty development activities planned for the current year. Staff development teams employed by the school district and Regional Education Service Centers generally plan and publish schedules that include a wide range of professional development offerings. These opportunities may range from short-term workshops to semester- or year-long courses of study, such as the state-initiated reading and math academies. Some are presented in centralized locations whereas others are offered at campus sites. The information presented may be content specific or cross-disciplinary. Teachers should plan to locate these publications and reserve a place for any sessions that seem appropriate. The more popular sessions often fill very quickly.

Based on the results of the Campus Improvement Plan, some workshops and focused training sessions are made available to all teachers. Other topics, however, are geared to particular grade levels or academic areas. Teachers are required to attend particular professional development sessions, but participation in other activities may be voluntary.

Teacher study groups serve as alternative approaches to improving professional knowledge and skills (Jenlink & Kinnucan-Welsch, 2001). A group of like-minded teachers meet regularly to investigate new curriculum content or to read and discuss current literature, with the purpose of analyzing and applying new teaching strategies. The group provides a structure for study, a sounding board for new ideas, and support for experimentation. For example, a team of teachers might read current books and articles related to research on brain development and then discuss methods for changing curriculum development at their grade levels.

The formation of reflective practice groups is another approach that emphasizes effective teaching to increase student achievement (Chase et al., 2001). Such groups may include new teachers, their mentors, veteran teachers, administrators, and teacher educators. Members tell stories about their teaching or share critical teaching moments. Then they ask for critical feedback from group members in a setting that ensures confidentiality.

Participation in **action research** provides a direct approach to augmenting a teacher's own professional knowledge and improving classroom teaching. With the support of critical peers, a university instructor, and/or an outside researcher, teachers can systematically investigate specific professional problems. Using a basic action research routine, teachers identify classroom concerns, hypothesize possible solutions, generate theories that interpret and explain the situation, select and implement a plan of action, and evaluate the results (Stringer, 1996). Because teachers focus on their own practices, the outcomes are seen as having an immediate impact on students while improving the teachers' confidence and sense of professionalism (Feldman & Atkin, 1995).

Teacher induction programs. Teacher induction programs are designed to assist new teachers in adjusting to the school culture by providing orientation to policies and procedures, as well as explanations of the unique history and customs of the campus (Ganser, 1995). An on-site or traveling mentor who is readily available to answer questions and alleviate concerns provides much-needed guidance during the survival phase of teaching (Baptiste & Sheerer, 1997).

The Texas Beginning Educator Support System (TxBESS) is a pilot program of teacher induction sponsored by the State Board for Educator Certification (2001). A local support team that consists of an experienced teacher-mentor, the principal, and a representative from a teacher preparation program provides on-the-job training to ensure effective teaching practices and to "improve the ability to work successfully with diverse children and communities" (State Board for Educator Certification, 2001, p. 1). New teachers are also provided with formative feedback to promote professional growth.

Universities. Credit courses are a Teacher Education Agency approved source of professional development. One semester hour of credit is equivalent to 15 CPE clock hours, and a 3-hour course counts as 45 CPE clock hours. Graduate and undergraduate course selections should be directly related to the teacher's content area, research, and best practice in education, and/or the integration of technology. Many universities have optional online study courses that can be taken for credit or continuing education.

Distance education classes are available to teachers who decide to take online courses offered by universities. These courses differ from the traditional classes offered on the university campus. Many completely online courses do not require that participants come to the university site for actual classroom instruction. For other courses, participants may be required to attend a limited number of university campus classes. In this situation, however, the majority of the instruction is completed online.

Universities and colleges regularly sponsor conferences with themes such as Early Literacy, At-Risk Learners, Bilingual Education, or Preventing Child Abuse. Flyers and announcements are often distributed through area school districts, educational cable programs, local newspapers, and radio stations.

Regional Education Service Centers. Professional coursework is also available through the 20 Regional Education Service Centers located throughout Texas. Each center provides activities that include coursework, workshops, and teacher training sessions. Programs at these centers offer a varied selection of professional development opportunities that allow teachers to update their knowledge and skills or gain new knowledge and skills.

Professional Organizations

A well-advised move toward professionalism for both preservice and new teachers is to join professional organizations. There are a variety of organizations designed specifically to meet the needs of educators.

Professional organizations present conferences each year. These conferences provide numerous sessions, panel discussions, poster presentations, research, and papers related to specific themes and topics. Teachers are encouraged to join and become active participants in professional organizations that offer contact with other professionals who have the same or similar interests. Information and discussions about current topics are frequently featured in the journals and newsletters of these organizations. Some organizations also provide Web sites that list clinics, symposiums, and online courses available to members. An additional benefit of membership is the option of pur-

chasing professional liability insurance, a necessity for all educators in these litigious times.

Professional journals and other publications keep educators well informed about current research and practice. Participation in conferences and symposiums offers valuable opportunities for networking with colleagues, gaining insight into policy decisions, and sharing successful educational strategies and programs. Some organizations also offer self-paced online learning modules focused on current topics such as differentiating instruction or incorporating multiple intelligences.

There are many choices to investigate. The National Education Association (NEA) boasts 2.6 million members. Founded in 1857, it is the oldest and largest organization supporting the cause of public education (National Education Association, 2000). The Texas State Teachers Association (TSTA) is an affiliate whose members across the state are teachers, librarians, counselors, support staff, administrators, and faculty. College and university students who plan to teach can join the Texas State Teachers Student Program (TSTA-SD), which has local chapters.

The American Federation of Teachers (AFT), organized in 1916, is a trade union representing workers in education, public service, and health care, with more than 1 million members nationwide. It is an affiliate of the AFL-CIO and a strong advocate for public education. The Texas Federation of Teachers (TFT) is the state affiliate organization.

Early childhood educators can choose to join the National Association for the Education of Young Children (NAEYC). This 75-year-old organization focuses on quality programs for children from birth through third grade (National Association for the Education of Young Children, 2001). The national headquarters in Washington, D.C. publishes a variety of professional books and videos, plus the journals *Young Children* and *Early Childhood Research Quarterly.* Annual conferences are the largest in North America, drawing more than 20,000 members. The position statement, entitled *Developmentally Appropriate Practice in Early Childhood Programs,* was adopted by the state department of education in Texas in 1994 (Bredekamp & Copple, 1997).

The Texas Association for the Education of Young Children (TAEYC) is located in Austin, Texas, with local affiliate chapters in communities throughout the state. The chapters provide additional opportunities for educators to come together for conferences, training sessions, socialization, celebrations of the Week of the Young Child, and advocacy on behalf of young children.

The Southern Early Childhood Association (SECA), located in Little Rock, Arkansas, is an organization of preschool, kindergarten, and primary teachers and administrators; caregivers and program directors; and individuals working with and for families. Texas is one of the 14 member states, with affiliation through TAEYC. SECA publishes the journal *Dimensions of Early Childhood,* position statements related to brain research, assessment, quality child care, and technology, as well as books and videos related to early childhood education.

Another organization that appeals to early childhood educators is the Association for Childhood Education International (ACEI), which was founded in 1892 as the International Kindergarten Union. The membership celebrates the Week of the Classroom Teacher and publishes *Childhood Education* and the *Journal of Research in Childhood Education,* as well as professional focus newsletters for teachers of infants and toddlers, Pre-K and K, and elementary students (ages 7–10). Books, brochures, video- and audiotapes, and position papers are some of the resources for educators distributed by the organization. Annual conferences are held in the United States and Canada, and world conferences and symposiums are convened in sites such as the Philippines, Chile, and China.

Additional professional organizations are designed to meet the needs of teachers in particular teaching fields and specializations. The following are some examples:

- American Alliance for Health, Physical Education, Recreation, and Dance
- Association for Supervision and Curriculum Development
- Council for Exceptional Children
- International Reading Association
- Music Teachers National Association
- National Art Association
- National Association for the Advancement of Computing in Education
- National Association for Bilingual Education
- National Association for Gifted Children
- National Association for Multicultural Education
- National Council for the Social Studies
- National Council of Teachers of English
- National Council of Teachers of Mathematics
- National Science Teachers Association

SUMMARY

Fulfilling the roles and responsibilities of a professional educator requires that teachers act and react appropriately with numerous individuals within and without the school community. Through the process of reflection, teachers become reflective practitioners who evaluate their effectiveness, participate in school and district activities, collaborate to enhance student achievement, and oversee their own professional development.

Beginning teachers have support systems that will help them to become well-trained and well-informed educators, able to instruct, tutor, coach, inform, and enlighten the public school children in Texas. To be of maximum value, these support systems require that teachers (a) develop reciprocal cooperative relationships, (b) understand and accept the unique contributions of others, (c) exhibit productive performance, (d) share ideas and visions, (e) solve problems and make decisions, and (f) become contributing members of teams.

Teachers, by themselves, cannot provide everything for all of their children, all of the time. However, when they join forces, combine efforts, and merge with other professionals, the chance that they will help more children more often becomes a reality.

GLOSSARY

action research   a method of investigating a problem in a school or classroom that involves the scientific processes of identifying, analyzing, planning, implementing, and evaluating problems, concerns, or educational questions. Teachers serve as the primary investigators to improve their own teaching practices.

administrators   superintendents, principals, assistant principals, instructional specialists, grade-level chairpersons, and supervisors who are essential to providing support for the personal and academic needs of students.

Campus Improvement Plan (CIP)   a stratagem for involving teachers in individual campus-level planning, evaluation, and decision-making processes at their own school.

collaboration   a group process that emphasizes a common vision and shared responsibility for planning and implementing goals.

Continuing Professional Education (CPE)   state requirements for certificate renewal specifying participation in approved learning experiences that improve and update an educator's knowledge and skills.

domains   specific areas of related information.

family liaisons   school representatives who serve as contacts and promote positive links between school personnel and the parents, grandparents, and relatives of enrolled children.

horizontal teaming   joint planning and decision making by teachers at the same grade level or in similar content area.

mentor   an experienced teacher or administrator who provides guidance and individualized assistance to promote retention and success for new teachers.

nonverbal communication   conversing with another individual without using spoken words (e.g., shaking head, raising eyebrows, nodding).

novice   a new or beginning teacher who has limited teaching experience.

parent educators   personnel who provide information about child growth and development and support for family members in their roles as primary caregivers of children.

professional development   activities that enhance teachers' personal knowledge, competence, expertise, and growth as educators.

Professional Development Appraisal System (PDAS)   a formal evaluation of a teacher's performance in the classroom in Texas.

protégé   a beginning teacher who benefits from the wisdom and guidance of a mentor.

reflection   giving serious thought or consideration to issues, activities, or events related to teaching and learning.

reflective practitioners   teachers who contemplate, look at again, or study their past teaching moments to enhance professional growth and student achievement.

reflective teaching   the natural outcome of teachers' re-examination and re-evaluation of their teaching.

reflective thinking   the process of probing, inspecting, and studying to improve one's teaching practice.

school community   individuals and organizations that assist one another in providing learning opportunities for students.

self-assessment, self-evaluation   teachers' rating, judging, or critiquing of their own performance, abilities, and effectiveness.

self-efficacy   effectiveness; the extent to which a teacher believes she or he can influence how well students learn.

site-based decision making   a procedure whereby teachers participate in the management, decision making, and governing of their own school and district.

specialists   individuals within the school community who have specific knowledge, understanding, and expertise in a particular area of information (e.g., psychologists and diagnosticians).

summative   a final, total evaluation of a teacher's performance at the end of a period of time (e.g., a school year).

support systems   individuals and organizations who are a source of strength, guidance, and encouragement for teachers and students.

teacher appraisal system   a procedure for the evaluation, assessment, and critiquing of teachers' abilities to provide meaningful learning outcomes for their students.

Teacher Self-Report Form   a requirement of PDAS that encourages teachers to look within themselves and examine closely their personal convictions; a personal, introspective, and informal evaluation or self-assessment.

team teaching   instruction provided by two or more teachers who share responsibility for planning and implementing learning experiences for the same class or group of students.

verbal communication   use of spoken words to transmit information to other individuals.

vertical teaming   joint planning and decision making across grade levels by teachers and other district employees whose focus is school and/or districtwide effectiveness.

SUGGESTED ACTIVITIES

1. Explore the Web sites for professional organizations. Choose two of the organizations that you find most interesting. You may want to select one that is geared toward your academic specialization and one for more generalized audiences. Create a chart or table to compare and contrast the following:

   - Mission statement
   - Target audience
   - History, background information
   - Location of headquarters
   - Benefits and services for members
   - State affiliates and/or local chapters
   - Cost of membership
   - Professional journals and/or newsletters (titles and purposes)
   - Publications (sample titles, range of topics)
   - Educational resources and products such as audio- and videotapes, brochures, posters
   - Position papers (sample titles, range of topics)
   - Legislative news and alerts
   - Policy initiatives, special projects
   - Job announcements and placement services
   - Opportunities for professional development through conferences, symposiums, leadership training sessions, discussion forums, and online courses.

2. Review a current issue of an educational journal published by one of the professional education organizations. Does the journal seem to focus more on research or practical applications in the teaching field? Check the table of contents. How many articles are there? What is the average length of an article? Make a list of the major topics in this issue. Is there an overall theme that connects the topics? Are there departments or specialized sections that appear to be printed regularly, such as letters from readers, tips for teachers, and association news? Are there photographs, illustrations, tables, and graphics? Does the journal contain advertisements? If so, what types of products are advertised? Are there book reviews, evaluations of software and technological resources, and/or recommendations of relevant Web sites? Are there notices of upcoming legislation or public policy reports? Read one of the articles. How can you use this information as a new teacher?

3. Write a letter to a friend who is a beginning teacher. Try to persuade her or him to enroll in a particular workshop or join a professional organization of your choice. Explain the benefits of participating with colleagues in professional development activities and accessing the latest resources relevant to your field. In sharing your enthusiasm for lifelong learning, you might invite your friend to attend a conference, join a study group, discuss a recent journal article, or enroll in an online course to enhance knowledge, pedagogical skills, and technological expertise.

4. Log on to the Internet, go to the Web site for the Texas Education Agency (www.tea.state.tx.us), and locate the Regional Education Service Center in your area. Visit the "Calendar of Events" to determine topics of workshops and training sessions offered this month. Check for events by subject area, by location, and by audience to find those most interesting to you. View the list of videoconferences and opportunities for distance learning, which may include a variety of virtual field trips designed for students enrolled in local school districts. Look through the "Online Materials Catalog" to discover the many instructional materials available. You will also find resources related to content areas, teaching and learning, assessment, and technology, as well as "Special Programs" and "Instructional Support." Write an overview of the professional development resources offered by your Regional Education Service Center, and

make a commitment to begin making use of the services.

5. The Commissioner of Education and the 15 members of the State Board of Education (SBOE) oversee the public education system in Texas. To discover who represents you in Austin, use the "Find Your Incumbent" page sponsored by the Texas Legislature Online. You can search by your home address or zip code. When you have found the SBOE member for your district, think about the most serious problems facing public education today. Using a problem-solving approach, list the five top priorities for improving education. Write a letter to your representative, listing and describing your specific recommendations for educational reform.

PRACTICE QUESTIONS

1. Ms. Gomez is a fourth-grade teacher who has been working conscientiously to create a classroom community of learners. Classroom routines were progressing smoothly until the entry of a new child, Jason, who lives with a foster family after having repeatedly suffered abuse at the hands of an out-of-work father. Jason has an extremely short fuse and can readily explode into tirades of expletives. Occasionally he pushes or strikes other students. With little exposure to abused children, Ms. Gomez is at a loss to determine how to handle this child, who is disrupting the classroom. Some appropriate sources of information and support are:

   A. The school counselor

   B. The foster parents

   C. A symposium on child abuse and neglect sponsored by the local college

   D. All of the above

2. Mr. Durham is an enthusiastic kindergarten teacher who is beginning his first year in a new school. He is planning to use journal writing with his kindergartners as part of his literacy program. He knows that the children do not already possess writing skills but is anx-ious to encourage drawing and invented spelling. During the first planning meeting with the kindergarten team, he shares his ideas with the other teachers. He is told flatly that the principal will not allow the use of journals, because writing is not included on the standardized tests given to kindergartners in their district. Only test-related objectives are emphasized on weekly lesson plans. Mr. Durham would be wise to do which of the following?

   A. Suggest that the team review articles and current research about the writing process to develop a body of knowledge that could serve as the basis for determining multiple strategies for teaching literacy, then present their recommendations to the principal for review and comment.

   B. Argue with the team, asserting his right to academic freedom.

   C. Turn in weekly lessons plans to the principal, being careful not to mention journal writing as a daily activity.

   D. File an application for transfer to another campus that would be more receptive to his ideas.

3. Ms. Jackson feels a little anxious and nervous because her first annual review has been scheduled in 4 weeks. Although she feels confident about the positive relationships she has established with her second-graders, she is concerned about the classroom observation by her assistant principal. Will her children behave, or will everything dissolve into chaos? Which would be the best way for Ms. Jackson to prepare for the evaluation?

   A. Ask her doctor for a prescription to keep her calm.

   B. Remind the children every day that her boss will be coming to visit, promising them a treat if they behave well.

   C. Ask her mentor teacher to observe her classroom and offer some specific suggestions for improvement.

   D. Be prepared to write a response to the evaluation that defends the effectiveness of her teaching strategies.

4. Ms. Lim is a new first-grade teacher with a busy schedule and a full classroom of active six-year-olds. She wants to make sure that they have a good foundation in basic skills and a positive attitude toward school. Ms. Lim has been asked to serve on the committee to investigate the mandatory requirement of uniforms for their campus. Meetings will be scheduled on the third Thursday of each month after dismissal of classes. She has a sinking feeling that she will never get her lesson plans completed if she gets involved in a potentially controversial issue. Which of the following would be the most appropriate action for Ms. Lim to take?

   A. Beg to be excused from serving because her own children have soccer practice on Thursdays.

   B. Attend the meetings but work on her lesson plans during the discussion times, thus optimizing her work time.

   C. Agree to participate but leave early so that she can finish the work that is her primary responsibility as a teacher.

   D. Approach the issues with an open mind and work collaboratively with peers and parents to find the best solution for the school.

5. Mr. Martinez has asked his mentor, Ms. Salazar, to critique his professional portfolio. Although he prepared a beginning portfolio as a university student, he is now ready to make revisions that will better represent his current strengths and challenges. Which of the following would *not* be a good choice to include in his teaching portfolio?

   A. Samples of student work

   B. His classroom management plan

   C. A videotaped lesson and some representative lesson plans

   D. His undergraduate university transcripts

Answers and Discussion

Answer 1: A teacher should seek the support of knowledgeable professionals in the school who have had experience in working with abused children and their families. The school counselor may be able to provide individual or group counseling, referrals, and suggestions for classroom adaptations while the child is adjusting to a new home and school environment. The foster parents will have information about the child's background and the types of strategies that have been successful in helping the child regain some self-control. A symposium on child abuse scheduled at a local college will provide access to experts in the field who can provide information and resources for teachers who are dealing with abused and neglected children. There are usually opportunities for question-and-answer sessions, as well as small-group workshops related to specific topics. The answer is *D*.

Answer 2: Teaching practices should be based on sound pedagogical knowledge and skills, not on personal preferences (*A*). A study group of kindergarten teachers can read and discuss current literature, make decisions based on best practices, and advocate effectively on behalf of their students. Answer *B* is an unacceptable approach because arguing with colleagues does not lead to supportive and cooperative relationships, but it may establish adversarial roles. Answer *C* represents a deliberate attempt to mislead the principal by omission and is therefore dishonest and unethical. Answer *D* is an option that may eventually have to be examined, but it is not the first step in solving a problem concerning differences of opinion. The answer is *A*.

Answer 3: A mentor teacher is assigned to a beginning teacher as a supportive guide who can provide advice and assistance to negotiate the first year of teaching. A classroom observation by the mentor can serve as a dress rehearsal, easing the beginning teacher's concerns about another adult in the classroom. The children can also get used to having someone else watching their daily activities. The experienced mentor can make suggestions based on the PDAS domains and review the Teacher's Self-Report Form, emphasizing areas of strength (*C*). Answer *A* does not address the problem, but advocates unhealthy approaches to handling predictable sources of stress. Answer *B* focuses on the children's behavior rather than the teacher's competence in addressing students' needs, managing the classroom environment, and designing effective instruction. Answer *D* takes a defensive role by assuming that the evaluation will be negative and that the evaluator will be unfair in assigning the ratings. On the other hand, a reflective practitioner is realistic about self-appraisal and open to constructive criticism from supervisors and informed peers. The answer is *C*.

Answer 4: Site-based decision making (SBDM) requires that many of the decisions about school policies be made at the campus level, allowing both local ownership and responsibility for the outcomes. It is important for new teachers, as well as experienced ones, to serve on schoolwide committees that make important decisions about programs and policies. Because evidence shows that implementing uniforms as dress codes can have a positive effect on student behavior and achievement, it is a critical issue that should be explored, with input from the teachers and community. Ms. Lim should accept her responsibility to investigate the issue and contribute to the decision-making process (*D*). Responses *A* and *C* wrongly suggest that the teacher has no obligations past dismissal time and that participation in school-based committees is optional and voluntary. Response *B* is incorrect because it demonstrates an unethical approach to service. The teacher attends in body but does not engage in the meaningful work of the campus committee. The correct answer is *D*.

Answer 5: His transcripts documented teacher preparation rather than in-job performance and thus are not a good choice for his current portfolio. A professional teaching portfolio should include items directly related to one's job responsibilities. A videotaped lesson and sample lesson plans demonstrate competence in instructional planning and delivery. Samples of student work provide concrete evidence of learning outcomes. A classroom management plan portrays the educator's ability to create a learning environment in which students can be successful. The correct answer is *D*.

WEB LINKS

If a site is no longer operational, use key words from this chapter.

www.acei.org

Association for Childhood Education International

www.cec.sped.org

Council for Exceptional Children

www.ericsp.org

Educational Resources Information Center

www.ericeece.org

ERIC Clearinghouse on Elementary and Early Childhood Education

www.naeyc.org

National Association for the Education of Young Children

www.nea.org

National Education Association

www.seca50.org

Southern Early Childhood Association

www.texasaeyc.org

Texas Association for the Education of Young Children

www.tft.org

Texas Federation of Teachers

www.tsta.org

Texas State Teachers Association

REFERENCES

Airasian, P., & Gullickson, A. (1997). *Teacher self-evaluation tool kit.* Thousand Oaks, CA: Corwin Press, Inc.

Ayers, W. (1989). Headaches: On teaching and teacher education. *Action in Teacher Education, 11*(2), 1–7.

Baptitste, N., & Sheerer, M. (1997). Negotiating the challenges of the "survival" stage of professional development. *Early Childhood Education Journal, 24*(4), 265–267.

Borko, H., Michalec, P., Timmons, M., & Siddle, J. (1997). Student teaching portfolios: A tool for promoting reflective practice. *Journal of Teacher Education, 48*(5), 345–357.

Bredekamp, S., & Copple, S. (Eds) (1997). *Developmentally appropriate practice in early childhood programs.* (Rev. ed.) Washington, DC: National Association for the Education of Young Children.

Chase, B., Germundsen, R., Brownstein, J., & Distad, L. (2001). Making the connection between increased student learning and reflective practice. *Educational Horizons, 48*(3), 143–147.

Christiansen, H., Goulet, L., Krentz, C., & Maers, M. (1997). *Recreating relationships: Collaboration and educational reform.* Albany, NY: State University of New York Press.

Collier, S. (1997, November). Theories of learning: Reflective thought in teacher education. Paper presented at the Annual Meeting of the Mid-South Educational Research Association, Memphis, TN.

Cunningham, W., & Gresso, D. (1993). *Cultural leadership: The culture of excellence in education.* Needham, MA: Allyn and Bacon.

Darling-Hammond, L., & McLaughlin, M. (1995). Policies that support professional development in an era of reform. *Phi Delta Kappan, 76*(8), 597–604.

Dewey, J. (1933). *How we think.* Boston, MA: D. C. Heath and Company.

Dieker, L., & Monda-Amaya, L. (1995). Reflective teaching: A process for analyzing journals of preservice educators. *Teacher Education and Special Education, 18*(4), 240–252.

Dougherty, J. (1997). *Four philosophies that shape the middle school,* (Fastback No. 410). Bloomington, IN: Phi Delta Kappan Educational Foundation.

Feldman, A., & Atkin, J. M. (1995). Embedding action research in professional practice. In S. E. Noffek & R. B. Stevenson, (Eds.), *Educational action research: Becoming practically critical* (pp. 127–137). New York: Teachers College Press.

Galvez-Martin, B., Bowman, C., & Morrison, M. (1998). An exploratory study of the level of reflection attained by preservice teachers. *Mid-Western Educational Researcher, 11*(2), 9–17.

Ganser, T. (1995). A road map for designing quality mentoring programs for beginning teachers. Paper presented at the annual conference of the Wisconsin Association for Middle Level Education, Stevens Point, WI. (ERIC Document Reproduction Service No. ED 394 932)

Gayfer, M., ed. (1991). *The multi-age classroom: myth and reality.* Toronto, Ontario: Canadian Education Association.

Gordon, S. P., & Maxey, S. (2000). *How to help beginning teachers succeed.* (3rd ed.). Alexandria, VA: Association for Supervision and Curriculum Development.

Halford, J. M. (1999). Easing the way for new teachers. In M. Sherer, (Ed.), *A better beginning: Supporting and mentoring new teachers* (pp. 13–18). Alexandria, VA: Association for Supervision and Curriculum Development.

Jenlink, P. M., & Kinnucan-Welsch, K. (2001). Case stories of facilitating professional development. *Teaching and Teacher Education, 17*(6), 705–724.

Katz, L. G. (1972). Developmental stages of preschool teachers. *Elementary School Journal, 23*(1), 50–51.

Katz, L. G. (1977). *Talks with teachers: Reflections on early childhood education.* Washington, DC: National Association for the Education of Young Children.

Katz, L. G., Evangelou, D., & Hartman, J. A. (1990). *The case for mixed-age grouping in early education.* Washington, DC: National Association for the Education of Young Children.

Kruse, S. (1997). Reflective activity in practice: Vignettes of teachers' deliberative work. *Journal of Research and Development in Education 31*(1), 46–60.

Lakein, A. E. (1999). How to help a new teacher by being a buddy. In M. Sherer, (Ed.), *A better beginning: Supporting and mentoring new teachers* (pp. 85–89). Alexandria, VA: Association for Supervision and Curriculum Development.

Lieberman, A. (1995). Practices that support teacher development. *Phi Delta Kappan, 76*(8), 591–596.

Maslow, A. (1954). *Motivation and personality.* New York: Harper & Row.

Moallem, M. (1997). The content and nature of reflective teaching: A case of an expert middle school science teacher. *The Clearing House, 70*(3), 143–150.

Moir, E. (1999). The stages of a teacher's first year. In M. Sherer, (Ed.), *A better beginning: Supporting and mentoring new teachers* (pp. 19–23). Alexandria, VA: Association for Supervision and Curriculum Development.

Moore, L., & Brown, D. L. (1995, April). Mixed-age grouping program evaluation revisited: Developmentally appropriate practices at work. Paper presented at the annual conference of the American Educational Research Association, San Francisco, CA.

Moore, L., & Brown, D. L. (1996). The mixed-age approach: A public school perspective. *Dimensions of Early Childhood, 24*(2), 4–10.

Morgan, J., & Ashbaker, B. Y. (2001). *A teacher's guide to working with paraeducators and other classroom aides.* Alexandria, VA: Association for Supervision and Curriculum Development.

National Association for the Education of Young Children. (2001). *NAEYC at 75: 1926–2001, reflections on the past, challenges for the future.* Washington, DC: NAEYC.

National Education Association. (2000). *2000–2001 NEA Handbook.* Annapolis Junction, MD: NEA.

North Carolina Department of Public Instruction. (2000). *Mentoring North Carolina novice teachers.* Raleigh, NC: North Carolina State Board of Education.

Ogden, C., & Claus, J. (1997). Reflection as a natural element of service: Service learning for youth empowerment. *Equity & Excellence in Education, 30*(1), 72–80.

Olebe, M. (2001). A decade of policy support for California's new teachers: The beginning teacher support and assessment program. *Teacher Education Quarterly, 28*(1), 71–84.

Portner, H. (1998). *Mentoring new teachers.* Thousand Oaks, CA: Corwin Press, Inc.

Pultorak, E. (1993). Facilitating reflective thought in novice teachers. *Journal of Teacher Education, 44*(4), 288–295.

Schon, D. (1983). *The reflective practitioner.* New York: Basic Books.

Shulman, L. (1987). Knowledge and teaching: Foundations of the new reform. *Harvard Educational Review, 57*(1), 1–20.

Sparks, D., & Loucks-Horsley, S. (1989). Five models of staff development for teachers. *Journal of Staff Development, 10*(4), 40–57.

State Board for Educator Certification. (2001a). *SBEC-TxBESS.* Retrieved Nov. 29, 2001, from State Board of Educator Certification Web site: http://www.SBEC.state.tx.us/txbess.htm

State Board for Educator Certification. (2001b). *Standard certificate renewal and continuing professional education requirements: Classroom teacher.* Retrieved Nov. 29, 2001, from State Board of Educator Certification Web site: http://www.SBEC.state.tx.us/certinfo/certren.htm

Stringer, E. T. (1996). *Action research: A handbook for practitioners.* Thousand Oaks, CA: Sage Publications.

Texas Education Agency. (1992). *Resource guide on site-based decision making and district and campus planning.* Austin, TX: TEA.

Texas Education Agency. (1995). *Learner-centered schools for Texas: A vision for Texas educators.* Austin, TX: TEA.

Texas Education Agency. (1997). *PDAS implementation manual for appraisers and teachers.* Austin, TX: TEA.

Young, T. A., & Crain, C. L. (1993). Helping new teachers: The performance enhancement model. *Clearing House, 66*(3), 174–77.

Competency 13

The teacher understands and adheres to legal and ethical requirements for educators and is knowledgeable of the structure of education in Texas.

The beginning teacher:

- Knows legal requirements for educators (e.g., those related to special education, students' and families' rights, student discipline, equity, child abuse) and adheres to legal guidelines in education-related situations.

- Knows and adheres to legal and ethical requirements regarding the use of educational resources and technologies (e.g., copyright, Fair Use, data security, privacy, acceptable use policies).

- Applies knowledge of ethical guidelines for educators in Texas (e.g., those related to confidentiality, interactions with students and others in the school community), including policies and procedures described in the *Code of Ethics and Standard Practices for Texas Educators.*

- Follows procedures and requirements for maintaining accurate student records.

- Understands the importance of and adheres to required procedures for administering state- and district-mandated assessments.

- Uses knowledge of the structure of the state education system, including relationships among campus, local, and state components, to seek information and assistance.

- Advocates for students and for the profession in various situations.

Chapter 19

Understanding Legal and Ethical Requirements and the Structure of Education in Texas

GARY R. CLAY

Houston Baptist University

TERMS TO KNOW

Acceptable use policy

Admission, Review, and Dismissal (ARD) Committee

Commissioner of education

Educators' Code of Ethics

Fair use doctrine

Family Educational Rights and Privacy Act (FERPA)

Free and appropriate public education (FAPE)

Inclusion

Individual Educational Plan (IEP)

Individuals with Disabilities Education Act (IDEA)

Least restrictive environment (LRE)

Local school board

State Board for Educator Certification (SBEC)

State Board of Education (SBOE)

Superintendent

Texas Education Agency (TEA)

Competency 13 of the Pedagogy and Professional Responsibilities for those who are seeking to be certified in Early Childhood through Grade 4 in Texas relates to fulfilling professional, legal, and ethical responsibilities. This chapter addresses skills and knowledge that teachers should possess in adhering to legal and ethical duties, along with information that enhances understanding of the structure of state and local educational systems in Texas.

An expectation of those who choose to become teachers is professional and ethical conduct. To act as professionals, it is necessary that beginning teachers have a clear understanding of the particular constraints and responsibilities that are in place in laws, regulations, and codes that govern the profession of teaching in Texas. Additionally, teachers should know the structure of education in their state, local district, and school so that they follow appropriate procedures when seeking information or assistance.

LEGAL REQUIREMENTS FOR EDUCATORS

Teachers in Texas should be familiar with the laws and policy directives that influence their employment and should always seek to be in compliance. These laws and policies have been put into place not only for the protection of children and their caregivers, but also for the protection of teachers, administrators, and other citizens (for example, authors and composers in regard to copyright law and other areas). Both district and campus administrators have responsibilities to assist teachers with understanding their responsibilities in legal areas and should be a ready resource for those who have questions or need assistance. Teachers should be regularly updated on any changes in laws and

policies by their employing districts and/or schools and should never hesitate to seek advice when in doubt about appropriate and legal conduct. When a question arises, teachers should consult with a campus administrator for direction or advice without hesitation. If the administrator needs legal advice to respond to a question, the district will contact attorneys.

A few words of advice and comfort, especially to beginning teachers, are in order. Teachers do not need detailed or expert knowledge of educational laws to be successful and effective. Being aware of the major areas discussed in this chapter will provide a basic understanding of teacher-related legal issues and guide teachers in their actions and decisions. An excellent resource for Texas teachers is *The Legal Handbook for Texas Teachers* by Fernando C. Gomez and Kenneth R. Craycraft (1998). Ordering information for this handbook is available from the publisher.

A wide range of state and federal laws related to education are enacted each year that legislators are in session. Additionally, state and federal agencies issue rules, policies, and procedures that implement or interpret the laws. Local districts may also enact policies that teachers must follow as a condition of their employment. This section addresses only selected areas that include legal requirements that all teachers should understand. One area that beginning teachers encounter early in their teaching is special education.

LAWS REGARDING SPECIAL EDUCATION

These laws are of particular importance to EC–4 teachers because children are most often tested and identified for special services in these early grade levels. In addition, more changes are usually made in children's programs (IEPs) at the earlier grade levels. Knowing the laws that pertain to special education helps teachers make sure that they navigate correctly through the process of ensuring that children receive the special help that they need and are guaranteed if identification is made.

The education of children with disabilities has been a requirement of schools for many years, beginning with the implementation of Public Law 94-142 (the Education for All Handicapped Children Act, passed in 1975). This law requires each school district to provide, at no cost to the parents or guardians, a **free and appropriate public education,** also referred to as **FAPE,** to all students between the ages of 3 and 22 who meet eligibility requirements and reside in the district. In 1997 Congress reauthorized federal laws related to special education by passing the **Individuals with Disabilities Education Act (IDEA).** Changes in federal law and regulations for special education are revised frequently. Although beginning teachers in Texas are not expected to have detailed knowledge in this area, they are expected to know general principles and procedures and understand that special education is tightly governed by law. Those with special education expertise on a campus can become invaluable resources for concerns and questions that new teachers may have.

Like many areas of education, special education has used acronyms and unique terms over the years to assist in communication. Beginning teachers should not hesitate to ask questions when new acronyms or terms are encountered or when clarification is needed about their responsibility related to the education of students in special education programs. Teachers should also help parents to understand the "jargon" often associated with special education so that caregivers may be full partners in the education process and not intimidated by their lack of understanding of terms or programs related to their child's education. Terms that describe children who have special needs have changed over the years. The most commonly accepted terms for identified children currently are *those with exceptionality* or *differently abled.* The

definition of special education has been expanded to include those identified as intellectually gifted. Special programs or services to address the needs of gifted students are required in Texas. This topic is addressed toward the end of this section.

Exceptionalities that teachers may encounter include learning disabilities, speech or language impairments, serious emotional disturbance, visual or hearing impairments, autism, orthopedic or other health impairments, and giftedness. Children with AIDS are considered to be in this group as well, although those with HIV are not. The district must offer a full range of programs to meet the special educational needs of students identified as having exceptionalities.

FAPE provides for educational instruction to accommodate the academic needs of students and for related services that may be required for a child to be able to maximize the instructional opportunities provided. Related services may include such programs or services as physical therapy, special transportation, psychological services, counseling services, parent counseling and training, and many more.

Before a child who is suspected of having an exceptionality may be placed in special education, an initial evaluation must be made, following a referral. The referral may be initiated by a teacher or parent and includes all information relevant to the child's performance and difficulties encountered in school. Teachers suspecting that they may want to initiate a referral are wise to begin documenting information about the child at once. When a referral is made, the district *must* conduct an assessment of the referred student within 60 calendar days. The child's parent(s) or legal caregiver(s) participate in the initial evaluation, and if a comprehensive evaluation is determined to be in order, signed consent is required of the parent. Trained assessment personnel at the campus or within the district conduct the assessment. When the assessment results are available, the district or campus *must* hold an **Admission, Review, and Dismissal (ARD) committee** meeting within 30 days to review the assessment data, determine the eligibility of the child, determine the appropriate placement and services to be provided, and develop an **Individual Educational Plan (IEP)** for the child. The IEP is a comprehensive plan that includes instructional objectives, identification of services needed to achieve the objectives, any modifications required, and other legally required components. Teachers are not at liberty to independently change any of these components.

The ARD Committee, which may also be known as the IEP Team, normally includes in its membership (a) representatives from the campus or district administration, (b) assessment personnel, (c) regular education teachers, (d) special education teachers, (e) the parent(s), and (f) the student (if age appropriate). Others who have needed expertise, interests, or can translate (if needed) may be invited to participate in the meeting, including those invited by parents. Beginning teachers should become knowledgeable of the legal guidelines and procedures related to the ARD committee because it is likely that they will serve on one or more ARD committees during the academic year. A great majority of referrals are made during the first few years of school, and it is usually a classroom teacher who initiates the process.

To begin the process, the teacher must formulate a description of the problems a child presents—academically, physically, or behaviorally. This involves data collection over time (observations, class work, portfolios, test scores from class and standardized tests, data from others who work with the child, etc.). This data should also include documentation of any successful and unsuccessful interventions that the teacher or others have implemented. For students with emerging English skills, data should include results of testing in their native language. With this data in hand, a school is ready for a prereferral meeting. At this meeting with caregivers, it is normally determined whether the case will move into testing and/or interventions will be delivered.

If a child meets the eligibility criteria, options for services range from continued placement in the regular classroom (with consultative services from special education personnel for the teacher) to a range of more restrictive environments, according to the needs of the child. The applicable law states that children eligible for special education services should be educated in the **least restrictive environment (LRE)** possible. The placement of students is determined by the ARD Committee, and inclusion or mainstreaming is encouraged whenever deemed appropriate. **Inclusion,** also known as *mainstreaming,* is a philosophy and practice that allows special education students to be included, as much as possible, in the regular educational environment. Regular education teachers must be well informed and supported to make inclusion successful for all concerned.

After children are admitted and begin receiving services, the ARD Committee must monitor their educational progress. The committee must meet at least annually to review the progress of the child and the services provided. The ARD can meet more frequently as needed, and any member of the committee can request a meeting. Required procedures for notification of all members apply. The ARD Committee also has the authority to dismiss a student from special education. Before dismissal, however, the committee must determine that services are no longer required for the child's academic progress. The committee or special education staff at the campus must monitor the child's progress for at least a year following dismissal to ensure that he or she is academically successful.

The provision of special education services involves many procedures guided by laws and administrative regulation. Teachers must be especially careful to carry out their responsibilities set out by the IEP and the ARD Committees. The IEP is considered a legal document, and teachers *must* implement the IEP to the best of their ability or risk placing themselves or the district in legal jeopardy. Each campus normally has a person who is certified or has special training to oversee the special education program. When questions arise, teachers should never hesitate to contact their campus designee or the campus administrator.

Another area of exceptionality is intellectual giftedness. Children in Texas who are identified as gifted are served in programs for gifted and talented students or G/T. They may be referred for screening by parents, teachers, or other educators. Multiple measures must be used to determine eligibility for placement in programs that can vary in method of organization from district to district. In Texas, programs for children identified as gifted are required for all schools in grades kindergarten through 12. Special funding is provided from the state to support G/T programs, and teachers must have specialized training before teaching classes that include children identified as G/T students. Beginning teachers should determine how their school and district identify and serve gifted students.

A special population of children that is rapidly growing in Texas consists of those whose home or native language is not English. Legal rules and procedures for identifying, serving, and monitoring the academic progress of these children are similar to those for students in special education. Children who are determined to be emerging English speakers or limited English proficient (LEP) are served in bilingual education or English as a Second Language (ESL) programs. LEP designates that a child's primary language is not English, and he or she has difficulties performing class work in English. Bilingual programs offer teaching in both the primary language and English for many subject areas. Children are placed in a separate classroom where the two languages are used in instruction, and there is emphasis on retaining the native language as well as learning English. ESL programs focus on mainstreaming children into regular classrooms as much as possible, with supporting techniques to help them function in English as soon as possible. Children with a different first languages are often "pulled out" of their regular classroom together for special ESL reading and language arts instruction in English at some point each day. Schools with more than 20 identified LEP children must have one or both of these programs. Children are usually identified as speaking another language at home when caregivers (or older children) fill out a required Home Language Survey for school check-in, although other testing may also apply. Parents must be informed of the benefits of a special program within 10 days of identification, and placement should occur within 4 weeks of initial enrollment in a school district. Parental permission is *required* for placement in a bilingual or ESL program. Schools must have in place legally required placement and exit procedures, and a certified teacher must be hired for ESL or bilingual services. Children are reviewed at the end of each year and assessed for placement and for possible special accommodation in testing by a language proficiency assessment committee consisting of a professional bilingual educator, a professional transitional language educator, a parent of an LEP student, and a campus administrator. Children who are placed in a program may not exit from prekindergarten through first grade. All teachers should be familiar with the way these programs operate to provide necessary support and proper academic instruction as a child makes the transition to the English language.

LAWS FOR TEACHERS

The rights of all children and their families must be understood and respected—not only those in special populations. Parents and legally appointed caregivers have rights set out in law regarding the education of their children and must be seen as integral partners in the education process. People other than the child's parents who may have these rights include foster parents, court-appointed legal guardians, and other family members who have been court appointed to assume parental responsibility. In the case of divorced parents, the court most often determines the rights of the respective parents. Frequently one parent is designated as the custodial parent and has legal parental authority. Campus administrators should have on file at the campus the appropriate legal documents when parental authority is in question. Teachers must be extremely cautious of anyone to whom they release a child in their care. Unfortunately, schools and teachers can become embroiled in legalities when a noncustodial parent takes a child from a classroom. Too frequently, children are abducted from schools by noncustodial parents, or more seriously, by those who may seek to do harm to children or their parents. Teachers are wise not to release children if there is any question on guardianship. Most school districts require that parents obtain through the office a release that must be presented to the teacher if they are removing a child for any reason during the school day.

Teachers and schools have been legally authorized to act in the place of parents during the time children are under their care and control. Teachers of young children must exercise extra caution to monitor the location and safety of their children at all times. School dismissal time is a particularly vulnerable time for children. Teachers must monitor students until they are safely on the correct bus or with the appropriate person for leaving school. Campuses normally have in place a procedure for dismissal that provides supervision for children, but teachers should always err on the side of caution when questions arise. Teachers, in summary, have the legal and moral duty to monitor and account for their assigned children at all times. A teacher should immediately check with the principal or other appropriate administrator(s) when any questions about a child arise in this area.

Another legality entitles a parent or legal caregiver access all written school records that pertain to his or her child, including test scores, grades, disciplinary records, and teacher evaluations of the child. This type of information is confidential. Personally identifiable information about a child cannot be shared with outsiders without the consent of caregivers. Caregivers also are entitled to review all teaching materials, including textbooks and other teaching materials and state assessment instruments, and to review each test administered to his or her child after the test is given. More about these rights is discussed in this chapter under the Family Educational Rights and Privacy Act (FERPA). Written consent must be obtained for any specialized testing, for videotaping a child, and for recording a child's voice other than for a teacher's own self-educational purposes. A parent or legal caregiver is entitled to remove the child temporarily from a class or other school activity

without penalty when the parent's religious or moral beliefs are in conflict.

Beginning teachers also must understand the legal issues related to student discipline. Teachers of children in the early grades encounter fewer cases of severe discipline problems compared with their colleagues in middle and upper grades. However, all teachers should be familiar with the concept of "due process" in their district's code of student conduct, a document that communicates the standard for student conduct in the district. Teachers are expected to document violations of the code of conduct and submit that documentation of the violation to the principal. Teachers are provided, through law, the right to remove from class children who continually or seriously disrupt learning, but carefully guarded procedures that must be followed are attached to this. Teachers also should remember that grades cannot be tied to bad behavior. If a child has bad behavior, grades in conduct can be lowered or other punishment found, but academic grades must stand on their own merit.

Another area of legal concern is corporal punishment. Reasonable corporal punishment is permitted in Texas schools, but many districts have prohibited its use. Educational researchers in psychology have found that corporal punishment is problematic in many ways other than legally, so even if a district allows corporal punishment, it should be used only as a last resort. If considering this type of punishment as an option, teachers must first determine the district policy and the required guidelines. They must adhere strictly to those guidelines and realize that they may be liable and subject to charges of child abuse if they use excessive force. Normally if a district allows corporal punishment at all, other disciplinary methods must be tried and documented first, parents must approve, the instrument must be approved, and only designated school personnel are allowed to administer it; however, a district may have additional restrictions. Those administering corporal punishment must not do so for spite, malice, or revenge, and this punishment should not be unreasonable in terms of the misbehavior. Schools must always consider gender, age, size, physical condition, and appropriate parts of the body when corporal punishment is administered. Corporal punishment can lead to permanent injury. The best advice for teachers, especially those of younger children, is not to consider this method of discipline as an option.

It is wise to remember that children have a right to due process. Even young children may occasionally be suspended for their actions. If suspension is for a particular incident, the reporting teacher should be sure to immediately give a written description (along with witnesses, etc.). Parents have a right to request a hearing with legal counsel, if desired, with the right to appeal.

Students are guaranteed protection from discrimination and violations of their civil rights by a series of state and federal laws. Children also have access to equal educational opportunities in the schools. This simply means that the teacher cannot refuse to permit a child to participate in any school program or activity because of the child's race, religion, gender, national origin, or disability, nor can a teacher force a child to participate in certain activities when they conflict with religious beliefs. For example, a teacher cannot require that a child stand for the pledge if this conflicts with the child's religious beliefs (teachers should always check with parents on this issue). Teachers cannot *promote* worship of any kind in public schools, and teacher-led prayer is not permitted in the classroom. Although teachers are allowed to talk about religion in the context of history and culture, they must show respect to their children at all times. Any negative reaction or evidence of prejudice to a child's gender, race, religion, or disability is inappropriate. Such behavior may place the teacher in legal jeopardy and be an embarrassment to the school and community. Maintenance of equity for all children in the school and in the classroom is important. A federal law, Title IX of the Education Amendments of 1972, requires gender equity in all areas of the school's operation. Teachers of younger children should exercise caution in differentiating assignments or activities based on gender. Reflective teachers regularly review their expectations for all children and analyze their instructional practices to ensure equity for all groups within the class.

Yet another important area of legal responsibility for teachers relates to the requirement set out in law for reporting child abuse or neglect. The Texas Classroom Teachers Association's *Survival Guide* (2001) provides a good overview of this topic, along with other education-related topics that are important for Texas teachers. Texas law requires that any professional who suspects that a child is being abused or neglected must make a report to Child Protective Services (offices are located in each county in the state) or to any local or state law enforcement agency within 48 hours of first suspecting the abuse or neglect. An abuse hotline set up in Austin is a source for more information and reporting guidelines (800-252-5400). It is important to remember that reports must be made of *any* suspected abuse or neglect, not only acts of physical abuse. At the extreme, a child's life may be at stake. No teacher wants to feel guilty because he or she might have stopped terrible events from occurring. Failure to report is a Class B misdemeanor. The identity of the professional who reports is kept confidential, and teachers cannot be held liable for false reports unless the act of informing is determined to be a malicious act. Teachers should be informed by the district of child abuse and neglect reporting requirements and told where to direct the reports. As a professional courtesy, teachers should inform an administrator of suspicions of abuse; however, this does not satisfy the mandate to report within 48 hours. Some districts may even have immediate response teams that help intervene.

Teachers in Texas should understand that they have a degree of immunity granted by the Texas Education Code and are not personally liable for acts that fall within the scope of their professional position. Society, however, expects them to protect children from injury by taking "reasonable care." In general, teachers are granted immunity while performing their expected duties, but there are three general limits to this liability. Teachers should understand each area of limitation clearly. The first involves *negligence*. A teacher who acts in a negligent manner may be found liable for that negligence. This may occur, for instance, when a teacher sees a situation that seems dangerous but does nothing, and subsequently a child is hurt. As another example, a teacher who is responsible for monitoring at recess and leaves children unsupervised to go inside the building may be proved negligent should a child be injured. A second area of limited liability is the use of *excessive force* when disciplining children. This concept is fairly straightforward, meaning that a teacher must not use more force than is necessary to stop a child from injuring others or him- or herself when restraining or otherwise managing a child. Teachers of young children are nearly always perceived as stronger than their charges, so it is particularly important to be careful when restraining or disciplining a child. Children can, at times, become very physical. Any time a teacher must restrain a child from physically hurting him- or herself or others, the child should be taken to the nurse to determine whether there are injuries from being held. The third limit to a teacher's immunity relates to the *operation of a motor vehicle*. Teachers can be held personally liable for what may happen when transporting children in their personal vehicles or in school-owned vehicles. The best advice is not to transport children. Even when children are left late at school and it seems like the easiest and most correct thing to do, children should not be in a teacher's private vehicle. There is a self-protection issue for teachers as well (to avoid any charges of sexual abuse when a child and a teacher are alone in a car). However, children should not be left sitting on the school steps alone, either. Call parents, contact an administrator, or wait. Even permission slips and the like do not protect teachers from expensive negligence suits should a child be injured in a teacher's personal vehicle.

An area with legal implications that teachers often encounter is the use of copyrighted materials created by others. The **fair use doctrine** is an exception to an author's or creator's exclusive right of use. This doctrine allows limited use of a copyrighted work by teachers without the express permission of the creator. As an example of "fair use," teachers may make a single copy of a short article from a newspaper or periodical for use in teaching, but multiple copies of works must always adhere to *standards of brevity* (word length is stipulated for each type of work), *spontaneity*, and *cumulative effect*. Thus a short poem or parts of a poem, essay, story, cartoon, and so forth may be copied if the teacher fortuitously finds something that will add much to a class. Yet creating one's own anthology, for example, is not allowed, nor can a teacher use multiple copies of the same author's work. Only one teacher in a school may copy a particular work for one class (and not more than nine times during the year), and teachers may not copy "consumable" material such as workbooks or worksheets unless given express permission by the creator or publisher of the material. Often materials sold in teachers' supply businesses are published for teacher use, and the purchase of the materials is specifically for multiple copies to be made for classroom purposes. However, it is always best to verify this before making copies for students or others.

Copyright laws apply to music and video as well. For example, teachers and children may not copy music at random, add copyrighted music to Web pages without permission, or copy music for use in class at random, although there are fair use rules as well. Programs can be videotaped for noncommercial use in the classroom, but they must be watched only once and within 10 days for presentation purposes. A tape may be viewed one other time by a class for "instructional reinforcement," and it must be erased or taped over within 45 days. A school should record only programs requested specifically by teachers. Schools may not record at random with the possibility that a teacher might want a tape at some future time. Computer software can be copied only as a backup (one copy only). When a teacher wishes to load multiple copies into many classroom computers, a site license must be obtained. Copying software programs not covered by a school license is not acceptable. One backup copy of a program can be made by an individual purchaser. Software is "authored," so copying infringes upon the rights of an author or company to make money from the fruits of their labor. When in doubt, check before copying any materials, for there are increasingly heavy fines related to copyright infringement. Permission for teachers is often given.

With the growing availability and use of technology in schools, teachers must become familiar with and follow the district's **acceptable use policy.** This policy outlines the district's expectations related to use of school resources, particularly computers and Internet resources. The teacher agrees by signature to abide by the policy. Normally students must agree to follow the same guidelines in the acceptable use policy. With the increasing availability and use of Internet resources and the presence of inappropriate material, teachers have a responsibility to monitor children's use of the computer carefully. It is best not to allow children to use computers unsupervised and to monitor children's use of all instructional resources regularly. If computers are in centers, be sure that the screens can be seen easily by the teacher in most parts of the room. Many school districts also require permission letters from caregivers for children to use computers. If a district has such a policy, teachers must follow local guidelines.

These two areas (use of copyrighted materials and compliance with acceptable use policies) are most often self-monitored by teachers, who demonstrate ethical conduct when they follow the law even though supervision by others is not routinely conducted. The understanding of and adherence to ethical guidelines are indicators of professionalism for Texas educators.

Young children are not often involved in personal freedom of expression issues, but occasionally a family challenges a district's dress code. Dress can sometimes be seen as personal freedom of expression, such as in a recent elementary boy's challenge concerning an earring in a Texas elementary school. However, clothing that depicts obscene messages, gang messages, and so on, is usually upheld as not suitable for school, as is clothing that threatens management, health, and safety. When in doubt, ask for administrative direction.

ETHICAL GUIDELINES FOR EDUCATORS IN TEXAS

A code of ethics has been developed that sets standards and expectations for ethical practice by Texas teachers. The State Board for Educator Certification (SBEC) was responsible by law for the development and adoption of the Educator's Code of Ethics and Standard Practices for Texas Educators. The board also enforces the ethics code for purposes related to certification disciplinary proceedings.

Educators' Code of Ethics

The Texas educator shall comply with standard practices and ethical conduct toward students, professional colleagues, school officials, parents, and members of the community and shall safeguard academic freedom. The Texas educator, in maintaining the dignity of the profession, shall respect and obey the law, demonstrate personal integrity, and exemplify honesty. The Texas educator, in exemplifying ethical relations with colleagues, shall extend just and equitable treatment to all members of the profession. The Texas educator, in accepting a position of public trust, shall measure success by the progress of each student toward realization of his or her potential as an effective citizen. The Texas educator, in fulfilling responsibilities in the community, shall cooperate with parents and others to improve the public schools of the community.

ENFORCEABLE STANDARDS

I. Professional Ethical Conduct, Practices and Performance.

Standard 1.1. The educator shall not knowingly engage in deceptive practices regarding official policies of the school district or educational institution.

Standard 1.2. The educator shall not knowingly misappropriate, divert or use monies, personnel, property or equipment committed to his or her charge for personal gain or advantage.

Standard 1.3. The educator shall not submit fraudulent requests for reinbursement, expenses or pay.

Standard 1.4. The educator shall not use institutional or professional privileges for personal or partisan advantage.

Standard 1.5. The educator shall neither accept nor offer gratuities, gifts, or favors that impair professional judgment or to obtain special advantage. This standard shall not restrict the acceptance of gifts or tokens offered and accepted openly from students, parents or other persons or organizations in recognition or appreciation of service.

Standard 1.6. The educator shall not falsify records, or direct or coerce others to do so.

Standard 1.7. The educator shall comply with state regulations, written local school board policies and other applicable state and federal laws.

Standard 1.8. The educator shall apply for, accept, offer, or assign a position or a responsibility on the basis of professional qualifications.

II. Ethical Conduct Toward Professional Colleagues.

Standard 2.1. The educator shall not reveal confidential health or personnel information concerning colleagues unless disclosure serves lawful professional purposes or is required by law.

Standard 2.2. The educator shall not harm others by knowingly making false statements about a colleague or the school system.

Standard 2.3. The educator shall adhere to written local school board policies and state and federal laws regarding the hiring, evaluation, and dismissal of personnel.

Standard 2.4. The educator shall not interfere with a colleague's exercise of political, professional or citizenship rights and responsibilities.

Standard 2.5. The educator shall not discriminate against or coerce a colleague on the basis of race, color, religion, national origin, age, sex, disability, or family status.

Standard 2.6. The educator shall not use coercive means or promise of special treatment in order to influence professional decisions or colleagues.

Standard 2.7. The educator shall not retaliate against any individual who has filed a complaint with the SBEC under this chapter.

III. Ethical Conduct Toward Students.

Standard 3.1. The educator shall not reveal confidential information concerning students unless disclosure serves lawful professional purposes or is required by law.

Standard 3.2. The educator shall not knowingly treat a student in a manner that adversely affects the student's learning, physical health, mental health or safety.

Standard 3.3. The educator shall not deliberately or knowingly misrepresent facts regarding a student.

Standard 3.4. The educator shall not exclude a student from participation in a program, deny benefits to a student, or grant an advantage to a student on the basis of race, color, sex, disability, national origin, religion, or family status.

Standard 3.5. The educator shall not engage in physical mistreatment of a student.

Standard 3.6. The educator shall not solicit or engage in sexual conduct or a romantic relationship with a student.

Standard 3.7. The educator shall not furnish alcohol or illegal/unauthorized drugs to any student or knowingly allow any student to consume alcohol or illegal/unauthorized drugs in the presence of the educator.

A complaint alleging a violation of the Code of Ethics may be formally submitted by an educator or the parent or legal guardian of a student to the State Board for Educator Certification. The complaint is reviewed by the state board (SBEC) to determine whether it meets the legal criteria for a valid complaint of "unprofessional practice" and must be acted upon with 130 calendar days. If the SBEC finds that the educator has violated the Code of Ethics, it can sanction his or her certificate up to and including revocation.

As generalized above, a teacher can be dismissed for incompetence, insubordination, immoral conduct, unprofessional conduct, and good and just cause. A teacher can also be let go as a result of a decreasing student population (reduction in force). Normally incompetence refers to lack of knowledge in a subject area(s), but it can also delve into other teacher duties such as assessment, management, and so forth, as seen over time. A teacher who willfully disregards school regulations or reasonable administrative orders may be asked to leave for insubordination. Immoral conduct may cover areas of sexual misconduct with a student, criminal behavior, and other dishonesty. Although many of the rules that applied in the past to teachers, particularly for women (no marriage, no dating, no lipstick, no leaving town without permission, and so forth), are no more, all teachers still have a professional responsibility to be role models for the children they teach and to provide an environment that they would want for their own children.

Teachers may not think in terms of legalities when they sign contracts. However, a teaching contract is a legal document, and teachers can be sanctioned for breaking it. For instance, teachers are required to keep records on students, and their pay can be withheld for not reporting attendance records and grades and for not returning textbooks. New teachers sign probationary contracts for 3 years. School districts also have legal guidelines that they must follow carefully in issuing and maintaining contracts. Districts must, for example, follow guidelines for teacher assessment closely. Each year, teachers must be informed of current appraisal procedures. If appraisals do not go well, the district and the teacher must follow strict legal guidelines and time periods for notification, remediation, and so forth prior to dismissal. It is worth-

while for all teachers to pay close attention to these details, for arbitrarily breaking a contract or dismissal by a school district may hinder their ability to teach again.

FERPA

One area of ethical conduct by teachers relates to maintaining confidentiality. The **Family Educational Rights and Privacy Act (FERPA)** of 1974 is a federal law that sets out the requirements to protect the privacy of parents or legal caregivers and children. This law, also known as the Buckley Amendment, empowers parents and children with rights including the necessity for signed consent before personally identifiable information may be released. The results of individual student performance on tests are confidential and may be released only to the child, his or her parent or guardian, and the education staff directly involved with the student's educational program. An example of a practice teachers may use that likely violates the protections of FERPA is the practice of having children grade other children's work and then call out scores for the teacher to record. This practice is not advised and is currently under review by federal courts. As a practical matter, teachers must be careful how they handle student-related information and with whom they discuss personal information or the academic records of their children. Teachers must respect the privacy of student information and follow school or district procedures for protecting the confidentiality of student records. They should also avoid talking about children's (or the family's) personal business within earshot of anyone without a specific "need to know."

Teachers have an ethical responsibility to be advocates for their students and for the profession of teaching. Holding a position of trust, they should always view the best interests of their children as their first priority and make every effort to ensure that each child has the opportunity to achieve to his or her full potential. Teachers are often viewed by parents, family members, and friends as the primary sources of information and views about the school or educational issues. They should continue to grow professionally, be aware of current educational issues, and take advantage of the opportunity to advance the cause of education, sharing the "good news" about Texas schools.

Maintaining Accurate Student Records

As mentioned earlier, it is a legal and ethical responsibility of teachers in Texas to maintain accurate student records. Teachers must follow school or district procedures in completing student records, securely storing those records, and following FERPA guidelines in communicating the information contained in student records. Teachers should never leave student records on their desk or workspace, where children or other unauthorized people may have access to or view them. Some student records, often referred to as "permanent file," "cumulative records," or "cum. file," are kept in a secure location, normally in an administrative area. These files contain all personal information, test records, prior school and grade records, copies of past report cards, and any other records deemed confidential. Teachers can access these records for children in their class to assist in the planning of instructional programs, but they should maintain security for the records at all times. Teaches are responsible for comments in student records and should remember that these comments should be fair and accurate, as they are open to challenge.

Another record for which teachers are responsible is their grade book. This record can be maintained either electronically or in writing. It is important to maintain accurate grades and attendance records to support reports to parents and as a source for funding (attendance) from the state for the district. If teachers enter grades or other student records electronically, they should back up the records in case of computer problems. Losing a grade book is a serious problem, so teachers should take care to keep them safe and secure at all times. Although excessive paperwork demands are a reality, the *accuracy* of records is a direct

responsibility of the teacher and should be given the highest priority.

When sharing student information with a child's parent or guardian, teachers must remember not to reveal the grades of other children, to protect privacy rights guaranteed by FERPA. They should not even cover names of children so that parents can compare their child's grades with others in the class (the parents might figure out, alphabetically, to whom some grades belong).

A matter related to the accuracy of records is the expectation and legal requirement for teachers to follow all required procedures for administering state- and district-mandated assessments. With the "high stakes" associated with assessment results, teachers feel a heightened sense of accountability for their students' achievement and growth in skills and knowledge while in their class. Specific guidelines exist for test administration, test security, and the handling of test materials. Teachers must have training related to these issues and must always abide by the required guidelines. Any violations of test security or guidelines for administration may be considered a violation of the code of ethics and law. A teacher who commits such acts risks legal action and potential loss of his or her teaching certificate.

STRUCTURE OF THE TEXAS EDUCATION SYSTEM

The competency addressed in this chapter focuses on teaching in Texas. It is important for Texas teachers to have a general understanding of how education is organized so that they can recognize the types of authority and decision-making structures within the system. Beginning teachers need to understand how system components are related and how best to seek information and assistance in addressing issues that might arise.

Under the United States Constitution, education is a state function. However, the federal government has a significant role in the operation of education if the state or district accepts federal funds for operating educational programs. If federal funds are accepted, the educational entity must comply with the requirements of federal laws and abide by the regulations of federal agencies such as the U.S. Department of Education.

In Texas, the legislature has established school districts and a central education authority, the **Texas Education Agency (TEA),** to organize and administer the educational programs of the state. TEA is located in Austin, and its management rests with the **commissioner of education.** The commissioner is viewed as the chief educational officer of the state and is appointed by the governor and confirmed by the Texas Senate. He or she has a number of duties prescribed by law, including the development of rules and regulations for the implementation of legislation related to education. The Commissioner works directly with the **State Board of Education (SBOE),** a statewide policy board made up of 15 members elected by district for 6-year terms. The SBOE is somewhat comparable to the local school board. The governor appoints the chairperson of the board from the membership.

Another state agency directly involved with education, particularly with new teachers, is the **State Board for Educator Certification (SBEC).** The agency is governed of 15 members who are appointed by elected officials and responsible for the oversight of all aspects of public educator certification, continuing education requirements, and standards of professional conduct. Through its staff the board oversees the implementation of certification rules and is the agency to which a teacher applies for certification. SBEC also governs all aspects of teacher assessments and accredits teacher preparation programs in the state.

At the local district level, the key leadership entities are the local board of education, the superintendent of the school district, districtwide administrators with specific responsibilities, and campus principals. The **local school board** oversees the operation of schools in a local community. Members of the board are elected and have the title of *trustee.* The board's primary tasks include adopting policies for district operation,

establishing goals for the district, approving an annual budget, setting the tax rate for the district, and employing and evaluating the superintendent. The board must meet and take action as a body in compliance with the Texas Open Meetings Law. No individual member has any authority to speak for or act on behalf of the board. Teachers and community members often attend meetings of the local board, and agendas frequently recognize or honor achievement by teachers, students, schools, or volunteers. Teachers in Texas should consider attending meetings of the local board to see firsthand how the business of the district is conducted. Texas teachers are expected to follow the policies adopted by the local board.

The policies of the board are communicated to the employees of the district by the **superintendent,** who serves as the chief administrative officer and educational leader of the district. One or more administrators may hold districtwide responsibilities for areas that may impact teachers. Examples include those responsible for curriculum, personnel, and finance.

The primary person to whom teachers are directly responsible is the campus principal. The principal is responsible for the daily operation of the individual school, and for its staff and children. In compliance with laws, state regulations, and district policies, the principal establishes procedures for the efficient operation of the school and has the primary responsibility for the employment, supervision, and professional development of the staff. The principal is viewed as the instructional leader of the campus and the spokesperson and primary contact for parents and the community. Schools may also have assistant principals, who have administrative functions designated by the principal.

Teachers should understand the hierarchy of authority in the local district when seeking advice or assistance. In general, it is appropriate to seek direction from the immediate supervisor, most often the campus principal. Teachers may seek additional assistance from other sources as directed by the principal and should always follow the chain of command. Thus the teacher is responsible to the principal, who is primarily responsible to the superintendent. The superintendent is responsible to the local board. The local district is accountable for following state laws and regulations in implementing the programs of the district. Texas has also encouraged teacher participation in site-based management. Rather than having administrators make decisions for all district schools in an umbrella fashion, teachers are asked to serve on individual school teams that generate many building-level policies, particularly for improvement purposes. However, they must remember that district, state, and national policies and laws always come first.

SUMMARY

This chapter has addressed the legal and ethical requirements of teaching in Texas and has provided a brief overview of the structure of education in the state. In summary, teachers in Texas should have a basic understanding of the key legal and ethical issues that impact their function as EC–4 teachers. Knowledge placed in practice ensures that their daily decisions and interactions with others are in compliance with educational law and the Educators' Code of Ethics. Additionally, understanding the organization and operation of state, local, and campus systems is invaluable for teachers seeking information or assistance in addressing issues. Teachers who are informed on the issues addressed in this chapter will be better equipped to prepare children in Texas today to be productive and educated citizens in the twenty-first century.

GLOSSARY

acceptable use policy   a statement of expectations for how students and faculty will use school resources, procedures they are expected to follow, and consequences when expectations and procedures are violated. This policy is most commonly associated with the use of computers and Internet resources.

Admission, Review, and Dismissal (ARD) Committee   a committee who determines eligibility for special education services, who creates, reviews, and modifies the child's IEP, and who may decide the child no longer requires special services; also known as the IEP team.

commissioner of education   the chief educational officer in the state of Texas. He or she is appointed by the governor and has administrative responsibility for the Texas Education Agency and for overseeing the implementation of legislation into school and district operations.

Educators' Code of Ethics   standards of ethical conduct for educators, violation of which may subject educators to disciplinary action. The code is developed by the State Board for Educator Certification.

fair use doctrine   a component of federal law related to copyrights. It allows specified copying privileges of a copyrighted work for teaching purposes.

Family Educational Rights and Privacy Act (FERPA)   relates to a family's and a child's right to confidentiality concerning school information and records.

Free and appropriate public education (FAPE)   the provision of IDEA that guarantees special education and related services to children with disabilities at public cost.

inclusion   refers to a philosophy and resulting practice associated with the education of special education students in regular education settings to the extent appropriate for each special education child.

Individual Educational Plan (IEP)   a plan or program for meeting the specific educational needs of each special education child. This plan is developed by the Admission, Review, and Dismissal Committee or team.

Individuals with Disabilities Education Act (IDEA)   a federal far-reaching law that requires the provision of special education and services for children with disabilities.

Least restrictive environment (LRE)   a principle outlined in IDEA that requires students in special education to be educated in settings that allow them to function to their maximum capabilities, based on their IEP (normally with the maximum possible placement in a regular classroom).

local school board   the community elected board that oversees the operation of schools in the local school district. The board has a number of specific responsibilities set out in law related to policy adoption and budgetary areas.

State Board for Educator Certification (SBEC)
an appointed board that has responsibility for all rules related to educator certification, teacher preparation programs, and the Educators' Code of Ethics.

State Board of Education (SBOE)   the state-level elected body that has specific areas of responsibility for education in the state. It is analogous to the local school board, but at the state level.

superintendent   the chief educational leader in the local school district. He or she is employed by the local school board and has responsibility for the provision of quality educational offerings in the district in compliance with all laws, regulations, and policies.

Texas Education Agency   the administrative state agency that assists in the development and enforcement of regulations required by education laws. It is directed by the commissioner of education.

SUGGESTED ACTIVITIES

To apply the concepts and information presented in this chapter, the beginning teachers in Texas may consider the following activities:

1. Explore the Web sites referenced in this chapter.

2. Regularly read newspapers, new magazines, journals, and other publications for current information related to legal and ethical topics on educational issues. Select an article and discuss your personal feelings about it, along with the guidelines of the law and/or policies that apply.

3. Discuss with a campus administrator how the district organizational chart is arranged. Determine what positions and departments exist at the central administrative office to assist teachers and the schools.

4. Meet all of the personnel on your campus who deal with special populations and be well prepared before the first ARD meeting that you attend. Ask to attend an ARD meeting as an observer before you attend as a member of the committee.

5. Attend the meeting of a local board of education.

6. Volunteer to serve on campus or district committees when the opportunity is presented. If

you are in a field-experience phase, ask your mentor or another teacher who serves if you can attend as a guest.

7. Carefully review all materials provided for you at the time of employment by the district. Carefully review the personnel handbook, which often contains many of the policies and procedures referenced in this chapter. If you are in a field-experience phase, go by your district's office and ask for a copy of the application packet, handbook, and so forth to review.

8. Obtain a copy of the teacher assessment instrument used in your district (most Texas districts, though not all, use the PDAS). Look closely at the timeline polices that regulate assessment in your district. Note, for example, how many working days you have to answer an assessor's comments if you want to dispute a rating.

9. Write a letter to the proper representative regarding an educational law or issue about which you have strong feelings. Explain your concerns clearly.

PRACTICE QUESTIONS

1. Ms. Sandoval had just completed her third week as a new teacher at Valley View Primary School. The first weeks had passed quickly and smoothly, although they were a bit hectic as she had expected. She graduated last spring from State University's program for teacher education and felt well prepared to be a successful teacher. Her student teaching experience, along with field experiences in her program, offered her good opportunities to see what was necessary to be an effective teacher and practice some of the required skills.

   Stopping by the teachers' workroom to get a soft drink at the end of the day, she sat down for a few minutes to look through some of the mail she had just picked up. Several teachers were in the workroom, and she couldn't help overhearing some of the conversations taking place. One teacher was discussing with another some information about a child in one of his classes who had to have special modifications because of the student's IEP. This conversation reminded Ms. Sandoval that one of the children in her class also had an IEP that she would have to investigate. Who determines what is included in the student's Individual Educational Plan (IEP)?

A. The student's teachers from last year

B. The counselor, in consultation with the parents

C. The Admission, Review, and Dismissal Committee

D. The student's current teachers

2. The Individual Educational Plan might specify that the special education student should receive some services in a regular education classroom so as to maximize his or her education. The philosophy that students should be mainstreamed to the appropriate extent is known as:

A. IDEA

B. Inclusion

C. Multidisciplinary

D. FAPE

3. Ms. Sandoval's grade-level chair asked that she stop by her room tomorrow. A parent was concerned about her child's grades. The parent wanted to examine the grades earned currently in the year, along with those of other students so that she could compare her child's standing to that of others in the class. According to the Family Educational Rights and Privacy Act (FERPA), the parent has the right to:

A. Review the grades of her child.

B. Make an appointment with the principal.

C. Take her child out of the class if not satisfied.

D. Look at the grades of all students if the teacher covers the names of the other students.

4. Two teachers sitting near Ms. Sandoval were discussing their students in a negative manner, and she recognized immediately that the comments were inappropriate. Reflecting later on what she had heard, she tried to recall which parts might be described as unprofessional. A

list of appropriate, professional conduct and practices can be found in which of the following documents?

A. The Code of Ethics and Standard Practices for Texas Educators

B. The employment contract signed by the teacher

C. The district policy handbook

D. The campus teacher handbook

5. One of the items in Ms. Sandoval's mailbox was an invitation to a workshop to be held in about 6 weeks. The workshop topic sounded appealing, and the speaker had a national reputation. Knowing that she had to continue her professional development and that the workshop would count for the staff development hours needed for certificate renewal, she decided to go. She could see one problem— the workshop was scheduled for a school day. What is the *first* thing Ms. Sandoval should do related to the workshop?

A. Send in the reservation so that a place would be held for her.

B. Arrange for a good substitute teacher to cover her class for the day.

C. Request permission from her principal to attend the workshop.

D. Send a letter to the local school board requesting permission to attend the workshop.

Answers and Discussion

Answer 1: Federal law and regulations prescribe the rules associated with special education, and the determination of the components of the student's Individual Educational Plan (IEP) is the responsibility of the Admission, Review, and Dismissal (ARD) Committee or team. The child's former and current teachers may have relevant contributions to the committee's decision but do not have the authority to determine what will be included in the plan. They or the counselor may serve as a member of a current committee (which, in a legally called meeting, may make changes in the IEP). However, the teacher is required to follow the IEP to the best of his or her ability. The parent is required by regulation to participate in the decision-making process as a member of the ARD committee or team. The answer is *C*.

Answer 2: "Inclusion" is the term for the philosophy and practices described in the question. IDEA and FAPE are acronyms associated with special education. See the Glossary of this chapter for definitions. Multidisciplinary does not directly deal with special education but refers to planning, instruction, or curriculum that includes several curriculum areas. The answer is *B*.

Answer 3: The parent or legal caregiver has the right, as guaranteed by FERPA, to review the grades and other educational records of her child. A parent can certainly request an appointment with the principal or request to remove her child from a class, but neither item is related to FERPA. A teacher should never share with a parent the individual grades of students other than her own child. A teacher could tell the parent the class range of scores or a class average. Even with the names covered, a parent or caregiver might discern the identity of other children in the class. The best practice is to transfer the grades from the grade book to another document for sharing with the parent or caregiver. The answer is *A*.

Answer 4: The Code of Ethics is the document listing ethical and standard practices for educators. The other documents contain relevant and important information for the teacher but would likely not have the code included. The code may be accessed at the State Board for Educator Certification Web site, www.sbec.tx.state.us. The answer is *A*.

Answer 5: Teachers should understand the organizational structure of authority in the district and the local school. The principal, as the primary supervisor of the teachers on campus, is the correct person to contact. Among the choices provided, the teacher should first obtain permission from the principal. The answer is *C*.

WEB LINKS

If a site is no longer operational, use key words from this chapter.

www.tea.state.tx.us

This is the Web address for the Texas Education Agency. It includes current school-related laws and regulations, campus and district data, curriculum and assessment information, accountability and accreditation information, and information on special programs. The site has links to other education sites.

www.sbec.state.tx.us

This is the Web site for the State Board for Educator Certification and includes information related to licensing, certification, testing for certification, Educators' Code of Ethics, and applicable rules.

www.ed.gov

This is the Department of Education's primary Web site. It specifies a wide variety of topics useful to teachers and links to related agencies.

www.tea.state.tx.us/curriculum/bilingual.html

The site contain extensive information on bilingual and ESL policies and rulings.

REFERENCES

Gomez, F. C., & Craycraft, K. R. (1998). *The legal handbook for Texas teachers.* Bulverde, TX: OMNI Publishers.

Texas Classroom Teachers Association. (2001). *Survival guide.* (Brochure). Austin, TX: Author.

Chapter 20

Study and Test-Taking Skills: Preparing for and Taking the Test

JANICE L. NATH

University of Houston—Downtown

CYNTHIA G. HENRY

Throughout this book we have provided information that you will need both to pass the EC–4 Pedagogy and Professional Responsibilities (PPR) TExES and to better teach young children. We know that test-taking skills and special preparation for this test can help determine how well you do, and this chapter can help you.

Four areas need your attention: (1) completing your registration correctly, (2) preparing for the day of the test, (3) developing a mindset for the test, and (4) making realistic study plans.

REGISTRATION

Make sure that you are eligible to take this test. If you are completing an approved EC-4 Texas educator preparation program or are certified in another state or country and seeking Texas certification, this TExES is most likely needed for certification. If you are in a preparation program for educators in Texas, there may be additional prerequisites for registration. Check with your certification office about your status in your program, and do it early. Teachers on emergency certificates sometimes let their time run out without completing prerequisites and discover too late that they are not permitted to take the test. Preparation entities do not often bend rules.

The deadlines for submitting your application are posted on the State Board for Educator Certification (SBEC) Web site (www.sbec.state.tx.us). Colleges of education should also have these deadlines posted, along with available registration booklets. SBEC is planning to offer online registration in the near future, although specific details were not available at the time of publication. Watch closely for this opportunity, for it may ease the process of registration. Fees for this test vary depending on whether deadlines are met. Postmarking your application early will save you money. Teachers or teacher candidates from out of state should request a registration booklet from the SBEC Web site, by phone, or by use of the email address listed at the close of this chapter. State deadlines are absolutely fixed! There are no exceptions on the final deadline for a testing date and a certification officer can do nothing should you miss it.

If you are from a Texas university, your certification officer must currently affix a bar code to your application, registering your university program and indicating that you are ready to take the test. Always check ahead, as quite often university deadlines are several weeks *ahead* of the state deadline. This enables your certification officer to see whether you have completed all program requirements. Your program is accountable for your test scores, so certification offices can be quite strict in checking your eligibility to test. Because your certification officer may be very busy during this time, do not wait to ask questions that may affect your test date. Ask early! The responsibility is yours. Each time you test or retest for any state teachers' test, you must go through the application process. Out-of-state applicants should contact the State Board for Educator Certification (SBEC) Information and Support Center listed at the end of this chapter.

Register for only one test per testing date. Many think that it is easy to take two or even three tests on the same day, but research has shown that this is risky. These tests are very long, and your concentration will suffer. If you plan your testing well in advance, you will not need to take more than one test per day.

Payment must accompany your registration application. A money order made out to NES is the best way for your application and scores to clear. If you write a check, be very sure that it will clear. If it does not, the state will return your application, and you will lose your testing date. One candidate's bank made a mistake and refused her check. Even though the bank was at fault and sent a letter to NES confirming this, the candidate's scores had already been deleted from the computer and could not be retrieved. When online registration begins, a credit card should be accepted.

Complete all parts of the registration form carefully. It will be returned if any blanks are not completed and/or if it is not signed, and you will probably lose your testing date or have to pay a late charge. Also, be very careful to complete the form accurately. The state continuously gathers information for state-based information banks, and their computers may compare information. If there are items that do not match, your application could be questioned and/or returned. If you will be moving between the time you test and the time you receive your score, put a more permanent address (for example, your parents' home) on the application. Do not forget to put a stamp on your envelope. Many students forget this, and their university office cannot provide stamps.

Call NES if you have sent your registration in plenty of time but have not received your admission before the late deadline. If they have not received it, you could still register late. Check the information sent back to you from NES for accuracy. They may not have given you the time or place that you requested on your form, and if you show up at a wrong site or time, you will not be allowed to test. If numbers do not match on your identification, you may not be able to test, or your scores may be reported as someone else's. Finally, double-check the test that you requested on your admission ticket. One candidate signed up for a test and prepared for it, but when he arrived at the site, they handed him a completely different test (out of his field). He had not seen the mistake on the admission ticket and no extra tests are brought to a site! No matter that it wasn't his fault, his preparation and testing day were wasted. Double-check everything in time for changes to be made.

Figure 20-1 is a checklist for registration. Things change often, so *please double-check* with the latest Registration Bulletin or Web site for current procedures. Read everything that applies to you—carefully.

PREPARING FOR TEST DAY

All of us have taken enough tests to know typical advice given to test takers. This section also includes a few guidelines specific to this test.

Anxiety can cause test-takers to "have an edge" or, conversely, can cause failure. A bit of anxiety can help motivate, but too much anxiety is counterproductive. Allowing plenty of time for arrival at the test site can help test takers feel calm and confident. One way to prepare for the test day is to begin several days in advance. If a test site is not familiar to you, drive there before the actual test day, and keep a map in the car with the site clearly marked. Some sites may be far enough from your home for you to consider driving there the night before and spending the night nearby. If so, arrange accommodations well in advance to avoid problems. The alternative could be an extremely tense, harried early morning drive. In the past, test takers had to arrive by 7:30 for the morning test (1:30 for the afternoon test). Check the time on your admission ticket. If you live far away, requesting an afternoon testing session may be the best plan. Also, be sure to check the gas in your car so that you do not have to worry about finding a service station on the way to a site or spending extra moments for fueling. Proctors have a definite cutoff time, and no refunds are given for latecomers.

Have all of your supplies ready and in the car the night before (see Figure 2-2). Rushing around late on the night before the test (or worse, the morning of the test) can create a frantic feeling that is hard to overcome. You will need your admission/acceptance ticket, two pieces of identification (one must be a government issue with a picture), pencils, and erasers. Other things might include a jacket, an accurate watch, and some food and/or beverages. A complete list of items needed (and those prohibited) can be found in your Registration Bulletin and are listed later in this chapter. Be sure to use the current bulletin because

Checklist for Registration

___ Checked the state deadline for registration

___ Checked early with certification office (or SBEC, if out-of-state) for eligibility

___ Obtained registration form

___ Checked deadline for obtaining bar code (if applicable)

___ Obtained money order (preferred) or wrote check

___ Completed all parts of registration form correctly

___ Registration form signed

___ For Texas university students (obtained and affixed): bar-code to registration form (or handed to university for certification officer to send)

___ Placed stamp placed on envelope

___ Confirmed test site, test time, correct test, ID numbers, and so forth, confirmed by information letter/admission ticket from NES and double-checked

Figure 20-1 A checklist to follow in registering for the test (Be sure to watch for online registration).

changes may have been made since the publication of this book.

A good night's sleep is essential to getting through this long reading test. Some people are very nervous sleepers when they know they must get up for a test early in the morning. If this describes you, set two alarms to avoid checking the clock during the night. Partying the night before or staying up late for any reason can make a crucial difference in your concentration level. Arrange early in your schedule for this to be a testing day *only*. Do not plan to be at an event (such as being a wedding party member or scheduling a plane departure) that would require you to rush to finish early or that would be exciting enough to break your concentration during the test. At more than $70 a try and with available testing days so far apart, it makes sense to take the test seriously in every respect. Even one point can make the difference between passing and failing. For a morning test, you should be in bed and asleep by at least 10:00 the night before.

Breakfast and/or lunch (for an afternoon test) is another important part of test preparation. You may need the entire 5 hours allowed to finish your test. Near the end of that time, your energy level may wane, causing a loss of concentration. Plan a moderate breakfast for a morning test and a moderate lunch for an afternoon test. Too heavy a meal may make you drowsy. A lull in your concentration, from being tired from lack of sleep, can make a difference in your getting that one point you need to pass. Foods high in protein and low in carbohydrates are recommended by nutritionists for optimal mental alertness (lean meats, fish, green and leafy vegetables, and peanuts; avoid cereals, pastas, potatoes, and breads). Testing sites are often in high schools or other areas in which "quick fix" snack and beverage machines are available, but prepare for nonavailability by eating a proper meal before your test. Backpacks, sacks, and so forth, have not been allowed in the testing rooms in the past, so you may want to stick an energy bar and a bottle of water or juice in your pocket or purse for a midtest "pick-me-up." Eating, drinking, and smoking are not allowed inside the testing room or area, so you may want to take a quick break to have your snack outside. You might attempt to persuade yourself that a large dose of caffeine before or during this test will help to keep you awake and alert, but it can actually impair concentration by leaving you jittery and, of course, interrupt your

A Checklist of Items to Have in the Car

___ Admission/acceptance ticket(s). Each test has its own ticket. If you are taking two tests, you must have both tickets. Read all the information carefully for site locations and times because NES does not have to give you the first site and/or time you requested.

___ Map that shows the test site location (if needed).

___ Two pieces of identification, one with a picture (one government issued, bearing your signature and picture, such as a driver's license or passport) and another (university ID, social security card, credit card, employee card, etc.).

___ Pencils (No. 2 are best).

___ Accurate watch that does not beep on the hour.

___ Energy bar.

___ Juice or bottled water.

___ Layers of clothing or jacket.

___ Lunch (if taking more than one test)

Figure 20-2 A checklist of items to take on test day.

test with multiple trips to the restroom. If you are taking two tests on one day (and we hope you are not), it may be worth taking a lunch and leaving it in a cooler in your car. Testing sites may not be located close to fast-food restaurants, and other test takers may be trying to get a quick lunch, too, crowding the time you have between tests. You do not want to worry about finishing your first test quickly to get lunch and then return by the next test's starting time.

Another important part of test taking is the temperature variant. We urge you to wear layers of clothing and/or a jacket no matter what the season. Those who set up testing sites often anticipate many, people in a room, so the temperature may be quite low upon your arrival. In fact, it may seem to be "freezing!" However, as people fill the room, the temperature will rise. Dress in loose-fitting, comfortable clothes.

Parking is sometimes limited, and test takers may be forced to park some distance away. We have heard a few reports of teacher candidates who arrived early but had to park far away, thus having to rush to get to the registration area on time. They were out of breath and anxiety ridden by the time they sat down to test. Again, allow enough time for driving and parking close to the site! Even if you have to sit in your car for a bit with a newspaper, novel, or review material, it is better than arriving late and in a frantic state.

When you have checked in, take your seat. Be sure to sit in your assigned seat (if applicable). Do not be creative in seat selection, because it may make a difference on your reported scores. Listen carefully for instructions. If there are further written instructions, read them carefully. Even if you have taken a practice examination, some things may have changed.

Figure 20-3 is a checklist of items that are prohibited during the test. If you bring communication devices (particularly cell phones) into the testing room, your scores can be canceled. Rather than worry about your phone during the test, leave it in the car.

Texas does make special accommodations for those with disabilities. However, you must apply for them early so that the testing site can be prepared for you, and documentation is required in most cases. Please make sure that you do this at the time of registration.

THE TEST

We want to remind you again not to sign up for multiple tests. Research continues to show that those who attempt multiple tests often do not pass one or both of their tests. If you have signed up for more than one and you find that you really do not have the energy to continue after a full morning, it may be to your benefit, psychologically, to forfeit your afternoon test. You will not receive a refund, but it may better serve you to come back fresh on the next test date rather than fail due to fatigue. If you do have to take two tests, do not let the fact that you have an afternoon test affect your morning test by making you rush or putting you in a bad frame of mind. Again, the best advice is to take only one test per day.

When Texas first instituted a test for teachers, the test consisted mainly of recall questions. For example:

Whose theory included a close examination of children's developmental levels?

A. *Piaget*

B. *Bloom*

C. *Jamison*

D. *Jones*

Either you knew the answer or you didn't. In many ways, taking the test is easier now—and in others, it is harder. There is no longer a list of names, dates, and so forth to memorize. Texas now tests through its competencies the skills, knowledge, attitudes, and philosophies that it wants in its teachers.

Match Your Answer to the Competencies

If you want to pass, do not answer in any way other than that aligned with the Texas philosophies through the competencies! For example, let

backpacks	briefcases	cell phones	pagers
beeping watches	packages	slide rules	highlighters
cameras	tape recorders	notebooks	textbooks
scratch paper	dictionaries	spell checkers	calculators
audiotapes	written materials		

Figure 20-3 Checklist of prohibited Iitems.

us look at the issues of classroom arrangement and student grouping. You may have grown up in a school where children sat quietly at traditionally arranged individual desks and where cooperative groups were never used. This arrangement may have worked successfully for you already, and you may (though we hope that you do not) believe that it is the correct way to run your classroom. The competencies tell us, however, that Texas wants us to use cooperative groups often—where children learn through interactions and talking to each other. This is not the time to engage in a battle of philosophies with the state. Answer the way that the competencies are stated.

Answering questions in accordance with the competencies may be particularly difficult if you went to school in another country or even to a strict private school where many experiences are in direct opposition to the competencies. If this is the case, be very sure that you understand the importance of matching your answers on this test to those of the Texas competencies rather than to those of your experience. Others who may have difficulty in matching their views with these competencies are those who already teach in schools where these Texas philosophies are not often seen. In many schools in PPR and other areas, these competencies are not a part of daily school life. We hope that you do not see schools that are gloomy places for children, with negative actions by teachers who say that their ways are examples of "what needs to be done in the real world." If you have never known a school that is a wonderful and positive place for all kinds of students and teachers and you persist in answering in ways that are contrary to the competencies, you will not succeed on this test. A good question to ask yourself

as you select you answer is, *"What does Texas say it wants a teacher to do in this situation?"*

This test is written with several strong values or biases: Texas wants its teachers to be student-centered, use cooperative groups when appropriate, teach multiculturally, give students responsibility and choice in their own instruction, and use multiple resources (especially technology and human resources). Look closely for those values as you select your answers.

Test Format and Testing Hints

Teacher decision sets. Now that you understand the importance of aligning your answers with the views of Texas, let us continue to look at the test layout more carefully. It is critical that you understand the amount of reading comprehension required for passing this test. The test is organized into large reading blocks, or "Teacher Decision Sets," although some shorter formats are included. Each Teacher Decision Set, or school scenario, is introduced with several paragraphs—perhaps a half page of reading. This is followed by a number of questions, usually several pages in length, all related to the opening situation. The questions may include several paragraphs that introduce new information into the scenario. Competencies are mixed at random throughout the test.

Slower readers. If you are a slower reader or an ESL learner with difficulty reading rapidly in English, you will have to keep a close eye on your time. Prepare thoroughly by learning the terms listed in the competencies and those in boldface in the chapters of this book. Practice your reading skills so that you can get through the vast amount of reading on this 5-hour test. If your university or certifying agency gives a practice test, you should take it (more than once, if possible). It will help you gauge the time involved in reading and answering this type of lengthy test. If reading rapidly is difficult, review by rereading the chapters in this book and other teacher education texts, answering questions from the chapters. Carefully establish and maintain a long-term study program (see hints later in this chapter).

Reading the questions. Some tips for answering the actual questions on the examination may be of help. First, be sure to read the opening scenario *carefully*. This will set the stage for the next few pages of the test. One strategy that you may have used on other tests is to read all of the questions before you read the scenario, yet this may be an *inappropriate* strategy for this test. Why? Remember that most of this test is written in Teacher Decision Sets, in which a number of subsets of questions follow an introductory reading selection. Events or information introduced in the opening scenario often continue throughout a Teacher Decision Set in the various questions under each set, and information is added as the set develops. If you read *all* questions belonging to the Teacher Decision Set, you may find that it is time-consuming and confusing, and that you miss important information added along the way. It *can* be a good strategy to read the questions that belong to each *smaller* scenario after the stage has been set by the introduction.

Don't skip questions. Answer each question as you come to it. Even if you are not sure, choose an answer and mark it so that if time runs out, you will have selected a good possibility. Your first inclination is often your best answer, so put *something* down. Try not to skip questions on this test. The time that it takes you to go back into each scenario to find skipped questions can be overwhelming.

Mark on the test. This examination is written in multiple-choice format. The answers are designed to make you think by recalling, analyzing, and evaluating information, and finally applying it to the current scenario. As you read the scenario and questions, underline key information and circle key words or phrases that you have seen in the competencies. Also, carefully underline or circle words and phrases that may negate an answer (*not, never,* etc.), as well as words that would change an answer (*always, frequently, first, never, best,* etc.).

Visualize. Try to picture the situation as it unfolds (as in a movie) so that you can visualize exactly what is happening. Cut out distracting parts that have no bearing on the question (cut to the chase!) so that your focus remains only on relevant details.

Eliminate. Read all of the answer choices before making your selection. There are usually four answers from which to select, and you are to mark your answer on a separate scantron. The process of elimination will help you considerably. As you read a question, you may find that one or two answers clearly stand out as incorrect. Put an "X" by those, and do not waste further time on them. Two answers, however, often are straight from the competencies and clearly sound correct, according to the views of Texas.

Does the answer really match the question? When you have narrowed your options, go back to the question and determine exactly what it is that the question is asking. Two or more answers may sound good, but only one will be correct. Many of the distracters are designed to be inviting. They are written in excellent educational terms and may sound like information from the competencies—*but they do not match the question!* Quite often this is where people make mistakes, particularly if they are in a hurry. A very good strategy is to ask yourself, "Does the selection I made *really* answer the question that was asked?" There are also some very tricky differences to discern between two of the best answers. For example, let us look at the following question:

Mr. Nguyen wanted his students to help the librarian select new books and games to be made available through a large PTO gift. He proposed that his fourth graders read and review some of the books from ordering lists, and that some games from the list also be available to be played and evaluated. He planned for his class to survey teachers and children from first, second, and third grades to determine their favorite authors and games, and then to present the survey to the librarian. He went to the principal, librarian, and grade-level committees to ask whether this was feasible. In doing this, he showed that he could:

A. Continue professional development by seeking direction from other professionals

B. Collaborate with others for his lesson objectives

C. Communicate with others to accomplish educational goals

D. Demonstrate to students how collaboration accomplishes objectives in the real world

Let us analyze this problem. Answer *A* is not correct, because: (1) he is not seeking direction for his plan, rather asking only for time and permission to run his surveys, and (2) there is nothing having to do with professional development in his actions. Therefore, we can put an "X" by that answer. Answer *D* is also not applicable, because there is no mention that the students could know that he went to talk with these other professionals. There is some distraction here, though. We know that Texas wants its teachers to continue professional development and to show how school relates to the real world, so we see that answers *A* and *D* are both written nicely to draw us in. However, we are left with answers *B* and *C,* both of which also sound very good. We know that Texas wants us to collaborate with others (straight from the competencies), so we could be drawn to answer *B,* but if we look a bit more closely, there really is no collaboration going on here. Collaboration means that others contribute. Mr. Nguyen is simply communicating his proposition to the other parties. He already has his ideas, and rather than asking others to work together with him to design his lessons, he wants permission to implement them. His ideas also involve

more than one lesson's objectives (this would no doubt be a series of lessons), so the proposition would be for a broader set of goals. He is simply communicating with others (answer *C*). These are small details, but taking the answers apart in this way is what you must do to pass the test.

If you can't prove it happened, it isn't the answer. We can use the question above to eliminate distracters, using this strategy. For example, *D* could be eliminated immediately because nothing in the paragraph indicated that Mr. Nguyen had ever told his class about talking with other teachers. Also, there was no professional development, as stated before. Look for things that did not happen, and "X them out!"

Determine which competency is being tested. Another strategy is to try to discern exactly which competency or part of a competency the question is trying to test. If you can determine this, you can often select an answer easily. If you know the language of the competencies very well, it will be easier for you to analyze the possible answers. For example, if you can determine that a question is testing Competency 3, and you know that some key concepts of that competency are developing clear, relevant, meaningful, and age-appropriate goals and objectives that can be assessed, the correct answer might be very obvious. Let us look at an example of using this technique with another competency.

Miss Huff was a new teacher who grew up in another area of the county. She was having difficulties with one of her third graders, Jorge. She went to ask her mentor, Ms. Faseler, what she should do because she was sure that Jorge was lying to her constantly. "The last time I asked him whether he was the one who was making all those noises during class, I told him to look at me and tell me that he didn't do it. He kept saying that he didn't, but I knew he must be lying because he wouldn't look me in the eye. What am I going to do with him? He just looks down—as though he is guilty." Ms. Faseler told Miss Huff that often Hispanic and Asian children will not look directly at an adult (especially a teacher or parent) and that this behavior is a sign of respect for their elders—whereas in middle-class White culture, it is taken to mean "guilty" if someone refuses to make eye contact.

The next time that Miss Huff wanted to question Jorge about his behavior, she had him wait after school and sit down beside her rather than across from her. Through questions, she calmly asked him to tell her about what had happened. She was pleasantly surprised that they actually had a nice conversation, and she was enlightened in several areas of classroom behavior. She used this information the next day to make some changes that improved the entire classroom environment. This teacher now understands that:

A. Collaboration with other professionals increases learning and a sense of a community of learners.

B. Students develop in different ways, according to their culture.

C. Establishing management techniques through collaboration is mutually supportive.

D. Being sensitive to nonverbal cues is an important part of communication in a classroom of learners.

All of these sound as though they could be correct, so let's use our analysis procedure. First, let us eliminate! Answer *A* cannot be the correct answer, because they are not really talking about increasing *learning*. In addition, there was really no collaboration, because Miss Huff simply received information from Ms. Faseler rather than equal contribution. The answer cannot be *B,* because there are no developmental problems being discussed—even though we could be distracted about the cultural issue, especially because this is the only reference to culture in all of the answers. Now let us closely examine the remaining two items by looking at the question to see from which competency the question has been taken. Certainly there is a management issue, but there was mentoring rather than collaboration happening between the two teachers. There were really no management techniques discussed in the entire conversation with Ms. Faseler—as answer *C* states. It was a com-munication issue. The main thrust of the question involved Miss Huff's misreading of a student's nonverbal cues. Answer *D* is correct because she used her new information to question Jorge with supportive strategies. Competency 7 states, "The beginning teacher practices effective communication techniques and interpersonal skills (including both verbal and nonverbal skills …)." When we can analyze the main idea of the scenario, the questions, and the possible answers, it is easier to go to the language of the competencies and pick out the answer. We must certainly know those competencies and their language well!

Look for "Texasland." Another strategy that may work well for you is to select the "rainbows and flowers" answer that signifies the most wonderful answer possible for children. In Disneyland, for example, all reality is suspended and everything is possible. In real life, however, we know that not every school has abundant technology, for example, or a number of teachers who are eager to collaborate, or the money to take children on field trips, and so on, so you may be hesitant to pick answers that do not seem true to all schools. Suspend that thought, however, for in the "Texasland" of the test, all is possible. Pick the answer that would be best for children.

Buy into the competencies. The best strategy is to *become* a teacher who follows these competencies. Selecting the best answer for children then becomes natural. Although resources do not come to every school, teachers who follow these competencies do create wonderful places for children. Texas did not create these competencies just to irritate teacher candidates—the competencies represent researched best practice.

Remember that not all of these test-taking strategies may work well for you. We have listed several that may be helpful, but if you find that a strategy is not suited to you, go on to another. Practicing with questions from these chapters or from the practice examination (which can be downloaded from the SBEC Web site) will show you which strategies are the best for you.

Marking your scantron. Test takers often make mistakes that are very easy to control—yet cost points. Not bearing down hard enough to ensure that a clear mark is made, not erasing clearly, not coloring in a full circle, or marking outside the lines on your answer sheet can cause the grading machine to read your answer incorrectly. If you do not want to worry about these mistakes during the test, allow several minutes at the end to go back over your scantron and correct these types of marks. Better yet, be careful in marking each answer the first time. If you run completely out of time and later believe that your graded scantron might have been misread because of marking errors, you may want to have your test rescored by hand. The cost is about $25, and the information and form for requesting a rescoring is in your registration booklet. It is unlikely that many items will have been misread, so this is suggested only if you have a question about the state of your scantron *and* if your score was within a very few points of passing.

Another common scantron mistake is mismatching the number of the question in your test booklet with that on your scantron. Be sure to stop every so often to ensure that you are on the same numbers on both your test and the scantron. Two good places to check are at the end of each Teacher Decision Set and when you begin a new column on your scantron. Catching a mismatch after completing a good portion of the test or not catching a mismatch at all can be devastating! Mismatching can also happen when you want to skip a question and come back to it later. A better suggestion is not to skip questions. Answer every question as you come to it, but put a light mark beside those that you wish to revisit if time remains (better yet, also put a large check beside them in your booklet). If you skip many questions, you will find yourself rereading practically the entire test! It will also be very confusing to try to reinsert yourself into each scenario. Your first inclination is often the best answer, so go ahead and take your "best shot" the first time. Come back to those that you have marked later, time permitting. Be sure to erase all extraneous marks on your scantron. Another good strategy is to mark your answer on both the scantron and in your test booklet. That way, if you have made a mistake on your scantron, you will still have a record of your answer choices on your test booklet.

Timing your test. Time may or may not be a concern for you. The number of items varies from test to test and item to item. Your certification entity may have prepared you to take a test of 150 items, but there may be only 100 items on the test you are given on test day—or there may be 180. Before you begin, check the number of questions you have been given so that you will know how to divide your time. If there are 100 items, you know that you should be covering 20 to 23 items per hour, factoring in some breaks. If there are more items, divide your time accordingly. Plan your breaks well. Taking a short break every hour is usually more profitable than plowing through the bulk of the test before stopping. Physical exercises developed for long flights (stretches in place and isometrics) can be helpful, or lay your head down for a minute or so, being careful not to doze off. Do keep an eye on your watch so that you will not be surprised by the passing of time. We advise you to bring a nonbeeping watch that keeps accurate time because the clock in your testing room may not be accurate or visible from where you are seated. Be sure that there is time to mark every answer. You are penalized for wrong answers and blanks but not for guesses (if they turn out to be correct). If you run out of time at the end, quickly mark all remaining blanks with *any* answer. Do try to leave enough time to recheck your scantron for stray marks and incomplete circles.

Test anxiety. As noted earlier, text anxiety can be a debilitating part of test taking. Here are some suggestions to help combat these feelings. Arranging your day such that your focus is on *only* the test, rather than on another big event immediately after the test, should help you remain calm. If you have followed our suggestions about arriving in plenty of time with your supplies, you are one step ahead of test anxiety. Allocating your time and breaks according to the number of questions and maintaining a schedule accordingly, so that you will not run out of time, should help reduce your anxiety. If it makes you nervous that someone seated near you is noisy, you may want to ask a proctor whether you can move—or ask the proctor to request that the person be quiet (do not say anything to another test taker yourself because any communication may be misinterpreted as cheating). Overall, the best strategy is to know your materials very well and to practice with the terms and the test format as often as possible. The following is a discussion of a long-term study plan that can help you feel confident in your knowledge.

LONG-TERM STUDY PLANS

The amount of material in this book is extensive, and it may seem overwhelming at first. Breaking the information down into smaller, more manageable steps is a key to preparation.

Time management. It is easy to let time slip away and find yourself with only a few weeks or days before your test. This can certainly cause anxiety, so try to avoid it by setting up manageable goals for study time. The amount of time that you set aside will depend on the time you have prior to your test date. For example, if you begin to study for the examination 4 months before the test, plan to study about 3 days a week for 30 minutes to an hour. If you have only a month or two, you will have to study more often and for longer periods of time. Both can be fairly manageable, but keep to your schedule. Write your study times on your calendar as you would for any appointment. This will help to remind you each week and emphasize the importance of this time. Using the same time each day or evening for study will help to establish a more consistent routine.

How to study. Everyone has a favorite learning style. If you need to be cozy on your favorite couch, with low light and no sound at all, or if you cannot seem to learn without sitting at your desk with the radio on, find that spot! Our brains are strange in many ways. Remembering the first and last items that we read is much easier for us than remembering information we read in the middle. What does this mean for our study habits? It is best to take frequent breaks so that your brain has a chance to "begin and end" more often, thereby cutting out the "forgettable middles." A brief 2-to 5-minute break is often what is needed to make that happen. Stretch, do an exercise set or so, get up for a drink or snack, listen to a song, pet your animal, or close your eyes for a second to rest your mind just long enough to help absorb the material you have read. You know your own body rhythms. Try to schedule your study time when you are energetic rather than tired.

How much is enough? This question is one we often ask when faced with a heavy workload. Setting a goal on how much to accomplish each time helps overcome study blocks. Again, look at the time you have and divide your pages into the days you have set aside. A reasonable amount of work for long-term study should be about 5 to 10 pages each period, with time to review some of the pages you studied earlier. You may also want to work through some practice questions each time. More practice questions can be downloaded from the SBEC Web site.

Materials management. Disorganization can cause us to waste time. It takes time to locate study materials, books, and so forth each time we want to use them, and this can be used as a subconscious avoidance technique. If there is one place where you can keep your test materials, you will find it easier to begin studying because no time is wasted in finding what you need.

Organization of materials is also important. Using different-colored file folders, coded labels, and so forth makes it easy to locate just what you want. You may want to organize your materials by competency or by another system such as "Know," "Need to Know," and "Still to Learn."

Study environment. Temperature affects our mental alertness. Keeping the room at around 68 degrees can help maintain concentration and memory. A study area free of visual distractions can also be helpful—a blank wall can be more conducive than a wall of bright posters or pictures. Lighting also makes a difference. Many people do not study well in soft light, which can increase mental fatigue (although a few are low-light learners).

Use your senses and memory techniques.
There is a large amount of material to remember for this test. Try to use as many sensory avenues as possible to help you remember the main concepts. One idea is to paraphrase each competency and put that information on index cards to help memorize the important concepts. Cards are also an excellent way to review the "Terms to Know" at the beginning of each chapter in this book and those found in the Glossary at the end of each chapter. It is difficult to understand the questions if you do not have the vocabulary. Use these in a typical flashcard way or in a matching game.

Another method, called the memory model technique, comes in handy. To demonstrate this technique let us use Competency 3, which addresses key concepts about "Designing Coherent Instruction." This technique requires creating a "ridiculous" visual image. To remember some of these issues you might draw a map of Texas (for the TEKS), holding a mirror that stands for instruction that enhances "reflection." The map can be shown holding the reins of a horse (representing horse sense or "logical sequencing of planning"), and on the horse are strapped some computers (for supporting resources). In the back of this image, a rainbow stretches across the sky, marked with math, language arts, science, and so on, instead of the colors (for a designing instruction that "stretches across disciplines"). The hand holding the reins of the horse has a huge wrist watch, indicating the allocation of time during lessons . . . and so forth. A simpler technique is to rhyme each competency number with a word that jogs your memory. For example, one = run, and Competency One reminds us that children must crawl before they can walk before they can run

(children go through developmental stages). Memory techniques are very personal, so try to make up tricks that make sense to you. This is a good technique because you "wrestle" with the material in creating your memory picture, but then it also flashes easily into your head because it is easy to visualize a ridiculous association.

Mnemonics are helpful as well. KCAASE for the six levels of Bloom's taxonomy may become "knowing combinations alleviates anxiety—simply and effectively" (*knowing* for knowledge level, *combinations* for comprehension, *alleviates* for application, *anxiety* for analysis, *simply* for synthesis, and *effectively* for evaluation). You might use the positive educational phrase that is PPR based— "knowing children and always supporting everyone"—as your key phrase for the first letter of each of Bloom's taxonomy levels. This must make sense for you, so either design your own phrases or take someone else's that work for you.

Another method that can help you internalize concepts is to make up your own PPR questions. Creating them will help you think as the test developers do, and you may be surprised at how closely your questions match those of the real test.

Talk concepts over with yourself when you are alone in the car. You will "hear" them often, and nobody will know that you are not singing along with the radio.

Make the most of your time. Focusing on the materials is to your advantage, so focus *all* of your attention when studying. Changing topics can help keep your mind fresh and maintain alertness when your attention is waning. Taking notes or underlining as you read also helps you to focus on what seems really important. As you come to a term or concept, try to visualize a classroom example. Note that example beside the term or concept. These techniques can stop you from arriving at the end of your reading and wondering what you have just read. Do not go past your time allotments too often, especially when you are feeling tired and irritated with your learning abilities. "Making a deal" to reward yourself at the end of your study period can be quite effective. Plan to do something enjoyable after your sessions! Hard work and commitment are required to "stay with it." This is one way to make it happen. Use a bit of psychology on yourself by trying to begin and end on a positive note. In other words, visualize yourself confident and ready for the test because you have completed your study goals regularly. See yourself with your certification in your hand!

Study groups. You may be with a group of teachers from your school or district who all need to pass this test to continue teaching, or you may be in a preservice program with fellow students who are all facing this examination. Study groups can be a great source of support and learning for you. Try to organize or become a part of such a group. Several minds can offer new insight into the materials and ways to approach certain questions. Just discussing the concepts of the test engages you in the material in an active way, and we all know that teaching other people (which you will do in a group) is also one of the best ways to learn. Working in a group often seems less like "work" when it comes to studying, so your energy often stays at a higher level. Put up notices at your school, university, or district to see whether you can organize or gain access to a study group for this test. Going over concepts, generating practice questions and answers, and talking over test-taking skills with others is a most effective way of preparing for this important examination.

Test review sessions. Attending a commercially sponsored review session may be a sound investment if you have not been recently prepared by a college of education or did not do well by the second time you took the test. These sessions can offer additional insights into the material and an opportunity to work with a practice examination that closely matches the real test. Regional service centers, school districts, universities, and others may offer these sessions. Find out about them early, however, because some are limited in size, and universities may limit their sessions to their students only. If you are unable to find a group in your area, you may want to establish an online review with someone who is farther away but with whom you can still maintain computer study time.

CONTACT NUMBERS

If you have questions about completing the forms, payment, test dates, registration deadlines, admission tickets, score reports, study guides, or ordering registration bulletins, you may call or write:

TExES Examination
National Evaluation Systems, Inc.
P. O. Box 140467
Austin, TX 78714-0467
Telephone: 512-927-5151
Telecommunications for the Deaf:
512-926-1248

If you have certification questions or questions about which tests you need, you may call or write:

State Board for Educator Certification Information and Support Center (SBEC ISC)
1001 Trinity Street
Austin, TX 78701
Telephone: 888-863-5880 (toll free)
Email address: sbec@sbec.state.tx.us
Web site: http://www.sbec.state.tx.us

Telephone numbers, addresses, and email addresses sometimes change, so you may have to call telephone information or do another computer search.

This is certainly not the first test that you will have taken. It is, however, one of the most important—for it opens the door to the very important career that you have chosen. Texas and its children need you! Prepare well so that you do not have to worry or spend more money to register again. Follow a study plan, have your paperwork in order for registration, approach the test with the "Texas frame of mind," and use all of your test-taking skills. You should do well! With the knowledge and skills you have gained, you will be ready to enter a classroom as a competent and confident educator of young children.

Index